PUBLICATIONS

OF THE

NAVY RECORDS SOCIETY

VOL. 134

THE SOMERVILLE PAPERS
Selections from the Private and Official
Correspondence of
Admiral of the Fleet Sir James Somerville

The NAVY RECORDS SOCIETY was established in 1893 for the purpose of printing unpublished manuscripts and rare works of naval interest. The Society is open to all who are interested in naval history, and any person wishing to become a member should apply to the Hon. Secretary, Deputy Chief Credit Officer, BZW Ltd, First Floor, St Mary's Court, Lower Thames Street, London EC3R 6JN. The annual subscription is £30, which entitles the member to receive one free copy of each work issued by the Society in that year, and to buy earlier issues at much reduced prices.

SUBSCRIPTIONS and orders for back volumes should be sent to the Membership Secretary, 5 Goodwood Close, Midhurst, Sussex GU29 9JG.

THE COUNCIL OF THE NAVY RECORDS SOCIETY wish it to be clearly understood that they are not answerable for any opinions and observations which may appear in the Society's publications. For these the editors of the several works are entirely responsible.

Admiral of the Fleet Sir James Somerville, GCB, GBE, DSO

THE SOMERVILLE PAPERS

Selections from the Private and Official
Correspondence of Admiral of the Fleet Sir James
Somerville, G.C.B., G.B.E., D.S.O.

edited by

MICHAEL SIMPSON, M.A., M. Litt., F.R. HIST. S.
Senior Lecturer in History, University of Wales, Swansea

with the assistance of

JOHN SOMERVILLE, C.B., C.B.E.

PUBLISHED BY SCOLAR PRESS
FOR THE NAVY RECORDS SOCIETY
1995

Published by
SCOLAR PRESS
Gower House
Croft Road
Aldershot
Hants GU11 3HR
England

Ashgate Publishing Company
Old Post Road
Brookfield
Vermont 05036
USA

British Library Cataloguing in Publication Data

Somerville, James
  Somerville Papers: Selections from the Private and Official Correspondence
  of Admiral of the Fleet Sir James Somerville, GCB, GBE, DSO. – (Navy
  Records Series; Vol. 134) I. Title   II. Simpson, Michael   III. Somerville,
  John   IV. Series 359.331092

Library of Congress Cataloging-in-Publication Data

Somerville, James, Sir
  The Somerville papers: selections from the private and official
  correspondence of Admiral of the Fleet Sir James Somerville, GCB,
  GBE, DSO / edited by Michael Simpson, with the assistance of John
  Somerville.
      p.   cm. – (Publications of the Navy Records Society ; vol. 134)
  Includes index.
  ISBN 1-85928-207-5 (hardback)
      1. Somerville, James, Sir — Correspondence. 2. Great
  Britain—History; Naval —20th century—Sources. 3. Admirals—Great
  Britain—Correspondence.   I. Simpson, Michael.   II. Somerville,
  John.   III. Navy Records Society (Great Britain) IV. Title.
  V. Series.
  DA89.1.S6A4 1995
  941.08'092—dc20   95–2621
                       CIP

ISBN 1 85928 207 5

Phototypeset by Raven Typesetters, Chester
Printed and bound in Great Britain by the University Press, Cambridge

CONTENTS

MAPS AND ILLUSTRATIONS

Frontispiece
Admiral of the Fleet Sir James Somerville, GCB, GBE, DSO

Maps

PREFACE

Admiral of the Fleet Sir James Somerville is not one of the best remembered British naval commanders of the Second World War. However, apart from Lords Cunningham and Fraser, no British flag officer rivalled Somerville's experience of widely different high commands – Force H, the Eastern Fleet and the British Admiralty Delegation in Washington – and none held continuous sea commands for as long as he did (June 1940 to August 1944).

Somerville began his wartime high commands in dramatic if distressing fashion with the bombardment of the French Fleet by Force H at Mers-el-Kebir (July 1940), ran numerous convoys to Malta, raided Genoa, Sardinia and Sicily, and it was aircraft from Force H which crippled the *Bismarck*. Following the loss of the *Prince of Wales* and *Repulse* and the debâcle in the Java Sea, he took command of the new Eastern Fleet in March 1942. For more than two years, he defended the sea lanes to India, the Gulf, Suez and Australasia and at the last harried and bombed Japanese bases. At both the outset and the end of his tour of duty, he commanded Britain's largest fleet. As the focus of the naval war shifted towards the Pacific, he was aptly if reluctantly cast as the Head of the British Admiralty Delegation in Washington, taking up the appointment in October 1944 and returning home in December 1945. Not only did Somerville command large forces in vital theatres, engaging the enemy as frequently and as closely as his elusive foes and his own meagre resources permitted, but he also led the Navy into the age of radar and became the Royal Navy's first true 'air admiral'. Often at odds with Government and Admiralty policy, he was nevertheless well liked by those who served under him.

For the most part, the documents in this selection are drawn from the Admiral's papers held in the Churchill Archives Centre at Churchill College, Cambridge. They have been supplemented by documents from the papers of Lord Cunningham and Admirals Pound, Willis, North, Tennant and Edwards, and Mrs Joan Bright Astley of the War Cabinet Office. I have also used a number of other collections for background purposes, for example, the papers of Admirals Blake, Whitworth and

Willis, Captain S. W. Roskill, and the contemporaneous First Lord, Viscount Alexander of Hillsborough, together with some Admiralty records. The object has been to establish Somerville's own perspective on the war at sea and on the problems of high command. I have used the most informative sources available for each event or topic and this accounts for the rapid transitions from *Reports of Proceedings* to letters and diary entries. The Somerville papers, rich and comprehensive during his Force H and Eastern Fleet days, become rather thin in the later months of 1945, when he was head of the British Admiralty Delegation in Washington, and I have been unable to discover meatier material in other collections or in the Public Record Office.

Somerville entered the Royal Navy in 1897 and had a distinguished career during the First World War as a wireless specialist and an officer of exceptional promise. Between the Wars he held successful commands of the Signal Division and Personal Services and three battleships. Promoted rear admiral in 1933 while serving as Commodore, RN Barracks, Portsmouth, his first sea-going flag appointment was in 1936, when he became Rear Admiral (D), Mediterranean Fleet, an appointment coinciding with the outbreak of the Spanish Civil War. It is with this appointment that Part One begins; there is an amusing portrait of the Coronation Review of 1937 and some material on Dunkirk but there are no papers of any significance on either his command of the East Indies Station (1938–39) or his pioneering work in naval radar. Part Two is wholly concerned with his command of Force H. Part Three deals with his command of the Eastern Fleet, and Part Four concerns the finale to his naval career, probably the least congenial of all his major appointments, the headship of the British Admiralty Delegation in Washington.

In accordance with the Society's tradition, the documents have been edited with as light a hand as possible. Punctuation has been left in its original form except where the occasional comma has been inserted to clarify meaning. Many documents are not reproduced in full and the passages omitted are indicated by an ellipsis (. . .). Many documents have numbered paragraphs and it will be obvious from the marginal numbers which paragraphs have been omitted. Missing words are indicated thus [–] or thus [–?]. Where a word is illegible a possible interpretation is indicated by [word?]. If a passage remains obscure after much editorial headscratching it is indicated thus [?] Place names are contemporaneous. All Admiralty communications originated from London and where possible the locations from which other messages were sent are indicated at the head of the document, though in the case of Force H I have noted the ship only in the cases of change of flagship. Biographical details have been drawn from the *Navy List*, the *Dictionary of National Biography*,

Who Was Who and A.J.P. Taylor's *English History 1914–1945* and other sources. Details of foreign officers' careers have been obtained from the naval historical branches in France, Germany, Norway and the United States. Information on ships and aircraft has been drawn from *Jane's Fighting Ships, Lloyd's Register of Shipping, Aircraft of World War II* (by K. Munson), *A Dictionary of Ships of the Royal Navy in the Second World War* (by J. Young), *The Directory of Shipowners, etc., 1944* and other sources. Dates given are for completion in the case of ships and first flight for aircraft. The numerals in square brackets in the introductory essays refer to the documents in the text.

ACKNOWLEDGEMENTS

I owe a particular debt to John Somerville and his wife Elizabeth for their warm encouragement, unstinted co-operation and assistance and not least their generous hospitality. Over many years Commander Somerville has undertaken the tedious task of unscrambling his father's tiny and almost illegible hand and making transcriptions for such scholars as Captain Stephen Roskill and Professor Arthur Marder. He has kindly made a number of new transcriptions for this volume and I have added a few of my own. He has given me unrestricted access to his father's papers, on deposit at the Churchill Archives Centre, Churchill College, Cambridge, and has also made available a number of other notes and papers in his own possession.

Like all editors and authors, I am deeply indebted to numerous archivists and librarians, the unseen engine room staff of any substantial historical enterprise. In particular I should like to thank Mr Corelli Barnett, Keeper of the Archives at the Churchill Archives Centre, and all of his colleagues, past and present. Their cheerful assistance is rendered with such quiet efficiency that they deserve the title 'the silent service'. Mr R.W.A. Suddaby, Keeper of the Archives at the Imperial War Museum, drew my attention to a number of collections held there and kindly made them available to me. The staffs of the Manuscripts Division of the British Library (Admiral of the Fleet Viscount Cunningham's papers) and the Public Record Office at Kew have also met my requests with courtesy and promptness. I have enjoyed particularly working in the Library of the National Maritime Museum at Greenwich, staffed by the pleasantest and most helpful librarians and archivists I have ever encountered.

I am grateful to the Archivo Historico Nacional at Salamanca and the historical branches of the French, German, Italian, Norwegian and United States Navies for specific information about officers from those countries.

Mr Guy Lewis, Cartographer in the Department of Geography, University of Wales, Swansea, has once again drawn maps of superb quality. My colleague the late Dr Pat Lewis, of the School of European

Languages, very kindly provided accurate translations of documents in French. My daughter Alison used her expertise in Spanish and French to good effect on several occasions. I have benefited from discussions with my colleague Dr Julian Jackson. My head of department, Professor Muriel Chamberlain, has given my research considerable support. My colleagues in the Society for Nautical Research and the Navy Records Society have once again been generous with their advice, information and encouragement. In particular, I should like to thank Dr Evan Davies, Mr G.L. Green, Mr Eric Grove, Commander Derek Howse, Dr Roger Knight, Mr Allan Pearsall, Lieut-Cdr Lawrence Phillips and Professor Bryan Ranft. Warm thanks are due also to the Publications Committee of the Navy Records Society, and especially its Chairman, Captain A.B. Sainsbury, for its encouragement to study the Somerville and Cunningham papers; Captain Sainsbury has also made a number of very helpful comments on a part of the draft. I have benefited greatly from the careful editing, sage advice and prompt attention of the Society's modest, courteous, painstaking and experienced Honorary General Editor, Mr Tony Ryan. I am especially grateful to the Twenty-Seven Foundation for shouldering the main burden of the research costs, and to the British Academy and the Research Support Fund of the University of Wales, Swansea for additional financial assistance.

After more than 30 years as an author's spouse, my wife still summons up apparently inexhaustible reserves of patience, support and love; this brief note is small recompense.

Michael Simpson

GLOSSARY OF ABBREVIATIONS

A/A	Anti-Aircraft
AAC	Army Air Corps
AAF	[US] Army Air Force
ABC	Admiral of the Fleet Sir Andrew B. Cunningham
ABDA	Australian British Dutch American [Supreme Command, SE Asia, 1942]
a/c	aircraft
ACM	Air Chief Marshal
ACNAS	Admiral Commanding North Atlantic Station
ACNB	Admiral, Commonwealth Naval Board [Australia]
ACNO	Assistant Chief of Naval Operations [US Navy]
ACNS	Assistant Chief of Naval Staff
	(H) : Home
	(F) : Foreign
	(U) : Trade & U-boat Warfare
ACOS (P)	Assistant Chief of Staff (Plans)
ADC	Aide de Camp
ADCNO (Air)	Assistant Deputy Chief of Naval Operations (Air) [US Navy]
Adm	Admiral
Admy	Admiralty
ADP	Assistant Director of Plans
ADPD	Assistant Director Plans Division
AEF	American Expeditionary Force
ALT	Air Launched Torpedo
AM	Air Marshal
Amb	Ambassador
AMC	Armed Merchant Cruiser
ANCXF	Allied Naval Commander Expeditionary Force
AOC	Air Officer Commanding
A/S	Anti-Submarine
ASV	Air to Surface Vessel [radar]
ASW	Anti-Submarine Warfare

A/SWD	Anti-Submarine Warfare Division
Atl	Atlantic
A/U	Anti-U-boat
AVM	Air Vice Marshal
BAD	British Admiralty Delegation [Washington, DC]
BAMR	British Admiralty Matériel Representative [Washington]
BASR	British Admiralty Supply Representative [Washington]
BatDiv	Battleship Division [US]
BB	Battleship
BCS	Battle Cruiser Squadron
Bde	Brigade
BEF	British Expeditionary Force
BF	Admiral Sir Bruce Fraser
Bn	Battalion
BOT	Board of Trade
BPF	British Pacific Fleet
Brig	Brigadier
BS	Battle Squadron
B/S	Battleship
Bur Nav	Bureau of Navigation [or Eng: Engineering; Ord: Ordnance] [US Navy Department]
C/A	Aircraft Carrier
Capt	Captain (D): Destroyers; (S) Submarines
CAS	Chief of the Air Staff
CCS	Combined Chiefs of Staff [UK & US]
Cdr	Commander
Cdre	Commodore 1 Cl: First Class; 2 Cl: Second Class
C Ex	Chancellor of the Exchequer
Ch d' A	Chargé d' Affaires
CID	Committee of Imperial Defence
CIGS	Chief of the Imperial General Staff
C-in-C EI	Commander-in-Chief East Indies
C-in-C SA	Commander-in-Chief South Atlantic
CINCPAC	Commander-in-Chief Pacific [US Navy]
Cmd	Command
Cmdt	Commandant
CNO	Chief of Naval Operations [US Navy]
CNSO	Chief Naval Staff Officer
Cntrlr	Controller
CO	Commanding Officer

COHQ	Combined Operations Head Quarters
COIS	Chief of Intelligence Staff
Col	Colonel
Comb Ops	Combined Operations
COMINCH	Commander-in-Chief, US Fleet
Con	Conservative
COS	Chiefs of Staff Committee; Chief of Staff
CruDiv	Cruiser Division
CS	Cruiser Squadron
CSO	Chief Staff Officer
CTF	Carrier Task Force
CV	Fleet Aircraft Carrier
CVL	Light Fleet Carrier
CVE	Escort Carrier
DAAG	Director of Anti-Aircraft Gunnery
DAQMG	Deputy Assistant Quarter-Master General
DASD	Director of Anti-Submarine Division
D/B	Dive Bomber
DCAS	Deputy Chief of Air Staff
DCNO (Air)	Deputy Chief of Naval Operations (Air) [US Navy]
DCNO (O)	Deputy Chief of Naval Operations (Ordnance) [US Navy]
DCNS	Deputy Chief of Naval Staff
DCOS	Deputy Chief of Staff
DD	Destroyer
DDGD (A)	Deputy Director Gunnery Division (Air)
DDPD	Deputy Director Plans Division
DDPS	Deputy Director Planning Section
DDSD	Deputy Director Signal Division
DEMS	Defensively Equipped Merchant Ship
DesDiv	Destroyer Division
DF	Destroyer Flotilla
D/F	Direction Finding
DLDD	Director of Local Defence Division
DMI	Director of Military Intelligence
DNAD	Director of Naval Air Division
DN Eqpt	Director of Naval Equipment
DNI	Director of Naval Intelligence
DNO	Director of Naval Ordnance
DOD	Director of Operations Division
DOIS	Director of Intelligence Section

DPS	Director of Personal Services
DSD	Director of Signal Division
DTSD	Director of Training and Staff Duties
DUKW	D[1942]U[utility]K[front wheel drive]W[six wheels]: amphibious vehicle
DY	Dock Yard
EF	Eastern Fleet
EO	Executive Officer
FAA	Fleet Air Arm
FDR	President Franklin D. Roosevelt
FDO	Fleet Dental Officer
FEO	Fleet Engineer Officer
FGO	Fleet Gunnery Officer
FM	Field Marshal
FMF	Force Maritime Français
FNO	Fleet Navigation Officer
FOC	Flag Officer Commanding
FOCNA	Flag Officer Commanding North Atlantic
FOCRIN	Flag Officer Commanding Royal Indian Navy
FO (D)	Flag Officer (Destroyers)
FOIC	Flag Officer in Charge
For Sec/FS	Foreign Secretary
FSL	First Sea Lord
FS & W/TO	Fleet or Flotilla Signal and Wireless Telegraphy Officer
FTO	Fleet or Flotilla Torpedo Officer
Gen	General
GHQ	General Head Quarters
GO	Gunnery Officer
GOC	General Officer Commanding
Gov-Gen	Governor-General
GP	General Purpose
G/R	General Reconnaissance
GS	General Staff
GSO	General Staff Officer
gt	gross tonnage
Gun O	Gunnery Officer
HAA	Heavy Anti-Aircraft gun
HE	High Explosive
HDML	Harbour Defence Motor Launch
HMG	His Majesty's Government
HMSO	Her Majesty's Stationery Office

i/c	in command
IDC	Imperial Defence College
Inspr	Inspector
JCS	Joint Chiefs of Staff [USA]
JSM	Joint Staff Mission [of UK armed services in Washington]
k	knots
L	[Destroyer Flotilla] Leader
LAA	Light Anti-Aircraft gun
Lab	Labour
LDD	Local Defence Division
LDV	Local Defence Volunteers
Lia O	Liaison Officer
Lib	Liberal
Lieut, Lt	Lieutenant
LS (I)	Landing Ship (Infantry)
LS (L)	Landing Ship (Large)
Lt-Cdr	Lieutenant-Commander
Lt-Col	Lieutenant-Colonel
Lt-Gen	Lieutenant-General
Maj	Major
Maj-Gen	Major-General
Mdshpmn	Midshipman
Med	Mediterranean
mg	machine gun
Mil	Military
Minr	Minister
ML	Motor Launch
M/L	Mine Laying
MNBDO	Mobile Naval Base Defence Organisation
MOI	Ministry of Information
M/R	Medium Range
M/S	Mine Sweeping
MT	Mechanical Transport ship
MV	Motor Vessel
MTB	Motor Torpedo Boat
MWT	Ministry of War Transport
NA	Naval Attaché
NAS	North Atlantic Station
Nav O	Navigating Officer
NAWI	North America and West Indies Station
ND	US Navy Department

NLO	Naval Liaison Officer
NID	Naval Intelligence Division
NOIC	Naval Officer in Charge
OC	Officer Commanding
OD	Operations Division
ONO	Office of Naval Operations [US Navy]
PD	Plans Division
PM	Prime Minister
PPS	Parliamentary Private Secretary
PRU	Photographic Reconnaissance Unit
PSD	Personal Services Division
(R)	Repeated
RA	Rear Admiral (A): Air; (D): Destroyers; (Q): Quartermaster
RA	Royal Artillery
RAN	Royal Australian Navy
RANASIO	Rear Admiral Naval Air Stations Indian Ocean
RCN	Royal Canadian Navy
RDF	Radio Direction Finding [radar]
RE	Royal Engineers
Res	Reserve
Ret List	Retired List
RFC	Royal Flying Corps
RFA	Royal Fleet Auxiliary
RIN	Royal Indian Navy
RM	Royal Marines
RME	Royal Marine Engineers
RNC	Royal Naval College
RNR	Royal Naval Reserve
RNSC	Royal Naval Staff College
RNVR	Royal Naval Volunteer Reserve
RNZN	Royal New Zealand Navy
RSig (TA)	Royal Signals (Territorial Army)
R/T	Radio Telephony
R/V	Rendezvous
SAAF	South African Air Force
SAC	Supreme Allied Commander
SACSEA	Supreme Allied Commander South East Asia
SAP	Semi-Armour Piercing
SBNO	Senior British Naval Officer
SD (Y)	Signal Division (Y) [intelligence gathering]
SEAC	South East Asia Command

Sec St	Secretary of State
SF	Submarine Flotilla
SGO	Senior Gunnery Officer
Sig O	Signal Officer
S/M	Submarine
SN	Steam Navigation
SNO	Senior Naval Officer
SO	Staff Officer (I): Intelligence; (O): Operations; (P): Plans
SOE	Special Operations Executive
Sqdn	Squadron
Sqdn Ldr	Squadron Leader
SS	Steam Ship
t	tonnage [displacement]
TA	Territorial Army
T/B	Torpedo Bomber
TBS	A very high frequency voice communication system
TF	Task Force
TL	Their Lordships
TMD	Torpedoes and Mining Division
TOO	Time of Origin
TSD	Training and Staff Duties
TSR	Torpedo Spotter Reconnaissance
tt	torpedo tubes
USec	Under Secretary
USNLO	US Naval Liaison Officer
VA	Vice Admiral
VACAC	Vice Admiral Aircraft Carriers
VACNA	Vice Admiral Commanding North Atlantic
VC	Victoria Cross
VCIGS	Vice Chief of Imperial General Staff
VCNS	Vice Chief of Naval Staff
VPres	Vice President [of the United States]
V/S	Visual Signalling
WO	Warrant Officer
WRNS	Women's Royal Naval Service
W/T	Wireless Telegraphy
1st Lord	First Lord of the Admiralty
1SL, 2SL, etc.	First, Second, etc. Sea Lords

CHRONOLOGY OF THE LIFE AND CAREER OF ADMIRAL OF THE FLEET SIR JAMES SOMERVILLE

(From Admiral Somerville's service record in ADM 196/47, Public Record Office, and other sources.)

17 July 1882	Born.
15 January 1897	Entered *Britannia*, Dartmouth as a cadet.
1 June 1898	Appointed to *Magnificent*.
15 June 1898	Became a Midshipman.
28 March 1899	Appointed to *Warspite*, Pacific Station.
15 December 1901	Promoted Acting Sub-Lieutenant.
30 April 1903	Served aboard *Sturgeon*, *Triumph* and *Tiger*.
5 October 1903	Appointed to *Pegasus*, Mediterranean Fleet.
15 March 1904	Promoted Lieutenant.
March 1904	Appointed to *Kent*.
29 October 1904	Appointed to *Sutlej*, Home Fleet (to 18 November 1904); China Station (19 November 1904–6 May 1906).
May 1906	Aboard *St George* for manoeuvres.
30 July 1906	Appointed to *Devonshire*.
2 September 1907	Appointed to *Vernon*; qualified as a torpedo officer and wireless telegraphy specialist.
12 June 1909	Appointed to *Goliath* for W/T duties on staff of Rear Admiral Jerram.
7 October 1909	Appointed to *Vivid* for eventual transfer to *Vanguard*, as torpedo and W/T officer.
3 January 1912	Appointed to *Vernon* for experiments with Poulsen W/T system and general W/T duties.

15 March 1912	Promoted Lieutenant-Commander.
January 1913	Married Mary Kerr Main.
8 May 1914	Appointed to *Vindictive* as W/T officer.
9 July 1914	Appointed to *Marlborough* and as W/T officer, 1st Battle Squadron.
20 December 1914	Appointed to *Lord Nelson* as W/T officer on staff of Vice Admiral Sir Lewis Bayly, C-in-C, Channel Fleet (succeeded on 17 January 1915 by Vice Admiral Sir A.E. Bethell).
February 1915	Transferred to *Prince of Wales*.
21 March 1915	Appointed to *Egmont* as W/T officer.
13 May 1915	Appointed to *Lord Nelson* on staff of Vice Admiral John de Robeck, C-in-C, Eastern Mediterranean Squadron.
31 December 1915	Promoted Commander.
14 March 1916	Appointed DSO for exceptionally able service as a communications officer (ship to shore) in Gallipoli operations.
3 November 1916	Appointed to *Vernon* for Signal School.
January 1917	Appointed to *King George V*, flagship, 2nd Battle Squadron, as Fleet W/T Officer, Grand Fleet.
1917	Son John born.
December 1917	Experimental Commander, Signal School, Portsmouth.
1920	Daughter Rachel born.
5 March 1920	Appointed to *Ajax*, Mediterranean Fleet, as Executive Officer.
October 1921	Appointed to *Emperor of India*, Mediterranean Fleet.
31 December 1921	Promoted Captain.
1 April 1922	Appointed Deputy Director, Signal Division, Admiralty.
20 August 1922	Appointed to *Benbow*, Mediterranean Fleet, in command and as Flag Captain to Rear Admiral John D. Kelly and later Rear Admiral Hugh D.R. Watson, 4th Battle Squadron.

7 February 1925	Appointed Director, Signal Division, Admiralty.
23 March 1927	Appointed to *Victory* for Senior Officers' Tactical Course.
6 May 1927	Appointed to *Barham* in command and as Flag Captain and Chief of Staff to Vice Admiral John D. Kelly; transferred to *Warspite* and (1 September 1928) back to *Barham*.
1 June 1929	Appointed to the staff of the Imperial Defence College.
21 September 1931	Appointed to *Victory* for Tactical Course.
28 December 1931	*Norfolk* in command; with Captain John Tovey investigated lower deck complaints after Invergordon Mutiny.
14 October 1932	Appointed to *Victory* as Commodore (2nd Class), RN Barracks, Portsmouth.
12 October 1933	Promoted Rear Admiral.
11 May 1934	Appointed Director of Personal Services, Admiralty.
1 January 1935	Appointed CB.
25 February 1936	Appointed to *Victory* for Senior Officers' Tactical Course.
8 April 1936	Hoisted flag aboard *Galatea* as Rear Admiral (D), Mediterranean Fleet.
July 1936	Outbreak of Spanish Civil War; constantly occupied off Spain's Mediterranean coasts.
May 1937	Guest on board Royal Yacht *Victoria and Albert* at Coronation Naval Review, Spithead.
11 September 1937	Promoted Vice Admiral.
1 October 1938	Succeeded Vice Admiral Sir Alexander Ramsay as C-in-C, East Indies Station.
12 April 1939	Invalided home with suspected pulmonary tuberculosis.
8 June 1939	Knighted (KCB).
31 July 1939	Placed on retired list on grounds of ill health.
2 September 1939	Made first BBC Broadcast.

6 September 1939	Joined Admiralty for special service in Signal Division; Chairman, Inter-Service Committee for Radio Interception.
1 January 1940	Joined Department of Anti-Aircraft Weapons and Devices, Admiralty.
27 May 1940	Joined *Lynx* (Dover) to assist Vice Admiral Sir Bertram Ramsay with operation DYNAMO (evacuation of BEF).
5 June 1940	Appointed Inspector of A/A Weapons and Devices.
27 June 1940	Appointed to command Force H.
1 July 1940	Assumed command of Force H.
3 July 1940	Commanded Force H in bombardment of French Fleet, Mers-el-Kebir.
6 July 1940	Disablement of *Dunkerque*, Mers-el-Kebir, by *Ark Royal*'s aircraft.
27 November 1940	Action against Italian Fleet off Cape Spartivento.
9 February 1941	Bombardment of Genoa.
24–27 May 1941	Pursuit and sinking of *Bismarck*.
21–27 July 1941	SUBSTANCE convoy to Malta.
27–28 September 1941	HALBERD convoy to Malta
13–14 November 1941	Loss of *Ark Royal*.
6 January 1942	Left Force H.
12 February 1942	Appointed C-in-C, Eastern Fleet.
17 February 1942	Sailed from Clyde in *Formidable*.
28 March 1942	Hoisted flag at Colombo.
30 March–9 April 1942	Japanese raids on Eastern Fleet, Ceylon and shipping in Indian Ocean.
6 April 1942	Promoted Admiral on the Retired List.
May 1942	Operation IRONCLAD (seizure of Madagascar).
May 1942–September 1943	Eastern Fleet based at Kilindini, Kenya.
September 1943	Eastern Fleet returned to Ceylon.
7 October 1943	Admiral Lord Louis Mountbatten arrived in Delhi as Supreme Allied Commander, South East Asia.
19 April 1944	Aircraft from *Illustrious* and *Saratoga* attacked Sabang, off Sumatra.

17 May 1944	Carrier planes attacked Sourabaya, Java.
25 July 1944	Eastern Fleet air and surface ship bombardment of Sabang.
10 August 1944	Restored to Active List.
22 August 1944	Promoted GCB.
23 August 1944	Turned over Eastern Fleet to Admiral Sir Bruce Fraser.
27 October 1944	Took over as head of the British Admiralty Delegation in Washington.
8 May 1945	VE-Day. Promoted Admiral of the Fleet.
15 August 1945	VJ-Day.
18 August 1945	Lady Somerville died.
16 December 1945	Left Washington.
1 January 1946	Promoted GBE.
21 January 1946	Appointed to Admiralty for special service.
27 April 1946	End of active service.
August 1946	Appointed Lord-Lieutenant of Somerset.
19 March 1949	Died at Dinder.

PART I

FLAG COMMANDS AND OTHER ACTIVE SERVICE
April 1936–June 1940

INTRODUCTION

James Fownes Somerville, born in 1882, was descended from a long line of country gentlemen. He grew up on the family estate at Dinder, near Wells in Somerset, developing a love of the countryside, its pursuits and its people. Though he was an infrequent visitor to his ancestral estate after he entered *Britannia* in 1897, he yearned always for the life of a country squire and it exercised almost as much of a pull on him as the development of his naval career. It was only after his retirement from the Royal Navy in 1946 that he was able to settle down at Dinder, in a very different rural milieu and for only three crowded years.[1]

In his mature years James Somerville came to be known as an extrovert figure, full of boisterous and often bawdy humour, an inspiring and ebullient leader of men and a man of apparently inexhaustible energy. Though his love of fun was inherent, his outgoing personality was acquired deliberately, as part of his perception of what was required of a commander. As a young man, he was on the small and slight side and his subsequent zest and drive might have been intended to prove to himself and others that he was capable of making good in his chosen career.

It seems that James himself chose the Navy as his career, thus perpetuating a strong thread of naval history in the family, including connections with the redoubtable Hood family. In his term in *Britannia*, which he joined in January 1897 at the age of fourteen, were a number of boys later to achieve flag rank, including Admiral Sir Charles Little[2] and most notably Admiral of the Fleet Viscount Cunningham of Hyndhope,[3] who

---

[1]There is one biography of Somerville, *Fighting Admiral: The Life of Admiral of the Fleet Sir James Somerville* (London: Evans Bros., 1961), by the distinguished escort group commander and well-known writer on naval history, Captain Donald Macintyre.

[2]Adm Sir Charles Little: Capt 1917; RA 1929; VA 1933; Adm 1937; 2SL, 1938–41; Head, BAD, Washington, 1941–2; C-in-C, Portsmouth, 1942.

[3]Adm of the Fleet Viscount Cunningham of Hyndhope (Andrew Browne Cunningham, 1883–1963): joined *Britannia* 1897; Mdshpmn 1898; S African War 1900; Lieut 1904; destroyer cmds 1908–19; Cdr 1915; Med 1913–18; Grand F 1918; Baltic 1919; Capt 1920; Capt (D), 6 & 1DFs, 1922; Capt-in-Charge, Port Edgar, 1924–5; Flag Capt & COS, *Calcutta* & *Despatch*, N Am. & WI, 1926–8; IDC 1929; CO, *Rodney* 1929–30; Cdre, Chatham Barracks, 1931; RA 1932; RA (D), Med F, 1934–6; VA 1936; VA, BCS & 2nd-in-C, Med F 1937–8; DCNS 1938–9; Actg Adm & C-in-C, Med, June 1939–April 1942; Adm, Jan 1941; Head, BAD, 1942; N C-in-C, TORCH, Nov 1942; C-in-C, Med, Jan–Oct 1943; Adm of Fleet, Jan 1943; 1SL Oct 1943–June 1946; Viscount 1946; autobiography, *A Sailor's Odyssey* (London: Hutchinson, 1951). An edition of his papers, by the editor of this volume, will form forthcoming volumes in this series.

remained a close friend throughout Somerville's life. James's first appointment as a Midshipman was to HMS *Magnificent*[1] in June 1898 and over the next few years he served in several ships of different types and on the Home, Mediterranean, Pacific and China Stations. It was on the Pacific Station, while serving aboard *Warspite*[2] that he contracted typhoid and narrowly escaped death, chiefly, it seems, by his own will to live. Promoted Acting Sub-Lieutenant in 1901, he became a Lieutenant in 1904, his exceptional promise having been noted by all of his commanding officers. Their reports drew attention to his all-round ability, zeal, tact, organising skills, determination and good judgment. In particular they noted his gift for scientific and technical studies, most conspicuously the then novel subject of wireless telegraphy. In 1907 he joined *Vernon*,[3] qualifying as a torpedo specialist, with a particular interest in radio communications. He was promoted Lieutenant-Commander in 1912 and all of his appointments between 1909 and 1920 were as a W/T specialist. He had further spells at *Vernon* to conduct experiments with the Poulsen radio transmitting system and during the Great War he served as Fleet W/T Officer in the Channel Fleet (1914–15), the Eastern Mediterranean Squadron (1915–16) and the Grand Fleet (1917–18). In the Mediterranean he served under Vice Admiral John de Robeck,[4] who quickly noted his promise and constantly recommended his accelerated promotion. Somerville was promoted Commander in December 1915. De Robeck's force supported the Gallipoli landings and carried out the eventual evacuation of the peninsula. For outstanding service in maintaining communications between the fleet and the forces ashore, under constant fire and the other hazards of an opposed landing and a fighting retreat, Somerville was awarded the DSO in 1916.

Somerville had married Mary Kerr Main, a colonel's daughter, in 1913. Mollie Somerville came from Hampshire, within striking distance of both London and Portsmouth and it was at Curdridge near Southampton that the Somervilles settled – in so far as a naval family settles anywhere. James was never entirely happy in Hampshire – he hankered always after more rustic Somerset. A devoted couple, James and Mollie corresponded almost daily when they were apart, which was more often that not. Their son John followed his father into the Navy,

---

[1]*Magnificent*: 1895, 14,900t, 4×12in, 12×6in, 5tt, 16.5k.

[2]*Warspite*: 1884, 8400t, 4×9.2in 10×6in, 6tt, 17k.

[3]*Vernon*: the Navy's torpedo school, which housed the early radio training and development establishment.

[4]Adm of the Fleet Sir John De Robeck (1862–1928): *Britannia* 1875–7; China and Newfoundland service; highly effective instr; CO *Pyramus*; Capt 1902; Insping Capt of Trng Ships; RA 1911; Adm of Patrols, Home Waters; 9 CS 1914; VA 1914; 2nd-in-C, Dardanelles 1915 & i/c March 1915; VA, 2BS, Grand F 1916–19; C-in-C, Med 1919–22; Adm 1920; C-in-C, Atl F 1922–4; Adm of Fleet 1925.

served in destroyers during the Second World War and similarly developed a talent for communications work. After the war, he left the Navy and had a distinguished career at GCHQ. His wife Elizabeth, who served ashore in the Eastern Fleet as a WRNS, is the daughter of Vice Admiral C.R. Payne.[1] Rachel Somerville also served as a WRNS officer in the Second World War and at the end of the war was with her father at the British Admiralty Delegation in Washington. Lady Somerville fell critically ill in August 1945 and Sir James flew home to be with her; unfortunately she did not recover and died a few days after VJ-Day.

After the First World War, Somerville gained command experience, first as executive officer of the battleship *Ajax*,[2] which was serving with the Mediterranean Fleet, transferring later to the flagship *Emperor of India*.[3] In December 1921 he was promoted Captain and spent 18 months as Deputy Director of the Signal Division at the Admiralty. Returning to the Mediterranean, he took up his first command, the battleship *Benbow*.[4] He was also Flag Captain to his old mentor, Rear Admiral John D. Kelly,[5] and his successor Rear Admiral Hugh Watson.[6] Though he was a highly successful big ship captain, earning further plaudits from Kelly, he experienced three spells of serious illness during the early twenties – pneumonia and typhoid in 1923 and a hernia in 1925. Despite 'grave anxiety' over his pneumonia, he once again recovered strongly and went on to head the Signal Division between 1925 and 1927. During this time he represented the Admiralty on the Radio Research Board and on a committee supervising the training of telegraphists. The Board of Trade expressed its 'high appreciation' of his services on the government's Wireless Direction Finding Committee, particularly for his work as chairman of the sub-committee on Marine Direction Finding. In 1927, after taking the Senior Officers' Tactical Course, he returned to the Mediterranean in command of *Barham*,[7] once again serving as Flag Captain and Chief of Staff to Kelly, now a Vice Admiral. In 1928 he transferred to *Barham*'s sister ship *Warspite*[8] and when she was badly

[1]Vice Adm C.R. Payne: Capt 1912; RA 1923; VA 1928; Ret List.
[2]*Ajax*: 1913, 23,000t, 10×13.5in, 14×4in, 2tt, 21k.
[3]*Emperor of India*: 1914, 25,000t, 10×13.5in, 12×6in, 4tt, 21k.
[4]*Benbow*: as 3.
[5]Adm of the Fleet Sir John D. Kelly (1871–1936): ent RN 1884; Lt 1893; Cdr 1904; Capt 1911; CO, *Dublin* 1914; chased *Goeben & Breslau*; Dardanelles 1915; *Devonshire, Weymouth, Princess Royal*; DOD 1919; RA 1921; RA, 4BS, Home F 1922–3; 4SL 1924; VA 1926; 1BS & 2nd-in-C, Med F 1927–9; Adm Cmdg Reserves 1929–31; Adm 1930; C-in-C, Atl F, foll Invergordon Mutiny, 1931–3; C-in-C Portsmouth 1934–6; Adm of Fleet 1936; elder bro of Adm Sir W. A. Howard Kelly.
[6]Rear Adm (later Adm Sir) Hugh Watson: Capt 1908; RA 1920; VA 1925; Adm 1929.
[7]*Barham*: 1916, 31,100t, 8×15in, 12×6in, 8×4in. 24k; sunk E Med, 25 Nov 1941, *U331*.
[8]*Warspite*: 1915; 30,600t, 8×15in, 12×6in, 24k; extensively modernised 1937–40, with 20×4.5in AA, 32,700t.

damaged on an uncharted rock (no blame was attached to him) he returned to *Barham*, buoyed by further outstanding reports from Kelly. In June 1929 he was seconded to the Imperial Defence College as an instructor and followed this with a further tactical course. Following the Invergordon Mutiny in 1931, Admiral Kelly was appointed C-in-C, Home Fleet. As a Kelly protege, Somerville, together with Captain John Tovey,[1] was given the task of investigating lower deck conditions and complaints and then recommending reforms, and also commanded the heavy cruiser *Norfolk*.[2] Following his cogent and sympathetic report, he was appointed Commodore of the naval barracks at Portsmouth in October 1932. During his time at Portsmouth he helped to set up a Naval Tailors' Association and the Royal Naval Housing Association, which drastically improved the domestic economy of many ratings' families. In 1933 he was promoted Rear Admiral, returning to the Admiralty in May 1934 as Director of Personal Services.

Somerville's first flag command was a daunting one – Rear Admiral (Destroyers), Mediterranean Fleet, flying his flag in the new light cruiser *Galatea*.[3] Unlike his predecessor, Somerville had no first hand acquaintance with the rather clannish world of destroyers. When Somerville took up his duties in April 1936, the Mediterranean had become a diplomatic earthquake zone. At the eastern end, under the frustrated gaze of the Mediterranean Fleet, Italy was subduing Abyssinia. In the west, Spain was on the verge of civil war, a conflict which embroiled in some degree all of the major European powers and at times threatened to act as the touchpaper for a general European war. The Spanish imbroglio placed a great strain on the Mediterranean Fleet's flotilla craft and for two years Somerville was generally the Senior British Naval Officer off Spain's Mediterranean coasts, more diplomat than warrior. Much the most challenging feature of Somerville's appointment was that he was following the Royal Navy's most outstanding destroyer leader, Rear Admiral Andrew Cunningham. It was, therefore, an appointment well calculated to test to the full his capacity for high command. It is thus appropriate to begin the documentary selection with this appointment.

As the crisis in the eastern Mediterranean caused by Italian aggression against Ethiopia began to fade in the summer of 1936, it was succeeded by a fresh altercation at the western end. On 31 July Somerville and his

---

[1] Adm of the Fleet Lord (John C.) Tovey (1885–1971): *Britannia* 1900; CO *Jackal* 1915; *Onslow* 1916; distinguished service at Jutland; Cdr 1916; *Ursa* 1917; *Wolfhound*; RNSC, Greenwich 1919–20; OD 1920–2; Capt 1923; Capt (D) 1923–5; IDC 1927; N Asst to 2SL 1928–30; *Rodney* 1932–4; Cdre RN Barracks, Chatham 1935; RA 1936; RA (D), Med F 1938; VA 1939; 2nd-in-C, Med F 1940; Actg Adm & C-in-C, Home F 1940–3; Adm 1942; C-in-C Nore 1943; Adm of F 1943.
[2] *Norfolk*: 1930; 9925t, 8×8in, 8×4in, 8tt, 32.25k.
[3] *Galatea*: 1935, 5250t, 6×6in, 8×4in, 6tt, 32.25k; sunk E Med, 15 Dec 1941, *U557*.

flagship *Galatea*, with the C-in-C, Mediterranean, Admiral Sir Dudley Pound,[1] on board, left Malta for Spanish waters, following news of civil war in Spain and, more urgently, the possibility of hostilities in the international port of Tangier. For the next two years, most of Somerville's time was occupied in protecting British interests in western Mediterranean waters. His tasks were to safeguard the lives of British citizens, ensure that British merchantmen proceeded unhindered about their lawful business, prevent gun-running, enforce international law and maintain the Royal Navy's long tradition of humanitarian relief. Like most civil wars, the conflict in Spain was extremely bitter and savage. The situation was complicated by the difficulty of establishing the legitimacy of local commanders and civil authorities. Further twists were added by the intervention of the Russians on the Government, or Republican, side, and of the Italians and Germans in support of General Franco[2] and the Falangists; ostensibly, all foreign participants were 'volunteers', a transparent disguise quickly penetrated by Somerville and other shrewd observers. The British were the most resolutely neutral of the great powers and this stance defined Somerville's conduct.

Somerville in *Galatea* and destroyers of his flotillas were constantly at sea, visiting the major ports of mainland Spain, the Balearic Islands, Tangier and the Spanish enclaves in North Africa. Like countless Royal Navy officers before him, Somerville was called upon to exercise all his reserves of humour, tact, judgment, patience and firmness. His knowledge of international law was examined constantly and exhaustively, as was his ability to liaise effectively with HM diplomatic corps, both sides in the conflict and the often slippery and meddlesome foreign naval officers and diplomats. Somerville never put a foot wrong, despite having to make many important decisions without reference to Pound or other higher authorities.

From the beginning Somerville took a blunt, no-nonsense line typical of a bluff seaman. He had absolute clarity of purpose and the resolution to carry it out, whereas most of those around him, naval or civilian, seemed to exhibit weakness, deceitfulness or opportunism; his contempt for them is evident in his letters to his wife [1–4], though his reports to

---

[1]Adm of the Fleet Sir A. Dudley P.R. Pound (1877–1943): *Britannia* 1891; Mdshpmn, Channel & China; CO of a torpedo boat 1897; torpedo splist; Cdr 1909; Instr, N Staff Coll 1913–14; Capt, Admy 1914; CO *Colossus*, Jutland, 1916; DOD (H) 1917; *Repulse* 1920–22; DPD 1922; COS, Med F 1925; RA 1926; ACNS 1927–9; BCS 1929; VA 1930; 2SL 1932; Adm 1935; C-in-C Med 1936–9; 1SL 1939–43.

[2]Gen Francisco Franco Y Bahamonde (1892–1975): COS Spanish Army 1936; sent to Canaries command by Govt 1936; part of right wing armed rising plot June 1936; flew to N Africa July 1936; aided in crossing to Spain by German & Italian aircraft; dictator of Spain 1939–75.

Pound [5, 7, 13, 14] were more circumspect. His distaste for the Republican side was marked [1, 2, 6], not unexpectedly given his social and professional background and the Republicans' predilection for murdering their officers. Nevertheless, in practice, Somerville was scrupulously even-handed in insisting on adherence by both parties to international law [1–14]. He struck up cordial relationships with both Spanish and foreign officers, even though situations were often delicate and he had to register protests at incidents affecting British merchant vessels [5, 8]. From time to time his unquenchable humour shone through, despite the difficult and often horrific situations with which he was confronted, such as the sinking of merchant ships by 'unknown' submarines, the bombing of civilian targets and the murder of naval officers by radical ships' companies, leaving him to rescue the widows and children [11–14]. Another rescue, of the crew of the Nationalist cruiser *Baleares*[1] by two of his destroyers, represented an extraordinarily fine piece of seamanship in highly dangerous conditions, superb testimony to the professional skill, courage, determination and humanity of the officers and men of the Royal Navy [15]. One of the few light spots in this phase of Somerville's career was the Coronation Naval Review, where his humour and charm came fully into play [10].

Following two arduous years in the bullring atmosphere of Mediterranean Spain, Somerville, now a Vice Admiral, went to the equally demanding East Indies Station. There, the problems were those of vast distances, incessant social engagements and the enervating climate. Constitutionally incapable of relaxing his pace to match the conditions, after a few months on the station, he was invalided home in April 1939. After spells in three naval hospitals, he was judged tubercular by three wise men at Chatham and compulsorily retired, despite his angry protests that the disease was safely in the past, a conviction shared by two Harley Street specialists whom he engaged.

Somerville went on the Retired List just a month before war broke out in Europe and on its eve he began what was to prove a highly popular series of radio commentaries on the war, strategy and sea power. Once the war began, the Admiralty called upon his considerable expertise in electronics and communications [16]. For six months, showing no sign of the fatigue associated with tuberculosis, he toured the country testing and developing radar and was largely responsible for ensuring that the Navy acquired sets at an early stage. Commander Howse, the historian of radar in the Royal Navy, has written that 'Much of the credit for the

[1]*Baleares*: 1936, 10, 670t, 8×8in, 8×4.7in, 12tt, 33k; hit by 2 torpedoes & a 6in shell in brief action with Govt cruisers & destroyers from Cartagena, while escorting Palma–N Africa convoy, 6 March 1938, later sank.

remarkable speed with which ships were equipped with radar during 1940 and 1941 must go to Somerville – in Watson-Watt's words, "the foster-father of naval radar" '.[1] Later, he headed an Admiralty section on Anti-Aircraft Weapons and Devices, which allowed him considerable latitude and suited his ebullient and energetic nature. His stamina, experience, decisiveness and capacity for leadership were put to an even sterner test when he became, somewhat accidentally, one of the key figures in operation DYNAMO, the evacuation of Allied forces from France in late May and early June 1940. He relieved Admiral Ramsay, commanding the Dover Straits,[2] for brief spells and in a few pithy sentences conveyed the stoicism at Calais, the scarcely tolerable strain imposed on flotilla craft and other small vessels, the incessant air raids and the breathless uncertainty of those days of unparalleled anxiety [17–19]. In the saga of providential delivery from utter disaster, Somerville played a characteristically vigorous and vital part, as Ramsay's tribute acknowledged [20].

The termination of operation DYNAMO was followed swiftly by France's total collapse and the signing of an armistice with Germany and Italy, which had joined the war in the hour of her neighbour's defeat. Not only did Britain now face a second enemy and a Mediterranean conflict without the assistance of her erstwhile ally, she could not be sure that the powerful French fleet would not be seized by the Axis powers, the terms of the armistice notwithstanding. Once again, Somerville's career took a dramatic turn and before June was out he was back in the western Mediterranean with a new flag command, Force H.

[1] I am greatly indebted to Cdr Derek Howse, author of the history of naval radar, for this information. See further D. Howse, *Radar at Sea: the Royal Navy in World War 2* (London: Macmillan, 1993), esp. pp. 11–12, 24, 32–44, 62. It is a matter of regret that no documents on Somerville's radar work suitable for reproduction are extant.

[2] Adm Sir Bertram Home Ramsay (1883–1945): *Britannia* 1898; NA & WI, E Indies stations; Somaliland expedition 1903–4; Lt 1904; signal splist; N War Coll 1913; Lt-Cdr 1914; Grand F 1914–15; *M25* 1915–17; Cdr 1916; *Broke* 1917–18; Flag Cdr to Jellicoe on Empire tour 1919–20; Med F 1920–3; Capt 1923; *Weymouth, Danae*; N War Coll 1927–9; *Kent*, China Sta 1929–31; IDC 1931–3; *Royal Sovereign* 1933–5; RA 1935; COS Home F but irritated by C-in-C (Adm Sir Roger Backhouse) & asked for relief Dec 1935; Ret List 1938; VA 1939; FO Dover 1939–42; FO & chief planner for Med landings 1942–3; planned NEPTUNE from Dec 1943 & ANXCF 1944–5; died in air accident, NW France, 2 Jan 1945.

1. *To his wife*

HMS *Galatea*, at sea,
31 July 1936

. . . The trouble is that the Spanish Navy – Communists – are using Tangier as a base and preventing Franco from taking troops across to Spain. By international convention Tangier is not to be used as a base for operations so we are going there to tell them to get to hell out of it or agree to have their machines and guns disabled. At least that is what DP[ound] wants to do but this is strictly entre nous. We are getting the anti-aircraft guns ready in case any of the Spanish aircraft attack us or ships in the vicinity. I wish they would as we would learn them a lesson all right but I'm afraid they won't.

2. *To his wife*

Tangier,
6 August 1936

About 3 p.m. one of the Spanish destroyers put to sea and we heard later of Franco's successful sortie across the straits from Ceuta to Algeciras when he managed to land some 2000 troops and a good deal of ammunition, etc. Apparently his ships were attacked by some of the submarines and the destroyers which use this place as a base, but they were driven off which just shows what a feeble lot they are, as they ought to have made mincemeat of Franco's party.

This morning the weather moderated a bit and we were able to establish communication though boat-work was still somewhat hazardous. I received a copy of a protest by General Franco against the use of Tangier by Spanish Government vessels and threatening if they did not cease he would take action against them here. I went over to see old Falangola[1] to find out how he reacted and was pleasantly surprised that he accepted my point of view, namely that until Franco is duly recognised as a belligerent it is not possible to deny the use of Tangier to Spanish Naval forces since technically no state of war exists until our respective Governments recognise Franco officially as a belligerent. He agreed that if Franco

[1]Rear Adm M. Falangola, Italian SNO, Tangier 1936.

attempted to attack the Spanish ships here it was our duty to defend the neutrality of Tangier and take action against him and finally that the continued presence of Spanish ships here constitutes a grave threat to the neutrality of Tangier. He tried to get me to agree that the Spanish ships were no longer acting under the orders of their Government and therefore had no *locus standi*. However I would not agree to this as I said I had no official evidence that such was the case. On the whole he was very fair-minded though of course he may be playing a double game. I happened to know that he and Rossi the Italian minister proposed visiting Franco at Ceuta yesterday and expressed my regrets that the weather had interfered with his 'excursion'. He spotted what I meant and with a twinkle in his eye he gave me an expressive shrug. Apparently he has found out that I go 'beetling'[1] and told me that it was 'Magnifico Splendido'. I don't think he can quite size me up and I'd love to see his reports on me to his Government. I went ashore to see Gye the Consul General[2] who was excessively diplomatic and nebulous. If we *do* have to take any action it's pretty clear that I shall have to take the lead as he's too damn slow for words . . .

3. To his wife

Tangier,
7 August 1936

Ever such a flap last night when Falangola's Flag Lieut came over to see me at 10.15 p.m. to report that an ultimatum had been received from General Franco to the effect that unless the Spanish ships were out of Tangier in 48 hours he would attack them. I said 'right ho' and that I was going to bed which I did but this morning I went over to see old Falangola and asked him what it was about. He was as slippery as an eel. Argued all round the corner until I pinned him down and said, 'What will you do, Admiral, if Franco starts bombing the Spanish ships in Tangier?' and he replied 'I will only shoot if bombs fall close to the *Savoia*[3] (his flagship). I told him I would shoot if bombs fell anywhere in the neutral territory of Tangier, which seemed to disturb him. And when I suggested that we should put the wheels on our respective seaplanes, fly them to the civil aerodrome here and use them to pursue Mr Franco's

---

[1]'Beetling' referred to Somerville's habit when in harbour of going for an early morning row in his skiff or 'beetle'.

[2]Ernest F. Gye: b 1879; FO 1903; served in Tehran; Con Gen, Tangier. April 1933–Oct 1936; Minister Plenipotentiary, Caracas Oct 1936; ret Oct 1939.

[3]*Eugenio di Savoia*: 1936, 8997t, 8×6in, 6×3.9in, 6tt, 34.5k; surrendered to Med F 1943.

planes he nearly had a fit. He evidently doesn't mean to do anything that would upset Franco but at the same time is very embarrassed at not being able to carry out his bold declarations when there appeared to be no prospect of any action being required. I twitted him a bit on this and he pursed up his mouth and gave immense shrugs. . . . I then went to see Gye the Consul General and found him just off to a meeting of the Commission and wobbling like a jelly. 'We can't have bombs and things being dropped here, you know', etc. I only had 10 minutes with him in the car on the way to the meeting and said 'You don't mean to tell me that you won't insist on a reply being sent to Franco that if he dares to drop a bomb in Tangier or send a man across the border he will be repelled by every means at the disposal of the Commission?'. Eventually I got him to say that he would . . . I also asked him to get the Commission to recommend that Franco should be recognised by the Powers as a belligerent. Once this is done the Spanish ships have no right at all in here and we can kick them out.

I have advocated this consistently for the last five days and was rather interested to see a signal from DP to the Admiralty last night pressing that this should be done as soon as possible. It's high time we took a strong line with these bloody Spaniards. If anyone drops a brick near me he'll certainly know all about it. . . .

Just got the report of the Commission's meeting. Not a ruddy word about a strong answer to Franco. Apparently the Frenchman said he'd heard the Spanish Govt. had given orders to withdraw so the Spanish Minister is 'making enquiries' of the Captain of the *Tofino* and will report in due course at a later meeting this evening. Weak-kneed lot of rats. Suggestion made that if order is confirmed we should enforce it. I don't believe it's legal to do so until Franco is recognised as a belligerent. Anyway the Commission accepted that part of my minute to Gye and have recommended early recognition. All bar the Spaniard who of course would not agree.

4.   *To his wife*

Tangier,
8 August 1936

A somewhat strenuous time since I last wrote. . . . Rossi broke the news to me that it would be necessary to call a meeting of the Committee of Control at 10 p.m. to consider the Franco ultimatum and that the Senior Naval Officers would be asked to attend at 11 p.m. to consider 'certain technical aspects'. . . .

De Lanley[1] – poor old boy – greeted me in a lousy suit of whites. He was very disturbed at the Franco ultimatum but told me 'in confidence' that if the Franco planes come over to bomb Spanish ships he would not fire a shot. I told him I regretted the lack of support from himself and Falangola but I should open fire immediately and no doubt he would be credited with part of the bombardment! He had some *very* confused ideas on international law which he expounded.

At ... 11.20 ... we were summoned to the meeting. We sat until 1.15 a.m. this morning and never have I seen such a spineless ignorant crowd. They all talked voluble French which I found difficulty in following but when it came to the legal aspects I insisted on talking English and set about them good and hearty. The Spanish minister was frightfully bucked when I said the Commission had no legal right to eject the Spanish ships. But when he argued that the *Tofino* was only a surveying ship ... I said it was 'fantastique', that I personally had observed her victualling the submarines and I was absolutely satisfied she was a Spanish war vessel actively engaged in hostilities. He looked at me as if I'd murdered his grandmother. Gye was a proper 'yes' man and did nothing to support me except to translate my statements into French. Eventually they accepted my point of view that until Franco was recognised as a belligerent we could only *request* Spanish ships to leave and that even if they disobeyed the order of their Govt. to this effect we had no right to enforce it. I then asked what action this Commission wished us to take if Franco bombed Spanish ships at Tangier. Although I repeated this question on three occasions I could get no reply. It was finally agreed that a joint body of officers from the ships should board *Tofino* this morning and on behalf of the Committee request her to leave. After the meeting I told Gye that it was the most spineless gathering of windbags I'd ever met. Rossi was off to interview Franco at Tetuan this morning but no one knew what he was going to say to him and I am positive it will be merely that the Committee is taking all steps to effect the removal of Spanish ships from Tangier. Actually at 2.20 a.m. just after I got back to the ship we received a message that the *Tofino* was leaving today by order of the Spanish Govt. and that the submarines would not return. This practically finished the crisis at Tangier but leaves a damn bad taste in my mouth. The Committee ought to have told Franco to go to hell and Falangola and de Lanley ought to have declared their readiness to assist me in repelling any direct military threat by Franco.

---

[1]Capt J. F. M. Bahezre de Lanley, French Navy: b 1884; ent navy 1902; Capitaine de Frégate 1926; Capitaine de Vaisseau 1933; cmded 5 ships 1918–34, inc *Suffren* 1934–6; ret list 1937.

5. *To Admiral Sir Dudley Pound*

HMS *Galatea*, at sea,
9 August 1936

Report on a Visit to Tangier

2. . . . The following vessels were in harbour:–

HMS *Brilliant*
Italian Cruiser *Eugenio di Savoia*, flying the Flag of Rear Admiral
M. Falangola
Italian Cable Ship *Citta di Milano*
French Cruiser *Suffren*
Portuguese Destroyers *Dao* and *Tejo*
Spanish (Government) TB 15 and Surveying Ship *Tofino*[1]

4. The following day, 2 August, the Levanter[2] had diminished in violence, and at 1000 I called on Admiral Falangola, and received calls from the Captains of *Suffren* and *Tejo*. I also called on HBM Consul General. I took the opportunity of discussing the situation at Tangier with these four Officers and forwarded a report of the conversations to you.
6. At 0910 on 4 August, HBM Consul General returned my call and later, in his company, I called on the President of the Commission of Control (Signor Rossi, the Italian Consul General); the Administrator (M. Le Fure) and the Mendoub (Sultan's representative). . . .
7. On 5 August I received a message from Rear Admiral, Gibraltar,[3] that bombs had fallen near British SS *Hedon* and Dutch SS *Zonnewyer*[4] three to four miles E of Europa Point. He asked that General Franco should be reminded of the protest of 22 July and that this protest should be vigorously renewed and assurances asked for that indiscriminate bombing should cease forthwith. This message was passed to HBM Consul General for transmission to General Franco.
10. At 1130, Captain (D), 4th Flotilla, arrived at Tangier in *Keith* from Gibraltar, bringing with him Lt-Col Burney of the Gordon Highlanders

[1]*Brilliant*: 1931, 1360t, 4×4.7in, 8tt, 35k.
Citta di Milano: unidentified.
Suffren: 1930, 10,000t, 8×8in, 8×3in, 6tt, 31.3k.
Dao, Tejo: 1935–6, 1219t, 4×4.7in, 4tt, 36k.
TB15: *c*. 1915, 177t, 3tt.
[2]The Levanter is a strong, swirling wind of the W Mediterranean.
[3]Vice Adm James M. Pipon: Capt 1920; RA 1932; RAIC & Adm Supt, Gibraltar, 1935–7; Ret List 1936; SBNO, S C Australia 1940–1; FOIC Southampton 1942–4.
[4]Probably *Zonnewijk*: 1928, 4499gt, NV Stoom Maats, Rotterdam. *Hedon* unidentified.

and General Staff Officer Major Martin, RA. These Officers lunched with me and in the afternoon the two Military Officers and my Squadron Gunnery Officer proceeded ashore to consider the best means of defence of the British Consulate General and the Villa de France Hotel in the event of an internal rising in Tangier. They returned to *Keith* at 1600 and the latter sailed for Gibraltar at 1630.[1]

11.   Consequent on your message timed 2211 of 8 August, *Galatea* sailed from Tangier at 0800 today, Sunday, 9 August, patrolled the Straits at Gibraltar and arrived at Gibraltar at 1400.

6.   *To his wife*

Palma, Majorca,
17 August 1936

. . . We left Gib. at 9 a.m. on Friday and after we had cleared the harbour I announced that we were bound for Palma and not Valencia as everyone thought. Just south of Europa Point we sighted *Lepanto*[2] – a Spanish Government destroyer – on patrol. She seemed a bit close to the 3 mile limit so I steered down towards her and she sheered off and finally we were both steaming E at about 15 knots, *Lepanto* being about 1½ miles on our starboard beam. At 9.30 a large aircraft passed overhead steering towards Spain and then turned and came back. No sooner did *Lepanto* spot her than she went to action stations, increased speed and closed to within 7 cables of us. The idea was quite obvious – she was afraid of being bombed and thought if she closed us the aircraft would hesitate to drop any bombs for fear of hitting us. I at once told *Galatea* to alter course to the northward and increase speed so as to shake off *Lepanto*. The latter did not have the nerve to follow us in this manoeuvre and sheered off at full speed to the southward. After that we had a dull trip to Palma where we arrived at 4.30 p.m. on Saturday 15. Here we

[1]Capt (D), 4DF, was Denis W. Boyd: Capt 1931; Capt (D) 4DF 1936; *Vernon* i/c 1938; *Illustrious* 1940; Actg RA (A) Med F April 1941; RA July 1941; RA (A) Eastern F 1942; 5SL & Chief N Air Eqpt 1943; VA June 1944; Adm (A) June 1945; C-in-C BPF June 1946.

Lt-Col G. T. Burney: 2Lt 1909; Lt 1910; W Africa 1912–18; W Front 1918; Capt 1915; Maj 1923; W Africa 1924–30; Lt-Col 1934; Col 1937; Temp Brig 1939.

Major G. N. C. Martin RA: 2Lt 1912; W Front 1914–18; Lt 1915; Capt 1916; SO, N Cmd 1928–31; Maj 1930; R Mil Coll, Canada 1931–3; WO 1934–5; GSO, Gibraltar 1935–8; Lt-Col 1938; Col 1940; Temp Brig 1941; Brig W Cmd 1943.

The Sqdn Gunnery Officer was Cdr (later Rear Adm) Sir, Anthony Wass Buzzard, Bt: Lt-Cdr & SO (O) to RA (D), Med F 1934; Cdr 1936 & SGO; PD 1937–40; CO *Gurkha* 1940; SO (O) Force H June 1940; Capt 1941; PD 1942; *Glory* 1944.

[2]*Lepanto*: 1930, 1676t, 4×4.7in, 6tt, 36k.

found an Italian destroyer, the *Maestrale* commanded by a Captain Biancheri and soon after we had anchored the British Vice Consul came on board. He is a retired Lt-Cdr Hillgarth[1] and seems quite a nice chap. He told us that an attack by Government forces on the island of Majorca was imminent. The Government held Minorca and Iviza and have command of the sea as the only ships Franco has are in the north of Spain. The people of Majorca are very conservative and have no use at all for Communists. About 10,000 are armed and they have plenty of ammunition while Palma itself is defended by a number of forts. He expected the attack would take place on Sunday morning and showed me the points on the map where landings were expected. This put me in rather an awkward position because if the Spanish ships entered the bay and engaged the forts, *Galatea* would be in the middle of the battlefield and would either obstruct the fire of the attackers or else be shot up without any legal right of reply. I decided eventually to have steam ready at daylight so as to weigh and proceed out of harbour directly there was any sign of an attack on Palma developing. I informed *Maestrale* of my intention and he replied at first that he would not leave himself as he thought that being a destroyer he might be shot at by the forts. However he changed his mind later and said he would come to sea with me so I told him I'd hold his hand and see he came to no harm.

Next morning there was no sign of an attack and at 10 a.m. Captain Biancheri came to call on me. A nice rather oldish man who speaks a little English. Knew quite a number of English officers. Whilst he was on board we got news that a landing had been effected by from one to two thousand Government troops at an unexpected point about 20 miles to the E of Palma but that the local defence forces had been rushed out to the threatened point and they reckoned they had the situation in hand. There were rumours of three other attempted landings but these Hillgarth was not able to confirm so I sent Buzzard ashore with him to get news. At 11 a.m. I went away in the galley under sail to return Biancheri's call. . . .

In the afternoon the beetle was nearly responsible for an international incident. I went for a pull inside the breakwater and towards the landing place and was on my way back when I saw several guards running and whistling and pointing to the landing place and eventually one damned fellow loosed off his rifle. I didn't see any splash near the beetle so presume he fired over my head but he gesticulated violently so I lay on my

[1]Capt Alan Hillgarth: Mshpmn, *Wolverine*, Dardanelles – seriously wounded; Lt-Cdr 1927; Ret List; Vice-Con, Palma 1932; Con 1937; Actg Capt (ret) 30 Aug 1939 & Asst NA Madrid; NA Feb 1940–Oct 1943; COIS, Eastern F 1943–4.
Maestrale: 1934, 1641t, 4×4.7in, 6tt, 38k; scut Sept 1943.

oars. He then waved for me to go to the landing place but as I saw the Captain of the Port's motor boat being manned I just stayed where I was and waited for the boat to come up to me. None of them could speak French or English so I got on board the motor boat and made them tow the beetle and returned to the landing place. There I found a Spanish sailor who spoke French, told him who I was and demanded the reason for this unpardonable outrage. The Captain of the Port was most apologetic and said there was a strict order that no pulling boats were allowed in the inner harbour. I asked him why the hell I had not been notified of this when he boarded the ship on arrival. He then offered to take me back to *Galatea* in his motor boat but I said 'No'; I'd pulled in and I'd damn well pull out – which I did. Although they ought to have notified us of the order it was not altogether their fault because beetle had no ensign. I'm having one made for her so as to avoid such incidents in future.

In the afternoon a second Italian destroyer arrived so I asked both Captains to dine with me last night whilst the wardroom asked the wardroom officers to supper and the flicks. . . . It really was most entertaining to find two foreign officers with an outlook so very much like our own. Buzzard returned with the consul at 8.30 p.m. having been out to see the battle. They were arrested and taken before the Commandant but released with apologies. . . .

Later. Just had Hillgarth on board and it appears that the first reports are wrong. They have not all been driven back to their ships and there are still quite a number ashore under the protection of the ships' guns. . . . The situation is so confused that I shall take *Galatea* out tomorrow and go and see for myself just what is happening so that I can judge whether Palma is likely to be captured by these damn reds and arrange evacuation accordingly. I hear they only started moving their howitzers out at 8 a.m. this morning! They ought to have moved them last night at the latest. . . .

P.S. Just got a statement from Admiralty on the legal aspects – almost word for word what I gave DP and which he was inclined to disagree with at first.

7.   To Pound

Iviza,
21 August 1936

Report of Visit to Majorca

4.   *Galatea* arrived at Palma the following day [15 August] at 1545, steering directly up the centre of the bay in view of Vice Admiral 1st Cruiser Squadron's[1] message timed 1145 dated 13 August and also because a warning broadcast signal in Spanish concerning the presence of mines had been received. Just before entering the bay a foreign cruiser hull down and steering a south-westerly course was passed. This subsequently proved to be the Italian *Fiume*[2] which had called at Palma for a few hours only. The only foreign war vessel present was the Italian destroyer *Maestrale* . . .

11.   At 0430 on 18 August, *Galatea* sailed to cruise up the eastern coast of the Island ostensibly to warn any British merchant ships to keep well clear of the area of operations, but actually to obtain more accurate information as to the situation. . . .

13.   At 0700 on 19 August a message was conveyed to me by Cdr Margottini that he had received information of a possible sea and air bombardment of Palma which would take place at 1300. I gave orders that *Galatea* was to be at two hours' notice.

14.   At 0800 *Deutschland*, flying the Flag of Rear Admiral Rolf Carls,[3] arrived and anchored. Rear Admiral Carls called on me at 0930 and I arranged for Cdr Margottini to be present in order to discuss the action which should be taken if the threat of bombardment materialised. I proposed that the foreign Consuls should be warned and that the foreign warships should be ready to leave harbour by 1230 at the latest or earlier if Spanish Government vessels were sighted approaching Palma. This

---

[1]Vice Adm (later Adm) Sir Max Horton (1883–1951): *Britannia* 1898; CO *A1* & s/m splist; later *C8*, *D6*; great success with *E9* 1914; *J6* 1915; *M1* 1917; CO, S/M flotilla, Baltic 1919–20; Capt 1920; 'K' boat flotilla 1922; Asst Dir Mobilisation; COS to Admiral Keyes, C-in-C Portsmouth; *Resolution*, Med F; RA 1932; 2nd-in-C, Home F 1934–5; 1CS, Med F 1935; VA 1936; Res F 1937–9; N Patrol 1939; FO S/M Jan 1940; refused C-in-C Home F Oct 1940 because he wanted control of RAF Coastal Cmd; C-in-C W Approaches Nov 1942–5.

[2]*Fiume*: 1931, 11,500t, 8×8in, 12×3.9in, 32k; sunk Matapan, 29 March 1941.

[3]Rear Adm (later Generaladmiral) Rolf Carls (1885–1945): ent navy 1903; Lt 1906; much sea service 1914–18, inc cmd of *U9* & *U124*; Kapitan zur See 1930, *Hessen* 1932–3; RA 1934; i/c German ships in Spanish waters 1936–7; VA 1937; Adm 1937; C-in-C East 1938–40; C-in-C North 1940–3; Generaladmiral 1940.

Deutschland: 1933, 12,000t+, 6×11in, 8×5.9in, 6×4.1in, 8tt, 26k; *Lützow* 1940; put out of action by RAF 16 April 1945; scuttled 3 May 1945.

proposal was concurred in and Admiral Carls informed me that *Deutschland* would take station astern of *Galatea* on which Cdr Margottini added that he would take the rear ship of the line.

16. *Galatea*, *Deutschland* and *Malocelle* weighed and proceeded at 1230, the foreign ships taking up and maintaining very good station on *Galatea*. Course was set to a point just clear of territorial waters and subsequently the 'international squadron' patrolled at 10 knots . . .

17. At 1545 *Garland*[1] was sighted and ordered to prolong the line astern.

19. At 1730 I proposed to the other foreign Commanders that, if no Spanish Government vessels were sighted by 1800, we should return to harbour . . .

21. By 1800 I appreciated that the signal from Alberto Bayo[2] was probably intended as a general warning of bombardment and was not restricted to bombardment at a particular time. I accordingly invited Admiral Carls and Cdr Margottini to dine with me in order to discuss future action. . . .

22. At the discussion which took place the Officers frankly admitted that their sympathies were entirely with the Rebels and they recognised that the British were the only people who could be regarded as strictly neutral in the present situation. I judged these admissions to mean that any views expressed by me on the situation would be accepted by them as being those of a strict neutral. I expressed the view that if Alberto Bayo was acting under the authority of the Spanish Government we should certainly comply with his request which was perfectly legitimate. Admiral Carls and Cdr Margottini questioned whether Bayo was acting under the orders of the Spanish Government. . . .

24. At 0435 on 20 August I received your message that *Galatea* was to sail forthwith. . . .

25. *Griffin*[3] arrived from Malta at 0700 and went alongside *Garland*. After turning over duties, *Garland* sailed for Malta at 0745 and *Griffin* subsequently proceeded to join Vice Admiral Commanding 1st Cruiser Squadron, at Barcelona, at 1315.

26. USS *Quincy* arrived off Palma Bay at 0630 and stopped so that I could acquaint her Captain with the situation. She then proceeded to Palma to prepare her Nationals for evacuation which was to be carried out by *Oklahoma*; the latter arrived at 0930.[4]

[1]*Malocelle*: 1930, 1944t, 6×4.7in, 4–6tt, 38k; mined 1943.
  Garland: 1936, 1335t, 4×4.7in, 8tt, 36k; manned by Polish Navy in WW2.
  [2]Alberto Bayo: Spanish Air Force Capt; Republican cdr Ibiza & Mallorca, Aug 1936; later guerilla cdr, C Spain; in 1960s, Gen in Cuban Army.
  [3]*Griffin*: 1936, 1335t, 4×4.7in, 8tt, 36k; RCN 1943.
  [4]*Oklahoma*: 1914, 29,000t, 10×14in, 24×5in, 20k; sunk Pearl Harbor, 7 Dec 1941; raised & scrapped.
  Quincy: 1935, 9375t, 9×8in, 8×5in, 32.7k; sunk Savo Island, 9 Aug 1942.

27. *Galatea* remained off Palma until 1300 when she proceeded up the east coast of the Island so that I could obtain information as to progress of the attack by the Government forces. . . .

8. *To Senior Spanish Naval Officers, Cartagena and Malaga*

HMS *Galatea.*
24 August 1936

I am directed by the British Naval Commander-in-Chief, Admiral Sir Dudley Pound, KCB, to inform you that:–

(a) Two British Merchant vessels, SS *Marklyn* and SS *Gibel Zerjon*,[1] were unlawfully stopped and boarded on the high seas by warships acting under the orders of the Spanish Government on 16 and 23 August respectively;

(b) In the opinion of His Britannic Majesty's Government, the present situation does not confer on warships acting under the orders of the Spanish Government any right to stop British Merchant vessels on the high seas – that is, on the sea at any point distant more than three miles from the coast of Spain or Spanish possessions;

(c) The Commander-in-Chief fully recognises the difficult task with which the warships of the Spanish Government are faced but he desires it to be most clearly understood that this affords no pretext for illegal acts of the nature quoted above.

2. I am instructed to obtain from you an assurance in writing that such acts shall cease forthwith, and to notify you that any recurrence will immediately be resisted by the ships of His Britannic Majesty, who will not hesitate to open fire if necessary in order to protect ships under the British Flag from illegal interference.

9. *To his wife*

HMS *Galatea*, Spithead,
21 May 1937

The Evening of the Coronation Review

. . . After a bit we moved up on the Promenade deck [of the Royal Yacht *Victoria and Albert*] and I found myself next to the Queen and

[1]*Marklyn*: 1918, 3090gt, Martyn & Martyn, Cardiff.
Gibel Zerjon: 1903, 1435gt, M H Bland, Gibraltar.

little [Princess] Elizabeth and rather apart from the others. The Queen's a little duck. She looked at me and then asked which was my ship and so on and finally said 'The only really pretty ships are the destroyers'. I said 'I presume you mean the ones painted a delicate shade of grey' and she said 'Yes, of course' and I asked if she didn't think they were *much* nicer than the dark grey ones and she quite agreed. Then [Princess] Elizabeth piped up and said 'Mummy, we must be frightfully careful the rocket sticks don't hit us' so I told her she could put my boat cloak over her head and then she'd be quite safe. She's a nice little girl with charming manners. Then the Queen said 'Do you think *Galatea* is really a pretty ship with those very straight funnels?' and I said, no, she wasn't perhaps the prettiest ship at the Review but she was *much* the cleanest. 'Is she really?' said the little Queen suitably impressed and then I heard a loud 'Hee Hee' just behind and old Cork[1] stepped forward and said 'Really Ma'am, you mustn't believe anything Admiral Somerville tells you'. 'But I think his ships are lovely,' said the Queen, 'only why are those two destroyers there so much duller than the others?', pointing to two astern of *Galatea*. 'Well done, Ma'am,' said old Cork, 'What's he going to say to that?' 'Oh, those two,' I answered, 'I admit they leave something to be desired, but those happen to be the two Canadian destroyers and they don't belong to me'. 'Well, what about that other ship with half her lights out; that's one of yours, I'm sure.' 'No, sir,' I replied, 'that happens to be *Indus*[2] of the Royal Indian Navy'. 'Well that shows,' said the Queen, 'that all Admiral Somerville's ships are quite perfect'. Just then we heard a lot of cheering coming from the direction of *Galatea* and the destroyers. 'Who is that cheering?' asked the Queen. 'I must accept responsibility,' I answered, 'but I assume it is only because my destroyers find it quite impossible to restrain their feelings of loyalty'. 'Well Ma'am,' said Cork, 'I give it up'. Just then little Elizabeth said 'Oh Mummy look at the time' (it was just on 11 p.m.), so I asked her if she'd ever been up so late before, and she said 'No – don't you *love* staying up late?' and I said no, I hated it and was always glad when my Nanny came to take me to bed. 'Oh I'm not,' said little Elizabeth. It really was rather amusing having this sort of little family talk. I tried to get away once but the Queen said 'Oh please don't go, I want to hear some more'. I think she rather liked having her leg pulled. . . . I didn't talk to the King at all

[1]Adm of the Fleet the Earl of Cork & Orerry (W. H. D. Boyle, 8th Earl, 1873–1967): *Britannia* 1887; NID 1909–11; Capt 1913; NA, Rome 1913–15; CO *Fox*, Red Sea; *Repulse* 1917; *Lion* 1918; Cdre 1918; RA 1923 & 2nd-in-C, 1BS, Atl F; 1CS, Med F; VA 1928 & Res F; Pres, RNC Greenwich; Adm 1932; C-in-C Home F 1933–4; C-in-C Portsmouth 1935–7; Adm of Fleet 1938; FO, Narvik, 1940, & in o/a cmd; Pres, Shaftesbury Homes & *Arethusa* TS 1942–53.
[2]*Indus*: 1934, 1190t, 2×4.7in, 16.5k.

except just at the end when he came up and said to the Queen, 'Well, I do think this has been a lovely day and I have enjoyed it'. The Queen said 'Yes, so have I' and then to bring me in she said 'Admiral Somerville has been telling me all about the ships' – with a twinkle in her eye. 'Oh that's very kind of him,' said the King and then she and old Cork looked at one another and laughed and I broke away.

10.   *Commanding Officer, HMS* Grenade, *to Somerville*

Tangier,
24 June 1937

2.   . . . the Consul General . . . stated that there have recently been some anti-British demonstrations in the Spanish Zone of Morocco. On Wednesday, 23 June, he visited the High Commissioner, Tetuan, who informed him, gratuitously, that he was strongly of the opinion that a friendly and unofficial visit to Ceuta by one of HM Ships would greatly help to reduce the local anti-British feelings in the Spanish Zone. Further, that permission for such a visit would be readily granted.
4.   The Consul General believes that the higher officials in the Spanish Zone are not really anti-British but that, through lack of opportunity of indicating their feelings in this respect, they have little influence over the young and irresponsible element which is thought to be responsible for the anti-British demonstrations. He considers that an unofficial visit to Ceuta by one of HM Ships would cause an appreciable improvement in our relations in the Spanish Zone.[1]

11.   *To his wife*

Valencia,
19 August 1937

A most awkward thing has happened. Late yesterday afternoon whilst I was away in the beetle a motor boat arrived alongside *Galatea* with a Spanish officer who in very bad French claimed asylum as a political refugee on the score that his life was in imminent danger. . . .

It's nasty business altogether. If I take him away and save his life for certain the Reds are practically sure to take steps which will prevent us saving other people far more worthy of consideration. Still no one likes

[1]See No. 13. *Grenade*: 1936, 1335t, 4×4.7in, 8tt, 35.5k; sunk off Dunkirk, May 1940, Ger a/c.

to send a poor fellow back to what can't be far off death and me least of all. How I loathe this damn Spain and all the doings here. It's all indescribably filthy.

At the moment there are about 15 widows and 20 orphans of Spanish Naval Officers, murdered at Cartagena, on our quarter-deck camped out waiting to be taken by us to Palma tonight. One simply can't listen to their stories of all the horrors as it's too depressing.

On top of it all there's the most tremendous sort of Scirocco[1] and not a breath of air and the temperature of my cabin is rising every moment as we raise steam.

At Palma I shall have some difficult negotiations with the Spanish and Italian Admirals and in this hot weather my brain simply doesn't work. I shall be thankful to see the last of this lousy Mediterranean and all its work.

12. *To his wife*

Palma,
22 August 1937

We left Valencia on Thursday night with our odd collection of widows and children camped out on the quarter-deck. One of the babies cried a bit at first but by 10.30 p.m. when I took a peep at them they were all asleep, worn out after their fearful trip from Cartagena and long wait at the landing place at Valencia. ...

We got to Palma after a fine smooth trip at 8.30 a.m. and I spent the forenoon in company with Hillgarth calling on the Governor, Admiral, etc., and also had a call from the Italian Admiral. I rubbed into them that if British merchant ships were attacked by submarines in the Eastern area I had absolute confidence I should have no difficulty in hunting and destroying the submarine, more especially as I had been connected for many years with the development of anti-submarine devices. Incidentally after we left Palma we sighted a darkened submarine on the surface about a mile away. We put a searchlight on her but she dived before we could identify her. I got a lot of very interesting and highly confidential information from the Spanish Admiral[2] who always treats me as a bosom friend. He told me his people had the strictest orders not to attack British ships. The difficulty is that so many Red ships are now going about disguised as British ships. ...

[1] A hot, dry, swirling wind from N Africa.
[2] Probably Adm Francisco Bastarreche, C-in-C, Nationalist naval forces at Palma.

13.   *To Pound*

Galatea, at sea,
24 November 1937

Report on a Visit to Cadiz

2.   *Galatea* sailed from Gibraltar at 0500 on 23 November and arrived at Cadiz 1000 on the same day . . .

3.   *Deutschland* and *Möwe*[1] were sighted underway to the southwestward of Cadiz.

8.   The [Spanish] Admiral said that night exercises and night firing by HM Ships in the area suggested, viz., S of latitude 35° 30'N and W of longitude 6° 40'W, would be unlikely to interfere with any operations by Nationalist ships. He would be grateful, however, if a few days' notice could be given of the intention of carrying out such practices in order to remove any danger of encountering darkened Nationalist war vessels.

9.   Other matters referred to during the interview are as follows:–

Visit to Ceuta. This has given great satisfaction and according to the Admiral will serve to extend and consolidate the good relations which have existed between the British and Nationalist Senior Officers at Palma. It will also facilitate the adjustment of any difficulties which may arise in the future.

Carriage of munitions to Spain. The Admiral considers that a number of ships are now trading from the Baltic and North European ports to Spain with munitions and enquired how, in the case of British ships, information concerning their movements could be conveyed to the British Naval Authorities. I replied that intelligence of this nature could be transmitted via Algeciras to the SO(I), Gibraltar, and that this line of communication has been in use for some time. In connection with these reports I referred to the case of the *Euphorbia*[2] and pointed out that such large expenditures of fuel could not be justified unless suspicions concerning the cargo were based on positive and accurate information. I asked that in future it should be stated clearly whether a suspicion only existed or whether definite information was available that ships had munitions on board. The Admiral appeared to appreciate that we could not be expected to embark on many more of these expensive wild goose chases. He is establishing a daylight air reconnaissance over the

---

[1]*Möwe*: 1926, 800t, 3×4.1in, 6tt, 33k; sunk by RAF, Le Havre, 14 June 1944.
[2]*Euphorbia*: 1924, 3380gt, 10k, J Robinson & Sons; a suspected gun runner; 2 destroyers sent to intercept.

western approach to the Straits in order to locate and report ships which are believed to be carrying munitions. . . .

Safety Anchorages. The Admiral again raised the question of the use which is being made by Merchant Ships at Valencia and Barcelona of the safety anchorages and asked what action could be taken in the matter. I suggested that a reminder, generally promulgated, to the effect that these safety anchorages were intended only for foreign war vessels and that no assurance could be given concerning the safety of Merchant vessels anchored in these areas, would probably have the desired effect. (It is, of course, obvious that if foreign men-of-war are present, adjacent Merchant Ships will be safe, but this point was not raised by the Admiral).

Attacks on ships without lights. The Admiral asked if it would be in order to attack without warning any ships who were not burning navigation lights, on the grounds that it was not lawful for ships to navigate in this manner. I told the Admiral that this would be unjustifiable and that the only penalty such vessels could incur would be as the result of collisions caused by lack of displaying the authorised navigation lights.

Exchange of Red and White Families. The Admiral asked me to assist if possible in promoting the exchange of certain Red families from Ferrol and Cadiz whose husbands are at Cartagena, with White families of Naval Officers who had been murdered at Cartagena. I promised to do what I could in the matter.

10.   *General.* According to the Vice Consul,[1] the Germans are held in great esteem in Cadiz and the Italians enjoy a fair measure of popularity. This appears to be in opposition to the views expressed by the High Commissioner and other Spanish Officers at Ceuta.

14.   *To Pound*

Galatea, at sea,
27 March 1938

Report on a Visit to Palma

2.   *Galatea* sailed from Gibraltar for Palma at 0700 on 25 March, and arrived without incident at 0900 on 26 March.

12.   As a result of this interview[2] I gained the impression that no further

---

[1]Robert A. Black: Consular service from 1920; Actg Vice-Con, Cadiz 1933–6; Pro-Con, Nov 1937.

[2]Presumably with the Nationalist Adm; the submarines were Italian.

submarine incidents are likely to occur. Italian manned aircraft continue to be the main difficulty but I have reason to believe that, as the result of the outcry caused by the bombing at Barcelona, the Italians will feel the need for greater circumspection. On the other hand they obviously dislike the good feeling which exists between the Spanish and British Naval Officers at Palma. To provoke incidents with British ships may well be a part of Italian policy in the hope that the subsequent protest and action of our patrols will tend to antagonise the Nationalists. I judged that Admiral Moreno is under no illusions on this score, and it seems possible that during his visit to Salamanca,[1] General Franco will be fully informed of the situation.

15. *Aide Memoire on the Rescue of Survivors of Baleares, 6 March 1938*

27 March 1938

4.   After picking up the men around *Kempenfelt*,[2] the Commanding Officer[3] decided to try and place his ship alongside to try and take off men on Quarter Deck. *Baleares* at this time had a list to starboard of 10°, was down by the bows, and port propellors were half above the water.

5.   An attempt was made to place the ship bow to stern to avoid propellors. This had to be abandoned owing to steel girders projecting at fore end of wreck which would have ripped open *Kempenfelt*. *Kempenfelt* was then brought in at an angle and placed with her bows alongside port side of *Baleares*, between propellers. *Baleares* was drifting so rapidly before the wind that this position could not be maintained and *Kempenfelt* was in danger of being ripped open by propellors and wrecked. A number of men who lowered themselves from the Quarter Deck of *Baleares* were taken out of the water. At this time *Baleares* showed no signs of sinking or capsizing. A second attempt was made and *Kempenfelt* was placed alongside *Baleares* abaft of the propellors and wires passed inboard. No sooner had she been secured than *Baleares* began to capsize to starboard and at 5.08 a.m. she disappeared.

[1] The Nationalist HQ.
[2] *Kempenfelt*: (L), 1932, 1390t, 4×4.7in, 8tt, 35.75k; RCN *Assiniboine* 1939; wrecked St. Lawrence 1945.
[3] Capt. (later Adm of the Fleet Sir) Rhoderick R. McGrigor (1893–1959): in destroyers, Dardanelles & Jutland, etc 1914–18; torpedo splist; Capt 1933; Cdre 1 CI & COS to C-in-C China Sta (Adm Sir Percy Noble) & *Kent* i/c 1938–40; *Renown* Feb–Sept 1941; RA & ACNS (Weapons) 1941; Sicily ldgs & SNO S Italy 1943; 1CS Home F 1944–5; VCNS 1945–8; Adm & C-in-C Home F 1948–50; C-in-C Plymouth 1950–1; 1SL 1951–5; Adm of F 1953.

Kempenfelt and *Boreas*[1] at once moved into the mass of struggling men in the water and large numbers were rescued. Officers and men of both ships went overboard to assist in rescue. The work of rescue was much impeded by oil fuel which covered boats, ropes and survivors.

16.   *To Acting Admiral Sir Andrew Cunningham*

Signal Division,
The Admiralty,
12 February 1940

... I was roped in for RDF[2] directly the war started. Well that sounds rather a limited split arsed mechanic's job but in fact it involved acting as a sort of unofficial liaison with the fighter command. The latter have expanded so much that they simply haven't got the chaps at the top they ought to have. I found that by going round all their stations myself I was able to get much more of a move on than by merely urging the Stanmore[3] people.

A/S on the whole seems to be holding its own pretty well though there have been occasional breaks. Still I reckon the score is probably nearer 40 than 30[4]. But the little boats are having a hard time of it and I'm not quite sure old Charles Forbes[5] is quite human enough. I feel that, when in harbour, everything possible should be done to give them as good an ease off as possible.

My job takes me all round everywhere so I see and hear a good deal of what is going on. Martin Nasmith[6] has a very good party in the Western Approaches. It is a pity it's not so good elsewhere.

You may have seen that my job has been expanded into A/A weapons and devices! Captain of Whaley[7] was carried off in a faint when he saw

---

[1] *Boreas*: 1931, 1360t, 4×4.7in, 8tt, 35k; *Salaamis*, R Hellenic N 1944.
[2] Radar was known initially as RDF or 'radio direction finding' for security purposes.
[3] An RAF station.
[4] The true figure was 13.
[5] Adm of the Fleet Sir Charles Forbes (1880–1960): *Britannia* 1894; Lt 1901; gunnery splist; Cdr 1912; Flag Cdr, *Iron Duke*, 1915; at Dardanelles & Jutland; Grand F staff; Capt *Galatea*, 1917, later of *Queen Elizabeth* & *Iron Duke;* DNO 1925–8; RA 1928; RA (D), Med F 1930–1; VA, 3SL & Cntrlr 1934; VA, 1BS, Med F 1934; Adm 1936; C-in-C Home F April 1938–Oct 1940; Adm of Fleet 1940; C-in-C Plymouth 1941–3.
[6] Adm Sir Martin E. Dunbar-Nasmith (1883–1965): Lt & CO, *E11*, won VC in Dardanelles 1915; Capt 1916; Capt, S/M flotilla, SW Ireland 1918; Capt, *Britannia* 1926–8; RA 1928; RA S/M 1929–31; VA 1932; C-in-C, E Indies 1932–4; 2SL 1935–8; Adm 1936; C-in-C Plymouth & W Approaches 1938–41; FOIC London 1942–6.
[7] HMS *Excellent*, the Whale Island Gunnery School. The Captain (later Vice Adm Sir Arthur) was A. F. E. Palliser, who had many subsequent dealings with Somerville: Capt, *Excellent*, 1938–41; Capt, *Malaya*, Force H, Feb 1941; RA Aug 1941; COS, Eastern F Dec 1941; Dep N Cdr, ABDA; RIN June 1943; VA Feb 1944 & Home F CS; 4SL March 1944; C-in-C, E Indies Sept 1945.

it! I'm off to the East Coast and shall be at sea in the A/A ships and escort vessels for a bit so as to see just what *does* happen. We've got some rather pleasing dirt coming along which ought to tease the bloody Huns quite a bit.

In the workhouse everyone is very immersed. DP seems to be bearing up. Tom Phillips[1] always looks like death and tries to do too much. Curious shadows move behind the throne – Bill Tennant, Grantham,[2] etc. A good deal of the work that goes on is like charity – don't let your left hand, etc.

Here again I find I can be of use. My job lets me butt in everywhere so like a bloody bee I carry somebody's problem on my backside and fertilise some other bloke's idea. But of course all this is gradually getting better. The fundamental trouble is that the men at the top will *not* leave details to subordinates. Their fatal remark – 'Let me see the signal before you send it' – damns so many of us. The leaders ought to decide the policy, the juniors execute it.

17. *Somerville's notes on the evacuation of Dunkirk and Calais*

24–28 May 1940

24 May

Brigadier Nicolson[3] at Calais reports that his anti-tank guns cannot stop the German tanks. Prime Minister[4] directed that Naval 12-pounders

---

[1]Actg Vice Adm (later Actg Adm) Sir Tom S. V. Phillips: ent RN 1903; Lt 1908; Dardanelles & Far E 1914–18; Actg Capt *Lancaster* & *Eurylaus* 1918; Staff Coll 1919; Br N Rep, League of Nations 1919–22; Cdr 1921; PD 1922–4; Staff, Med F 1925–8; Capt 1927; Capt (D) 6DF 1928–30; ADPD 1930–2; *Hawkins* 1932–5; DP 1935–8; Cdre (D) Home F 1938–9; RA & VCNS 1939; Actg VA 1940; C-in-C Eastern F autumn 1941; lost in *Prince of Wales*, 10 Dec 1941.

[2]Capt (later Adm Sir) William G. Tennant (1890–1963): ent RN 1905; Navigator 1912; N Sea & Med 1914–18; Nav O, *Renown*; Navigation Sch; Nav O, *Repulse*; Cdr, *Sussex*; Staff Coll; Capt 1932; IDC 1939; Capt *Arethusa*; CSO to 1SL; SNO, Dunkirk May–June 1940; Capt *Repulse* May–Dec 1941; RA, 4CS, Eastern F, Feb 1942; RA i/c Mulberry harbours, NEPTUNE; Actg VA & FO, Levant & E Med Oct 1944; FO Egypt; C-in-C N A & WI 1946–9.

Capt (later Adm Sir) Guy Grantham: Capt 1937; Admiralty 1939; Naval Asst to 1SL 1940; Capt *Phoebe* June 1940; Capt & CSO, 15CS, *Cleopatra* March 1942; *Indomitable* Aug 1943 & COS, RA Home F Carriers; DPD April 1944; VCNS 1954; C-in-C Med 1955.

[3]Brig. Nicolson: Lt 1909; Capt 1912; Maj 1922; Lt-Col 1929; CO, Calais Garrison, May 1940.

[4]Rt Hon (later Sir) Winston L. S. Churchill (1874–1965): cavalry officer, India & Sudan, 1890s; war correspondent, Cuba & S Africa 1898–1900; Con, later Lib, MP 1900–22 & Con 1924–64; Pres, Bd of Trade, Home Sec, 1st Lord of Admiralty, 1906–15; Lt-Col on W Front 1915–16; Min Munitions, Sec State for War & Air, & Cols, 1917–22; C of Ex 1924–29; pol wilderness over India question 1931–9; 1st Lord 3 Sept 1939–10 May 1940; succ N. Chamberlain as PM May 1940; Ldr of Oppn July 1945–51; PM 1951–5.

should be mounted on lorries at Portsmouth and sent over to Calais by train ferry from Folkestone. In my capacity as Director of Anti-Aircraft Weapons and Devices I was requested to accelerate the arrival of these guns as much as possible. We left London by car at 10 a.m. and got to Dover at 6 p.m. Saw Admiral Ramsay and General Lloyd[1] who reported it was very bad and they thought it was probably too late to get guns into Calais. I decided to go over and see for myself and embarked in *Verity* (Lt-Cdr Black).[2] We sailed at 11.30 p.m. after having embarked 80 marines and some ammunition.

25 May

We arrived at Calais after an uneventful passage at 1.30 a.m.; an overcast sky with a three-quarter moon hidden by the clouds giving fairly good visibility. Just before we entered harbour we heard an aircraft circling overhead but could not see it. As we were passing our wires ashore to berth alongside the railway jetty a 5.9" battery opened fire. The first salvo was short but the next three salvoes straddled the ship and one or two men were wounded by splinters. Gave orders to cast off and go astern and find a better billet. The battery continued to fire after we left which suggested our movement had not been detected; eventually we berthed alongside another wharf behind a coal dump which we hoped would hide us from the battery. The battery was now firing apparently on the Blue train drawn up at the station and this was soon knocked to pieces. When fire ceased after about 10 minutes, Commodore Gandell,[3] the SNO at Calais, met me on the jetty and took me to Brig Nicolson's HQ. These were in a cellar under the railway station, lit by a few candles and filled with exhausted officers and men fast asleep except for the Staff Officers and telephonists actually on duty. I woke Nicolson who at once asked if we had come to bring them off. I had to inform him that this was not the case but that I had received a telephone message from the Prime Minister before leaving Dover that it was essential that the garrison at Calais should fight to the last in order to hold up the advance of the Germans which was threatening to cut off the BEF from their last remaining base at Dunkirk. Nicolson appeared to be quite unperturbed saying that he anticipated that he might get these orders and then showed

---

[1]Gen Lloyd: Coldstream Gds; 2Lt 1910; France 1914–18; Maj 1922; SO London Dist 1920; Col 1933 & CO, Cldstrm Gds; WO 1934–6; Brig, GS, Egypt 1936–8; Brig Cdr, Aldershot 1938; Maj-Gen 1938; Maj-Gen Home Cmd 1940; Lt-Gen Feb 1941.

[2]Lt-Cdr A. R. M. Black: Lt-Cdr 1927; *Verity* 1939; *Tyne* 1943; Ret List; Actg Cdr, *Eland* & staff of FO, W Africa, Feb 1945.

Verity: 1919, 1120t, 4×4.7in, 3tt, 31k.

[3]Cdre W. P. Gandell: Cdr 1919; Capt Ret List 1931; SNO Calais May 1940; Sea Tpt Div 1940; Cdre, *Drake* 1941–5; *Emerald* i/c March 1945.

me on the map what he proposed to do, i.e. to retire if possible to the Citadel and hold out there as long as possible. I told Nicolson that in my opinion it was essential that I should order *Verity* and *Wolfhound*,[1] another destroyer in harbour, to sail as otherwise they would certainly be knocked out by the German batteries at daylight. Nicolson said this would remove his only wireless communication with Dover but I pointed out that I had seen a wireless van in the station which had not been knocked out and I was fortunately able to give him the wavelength on which Dover was working as I had happened to pass the wireless van at Dover on my way down to *Verity*. On my return to the jetty I found that through some mistaken order *Verity* had sailed so I embarked on *Wolfhound* and left finally at 3 a.m., reaching Dover at 4.30 a.m.

After telephoning a report of the situation at Calais to the Admiralty and after seeing Admiral Ramsay I had a couple of hours' sleep and then went to Hawkinge[2] where a wireless intercepting station had just been established with the object of reading the plain language German messages made by the enemy's aircraft and tanks. This happened to be also part of my business as I was Chairman of the Inter-service Committee concerned with the direction of wireless interception. Got to bed finally at midnight. At about 12.30 a.m. there was a heavy air raid on Dover. A few bombs were dropped but most of the aircraft appeared to be trying to to lay magnetic mines in the harbour. While looking out of the window watching the raid I saw an aircraft carrying a magnetic mine hit by anti-aircraft fire and explode with a tremendous explosion in mid air.

26 May

At 6 a.m. I relieved Admiral Ramsay and dealt with the various movements of destroyers and other craft that were trying to support our forces at Calais and finally left at 12.40 p.m. for London where I was required to give a personal report. I saw Mr Alexander, the First Lord,[3] who appeared to be very depressed and said the BEF would have to be evacuated. I also saw Admiral Pound and Phillips the DCNS who told me that orders had been given that the evacuation of the BEF was to start that night. As I knew Admiral Ramsay was feeling the strain of being continually on duty I suggested I should go to Dover to lend him a hand. This was agreed to and I finally left at 9.30 p.m. with a Wren driving my car.

---

[1]*Wolfhound*: 1918, 1100t, 4×4inHA, 28k.

[2]RAF fighter station in Kent.

[3]Albert Victor (later Earl, of Hillsborough) Alexander (1885–1965): local govt officer; NALGO; Capt, Artists' Rifles, WW1; lay preacher; prominent in co-op. movt; Lab MP Hillsborough, Sheffield 1922–31 & 1935–50; Parl Sec, Bd of Trade 1924; 1st Lord 1929–31 & May 1940–Dec 1946; Min Defence 1946; Chllr of Duchy of Lancaster & Vsct 1950; Lab Ldr, Lords 1955; Earl 1963.

Unfortunately as it got dark I found she could not see in the dark and as I was too sleepy to drive myself we had to put up at a roadhouse until daylight at 4.30 a.m.

27 May

I reached Dover at 6 a.m. and at once took over from Admiral Ramsay in order that he might have some rest. Found that the German guns on the coast were in action as far as Gravelines and that *Verity* and a transport had been hit and had had to turn back. They had been endeavouring to get to Dunkirk by the southern channel which passes within range of the guns in the vicinity of Calais. The officers from GHQ arrived during the afternoon and reported that the main body of the BEF were completely cut off from Dunkirk and that we should be lucky if we got 25,000 men off altogether. In view of this information every small boat and craft of every description which had been arriving at Dover in response to urgent requests for boats were sent over at once to the beaches to bring off our men. Heard that there was some trouble in the *Verity* which had had an exceedingly trying time for the last three weeks in addition to some casualties, including her Captain that morning. I went on board and addressed the men and managed to get them into a fairly cheerful frame of mind. Captain Tennant had been appointed as SNO Dunkirk and had sent a signal over to say that in view of the bombing of the harbour there most of the evacuation would have to take place from the beaches.

28 May

I relieved Admiral Ramsay at 1 a.m. and found a message from Tennant who said things had quieted down a bit. He asked that all personnel ships should be sent over as quickly as possible and said that it did not appear that the BEF were actually cut off from Dunkirk. This was confirmed later in the day by our intercepted messages from German aeroplanes by means of which we were able to plot the position of our own and the enemy troops. From this picture it seemed clear that the way was still open to Dunkirk. At this time we appeared to have no communication at all with GHQ which under the circumstances seemed quite fantastic. Received reports from Tennant that the troops on the beaches were short of water and food and asking if these might be sent over in the small boats and other craft taking part in the evacuation.

18.   *To his wife*

Dover,
29 May 1940

Under pressure from Admiralty and Ministry of Information I've agreed to broadcast tomorrow Thursday at 9.15 p.m. It's been impossible really to write up anything worth listening to at all but they say it doesn't matter. Things are very strenuous here and one doesn't get much sleep. My trip to Calais was necessary but don't worry – I'm stuck here until this particular business is over. And a pretty grim business it is too but I can't tell you much about it. Directly it's over I shall try to get down to you for 2 or 3 days as I shall want a rest. But I'm keeping quite fit and see Arthur[1] at times. The news is of course damn black but we're doing our best to make it less so.

19.   *To his wife*

Dover,
30 May 1940

We're having a hell of a time as you may imagine and it's not at all easy for us. A tremendous task we've been given and personally I think we're doing much better than I expected. Not so the poor soldiers across the water but one must make allowances for them in view of their deplorable situation. Thank God there's some fog today and so far the bombing does not appear to have been at all bad. It was frightful yesterday.

The chief trouble is to get any sleep but I manage odd half hours and 2–3 hours each night. Glad to hear you've got so much to do as it helps to keep one's mind off it. Reggie Parish[2] came in just now absolutely dead to the world. I never saw anyone so played out. I believe his officers and men are equally done in so I'm not sending him to sea though we are sorely in need of destroyers. Spoke to Bill Adam[3] and Lord Gort[4] on the

---

[1]Col Arthur K. Main, his brother in law: b 1881; cmnd 1900; Col 1923; ret as staff officer March 1937; OC Dover Sept 1939.

[2]Lt-Cdr F. R. W. Parish: Lt-Cdr 1935; *Vivacious* 1939; Cdr June 1940; LDD 1940–2; *Ceylon*1943–4; 2 Bn, RME 1945.

[3]Probably Lt-Gen Sir Ronald F. Adam, a Corps commander in the BEF.

[4]Gen (later Field Marshal) the Viscount Gort, VC (1886–1946): Grenadier Gds 1905; Capt 1914 & ADC to Gen Haig; Lt-Col 1917; VC 1918; Staff Coll 1919–21; Col 1925; India 1932; Cmdt, Staff Coll 1936; Gen & CIGS 1937; C-in-C BEF Sept 1939–June 1940; Inspr-Gen 1940–1; Govr & C-in-C Gibraltar 1941, & Malta May 1942–4; FM 1943; H Cmnr & C-in-C, Palestine & Trans-Jordan 1944–5.

telephone just now. Former sounded very nervy and bad tempered, latter was quite cool and pleasant. They must be having the hell of a time. Winston and I usually hold light converse on the telephone at 6.30 a.m. As he always has his teeth out then it's not so easy.

20. *Vice Admiral Ramsay's Report on Operation DYNAMO*

18 June 1940

. . . I would like to pay tribute to the valuable support and assistance which I received throughout the whole course of the evacuation from Vice Admiral Sir James Somerville, KCB, DSO, who was appointed to HMS *Lynx* for special service in connection with the evacuation. The attributes of this officer for initiative and resource are well known throughout the Service, but I venture to express the opinion that never in the course of his long and distinguished career have they been put to better use than during the operations for the evacuation of the Allied Armies from Dunkirk.[1] . . .

[1] *Lynx*: name of RN HQ, Dover.

PART II

FORCE H
June 1940–January 1942

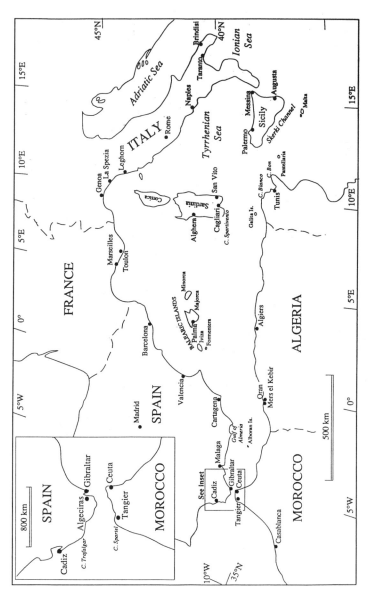

The Western Mediterranean, 1940–1942

INTRODUCTION

The collapse of France and the accompanying entry of Italy into the war posed several strategic problems for Britain. She had to decide whether Italy constituted a significant threat requiring the commitment of substantial forces to counter and defeat it. She had to weigh the consequences of the loss of the French fleet, which had taken the principal responsibility for the security of the western Mediterranean. She had to consider how secure was her own historic base at Gibraltar. The fall of France and the belligerence of Italy might well draw Franco's Spain into the conflict on the Axis side, with obvious implications for the Rock's defence. A failure to guard the Straits might lead to the Italian fleet sortieing into the Atlantic. Finally, she was apprehensive about the future of the French warships. It was conceivable either that Germany and Italy might break their word and seize the ships for their own use, or that a collaborationist Vichy regime might permit such use, together with port facilities, or even enter the war on the Axis side. Though Italy had been increasingly aggressive in the Mediterranean (termed by Mussolini 'Mare Nostrum') since 1935, seeking to undermine the British position everywhere, British policy up to Mussolini's jackal-like entry into the war had been to appease Italy, or at least to hope that she would remain neutral.[1] Such plans as had been made to deal with her belligerence rested heavily on French strength in the region. The situation which arose in June 1940 was, therefore, unexpected and moreover there was little time to take a cool, considered view as to what should be done. Policy and strategy had to be made virtually on the hoof.

It was in these circumstances that Force H was created, under Somerville's command, on 27 June 1940 [21]. Though it was envisaged as a permanent force based on Gibraltar, its initial function was to either neutralise or win over the French warships in the Algerians ports of Oran and Mers-el-Kebir. Following this delicate task, Force H was to secure the western gateway of the Mediterranean against hostile vessels. At Gibraltar, it was handily placed to seize the Atlantic islands of Portugal

---

[1] See A. Clayton, *The British Empire as a Superpower, 1919–1939* (Athens, Ga.: U of Georgia Pr., 1986), pp. 335–46, 357–62, 370–1.

and Spain and to defend trade in the central Atlantic. It could interdict French commerce to ensure that contraband did not reach the Axis. Opportunities to singe the King of Italy's moustache would be seized, with the object in part of impressing a former victim of singeing, Spain, with Britain's continuing strength and determination and deterring Franco from making common cause with the Axis. It was intended to concert operations with the Mediterranean Fleet, especially the running of convoys to Malta and Alexandria. Though Force H was under the direct control of the Admiralty, a *modus vivendi* would have to be struck by its commander with the Flag Officer Commanding North Atlantic, Vice Admiral Sir Dudley North.[1]

Such varied, substantial and difficult tasks called for leadership of vigour, tact, boldness, strategic vision and fine judgment. Somerville's previous flag appointments had demonstrated his possession of these qualities. He had recent experience of the western Mediterranean and of dealing with the Spaniards. His wartime service had confirmed his physical fitness. No doubt the Admiralty took these factors into account but it is more likely that his selection was due to the fact that he was the only senior flag officer with recent sea-going experience readily available.

As Somerville hastened to Gibraltar, the Admiralty began to define its policy towards the French fleet, the most powerful units of which were in Mers-el-Kebir. While the old battleships *Bretagne* and *Provence* were of little fighting value, the new battlecruisers *Dunkerque* and *Strasbourg* were formidable ships which in the hands of our enemies would probably turn the naval balance in Europe against us. The French also had numerous modern, fast and well-armed cruisers and outsized destroyers. Of almost equal concern were the two unfinished battleships *Jean Bart*. at Casablanca and *Richelieu*, at Dakar.[2] The French Navy was well organised, well disciplined and, with the exception of one or two senior officers,[3] fiercely loyal to Admiral Darlan.[4] Though exhibiting at times a

---

[1]Vice Adm (later Adm) Sir Dudley North (1881–1961); *Britannia* 1896; Lt 1903; Heligoland 1914; Cdr 1915; Dogger Bank 1915; Jutland 1916; Capt 1919; commanded 'C' class cruisers 1922–4; Royal tours; Flag Capt Atl & Res Fleets; DOD 1930; RA 1932 & COS to Adm Sir John D. Kelly, C-in-C, Home F; cmded Royal yachts 1934; VA 1936; FOCNA Nov 1939–Nov 1940; Home Guard; FO, Yarmouth, rank of RA (ret) 1942; Adm Cmdg Royal Yachts 1946–7.

[2]*Bretagne, Provence*: 1913, 22,189t, 10×13.4in, 14×5.5in, 21k.
Dunkerque, Strasbourg: 1937 & 1938, 26,500t, 8×13in, 16×5.1in, 29.5k.
Richelieu, Jean Bart: 35,000t+, 8×15in, 9×6in, 12×3.9in, 30k.

[3]The C-in-C Toulon, Admiral de la Borde, for example.

[4]Admiral Jean Darlan, sometimes regarded as the father of the modern French Navy; head of Navy 1939–40; assassinated in Algiers Dec 1942, when co-operating with Allies following invasion.

not-unsurprising residual Anglophobia, Darlan and his Navy had co-operated effectively with the Royal Navy during the 'phoney war'.

Once France's collapse seemed likely, the British Government and Admiralty became anxious about the fate of Europe's second largest fleet. Initially, they urged Darlan to continue the fight from British ports and this remained likely until 17 June; in any case, Darlan repeatedly assured Churchill, Alexander and Pound that the ships would not be allowed to fall intact into Axis hands. Pound felt that he could be trusted. There matters might have rested had Darlan not joined Pétain's cabinet on 17 June as Minister of Marine, thus identifying himself, in British eyes, with the collaborators.[1] Furthermore, from 23 June the British Government lost contact with the Vichy regime and there were disturbing signs that the Germans were sending messages to the French fleet in Darlan's name. The final armistice terms of 1 July indicated that all ships should return to their metropolitan home ports. Even if many units were permitted for the time being to remain in colonial harbours, pressure might be put on Vichy to recall them at a later date. Hitler's proven untrustworthiness and his capacity for swift *coups de main* led the British to believe that he would break the terms of the armistice when it suited him and seize the fleet. French insistence that they would scuttle their ships if such a threat materialised seemed hopelessly naïve; moreover, ships scuttled in shallow water could be easily raised. Against these fears, all the Naval Liaison Officers' reports minimised the threat of Axis seizure. Moreover, Hitler knew the ships were beyond his immediate control and that, together with the colonies, they gave the French bargaining counters. He wished to be lenient with France, in part to secure her co-operation, partly to erase her from his military agenda and finally because he hoped for an early peace with Britain. The Admiralty was not reassured and the Cabinet took the rather exaggerated view that the enemy's acquisition of major units 'would determine the whole course of the war'.[2]

Threatened with invasion and challenged by Mussolini, the British felt there was no time to lose in settling the issue. Initially, service opinion opposed the use of force because it might lead to more severe British than French losses and might align France with the Axis, though Pound

---

[1]Marshal Pétain, hero of France's resistance in Great War; PM June 1940; signed armistice with Germany & Italy; headed Vichy Govt 1940–4; imprisoned after war.

On the whole issue of the French Fleet in the spring and summer of 1940, E. M. Gates, *End of the Affair: The Collapse of the Anglo-French Alliance, 1939–1940* (London: Allen & Unwin, 1981), pp. 329–72, affords a detailed treatment and a cogent analysis; on Darlan's change of attitude, see p. 333.

[2]F. H. Hinsley, *British Intelligence in the Second World War*, vol 1 (London: HMSO, 1979), p. 152.

believed the imposition of a British blockade on France would probably do so in any case. After three weeks of deliberation, however, Pound suggested 'a surprise attack carried out at dawn and without any form of prior notification'. Churchill, though more circumspect, argued that on a question 'so vital to the safety of the whole British Empire we couldn't afford to rely on the word of Admiral Darlan'.[1] With one eye cocked in the direction of America, the Prime Minister was no doubt relieved to learn from the British Ambassador in Washington, Lord Lothian,[2] that President Roosevelt[3] and the American public would approve a British seizure of the ships. Furthermore, Churchill, anxiously awaiting a positive response from Roosevelt to his request in May for 50 over-age destroyers, was aware that the United States would require solid evidence of both Britain's will and capacity to fight on before handing them over. A short, sharp, decisive action (hopefully bloodless) against the French fleet would fit the bill. Having secured Cabinet and Admiralty support, Churchill moved at once to safeguard the Empire, frustrate Hitler and Mussolini and impress the world.

Between 27 June and 3 July, Somerville's instructions were revised almost daily, each refinement limiting further his freedom of manoeuvre [21–23, 27–30]. At first, he was convinced that force would be unnecessary as well as undesirable. Those with whom he discussed the proposed operation CATAPULT – North, Vice Admiral Wells, Captain Holland, his chosen emissary, and Lt-Cdrs Spearman and Davies, two former liaison officers with the French Navy – all viewed the use of force as disastrous, guaranteed to rebound against us militarily and internationally, and in any case unnecessary. All trusted the French to deny their ships to the enemy.[4]

---

[1]M. Gilbert, *Winston S. Churchill:*, vol 6, *Finest Hour, 1939–1941* (London: Heinemann, 1983), pp. 481, 590, 596. See also undated notes in Pound papers, DUPO 5/1, Churchill Archives Centre.

[2]Philip H. Kerr, Marquis of Lothian (1882–1940): jnlst, col civ svt; protégé of Milner & Lloyd George; Lib poln; Chllr, Duchy of Lancaster 1931; USec St, India 1931–2; prominent appeaser; Amb, Washington, May 1939–Dec 1940; died in office.

[3]Franklin D. Roosevelt (1882–1945): country gentleman from upstate New York; Democrat; NY St Sen 1911–13; Asst Sec Navy 1913–20; VPres cand 1920; polio 1921; Govr New York 1929–32; President March 1933–April 1945; won record four terms and inspired New Deal; disciple of Woodrow Wilson on League of Nations.

[4]Vice Adm L. V. ('Nutty') Wells: Capt 1924; RA 1936; cmded carriers, Home F 1937–40; VA 1939; VACAC, Force H, June–Aug 1940; FOC Orkney & Shetland 1941; Ret List 1943; FOIC Aberdeen 1943–5.

Capt Cedric S. Holland: Capt 1932; NA Paris, Brussels, The Hague Jan 1938–May 1940; Capt *Ark Royal* June 1940–April 1941; Capt *Cormorant* (Gibraltar HQ) May 1941; DSD 1942: RA June 1942; RA (Q) Eastern F Nov 1943; VA June 1945, on Ret List.

Lt-Cdr A. Y. Spearman: Lt-Cdr 1935; *Resource* 1938; NLO (Sud), Bizerta 1940; *Curacoa* 1941–2; lost when she was cut in half by *Queen Mary* 2 Oct 1942.

Lt-Cdr G. P. S. Davies: Lt-Cdr 1935; *Tribune*, i/c, commissioning 1938–9; SO (O), *Cyclops* July 1940; *Dolphin* 1942; Cdr 1942; SO (O) II & SO (S/M), BPF, Sydney 1945.

Somerville's powerful but rather scratch force arrived off Oran early on 3 July. His negotiators, Holland, Spearman and Davies, were fluent in French and well acquainted with the French Navy, particularly its senior officers. Holland, lately Naval Attaché in Paris, was a man of patience, courtesy and ability, seemingly the perfect emissary. However, he was deeply and sentimentally Francophile, a trait noted by the DNI, Admiral Godfrey,[1] and communicated to Pound (though not, it appears, to Somerville). The French C-in-C, Admiral Gensoul,[2] may have been offended at having to deal with an officer of inferior rank. Lord Cunningham suggested after the war that Somerville should have gone himself, as 'few could resist James's blandishments'. Aside from the likelihood that Gensoul was proof against anyone's charms, Somerville would have been foolish to cut himself off from instant communication with London, nor would the Admiralty have permitted it. Of the other flag officers available, North had conferred with Gensoul on 24 June, when the latter had reiterated Darlan's assurances. However, he seems not to have had Pound's full confidence, while Wells appears not to have enjoyed Somerville's confidence.[3]

The French were sincere in their assertions that their ships would not be allowed to fall intact into Axis hands. Most French officers were equally certain that they must give the enemy no pretext either for seizure or for retaliation against sailors' families. The vast majority regarded Vichy as the legitimate government and remained personally loyal to Darlan. They expected Britain herself to be defeated in a matter of weeks and thus saw little point in aligning themselves with the Royal Navy. Moreover, Britain's support for de Gaulle,[4] who was either unknown in or disliked by the Navy, irritated them and they were further enraged by the forcible seizure of French ships in British ports on 2 July. They castigated Britain for her ineffectual support before Dunkirk and for her alleged desertion of her ally after it. Finally, they were incensed

[1]Adm John H. Godfrey: Capt 1928; *Repulse* 1937; RA 1939: DNI 1939–42; VA & FOCRIN 1943–6.

[2]Adm Marcel-Bruno Gensoul (1880–1973): ent navy 1898; Lt de V 1911; torpedo specialist; Med 1914–18; staff work 1922; N War Coll 1926; Capt de V 1927 & CO *Bretagne*; *Provence* 1929; RA 1932; 3rd Light Sqdn 1934; VA 1937; Préfet Maritime, Toulon; C-in-C, Atl Sqdn 1938; C-in-C Atl F 1939; Adm July 1940; Inspr Gen, Maritime Forces & Chief C Marine Works Service; Ret List Oct 1942.

[3]Cunningham to Godfrey, *c*. 17 May 1959, CUNN 5/4, Churchill Archives Centre, Cambridge.

[4]Gen Charles de Gaulle (1890–1970): École Mil 1909; W Front; staff & instr appts; i/c armr fmtns 1937–40; jun gen & minr in Reynaud Govt 1940; escaped to UK & headed Free French forces & govt; restored French Govt in Paris 1944; headed govt until 1946; came out of retirement to lead Fifth Republic following debâcle in Algeria 1958; ousted by popular discontent 1968.

at Britain's prompt imposition of a blockade even on unoccupied France. Most of them wanted to sit out the war, preferably at home, and many were repatriated.

Admiral Gensoul, who had told North that he would remain in North Africa and would neither join the British nor allow his ships to fall into enemy hands, was totally loyal to the Pétain government and to Darlan. He appears to have been a man of principle, though somewhat slow and of limited vision. Adhering faithfully to his orders and to the terms of the armistice, he felt he had given the British all the assurances they could possibly require. He refused to see Holland until mid-afternoon and his communications with Somerville via his subordinates offered no way forward [31]. Angered by British behaviour elsewhere, he was further enraged by the deployment of a menacing force more powerful than his own and, moreover, one which enjoyed all the tactical advantages. When French ships appeared to be getting under way, Somerville mined the exit channel; as negotiations were still in progress, Gensoul was annoyed by this and Cunningham suggested later that Somerville had prejudiced the talks by this action. However, Somerville was caught between two stools; he was under orders to prevent the French escaping *and* to negotiate a settlement. Furthermore, at Alexandria, Cunningham also took threatening steps while continuing to negotiate.[1]

Since nothing had been achieved before Holland met Gensoul in person, everything now hung on this encounter. Gensoul was not in the best frame of mind but Holland persevered. According to Holland, it was at this point that Gensoul realised that the British would use force if talks failed and therefore made the proposal for demilitarisation in North Africa, with the assurance that he would go to Martinique should the Axis threaten his ships. He pointed out that discharge of non-essential personnel had begun and took Holland into his confidence by showing him Darlan's final instructions, with his reiterated command not to allow the Axis to obtain the ships intact [32–35]. Doubts remain about the genuineness of Gensoul's proposals; he might have been playing for time until he could sortie, link up with approaching cruiser reinforcements from Algiers and slip away to Toulon under cover of darkness. However, the proposals were similar to those accepted at Alexandria, they had been put forward by Pound himself at one stage and they were the most hopeful signs in a long, wearisome day. Nevertheless, they were outside the bounds of Somerville's remit and they were inadequate for the Mers-el-Kebir situation. Alexandria was a British base; demili-

---

[1] See *A Sailor's Odyssey*, pp. 243–56.

tarisation could be monitored constantly and the Axis would be unable to seize the ships. At Mers-el Kebir, the French would have to be taken at their word, and Vichy might make a new deal with the enemy which would release the ships to the Axis. A sudden Axis descent on Algeria might prevent the ships from sailing to Martinique, as happened at Toulon in November 1942. In any case, there was no time to ponder, for light and fuel were running out for the British, French reinforcements were arriving and London was demanding an immediate and satisfactory conclusion. Boxed in by time, Churchillian implacability, French intransigence and other operational constraints, Somerville had no option but to open fire.

After ten minutes of capital ship broadsides, to which the immobile French replied only ineffectively, Force H had blown up the *Bretagne*, severely damaged the *Provence* and forced the *Dunkerque* to beach herself. Almost 1300 French seamen were killed and 350 injured. Somerville ceased fire to allow the French to abandon their ships but shortly afterwards the undamaged *Strasbourg*, accompanied by five large destroyers, got clean away. Despite gallant but fruitless attacks by *Ark Royal*'s aircraft,[1] they escaped to Toulon, in unoccupied France but still within the enemy's grasp. Apart from a torpedo bomber *coup de grâce* attack on the grounded *Dunkerque* [42, 43] on 6 July, that was the macabre and disappointing end to a distressful day for both British and French; no one was more distraught than Somerville himself [36, 37, 39, 40, 41].

Could bloodshed have been avoided? There is no clear cut answer. Both international and local factors entered into the situation and there were severe constraints of time, different cultures, strong personalities and communications difficulties, all in play at the same time (language, mercifully, seems not to have been a barrier).Churchill is usually singled out as the principal villain, attacked for haste, intransigence and a petulant demand for a demonstration of British resolve and might to influence his own people, the enemy, the Spaniards and (especially) the Americans. Apart from the fact that Churchill was strongly Francophile, he hesitated for three weeks before making up his mind; having done so, he was well aware of the likely outcome but, said Ismay, he 'never flinched'.[2] Moreover, his Cabinet and his service advisors, at least at home, were unanimous in their support. 'Certainly no more distasteful

---

[1] It was thought at the time that *Strasbourg* had suffered damage from the air attacks but she escaped unharmed.

Ark Royal: 1938, 22,000t, 60 a/c, 16×4.5in, 31k; sunk W Med 14 Nov 1941, *U81*.

[2] A. J. Marder, *From the Dardanelles to Oran: Studies of the Royal Navy in War and Peace, 1915–1940* (London, Oxford U Pr, 1974), p. 236.

decision was ever taken by a British Cabinet', claimed Rohan Butler, 'and its execution went sorely against the grain of the Navy'.[1]

The Navy afloat was at odds with the Admiralty. Cunningham claimed that '90% of senior naval officers' thought the use of force was 'a ghastly error'.[2] Admiral North bravely if unwisely wrote a letter of protest to the Admiralty. Somerville's own feelings are revealed starkly in his letters to his wife. For immediate solace, he sought out the Reverend Knight-Adkin, former Chaplain to the Fleet and currently Dean of Gibraltar. Yet Somerville had strained his orders, daylight and the Government's patience to the absolute limit and effected a minimum bombardment; it is impossible to see what more he could have done. Holland, a most reluctant envoy, has been criticised for not emphasising firmly and early enough the determination of the British to settle the issue by force if necessary; that may be true, though conveying the grim message to Gensoul was hampered by the latter's reliance on intermediaries. When at last Holland saw Gensoul, the truth dawned on the French Admiral quickly enough.[3]

Gensoul erred first in not seeing Holland during the forenoon; it required little imagination to see that force was at least a distinct possibility if talks were not held, especially as the British had used rough hands on French ships elsewhere. His second error, when offered several options, was to inform the Ministry of Marine only that he had been presented with an ultimatum to sink his ships in six hours or be sunk. Not unnaturally, he was ordered to resist both courses.[4]

Had Gensoul seen Holland during the forenoon and made his demilitarisation proposal at that point, all parties would have had sufficient time to reflect upon it, suggest amendments and *perhaps* arrive at a peaceful settlement. Pound had in fact sounded out the War Cabinet on demilitarisation in North Africa; unfortunately, this was rejected as a sign of weakness.[5] It was not possible to wait another day as the French might have slipped out at night. The blame cannot be heaped upon any one head, nor upon one nation. The tragedy was the result of many factors converging on 3 July. Marder spoke of 'a case of right versus right' and concluded that, while the French probably could have been trusted, and that the Germans would have been unlikely to acquire the ships, the

[1]J. R. M. Butler, *Grand Strategy*, vol 2 (London: HMSO, 1957), p. 226.

[2]Cunningham to Adm of the Fleet Lord Fraser, 9 Jan 1950, quoted in S.W. Roskill, *Churchill and the Admirals* (London: Collins, 1977), p. 158. See also Cunningham to Godfrey, c. 17 May, c. 5 Aug 1959, 26 April 1960, CUNN 5/4, Churchill A C.

[3]Marder, *Dardanelles to Oran*, p. 240.

[4]Marder, *Dardanelles to Oran*, pp. 240–6; P. M. H. Bell, *A Certain Eventuality: Britain and the Fall of France*, Aldershot: Saxon House, 1974, p. 155; Gates, p. 361.

[5]Roskill, *Churchill and the Admirals*, pp. 157–8.

British 'action is both intelligible and defensible' in the light of available information.[1] Matters were not helped by a total breakdown in communications between London and Vichy. Butler has argued that

> In view of the tense emotional atmosphere then enveloping both parties it seems unlikely that force could have been avoided. . . . It was from the British point of view a balance of risks: the risk of allowing these all-important ships to fall into enemy hands and the risk of driving the French into the enemy camp.[2]

There is some truth in this judgment but one has to consider the ultimate balance sheet before one can come to as final a conclusion as is possible in these muddy waters. Considered in isolation, the action at Mers-el-Kebir was botched. *Strasbourg* escaped and went just where the British did not want her to go. Somerville, as he acknowledged, was to blame for this major setback. He withdrew too far to the west after ceasing his bombardment, unwisely trusted in the mining to block the exit channel and then discounted early reports of *Strasbourg*'s sortie [31]. *Dunkerque,* though put out of action for 18 months, ultimately joined her sister ship in Toulon. The 1600 French casualties generated a vast wail of bitterness, echoes of which remain, and Vichy broadcast with grim relish the latest example of Albion's characteristic perfidy. Demilitarisation of other French naval units was halted, North Africa confirmed its allegiance to Vichy, and resistance to de Gaulle and his British sponsors at Dakar in September 1940 was virtually guaranteed, as was hostility to the Anglo-American invasion of North Africa in November 1942. The firing at Mers-el-Kebir very nearly wrecked Cunningham's agreement with Godfroy[3] at Alexandria; the laborious knife-edge negotiations had to be repeated, fortunately with success. Somerville's base at Gibraltar was the target for French reconnaissance and bombing raids over the next few months. Vichy and the British played a tedious, apparently meaningless, cat-and-mouse game in the western Mediterranean for the next two and a half years, while events of great moment swirled around them. Somerville's bombardment opened up the possibility of Vichy offering the Axis use of French ports, at home and abroad, for surface raiders and U-boats.

On the positive side, the BBC claimed widespread public support for the action, British diplomats in Madrid reported that the Spaniards were

---

[1]Marder, *Dardanelles to Oran*, pp. 283–8; Bell (p. 155) suggests that the difference between the British and French positions 'appeared to be one of timing'.

[2]Butler, *Grand Strategy*, 2, p. 226.

[3]Vice Adm R.E. Godfroy, cmdr, French sqdn, Alexandria; accepted demilitarisation but joined Allies 1943.

suitably impressed by the show of muscle and grit, and Roosevelt's personal envoy and factotum, Harry Hopkins[1] claimed that the President and the American public were now convinced that Britain would fight on. Militarily, while the bombardment was only a partial success, taken together with actions against French units elsewhere in the summer of 1940, the British enjoyed spectacular success. By the end of September, of nine French capital ships extant in June, only *Strasbourg* was seaworthy. The carrier *Béarn*[2] was confined to Martinique and only cruisers and destroyers, scattered between Toulon and several North African ports, remained to irritate Britannia.

It was the conviction of Somerville and his brother officers that 'the affair was a deplorable blunder'.[3] On balance, the British lost more than they gained. Their hands were stained with the blood of their late ally. They lost whatever opportunity there was to persuade French Africa to continue the fight against fascism and very nearly caused Vichy to join the enemy. Most of those involved in the fruitless negotiations believed, then and for ever afterwards, that given more time an amicable agreement could have been reached. That would have taken another day, at least; in the meantime, Gensoul would have had to undertake not to leave harbour. This he might well have agreed to and honoured his bond. The likely outcome then would have been demilitarisation in North African ports, possibly with periodic British inspections. Pound had believed, at least initially, that Britain was more likely to gain her ends by trust than force. However, all this is speculation. The actual situation was fraught with fear, emotion, tension, haste, scepticism and distrust; taken together, they left precious little room for a peaceful outcome.[4]

Contretemps with Vichy were to drag on wearily and often pointlessly for over two years, until they were bloodily and finally resolved following the TORCH landings of November 1942. The Vichy government attempted to carry on life as a neutral country, conducting trade with its North African colonies and other parts of the world, though organising

---

[1]Harry L. Hopkins (1890–1946): soc wkr, New York City; headed New Deal relief programmes 1933–8; Sec of Commerce 1938–40; pers asst to & roving ambassador for Roosevelt 1940–5; headed Lend-Lease 1941. Gilbert, *Finest Hour*, pp. 643–4.

[2]*Béarn*: 1927, 22,146t, 40 a/c, 4×5in, 21.5k.

[3]Butler, *Grand Strategy*, 2, p. 226. See also Vice Adm Sir Geoffrey Blake to Pound, 10 Oct 1940, and to Donald MacLachlan, 12 Sept 1967, BLE 9, National Maritime Museum.

[4]For fuller discussions of the affair, see: Marder, *Dardanelles to Oran*, pp. 179–288; Roskill, *Churchill and the Admirals*, pp. 151–60; Hinsley, *British Intelligence*, vol 1, pp. 149–53; Butler, *Grand Strategy*, 2, pp. 205–6, 209, 218, 221, 222–7, 229. Charles Morgan, 'Oran, 3 July 1940', paper for NID, in possession of J. Somerville. For the French point of view, see E. H. Jenkins, *A History of the French Navy* (London: MacDonald & Jane's, 1973), pp. 320–5.

most of its shipping into convoys. It insisted on moving its warships about as it judged necessary, it flew reconnaissance planes over the Mediterranean, vigorously defended its territorial waters and air space, regularly kept an eye on the harbour at Gibraltar and retaliated against hostile British behaviour with occasional bombing raids on the Rock. For their part, the British authorities were determined that Vichy should not become a front for Axis breaches of the blockade; they insisted, therefore, on their right to search French merchantmen, if necessary applying force and seizing ships within French territorial waters. The British also supported Gaullist attempts to wrest control of French African colonies from Vichy or other non-combatant regimes. In the implementation of these policies, Gibraltar, Force H and Somerville became key factors.[1]

For the rest of the summer of 1940, British attention focused on the West African colonies, which de Gaulle hoped to persuade to join the Free French cause. The principal object of the haughty general and his British supporters was the strategic base of Dakar. It would have been logical for Somerville and Force H to supply the naval support for operations off the African Atlantic coast and indeed he was ordered, immediately after the air strike to fully disable *Dunkerque*, to carry out a similar attack on the almost-completed battleship *Richelieu* at Dakar. This was quickly rescinded and the operation allotted to another task force, possibly because it was felt Somerville was not in the right frame of mind for further vigorous action against the French [44] but also because Force H was required to support operations by the Mediterranean Fleet.[2] Though some of his ships were loaned to forces operating against the French colonies, he took no part in the assaults, to his undoubted relief [65].

For the rest of his time in Force H, however, he was to be plagued by a series of incidents with Vichy forced on him by the policy makers in London. The first arose from the operation against Dakar in September 1940, MENACE. This was conducted by an independent naval and military force though it contained *Ark Royal* and some of the Force H destroyers. Neither Somerville nor North were privy to the plans or to the general policy towards Vichy underlying them. As a result, events occurred which were to deprive North of his command and his professional reputation and might well have finished Somerville's career, too. On the evening of 9 September, the Consul-General at Tangier reported

[1]Marder, *Dardanelles to Oran*, pp. 272–4; S. W. Roskill, *The War at Sea*, vol 1 (London: HMSO, 1954), pp. 272–6; Butler, *Grand Strategy*, 2, pp. 232–3.
[2]D. Brown, 'Admiral of the Fleet Sir James Somerville', in S. Howarth, ed., *Men of War: Great Naval Leaders of World War II* (London: Weidenfeld & Nicolson, 1992), p. 460.

the imminent passage from the Mediterranean into the Atlantic of a French squadron, information confirmed by the French themselves in a message to the British Naval Attaché in Madrid communicated to the Admiralty on the evening of 10 September. Somerville and North received these messages, the one from Madrid only at 0800 on 11 September, some three hours after a British destroyer had sighted the French ships. North saw no need for action but Somerville ordered *Renown* and the one available destroyer to come to one hour's notice for full speed. He did not proceed to sea because he lacked a proper screen, because he would have been unable to surprise the French squadron and because he assumed that the Admiralty, being in receipt of the same messages but at a much earlier time, would have instructed him further. Since the Oran affair, British policy towards Vichy appeared to be extremely restrained; neither Somerville nor North knew of any change in this line. Thus they allowed the French to proceed to what they judged, correctly, was a West African destination [58].

In the afternoon of 11 September the Admiralty ordered Somerville to intercept the French and inform them that, while they might proceed to Casablanca, they could not make for Dakar, the object of operation MENACE. It was too late and Somerville's force too limited to prevent the French going where they pleased, though he disposed his ships as effectively as he could. The French duly reached Dakar unseen, though Force H continued to sweep to prevent further egress of French vessels from the Mediterranean [62]. Admiralty policy, unforgivably hazy at the outset, continued to be made in an *ad-hoc* manner and Gibraltar was left uncertain about its aims, the progress of MENACE and the general attitude to Vichy [59–68]. For two weeks, Force H was reduced to chasing shadows, as doubts about the whereabouts of *Richelieu, Strasbourg* and other French units gave rise to Admiralty orders to prevent them going to Biscay ports.

Somerville was exasperated, justifiably, by 'this French stuff', for several reasons. In the first place, Britain's enemy in that region was Italy and it made sense to concentrate such forces as we had against her. Secondly, given our parlous position, it was sheer lunacy to provoke Vichy to the point of belligerence without good cause. Thirdly, HM Government was economical with the truth to the extent that the authorities at Gibraltar were left ignorant of both our general policy towards Vichy and of operation MENACE. Fourthly, French retaliation took an obvious form – constant air surveillance of Gibraltar and the Straits, followed by heavy air attacks on the naval base, which had no fighter protection and grossly inadequate (and inefficient) anti-aircraft defence. Finally, Somerville's men and ships were being run down in a fruitless campaign when they should have been conserving their strength and training for action against the real enemy. Somerville reserved his vitriol for his letters to his wife [59–61, 65–67] but in his communications to the Admiralty he insisted on having full information and precise instructions. Though his requests were ultimately met, he remained convinced that our policy towards Vichy was misconceived.

Though Somerville's hectic activity ceased after the abandonment of MENACE on 25 September, the repercussions of the Dakar fiasco were to ripple through the highest ranks of the Royal Navy and successive governments for a quarter of a century. It was only after the failure of MENACE that London began to enquire into the reasons why –a procedure which seemed, then and now, little more than a search for scapegoats [78]. In particular, Admiral Sir Dudley North, Admiral Commanding, North Atlantic Station, was singled out for blame and relieved of his post with effect from the end of the year; he was not offered a further appointment. The Admiralty's charge was that he should have ordered *Renown* and destroyers to sea to intercept the French squadron directly he received the message from Madrid, just after midnight on 11 September; had Force H sailed by about 0400, the interception probably could have taken place. The Admiralty considered further that he should have anticipated that Dakar was the likely destination of the French ships, that their arrival would prejudice the success of MENACE and that he should have acted immediately and on his own initiative, without reference to the Admiralty. The case against North is not the direct concern of this work except in so far as it affected Somerville. He was involved in that the British ships to be used came under his tactical command and, moreover, he was incensed at the treatment of his friend North, both because of its unfair and peremptory nature and because of his conviction that, if blame was to be attached it should more accurately fall on Somerville himself [81, 83, 84].

Somerville argued that Force H was an independent command under his control and responsible directly to the Admiralty. North had no authority over it; at most, there was an informal agreement between the two admirals that destroyers of the 13th Flotilla (under North) and the 8th Flotilla (belonging to Force H) could be called upon by either commander as required. Both North and Somerville had been convinced that, had the Admiralty wanted the French ships to be intercepted, they had ample time in which to order action based on the information received from Tangier and Madrid [58, 77]. Though Somerville continued to assert that he, not North, was the responsible officer [84], the Admiralty went to considerable lengths to absolve him of all blame and to continue with its persecution of North, who was refused a court martial or any

other enquiry in which he could state his case [99]. Apart from
Somerville, several other admirals, including Sir Andrew Cunningham,
protested against the treatment of North [97, 157, 158, 183]. There was
no prospect of justice while Pound remained First Sea Lord but when
Cunningham succeeded him in October 1943, North promptly requested
a proper hearing [86, 87], again to no avail; neither the First Lord,
Alexander, nor the Prime Minister, Churchill, were willing to concede
that an error had been made, still less that an injustice had been committed. It took many years of postwar campaigning by Cunningham and
other Admirals of the Fleet – and Churchill's retirement from politics –
before North's name was cleared.

North *was* unfairly censured and the episode reflected no credit on
Churchill, Alexander and Pound; it was much the worst case of its kind
in the Royal Navy during the war. Churchill, as later events in
Somerville's career, among others, were to show, was always quick to
demand instant retribution if an admiral did not behave with the *élan* the
Prime Minister considered necessary, regardless of the circumstances,
the wider strategic context or the simple justice of a fair hearing. Had
MENACE succeeded, it is likely that nothing more would have been
heard of the failure to intercept the French cruisers. The MENACE
fiasco demanded that someone's head should roll. That it was North's
had little to do with the actual events in question and more to do with the
need to identify a scapegoat. North had lost the confidence of Alexander
and Churchill (though not entirely that of Pound, who resisted their call
for North's immediate relief) as a result of his vigorous dissent from the
use of force at Mers-el-Kebir; thereafter Alexander and Churchill were
waiting for an appropriate opportunity to dismiss him.[1]

The fault lay almost entirely with the Admiralty. It had failed to define
the relationship between North's command and Force H, a consequence
no doubt of the haste with which the latter was formed. It failed to ensure
that North and Somerville had clear and comprehensive instructions on
the treatment of French naval and mercantile vessels. It failed to inform
them fully about the nature of operation MENACE and how that
changed existing policy. Finally, it failed, through its own internal inefficiency, to react promptly to the messages from Tangier and Madrid. The
stolid refusal of the authorities to give North a fair hearing suggests that
they felt uncomfortable at their own behaviour. Somerville had taken as
much and as prompt action as he could have been expected reasonably to

---

[1]The athoritative work on the whole episode is A. J. Marder, *Operation Menace: The
Dakar Expedition and the Dudley North Affair* (London: Oxford U Pr, 1976). See also
Blake, n.d., BLE 9; Gilbert, *Finest Hour*, 720–2, 748, 787–90, 804–8; Roskill, *War at Sea*,
1, pp. 308–20, and *Churchill and the Admirals*, pp. 159–67.

do. He and North took counsel together and were both of the opinion that instant readiness for sea, together with air surveillance of the French voyage, was as far as current policy required them to go.

Even after the Dakar affair had subsided, Somerville continued to suffer exasperation, diversions, air observations and bombing attacks as a result of our policy of treating Vichy France as an Axis puppet (which was not entirely the case, the Vichy government steering a more independent course than was appreciated by Britain). From time to time, Force H was alerted to the possibility that one or more of the modern French capital ships might run for a German-held metropolitan port [91–3, 99, 150, 163]. The British Government's determination to enforce its blockade of Axis-dominated Europe led to operation RATION, a standing policy of seizing French merchantmen and escorting them into Gibraltar, to be searched for contraband.[1] Somerville was instructed, to his considerable disgust, to prosecute the policy with vigour, even intercepting escorted convoys, being prepared to use force and to invade French territorial waters [92–4, 99, 100, 104, 127, 131–5, 149]. He never accepted the necessity of the policy and protested frequently that it exposed his ships to unwarranted wear and tear, as well as damage by bombing, Gibraltar being a plump and soft target for French reprisals even for events at the eastern end of the Mediterranean [163, 164]. Provoking Vichy could have made her a full belligerent; indeed, the relative restraint of the French was remarkable. The Royal Navy was, of course, only the agent of Government and it seems that the Admiralty was as anxious as Somerville to reduce our commitments, safeguard Gibraltar and achieve a *modus vivendi* with Vichy. A complete blockade of French Mediterranean ports was impossible and all that could be achieved was harassment and an occasional reminder that Vichy should behave itself. Overall, however, the policy was sheer lunacy. Somerville and other admirals in the Mediterranean were right – Vichy should have been left alone unless there was clear evidence of blockade running for the enemy; resources, limited as they were, should have been concentrated on the Italians.

The British were worried also about the strong possibility of Spain's participation in the war on the Axis side. However, despite Franco's keen desire to fight, he was restrained by the need to consolidate his hold on power, by 'Spanish war-weariness and economic weakness' and, most significantly, by Hitler's refusal to grant him French colonial territories and furnish him with vital supplies. Hitler, who despised Franco, believed that Spain would be a liability rather than an asset, though he

[1]Butler, *Grand Strategy*, 2, pp. 232–3, 406–8, 427–30, 434–7.

devised a plan (FELIX) to drive through the peninsula and occupy Portugal, Gibraltar and the Iberian Atlantic islands. To remove the threat of Spanish belligerency, Britain, with American assistance, used a carrot-and-stick policy, giving Spain economic aid in return for good behaviour. The British Ambassador, the former Foreign Secretary Sir Samuel Hoare, redeemed his tarnished reputation by his adroit and sensitive diplomacy.[1]

The authorities at Gibraltar, including Somerville, played their part in maintaining amicable relations with the Spaniards. Here Somerville's recent experience of Spanish conditions and service and civilian leaders was invaluable, as were his bonhomie and shrewdness. The Governor of nearby Algeciras paid regular visits to the Rock, where he was always welcomed by the Governor and the military and naval commanders, generally being invited to visit ships of Force H [54, 146, 174, 184]. Efforts were made to impress the Spaniards with British naval power, partly to counter extensive Italian propaganda, evidently with some success [180, 181] and Somerville himself kept closely in touch with Spanish political developments via Hoare and the Naval Attaché in Madrid, Captain Alan Hillgarth, whom he had met in Majorca in 1936. Nevertheless, the British did not trust fully the smile on the Spanish face. Contingency plans were laid not only for a possible siege of between two and six months but also for counter attacks on Spanish ports and naval forces and Atlantic islands, together with alternative bases to Gibraltar, which was expected to become untenable for the Navy in a war with Spain [48, 53, 147].

The defences of Gibraltar against the current threats from the Italians and the Vichy French exercised Somerville considerably. When he arrived with Force H in June 1940, there were no fighters, few anti-aircraft guns and no radar; moreover, neither the fortress guns nor the anti-aircraft weapons were at all efficient, as both practice and real tests quickly demonstrated. Somerville agitated constantly for better training and direction of the Rock's gun defences and took the initiative in setting up the base's radar set [48, 54, 57, 133, 146, 147, 193]. Little progress seems to have been made until the arrival in May 1941 of a new Governor, Field Marshal Viscount Gort, who got on with Somerville

---

[1]Butler, *Grand Strategy*, 2, pp. 238–9, 358–60, 430–4, and see especially P. Preston, *Franco: A Biography* (London: Harper Collins, 1993), pp. 124–5, 355–450.

Sir Samuel Hoare (Viscount Templewood, 1880–1959): Con MP, Chelsea, 1910–44; army service, Russia & Italy 1914–18; Sec State for Air 1922–4; Sec State for India 1931; For Sec 1935; rsgnd foll furore over Hoare-Laval Pact; 1st Lord 1936; Home Sec 1937; Lord Privy Seal 1939; Sec State for Air 1940; Amb to Spain 1940–4; Vsct 1944; a skilful and successful envoy.

extremely well and set about galvanising the soldiers on the Rock [165]. Nor were the harbour defences and facilities adequate for the heavy pressures placed on Gibraltar by the permanent presence of a substantial naval force including two capital ships, augmented greatly at frequent intervals by both naval and merchant vessels forming convoys and escorts for the 'club runs' to Malta and points east. One relief was the early completion of a dock capable of taking a capital ship but this was partially nullified by a grave shortage of skilled dockyard hands [90, 92]. The crowded harbour was a tempting target not only for French and Italian bombers, though fortunately they never hit any ships, but also for Italian human torpedoes. This was a genre of warfare in which the Italians specialised and excelled and, apart from their successful attack on the Mediterranean Fleet battleships in Alexandria in December 1941, they made two attacks on Gibraltar, though luckily not damaging their principal targets, the major warships [93, 184]; nevertheless, the doubtful security of his anchorage was an additional worry for Somerville.

Had Gibraltar come under siege, one of the alternative bases for Force H would have been the Portuguese Azores Islands. They occupied a strategic spot in the central Atlantic, a useful refuelling base for both transatlantic and north–south shipping, a possible maritime air reconnaissance station and a point from which surveillance could be kept on the Straits of Gibraltar. From time to time, British intelligence warned of a German expedition from Bordeaux to seize the islands and Force H was employed on several occasions to patrol round the islands to intercept any such attempt. Should the Germans achieve a surprise landing, operation ALLOY was devised to drive them out and secure the islands for our own use. The diplomatic context was delicate; Portugal, though our oldest ally[1] was neutral in this war, unlike the Great War, when she had fought against Germany and thus made the Azores available to the Allies. The British were unsure of their welcome should they attempt to seize the islands ahead of the Germans. As it happened, the Germans never descended on the islands, judging that though they might seize them unopposed, they could neither supply nor retain them in the face of superior British sea power. Ultimately, in 1943, combined Anglo-American pressure made the islands available to Allied escort vessels and reconnaissance aircraft but in Somerville's time with Force H, keeping a weather eye on this desirable property was yet one more burden for his small force [76, 89, 92, 93, 96, 123].

The watching brief kept by Force H on the Azores is a reminder that it was seen by the Admiralty as just as much an Atlantic force as a

---

[1] By a treaty of 1373.

Mediterranean one. From time to time, the appearance of German surface raiders in the central Atlantic brought Somerville rushing westward
to defend the sea lanes from home ports to Gibraltar, Freetown and the
Cape. Although he never caught one of the raiders (by the time enemy
reports were received at Gibraltar, the raider had left the area), he
escorted convoys and rounded up scattered merchantmen, in the process
destroying some German blockade runners and prizes [93, 96, 123,
127–31, 145–49, 152, 167].

The greatest of all raider hunts in which Force H was involved was
that for the German super-battleship *Bismarck* in May 1941. Fresh from
working up in the Baltic, *Bismarck*, in company with the heavy cruiser
Prinz Eugen,[1] had sailed from Norway on 21 May. Effective aerial
reconnaissance had charted their brief sojourn in Norwegian waters and
had enabled the C-in-C, Home Fleet, Admiral Sir John Tovey, to dispose
his scouting and heavy forces to shadow and then intercept the raiders.
On his own initiative, Somerville, in harbour at Gibraltar, had brought
Force H to two hours' notice for full steam on receiving the first report
that the enemy had been sighted off Greenland. Just after midnight on 24
May, the Admiralty ordered him to sea to protect a convoy bound for the
Middle East via the Cape [160]. Following the sinking of *Hood* [158]
around dawn on 24 May, the failure of *Victorious*'s[2] aircraft to slow
down *Bismarck* and the loss of contact by the shadowing cruisers early
on 25 May, Somerville was ordered by the Admiralty to search for the
enemy on the assumption that *Bismarck*, known to be damaged, was
heading for Brest, a deduction he had already made.

Now came Force H's finest hour, one in which the Royal Navy's pride
and prestige were retrieved from what seemed likely, early on 25 May,
to become one of its greatest and most embarrassing catastrophes.
Somerville was in his element; his 'running commentary' letter to his
wife [159] conveys the drama of the chase and his own relish for it, as
well as the problems he faced. First of all, *Bismarck* had still to be redis-
covered. Secondly, her destination, course and speed had to be determined. Thirdly, Somerville had to keep his distance, since *Renown* could
not engage in a surface action; the purpose of committing Force H to the
chase was, assuming its discovery of *Bismarck*, to launch *Ark Royal*'s
torpedo bombers at her in the by now desperate hope that they could
accomplish the designed function of the Fleet Air Arm, namely, to so

---

[1]*Bismarck*: 1941, 42,000t+, 8×15in, 12×5.9in, 16×4.1in, *c*. 30k.
  Prinz Eugen: 1940, c12,000t, 8×8in, 12×4.1in, 12tt, 32k; captured after war, expended
at Bikini atomic tests 1946.
  [2]*Hood*: 1920, 42,100t, 8×15in, 12×5.5in, 8×4in, 6tt, 31k.
  Victorious: 1941, 23,000t, 54 aircraft, 16×4.5in, 31k.

slow down the enemy as to hand her on a plate to the pursuing superior forces of the Home Fleet. Should the airmen fail, *Bismarck* would make Brest safely, there to join up with *Gneisenau* and *Scharnhorst*[1] to form a squadron likely to prove superior to most combinations of capital ships the Royal Navy could bring against them. A further worry for Somerville was that the two battlecruisers would sortie to assist *Bismarck*'s dash for safety. Somerville also needed to be at peak alertness but rest was difficult given the fraught situation and the rough weather. The weather on 26 May was in fact the worst of his problems [161]. Not only did it make take off and landing conditions distinctly dangerous, the dense cloud cover almost down to sea level rendered the sighting of *Bismarck* immensely difficult. However, Somerville's insistence on continuous training now began to pay dividends, for *Ark Royal*'s reconnaissance planes spotted and tracked *Bismarck*, supported later by *Sheffield*.[2] The torpedo bombers which followed nearly compounded the developing British fiasco as they launched their torpedoes at *Sheffield*, a function both of foul weather and also of a communications failure, the crews not having been informed of *Sheffield*'s detachment to shadow; Somerville must take some of the blame for not ensuring that the detachment was signalled to all parties. However, the second attack was decisive; *Bismarck*'s steering was crippled in a determined if fragmented attack, *Ark Royal*'s Swordfish having at last hit a moving target. Though Force H's part was by no means over, the main action was now between Tovey's battleships and the wayward enemy. Lack of communications from the C-in-C led Somerville to launch a third strike, which arrived to see the surface forces deliver the *coup de grâce* on the morning of 27 May. Force H, evading bombs and U-boats,[3] and lacking a destroyer screen for the past 48 hours, made for Gibraltar. Thus ended a chase unparalleled in naval history since the French went to Martinique and back with Nelson on their trail.

The analysis of the hunt for the *Bismarck* does not properly belong here[4] but it is appropriate to discuss the contribution of Somerville and Force H. In the first place, Somerville's strategic sense was acute enough to realise his squadron might be needed and secondly he assessed correctly *Bismarck*'s destination. Thirdly, his training and direction of *Ark*

---

[1]*Gneisenau, Scharnhorst*: 1938 & 1939, 26,000t, 9×11in, 12×5.9in, 14×4.1in, *c.* 29k; *Gneisenau* sunk by aircraft, Gdynia, 1945; *Scharnhorst* sunk by Home F 26 Dec 1943.

[2]*Sheffield*: 1937, 9100t, 12×6in, 8×4in, 6tt, 32k.

[3]On the evening of 26 May, *U556*, having expended all her torpedoes, was unable to attack *Renown* and *Ark Royal*, though she had them in her sights.

[4]C. Barnett, *Engage the Enemy More Closely: the Royal Navy in the Second World War* (London: Hodder & Stoughton, 1991), pp. 278–316, is the most recent account.

Royal's limited and obsolescent air power demonstrated his grasp of its capacities for search and attack. Hitting a moving warship in atrocious weather and through a dense barrage of flak demanded immense courage, high skill, determination and experience. Whereas *Victorious*'s aircrews were novices, *Ark Royal*'s were comparative veterans. Their aircraft were already museum pieces in most respects but the Swordfish's lack of speed, together with its sturdiness, was in fact an immense advantage, first in enabling it to take off and land in conditions which probably no other carrier plane in the world could have mastered, and secondly in misleading the *Bismarck*'s gunners, who calculated on the basis of a somewhat faster airspeed. Had Somerville's force not held and slowed *Bismarck*, Tovey would either have failed to catch her at sea or had to abandon the chase through shortage of fuel. The C-in-C paid a generous and appropriate tribute to Somerville and Force H, who had been instrumental in transforming tragedy into triumph.[1]

Somerville had brushes with raiders beneath the waves, too. It is difficult to discern his anti-submarine doctrine. Like many other senior commanders, he appears to have been attracted to hunting, though he recognised that it generally paid no dividends [44, 46, 64, 199, 200, 204]. Certainly, most of the German and Italian U-boats destroyed in the Western Mediterranean and the approaches to the Straits of Gibraltar were despatched in the neighbourhood of either convoys or fleets. He paid a great deal of attention to anti-submarine training; there had been an early indication (the sinking of HMS *Escort*, 11 July 1940, 44–46) of the need to do so. Initial hunts and attacks on submarines were fruitless [44, 68, 89, 121] but a combined air and sea hunt netted two victims in October 1940 [91, 92] and there were other successful chance encounters [166, 174, 185, 199, 205, 207]. He used submarines attached to the station as 'clockwork mice' [48] and when *Ark Royal* was at sea, Swordfish flew regular anti-submarine patrols [51, 94, 96, 100, etc.] Frequent requests were made for co-operation from 200 Group RAF [48, 68, 94]. Though there were regularly 10–16 Italian submarines in the western basin, it was not until German U-boats arrived in October 1941[2] that Force H was under serious threat [188]. Air and surface support was given to convoys in the vicinity of Gibraltar [189, 192]. The skill and determination of German U-boats was amply demonstrated by the sinking of *Ark Royal* (13–14 November 1941), despite Somerville's heightened warnings to be vigilant, and a sizeable screen [194–198].

---

[1]In his report; see B. B. Schofield, *The Loss of the Bismarck* (London: Ian Allan, 1972), p. 70: 'Force H was handled with conspicuous skill throughout by Vice Admiral Sir James F. Somerville, KCB, DSO, and contributed a vital share in its successful conclusion'.
[2]Roskill, *War at Sea*, 1, p. 293.

Though Force H made regular forays into the Atlantic, its main function was to control the western basin of the Mediterranean, enable supplies and reinforcements to reach Malta and the eastern basin, and to co-operate with the Mediterranean Fleet (at Alexandria) in attacking Italian targets ashore and Italian ships at sea. Nevertheless, its role was essentially defensive, as it had very limited offensive power. The flagship for most of Somerville's time, *Renown*, though modernised, was no match for the new or modernised Italian battleships, while the new fleet carrier *Ark Royal*, though designed to carry 60 aircraft, seems never to have had more than 30 torpedo spotter reconnaissance and 24 fighters. A modern cruiser, albeit only a 6-inch gunned ship, and a flotilla of modern destroyers made up the regular Force H, though it could be augmented quickly for special operations. Apart from the fact that it had many other calls on its services and thus could give only intermittent attention to the Italians, it was at least two days' steaming from potential targets and it lacked adequate intelligence and reconnaissance of the enemy's movements [104, 182]. Furthermore, Somerville was under the Admiralty's direct strategic control and lacked the freedom of action enjoyed by a Commander-in-Chief.[1] The Italians enjoyed numerous advantages – several bases, full repair facilities, operations in home waters, the strategic facility of switching the weight of their forces from the eastern to the western basin at the drop of a hat, and numerous agents in Spain and North Africa assiduously reporting every movement of the British forces. Their ships outnumbered the British in every category except carriers; they were all modern or modernised, fast and well armed. Though the Italians lacked carriers, they had the inestimable benefit of a large metropolitan air force which enabled them to watch virtually every corner of the Mediterranean and to assemble substantial concentrations of both high level and torpedo bombers, supported by fighters. Their home waters were thickly sown with mines and they had a well-drilled force of motor torpedo (E) boats. Of their large submarine force, several were equipped to handle the human torpedoes or chariots, in the use of which the Italians were both expert and brave. Nevertheless, the Italians too suffered from a multiplicity of maritime obligations, for they had to defend their communications to Libya, Greece, Albania and the Dodecanese and they had to contend with well-handled British naval forces on both flanks. Two weaknesses seriously affected their ability and willingness to commit themselves to fleet actions against even inferior British forces. They were extremely short of oil fuel and they could not easily replace lost warships. Moreover, despite the disparity in

[1]See Blake, n.d., BLE 9.

strength, Somerville enjoyed some advantages over the Italians. He knew the waters of the western basin intimately, he was on excellent terms with Cunningham in the east, he was a first-rate trainer, technically aware and a charismatic, imaginative and aggressive leader, able to build on a tradition of invincibility and superiority of enormous depth and vast psychological importance. His force was also modern or modernised, though it conceded several knots to the Italians, the *Ark Royal* was a constant bogey to the Italians and *Sheffield* was equipped with radar, a facility never enjoyed by the Italians [93, 139]. Nevertheless, Somerville's awareness that *Ark Royal* was his trump card made him reluctant to expose her to unjustified risks and he recognised that she would be the prime target of the Italian bombers. Her Swordfish could not operate in daylight against fighter cover and her fighters, both Skuas and the Fulmars[1] which replaced them, were slow and clumsy compared with shore-based aircraft [94, 139, 158, 169]. He was always uneasy, too, about the Italians' ability to concentrate overwhelming forces against him [96, 97, 99, 100, 101, 102, 104, 119, 122, 126, 127, 138, 154]. He requested additional forces for operations to the eastward, called for submarines to be stationed at Gibraltar [52, 56, 178][2] and worked hard to develop good co-operation with 200 Group RAF Gibraltar and the Malta air reconnaissance unit [48, 62, 68, 91, 92, 94, 96, 122, 168, 169, 173, 182, 185, 186, 195, 199].

When Force H went eastward, Somerville's defensive arrangements always followed the same pattern. Ships were formed into a cruising order which placed the heavy vessels at the centre, where their concentrated A/A fire offered the vulnerable carrier maximum support; destroyers formed an anti-submarine screen and outer A/A barrage. Swordfish reconnaissances covered sectors ahead of the force and other planes performed close range anti-submarine roles, while at least one section of fighters were kept aloft. If shadowers were detected by radar, the set was then used to direct fighters onto the target, with the aim of destroying it before a sighting report could be made to the Italian bomber force. Should high level bombers appear, they were engaged by fighters outside the screen and if they succeeded in attacking the fleet, ships concentrated their fire, ensuring all guns were bearing but retaining enough sea

---

[1]Fairey Swordfish: 1934, 1 torpedo or 1500lb bombs, 2mg, 138mph.
  Blackburn Skua: fighter/dive bomber, 1938, 5mg, 500lb bombs, 225 mph.
  Fairey Fulmar: 1940, 8mg, 280mph.
[2]There seem to have been at least two submarines at Gibraltar most of the time but it was not until April 1941 that a proper flotilla (the 8th) was based there, with a depot ship, *Maidstone*.

room to take avoiding action. Though Italian high level bombing was probably better than any other air force's, it rarely succeeded in hitting its targets and therefore Force H could hope to escape unscathed, though suffering near misses [55, 56, 94, 95, 100, 137, 156]. After several fruit-less attempts from 10,000 feet or so, the Italians then concentrated on wave-skimming torpedo attacks, delivered with courage and skill. These were much more difficult to fend off, as torpedo drops and runs were often unseen and unpredictable and frequently delivered simultaneously from several angles. Heavy ships had to be adroit at combing the tracks of torpedoes but, although low level attacks were harder for fighters to deal with, they did allow low elevation main armaments to join in the barrage, which was frequently impenetrable and inflicted heavy casual-ties on the Italian torpedo bombers, which nevertheless scored more successes that their high level counterparts [90, 156–58, 173, 186]. Though barrage fire was effective at low altitudes, the force's A/A gun-nery was generally disappointing to Somerville, fire being usually below and behind the attackers [44, 94, 95, 100, 102]. After some six months' practice and head scratching, the standard did improve somewhat [137, 138].

Most of Somerville's Mediterranean operations were defensive, gen-erally escorting convoys to Malta, and he had neither the time nor the resources for a sustained and significant assault on the Italians. For the most part, attacks on Italian targets were by-products of 'club runs' to Malta. The range of objectives was effectively limited to airfields and other defence facilities in Sicily and Sardinia, since an approach too close to mainland Italy would expose the force to mines, fast attack craft, heavier than normal air bombardment and the full weight of the Italian Fleet in restricted waters. Somerville judged that no metropolitan targets would justify the inordinate risks Force H would have to run. Thus, Cagliari and Alghero airfields, together with harbours, a dam and a cork wood, received such force as Somerville's limited offensive capacity could muster – never more than a dozen Swordfish, attacking at night so as not to expose them to fighter attack [42, 44–46, 49–51, 55, 94, 95, 122, 156, 175]. Given such small numbers of aircraft and the somewhat derisory bombload (about 1000 lbs.) carried by the Swordfish, the raids were essentially strafes rather than saturation bombing and had only temporary effect rather than strategic impact. Though *Ark Royal* was equipped initially with the Skua, a fighter-dive bomber, only once was it used in the bombing role and Somerville saw little possibility for its reg-ular employment in that mode [100, 139]. The Skua was replaced by the end of 1940 by the Fulmar, a fighter-reconnaissance plane, faster and more heavily armed. In view of the dramatic successes against ships of the Ju 87 dive bomber,[1] Somerville may have been a little hasty in letting his Skuas go; a dozen well trained dive bombers, used in conjunction with Swordfish torpedo bombers in attacks on enemy warships, would have given him another attacking option.

The one solely offensive sortie undertaken by Force H was the bombardment of Genoa in February 1941. Both Cunningham and the Admiralty had urged Somerville to attack mainland Italian targets but he had judged, correctly, that the likely gains did not justify the extreme risks of operating under the enemy's nose [42, 44, 118, 121, 155, 191]. By early 1941, however, it was considered essential to draw off the enemy's growing air power from southern airfields and thus Somerville planned a bombardment of Genoa together with an ancillary air strike against a refinery at Leghorn. The first attempt was frustrated by bad weather [139, 140] but a second effort was made shortly afterwards [141–44]. Elaborate precautions were taken to conceal the object of Force H's eastward foray; these and heavy weather succeeded in wrong-footing the Italians and Somerville sneaked in to deliver a resounding and generally accurate bombardment, getting clean away without damage to his force. Hits were scored on harbour installations, communications and factories but the battleship *Caio Duilio*,[2] in dry dock after damage received at Taranto, was not spotted and the air attack on Leghorn achieved little. Genoa was shaken but did not suffer irreparable damage and there seems to have been no significant redistribution of Italian aircraft. Singeing the King of Italy's moustache delighted Churchill and the media but it might well have resulted in the disaster Somerville had feared. The Italians knew Force H was out but assumed it was running another Malta convoy; in any case, lack of air and sea co-operation meant that they could not locate the British fleet. However, British intelligence failed to spot the departure of an Italian fleet of three battleships, three heavy cruisers and seven destroyers from Spezia. On Somerville's return leg, the two fleets passed each other at a distance of 30 miles, each unaware of the other's proximity. More typical of 'the fertile imagination of Admiral Somerville' was his instigation of a minelaying expedition off the Italian coast by the fast minelayer *Manxman*[3] in August 1941; the mines, however, were quickly discovered and swept up [176, 178].

As with Cunningham and the Mediterranean Fleet at Alexandria, much of Somerville's time was taken up with the supply and reinforce-

---

[1]Junkers Ju87: 1935, 4mg, 1540 lb of bombs, 255mph; the 'Stuka'.
[2]*Caio Duilio*: 1915, rebuilt 1937–40, 26434t, 10×12.6in, 12×5.3in, 10×3.5in, 26k.
[3]*Manxman*: 1941, 4000t, 156 mines, 8×4in, 40k.

ment of Malta and the accompanying transfer of both warships and merchantmen to and from the eastern Mediterranean. Whether the British should have committed so much of their scarce resources to 'the Verdun of the Mediterranean', and indeed to the middle theatre in general, is a subject better discussed elsewhere.[1] Somerville himself never questioned our Mediterranean strategy in general or the necessity of sustaining Malta in particular, despite the high cost in ships, planes, equipment and lives entailed. Succouring Malta was a symbol of our general resistance to the braggadoccio Mussolini just off his own coast. We owed it to the gallant and loyal Maltese to hold on to the island at all costs. Properly defended it could become an advanced striking base, against the Italian mainland but more particularly interdicting his traffic to Libya. It was equally important as a link in British reconnaissance and, bombing permitting, a repair and refuelling centre for both ships and aircraft. Whether it could ever fulfil these roles with reasonable success and for any length of time in a conflict with Italy was doubtful. Before the war, both the Army and the RAF had concluded that Malta was indefensible; the Navy, whose main base it was, emphatically disagreed. Belatedly, Malta's defences were improved from July 1937 but by the time of Italy's entrance into the war, it had only eight light and 34 heavy A/A guns, one radar set and three spare Fleet Air Arm Sea Gladiators, hastily assembled and forming the only fighter defence.[2] There were few reconnaissance aircraft, no air or surface striking forces and only a handful of submarines; nor were there sufficient troops to repel a landing. Regular trips with reinforcements of men and material, together with food and fuel, would be required, preferably from both ends of the Mediterranean; in any case, Force H would have to co-operate closely with the Mediterranean Fleet. Not only would this involve large numbers of warships of all classes, often drawn from the Home Fleet and thus limiting its operations, it demanded the deployment of merchantmen of good carrying capacity and high speed (at least 15 knots), of which there were few available and those in constant demand elsewhere.

The Government's decision to wage a major war against Italy, taken in the light of our general global obligations (particularly to the Empire), our vital oil interests in the Middle East and our inability to engage our enemies offensively in any significant manner elsewhere, led to hasty efforts to build up Malta's air and ground defences, provision it against

[1]Barnett, *Engage the Enemy More Closely*, has argued cogently that the Mediterranean strategy was a great mistake.
[2]Gloster Sea Gladiator: 1934, 4mg, 253mph. Barnett, *Engage the Enemy More Closely*, p. 225.

the expected siege, and to rush troops, planes, trucks and tanks to Egypt – which meant sending them through the Mediterranean, as the alternative route round the Cape involved a voyage of months and 22,000 miles, almost ten times the time and distance. Over the years 1940–42, most supplies and men did go via the Cape, with planes going overland from West Africa but on two occasions impending British offensives led to the despatch of important convoys through the Mediterranean.

Between July 1940 and November 1941, Somerville conducted no less than 20 'club runs' with convoys for Malta and/or Alexandria, or with warship reinforcements for the Mediterranean Fleet, or bringing back both merchantmen and warships from the eastern Mediterranean. On 31 July, operation HURRY delivered Hurricanes to Malta, Force H attacking Cagliari *en route* [49–51]. A month later, HATS essayed a motor transport and tank convoy through the Mediterranean, together with reinforcements for the Mediterranean Fleet; this was opposed by naval leaders at home and in the Mediterranean but Churchill insisted on risking the direct voyage in order to get the vital equipment to Egypt in time for Wavell's first offensive; fortunately, it was a brilliant success [52, 55]. Operation COAT, beginning on 7 November, passed more reinforcements through to Cunningham, together with troops for Malta [94, 95]. On 15 November, WHITE attempted to get more Hurricanes to Malta but more than half failed to arrive [96–99]. More troops were sent to Malta in COLLAR, together with three MT ships for the Middle East and corvettes for the Mediterranean Fleet; this led to a brief, inconclusive encounter with the Italian Fleet off Cape Spartivento on 27 November, which resulted in Somerville facing a Board of Inquiry (see below, 100–117). On 20 December there began HIDE, designed to bring *Malaya*[1] and the MT ships from COLLAR back to Gibraltar [121, 124, 125]. In January 1941, Somerville escorted four MT ships to the east and flew off Swordfish for Malta {136–38]. In the spring, there were more Hurricanes for Malta [154] and in May the TIGER convoy with important cargoes for Egypt, about which Churchill was said to be 'very nervous' [155–57]. In June there were no less than three trips with Hurricanes for Malta [162, 164, 165, 167]. More Swordfish, troops and other equipment were sent to Malta in SUBSTANCE in July; this encountered fierce air attacks [168, 171–73, 177]. Troops whose cruiser, *Manchester* and transport *Leinster*[2] had been unable to reach Malta were ferried there in other ships later in the month and opportunity was taken to bomb Alghero airfield [174]. The next operation was not a convoy but

---

[1]*Malaya*: 1916, 31,000t, 8×15in, 12×6in, 8×4in, *c*. 24k.
[2]*Manchester*: 1938, 9400t, 12×6in,, 8×4in, 6tt, 32k; sunk on Malta convoy 1942.
Leinster: 1937, 4302gt, 17k, B&I Line.

Manxman's minelaying expedition, dovetailed with an air attack on some cork woods [176–80]. In September there were two more flights of Hurricanes to Malta [181] and at the end of the month the greatest convoy in the series thus far, with a much augmented Force H and no less than nine merchant ships, together with reinforcements for the Mediterranean Fleet and the independent return of merchant vessels from earlier convoys. A momentary brush with the Italian Fleet was accompanied by heavy air attacks, in the course of which Somerville's flagship, *Nelson*,[1] was torpedoed and had to limp home to Gibraltar [182, 184–86, 188]. CALLBOY, which began on 16 October, was another celebrated operation since it flew 14 Swordfish to Malta and escorted there the famous Force K, a *force de raid* of two light cruisers and two destroyers, intended to prey on Italian convoys to Libya [190]. On 10 November, Somerville set out on yet another Hurricane ferry trip but on his return from Malta and just short of his home base, *Ark Royal* was torpedoed and, despite herculaean efforts to save her, she eventually capsized and sank [194–98]. Somerville left Force H a few weeks later, the last voyage east during his command being one which he did not accompany, that of four destroyers which, *en route* to join Cunningham, surprised a superior Italian force and sank two cruisers and a destroyer [205].

The convoy operations were planned with extreme care. Elaborate measures of deception were undertaken at Gibraltar. Attempts were made to disguise the nature and scale of cargoes and bodies of troops and when Force H and its charges set off, course was often set to the west, the convoy doubling back into the Mediterranean under cover of dark, though Somerville doubted that these ruses succeeded on many occasions. Force H often acted as distant support for the convoy and its close escort and in any case turned back before the Narrows, leaving the convoy or reinforcements to negotiate the shallow, mine-strewn, aircraft-haunted, E-boat-plagued waters around Malta. If the convoy was continuing to Alexandria, Cunningham and the Mediterranean Fleet would meet it east of Malta. Somerville tried to avoid moonlit nights and prayed for thick cloud to frustrate Italian reconnaissance. Most convoys were detected and attacked from the air but the weather helped several to enjoy total immunity. The most serious threat was from Italian torpedo bombers and Somerville was fortunate that the Luftwaffe, which visited such immense destruction on the Mediterranean Fleet and merchantmen in its care, attacked Force H only twice, once being driven off by fighters and achieving only near misses on the second occasion. By a combina-

[1]*Nelson*: 1927, 33,950t, 9×16in, 12×6in, 6×4.7in, 2tt, 23k.

tion of good fortune, immaculate planning, dedicated training, the maximum exploitation of the force's principal assets – speed, cohesion, radar and its carrier-borne reconnaissance and air defence – and the shrewd, charismatic and authoritative leadership of its admiral, Force H delivered the goods with but token losses among merchantmen, warships and aircraft.[1] It had helped to supply the armoured forces which spearheaded two Western Desert offensives, and it had raised Malta's defences by August 1941 to a tolerable level; there were then 22,000 troops on the islands, with 118 light and 112 heavy A/A guns, 75 serviceable Hurricanes, and supply levels ranging from eight to fifteen months.[2] It provided Swordfish and surface craft to enhance Malta's offensive role and having taken a total of 38 merchant ships eastward, it ensured the safe return of the vast majority of them.

On only one occasion did Somerville have to justify his tactics on these 'club runs'. The COLLAR convoy which departed from Gibraltar on 25 November 1940 with troops for Malta, corvettes for the Mediterranean Fleet and three MT vessels for the Middle East, clashed briefly with the Italian Fleet off Cape Spartivento. As COLLAR took place a few days after the Mediterranean Fleet's skilful attack on Taranto, in which three of Italy's six battleships were put out of action, Somerville expected the Italian Fleet to exact revenge against his force. He was ill-served by shore-based reconnaissance and by intelligence and did not know the whereabouts or intentions of the Italian forces, which could still overwhelm him. The Italians did in fact put to sea and were reported by British aircraft early on 27 November, south of Sardinia and shaping to intercept the British fleet by about noon. Their force consisted of the new battleship *Vittorio Veneto*, the modernised Great War dreadnought *Giulio Cesare*,[3] seven 8-inch gun cruisers and 16 destroyers. They were thus greatly superior to Somerville's force, formed by the battlecruiser *Renown,* the carrier *Ark Royal*, three of the new 'Town' class cruisers and an old light cruiser, and ten destroyers. The force was handicapped by the presence of large numbers of troops on two of the cruisers, four slow corvettes and three MT ships, though it was due to be reinforced in the afternoon by the unmodernised battleship *Ramillies*, a heavy cruiser, a light cruiser, an A/A ship and four destroyers which

---

[1]The most serious loss was *Ark Royal*; otherwise only two destroyers, two merchant vessels and a score of aircraft were lost.

[2]I.S.O. Playfair, *The Mediterranean and Middle East*, vol 2 (London: HMSO, 1956), pp. 269–70.

[3]*Vittorio Veneto*: 1940, 41,000t, 9×15in, 12×6in, 12×3.5in, 30; surrendered at Malta 1943.

Giulio Cesare: 1914, rebuilt 1933–7, 26,140t, 10×12.6in, 12×4.7in, 8×3.9in 26k; transferred to USSR after surrender.

were being sailed westward from Alexandria.[1] Some ships were suffering from defects. As usual, Somerville placed his main force to the north of the convoy, ready to foil any surface attack on the MT ships and flew constant reconnaissances, anti-submarine and fighter patrols. The corvettes had already dropped astern of the convoy and had to be left to make their own way eastwards. Force H could not escape battle with a superior force and the Italians should have been able to win a decisive victory.

That they did not was due in part to their own shortcomings. The Italians could not afford further damage to their capital ships. This inducement to caution was strengthened by the enemy's rather exaggerated fear of *Ark Royal*'s striking force, by his (incorrect) belief that the British force was stronger than his own, and by the irresolution which characterised most Italian surface operations. Nevertheless, Somerville played his weak hand superbly, maximising his strengths and hiding his weaknesses. First, he recognised that he must take a Nelsonian course and concentrate his strongest units for an attack upon the enemy line, hoping to drive him away from the convoy. Secondly, his weaker ships now formed the convoy's escort and led it further to the south, increasing the distance between it and the enemy. Thirdly, the carrier was detached with two destroyers and ordered to launch a torpedo bomber attack with the object of slowing down the enemy, thus removing his advantage in speed and bringing him within range of the British guns. Somerville thus calculated that boldness and resolution might disrupt the enemy, inflict substantial damage upon him and reinforce the moral ascendancy seized so brilliantly by Cunningham in the eastern basin. His principal task, however, remained the safe delivery of the MT ships and the corvettes and the shepherding of *Ramillies*'s force back to Gibraltar; the clash, therefore, was always likely to be a skirmish rather than a battle. Were he to stand and fight the main Italian force, enemy bombers, light craft or cruisers might seize the opportunity to annihilate the convoy once Somerville was distracted and drawn away from it.

The junction with *Ramillies* (Force D) was effected at about 1130 and the action commenced nearly an hour later, at an extreme range, which was never materially reduced, since the Italians, after opening fire, retired at once behind a smoke screen, from which they emerged only briefly at 1250. While Somerville was anxious to close the range, he found it difficult to do so owing to the Italians' superior speed and disinclination to force an action, their effective smokescreen and the necessity of keeping his own cruisers out of range of the enemy battleships

[1]*Ramillies*: 1917, 29,150t, 8×15in, 12×6in, 8×4in, *c*. 20k.

and heavy cruisers. In addition, though *Renown* could match the Italian battleships for speed and range, she was but lightly armoured and her consort, *Ramillies*, was about 10 knots slower and her guns had a much inferior range. It was therefore virtually impossible for Somerville to operate his two capital ships together, yet if he failed to do so, he might be defeated in detail. The exchange of fire had ceased by 1310 and Somerville, observing that the enemy was still drawing away from him, had now to decide whether further pursuit was both worth while and safe, both for the warships and the convoy. It seemed clear that the Swordfish had failed to slow the enemy sufficiently; in fact, although one hit on the *Vittorio Veneto* was claimed, the report was false. A later report of a cruiser stopped led to a Skua dive bomber force being sent off to attack her, together with a second torpedo strike against the Italian battleships. Neither attack was successful, though again one hit was claimed, on a group of three cruisers.

When the gunnery exchanges ceased, Somerville reconsidered his position. Not only had the engagement drawn him away from his convoy, it had also brought him within 30 miles of enemy territory. Air attack was certain; mines, E-boats and submarines were also likely perils. He was willing to risk such dangers if there was a reasonable hope of catching a sizeable part of the enemy force. With reluctance, he decided that the enemy still had a good margin of speed and would reach his bases without difficulty. The risk of serious damage to his own ships in a forlorn pursuit was not justifiable and the more time he spent on such a fruitless errand would mean a longer return voyage to the convoy, which might itself come under attack from superior forces. As the convoy was several hours' steaming away, it was necessary to make an early decision to return in order to join it before dark. The return journey was punctuated by Italian high level bombing raids, which caused no damage, and the convoy was safely regained; thence, the ships for Malta were covered and thereafter the return voyage to Gibraltar was undertaken without incident [100].

While still at sea, Somerville had made a brief report of the action to the Admiralty. Even as Force H made a triumphant return to Gibraltar, a Board of Enquiry was on its way to investigate the abandonment of the chase, London evidently feeling that there was a case to answer [102, 103]. The Board, under Lord Cork, was ordered by the First Lord, Alexander, supported by Pound, though it seems clear that Churchill was the prodding force behind it. Somerville's reluctance to use force at Mers-el-Kebir and his frankness in criticising proposed operations had created in London a desire to dismiss him when a good opportunity to do so offered itself. Acting on Somerville's initial summary, the authorities at home ordered the Board of Enquiry, apparently confident that it would reveal the Admiral's lack of fighting spirit and misjudgment of his task. Arrangements were made for him to be succeeded by Vice Admiral Harwood, of River Plate fame[1] and thus a current favourite of the Prime Minister; a letter informing Somerville that he was to be relieved was prepared. Pound's role in these discreditable proceedings is unclear. He may have suggested the enquiry and instigated it so hastily in order to forestall even more iniquitous action by the politicians. Pound's subsequent support of Somerville and his somewhat lame and evasive replies to Somerville and Cunningham [105, 120] suggest that he was opposed to his political masters but, characteristically, frustrated their desires by indirect means rather than the blunt adversarial style favoured by his successor, Cunningham.[2]

The Board sat for five days, a tedious, sterile and irritating time for Somerville. It seems to have been a rambling and often irrelevant affair. Somerville, deeply suspicious of Cork's competence and impartiality, had the firm support of his captains, who were as enraged as their Admiral at the Admiralty's peremptory action. He stood firmly by the decision he had made on the early afternoon of 27 November, that his chief responsibility was to cover the passage of the convoy to Malta and that there was danger only to his own forces in further pursuit of the fleeing Italian fleet. He vented his anger at the inordinate haste of the enquiry, convened before his full report had been received, both to the Board of Enquiry itself and to the Admiralty [107, 108]. Somerville's observations are notable for their clarity of expression and purpose, and the confidence and vigour with which he gave his evidence had a favourable effect on the Board, which fully endorsed his actions and thus embarrassed Churchill and Alexander. The Admiralty was left with little room for criticism but, as Somerville recognised, they had to say something, however limp, to justify their extraordinary and absurd action [115], which merely gave Somerville a further opportunity for a devastating counter attack [116]. The indications are that senior officers at the Admiralty supported Somerville and were equally appalled at the

[1]Vice Adm (later Adm) Sir Henry Harwood: Capt 1928; Capt *Exeter* 1936; Cdre S American Div 1939; immed after Battle of R Plate, Dec 1939, RA; ACNS (F) Dec 1940 & VA; C-in-C Med March 1942; C-in-C Levant Feb 1943; invalided home March 1943 but undermined by unsubstantiated charges of lethargy by Gen Montgomery; FOIC Orkney & Shetland April 1944; Ret List Aug 1945.

[2]New assessments of Pound and Cunningham by Robin Brodhurst and the present editor respectively will appear shortly, in M. H. Murfett, ed., *From Fisher to Mountbatten: First Sea Lords of the Twentieth Century* (New York: Praeger). Pound has been criticised heavily by Roskill, *Churchill and the Admirals*, and defended by Marder, *From the Dardanelles to Oran*.

despatch of a board of enquiry [113, 119]. Cunningham, too, was out-spoken in his criticism [120] and not surprisingly North shared Somerville's indignation [103].

It may be that the despatch post haste of Cork was an adroit move on Pound's part to outmanoeuvre Churchill and Alexander and thus keep Somerville in his command. If this was the case, then it succeeded – but at a price. Thereafter Somerville seems, understandably, to have lost confidence in Pound. He was already suspicious of Churchill's behaviour and he held Rear Admiral Tom Phillips, the Vice Chief of Naval Staff, in low regard. Several days which ought to have been devoted to training and to planning future operations were wasted in a wholly unnecessary hearing. The Admiralty was further embarrassed when the letter relieving Somerville was actually despatched to him and then had to be retrieved unopened;[1] it was a final example of London's despicable and inept behaviour throughout the matter. The only good purpose it served was to enhance the already strong bond between Somerville and the men of Force H. Had this trust not existed, the confidence of Somerville's captains and their crews in their flag officer might have been undermined fatally by the crass and unwarranted behaviour of the Admiralty. If such peremptory action were to become a habit, then fleet commanders would become inhibited and morale in the Senior Service would plunge. Fortunately, Lord Cork's sensible and resounding support for Somerville's actions [107, 110, 114] seems to have taught the Admiralty a lesson, though not one to which it admitted; at any rate, the Spartivento enquiry was, thankfully, an isolated incident.

Somerville had made optimum use of his inferior forces and in particular wielded the one advantage he had, *Ark Royal*'s striking force, to maximum effect; the carrier did exceptionally well to put into the air, in addition to the usual shadowers, anti-submarine and fighter patrols, no less than three attacking forces. He judged almost to perfection the moment to break off the pursuit, both with regard to fulfilling his primary obligation, the support of the convoy, and to safeguarding his own force from attacks in inshore waters where it would have been at grave risk with no opportunity of inflicting damage on the enemy's main body. Reports of serious damage to the enemy reached him late but were in any case unfounded; on the information at his command at the moment at which he had to decide whether to continue the pursuit or to return to his convoy, he took the right decision.

[1]On this, see Churchill to Alexander, 20 Jan 1941: 'I am glad to learn from the First Sea Lord that the letter relieving Admiral Somerville has not yet gone. In view of all the circumstances, I think the question might be reviewed.' in AVAR 5/5/4, Alexander Papers, Churchill A C. Also see Blake to Pound, 1 Dec 1940, BLE 9.

A year later, another inquiry was set in motion by the loss of *Ark Royal*. Early in October, 1941, Somerville had been informed that Enigma decrypts revealed the presence of German U-boats in the Mediterranean [188]; their general patrol areas were known and it was also known that shore-based agents were reporting British maritime activities to them.[1] Thus alerted, Somerville instructed his ships to be more vigilant and put into practice more elaborate anti-submarine precautions. When Force H sailed for Malta on 10 November with *Argus*[2] and *Ark Royal* and more Hurricanes for the islands, the screen was primed for anti-submarine operations and aircraft, both shore-based and carrier-borne, patrolled overhead. The force zig-zagged and the Hurricanes were flown off on 12 November, after which course was set for Gibraltar. On 13 November, during the final approach to the Rock, several Swordfish flew anti-submarine patrols, both distant and local, Somerville again warned his ships of the likely presence of U-boats and course was altered to throw the enemy off the scent and Gibraltar was approached by a route not normally employed. There were several reports of contacts by the destroyers but nothing was held or confirmed. In mid-afternoon, *Ark Royal* was performing flying operations and was thus at her most vulnerable, though she was, as Somerville strictly enjoined, inside the destroyer screen. At 1545, she was struck on the starboard (i.e., island) side by a single torpedo fired by *U-81* (*U-205* may also have attacked simultaneously but scored no hits). At once, Force H went into emergency drill, *Malaya* (Somerville's current flagship) and *Argus* returning to Gibraltar at their best speeds while the destroyer screen either assisted *Ark Royal* or hunted for the U-boat. Before reaching Gibraltar, Somerville requested from the base a salvage and escort armada approaching Dunkirk proportions and himself returned to the scene on a destroyer, arriving there in the dark. He stationed anti-submarine craft to ward off further attacks on the stricken carrier and monitored the attempts to save the ship by pumping, efforts to raise steam and power, and by towing. Before midnight, these strenuous endeavours appeared to be succeeding but the outbreak of fire and the steepening list put paid to the gallant salvage mission. The list, which had developed immediately after the torpedo struck, had reached over 35° by 0430 and the remaining crew were taken off. *Ark Royal* finally capsized and sank at 0620 on 14 November, nearly 15 hours after being hit and within 25 miles of Gibraltar [194–96].

---

[1]Hinsley, *British Intelligence*, 1, p. 327, states that Enigma decrypts had revealed the presence of U-boats in the Mediterranean and their approximate patrol areas and that agents were known to be reporting British movements.
[2]*Argus*: 1918, 14,450t, 12–20 aircraft, 6×4in, 20k.

It was a chastened Somerville and Force H which returned to Gibraltar in the forenoon of 14 November. *Ark Royal* was the key member of what had become something of a family, she was the core unit of Force H, the Royal Navy's most up to date ship on the outbreak of war, the survivor of numerous attempts to sink her by bomb, torpedo and propaganda, and a veteran of operations in the North Sea, the Atlantic and the western Mediterranean. Somerville felt a particular attachment to her, for he was familiar with her aircrews, had flown several times from her deck and had regarded her as his trump card against the Italians. He had taken exceptional steps to protect her, refusing to risk her in operations of little moment and shielding her by both destroyers and her own anti-submarine aircraft. It was ironic that she was sunk when he had taken even more stringent precautions.

She succumbed to one torpedo hit which caught her amidships and apparently ripped a hole of enormous size in her unprotected hull. The list developed because water was able to travel up her funnel intakes and ultimately it flooded the boiler rooms and caused a fire, preventing steam and power being maintained. Another Board of Enquiry was convened at Gibraltar, with Admiral of the Fleet Sir Charles Forbes, then C-in-C, Plymouth, as president. As Somerville noted, the torpedo hit in the very worst spot, exposing what some termed a design fault, i.e., that the funnel uptakes could be flooded. It was an unforeseen weakness but what warship does not have shortcomings? All warships are compromises between the demands of endurance, speed, armament, protection, seaworthiness, and often also the Treasury and international arms agreements. The principal finding of the enquiry was that there were deficiencies in the damage control arrangements, compounded by premature evacuation of the boiler rooms. The commanding officer, Captain Maund, was summoned to a court martial at Portsmouth and, despite robust support from Somerville, was reprimanded for negligence and rose no further on the Active List, though he did distinguished work in Combined Operations during the remainder of the war.[1] Somerville sympathised with Maund's fear that the carrier might capsize quickly, so trapping hundreds of men, and while the court martial's decision may

---

[1]Capt L. E. H. Maund (1892–1957): Lt in destroyers 1914–18; *Scorpion* i/c 1918; Staff Coll 1923; N Asst Sec CID 1929–30; EO *Courageous* 1931–3; Capt 1934; ADP 1935; *Danae* 1936; Cdt Comb Ops Dec 1938; N COS Narvik 1940; COHQ; *Ark Royal* March 1941; CO, *Grebe* (N Air Sta, Egypt) Feb 1942; Actg RA, Dir Comb Ops Mid E & India May 1942; i/c unallocated landing ships & craft, *Dinosaur*, Scotland, Oct 1944. Brown's assertions (in Howarth, ed., *Men of War* p. 465) about *Ark Royal*'s lack of efficiency are patent nonsense. Barnett's analysis of her loss (in *Engage the Enemy More Closely*, pp. 372–4), though it has some technical justification, draws false conclusions; is one to assume that other navies' ships had no design faults?

have been unavoidable, Maund had been faced with an unenviable choice of evils, to hazard the ship or the lives of hundreds of his men [197, 198].

No blame was, or could possibly be, attached to Somerville himself. He had warned his force to be especially vigilant and he had adopted the fullest possible precautions. Once the carrier had been hit, there was little he could do except ensure that all possible salvage equipment reached her quickly and that she was screened against further attack. Had sufficient crew been left below immediately after the explosion to carry out counter flooding to correct the list, ensure all watertight doors were shut and regain steam and power, the likelihood is that she would have been saved, since she was so close to base and sea conditions were favourable for towing. Even more to the point was Somerville's belief that had the destroyer *Legion*[1] reported a hydrophone effect heard just before the torpedo struck (and which was probably the noise of the torpedo running), the fleet would have made an emergency turn away and the torpedo might then have missed [194, 198].

Force H was now reduced to something of a caricature of its great days. It had a flotilla of modern destroyers (now 'L' instead of 'F' class) and a good and efficient new light cruiser, *Hermione*,[2] though lacking *Sheffield*'s weight of broadside and endurance. In place of the outstanding pairing of *Renown* and *Ark Royal*, however, Somerville now had to make do with *Malaya*, an unmodernised battleship, capable of little more than 20 knots, deficient in main armament range, anti-aircraft weapons, protection and endurance, and *Argus*, even slower, capable of taking no more than a dozen planes and almost completely lacking in armour and armament. Somerville clearly regarded her as a liability [198] and he ventured to hope that *Malaya* was but a temporary resident [189]. New ships had to be drilled in Force H's ways and raised to its demanding standards; much of Somerville's remaining time in command was therefore spent in training. The arrival of the German U-boats also demanded additional escort, patrol and sweeping duties by FAA aircraft and the destroyers, thus frequently immobilising the heavy ships, whose utility in any case was much less than that of their predecessors [196, 198, 199, 200, 204, 205, 207]. In these circumstances, which compelled Somerville to remain in harbour for much of the time, he began to fret at his inactivity [202, 204] and to come to the conclusion that in the current situation it was undesirable to have two flag officers at Gibraltar [204]. Given the recent entry of Japan into the war and the loss, either

[1]*Legion*: 1941, 1920t, 6×4.7in, 8tt, 36.5k; lost by bombing, Malta 26 March 1942.
[2]*Hermione*: 1941, 5450t, 10×5.25in, 6tt, 33k; sunk S of Crete, 16 June 1942, *U205*.

permanently or for some months, of several capital ships and carriers, there was no possibility of reconstituting Force H around ships equivalent to *Renown* and *Ark Royal* in fighting value. It seemed an appropriate moment for Somerville to haul down his flag and, after a long overdue spell of leave at home, exercise his invaluable experience and well-honed talents on another challenge. He left Force H on 3 January 1942 [208], to universal and mutual expressions of regret.

A year after Spartivento, the Admiralty had no misgivings about Somerville's suitability for high command. The crippling of the *Bismarck*, the constant succouring of Malta, the bombardment of Genoa and numerous other successful operations had redeemed his reputation fully in their eyes, and in Churchill's, though such redemption was surely unnecessary. At all events, he was judged capable of taking on an even more daunting challenge, the command of the Eastern Fleet, a force designed to defend the Indian Ocean and our remaining Asian territories against the Japanese onslaught. During his 18 months in Force H, Somerville had not enjoyed the smoothest of relationships with the Government and the Admiralty, as his letters to his wife and other flag officers demonstrated [37, 49, 50, 60, 65, 66, 70, 71, 73, 78, 83, 88, 99, 105, 107, 112, 113, 125, 126, 129, 132, 134, 135, 141, 151, 158, 163, 179, 183, 191]. The lack of complete confidence was mutual and began at the outset of Somerville's command of Force H, with his reluctance to open fire on the French at Mers-el-Kebir, his efforts to moderate the British Government's policy and his belief that given more time bloodshed could have been avoided and a satisfactory solution agreed. The provocation of Vichy during the following 18 months earned his unreserved opposition to official policy. He complained frequently at being kept in the dark on general policy and operations in neighbouring commands. He opposed several operations either because they were in the realm of fantasy or because inadequate forces were available. The Admiralty seemed indifferent to his difficulties and gave him few words of praise for carrying out difficult tasks.

Somerville was always likely to have difficulties with the Prime Minister, as indeed were most military commanders. Churchill, the embodiment of national resistance and bold ripostes, was heavily influenced by the lack of enterprise and resolution allegedly displayed by the Army and the Navy in the First World War; the sailors' and soldiers' failure to capitalise on the Gallipoli initiative rankled particularly with him. He was determined that in this war the commanders of fleets and armies should act with dash and purpose and, once engaged with the enemy, battle on until a complete victory was secured. For all of his own military experience, deep knowledge of history and grasp of grand strategy, Churchill had neither interest in nor understanding of the many other factors in a military situation which might rule out the prosecution of an offensive, such as the obligation to protect a convoy or the shortage of fuel, bad weather or lack of air cover. His rich imagination conjured up 'wild schemes' [49], aided and abetted by his friend and Great War hero Roger Keyes [113, 132], who was almost equally irresponsible and short-sighted.[1] Though Churchill was now Prime Minister, he often acted as if he was still First Lord of the Admiralty and, like many other flag officers, Somerville felt that the new First Lord, Alexander, was merely a lackey of the Prime Minister [132]. Churchill's impractical proposals usually foundered on reasoned objections by his senior military advisors but he was apt to prod local commanders with detailed suggestions or demands for explanations for supposed shortcomings. Worst of all, he had a propensity for removing senior commanders summarily, without giving them an opportunity to state their case, and replacing them with one of his current favourites. The Cape Spartivento affair was a classic instance of his unreasonable behaviour, and his frequent inability to make sound judgments about a man's capacity to exercise high command is demonstrated by his desire to replace Somerville by Harwood [151]. British commanders in the Second World War, whether in Whitehall or elsewhere, found that one of their most time-consuming and delicate tasks was to 'manage Winston'. They chose different tactics. Pound was generally indirect, patient, skilful and often successful, whereas his successor Cunningham was blunt and uncompromising though not without subtlety on occasion – and at least equally successful.

Somerville had some prior experience of Churchill both as First Lord and as Prime Minister in the early months of the war and thus had a fair idea of what was expected of him and the likely consequences if he failed to meet the Premier's exacting standard of aggressive leadership. He evidently felt insecure during his first six months and when he was critical of operations suggested by Whitehall, or when he was unable to carry out an offensive operation, he braced himself for a blast of disapproval from Downing Street or even a peremptory recall [47,49, 65, 67, 102]. After surviving the Cape Spartivento enquiry, however, he seems

---

[1]Adm of the Fleet Sir Roger (later Lord) Keyes (1872–1945): ent RN 1885; gallantry in Boxer campaign, China 1900; NA, Vienna & Rome; Inspecting Capt of Submarines 1910–12; Cdre (S) 1912–15; COS to de Robeck, Dardanelles 1915; *Centurion* 1916–17; RA 4BS, Grand F June 1917; DP Oct 1917; VA Dover Jan 1918; raided Zeebrugge & Ostend April 1918; DCNS 1921; C-in-C Med 1925 – 28; Adm 1926; C-in-C Portsmouth 1929–31; Adm of Fleet 1930; ceased active service 1935; Con MP Portsmouth 1934–43; Director of Combined Operations 1940–1; Baron 1943. See Paul G. Halpern, ed., *The Keyes Papers*, 3 vols (London: Allen & Unwin for Navy Records Society, 1972–81).

to have felt more secure and continued to comment frankly on both general policy and proposed operations [113, 126, 129, 182, 183, 191]. An admiral from home confirmed that Churchill had instigated both North's relief and the Cork inquiry [179] and Somerville himself challenged Churchill on these two issues, though without any intelligible response from the old lion [183]. As Somerville's list of achievements became more and more impressive, however, Churchill, who had regarded him 'with a good deal less than complete confidence' after Mers-el-Kebir, came to feel that he was made of the right (i.e. Churchillian) stuff after all, praising his daring attack on Genoa and his 'skill and resolution' in fighting through the HALBERD convoy.[1]

Somerville's relations with the Admiralty were generally strained, for he had many complaints about Their Lordships' policies and behaviour. As he was not a Commander-in-Chief, he was subject to a high degree of Admiralty direction but felt that his instructions were too vague [59, 61, 73, 112, 141]. The Admiralty seemed unable or unwilling to comprehend the situation in which Force H had to operate [59, 88, 113, 125, 126, 151, 157]. He was frequently 'just left to grope in the dark' through lack of information about our foreign and strategic policies and about operations in adjoining areas, a failing on the part of the Admiralty which lessened the effectiveness of his force [60, 64, 71, 88]. Most of his exasperation with the Admiralty arose from its policy towards Vichy naval forces and merchant shipping, since it appeared to have have been devised without consideration for Vichy retaliation against Gibraltar and the ability of the French to concentrate superior forces against Force H, quite apart from distracting Somerville's scarce and overworked resources from the main enemy [60, 66, 70, 90, 91, 129, 134, 135, 149, 163]. Though he had begun his appointment on good terms with Pound, his regard for the First Sea Lord fell away rapidly, especially after the Cape Spartivento enquiry. He felt that Pound should have held up such action until a full report was available to the Government and he considered, too, that his fellow flag officers at the Admiralty had failed to support him on the issue [103, 105, 107, 108, 112]. He criticised Pound for failing to defend the Navy against Churchill and other politicians [113, 132] and identified the Vice Chief of Naval Staff, Rear Admiral Tom Phillips, as a particular menace, an armchair sailor without sea-going experience in this war, who wanted to supplant Somerville in Force H [151, 157].

With his fellow flag officers in the Mediterranean, Somerville had generally amicable relations, especially with Admiral North. They fash-

---

[1]Quoted in Roskill, *Churchill and the Admirals*, p. 186.

ioned a harmonious and effective working relationship in the absence of any Admiralty directive. The escape of the French warships, though it led to such a directive, defining precisely the roles of the Flag Officer in Charge, North Atlantic, and the Flag Officer, Force H, was due to Admiralty incompetence, not to any shortcomings in the informal relationship between North and Somerville. After North's removal at the end of 1940, Somerville continued to correspond with him throughout the rest of the war. He formed no such intimate relationship with North's successor, Vice Admiral Edward-Collins.[1] This may have been due in part to a natural resentment of anyone replacing North, and in such disagreeable circumstances. However, Somerville quickly came to the conclusion that Edward-Collins was incapable of working effectively with Force H and that he was slow and indecisive [132, 198, 204]; his references to Edward-Collins were rarely complimentary [158]. Cunningham was an old friend with much the same attitude towards Admiralty and Churchillian policies and proposals [70, 104, 126, 165, 182, 187, 191, 198, 206]. They gave each other moral support [50, 165, 196, 204] and co-operated closely in running convoys to and from Malta and Alexandria [52, 55, 94, 96, 121, 136, 138, 155, 168, 171, 177, 185, 188]. If possible, they undertook feints and diversionary operations to distract Italian attention from a more substantial undertaking [44, 139, 153, 154, 165, 176, 178, 179, 182, 184, 191, 196, 200]. They agreed that the use of force against the French Navy in July 1940 would be disastrous and both opposed the policy of interfering with Vichy shipping [23, 39, 99, 198]. Both were appalled at the treatment meted out to Sir Dudley North and continued to support his case [97]. Cunningham was equally outspoken in criticism of the Cape Spartivento enquiry [120]. Of the several flag officers from other commands who assisted in Mediterranean convoy operations, Somerville was certain that Syfret[2] was by far the best [170, 173, 177] and after his fine performance in SUBSTANCE, Somerville requested him for HALBERD [185]. Whether Syfret's recent experience of the western Mediterranean and Somerville's enthusiastic commendation influenced his appointment as Somerville's successor as Flag Officer in Command, Force H, is unknown but the selection earned Somerville's warm approval [203, 204, 208].

---

[1]Adm Sir George F. B. Edward-Collins: Capt 1923; RA 1935; RA 2CS April 1938; VA 1939; VACNA Jan 1941; Adm on Ret List Jan 1943; *Forte*, Falmouth Feb 1944.

[2]Rear Adm (later Adm Sir) E. Neville Syfret (1889–1971): *Britannia* 1904; Lt 1909; gunnery specialist; Harwich 1914–18; Cdr 1922; Capt 1929; *Rodney* 1939; Naval Sec to 1st Lord Nov 1939; RA 1940, 18 CS; cmded Force H, Jan 1942; seizure of Madagascar 1942; Malta convoys 1941–2; N African landings Nov 1942; VCNS & VA 1943; Adm 1946; C-in-C Home F 1945–8; Ret List 1948.

Somerville's period in command had been highly successful. In material terms, Force H had neutralised several elements of the French fleet and seized several Vichy merchantmen. It had shadowed and crippled the *Bismarck* at a critical stage of the operation, shepherded Atlantic convoys and stood guard against a German seizure of the Azores. It delivered well over 200 aircraft, thousands of troops and other vital supplies to Malta and escorted safely several convoys much of the way to Egypt. Italian morale had been shaken by the bombardment of Genoa, while several other ports and aerodromes had been raided successfully and at little cost. Several Italian and German submarines, a number of enemy merchant vessels and dozens of Italian aircraft had been destroyed for the loss of the carrier *Ark Royal* and two destroyers. Because of its many functions, Force H had little respite and it was difficult to effect repairs or spare ships for proper refits; it spent more than two-thirds of its time at sea and many of its units steamed up to 100,000 miles. What had begun in July 1940 as a scratch force hastily assembled to overawe the French fleet became within three months a well-integrated, well-drilled force with a high standard of efficiency and a buoyant morale, confident of executing effectively any task thrust upon it.

That Force H reached such an impressive level of cohesion, efficiency and spirit was due to the collective determination, courage and professionalism of its officers and men but above all to the leadership of Vice Admiral Somerville. Like most successful commanders, he set a formidable example of dedication, energy, efficiency, thoroughness and decisiveness and demanded much of his staff and captains. Somerville had evidently thought much about the nature of command. He was a highly visible, even flamboyant, certainly humorous commander, frequently visiting his ships and flying with his airmen; in the early morning, he was to be seen sculling round Gibraltar harbour in his 'beetle'. From the time he had first commanded a ship, some 20 years earlier, he had consciously cultivated a new, more extrovert persona which was somewhat at odds with the rather quieter manner of his youth. Not everyone appreciated his sense of humour, which could be coarse, and many of his subordinates could not keep pace with his speed of thought and decision, much to his exasperation. However, he understood the importance of stimulating efficiency and enthusiasm and maintaining morale by having regard for the needs of his men, going among them as often as brief sojourns in harbour allowed, and having a clear and firm sense of purpose at sea.

Somerville had clearly mastered the art of handling a fleet in various situations. Dispositions were thought out with great care and varied to meet changing conditions. He learned quickly what was required in the western Mediterranean under the threat of high level and torpedo bombers, E-boats and submarines. Changes of course and activity were made crisply and unobtrusively, often without signals. That this high degree of quiet efficiency was achieved within a few months of mostly hectic operations is a fine tribute to his insistence upon constant training, his ability to communicate clearly what he required and his breadth of understanding of what a fleet in modern conditions needed to learn. He knew that Force H would have to operate in hostile waters and under dangerous skies, against a variety of attackers and in the face of superior enemy forces. Thus a high standard of discipline and cohesion were essential if the force was to accomplish its objects at minimum cost. However, until the French fleet had been put out of action, there was no opportunity either to plan other operations or to train the force, which had, Somerville noted, serious shortcomings in fleet work, gunnery, night searching and cohesion [42, 44, 45]. The failure to destroy an Italian submarine which sank the destroyer *Escort* [46] indicated how much work needed to be done and Somerville pleaded with Pound for an opportunity to exercise his force, particularly the destroyers and submarines. The projected programme was disturbed by the diversion of screening vessels but, if ships could not proceed to sea, Somerville insisted that they should do what they could in harbour [48]. Most practising was undertaken on the return leg of convoys, indeed at any reasonably quiet time at sea [51, 54]. Operations revealed continuing deficiencies and the need to adopt new tactics and Somerville was always seeking to learn from operational experience. He emphasised the need for constant alertness and quick reactions [75] and deplored the requirement to intercept Vichy ships because it deprived his ships and men of vital rest and repair work on the eve of important convoys, when they would have to be fresh and eternally vigilant [100]. Constant changes in the ships allocated to Force H also reduced the squadron's homogeneity and efficiency [95]. Certain aspects of fleet work required constant attention. One of the gravest deficiencies revealed by early operations and never fully overcome was the ineffectiveness of anti-aircraft fire; it was generally too low and behind the attacking aircraft [102, 184], though some adjustments to height and range finding were made which led to a measurable improvement after about six months [136]. Given the large number of Italian submarines and the arrival of German U-boats in the autumn of 1941, anti-submarine training was another vital requirement; the numerous successes of Force H ships testified to the improvements effected, though Somerville clearly felt at the end of his stay in Force H that opportunities were still being missed because of lack of training [204]. As *Ark Royal* was Somerville's trump card, much of his attention was focused on improving her flying on and off efficiency and on drilling her fighter, dive bomber and torpedo squadrons, often flying with them himself [121, 147]. Constant changes of squadrons and air crew meant that the carrier's airmen were often novices and consequently performed inadequately on several occasions; fighters lacked the tactical expertise to bring down Italian bombers [94, 95] and the torpedo bombers were unable to hit moving warships [102, 117]. Not only did they practice torpedo attacks against their own ships [145], they also underwent night flying training [147]; Somerville was determined to be able to meet every eventuality. Even the Rock's coastal artillery was tested by Force H. It is probable that no other British fleet commander exercised his ships and aircraft with the regularity and intensity of Somerville; on just one day in September 1941, Force H, returning from delivering Hurricanes to Malta, was subjected to a dawn air launched torpedo exercise, fighter direction and interception training, ranging and inclination exercises, height finding exercises, destroyers firing at smoke bombs representing submarines, dummy dive bombing attacks, and other practices [181].

It was of considerable benefit to Force H that its commander was an all-rounder, a fine seaman, fleet handler, skilled leader of men, and a technical expert with a wide range of interests and knowledge. Having been one of the first officers to master the new medium of radio, he had taken a leading role in developing naval radar at the outbreak of the Second World War. When he joined Force H, he was thus quick to capitalise on the early air warning sets, recognising their value for picking up enemy aircraft at a distance and for guiding fighters onto them. For most of his time at Gibraltar, his only radar equipped ship was the cruiser *Sheffield* but if she was required for operations elsewhere, he was left blind and therefore requested sets for *Renown* and for two destroyers [93]. *Sheffield*'s set gave warning of approaching aircraft up to about 40 miles [114] but it was some time before British planes were fitted with IFF and thus distinguishable from those of the enemy [46]; this handicap was extremely tiresome, resulting in numerous false alarms [51]. However, Force H quickly gained confidence in radar's ability to prevent surprise attacks and soon learned the technique of vectoring fighters on to unseen enemy aircraft [55, 56, 94, 138, 185]. Radar was also used to make alterations of course to avoid detection by enemy reconnaissance planes [144]. By the spring of 1941, a number of Swordfish were also equipped with ASV radar, invaluable in the attacks on the *Bismarck* and U-boats [161, 200, 207]. The Italians, who did not possess radar, eventually devised a technique to avoid detection by flying low; reconnaissance planes remained on the horizon, made snap reports and flew off before being detected, while torpedo bombers also came in below the radar beam [181, 185]. While Somerville fostered the development of radar at sea and in the air, he did not neglect shore-based air warning systems, giving technical advice to the Gibraltar defences, taking vigorous steps to make the Rock's radar fully effective and chairing inter-service meetings on radar equipment [54, 57, 193, 208].

Somerville was less progressive in anti-submarine defence. While he operated Force H with a carefully organised screen and always flew air patrols, he retained, as did many senior officers, an addiction to destroyer sweeps and a Straits patrol. This predilection ignored the clear evidence of 1917–18, that the best means of destroying U-boats was by resolute, adequate and highly trained defence of convoys by escort vessels, supported by aircraft, preferably from an escort carrier; a classic demonstration of the basic principle of using the convoy as a bait to draw the U-boats to it, thus giving the defenders opportunities to detect and then attack the submarines, was given by convoy HG 76 in December 1941. This was escorted by the prototype escort carrier *Audacity*[1] and a variety of destroyers, sloops and corvettes, of which there were sufficient to enable groups of them to be detached to follow up contacts; despite the loss of *Audacity,* one escort vessel and an aircraft, four U-boats were sunk [205]. Somerville and the Flag Officer, North Atlantic, conducted several sweeps [46, 199], operated a permanent patrol in the Straits [133, 193, 198, 204 207] and used their destroyer flotillas in extended hunts after making initial contacts, generally accompanied by air searches [26, 58, 121, 204], but apart from one success [92], these proved fruitless. They failed to prevent Italian submarines sailing from the Mediterranean to Biscay ports or German U-boats from penetrating the Mediterranean in substantial numbers. They did operate under some handicaps; seasonal variations in sea conditions in the Straits, for example, created a layer of impenetrable heavy water which frustrated the Asdic operators [24, 51, 188]. Air patrols had only an ineffective anti-submarine bomb until late in 1941, when air-launched depth charges at last became available. Destroyers were overworked and could obtain little opportunity for rest, repair or practice. Though ships and aircraft attached to Gibraltar did achieve several successes against enemy submarines, they were almost all gained by chance encounters, alertness and skilful ship and plane handling [166, 174, 185, 199]. The German U-boats were more highly trained, had a better *esprit de corps* and were much more formidable than the numerous Italian boats and Somerville was rightly apprehensive of their entry into the western Mediterranean in

---

[1] *Audacity*: ex-German, prize Feb 1940, converted to escort carrier; 6000t, 6 aircraft, 16k; sunk by *U751* 21 Dec 1941.

the autumn of 1941 [188, 194–97, 204, 207]. Though he took elaborate precautions, even a sizeable screen accompanied by several patrolling aircraft did not prevent the torpedoing of *Ark Royal*. Somerville's anti-submarine precautions when Force H was at sea always included an adequate screen and a constant air patrol but he also called for flying boat support from Gibraltar and avoided being silhouetted at sundown or in moonlight [44, 48, 51, 55, 58, 68, 69, 94, 95, 173, 176, 177, 179, 188, 189, 200, 205, 207]. Only on a few occasions was he prepared to dispense with a screen, as when he had to operate in the Atlantic, where the heavy seas and lack of endurance of his destroyers meant that *Renown* and *Ark Royal* had to trust to their high speed, zig-zags and the carrier's aircraft [96, 130, 131].

Force H was built round *Ark Royal* and Somerville was just the man to make optimum use of the carrier. He had little experience of naval aviation before he was appointed to Force H but his characteristic interest in technical matters and new defence systems led him quickly to appreciate both the potentialities of naval aviation and the vulnerability of the carrier. *Ark Royal's* key function in his force was understood equally well by the Italians, who were wary of placing their heavy ships in range of her strike aircraft and whose air force made her their principal target, her bulk and her vast expanse of flight deck making her an attractive aiming point both for torpedo and high level bombers. Somerville was understandably nervous of exposing *Ark Royal* to enemy air and surface attacks and on several occasions turned down proposals by the Admiralty and Cunningham for attacks on defended shore targets as risks not commensurate with any possible gains [44, 46, 52, 91, 95, 118, 121, 155, 189]. *Ark Royal* did undertake several operations on bases and installations ashore but always flew off her aircraft in the dark, recovering them early in the morning and steaming quickly away from Italian territory. The major exception was the attack on the French fleet at Mers-el-Kebir, where the carrier's performance was astounding and demonstrated her versatility and high standard of operation for she was called upon to provide large numbers of aircraft simultaneously and for a variety of functions (reconnaissance, spotting for gunfire, mining, air defence of the fleet, escort fighters for bombing forces, bombing and torpedo attacks against the French ships in harbour and at sea, and anti-submarine patrols). The rapidly changing situations tested the flexibility of her flying arrangements to the utmost. Somerville was impressed with her capabilities and full of praise for her prompt responses to new demands [26, 40, 42, 43]. Several Swordfish attacks were made on Italian harbours, air stations, a dam and a cork wood. Except for the failure to damage the Tirso dam, the attacks were successful and achieved at low cost [51, 94, 140, 174, 175, 180]. In the force's bombardment of Genoa, *Ark Royal* provided reconnaissance and spotting aircraft and her planes also laid mines and attacked targets at Leghorn [139, 143, 144]. Her decisive role in the search for and destruction of the *Bismarck* [159, 161] has been discussed above.

Ark Royal's successes were achieved despite her small complement of aircraft (never more than 54, divided more or less evenly between fighters and torpedo-spotter-reconnaissance planes). Moreover, they were of antiquated design, slow, poorly armed and of limited carrying capacity, though sturdy and possessed of good endurance. This state of affairs is generally blamed on the dual control of naval aviation exercised by the Royal Navy and the RAF in the period 1918 to 1937, their mutual antagonism, and the RAF's indifference to or hostility towards naval aviation. There is some truth in this charge but one wonders whether a Fleet Air Arm under solely naval control would have fared much better, in respect of the number and quality of its carriers and planes and the development of tactical doctrine. Few senior figures in the Navy appeared to take a serious interest in air power at sea and almost none of the captains of the carriers had prior experience of naval aviation.

The role played by Ark Royal in Force H conformed to pre-war British fleet doctrine: her strike aircraft were intended to slow down the enemy heavy units and thus bring them within range of the force's capital ships. The small size of her air group precluded anything other than an ancillary role [43, 44, 51, 55, 94, 138]. The Fulmar was too slow to catch most enemy bombers in level flight but it compiled a formidable record against great odds and defended Force H and its many convoys extremely successfully against both high level and torpedo bombers and on one occasion a handful of them saw off a substantial group of Luftwaffe bombers [94, 137, 155, 157, 172, 173, 177, 190]. It was outfought only by the CR 42, a highly manoeuvrable biplane. The Fulmar was handicapped by the Navy's insistence that it should perform an additional role as a reconnaissance plane, though it was rarely used in that guise, and by the conviction that pilots were too fully occupied with flying the machine to navigate out of sight of their carrier. Pending the arrival of the substantially faster American single seat fighter, the Martlet, late in 1941, *Ark Royal* embarked three Sea Hurricanes, thoroughbred fighters of relatively high performance but short range[1]. It is not surprising that Somerville was somewhat puzzled as to how best to use them; he seems to have decided to keep them ranged on deck and

---

[1]Grumman Wildcat (Martlet): 1937, 4–6mg, 328mph.
Hawker Sea Hurricane: 1935, 8mg, 330mph.
Fiat CR42: 1939, 2mg, 267mph.

flown off only when an air attack was imminent. It is characteristic of him that he should be interested in the technique of operating them [168].

When Force H was at sea, the normal disposition of the carrier's aircraft was an anti-submarine patrol of two Swordfish during daylight hours, with a further six reconnoitring on a broad front ahead of the line of advance and to depths of 50–100 miles, with one section of fighters aloft to deal with shadowers and one or two sections ranged on deck; in areas close to the Italian coast, three sections were generally airborne [51, 55, 94, 100, 145, 149, 179]. Constant operations left little time for training and the frequent replacement of air crews meant that untried fliers had to be sent into combat, with less than satisfactory results [94, 100, 117, 177]; training had to be fitted in during the final approach to Gibraltar after an operation [42, 54, 94, 95, 145, 147]. After *Ark Royal* was lost, the old carrier *Argus* was re-equipped for operations with eight Swordfish and two Fulmars, [198, 199, 204, 207]. Events elsewhere deprived *Ark Royal* of a much needed refit and an opportunity to incorporate more modern equipment; the new carrier *Formidable,* which should have replaced her early in 1941, had to stand in for the damaged *Illustrious* in the eastern Mediterranean. It was intended later that *Indomitable*[1] should take her place but when relations with Japan deteriorated, she was earmarked for the Far East in August 1941 [138, 205].

Somerville was always eager to improve equipment and operating technique on board *Ark Royal*, inspecting an effective new crash barrier [94] and going aloft himself to test faster take-off procedures developed in the Mediterranean Fleet [146, 147]. He made detailed arrangements to coordinate air defence work with shore-based fighters from Malta and with the force's anti-aircraft barrage [179, 184, 185]. Only when *Renown* was absent on other duties did Somerville fly his flag in *Ark Royal* and it might be asked why an admiral so air-minded should have chosen to command his force from a conventional capital ship. Unlike *Ark Royal, Renown* was equipped as a flagship but in any case it was necessary for the carrier to operate independently when flying her aircraft on or off, which would naturally take Somerville away from the rest of the force. His practice was to lay down a broad tactical scheme in which the carrier's captain would then carry out his specific flying duties, thus enjoying a great deal of freedom of manoeuvre [117].

Within a very short time, Somerville came to have an extremely high regard for *Ark Royal,* her captains, Holland and Maund, and especially

---

[1]*Formidable, Illustrious, Indomitable*: 1940–1, 23,000t, 54–60 aircraft, 16×4.5in, 31k.

her fliers. He praised her achievements frequently [40, 42, 43, 51, 106, 155, 156, 157, 185] and often mentioned her airmen in despatches, recommending several for awards [43, 51, 55, 94, 155, 190]. He came to understand their problems intimately and had enormous sympathy for them [50, 95]. On several occasions he flew in a Swordfish, performing the telegraphist's duties with ease and impish delight, though his chief aim was more fundamental. 'I am convinced', he wrote, 'that when opportunity serves, it is most desirable that Senior Officers should take part in such practices in order that they may acquire a full appreciation of the problems which face the FAA pilots and observers' [119, 121]. His effort to understand the problems and possibilities of naval aviation earned the appreciation of *Ark Royal's* captain and ship's company and especially her airmen. Somerville's nephew Mark[1], an observer in a Fulmar who was later killed in action, wrote to him to express the universal feeling that

> the ship is now operating under a Flag Officer who not only understands the general aspect of naval aviation but who had also taken the trouble to investigate the practical and personal side of it, and thus understands the small difficulties which sometimes appear so trivial and yet which are, in reality, so important [122].

Of no other British flag officer of the time could that have been said.

Somerville was somewhat limited in the extent to which he could direct the operations of Force H. It was a detached squadron under the strategic control of the Admiralty and Their Lordships frequently instructed him to undertake operations with which he profoundly disagreed. He was particularly opposed to the use of force against Mers-el-Kebir and to the provocative interference with Vichy maritime traffic. The decisions to run convoys through the Mediterranean were made in London, though Somerville and Cunningham were consulted as to dates, the forces required and other details. Ships were taken from Force H for service elsewhere and, while Somerville could call upon the 13th Destroyer Flotilla, normally engaged on local patrol and escort duties, for major operations, by the same token, his own destroyers, the 8th Flotilla, were frequently employed on Straits patrols. Though the strategic direction of Force H was vested in London, Somerville and his staff had to plan the operations in detail. Unlike many flag officers, Somerville had the ability to delegate specific aspects of the plans to members of his staff, though he insisted on meticulous and clear orders

---

[1]Lieut Mark Somerville: Lt 1935; FAA, *Tamar* 30 Aug 1939, for misc service; joined *Ark Royal* as Observer with 808 Sqdn (Fulmars); killed in dogfight with Fiat CR42s 8 May 1941, during a Malta convoy operation.

and sought the advice of his captains and Admiral North [23, 26, 44, 63, 70, 86, 92, 94, 95, 98, 99, 100, 103, 107, 108, 142, 147, 178, 179, 184, 198, 199, 208]. A man with a quick and decisive mind, dynamic and firm of purpose, Somerville could be impatient with those of his subordinates who were slower and more deliberate, particularly at times of great pressure [59], and there is no doubt that he drove them hard and expected high standards of performance [75]. He could, however, smooth over fraught situations with his infectious good humour and in November 1940 recommended both his Chief of Staff, Captain Jeffrey, and his Staff Officer (Operations), Cdr Buzzard[1], for decorations for their 'valuable assistance' and 'excellent work' [94].

The constant operations in hostile waters, the lack of time in harbour, the unceasing planning for future sorties, the necessity to liaise with the other services, with diplomats and politicians and with the neighbouring Spaniards, the shortage of ships and aircraft, the need to train and adapt to new techniques and technology, all of this placed a great strain on Somerville, physically and mentally. For one who had been retired on grounds of ill health just a year earlier, Somerville showed no signs of fatigue or illness. He took what exercise he could when in harbour, walking up the Rock or rowing round the harbour in a skiff. Otherwise, he derived much pleasure from his cat Figaro and his canary Tweet. Mental relaxation was more difficult to obtain. It was not easy to shake off the enormous responsibility of high command, for ten or twenty precious ships and thousands of lives; the thought of dangerous and difficult operations to come must always have been in his mind. Somerville's situation was not helped by the absence of other sea-going Flag Officers, except on the largest operations. There was little he could do to devolve responsibility but while Admiral North was there, the two of them could share their troubles. The Dean of Gibraltar, the Reverend Knight-Adkin, a former Chaplain of the Fleet, was another with whom he could talk freely, but he, too, soon departed for England. For most of his time in Force H, Somerville had no one else at hand to whom he could unburden himself; his letters to his wife were generally his only means of laying bare his soul and they display vividly the loneliness of high command, with its moral as well as its material responsibilities [37, 39, 40, 45, 49, 50, 59, 60, 61, 65, 66, 69, 71, 78, 83, 88, 95, 98, 99, 101, 102, 103, 125, 126, 128, 129, 132, 134, 137, 141, 142, 143, 156, 195].

Despite the pressures to which he was subjected, Somerville nevertheless proved robust enough to carry out the multitude of tasks with which

[1]Capt Eric Gordon Jeffrey: Capt 1938; IDC course 1939; COS, Force H June 1940; died by his own hand 24 Oct 1941.

Force H was charged, welding a disparate collection of ships into a highly disciplined and efficient force, which had enormous respect for its commander and enjoyed his humorous sallies, as much a calculated device to sustain morale as a spontaneous expression of his own warm personality [95, 126]. The classic Force H formation was *Renown, Ark Royal, Sheffield* and the 8th Destroyer Flotilla of 'F' class ships; by the middle of November 1941, the squadron was a sad reflection of the over-stretched nature of the Royal Navy at that time. After the loss of *Ark Royal* and with most of its destroyers engaged on convoy operations and other anti-submarine work, it was virtually immobilised and much reduced both in cohesion and power. Somerville, mourning the loss of *Ark Royal,* the key ship in his force, fretted at his lack of sea-going activity and came to the conclusion that it was time for a change in command; there was little more he could accomplish in the circumstances. While his command of Force H ended in something of an anti-climax, through no fault of his own, he had displayed his remarkable ability to train a scratch force to a high standard, to exploit naval air power to the full and to adapt with speed and consummate skill to quickly changing demands. His leadership of Force H had demonstrated his fitness to command a fleet in all manner of operations, and in hostile waters in which his force was inferior in strength to the enemy. Given his record in Force H, it is not surprising that he was asked to take command of the new Eastern Fleet, hastily assembled after the sinking of *Prince of Wales* and *Repulse* to defend the Indian Ocean against the rampant Japanese forces pushing westward from the East Indies. On 3 January 1942, he sailed for Plymouth aboard the cruiser *Hermione,* arriving home on 7 January, almost 18 months after he had set off in *Arethusa*[1] to take command of Force H and write a chapter of our naval history as honourable as any in that long chronicle.

---

[1]*Arethusa*: 1935, 5220t, 6×6in, 8×4in, 6tt, 32.25k.

21.   *Report of Proceedings, 27 June–4 July 1940*

HMS *Hood*
26 July 1940

27 June

2.   At 1530 I was informed by the First Sea Lord that it had been decided to assemble a force at Gibraltar consisting of HM Ships *Hood*, *Valiant*, *Resolution*, *Nelson*, *Ark Royal*, *Arethusa*, *Enterprise*, *Delhi* and 10 destroyers, in addition to the 9 destroyers of the 13th. Destroyer Flotilla based on Gibraltar[1].

The initial task of this force, to be known as Force H, would be to secure the transfer, surrender or destruction of the French warships at Oran and Mers-el-Kebir, so as to ensure that these ships did not fall into German or Italian hands.

3.   At a later interview with the First Lord and the First Sea Lord, it was explained to me that whilst every preparation was to be made to employ force in order to complete the task of Force H, it was hoped that the necessity would not arise.

4.   The opinion I held after this meeting was that the French collapse was so complete and the will to fight so entirely extinguished, that it seemed highly improbable that the French would, in the last resort, resist by force the British demands.

28 June

5.   At 1300 I embarked with my staff on board *Arethusa* at Spithead. *Arethusa* sailed for Gibraltar at 1430, having embarked magnetic mines and other stores. Whilst on passage, provisional plans for dealing with the situation were prepared. . . .

---

[1] *Valiant*: 1916, modernised 1937–40, 31,520t, 8×15in, 20×4.5in, 24k.
Resolution: 1916, 29,150t, 8×15in, 12×6in, 8×4in, *c*. 20k.
Enterprise: 1926, 7580t, 7×6in, 3×4in, 16t, 33k.
Delhi: 1919, 4850t, 6×6in, 3×4in, 12tt, 29k; re-equipped in US *c*. 1942 with 6×5in AA.

29 June

6. . . . At 1445, I received Admiralty message 1346/29, ordering *Proteus* to patrol off Oran and *Pandora*[1] off Algiers to report any French movements but not to attack.

22.   *From the Admiralty*

30 June 1940

A.   After further consideration operation against Oran, which will be called CATAPULT, it is clear that alternative of either sinking their ships or being destroyed by gunfire has [such] grave disadvantages from French point of view that in either case they would not (R) not have their ships when peace is declared between the British Empire, Germany and Italy. Under armistice terms they would get them back.

B.   As we desire to prevent ships getting into German or Italian hands with as little trouble and bloodshed as possible, it is under consideration to give them three alternatives, as follows:–

1.   To steam their ships to a British port.
2.   To sink (R) sink their ships.
3.   To have their ships destroyed by gunfire.

C.   Your plan should be based on giving them the three alternatives.

You will be informed as soon as possible which alternatives HMG decides to give them.

D.   Should it be decided to give them the first alternative it would be necessary to ensure ships were in a condition neither to fight nor to run away and consequently they should only have sufficient hands on board for

1.   steam half boiler power
2.   visual signalling
3.   steering and anchoring the ship
4.   feeding officers and men
5.   possibly some ratings for other essential services
6.   submarines would have to be rendered innocuous by landing their torpedoes or pistols.

E.   It is realised that first alternative will prolong the operation as ships may be at as much as 8 hours' notice for steam.

[1]*Proteus, Pandora* (bombed Malta 1942): 1930, 1475/2040t, 8tt, 1×4in, 17.5/9 k.

F.   If the French agreed to first alternative, it is desirable that all ships should proceed to a British port rather than to Gibraltar.

G.   Request your remarks as to whether you see any insuperable difficulties in carrying out first alternative.

H.   As soon as you obtain information as to which ships are berthed you should report whether if alternative 3 has to be adopted there will be danger of loss of life to civilians from gunfire of our ships.

23.   *Report of Proceedings, 28 June–4 July* (cont.)

30 June

7.   At 0221, I received AM 0015/30, ordering the Vice Admiral Commanding Aircraft Carriers[1] to establish a destroyer patrol 30 miles W of Oran and that should *Dunkerque* and *Strasbourg* proceed to the westward they were to be captured and taken to the United Kingdom.

At 0429, I received AM 0135/30, instructing the Admiral Commanding North Atlantic Station to investigate the action which could be taken by Force H to neutralise bombardment in the event of Spain becoming hostile.

I was somewhat surprised at receiving this message, since I understood that a number of appreciations of the situation referred to had invariably reached the same conclusion, namely, that Gibraltar as a naval base would immediately become untenable, except, perhaps, for a few small craft and possibly submarines.

8.   ... At 1614, I received C-in-C, Mediterranean's message 1105/30, in which he expressed strong opposition to the proposal that ships at Alexandria should be seized forcibly,[2] and to the use of force at Oran, which he considered might have serious repercussions.

9.   At 1745, *Arethusa* arrived at Gibraltar and secured at Cormorant berth.

I called immediately on Admiral Sir Dudley North. He expressed grave concern at the proposal to use force against the French fleet and was strongly of the opinion that this should be avoided at all costs. Discussing AM 0135/30, he considered that since the Germans would be co-operating actively with the Spaniards, it was idle to suppose that Gibraltar could be used as a naval base. Engagement of shore batteries by ships and *Ark Royal*'s aircraft could only silence some of the batteries temporarily.

[1]Vice Admiral Wells.
[2]See *A Sailor's Odyssey*, pp. 245–6.

10.   I then called on HE the Governor,[1] who endorsed the views expressed by Admiral North concerning the continued use of Gibraltar as a naval base in the event of war with Spain.

11.   That evening I called a meeting of Flag Officers and senior COs to discuss the Oran operation.

VACAC considered that torpedo attack by aircraft would be difficult and unproductive unless anti-aircraft gunfire was first silenced. Net defences and the restricted area of the harbour appeared to rule out torpedo attack by destroyers.

It was decided finally that, in the case of Mers-el-Kebir, a round or two (aimed not to hit) should be fired to show we were in earnest, and if this failed to bring acceptance of our terms, a limited period of gunfire and/or bombing should be used to cause evacuation of the ships, final sinking being effected by torpedo-bomber attack or demolition, according to circumstances.

It was thought that to complete destruction by gunfire would require a great deal of ammunition and cause very great loss of life.

12.   In the case of Oran, it was agreed that gunfire would cause very severe civilian casualties and it was hoped that the action taken at Mers-el-Kebir would induce the French to scuttle their ships at Oran.

The view I held, and which was shared by others present at the meeting, was that it was highly improbable that the French would use force to resist our demands.

13.   After the conclusion of this meeting, Admiral North, Admiral Wells and Captain Holland all expressed themselves as strongly opposed to the use of force. They considered that there was little fear of the French allowing their ships to fall into German hands.

1 July

14.   At 0346 I received AM 0251/1, ordering *Nelson* to return to Scapa.

At 0410 received AM 0225/1, giving four alternatives to put before the French, namely

1.   to bring their ships to British harbours and fight with us,
2.   to steam their ships to a British port,
3.   to demilitarise their ships to our satisfaction,
4.   to sink their ships.

15.   . . . 0942 – I informed the Admiralty that I presumed that the final instructions for CATAPULT would contain orders as to the action to be taken should the French refuse all four alternatives. . . .

[1]Gen Viscount Dillon, formerly of the R Munster Fusiliers.

To this I received a reply at 1846, that it was the firm intention of HM
Government that, if the French would not accept the alternatives which
were being transmitted to me, their ships must be destroyed; my proposals were therefore not acceptable.

17.   I felt at this time that, although there was a possibility that the
French might be prepared to fight, it was improbable that they would do
so under the conditions which would obtain at Oran. At the worst, they
might fire a few token shots before abandoning their ships.

24.   To the Admiralty

Gibraltar,
1 July 1940

Earliest date CATAPULT can be put into effect is a.m. 3 July, V.A.
Force leaving harbour p.m. 2 July.

2.   Intend withdrawing patrols from Oran, Casablanca and Straits
Monday which should give me 5 destroyers of 13DF plus 6 others for
operation. Remainder making good defects or on urgent and minimum
convoy escort.

3.   Consider this destroyer force is sufficient in view of low standard of
Italian submarine efficiency and in spite gradual deterioration of Asdic
conditions in Straits of Gibraltar area.[1]

4.   My 1514/29 June. Now consider Holland should arrive Oran at dusk
2 July, and Force H daylight 3 July so that whatever alternative adopted
can be completed before dark.

25.   To the Admiralty

1 July 1940

I have had further opportunity to discuss situation with Holland,
Spearman and Davies and am impressed by their view that use of force
should be avoided at all costs.

They consider now armistice terms are known there is distinct possibility of French accepting first alternative. To achieve this and in accordance with their experience of French, they proposed Holland arrives
0800 [–?] and before sailing in [–?] plain language message address
Admiral Gensoul.

'The British Admiralty have sent Captain Holland to confer with you.

---

[1]A layer of dense water was present during the summer months and adversely affected
Asdic signals.

'The British Navy hope their proposals will enable you and your glorious French Navy once more to range yourselves side by side with them. In these circumstances your ships would remain yours and no one need have anxiety for the future. A British Fleet is at sea off Oran waiting to welcome you.'

One hour after Holland enters harbour Force H arrives off Oran and repeats same message addressed to French Admiral using signal projectors trained on as many ships as possible. This is to ensure purport of message is received by officers and men other than French Admiral.

If French refuse first alternative they consider second alternative must be amended as follows:–

French to proceed to sea with minimum steering party, i.e., DEMILI-TARISED, and allow themselves to be captured by Force H. Strictly ensure ships are to be returned to France on completion of hostilities. French can plead they acted under force and that therefore [they were] unable to contest British action.

Third and fourth alternatives to be in the form of invitation to French. Quote

'They hold strongly that offensive action on our part would immediately alienate all French wherever they are, and transfer defeated ally into an active enemy. They believe use of prestige would be enhanced if we withdraw from Oran without taking offensive action.'

These views based on very recent contacts of French Naval Authorities. Unless Their Lordships have more definite and [–?] information, I consider that the proposals merit very careful consideration.

Very early reply requested as possible acceptance of first or second alternative depends on immediate action.

26. *Report of Proceedings, 28 June–4 July* (cont.)

2 July

18. . . . 0640 – *Valiant, Foresight, Forester* and *Escort*[1] arrived at Gibraltar.
19. I held a meeting of Flag and Commanding Officers during the forenoon, at which the orders for operation CATAPULT were explained and discussed. As will be noted, the orders had to be framed in somewhat general terms, since the exact situation which would arise could not be foreseen.

---

[1]*Escort*: 1934, 1375t, 4×4.7in, 8tt, 36k; sunk 11 July 1940, Italian S/M *Marconi*. *Foresight* (sunk 1942, Ital a/c), *Forester*: 1935, 1375t, 4×4.7in, 8tt, 36k.

In the light of later events, it is clear that these orders did not make sufficient provision for dealing with any French ships that might attempt to leave harbour after the entrance had been mined and the ships subjected to bombardment.

It will be noted that the orders contain no reference to the laying of magnetic mines.

20.   I was informed by Vice Admiral [Wells] that aircraft could be armed with mines at short notice and the plan for laying at Mers-el-Kebir was discussed. It was not my intention, however, to lay mines, except as a last resort, since this would have prevented the French from accepting first or second alternatives and it would also have prevented the entrance of our destroyers with demolition parties.

22.   Captain Holland having expressed some doubts that Admiral Gensoul might be at pains to conceal from his officers and men the alternatives proposed for acceptance, I decided that *Foxhound* (the ship detailed to embark Captain Holland) as well as selected ships of Force H should signal the following message in French, using a signalling projector trained on *Dunkerque* and as many other ships as possible.

Pour Admiral Gensoul de Admiral Somerville.

Nous espérons trés sincerement séront acceptables et que nous vous trouverons à nos cotes.[1]

23.   . . . At 1500, destroyers left harbour to carry out A/S sweep of the approaches and Gibraltar Bay.

At 1525, *Proteus* was informed that Force H would be operating off Oran as from 0800, 3 July, and was instructed to take up a patrol position well clear to the northward.

24.   By 1700, Force H, consisting of the following ships

Hood (Flag of Flag Officer Commanding, Force H), *Ark Royal* (Flag of VAC Aircraft Carriers), *Valiant, Resolution, Arethusa, Enterprise, Faulknor* (Captain (D), 8th DF), *Foxhound, Fearless, Forester, Foresight, Escort, Keppel* (Captain (D), 13th DF), *Active, Wrestler, Vidette, Vortigern*[2] were clear of the harbour and course was shaped to the eastward at 17 knots, . . .

---

[1] 'For Admiral Gensoul from Admiral Somerville. We hope very sincerely these will be acceptable and that we shall find you on our side.'

[2] *Faulknor*: (L), 1935, 1475t, 5×4.7in, 8tt, 36k.

Foxhound, Fearless (lost, Malta convoy 1941): 1935, 1375t, 4×4.7in, 8tt, 36k.

Keppel: 1925, 1480t, 4×4.7in, 1×3in, 6tt, 31k.

Active: 1930, 1350t, 4×4.7in, 8tt, 35k.

Wrestler: 1918, 1100t, 4 (later 2)×4in, 28 (later 24.5)k; scrapped after mine damage 1944.

Vidette: 1918, 1090t, 4×4in, 28k.

Vortigern: 1918, 1090t, 3×4in, 3tt, 28k; sunk N Sea 1942, E-boat.

25.   At 2010, I informed Captain Holland the Admiralty had informed me that the French had a scheme for demilitarisation at two hours' notice. Should necessity arise, he was to question them on this and satisfy himself the proposed measures would be effective, that is, that the ships could not be ready for service again within 12 months, even with dockyard assistance.

26.   At 2247, . . . a torpedo exploded ahead of *Vortigern* . . . The U-boat was hunted by *Vortigern* and *Vidette* for 65 minutes, but without success.

27.   *From the Admiralty*

0103, 2 July 1940

HM Government have decided that the course to be adopted is as follows

A.   French Fleet at Oran and Mers-el-Kebir is to be given four alternatives:–

1.   To sail their ships to British harbours and continue to fight with us.
2.   To sail their ships with reduced crews to a British port from which the crews would be repatriated whenever desired or in the case of alternative (1) or (2) being adopted, the ships would be restored to France at the conclusion of the war or full compensation would be paid if they are damaged meanwhile. If the French Admiral adopts alternative (2), but asks that their ships should not (R) not be used by British during war, say we accept this condition for so long as Germany and Italy observe the armistice terms but we particularly do not (R) not wish to raise point ourselves.
3.   To sail their ships with reduced crews to some French port in West Indies such as Martinique. After arrival at this port they would either be demilitarised, to our satisfaction, if so desired, or be entrusted to the USA jurisdiction for the duration of the war. The crews would be repatriated.
4.   To sink (R) sink their ships.

B.   Should French Admiral refuse to accept all above alternatives and should he suggest he should demilitarise his ships at our satisfaction at their present berths, you are authorised to accept this further alternative provided you are satisfied that measures taken for demilitarisation can be carried out under your supervision within six hours and prevent ships being brought into service for at least one year, even at fully equipped dockyard port.

C.   if none of those alternatives are accepted by the French you are to endeavour to destroy (R) destroy ships in Mers-el-Kebir particularly *Dunkerque* and *Strasbourg* using all means at your disposal. Ships at Oran should also be destroyed if this will not (R) not entail any considerable loss of civilian life.

D.   Communication to be made to French Admiral as follows:–

1.   HM Government have sent me to inform you as follows:–

2.   They agreed to French Government approaching the German Government only on conditions before an armistice was concluded the French Fleet should be sent to British ports to prevent it falling into the hands of the enemy. The Council of Ministers declared on 18 June that before guilty of capitulation on land the French fleet would join up with British Force or sink (R) sink itself.

3.   While the present French [Government] may consider terms of their armistice with Germany and Italy are reconcilable with these undertakings, HM Government finds it impossible from our previous experience to believe Germany and Italy will not (R) not at any moment which suits them seize French warships and use them against Britain and allies. Italian armistice prescribes that French ships should return to metropolitan ports and under armistice France is required to yield up units for coast defence and minesweeping.

4.   It is impossible for us, your comrades up till now, to allow your fine ships to fall into power of German or Italian enemy. We are determined to fight on to the end, and if we win, as we think we shall, we shall never forget that France was our ally, that our interests are the same as hers, and that our common enemy is Germany. Should we conquer we solemnly declare we shall restore the greatness and territory of France. For this purpose we must be sure that the best ships of the French Navy will also not (R) not be used against us by the common foe.

5.   In these circumstances HM Government have instructed me to demand that French Fleet now at Mers-el-Kebir and Oran shall act in accordance with one of the following alternatives:–

(a)   Sail with us and continue to fight for victory against the Germans and the Italians.

(b)   Sail with reduced crews under our control to a British Port. The reduced crews will be repatriated at the earliest moment. If either of these courses is adopted by you we will return your ships to France at the conclusion of the war, or pay full compensation if they are damaged meanwhile.

(c)   Alternatively, if you feel bound to stipulate that your ships should not (R) not be used against Germans or Italians, for which these [alternatives?] break the armistice, then sail them with us with reduced crews to some French port in the West Indies, Martinique for instance, where they can be demilitarised to our satisfaction, or perhaps be entrusted to the USA, and remain safely until end of war, the crews being repatriated.

6.   If you refuse these fair offers, I must with profound regret require you to sink your ships within six hours. Finally, failing the above, I have the orders of HM Government to use whatever force may be necessary to prevent your ships from falling into German or Italian hands.

E.   It is most undesirable that you should have to deal with French Fleet at sea and consequently at about 12 hours' warning, as suggested in your 0812/1,[1] is not (R) not acceptable. Hence, you should arrive in the vicinity of Oran with your force at whatever time you select, and send your emissary ashore, subsequently taking such action you consider fit with your force in period before time limit given expires.

F.   If first alternative is accepted ships should proceed to a United Kingdom port unless French prefer Gibraltar.

G.   In view of strength of defences at Algiers and impossibility of avoiding destruction of town, it is not (R) not considered justifiable to carry out an operation against that place.

H.   These are your final instructions in case you find the French fleet in harbour which were decided on after receipt of your 1220/1.

I.   Further instructions follow as regards the action to be taken if French Fleet is at sea.

28.   *From the Admiralty*

0113, 2 July 1940

The following suggestions are merely intended to be a guide for your consideration in the event of a discussion arising and they are in no way (R) no way to affect your orders.

1.   On 18 June Darlan gave a personal promise to First Lord and First Sea Lord that French Fleet would never surrender to enemy.

2.   The French may argue that they will scuttle if Germans and Italians attempt to seize ships even in French metropolitan ports. But with

[1]See Document nos. 24 and 25.

French Army disarmed and Fleet laid up with reduced crews under German and Italian surveillance, there can be no (R) no certainty that, however resolute the attempt to destroy or sink any particular ship, it would be possible to forestall seizure by the enemy.

3.   Officers and men of any units fighting with us will receive British rates of pay and pensions, etc.

4.   Our recent naval successes against Italians show that vigorous action which would be possible with continued French collaboration would have greatest value in undermining Italian will to fight. We have now sunk or captured 10 Italian S/M's for certain and 5 possible and sunk a destroyer all in about a fortnight.[1]

5.   It is a delusion to believe that France can be restored by co-operation with the Axis. Armistice terms are not (R) NOT peace terms and *Mein Kampf* shows what treatment Hitler has in store for France. Whatever is left to France, if anything, will only be held on sufferance until Germany is defeated. How much better, therefore, to fight on with us for the restoration of the French Empire.

6.   If French Admiral replies to first overture by saying we have no (R) no need to worry since all arrangements have been made, you should reply 'How can you be sure that this will be effective? You may be relieved from your command, pressure may be put on [your] ships' companies and so on. The ships' companies may in any case be unwilling to scuttle in a French port for fear of immediate sentence by enemy. Therefore you must put your intentions into effect now and at this port, when blame will fall on us and not (R) not on your ships' companies'.

29.   *From the Admiralty*

2 July 1940

A.   The conditions under which you may meet French Fleet at sea are so varied that it is not (R) not possible to give you more than general instructions.

B.   What we particularly require is that *Dunkerque* and *Strasbourg* should not (R) NOT get into enemy control. Other modern units are important but less so.

C.   If French Fleet is either in V/S distance or in sight of your aircraft, some means must be found to order them to stop and if they fail to do so action must be taken to force them to do so either by gunfire [or by air attack?]

---

[1]The Italian s/m code had been broken, though this was a temporary success. The true total was nine.

D.   Once they have stopped, action must be taken as if they were in harbour except that should they finally suggest demilitarisation you should only accept on condition they return to Oran.

30.   *The Admiralty to Cunningham and Somerville*

3 July 1940

No time limit for acceptance of demands is contained in your instructions, but it is very important that operations should be completed during daylight hours today Wednesday.

31.   *Report of Proceedings, 28 June–4 July* (cont.)

3 July

28.   *Foxhound* was dispatched at 0300 to proceed ahead with Captain Holland and closed Cape Falcon at 0545. Communication was established with the Port War signal station and at 0558 permission was requested to enter the port.

A similar request was passed to the Admiral of the Port's signal station at 0620, together with the following message to Admiral Gensoul:–

L'Amirante Britannique envoie le commandant Holland conferer avec vous. La Marine Royale espère que les propositions vont vous permettre, la Marine Nationale Française vaillante et glorieuse, de se ranger à nos cotes.

En ce cas vos batiments resteraient toujours les votres et personne n'aurait besoin d'aucun anxiété dans l'avenir.

La Flotte Britannique est au large d'Oran pour vous accuellir.[1]

29.   Permission for *Foxhound* to enter was received at 0742 and 10 minutes later the pilot came aboard bringing instructions for *Foxhound* to proceed inside Mes-el-Kebir and to berth near *Dunkerque*. On the excuse that messages might have to be conveyed to the FOC Force H, and as a precaution against being prevented from sailing, the ship was, however, anchored at 0805 in a position 1.6 miles 115° from Mers-el-Kebir, outside the net.

30.   Five minutes later, the Flag Lieutenant[2] arrived alongside in the

---

[1]The English translation is given in No. 25, para. 2.
[2]Lieut de Vaisseau B. J. M. Dufay: b 1907; entered navy 1925; Lt de V 1934; Capt *Croix de Lorraine* 1945–6; Capt de Frégate 1948; *Beautemps Beupré* 1950–1; Capt de V 1955; TS *Étoile* 1957–9; Ret List 1961.

Admiral's barge and informed Captain Holland that the Admiral was unable to see him but would send his Chief of Staff.[1]

31.   At 0847, *Foxhound* received a signal requesting her to sail immediately. Captain Holland, accompanied by Lt-Cdr A.Y. Spearman (late British NLO (Sud) at Bizerta) at once embarked in *Foxhound*'s motorboat and *Foxhound* weighed with hands fallen in on deck.

32.   A reconnaissance aircraft had been flown off *Ark Royal* at 0630, and at 0835 this aircraft reported that the French battleships and cruisers appeared to be raising steam. Forty minutes later, a further report was made that the battleships were furling awnings.

33.   At 0910, Force H arrived off Oran and message 'F'[2] was signalled from *Hood*, *Valiant*, *Resolution*, *Arethusa* and *Enterprise* (see 22 above) by signal projectors trained on the French heavy ships.

Paravanes had been streamed at 0631 and hands closed up at action stations at 0830, but guns were kept trained fore and aft.

The visibility at this time was approximately six miles. The upperworks of the French heavy ships in Mers-el-Kebir were clearly visible over the breakwater . . .

34.   Meanwhile, Captain Holland had been met halfway between the inner boom and the breakwater by the Admiral's barge with the Flag Lieutenant on board. Captain Holland handed the Flag Lieutenant a copy of the proposals as contained in AM 0103/2[3] and informed him that he would wait for a reply. The proposals probably reached Admiral Gensoul at about 0935. At 0925, Captain Holland informed me that the Admiral was trying to avoid him and proposed sending his Chief of Staff.

35.   At about 1000, the Flag Lieutenant returned with a written reply[4] confirming the assurances already given. . . .

36.   Captain Holland had a long and friendly conversation with the Flag Lieutenant, at the conclusion of which the latter accepted a written statement which Captain Holland had prepared previously, and at 1050, returned to *Dunkerque*.

37.   As a result of this action, Admiral Gensoul's Chief of Staff brought out a written reply[5] reiterating the Admiral's previous statements . . . Captain Holland then returned to *Foxhound*, arriving on board at about 1125.

During this period, Force H was steaming to and fro across the Bay

[1]Unidentified
[2]The message printed in No. 26, para. 22.
[3]No. 27.
[4]No. 32.
[5]No. 33.

and making occasional legs to seaward. *Ark Royal* with her destroyer screen was acting independently as necessary for flying off aircraft.

38.　Meanwhile, further reports had been received in *Hood* from the reconnaissance aircraft, indicating that the destroyers in Mers-el-Kebir had furled awnings, that *Paris*[1] was hoisting boats and that the cruisers and destroyers were preparing for sea.

The aircraft was directed to watch the submarines in Oran, but reported there was, as yet, no sign of activity amongst them.

39.　On his return to *Foxhound*, Captain Holland received the message which I had transmitted at 1046, indicating that it was imperative that the French should know that I would not allow them to leave harbour unless the terms were accepted. This message was sent in by Lt-Cdr Spearman, who handed it to the Flag Lieutenant at 1140. At the same time, a message was passed to Admiral Gensoul by light informing him of the action being taken by Admiral Godfroy to demilitarise the French ships at Alexandria.

40.　At about 1200, *Foxhound* proceeded outside the outer boom in order to avoid having to run the gauntlet of the shore batteries should hostilities commence, whilst still remaining within easy touch of visual signalling with *Dunkerque*.

41.　*Foxhound*'s signal, summarising Admiral Gensoul's reply (37 above) and indicating the apparent intention of the French ships to put to sea and fight, was received in *Hood* at 1227. Orders were then given to mine the entrance to the port and the Admiralty informed that I was preparing to open fire at 1330. A signal was also made to *Foxhound* asking Captain Holland if, in the light of his discussions, he saw any alternative to opening fire with main armament.

42.　Captain Holland's reply to this signal, stating that he was waiting in visual signalling touch in case of acceptance before the expiration of time, left me in some doubt whether Admiral Gensoul had, in fact, been given a time limit in which to decide. A further signal was therefore made to *Foxhound* – 'Does anything you have said prevent me opening fire?'

43.　At 1307, minelaying aircraft were flown off with fighter escort and five mines were laid in the entrance to Mers-el-Kebir.

Shortly afterwards an aircraft report was received that the boom, which had been opened, was now closed and that boats had not yet been hoisted.

It appeared that the French had no immediate intention of proceeding

---

[1]As *Paris* was already in the UK, this must be a mistake; the old battleships at Mers-el-Kebir were *Provence* and *Bretagne*.

to sea and in consequence I decided to give them until 1500 to make a decision. I was strengthened in this decision by Captain Holland's reply to my last signal in which he suggested that the use of force might be avoided if *Foxhound* went in to visual signalling touch and asked if there was any further message.

44.   At 1340, *Foxhound* proceeded towards Mers-el-Kebir to keep in visual touch with *Dunkerque*. Five minutes later, an aircraft report was received that submarines were leaving Oran. *Vortigern* was therefore ordered to proceed toward the entrance to stop and, if necessary, to sink any submarine attempting to leave; aircraft were also ordered to attack in similar circumstances. Subsequent aircraft reports indicated that the submarines were merely shifting berth inside the harbour, presumably to obtain added protection from the mole.

45.   *Foxhound* was directed to instruct Admiral Gensoul to hoist a large square flag at the masthead if he accepted our terms. A further and final message was about to be passed to *Dunkerque*, when a signal was received from Admiral Gensoul at 1440 stating that he was ready to receive a delegate for honourable discussion.

I debated in my mind whether this was merely an excuse to gain time, but decided that it was quite possible Admiral Gensoul had only now realised it was my intention to use force if necessary.

46.   Permission was given for Captain Holland to proceed inshore and at 1506, accompanied by Lt-Cdr Davies, he embarked in *Foxhound*'s motor-boat at a point N of Mers-el-Kebir just clear of the minefield. This involved a passage of $7\frac{1}{2}$ miles, and it was not until 1615 that Captain Holland, after transferring to the Admiral's barge inside the net defences, arrived on board *Dunkerque*. . . . All ships were in an advanced state of readiness for sea, control positions manned and tugs standing by the stern of each battleship.

47.   In the meantime, aircraft had been flown off and two mines laid in the entrance to Oran harbour. *Wrestler* was ordered to relieve *Vortigern* off Oran harbour.

48.   Captain Holland was received very formally by Admiral Gensoul in the Admiral's cabin. The Admiral was extremely indignant at the presentation of an ultimatum and the mining of his harbour. After some considerable discussion, . . . Admiral Gensoul apparently first began to realise that force might really be used and it was at this stage that he produced a secret and personal copy of the orders received from and signed by Admiral Darlan . . . .[1]

When producing these orders, Admiral Gensoul asked and received

[1]See No. 34.

Captain Holland's assurances that the contents should not be disseminated, since otherwise immediate German or Italian action would occur.
49. Whilst this long discussion was taking place in the Admiral's cabin of *Dunkerque*, AM 1614/3 containing instructions to 'settle matters quickly or you will have reinforcements to deal with' was received at 1646 in *Hood*. A signal was immediately passed visually and by wireless to Admiral Gensoul, informing him that if the terms were not accepted, fire would be opened at 1730. Simultaneously, 'Preparative ANVIL at 1730' was made to all ships of Force H.
50. The message referred to reached Admiral Gensoul at 1715, whilst the discussion with Captain Holland was still proceeding. The latter then drafted a brief signal, which was shown to the Admiral, stating that the crews were being reduced and the ships would proceed to Martinique or the USA if threatened by the enemy. This was received in *Hood* at 1729, but as it did not comply with any of the conditions laid down, air striking forces were ordered to fly off and the battleships stood in to the coast.
51. Captain Holland finally left *Dunkerque* at 1725 and at the same time 'action stations' were sounded in the French ships. Transfer to *Foxhound*'s motor-boat was effected at 1735 and the boat proceeded clear of the net defences.
52. Fire was opened at maximum visibility range of 17,500 yards at 1754, employing GIC concentration with aircraft spotting. The line of fire was from the NW, so that the fire from the French ships was to some extent blanked by Mers-el-Kebir fort and risk of damage to civilian life and property reduced.
53. Simultaneously with opening fire, an aircraft report was received that the destroyers in Mers-el-Kebir were under way inside the boom.
54. At 1757, three minutes after opening fire, a very large explosion occurred inside the harbour, followed immediately by an immense column of smoke several hundred feet high. There would appear to be little doubt that this was caused by the blowing up of a battleship of the *Bretagne* class.[1] It was followed shortly afterwards by a similar but smaller explosion which was apparently a destroyer blowing up. By this time the harbour was clothed in smoke from explosions and fires, rendering direct spotting almost impossible and air spotting most difficult.
55. Enemy shore batteries opened fire about a minute after the first British salvo. These were promptly engaged by *Arethusa* but the range

---

[1]It was in fact *Bretagne*. In addition *Dunkerque* and *Provence* were heavily damaged and beached; *Commandante Teste* (aircraft tender, 1929, 10,000t, 26 seaplanes, 12×3.9in, 20.5k) was set on fire but managed to escape to Toulon; *Mogador* (a super-destroyer, 1938, 2884t, 8×5.5in,10tt, 38k) was heavily damaged. Of the almost 1400 French dead, 930 died in *Bretagne*.

was too great for *Enterprise*'s older guns. Shortly afterwards heavy projectiles commenced to fall near the battleships.

56.   Enemy fire was at first very short but improved considerably in accuracy subsequently, a number of main armament (probably 13.4 inch) projectiles falling close to all ships and in certain cases, straddling. No hits were incurred, but a number of splinters caused minor superficial damage in *Hood* and injuries to one officer and one rating.

57.   After firing a total of 36 15-inch salvoes, the fire from the French ships died down but the fire from the forts was becoming increasingly accurate. Course was altered 180° to port together and ships ordered to make smoke to avoid damage from the fire of the forts. Fire on the French ships ceased at 1804.

58.   My appreciation of the situation at this time was that resistance from the French ships had ceased and that by ceasing fire I should give them an opportunity to abandon their ships and thus avoid further loss of life. Since the French knew that the entrances to the harbour had been mined, I felt quite positive that no attempt would be made by them to put to sea.

59.   Force H proceeded to the westward with a view to taking up a position from which further bombardment of the French ships could be carried out if necessary, without causing casualties to men proceeding ashore in boats and without exposing the ships of Force H unduly to the fire of the forts.

60.   At 1732 I had received a report that there was activity at the aerodrome and in view of there being a pall of smoke now lying between Force H and the shore, I considered it desirable to stand out to seawards to avoid a surprise attack by aircraft under cover of the smoke.

61.   Repeated signals were now received from the shore visual and wireless stations requesting fire to be ceased, to which the reply was made – 'Unless I see your ships sinking, I shall open fire again'.

62.   At 1820 I received a report from *Ark Royal*'s aircraft that one *Dunkerque*[1] had left harbour and was going east. In view of other reports of movements which had been subsequently cancelled, the difficulty of observation owing to smoke and the certainty I entertained that the French would abandon their ships, I did not attach sufficient weight to this report.

It was not until a subsequent report, received at 1830, confirmed the escape of a battlecruiser and destroyers to the eastward that I decided to alter course to the east. The resultant delay in commencing the chase, though not appreciably affecting the situation, could have been avoided.

[1]Actually *Strasbourg*.

63. Meanwhile, at 1825, six Swordfish, armed with 250 lb SAP bombs, with Skua escort, had been flown off to attack the heavy ships in Mers-el-Kebir. Their departure had been delayed by the necessity of landing on a considerable number of other aircraft which had reached the limit of their fuel endurance. The striking force was now diverted and ordered to attack the battlecruiser already at sea.

65. At 1845, cruisers and destroyers were ordered to the van. At this time there was some doubt as to how many heavy ships had left harbour, but when it appeared that only one *Dunkerque* was actually at sea, *Hood* and light craft proceeded ahead, leaving the two battleships to follow unscreened.

66. The bombing attack on *Strasbourg* was well pressed home and met with heavy opposition. Although confirmation is lacking, it is believed that at least one hit with a 250 lb bomb was obtained.[1] Two Swordfish failed to return but their crews were picked up by *Wrestler*.

67. At 1914 a small boat flying a white flag and a White Ensign was sighted on the starboard bow. *Forester* was ordered to close, and picked up Captain Holland, Lt-Cdrs Spearman and Davies and the boat's crew. By this time *Hood* was working up to full power with *Arethusa*, *Enterprise* and destroyers in the van.

68. Between 1935 and 1945, a French destroyer proceeding W,[2] close to the coast inshore of the Force, was engaged at ranges of 12,000 to 18,000 yards by *Arethusa* and *Enterprise*; *Hood* and later *Valiant* also fired a few main armament salvoes.

At least three hits were observed and the destroyer turned back towards Oran. During this period torpedoes were reported approaching from starboard to port and course was altered away for four minutes.

69. Six Swordfish, armed with torpedoes, were flown off at 1950 with orders to press home an attack on the French battlecruiser, making use of the failing light.

70. All ships proceeded at their utmost speed until 2020, when I decided to abandon the chase. At this time *Strasbourg* and 11 destroyers were reported to be 25 miles ahead of *Hood*. From the reports received, I calculated that the Algiers force, which included several 8-inch and 6-inch cruisers and destroyers, would probably meet *Strasbourg* shortly after 2100.

I considered that a night contact and engagement under these conditions was not justifiable. I knew that neither the 13th nor the 8th Destroyer Flotillas had any recent experience of shadowing and since

[1] No hits were obtained.
[2] Unidentified.

the French were numerically superior, it appeared to me that the situation could be summed up as follows.

(i)   The prospects of locating and engaging the French battlecruiser at night were small.

(ii)   Force H would be at a disadvantage, being silhouetted against the afterglow.

(iii) The speed of advance was too high to allow the destroyers to spread.

(iv)   The fuel endurance of the 'V' and 'W' class destroyers would not permit of more than three hours' chase.

(v)   Unless *Hood* was in a position to support the advanced forces, the latter would be numerically much inferior to the French. This support could not be assured under night action conditions.

(vi)   I did not consider that the possible loss of British ships was justified as against the possibility of French ships being allowed to fall into German or Italian hands.

(vii) *Valiant* and *Resolution* were unscreened.

71.   Course was accordingly altered to the westward and the Admiralty informed that it was my intention to remain to the westward of Oran during the night and to carry out air attacks on the ships in harbour at dawn or as soon after as possible.

I discarded the alternative course of renewing the attack by gunfire owing to the limited endurance of the older destroyers and the greatly increased risk from submarines while bombarding.

72.   High angle fire was opened at intervals on French reconnaissance and bombing aircraft between 1930 and 2100. A few bombs were dropped, but except for four about 50 yards from *Wrestler*, all fell wide. No attacks were pressed home.

73.   The torpedo-bomber attack on *Strasbourg* took place at 2055, 20 minutes after sunset. This was very well carried out, the aircraft approaching from the land so that the target was silhouetted against the afterglow. Darkness and funnel smoke made observation difficult, but one explosion was seen under the stern and there is some evidence of a hit amidships. No casualties were sustained and no aircraft damaged.[1]

74.   *Proteus*, who had been instructed to proceed clear to the northward during the day, was ordered at 2150 to patrol off Cap de l'Aiguille and both *Proteus* and *Pandora* were ordered to attack any French ships encountered. *Pandora* was further informed that *Strasbourg* might arrive off Algiers after 2300.

---

[1] No hits obtained.

75.   Course was set during the night to reach position 36° 12'N, 1° 48'W at 0430, 4 July, at which time it was intended to fly off 12 Swordfish and 9 Skuas. Occasional fog persisted and shortly after 0400 the Force ran into thick fog. At 0630, VACAC reported that he had been forced to abandon the attack owing to weather conditions. In view of this, and also of a message I had received from Admiral Gensoul that his ships were *hors de combat* and that he was ordering personnel to evacuate their ships, I shaped course for Gibraltar, all ships being secured alongside by 1900, 4 July.

76.   During the operations on 3 July, 3 Swordfish and 2 Skuas were lost, but all crews were rescued with the exception of that of one Skua.

77.   Reviewing the operation in the light of what actually occurred, it is clear that I committed an error of judgment in proceeding so far to the westward after ceasing fire.

At the time, I was convinced that as the entrance to the harbour had been mined, the heavy explosions observed, coupled with the request of the shore stations to 'cease shelling', indicated quite clearly that the French intended to abandon their ships. The thought uppermost in my mind was how to complete my task without causing further loss of life to the ill-advised but very gallant Frenchmen and without bringing Force H under fire from the forts or subjecting it to attack from any of the submarines that might succeed in leaving Oran.

78.   I was also under the impression that a torpedo flight had either taken off or would shortly take off and would be in a position to complete the destruction of ships still afloat.

In this connection I must point out that the repeated postponement of ANVIL had seriously upset *Ark Royal*'s flying on and off programme. This I failed to appreciate at the time.

79.   Nevertheless, it is clear that by exercising better judgment I could have taken up a position which would have enabled me to cover the eastern approaches and at the same time to reach the selected bombarding position before darkness fell should further gunfire be required to complete the destruction of the French ships.

I am of the opinion, however, that my decision to abandon the chase of the *Strasbourg* at 2020 was correct.

80.   Although it is somewhat outside the scope of this report, it is, perhaps, not out of place to speculate whether the use of force might not have been avoided had Admiral Gensoul agreed to meet Captain Holland in the first instance. The final offer made by the French Admiral[1] was very near to a British alternative but differed, unfortu-

---

[1] See No. 35.

nately, in the proviso that the action proposed would not be carried into effect *unless* there was a danger of the French ships falling into the hands of the enemy.

Admiral Gensoul claimed that this danger was not imminent; we maintained that it was. I believe that given more time Captain Holland might have succeeded in converting Admiral Gensoul to our point of view. At the actual time when the French Admiral made his offer, it was already too late, since French reinforcements were approaching and the orders of HM Government were explicit that a decision had to be reached before dark.[1] . . .

32.   *From Admiral Gensoul*

3 July 1940

1.   The assurances given by Admiral Gensoul to Admiral Sir Dudley North remain the same. In any case, at any given moment, and any-where, and without orders from the French Admiralty, French warships will not be allowed to fall intact into the hands of the Germans or Italians.

2.   In view of the meaning and form of expression, the veritable ultima-tum which has been sent to Admiral Gensoul, French warships will meet force by force.

33.   *From Admiral Gensoul*

3 July 1940

1.   Admiral Gensoul can but confirm the reply already sent by Lieutenant du Vaisseau Dufay.

2.   Admiral Gensoul has decided to defend himself by every means possible.

3.   Admiral Gensoul wishes to draw Admiral Somerville's attention to the fact that the first shot fired against us will have the result of putting immediately the whole French Fleet against Great Britain, a result which is diametrically opposite to that which HM Government wishes.

[1]See No. 30.

34. *Copy of Secret and Personal Orders from Admiral Darlan handed to Captain Holland by Admiral Gensoul*

c. 23 June 1940

The clauses of the Armistice are notified to you *en claire* by other means. I take advantage of these last communications that I can send you in cypher to inform you of my ideas on the subject.

1.   Demobilised French warships should remain French under French Flag with reduced French crews and berthed in French metropolitan or colonial ports.

2.   Secret sabotage precautions should be taken so that neither enemy nor foreigner attempting to take the ship by force would be able to use her.

3.   If the Commission interprets the terms of the Armistice other than is shown in paragraph 1 at the moment of executing this new decision, warships should without orders be taken to the United States of America or scuttled if it is not possible to do otherwise, in order to deny them to the enemy. In no case must they be allowed to fall into enemy hands intact.

4.   Ships thus taking refuge in foreign lands must not be used in operations of war against Germany or Italy without the orders of the C-in-C, FMF.[1]

35.   *Final written statement from Admiral Gensoul*

1720, 3 July 1940

1.   The French Fleet must carry out the Armistice clauses on account of the consequences which might otherwise arise to Metropolitan France.

2.   The Fleet has received strict orders and these orders have been sent to all Commanding Officers so that if after the Armistice, the ships are threatened with falling into enemy hands they would be sent to the USA or scuttled.

3.   These orders will be carried out.

4.   Ships at Oran and Mers-el-Kebir have begun since yesterday, 2 July, their demobilisation (reduction of crews). Men from North Africa have been disembarked.

---

[1]Holland undertook not to disclose these orders, except to Somerville.

36.   *Pocket diary, 1940*

4 July

Owing to fog aircraft could not carry out attack on *Dunkerque* so proceeded towards Gib[raltar]. Patches of fog all forenoon. French naval forces released from Franco-Iti. armistice terms so it looks as if they will now be an active enemy. Destroyers got a contact about 20 miles from Gib. and attacked patches of oil. Arrived Gib. 5.40 and secured to Mole. Went to see Dudley and Nutty.[1] Both think affair frightful. Now have orders to take on *Richelieu* at Dakar. How I loathe it all. Held meeting of all COs to discuss programme. Lord Dillon to see me 9.30. He thinks quite right to have fired on French ships! Can't understand it. . . .

37.   *To his wife*

4 July 1940

. . . Expect you have heard about this battle at Oran. Before we left Gib. I *begged* the Admiralty not to go to the lengths of opening fire on the French as I felt sure it would be disastrous. Besides the idea of slaughtering our former allies (or being slaughtered by them) was most repugnant. However HM Govt. said they were determined I should sink the French ships if necessary, so I had no alternative.

I did my damnedest to make the French Admiral accept our conditions and kept on postponing the evil minute. . . .

Afraid I shall get a colossal raspberry from the Admiralty for letting the battlecruiser escape and not finishing off more French ships – we disposed of three or four big ships in the harbour I believe. In fact I shouldn't be surprised if I was relieved forthwith. I don't mind because it was an absolutely bloody business to shoot up these Frenchmen who showed the greatest gallantry. The truth is my heart wasn't in it and you're not allowed a heart in war.

But, as I warned the Admiralty, I think it was the biggest political blunder of modern times and I imagine will rouse the world against us.

Still, if it brings me back to you it will be some consolation, though I hate the idea of being regarded as the 'unskilled butcher of Oran' or something like that. Those are my reactions at the moment and I thought you'd like to know. It *was* a hateful business, but the French Admiral played me up all right by delaying and playing on my feelings to avoid killing a lot of Frenchmen.

[1] Adms North and Wells.

I was quite determined that I would not have any of my destroyers sunk or big ships seriously damaged in this beastly operation and I succeeded. Wonder if anyone will think I had cold feet? Shouldn't be surprised. But the truth was that the action left me quite unmoved. I just felt so damned angry at being called on to do such a lousy job. I never thought that they would fight in spite of what the French Admiral said. Hooky Holland acted as our delegate and I am quite sure put up the best possible case for accepting our terms. But the French were furious that we did not trust them to prevent the ships falling into German hands.

I'm sure myself we could have trusted them but even if we didn't I'd sooner that happened than that we should have to kill a lot of our former allies. We all feel thoroughly dirty and ashamed that the first time we should have been in action was an affair like this.

But I feel sure that I shall be blamed for bungling the job and I think I did. But to you I don't mind confessing I was halfhearted and you can't win an action that way. . . .

38.   *From Alexander and Pound*

0035, 5 July 1940

While we were sorry that you did not put *Dunkerque*[1] in the bag, we congratulate you on measure of success so far achieved. Request all under your command may be informed that Their Lordships appreciate efficiency with which bombardment was carried out. The Prime Minister wishes to be associated with the above.

39.   *To his wife*

5 July 1940

. . . You will have had a bellyful of my name on the wireless and in the papers and it all disgusts me because it is connected with this filthy business. And now I've got to do some more of it and kill a lot more French soldiers and probably a lot of civilians as well. I feel thoroughly depressed and unclean. Of course I'm only carrying out my orders but that doesn't seem to make it any better. . . .

I have now sent a message saying that further loss of French lives must inevitably provoke the French Navy into immediate and hostile action.

[1]Presumably they meant *Strasbourg*.

Dudley North is in entire agreement with me that the bombardment on Wednesday was bad enough, but to continue further action would be disastrous. Andrew Cunningham has said the same. It's all too bloody for words and I curse the day I was landed with this appointment. It all seemed so rosy and has all been so horrible.

Poor Hooky Holland is so upset that he's asked to be relieved of his command in *Ark Royal*. I persuaded him to withdraw it but have sent on a letter to the Admiralty saying in all fairness he ought to be relieved as the strain of it all after his close association with the French must inevitably prove too much for him.[1]

As for the future, I have no time to think of that at all. Old Dudley North has been *most* sympathetic and understanding. He feels as I do about the whole matter and is continually coming over to discuss matters.

40. *To his wife*

6 July 1940

. . . Just before we sailed last night I made a final appeal to the Admiralty pointing out that this second bombardment of *Dunkerque* at Oran would inevitably mean not only a lot more French officers and men but also civilians [would be killed?] as the ships were quite close to the town of St Andre. I said that the Wednesday action must have caused very heavy casualties and asked if some means couldn't be found to induce the French to demilitarise the ships to avoid further bloodshed.

Admiralty suggested my sending in a delegate to propose to the French they should do this and if they didn't agree I must bombard. I replied that the French would never receive a delegate after what has happened and that any warning to them would result in their attacking me with every submarine and aircraft available. Eventually at 3 a.m. this morning they said I could attack with torpedo aircraft only. Before they had turned down my suggestion to do so; they said it wouldn't be sufficiently effective.

Well it was a rush to organise it all in the hour or two available but *Ark Royal* did very well indeed and her first flight scored a complete surprise and got in 4 hits. Two other hits, one of which caused a large explosion, were obtained later. Two of our aircraft failed to return. The ships must be completely knocked out so that filthy job is over at last.

---

[1]Holland remained in command until April 1941. Cunningham thought him highly strung: Cunningham to Godfrey, *c.* 17 May 1959, CUNN 5/4, Churchill A C.

I hear from the Press that the French Government has severed diplomatic relations so what the hell have we gained by this monstrous business? I still simply can't understand how their minds are working at home. None of us can. It doesn't seem to worry the sailors at all as 'they never 'ad no use for them French bastards'. But to all of us Senior Officers it's simply incredible and revolting.

If I didn't feel that in war one can only have one loyalty and that is to the King and Government I shouldn't hesitate to ask to be relieved at once. But I feel it would be wrong and a stab at the country if I did.

Well I don't know what other butcher's work awaits me, but as things are it looks as if the French will actually declare war on us by now so then at least they will be legitimate enemies.

How are you darling? I hope all this won't worry you too much but I'd like you to know what's passing in my mind. . . .

41. *Memorial from Captain and Officers of* Dunkerque

July 1940

The Captain and Officers of the *Dunkerque* inform you of the deaths, for the honour of their flag, on 3 and 6 July, of nine officers and 200 men of their ship.

They return to you herewith the mementoes which they had from their comrades in arms of the British Royal Navy in whom they had put all their trust.

And they express to you on this occasion all their bitter sadness and disgust that these comrades did not hesitate to soil the glorious flag of St George with an indelible stain, that of murder.[1]

42. *To Vice Admiral Sir Geoffrey Blake*[2]

HMS *Hood*,
7 July 1940

I was much relieved when I got your signal to say that the second attack on *Dunkerque* could be carried out by the torpedo-bombers. She

---

[1]This is a translation from the French.
[2]Vice Adm Sir Geoffrey Blake (1882–1968): ent RN 1897; Lt 1904; gunnery specialist; Cdr 1914; Grand F 1914–18; Capt 1918; NA Washington 1919–21; *Queen Elizabeth* 1921–3; Naval War Coll 1923–5; Dep Dir & Dir, N Staff Coll 1925–9; Cdre NZ Sta 1929–32; RA 1931; 4SL 1932; VA 1935; BCS 1935–8; Ret List 1938 following serious illness; ACNS (F) 1940; FO Liaison with US Navy in European Waters 1941–5.

was so close to St André that we must have killed a lot of civilians had we bombarded.

From the accounts of the pilots and observers it is clear that six and possibly seven hits were obtained, all on the starboard side. One caused a large explosion which enveloped the ship in smoke. I think she can now be written off for this war.[1] *Ark Royal* did extremely well, as she had arranged to bomb the forts and protect the air spotters and fleet with fighters; at 0345 it had all to be reorganised.

I was thankful to find that we had lost no one in this operation as it was my fault it had to be carried out. . . .

Of course, I don't know all the facts but, from what Holland tells me, it does appear that if Gensoul had not been given an ultimatum we might have brought him round. He evidently had doubts whether Darlan was still a free agent and in view of Darlan's last certified orders, that the ships were *not* to fall into German hands, it does seem just possible that we might have brought him round to demilitarising at Martinique. But no doubt you had other information which showed that this was not the case. . . .

Taranto and Messina appear to be ruled out for torpedo-bomber attack, as even if the aircraft reached their objective, it is very doubtful if an attack could be brought off successfully. The very low performance of the Swordfish makes her such easy meat for shore-based fighters that unless the attack was carried out in the dark hours we should get none of them back. We're bound to be shadowed and bombed all day during the approach, and the flying-on lights would probably bring their bombers on to us if we attempted to land on at night. There are only six pilots who can do this at present.

The objection to Palermo is that the birds will probably have flown before we could get there. It's not possible to carry out a torpedo-bomber attack owing to the nature of the harbour and I take it that bombardment of the town itself is not recommended.

Mind you, I'm not suggesting for a moment that there are no suitable targets for us, but I do feel that the effect would be the opposite to what we want if the Italians seriously damage one of our ships and we fail to give them an effective crack. I must have time to study the matter more thoroughly and incidentally, to get this very varied Force together. The gunnery and fleet work leave a lot to be desired and the destroyers are not capable of night search at present. What we really want is a trip out to

---

[1]She was repaired by early 1942 and slipped away to Toulon, where she was scuttled along with other warships in Nov 1942 when the Germans occupied S France in retaliation for Allied landings in N Africa.

the west from Gibraltar where we can exercise for a couple of days, carry out a throw-off shoot, sleeve target practice, etc.

It is for that reason I thought I had better confine myself to bombing the seaplane base and submarine base and laying mines in Cagliari. It's a difficult place to bombard as you can see from the chart and the light would be all wrong for us in the early morning. . . .

But I quite realise that a bombardment gives a greater moral effect than bombing. Still, until I can make sure of getting on to the target, I feel it is not worth getting these ships holed so far from the base and no dock available when we get there.

43. *Report of Proceedings, 4–6 July 1940*

29 July 1940

4 July

2.   After return to Gibraltar at 1800 on 4 July, on completion of operation CATAPULT, all ships of Force H completed with fuel and ammunition and were ready to sail by 0530 on 5 July, to carry out operations against *Richelieu* at Dakar, should these be ordered.

3.   At 2240, in reply to AM 1929/4, I informed the Admiralty that from aircraft observation it was not possible to state the extent to which *Dunkerque* had been damaged in Mers-el-Kebir harbour, but that she was definitely aground.

5 July

4.   Between 0100 and 0200, unidentified aircraft dropped bombs and what was reported to be mines in the approaches to Gibraltar. Action was immediately taken by the ACNAS, to have the approaches swept by Double 'L' and Oropesa sweeps.

5.   At 0308 I received AM 0056/5, stating that unless I was certain that *Dunkerque* could not be refloated and repaired in less than a year, she should be subjected to further destruction by bombardment on 6 July, and this was to take precedence over the operation against *Richelieu*.

Plans were drawn up accordingly and at 1329 I informed the Admiralty that I intended using *Hood, Valiant, Ark Royal, Arethusa, Enterprise* and 10 destroyers for further operations against *Dunkerque* and that the bombardment was expected to commence at 0900 the following morning (6 July).

6.   During the forenoon of 5 July, I received through ACNAS, AM 2005/4, containing instructions regarding the attitude to be adopted by HM ships towards French warships. A report was received from

Pandora that she had sunk a French 6-inch cruiser of the *La Galissonnière* class.[1]

11.   Meanwhile, Force H (less *Resolution*) had put to sea and were clear of Gibraltar by 2000. After making a feint to the westward till after dark, course was shaped towards Oran and speed increased to 22, later 23 knots.

It is doubtful if the feint of a large force in the Straits achieves its object, since the very bright lights of Ceuta should enable any careful observer to mark the passage of large darkened ships.

6 July

12.   At 0250, I received AM 0224/6, cancelling the bombardment of *Dunkerque* and ordering continuous aircraft torpedo attack to be carried out until she was thoroughly damaged.

13.   This necessitated a complete reorganisation of the flying programme arranged by *Ark Royal* for bombardment. In spite of this and the time occupied in passing the signal to *Ark Royal* by shaded lamp, she reported she would be ready by 0515.

Accordingly, at 0520, . . . (that is, about 90 miles off Oran) torpedo-bomber striking forces were flown off from *Ark Royal* together with Skua aircraft to provide fighter protection, and three separate torpedo attacks were carried out on *Dunkerque*. . . .

14.   The following is a summary of the results of the attacks:–

(a)   *First attack* – by 6 aircraft; complete surprise achieved and no opposition. Four hits on starboard side amidships.

(b)   *Second attack* – by 3 aircraft; considerable opposition by A/A fire. One certain, two possible hits on starboard side.

(c)   *Third attack* – by 3 aircraft; heavy opposition by A/A fire and interference from enemy fighters. One doubtful hit on port side.

15.   At least 5 hits and possibly two others were therefore obtained on *Dunkerque* and I am satisfied that she has been put out of action for at least a year.

16.   Although a number of Swordfish were hit, all returned safely. All Skuas landed on with the exception of one which force-landed alongside *Ark Royal* due to damage received in contact with French fighters. Her crew was, however, picked up and there were no casualties to FAA personnel.

17.   Force H returned to Gibraltar at 1830, 6 July.

---

[1]Actually the sloop *Rigault de Genouilly*: 1932, 1969t, 3×5.5in, 14k. Lt-Cdr Linton, the CO of *Pandora* could be forgiven; the silhouettes were very similar.

18.   I consider that the flying-off of *Ark Royal*'s torpedo-bomber striking force at such short notice, after preparations had been made for a
very different operation, the successful manner in which the attacks
were carried out and the way in which the Skuas beat off the French
fighters, reflect great credit on the Commanding Officer and all concerned in *Ark Royal*.

19.   In particular, I would invite attention to VACAC's letter of 16 July
which gives the report of an encounter between a Swordfish and a
Dewoitine D520 aircraft. I concur that this was a very gallant action and
consider the services of Sub-Lt (A) R.B. Pearson[1] on this occasion
deserving of recognition.

I wish also to draw attention to the very able manner in which Lt-Cdr
J. W. Linton,[2] commanding HMS *Pandora*, carried out the attack on the
French *La Galisonnière* class cruiser. Considered as a successful subma-
rine operation, I consider that this also merits recognition.

44.   Report of Proceedings, 6–11 July 1940

6 July

2.   On arrival at Gibraltar at 1830 from the second attack on *Dunkerque*
(operation LEVER) . . . Force H refuelled and plans were prepared for
carrying out air attacks on *Richelieu* at Dakar in accordance with AM
1650/4.

7 July

6.   AM 0419/7, informing me that the operation against *Richelieu*
would be carried out by a squadron under the orders of *Hermes*,[3] was
received at 0720. This message also directed me to carry out an operation against the West coast of Italy, Sicily or possibly Sardinia, passing
to the southward of Sardinia to avoid provoking French action. It was
suggested that the force should consist of *Hood*, *Valiant*, *Ark Royal*,
Arethusa and 7 modern destroyers. The objective was left to my discretion, but T/B attack on ships at Taranto, Augusta or elsewhere was suggested. This operation was to coincide with an operation by the C-in-C,

---

[1]Dewoitine D520: 1938, 1 cannon, 4mg, 329mph.

   Sub-Lt (A) R. B. Pearson: S-Lt (A) 1938; 810 Sqdn, *Ark Royal*, April 1939; Lt (A) June
1940; 760 Sqdn, *Heron* (shore sta), May 1941; Actg Lt-Cdr (A) & CO 893 Sqdn Sept
1942; *Daedalus* (Lee) April 1944–5.

   [2]Lt-Cdr J. W. Linton: Lt-Cdr 1936; CO *Pandora* 1940; CO *Turbulent* Aug 1941; Cdr
Dec 1941; lost in Med March 1943; posthumous VC.

   [3]*Hermes*: 1923–4, 10,950t, 12 aircraft, 6×5.5in, 3×4in, 25k; sunk off Ceylon, 9 April
1942, Japanese naval a/c.

Mediterranean Fleet, of which I had at that time only partial knowledge, viz., that cover and escort were being afforded to a convoy proceeding from Alexandria to Malta.[1]

7.   It will be appreciated that at this time neither my staff nor I had had any opportunity to consider plans for operations on the Italian Coast, since our time had been fully occupied in current operations, and preparing for the Dakar operation.

8.   I convened a meeting with the VACAC, at which the Admiralty proposals were discussed, and asked C-in-C, Mediterranean Fleet, . . . for his views on these proposals. This crossed a message from C-in-C, Mediterranean Fleet, from which I learnt that he proposed to carry out an attack by FAA aircraft on enemy ships in Augusta, to be followed possibly by a bombardment of that port. He suggested that a similar operation might be carried out by Force H against ships in Naples, Trapani, Palermo or Messina in that order of preference. He did not advocate FAA attack on Taranto.

9.   An examination of these proposals showed that:–

(a)   It was most improbable that surprise could be achieved.
(b)   The striking force would be limited to 12 TSRs and 9 Skuas.
(c)   Only 5 destroyers of sufficient endurance to accompany the Force in the final stage and withdrawal were available.
(d)   Attacks could be carried out better from the East or Malta, thus avoiding capital ships proceeding into a dangerous area where they could not be used effectively.

10.   I informed Admiralty and C-in-C, Mediterranean Fleet, to this effect in my 1430/7, and stated that unless a favourable target was presented the operation would be limited to air attack on Cagliari where surprise might be achieved and the destroyers of the 13th Flotilla could be employed. I pointed out that this attack could only be a pinprick and it had the disadvantage of putting the Italians on their guard without achieving material results. As an alternative I suggested that 12 TSRs should be flown off from *Ark Royal* to proceed to Malta to launch attacks from there, the TSRs being retrieved subsequently.

11.   To C-in-C, Mediterranean's 1409/7 I replied at 1720/7 that lack of destroyers with sufficient endurance, and time to formulate proper plans, prevented me from undertaking the operations he suggested, and that Force H would sail a.m. on 8 July to carry out an air attack on Cagliari at dawn on 10th and thus cause a diversion.

---

[1]This was probably a convoy *from* Malta. If so, there were in fact two convoys, one fast, one slow, and the operation led to a clash between the Mediterranean Fleet and the Italian Fleet off Calabria on 9 July. See Cunningham, *A Sailor's Odyssey*, pp. 257–66.

8 July

14.   At 0157 I received AM 0055/8 suggesting that the moral effect would be greatly enhanced by the bombardment of the Naval Base or Elmas Air Station at Cagliari. This had already been considered but apart from the fact that time did not permit of any thorough examination of the problem or the preparation of proper plans it was clear that:–

(a)   Bombardment would have to take place in an area which was probably mined and within effective range of the coast defences.
(b)   No surprise could be achieved since daylight would be required in order to obtain aiming marks.
(c)   Air spotting could not be relied on owing to probable presence of enemy fighters.
(d)   Owing to lack of surprise ships would be exposed to prepared submarine and MTB attack during the final stages of the approach and whilst proceeding to a bombarding position.

15.   I therefore informed the Admiralty in my 0815/8 that unless there were strong political reasons for bombardment the results likely to be achieved were not commensurate with the risks.

16.   At 0700, Force H consisting of *Hood, Valiant, Resolution, Ark Royal, Arethusa, Enterprise, Delhi, Faulknor, Fearless, Forester, Foxhound, Escort, Wrestler, Velox, Vortigern, Active* and *Douglas*[1] sailed from Gibraltar and proceeded to the eastward.

19.   From 1545 to 1840 the Force was heavily bombed by Italian Savoia aircraft.[2] These attacks were delivered in three waves.

20.   The first attack at 1545 was carried out by two sub-flights of 3 aircraft. These aircraft were only sighted a few seconds before bombs fell and consequently were only engaged during their withdrawal.

21.   Immediately after this attack, a reconnaissance aircraft reported a submarine on the surface ahead of the Fleet. Course of the Fleet was altered as necessary. The submarine dived before an attack could be made.

22.   RDF reports of small numbers of aircraft were received from *Valiant* from 1614 onwards and at 1731 a report of a large number of aircraft approaching the Fleet was received.

23.   At 1750 some bombs were seen bursting in the sea about 5 miles SE from the Fleet. Shortly afterwards aircraft were seen approaching from that direction and were heavily engaged by the whole Fleet.

---

[1]*Velox*: 1918, 1090t, 4×4in, 28k.
Douglas: 1918, 1530t, 3×4.7in, 3tt, 31k.
[2]Probably Savoia SM79: 1935, 2750lb of bombs or 2 tpdos, 4mg, 270mph.

24.   At 1836 the third attack was carried out from the sun sector without positive warning from the RDF. The aircraft were however sighted and engaged before bomb release.

25.   It is estimated that about 40 aircraft took part in these attacks and over 100 bombs were dropped. The bombs were thought to be 500 lbs HE with thin metal casings and instantaneous fuses. All attacks were pressed home most determinedly and although no hits were obtained the accuracy of the bombing compared favourably with that of the Germans. It is estimated there were 12 near misses. All attacks were carried out at a height of 10,000–13,000 feet and bombs dropped in patterns using stick bombing.

26.   During the attack the mean course of the Fleet was 076°, speed 17 knots. Immediately after the first attack the line was staggered. During the attacks course was only altered sufficiently to open 'A' arcs of the long-range A/A armament.

27.   From our own aircraft it was learnt later that two enemy aircraft were shot down by fighters and two by gunfire. Three more were badly damaged and unlikely to reach their base. Four others were damaged. A good volume of A/A fire was developed but our fighters reported that bursts were generally on the short side.

28.   There were no casualties in Force H and only minor superficial damage from bomb splinters.

29.   As a result of this, our first contact with the Italian Air Force, it appeared to me that the prospects of *Ark Royal* escaping damage, whilst operating within 100 miles of the Sardinia coast the following morning were small. I conceived that it was highly improbable that Their Lordships would wish to have *Ark Royal* put out of action, with the possible loss of a large number of her aircraft, for a minor operation which was intended to act as a diversion.

30.   I therefore decided that at 2215 the Force should withdraw to the westward and proceed at its highest speed (20 knots) in order to increase the range from Sardinian aerodromes. Since the Force had been steering to the eastward until after dark I considered that the enemy would be kept in doubt as to the intentions of Force H and experience difficulty in locating it the following day.

11 July

37.   At 0325 a signal was received from *Forester* reporting that she was standing by *Escort* who had been torpedoed.[1] . . .

---

[1]By *Guglielmo Marconi*: 1940, 1190/1489, 8tt, 1×3.9in, 18/7k; lost Atl Nov 1941, cause unknown.

38.   On receipt of this report, *Faulknor* was ordered to close *Escort*, and ACNAS asked if he could send destroyers to assist in screening the Fleet into harbour.

39.   It was later ascertained that the explosions seen at 0215 were caused by the torpedoing of *Escort* and by *Forester* opening fire on a submarine. *Forester* sighted the submarine at short range on the surface on the starboard bow. She attacked with gunfire and attempted to ram. Depth charges were at 'safe' and could not be released in time.

40.   While *Forester* was attacking, the submarine crash dived and fired a torpedo from her stern tube. This, or a previous torpedo, hit *Escort*. No asdic contact was obtained at this time by either ship though the approaching torpedo was heard as hydrophonic effect in *Escort* immediately before the explosion. *Forester* continued to search for the submarine until informed by *Escort* that she had been torpedoed. *Forester* then closed and at 0300 obtained a firm contact and attacked with 6 depth charges set to 300 feet. No visible results were seen.

41.   After closing, *Forester* transferred *Escort*'s ship's company, with the exception of about 20 officers and men. Endeavour was then made to take *Escort* in tow, but this proved extremely difficult owing to *Escort*'s rudder being jammed. An attempt was then made to tow stern first, but at 1115 *Escort* sank.

42.   During the search for the submarine the remainder of Force H proceeded towards Gibraltar, entering harbour at 0830.

44.   After the Fleet had entered harbour, *Foxhound*, *Keppel* and *Foresight* were ordered to join Captain (D), 8th DF,[1] and hunt the submarine. . . .

45.   At 1332 two aircraft with Italian markings bombed the searching destroyers, 6 bombs falling near *Foxhound* without causing damage.

46.   The search was continued throughout the day, and night, and the following day but without success. Aircraft patrols were maintained over the searching destroyers during this period. . . .

45.   *To his wife*

10 July 1940

. . . I feel that some of the people at home will be thinking I hadn't got the guts to go on. Seems to me it required far more not to. I hate doing a thing which I feel in my bones is radically wrong and I also hate doing an

[1]Capt Anthony F. de Salis: Capt 1938; *Faulkner* & Capt (D) 8DF Feb 1940; TMD 1942; DTM 1944; *Sussex* Dec 1944.

operation like this before I've had a chance to get my force trained and on its toes. Apart from that some of the older destroyers I have carry so little oil that I'm always preoccupied about whether they can get back or not. . . . As regards myself you need have no fears because there is an immense Admiral's Conning Tower to which I retire in action with my staff. There is no sense in remaining out in the open and I get a better view from there than I do from my bridge. . . .

. . . The little boats have been doing nothing but convoy work up till now so they're a bit green at the Fleet stuff. What we want is a few days in harbour in which to be able to discuss things and really get together and I've not had a chance of that yet. . . .

46. *To Pound*

13 July 1940

Calling off the attack on Cagliari was a most distasteful decision to make but I felt it was most improbable you would want *Ark Royal* put out of action in view of our limited objective.

Valiant's RDF was reporting aircraft throughout the forenoon and early afternoon of 9 July, but owing to the absence of IFF in our aircraft, it was impossible to determine which were shadowing and the Skuas failed to locate any until later in the afternoon, when they shot one down. The first bombing attack at 1630 was unobserved until the bombs fell. It was a clear sky with a bright, high sun that made observation of aircraft very difficult. This attack was principally on *Ark Royal* and she had one or two very near misses. . . .

For the attack on Cagliari, Wells considered that *Ark Royal* must operate within 90 to 100 miles of the target and that flying off could not commence before 0215. This meant that flying on could not be completed before 0615. In view of the easterly wind it involved flying on towards the land and would bring Force H and *Ark Royal* under air attack for a period of 9 or 10 hours. Taking into consideration that we were only delivering an attack with 12 bombers and 3 minelayers, the best *Ark Royal* could do with[out] night flying pilots, it seemed quite obvious that the Italians would be almost certain to score more points than we should, by getting hits on *Ark Royal*.

. . . until I hear from you that I need not restrict *Ark Royal* to objectives of high military or political importance I do not feel justified in having her put out of action for such minor adventures.

The low endurance of the destroyers is a constant worry. I had to limit speed at night to 14 knots in order to have something in hand for a surface encounter. I think we shall have to oil at sea at night in spite of the risks, otherwise we shall never get anywhere.

The submarine which got *Escort* early this morning was on the surface. *Forester*, who was rear wing ship astern of *Escort*, saw the submarine on the surface at 0215, just after she had fired at *Escort* (or the battle squadron), turned towards and opened fire with 'B' gun, ran over the spot *but* the depth charges were not ready. It's maddening as we ought to have had the submarine for a certainty.

. . . I am, of course, investigating *Forester*'s failures to let go depth charges or to make any enemy report.

This shows how essential it is for the units of this force to be properly 'worked up'. Until they are, I can have no confidence that they are ready to do their stuff. . . .

All the Captains are crying out for an opportunity to exercise, so I am asking to be given a chance to do something if the situation admits. Out in the Atlantic, asdic conditions ought to be normal, but here they are very bad. A heavy layer at 90 feet gives the submarines complete cover and makes day hunting abortive. *Proteus* and *Pandora* are anxious to do some stalking and I am organising a drive of destroyers at night and up moon to see if we can catch anything on the surface. . . .

Officers and men of Force H are all in very good heart. The lack of mails and beer in the canteen are adverse factors but I hope they will be put right before long.

47. *To his wife*

24 July 1940

. . . I'm somewhat appalled at my apparent lack of foresight [at Mers-el-Kebir] though I appreciate of course how completely the French resistance took me by surprise. I never expected for one single moment that they would attempt to take their ships out of harbour under such conditions. Still I ought to have been prepared for it and wasn't. Don't know what view the Admiralty will take about it when they do get the report and I don't know that I mind much. I've had a run for my money anyway. . . .

I wonder whether this General de Gaulle will be able to do anything. He doesn't seem to be a very well known man or outstanding leader. It's a pity there's not someone who could really get the overseas French together. In France the Germans have evidently got the French entirely flattened out. What damned fools the French were not to go on fighting from N. Africa.

48. *Report of Proceedings, 11–30 July 1940*

2. Providing Force H was not required for some specific operation, it was my intention to carry out a programme of exercises and practices by the Force as a whole, with the object of welding a somewhat varied collection of ships into a homogenous fighting unit.

Unfortunately the departure of five destroyers of the 13th DF for the United Kingdom on 14 July so reduced the destroyer force available that the exercises had of necessity to be limited to individual practices by cruisers and destroyers, carried out in an area to the eastward of Gibraltar during the week commencing 15 July. These exercises included full calibre and sub calibre firing.

3. Ships in harbour were given daily communication exercises, height-finding and other air defence exercises . . . searchlight exercises against motorboats representing MTBs, concentration exercises with air spotting, etc.

Anti-submarine exercises were carried out by destroyers with *Proteus* and *Pandora*.

4. Much attention was paid to the development of the shore A/A defence organisation, which was not of a high standard. . . .

The frequent presence over the Rock of unidentified reconnaissance aircraft and two air raids during this period, though causing negligible damage, undoubtedly did much to bring home to the personnel concerned the importance of a very rapid improvement in this branch of the Gibraltar defences, and I am able to report that, as a result of the measures taken, the increase in efficiency has been marked, though it still falls below what I consider to be an acceptable standard.

7. I have been in frequent consultation with the ACNAS and the military C-in-C[1] over the question of the defence of Gibraltar in the event of the entry of Spain into the war, and the role of Force H if this should happen. . . . with particular reference to Force H, I stated:

> I consider every effort should be made to obtain advance information when Spain will declare war and Force H withdraw before and not after hostilities have commenced.

AM 1432/28 . . . expressed full agreement with this view. . . . Outline plans for attacks on Cadiz, Ferrol and/or Vigo . . . were forwarded in my 0700/31.

---

[1] Lt-Gen Sir Clive G. Liddell: Leics Regt; 2Lt 1902; Capt 1908; France 1914–16; WO 1916–19; Maj 1917; Staff Coll 1919–22; Col 1923; WO 1928–31; Maj-Gen 1933; S Cmd 1931–4; London Dist Div Cmd 1935; Lt-Gen 1938; Adj-Gen to Forces 1937; C-in-C Gibraltar July 1939; Gen Feb 1941.

9. ... I felt it incumbent to stress that the most important task of Force H appeared to be the control of the Straits and that no other demands on the Force, such as raiding the Italian coasts, should be allowed to endanger the fulfilment of this primary object, unless it was reasonably certain that such operations would be justified by the results likely to be achieved.

12. On 12 July was received AM 1405/21, instructing me to advise the Admiralty if it was my intention to take any part of Force H to sea during the week commencing 22 July, since it might be desired to combine such exercise with the interception of some important ships which were proceeding to Spanish ports. I replied at 2009 that insufficient destroyers were available to take the battleships to sea, but that it was my intention that *Ark Royal*, *Enterprise* and 3 destroyers should carry out exercises to the west on 23 and 24 July.

On receiving AM 0205/22 to the effect that *Ark Royal* should be screened by not less than 4 destroyers and that the 13th DF should be called upon if necessary, I replied that of the 10 remaining destroyers comprising the combined 8th and 13th Flotillas, three were under repair. To provide a continuous screen of four for *Ark Royal* therefore would have left only three for patrol duties and as a screen for three heavy ships if required in an emergency. Arrangements were made, however, to provide the fourth destroyer for passage out and back clear of the Straits.

13. At 2123 on 22 July, AM 2032/22 was received, ordering air attacks to be carried out on merchant shipping in Le Verdon Roads and at Bordeaux. ...

14. Owing to fog, the force was unable to sail at 0630 on 23rd as intended, and at 1020 I reported to Admiralty that while Le Verdon Roads was suitable for aircraft torpedo attack, Bordeaux was only suitable for bomb attack, which could be more suitably carried out from the UK. ...

15. *Ark Royal*, *Enterprise*, *Faulknor*, *Foresight*, *Escapade* and *Forester* accordingly left Gibraltar at 2200 on 23 July. At 0100 on 25 July AM 2355/24 was received in *Ark Royal*, cancelling the operation. ...

16. The importance of adequate air reconnaissance both to the W and E of Gibraltar is self evident. 200 Group in their signal 1042/30 addressed to the Air Ministry, have asked for the permanent allocation of two Sunderlands[1] for reconnaissance. In my signal 0529/4 August, I strongly supported this proposal. Unless air reconnaissance is available

---

[1]Short Sunderland: flying boat, 1937, 2000lb of bombs, 10–14mg, 213mph, 2980mls range.

to a sufficient depth, the risk of enemy vessels breaking in or out of the Straits is greatly increased during conditions of low visibility in the Straits. ...

49. *To his wife*

2 August 1940

I feel in a better temper than when I last wrote ... We went off on what promised to be a very difficult and sticky party on the 31st. The big idea was to give old Ma Ford some gales of wind, if you know what I mean. They had to go in a rather slow old cup of tea so it wasn't altogether a bright prospect with these Iti bombers buzzing round.[1]

However it's all gone off a treat so far. Ma has got his gales and we gave Cagliari aerodrome a damned good bombing which will learn them all right. It was so effective that we had no eggs on us at all today. Yesterday afternoon 16 of their big Savoias came out to do their stuff but our A/A gave them cold feet and the accuracy of their bombing was nothing like as good as last time. Our Skuas shot down 3 altogether whilst I saw another hit very hard by A/A fire and I think we peppered some more. At Cagliari we got 4 on the ground and some more probably in the hangars. So up to date it's been quite a good party. ...

I was also pleased to get a signal from Andrew B. [Cunningham]. He'd made out a plan which I'd torn to bits as it didn't seem to face up to the facts of the situation and I expected a torrent in reply from him and the Admiralty. Instead of which he entirely agreed with me and said he would modify his plan accordingly. It's been most unpleasant for me always having to pour water on these rather wild schemes but I believe now that he and the Admiralty are beginning to realise hard facts and what can be done and what should not. My responsibility is very heavy and I'm not prepared to be a 'yes man' so as to provide Winston with some squib to let off in the House.

As you can imagine it's an anxious time for me but that does not worry me unduly. It's no effort to me to act quickly, the only snag is that others don't always react quite quickly enough.

[1]Vice Adm (later Adm) Sir Wilbraham T. R. Ford: Capt 1922; RA 1932; VA & FOIC Malta 1937–41; Adm Dec 1941; C-in-C Rosyth April 1942–June 1944; Ret List June 1944.
The gales of wind were Hurricanes and the cup of tea was *Argus*.

50.   *To his wife*

5 August 1940

Well we got back all right from our expedition to Cagliari and delivery of goods to Ma Ford. Unfortunately we just couldn't make it Saturday night so I had a rather tiring and anxious extra night mucking about until daylight.

Apparently the Admiralty were pleased as I received Their Lordships' congratulations on a successful operation. Dear old Dudley North also sent me a very charming signal and Andrew B. came up with 'Nice work' to which I replied as a brother doorkeeper. 'To Gog from Magog: Thank you'.

Everyone seems pleased with the result of the operation and if we hadn't lost the crew of one aircraft we should have got away with a clean sheet. I think we must have shaken those ice creamers a bit.

About 2.30 a.m. in the pitch dark on Friday morning as we were mucking about only 100 miles or so off the Iti coast I thought of all the possibilities – destroyers, MTBs, submarines, cruisers, bombing attacks at daylight, etc., and began to feel that it was all a bit sticky and the temperature of my feet dropped appreciably.

And then in the pitch dark I saw a small shadow separate itself from the great shadow of the *Ark*. The first Swordfish taking off. And then I thought of those incredibly gallant chaps taking off in the pitch dark to fly 140 miles to a place they've never seen, to be shot up by A/A guns and dazzled by searchlights and then mark you to fly over the sea and find that tiny floating aerodrome with the knowledge that if they don't find it they're done.

Well that shook me up and I realised how small were my personal difficulties compared to theirs. The wind changed completely while they were away and some only just got back. It was an anxious time waiting for them but a heartening moment when they came trundling back one after the other under the low clouds.

. . . I can tell you now that I shall be transferring to *Renown* so address me there in future. She's been modernised and has first class A/A equipment – better than *Hood* so we ought to give the Iti planes a good knock next time we meet.

51.   *Report of Proceedings, 30 July –9 August 1940*

2.   At 0630 on 30 July, *Argus* arrived at Gibraltar in company with *Greyhound, Gallant, Encounter* and *Hotspur*, from the UK, bringing

with her 12 Hurricanes, 2 Skuas and RAF personnel and stores to be transferred to Malta by means of operation HURRY. . . .

7.   At 0800 on 31 July, Force H, consisting of *Hood, Valiant, Resolution, Ark Royal, Argus, Arethusa, Enterprise, Faulknor, Foxhound, Forester, Foresight, Hotspur, Greyhound, Gallant, Escapade, Encounter* and *Velox*,[1] sailed from Gibraltar and proceeded on a course 080°, speed 17 knots.

8.   At 0935, *Ark Royal* flew off two TSRs for anti-submarine patrol. . . .

At 1445, *Ark Royal* flew off 8 TSRs to carry out a parallel track search ahead, No. 200 Squadron at Gibraltar having provided the initial search.

At 1500 it became necessary to reduce the speed of the Fleet to 16 knots, as destroyers were bumping in the steep head sea and Asdic operation was being adversely affected.

9.   I had intended to alter to the westward immediately before dark and then turn back to the eastward after dark, with the object of avoiding the Fleet being silhouetted in the after-glow and thus facilitating attack by any submarines lying to the eastward. Owing to the adverse weather conditions and the necessity for making ground to the eastward, this intention had to be abandoned.

1 August

11.   At 0550 reconnaissance aircraft were flown off *Ark Royal* to search 100 miles to the eastward and to carry out normal A/S patrols. At 0800 the third degree of A/A readiness was assumed and three Skuas flown off to drive off shadowers.

From 0600 onwards, numerous RDF reports were received from *Valiant*. Some of these could be identified as our own aircraft, but the lack of IFF gave rise to many false alarms of incoming raids and imposed an unnecessary strain on the personnel.

14.   At 1230 the Fleet assumed the second degree of A/A readiness, took up open order and staggered the line in readiness for air attack. At 1710 6 additional Skuas were flown off to maintain a fighter patrol over the Fleet.

. . . at 1749, 8 aircraft in three sub-flights were sighted approaching from the port beam at a height of 12,000 feet. They were engaged by the Fleet, the fire of which appeared to be generally effective though, as usual, somewhat on the short side. Two aircraft were seen to turn away before reaching the bomb release position.

---

[1]*Escapade, Encounter* (lost, Java Sea, March 1942): 1934, 1375t, 4×4.7in, 8tt, 36k;

Greyhound (sunk off Crete May 1941, Ger a/c), *Gallant* (mined Malta Jan 1941): 1936, 1375t, 4×4.7in, 8tt, 36k.

Hotspur: 1936, 1340t, 4×4.7in, 8tt, 36k.

A few minutes later a second wave of 9 aircraft also in three sub-flights were sighted approaching on the port quarter. An emergency turn of 40° to port was at once executed to bring this attack abeam. Fire was opened and several aircraft were observed to sheer off before releasing their bombs. One aircraft appeared to be hit by A/A fire, making a sharp turn away with considerable smoke issuing from the tail.

15.   These attacks were not pressed home with the same determination as the attack delivered on 9 July. It is considered that this can be attributed to the marked improvement in A/A fire.

Some 80 bombs in all were dropped and appeared to be of the SAP type with delay fuses. One Savoia SM79 was shot down by 803 Squadron (Skuas).

16.   No further attacks took place and at 2045 Group I, consisting of *Hood, Ark Royal, Enterprise, Faulknor, Foxhound, Foresight* and *Forester* were detached and proceeded at 20 knots for flying off aircraft for the attack on Cagliari.

Group II, comprising the remainder of Force H, proceeded under *Valiant* to the eastward in order to fly off the Hurricanes at dawn. The position from which this would take place was dependent on the later weather reports from Malta, coupled with local wind observations.

At 2130, *Enterprise* was detached to carry out the diversionary operation SPARK[1] and subsequently to act in accordance with AM 1938/1, ... instructing me to take action to intercept the French ship *Gouverneur Général de Gueydon*, which was believed to have sailed from Algiers at 1600, 1 August, for Marseilles with M. Daladier[2] aboard.

17.   In view of *Oswald*'s message 1230/1 to Captain (S), 1st SF,[3] which was intercepted, and read as follows:–

Ship of [class] cruiser *Giovanni delle Bande Nere* passed northward through Straits of Messina at 0700. Four ships of [class] cruiser *Bolzano* or cruiser *Eugenio di Savoia*[4] escorted by destroyers passed through Straits of Messina northbound,

it appeared possible that these might be encountered during the night.

---

[1]Transmitting confusing radio messages.
[2]Edouard Daladier (1884–1970): Rad Socst Deputy; lecturer; Lt W Front 1914–18; Minr for Cols 1924; PM Jan–Oct 1933, 1934; Minr Natnl Defence; PM April 1938–March 1940; Minr War & For Affs ; jailed by Vichy; Deputy 1946–58.
Gouverneur Général de Gueydon: 1922, 4513t, CGT, Marseilles.
[3]*Oswald*: 1928, 1311/1831t, 8tt, 1×4in, 15/9k; sunk E of Sicily 1 Aug 1940, destroyer *Vivaldi*.
Captain (S), 1st SF was Captain S. M. Raw, based at Alexandria: Cdr 1933; Capt June 1940; *Medway* 1940; *Dolphin* 1942; *Phoebe* June 1943.
[4]*Giovanni delle Bande Nere*: 1931, 5069t, 8×6in, 6×3.9in, 4tt, 37k; sunk 1942, *Urge*.
Bolzano: 1933, 11,065t, 8×8in, 12×3.9in, 8tt, 34k; sunk La Spezia 1944.

In order to maintain contact during the night, preserve wireless silence and at the same time deal with conditions which would involve drastic alterations of course and speed during flying off operations, it had been arranged that during the approach destroyers would be stationed at maximum visibility distance ahead of the guide, 1500 yards apart. At 0200, without signal, *Ark Royal* would proceed ahead of *Hood* and the destroyers would drop back and prolong the line astern. *Ark Royal* would then shape course and speed as requisite for flying off, eventually closing Group II, the destroyers taking up screening position on *Ark Royal* when flying off was completed.

2 August

18.   These arrangements worked according to plan, and at 0320 *Ark Royal* commenced flying off the striking force consisting of 9 TSRs armed with bombs and 3 with mines. One aircraft crashed on taking off and fell into the sea.[1] . . .

19.   By this time the wind had shifted from S to the westward and was freshening. Owing to the change of wind, the air striking force was set to the southward and had some difficulty in locating the target. This delay caused the attack to be delivered in daylight instead of at dawn as was intended. From the reports received from the VAA, there is little doubt that the attack was carried out with great determination and was most successful despite heavy A/A fire and opposition from enemy fighters. Direct hits were obtained on 4 hangars, 2 of which were burning fiercely. At least 4 aircraft in the open were destroyed in addition to those in the hangars. Many aerodrome buildings were destroyed or badly damaged. Three mines were laid in the entrance at Cagliari harbour. One Swordfish made a forced landing at Elmas. . . .

20.   After flying off the air striking force, Group I altered course to the southward to rejoin Group II, *Ark Royal* continuing in the van. At 0445 *Ark Royal* flew off 5 TSRs to carry out a search from 065° to 100°, and 130° to 160°, the latter to ensure contact with Group II. Nine Skuas were also flown off to provide an escort for the returning striking force and a patrol over the Fleet.

21.   Group II . . . proceeded to the eastward, and adjusting speed so as to reach position 37° 40'N, 7° 20'E, by 0445. Difficulty was experienced in starting up one Skua and the flying off for the first flight did not take place until 0515. The second flight was ranged and flown off by 0600. The two Sunderlands which had flown from Gibraltar to provide additional escort for the Hurricanes were not sighted although they were picked up by the RDF screen.

[1]Crew lost, despite search.

22.   Group II was sighted at 0520 and Group I manoeuvred as requisite to maintain close support of Group II and at the same time to fly on and off *Ark Royal*'s aircraft. Visibility had deteriorated and the cloud ceiling was only about 4000 feet. At 0630 the first of the air striking force returned but it was not until 0720 that the last was flown on. . . . the aircraft were faced with a strong headwind. That the striking force succeeded in regaining their carrier under these most difficult conditions reflects great credit on the navigation of the aircraft.

23.   Several Italian aircraft were sighted by our aircraft during the morning, one of which was forced down, badly damaged, by Skuas. One submarine was sighted by a TSR aircraft about 60 miles E of Group I at 0530 but the aircraft had dropped her bombs and could not attack.

24.   By 0815, Group I had rejoined Group II. The force took up cruising disposition No. 5 and proceeded to the westward at its maximum speed (18 knots). *Ark Royal* flew off two TSRs, for A/S patrol and 6 Skuas for fighter patrol, 3 of which patrolled astern of the Fleet to drive off any shadowers. During the forenoon, *Valiant* reported several shadowers on the RDF screen and at 1000 aircraft were reported closing from the starboard beam. These aircraft were plotted in to 10 miles but then turned away and were lost. It appears possible that these were bombers which were unable to locate the Fleet. . . .

25.   At 0930 *Arethusa* was detached to intercept the *Gouverneur Général de Gueydon* . . . Four TSRs were flown off *Ark Royal* to assist in the search.

At 1000, *Enterprise*, who had proceeded to the N of Minorca to intercept the same ship, reported that there were two aircraft overhead. It appeared therefore, that operation SPARK had been successful as a diversion, but as *Enterprise* was unsupported I ordered her to proceed to Gibraltar passing W of the Balearics.

Neither *Enterprise* nor *Arethusa* sighted the *Governeur Général de Gueydon*.

26.   At 1250, Blue Section of 800 Squadron (Skuas) under Lieut G.R. Callingham[1] shot down a Cant Z506[2] in flames which was shadowing the Fleet from astern. It appears probable that after this the enemy aircraft lost touch with the Fleet.

4 August

29.   On arrival [at Gibraltar] all ships completed with fuel and ammunition, and at 2000, . . . the following ships sailed for the United Kingdom:–

---

[1]Lieut G. R. Callingham: Lt 1940; 800 Sqdn 1940; 880 Sqdn 1941; 882 Sqdn 1942; Actg Lt-Cdr BAD June 1943; Lt-Cdr 1945.
[2]Cant Z506: seaplane, 1937, 2645lb of bombs, 4mg, 217mph.

Hood, Valiant, Argus, Arethusa, Faulknor, Foresight, Forester, Foxhound, Escapade.

Owing to engine room defects *Fearless* was unable to sail with the remainder of the Force, but joined company the following day.

30.   In order to increase the effectiveness of the search for merchant vessels attempting to evade the blockade, . . . *Ark Royal, Enterprise* and the four modern destroyers of the 13th DF accompanied the Force to sea.

5 August

33.   During the afternoon, starting at 1400, a diverging search was carried out by 9 aircraft between 180° and 020° to depth of 100 miles. One of these aircraft at 1540 sighted and reported the Brazilian SS *Raoul Soares*,[1] 60 miles to the northward, and apparently making for Lisbon. *Enterprise* was detached to examine the vessel, . . .

6 August

34.   . . . I detached *Ark Royal, Enterprise* and the four destroyers of the 13th DF at 1050 with instructions to search for shipping and then return to Gibraltar.

35.   At 1350 a merchant ship was sighted on the port beam and *Arethusa* was ordered to investigate. She was found to be the Greek SS *Svoa Nicholas*[2] bound from Buenos Aires to Cork, with a cargo of grain, and had called at Las Palmas. She was allowed to proceed. . . .

7 August

37.   At 1115 a report was received from *Kingston Sapphire*[3] that she had been bombed in a position 100 miles ahead of the Fleet. RDF watch was set in *Valiant* but no indication of the presence of aircraft was obtained.

8 August

40.   At 1415 an incomplete W/T message was received from a shore station which led me to believe that *Laconia*[4] had been torpedoed in a position 25 miles to the eastward of *Hood*. *Foxhound* was therefore detached to search and assist, and ordered to report accordingly to the C-in-C, Western Approaches.[5] It subsequently transpired that the message

---

[1]*Raoul Soares*: 1900, 6003t.
[2]*Svoa Nicholas* unidentified.
[3]*Kingston Sapphire*: trawler, 1929, 356t, Kingston ST Co, Hull.
[4]*Laconia*: 1922, 19695t, 17k, Cunard White Star Line.
[5]Adm Dunbar-Nasmith.

referred to another unknown ship, and *Foxhound* rejoined the following morning, having found nothing.

9 August

44. HMS *Hood* arrived at Scapa at 0500 on 10 August.
Exercises and Practices
45. Opportunity was taken during the passage when weather and circumstances permitted to carry out much-needed exercises and practices.[1] ...
Conduct of Personnel
47. I have once more to record the admirable courage, endurance and skill displayed by the crews of the FAA aircraft operating from *Ark Royal*.

52.   *Notes of a meeting held in the First Sea Lord's room*

The Admiralty,
11 August 1940

Present

First Sea Lord, Vice Admiral Somerville, ACNS (F), DOD(F), Captain Jeffery, Cdr Buzzard, Cdr Secker.[2] ...

... The First Sea Lord expressed the opinion that, if he were considering the project from a purely military point of view, he would incline to sending the first two M/T ships round the Cape, thereby ensuring as far as possible their safe arrival at their final destination. The possibility of sending further M/T ships through the Mediterranean might then be considered in a separate operation to HATS.

Admiral Somerville, in reply to a question by the First Sea Lord, expressed the opinion that to attempt to pass even two M/T ships through to the Eastern Mediterranean in connection with operation HATS would add considerable difficulties to his operation owing to the resultant reduction in speed and the necessary splitting up of his forces. He was of the opinion that to attempt to pass more than two M/T ships through would be distinctly harzardous, and advocated most strongly that the M/T ships should be sent via the Cape, as he felt that to try and combine sailing them through the Mediterranean with operation HATS might

---

[1]Practices included dive bombing attacks by Skuas, night exercises and gunnery practice.
[2]Cdr D. H. Secker: Cdr 1936; Nav O, *Victoria & Albert* 1937; OD Jan 1940; *Daedalus* (Lee-on-Solent) 1941; OD Jan 1943.

well jeopardise that operation and hazard our own ships, more particularly the aircraft carriers. It was stated that C-in-C, Mediterranean, had pointed out that he could not wait outside Malta with M/T ships while *Valiant* was unloading guns, etc., for Malta, and it would therefore be necessary to send a third M/T ship with these latter stores. ACNS (F) said that he thought it was essential to remember the object of operation HATS. This was designed to reinforce the fleet in the Eastern Mediterranean, and the success of the whole operation would be hazarded by the addition of M/T ships. . . .

The First Sea Lord remarked that the urgency of the armoured brigade reaching Egypt was due to the desire to get it there before the big battle, which it was anticipated would start in the near future. . . .

Subsequent to the discussion of operation HATS, Admiral Somerville raised a number of other operations. He asked whether it would be possible to have one, or possibly more, submarines in the Western Mediterranean basin. The First Sea Lord stated that he did not think this would be possible for the present. It was very necessary to maintain the submarine strength in the Eastern Mediterranean particularly to attack convoys proceeding from Italy to Libya in the event of German troops being sent by this route.

Admiral Somerville also raised the question of some minelaying destroyers being added to his force, but was informed that the minelaying destroyers had a very extensive programme of minelaying to be carried out at home.

Admiral Somerville, referring to the primary object of Force H, questioned the advisability of jeopardising his ships, particularly *Ark Royal*, by operating off the Italian coast, and asked how far he was entitled to risk his ships in such operations.

The First Sea Lord, in reply, said that the matter would not arise for a month or so on account of operation HATS, and stated that it was the intention for the RAF to carry out fairly extensive bombing raids on Italy in the near future, and this might well alter the scale of bombing attack to which Force H would be subjected.

53. *Subjects of Interest to Senior Officer, Force H*

August 1940

Japanese participation in the war

(a) In the event of Japanese attack on Malaya, or, possibly NEIs, it is not the intention to send major units to the Far East.[1] It is probable that *Renown* and *Ark Royal* would be sent to Colombo to protect our trade routes, together with a reinforcement of cruisers and some destroyers.

(b) In the event of Japanese attack on Australasia the political necessity might arise to send our Fleet now in the Eastern Mediterranean to the Far East. In that case it would be hoped still to confine the Italian Fleet to the Mediterranean by detaching additional units from the Home Fleet, if the situation in Home Waters allowed, or by forming a squadron of 'R' class [battleships] at Gibraltar. *Renown* and *Ark Royal* might still be sent to the East Indies Station.

5. *Proposals for Mining Spanish Ports*
These have been forwarded in detail already.
6. *Proposals for attack against Spain*

(a) Plans for offensive action against Spanish ports and forces in the event of Spanish intervention . . . have been signalled to SO Force H. . . .

7. *General position as regards Gibraltar*

(a) Information re Spanish intentions. Communication with NA Madrid. Local information. Information from Tangier.
(b) Possibility of sabotage of batteries by agents.
(c) Air attack and defence.
  Vulnerability of ships.
  Hurricanes – operation of.
(d) Italian submarine activity.
(e) French activity at Casablanca.
(f) Italian air activities at Palma, Mallorca, with reference to bombing of Gibraltar.

---

[1]The British Government had been extremely ambivalent about the Far East for many years. Reluctant but vague commitments had been made to Australia and New Zealand about the despatch of a great fleet in the event of war with Japan, supposedly the main potential enemy in the inter-war years, though the Navy's vessels were not designed for an eastern war and the bases were virtually non-existent. By 1940 it was becoming apparent that the eastern Empire could not be defended.

8. *Alternative bases to Gibraltar*

(a) SO Force H has suggested Madeira as a base.

(b) Admiralty replied explaining the considerations affecting decision on Azores as refuelling base, and should Spain enter the war, of occupying the Cape Verde Islands to deny them to the enemy.

54. *Report of Proceedings, 10–25 August 1940*

2. HMS *Hood* arrived at Scapa [0500, 10 August] transfer the Flag of FOC Force H to HMS *Renown* . . .

3. At 0930, [10 August], I proceeded by air to London in company with my Chief of Staff, SO (P) and Flag Commander.[1]

6. At 1630, 13 August, *Renown*, escorted by *Bedouin, Punjabi, Mashona* and *Tartar*,[2] left Scapa for Gibraltar. The escort was to accompany the ship to the limit of the submarine area. . . .

7. . . . At 1059 [15 August] I received AM 1031/15, ordering *Renown* to remain in the vicinity of Iceland since the sailing of a German force from Norway in the very near future appeared to be a possibility. . . .

8. . . . At 0102, 16 August, *Renown* was ordered to return to Gibraltar . . .

At 2235, VAA, in *Ark Royal, Enterprise, Greyhound, Gallant, Hotspur, Encounter* and *Wrestler* sailed from Gibraltar to rendezvous with *Renown*. It was intended to carry out flying practices from *Ark Royal*, and to exercise Force H as a whole during the approach to Gibraltar, and also to intercept any merchant shipping bound for European ports.

11. At 0215 on 19 August, a shore broadcast was received stating that *Rowallan Castle* was being shelled by a raider. . . . The destroyer screen was ordered to return to Gibraltar to refuel and await orders whilst *Renown* and *Ark Royal* proceeded unscreened to the westward. Air search was carried out and it was not until 1050 that the AM was received stating that the *Circassia*[3] had reported shelling *Rowallan Castle*.

---

[1]Capt Jeffery, Cdr Buzzard, Lt-Cdr J. R. B. Longden: Lt-Cdr 1939; *Renown* 1940; *Nelson* 1941; *Mercury* 1942; Cdr Dec 1942; RCN 1943; *Mercury II* (Admy Sig Est, Petersfield) Feb 1944; *Mercury* 1945.

[2]*Renown*: 1916, extensively modernised 1936–9, 32,000t, 6×15in, 20×4.5in, 8tt, 29k.

Bedouin, Punjabi, Mashona, Tartar: 'Tribal' class, 1938–9, 1870t, 8×4.7in, 4tt, 36.5k; first three lost 1941–2.

[3]*Rowallan Castle*: 1939, 7798gt, 16.5k, Union-Castle Line.

Circassia: 1937, 11,137t, 16k, Anchor Line: serving as an AMC.

12.   Force H arrived at Gibraltar at 2000 on 20 August.

13.   Three air raid warnings were received during the night 20/21 August. During the first attack, bombs were dropped in the harbour about a cable and a half to the W of *Cormorant*.[1] The aircraft was picked up by searchlights just before bomb release but ships and A/A batteries were slow in opening fire. The target was subsequently held well and effectively engaged until brought down in the sea about 1½ miles W of Europa Point. Evidence available suggests that the aircraft was hit by 4.5" salvo from *Renown*, the right wing and part of the tail being shot away. Subsequent recovery of the wing proved the aircraft to be an Italian S82.[2] ...

While the efficiency of the shore A/A organisation is still below the standard considered satisfactory, a certain improvement is noticeable, particularly in the ability of the searchlights to pick up and hold the target.

14.   At 1130 on 21 August, I attended at Government House where the Military Governor of Algeciras,[3] who was paying an official call on HE the Governor of Gibraltar, was received. ...

At the request of HE the Governor and Admiral Sir Dudley North, I extended an invitation to the Military Governor to pay a visit to HMS *Ark Royal* on a future occasion. This was, in a sense, a *quid pro quo* for his concurrence in the use of the Racecourse by British fighter aircraft.

15.   I visited the Type 79Z RDF installation now erected and working on Spyglass Hill. I considered the results were disappointing, inasmuch as the land echoes are excessive and the amplitude of the aircraft echoes in proportion appears to be unduly small.

20.   ... I ... am more convinced than ever that until a really live and experienced A/A officer is sent out to take charge at Gibraltar, the A/A defences will not attain a satisfactory standard of efficiency.

21.   During the whole of the period under review in this Report, preparations were going forward for operations HATS and BONNET. I decided to take the whole of Force H participating in these operations into the Atlantic for the last two days of the passage of the Mediterranean reinforcements to Gibraltar, in order to exercise ships in company and rehearse certain phases of the operational plans.

22.   *Ark Royal, Enterprise, Gallant, Hotspur* and *Griffin* were sailed from Gibraltar at 0730 on 25 August in order to allow *Ark Royal* to carry out some much needed flying practice. ...

---

[1]*Cormorant* was RN HQ Gibraltar.

[2]Savoia SM82 was a transport, so it is likely this was an SM81: 1935, bomber, 4–5mg, 196mph.

[3]Gen Don Muñoz Grandes: Col & cdr of a Nationalist div 1937; Gen i/c a corps 1938; Capt-Gen & close associate of Franco 1939; later led Spanish Blue Div on Russian Front.

At 2030 I sailed in *Renown*, in company with *Velox, Encounter, Greyhound* and *Vidette* to rendezvous with the Mediterranean reinforcements on 27 August.

55.   *Report of Proceedings, 30 August–3 September 1940*

HMS *Renown*,
14 September 1940

30 August

At 0845 on 30 August, Force H (less *Resolution*) and reinforcements for the Eastern Mediterranean sailed from Gibraltar. The Force consisted of *Renown, Valiant, Illustrious* (flying the Flag of RAA, Mediterranean), *Ark Royal, Sheffield, Coventry, Calcutta, Faulknor* (Captain (D), 8th DF), *Fortune, Fury, Foresight, Firedrake, Forester, Encounter, Gallant* (Captain (D), 13th DF), *Greyhound, Hotspur, Griffin, Nubian, Mohawk, Janus, Hero, Wishart* and *Velox*.[1] Cruising Disposition No. 4 was assumed and course shaped to the eastward with the Force zig-zagging and maintaining a speed of advance of 15½ knots.

3.   Each carrier acted as fighter directing ship for its own fighters, *Illustrious* being free to use her own RDF set as occasion demanded. The remaining RDF ships were given the following sectors of responsibility:–

Sheffield between compass bearings of 335° through 090° to 185°.
Coventry between compass bearings of 175° through 270° to 005°.
Valiant all round look out with particular object of detecting aircraft not located by either *Coventry* or *Sheffield*.

6.   The above organisation worked most satisfactorily, and undoubtedly gave a feeling of confidence to the Fleet, in that surprise attack without prior RDF warning was most unlikely. Furthermore the use of W/T for passing RDF reports enabled fighters to be directed on to shadowers with the minimum delay.

---

[1]Formerly light cruisers (4190t, 5×6in, 29k), recently rearmed as AA ships, 8×4in: *Coventry*: 1918, 10×4in; sunk E Med 1942, German aircraft; *Calcutta*: 1919, 8×4in; sunk E Med 1941, German aircraft.
    Fortune, Fury (mined Channel 1944), *Firedrake* (sunk N Atlantic 1942 *U211*): 1935, 1375t, 4×4.7in, 8tt, 36k. *Hero*: 1936, 1340t, 4×4.7in, 8tt, 36k. *Nubian, Mohawk* (sunk C Med 1941, destroyer *Tarigo*): 'Tribals'. *Janus*: 1939, 1690t, 6×4.7in, 10tt, 36k; sunk Anzio 1944, Ger a/c. *Wishart*: 1920, 1150t, 4×4.7in, 3tt, 32k.

31 August

10.   At 0600 *Illustrious* flew off aircraft for night deck landing training, and at 0815 *Ark Royal* flew off 6 TSRs to carry out a parallel track search on a bearing of 060°.

11.   About 0920 *Ark Royal* intercepted Italian messages . . . These were decoded in *Renown* and found to be reports of a surface force consisting of 3 cruisers and 3 destroyers. . . .

12.   At 1000 the Fleet reduced speed and streamed paravanes, although no risks from mines were to be expected during this day, I considered it preferable to stream paravanes before the Fleet was liable to heavy air attack.

13.   At 1240 . . ., a fighter section of Skuas on patrol (Section Leader Lieut K. Spurway[1]) was ordered by *Ark Royal* to intercept an enemy shadowing aircraft reported by RDF. Interception took place at 1248 at a height of 10,000 feet 25 miles on the starboard bow of the fleet. The enemy was a Cant Z506B floatplane . . . After a chase of 55 miles 2 seconds' fire from the front guns of one Skua was sufficient to cause the enemy aircraft to catch fire and break up in the air. Two of the crew baled out on one parachute.

14.   At 1630, another section of Skuas (Section Leader Lieut J.M. Bruen) was similarly directed on to a shadower. The enemy plane was a Cant Z501 flying boat[2] . . . It was shot down at 1640 and the wreckage burnt so fiercely that it was seen from the Fleet.

15.   At 2150, . . . Force W, comprising *Velox* and *Wishart*, was detached for operation SQUAWK. This consisted of a diversion to the N of the Balearic Islands, during which, whilst still on a north-easterly course . . ., the two destroyers would transmit a series of messages by W/T.

16.   The object of this diversion was twofold, viz.:–

(i)   To mislead the enemy into thinking that the whole Force had maintained its north-easterly course towards the Gulf of Genoa during the night.

(ii)   To cover the transmission of course and speed signals of *Ark Royal* on low power W/T when altering course to fly off aircraft and shaping course for the flying on rendezvous after flying off was completed.

---

[1]Lieut K. Spurway: Lt (A) 1938; 800 Sqdn, *Ark Royal* April 1940; *Heron* April 1941; killed flying 12 Nov 1941.

[2]Lieut J. M. Bruen: Lt (A) 1934; *Ark Royal* June 1940; OC 803 Sqdn; *Formidable* 1941; Lt-Cdr *Daedalus* 1942; *Indomitable* 1942; *Shrike* (L'derry) 1943; Actg Cdr 1944.

Cant Z501: reconnaissance, 2–3mg, 171mph.

1 September

19.   At 0305, *Ark Royal* took station ahead of *Renown* and became Guide of the Fleet. Twenty minutes later, when 155 miles 264° from Cagliari the course of the Fleet was altered by W/T to fly off the air striking force for an attack on Elmas aerodrome. After flying off had been completed course was altered for the flying on position approximately 120 miles 226° from Cagliari.

20.   The striking force consisted of 9 Swordfish, each armed with 4×250 lb GP bombs and 8×25 lb incendiary bombs. Parachute flares were also carried. Weather conditions were good, the night though moonless being clear and starlit. The striking force formed up over flame floats dropped 10 miles from the fleet and proceeded in company towards Cagliari.

21.   At 0600 the aircraft attacked the aerodrome after establishing its position by dropping flares. Flares were however hardly required owing to the quality of the 'Flaming Onions'[1] which at that time lit up the aerodrome. Bombs were released at 3000 feet and hits observed on the barracks, aerodrome buildings and aircraft dispersed round the aerodrome. Several fires were seen to start. About 30 floatplanes were moored in the trot and about 40 aircraft dispersed round the aerodrome were sighted.

22.   During the dive to attack, the damage done by the previous raid carried out on 2 August could be clearly seen. Three hangars were complete ruins, whilst a fourth appeared to be in process of reconstruction.

24.   All aircraft returned safely, landing on about 0800. During the return journey the following were sighted by the striking force:–

(a) An enemy submarine on the surface . . . The submarine fired a yellow flare and dived when attacked by machine guns.

(b) A convoy of 7 merchant ships of 3000 to 4000 tons . . . steering N, speed 10 knots.

(c) A formation of 7 aircraft burning navigation lights . . .

25.   The position of the reported U-boat was 11 miles on the port quarter of the Fleet. *Greyhound* and *Hotspur* were despatched to attack with orders to rejoin at 0900. Although A/S aircraft saw a patch of oil in the position the U-boat was not located by the destroyers.

26.   No action was taken against the convoy as the proximity of enemy air bases and distance of convoy from the Fleet rendered either air or surface attack impracticable without prejudice to the safe but timely passage of Force F. Further, it was quite possible that the convoy was French.

---

[1] A form of Italian A/A.

28.   At 1030 course was altered to 080°. From this time onwards two fighter patrols, each of 6 aircraft, were maintained over the Fleet throughout the day.

29.   At 1630, *Illustrious* flew off 7 TSRs to carry out a search to the maximum depth to the eastward.

32.   At 2200, . . ., NE of Skerki Bank, Force F, consisting of *Illustrious*, *Valiant*, *Coventry*, *Calcutta*, *Nubian*, *Mohawk*, *Hero*, *Janus*, *Gallant*, *Griffin*, *Greyhound* and *Hotspur*, parted company without signal and proceeded to the south-eastward.

33.   The remainder of the Force after proceeding for a quarter of an hour to the northward (during which *Sheffield* and destroyers took up Night Cruising Disposition No. 15), altered course to the westward and increased speed to 24 knots so as to reach a suitable position for the second air strike on Cagliari. . . .

2 September

34.   At 0305 *Ark Royal* took station ahead of *Renown* and 15 minutes later altered course without signal as requisite for flying off aircraft.

35.   The striking force of 9 Swordfish were armed with 4 × 250 lb GP bombs and 20 lb Cooper or 25 lb incendiary bombs, in addition to parachute flares.

36.   Weather conditions were not good, the night being dark and hazy and the horizon bad.

37.   On reaching the vicinity of their objectives, the aerodrome and power station, the aircraft encountered a layer of cloud at 5000 feet and another layer at 4000 feet. The valleys appeared to be filled with mist or fog and low clouds. Parachute flares were dropped at intervals for a period of about 45 minutes in the hope of identifying the targets, but without success.

38.   Four aircraft attacked searchlights and apparently put one out of action. Two attacked what was thought to be a flare path which turned out to be a field 2 miles to the NW of the aerodrome. The 3 remaining aircraft jettisoned their bombs into the sea.

39.   During the attack aircraft encountered heavy but erratic A/A barrage fire. This fire was continued until the aircraft were over 17 miles from the aerodrome. It was apparent that the A/A defence had been increased since the last attack. Searchlights were few and ineffective and appeared to have no form of control.

40.   By 0800 all aircraft had landed on . . . and the force proceeded at 26 knots to the westward to get out of range of enemy air attack.

43.   During this operation the Force was in effective bombing range of Italian air bases for at least 48 hours. Heavy air attack had been antici-

pated and hoped for, since with the heavy A/A concentration and number of fighter patrols available, I felt it should be possible to deliver a blow to the Italian Air Force which might have a telling and lasting effect.

44.   The lack of surface and air opposition experienced was possibly due in part to the effect of the Balearic diversion and operation SQUAWK, and the failure of the bombers to attack due to a combination of:–

(a)   The summary destruction of shadowers on the first day.
(b)   The first attack on Elmas aerodrome.
(c)   The fear of the exceptionally heavy A/A and fighter concentration.

3 September

45.   Nothing further of interest occurred and the Force entered Gibraltar harbour at 1100 on 3 September.

46.   At 1645, *Gallant, Hotspur, Greyhound, Griffin* with *Garland* in company, left Malta, and after carrying out an A/S search to the S and W of Malta, sailed for Gibraltar where they arrived on 5 September. . . .

47.   I desire to bring to the notice of Their Lordships the names of Lt-Cdr Mervyn Johnstone and Lieut Terence Waters Brown Shaw, the pilot and observer respectively who led the striking forces to the attack on each occasion at Cagliari. These officers showed commendable determination coupled with accurate navigation in difficult circumstances.[1]

56.   *To Blake*

4 September 1940

. . . I am certain that keeping well locked up is the answer should the bombers be able to press home their attacks, since this ensures that every gun in the force is in action before the bombers can reach the point of bomb release. It's the ship or unit that becomes detached which is usually singled out for attack. By staggering the line and stationing cruisers and A/A ships on the bows and quarters, you get a compact formation which can be 'blued' in any direction to keep the 'A' arcs open.

Another striking point about the operation was the control of fighters

---

[1]Lt-Cdr Mervyn Johnstone: Lt 1931; Lt-Cdr Jan 1939; 810 Sqdn *Ark Royal*; *Stalker* (CVE) May 1942; Cdr (F) *Jackdaw* (Crail) May 1944.
  Lieut Terence W. B. Shaw: Lt 1933; Observer Lt *Peregrine* (Ford) 1939; 810 Sqdn *Ark Royal* June 1940; Lt-Cdr 1941; *Warspite* April 1942; Actg Cdr & Air SO *Illustrious* Eastern F Feb 1943; OIC, *Condor* (Arbroath), N Air Sig Sch Nov 1944.

by RDF. With four RDF ships we were able to control the fighters on to their targets and at the same time maintain a continuous all round search. ...

My object now during MENACE,[1] is to work up the night-fighting efficiency of *Renown*, *Sheffield* (when available) and the 13th DF. Once that is satisfactory, we should be in a position to carry out some productive raids in the Western basin as soon as the *Ark* returns.

I still feel there is scope for a couple of submarines at my end. A little interference with the Italian–Spanish trade might well absorb considerable Italian A/S forces in counter measures. ...

57.   *Report of Proceedings, 4–10 September 1940*

14 September 1940

6 September

6.   At 1800 *Ark Royal*, *Barham*, *Resolution*, *Faulknor*, *Fury*, *Fortune*, *Forester*, *Greyhound*, *Inglefield*, *Eclipse* and *Escapade* sailed for Freetown to take part in operation MENACE. *Echo*, delayed by a defect, sailed later to rendezvous with the detachment.[2]

9 September

9.   I inspected the FAA section established on the North Front and went up in a Swordfish in order to obtain a view of the harbour as seen from bombing aircraft. It was clear that, for high level bombing, ships alongside the Moles presented a difficult target. For dive bombing, however, the target presented is favourable.

10.   I witnessed further trials of the Type 79Z RDF set on shore and found that a punctured condensor had been the cause of poor operation in previous trials. The set now gives reasonably good indication of range up to 40 or 50 miles but the prevalence of land echoes makes it very difficult to obtain accurate bearings. As a means of medium distance warning of approach, the set now serves a useful purpose, but does not enable a long distance plot to be obtained. It appears that either a set with a shorter wavelength or else larger aerial arrays will be required to deal with the difficult local conditions for RDF. ...

---

[1]The operation against Dakar.
[2]*Eclipse* (mined Aegean 1943), *Echo*: 1934, 1375t, 4×4.7in, 8tt, 36k. *Inglefield*: L, 1937, 1455t, 5×4.7in, 10tt, 36k; sunk Anzio 1944, Ger a/c.

58.   *Report of Proceedings, 11–14 September 1940*

17 September 1940

11 September

2.   At 0510 a report was received from *Hotspur*, who was engaged with *Griffin* and *Encounter* in hunting a U-boat reported the previous day by air reconnaissance, that at 0445 she had sighted six ships, burning navigation lights, . . . steering 270° at high speed. This confirmed the intimation given in Consul-General, Tangier's[1] message 1824 of 9 September that French Naval Forces might proceed out of the Mediterranean, possibly within 72 hours following his message. It should be noted that the sources of this information had hitherto proved somewhat unreliable.

3.   I ordered *Renown* to be at one hour's notice for full speed, together with *Vidette*, the only available destroyer of the 13th DF.

4.   I considered proceeding to sea to the westward in *Renown* but decided that owing to lack of destroyer escort, this was inadvisable; further, it seemed unlikely that *Renown* could make sufficient ground to the W to avoid being sighted by the French Force. It seemed to me most improbable that the Force would proceed to a Bay Port and that Casablanca was the probable destination. So far as I was aware, it was not the policy of HM Government to interfere with the movements of French warships to French controlled ports. The possibility of this operation being connected with operation MENACE was considered but in view of the report from the Naval Attache at Madrid 1842/5, it appeared to me that quite possibly the French wished to remove these ships in order to prevent their seizure by the Germans in retaliation for any action taken by us at Dakar. The prolonged absence from Gibraltar of *Ark Royal* and other ships attached to Force H, together with the departure of *Barham*, must by this time have given rise to some conjecture that operations to the south were contemplated.

5.   In view of the Consul-General, Tangier's message 1842/9 and the Naval Attache, Madrid's 1809/10 (received by me at 0800, 11 September) I assumed that the Admiralty were fully aware of this movement of French ships and that had any action been required by me to intercept I should have received instructions to this effect. I assumed that, as no instructions had been given, it was the policy to avoid any incidents with the French at this juncture and that this movement was

---

[1]A. D. F. (later Sir Alvary) Gascoigne: b 1893; Army 1914–18; FO 1919; 2nd Sec FO 1925; Oslo Ch d'A 1928–30; Tehran 1930; Tokyo 1931; 1st Sec 1933; FO 1934; Ch d'A Budapest 1936–9; Con-Gen Tangier & Cnslr Aug 1939; Minr Hungary 1945; Amb Japan 1946; Amb Moscow 1951; Ret List 1953.

regarded as being favourable rather than unfavourable to our cause. At noon, therefore, I ordered *Renown* and the destroyers to revert to two hours' notice for steam.

7.   At 1406 I received AM 1347/11 ordering me to proceed to sea and endeavour to obtain contact with the French Force, and stating that further instructions would follow. *Renown, Griffin* and *Vidette* were ready to proceed at 1500 but *Velox* could not complete refuelling until 1640. By this time it was clear that if the destination of the French ships was Casablanca, they could not be intercepted before arrival.

8.   At 1546 I received AM 1429/11, giving further instructions. These were that the French Force was to be informed there was no objection to their proceeding to Casablanca, but they could not be permitted to go to Dakar which is under German influence, nor could they be permitted to proceed to Bay Ports since they are in German hands. Minimum force was to be used to enforce compliance with these instructions.

9.   *Renown, Griffin* and *Vidette* proceeded at 1600, being joined by *Velox* before clearing the Bay. From air reconnaissance it was now clear the French Force was proceeding to Casablanca. Course was therefore shaped to the south-westward at 24 knots keeping 30 miles from French territory. Shortly afterwards, the French Force was reported as having entered Casablanca at 1610.

10.   My appreciation of the situation at this stage was as follows. The French Force might complete with oil that evening and continue to the southward. To counter this high speed was necessary in order to reach an intercepting position. On the other hand, the French might remain at Casablanca for some days; in this case economy of fuel was essential in order to enable the patrol to be maintained.

12.   At 2104 I received AM 2006/11, instructing me to establish a patrol as necessary so that the French Force could be intercepted if they sailed southward from Casablanca. In view of the bright moonlight I considered it was undesirable to establish a close inshore patrol off Casablanca since the French had made it abundantly clear that they would open fire on any ships or aircraft within 20 miles of the coast. On account of the bright moonlight I also considered it undesirable that *Renown* should proceed unscreened. I therefore continued my course to the southward at 24 knots with a view to keeping ahead of the French Force should they proceed to Dakar. I anticipated that the situation would be clarified when I received the result of the dawn air reconnaissance.

13.   I informed Admiral Commanding, NAS, that it was essential that a dawn reconnaissance should be carried out over Casablanca throughout daylight hours.

12 September

17.   At 0923 when *Renown* was in position 32° 20'N, 10° 30'W, reconnaissance aircraft reported that 3 cruisers and 3 destroyers had been identified in Casablanca, and possibly more. I consequently altered course to the north-eastward to effect a rendezvous with the 3 additional destroyers (*Hotspur, Encounter* and *Wishart*), whom I had previously instructed to steer 220° at 16 knots.

18.   I reported to the Admiralty in message 1109/12 that it was my intention to carry out a line of bearing patrol between Cape Blanco and Agadir, steaming south by night and north by day, with the inshore destroyer 20 miles from the coast. I also reported that the weather was unsuitable for oiling at sea and consequently, unless it improved, two of my destroyers would have to leave patrol at dusk the following day and a third 24 hours later.

21.   The search was designed so that if the French Force left Casablanca after 2000, i.e., at dusk, and proceeded at 25 knots, the searching Force would be south of the French farthest-on position at daylight. With the limited force at my disposal it was appreciated that this search was by no means fully effective. In fact, if the French had adequate air reconnaissance, they would have little difficulty in evading my search.

13 September

26.   At 1001, I reported to the Admiralty that weather still prevented oiling the destroyers, with the consequence that the chances of intercepting the French Force with the units remaining after 2030 (when it would be necessary to detach two) would be much reduced. I suggested that to ensure interception a patrol should be established off Dakar. At 1408 I received a signal from the Admiral Commanding, NAS, that the air reports and photographs were still inconclusive.

27.   Two hours later, at 1620, I received an aircraft report that no cruisers were at Casablanca. I informed the Admiralty accordingly at 1643 and reported that I could either:–

(a)   Arrive Gibraltar with 3 destroyers, refuel and be ready for sea by 1500/14.
(b)   Arrive Freetown with 2 destroyers at 1200/19.
(c)   Arrive Freetown unescorted at 1000/16.

and intended to proceed as at (a) after 2000 since the maintenance of the patrol appeared to be no longer required.

28.   At 1947, I received AM 2335/13 directing me to proceed to

Gibraltar and complete with fuel. The Force then proceeded at the maximum speed that the weather permitted to Gibraltar. . . .

59. *To his wife*

12 September 1940

. . . at 1 p.m. they [the Admiralty] burst into song and we had to go out at full speed. Had the hell of a job to collect enough small ships to come with us and off we went at 4 p.m. with the usual vague and general orders that they mustn't go here or there and if necessary force must be used to stop them. Though how the hell I was expected to stop all six I don't know. . . .

. . . I simply loathe this French stuff as you don't know where you are and a wrong step might bring about all sorts of reactions. The people at home never seem to put themselves in my shoes and give me their ideas of what the situation is and what might be expected. . . .

The great thing is that Flags has found a beetle for me and for two mornings I've been able to have a pull before breakfast and felt all the better for it.

60. *To his wife*

14 September 1940

. . . Our gyrations make me quite giddy. Soon after midnight we were told to do what I'd proposed i.e. back to Dudley [North]. Admiralty also adopted a proposal I'd put yesterday to put some policemen off the door of the place the Frogs might be going to. They might have done it a bit earlier with advantage. . . .

Later: Nice breezy little message from the Admiralty to say that the operation down south may lead to Vichy Govt. declaring war on us and attacking Gib by air! Pleasant outlook I must say. And I wonder what the devil I'm supposed to do? Wander about the ocean like the Flying Dutchman I suppose. . . .

I hope to goodness the Vichy Government does not declare war – it would be just what the Germans would want and would make things extremely difficult for us. Seems to me our policy should be to avoid such a thing unless it's essential and I don't believe it is at the moment. We do truly have some damned awful problems to deal with in these sort of jobs and one gets so little help from the Admiralty. They never send me *their* appreciation of the situation and they must have far more information on which to base an opinion than I have. . . .

61. *To his wife*

17 September 1940

. . . After two nights in harbour here we are off again on another blasted French job. . . . I have no real information as to what it's all about, just vague hints and very airy general directions which seem to have little relation to the practical aspect of the situation. On top of it all a convoy arrived yesterday afternoon and seems to have brought no mail. . . . The French situation appears to be very involved and I rather guess that certain shows have come to nought. I was never in favour of them unless it was clear that all the conditions were propitious and said so whilst I was at home. The Spanish situation too is becoming more difficult owing to German pressure but I believe that if the Germans do invade Spain they may set up a guerilla campaign which would prove extremely troublesome to them.

62. *Report of Proceedings, 15–20 September 1940*

20 September 1940

15 September

3. . . . I . . . requested guidance as to what policy was to be pursued in the event of further French Forces attempting to leave the Mediterranean.

16 September

4. In reply to this signal, I was informed by AM 0145/16 that:–

(a) French Forces were to be shadowed if they left the Mediterranean and instructions regarding further action to be taken would then be given.
(b) A limit of 20 miles from French territory need not be adhered to, but it was desirable to avoid incidents at this juncture.

In view of the above, I made arrangements for *Renown* and 4 destroyers to be at two hours' notice for steam until the situation had clarified.

5. Information was received at 2054 that the presence of 3 French cruisers of *La Galissonnière* class at Dakar had definitely been estab-

lished. It seems possible now that these ships may have left Casablanca during the night of 11/12 September, when they could without difficulty have evaded *Renown*. It will be recalled that the air reconnaissance for Gibraltar reported these ships as being in harbour during the forenoon and afternoon of Thursday, 12 September. Subsequent interrogation of pilots and observers showed that this report was not based on positive identification. Had this been known on the forenoon of Thursday 12 September, it is possible that by continuing her southerly course *Renown* might have intercepted the French Force.

17 September

6.   At 0105 I received AM 2359/16, instructing *Renown* and destroyers to proceed to the southward of Casablanca to establish a patrol off that place if ordered.

My appreciation of the situation was as follows:–

(a)   it was not possible to maintain an effective patrol in the immediate vicinity of Casablanca even if the risk of incidents was accepted, since the French were able to engage our patrol with superior forces and drive them off.

(b)   By using *Tetrarch* and *Triton*[1] as close inshore patrols during the night, some degree of warning of the French leaving Casablanca might be obtained though the submarines would be exposed to considerable risk.

(c)   Owing to the superior speed and relative strength of the French Force, it was probable that night shadowing could not be guaranteed. It was therefore desirable that contact should take place in daylight hours, both for this reason and in view of the necessity for conveying the instructions of HM Government to the Senior Officer of the French Forces and taking measures to enforce them, either of which could be effected satisfactorily at night.

7.   In view of the above, it appeared to me that the best position for Force H to take up would be in the vicinity of the Canary Islands. Assuming that the French left Casablanca at night, they would pass this area in daylight. The lee afforded by the land would also facilitate refuelling of the destroyers.

These views were represented by me to the Admiralty in my message time 0337/17.

8.   . . . I was left in doubt whether MENACE had been abandoned. . . . I

---

[1]*Tetrarch* (lost off Sicily Nov 1941), *Triton* (lost S Adriatic Dec 1940): 1940, 1090/1575t, 10tt, 1×4in, 15.25/9k.

therefore asked . . . that I might be informed if operation MENACE was postponed or abandoned.

18 September

13.   At 0235 I received AM 2348/17 which ordered *Renown* and screen to cruise in a position to westward or south-westward of Straits ready to intercept French Force located by patrols in the Straits.

20.   During the evening I signalled my general intentions in cypher to the destroyers in company, as follows:–

If the French warships pass westwards through the Straits, the following are my intentions.

(i)   To obtain an assurance from them that they will not proceed beyond Casablanca.

(ii)   By day, assuming air reconnaissance, to steer to intercept with destroyers in company.

(iii)   By night, or if no air reconnaissance, destroyers will be spread to locate and shadow with *Renown* in support.

(iv)   When interception by *Renown* is assured, destroyers will be ordered to concentrate.

(v)   French will be requested to state destination and may be ordered to stop.

(vi)   If the order to stop is not complied with, *Renown* will fire rounds ahead to enforce compliance and if this does not succeed, French ships will be engaged.

(vii)   Destroyers are to take up position as ordered and to be ready to attack with torpedoes and guns as ordered.

21.   At 1742 I signalled to the Admiralty in my 1610/18, that taking all factors into consideration, I now considered that interception with French Forces was more likely to be achieved if *Renown* was stationed at Gibraltar. I also requested confirmation that the importance of preventing French Forces from reaching Dakar justified engaging equal or superior forces and night action.

24.   . . . air and surface reconnaissance with destroyers, trawlers and yachts to the eastward of Gibraltar gave a better prospect of success than keeping *Renown* in a relatively restricted area to the westward, particularly during the next few days of bright moonlight. The patrol to the westward might involve submarine attack and would employ destroyers uneconomically.[1]

---

[1] In these operations other French warships were sighted and occasionally fire was exchanged.

19 September

29.   At 1945 approval was received from the Admiralty for *Renown* to return to Gibraltar; course and speed were adjusted so as to arrive there at daylight 20 September, and to avoid convoy HG 44 which sailed from Gibraltar at 1800, 19 September. . . .

63.   *Report of Proceedings, 20–28 September*

29 September 1940

20 September

2.   At 1055 the extended patrol reported that an unknown destroyer (which it subsequently transpired was the French escort vessel *Élan*[1]) had been sighted 8 miles 340° Alboran Island steering 270°.

. . . No instructions having been received when *Élan* reached the Straits, she was allowed to proceed.

21 September

4.   . . . I considered it was necessary to obtain guidance as to whether it was intended to stop:–

(a)   All French war vessels
(b)   Only cruisers and above, or two or more destroyers
(c)   French merchant vessels escorted by one or more warships.

I embodied the above in my 1205 of 21 September to Admiralty. I also pointed out that owing to the lack of definite information concerning the situation at Dakar, it was difficult for me to appreciate when avoidance of incidents should take priority over control of movements of French warships.

5.   To this signal I received AM 0253/22 in reply, stating that French merchant vessels escorted were not to be interfered with and that if *Strasbourg* should pass through the Straits, she should be shadowed whether going north or south and prevented, after due warning, from proceeding north. If one or more cruisers, or four or more destroyers passed, they were to be shadowed and prevented from going north only. Throughout the preceding days I had felt the need for daily appreciations from the Admiralty of the French situation. A certain amount had been gleaned from intercepted signals, but generally speaking, both the Admiralty Commanding, NAS, and myself felt we were very much in

[1]*Élan*: 1938, 650t, 2×3.5in, 20k.

the dark as to what was actually happening and what developments of the situation could be anticipated.

23 September

7. This entire lack of information made it most difficult to judge what action might be required locally. After discussing with the Admiral Commanding, NAS, the latter sent a signal to the Admiralty repeated to FO (M)[1] (timed 1134 of 23 September) asking that both Admiral Commanding, NAS, and FOC, Force H, should be included in the address of Messages concerning the operation in progress. . . .

64. *To Blake*

24 September 1940

. . . Now about those French cruisers and destroyers – so far as I could judge the Admiralty had the warning from Tangier that a force would pass the Straits within the next 72 hours, this was followed by Hillgarth's formal notification from the French that the force would pass the Straits the following morning and finally we had the patrol report of sighting.

My instructions at the moment gave me no justification to stop them. In view of the reports that Vichy was coming our way a bit, I assumed that this movement was carried out with full approval of our Government.

It was unfortunate that three of our four destroyers were hunting a promising submarine contact off Alboran and that owing to defects, escort duties, etc., the available destroyers to screen *Renown* were reduced to two. But this is bound to happen unless one gets some notification that a situation is likely to arise.

When I put to sea and proceeded south of Casablanca, I should have had a chance, though not a good one, to intercept if I had not been deceived by the air report which stated positively that the French ships were in Dakar that forenoon and confirmed it again in the afternoon. Subsequent interrogation of the pilot and observer (RAF) showed that they *thought* they'd seen them.

When I was joined by three more destroyers that morning I was able to maintain a fair sweep but the speed of the French was such that it would have been pure chance if we'd succeeded in intercepting.

Subsequently I was very much in the dark as to what was happening

[1] FO (M) was Adm Ford at Malta.

and in view of a somewhat cryptic message about operations at Duala I had to ask whether MENACE was postponed and the Duala operations substituted.

Yesterday – the first day of MENACE – I had no news of what was happening down there until I got the BBC broadcast at 10.00 p.m. I think there must be a screw loose somewhere because I am sure it was appreciated that both Admiral Commanding North Atlantic and myself must know what is going on and what the policy is *vis à vis* French ships if we are to do our stuff properly.

Yesterday I was told at 1300 that *Renown* was to prepare for sea, which I assumed meant we were to be ready to leave at a moment's notice. I had already arranged to withdraw the Alboran patrol, which is quite unsupported, and for *Renown* to proceed to the westward where we would be in a position to head off French ships going north or to shadow *Strasbourg* if she appeared on the scene which I judged to be very doubtful. Since by 1800 I had received no orders I signalled my intention to proceed but was ordered to remain here.

I know how difficult it is for you to keep us informed of each move that takes place but I feel that a very short appreciation of how you judge the situation may develop would be of the greatest value. Then even if we have missed a number of signals we can still keep in the picture sufficiently.

The news from Dakar this morning does not seem too good. Forts v. ships in low visibility and hostile light craft and submarines on the move all create a very sticky situation. I am sure if anyone can handle it J.H.D. [Cunningham][1] is the chap.

Seems to me that these damn Frenchmen are quite prepared to fight us at any time though they won't fight the Germans. It certainly doesn't seem that Dakar had been properly salted beforehand, otherwise we should hardly have had so bad a reception. One can't help admiring the reply from Dakar to our ultimatum, ditto *Primaguet*'s reply to *Cornwall*, that if they had a fight the only winners would be the Germans.[2]

Well I hope it ends all right so that we can get busy again on these Italians. We've given them too long a stand off.

---

[1]Vice Adm (later Adm of the Fleet) Sir John H. D. Cunningham (1885–1962): *Britannia* 1900; Lt 1905; navigation specialist; Med & Grand F 1914–18; Cdr 1917; Cdr, Nav Sch 1922–3; Master of Fleet 1923; Capt 1924; staff commands; Naval War Coll; DP; *Adventure, Resolution*; RA 1936 & ACNS; ACNS (Air) & then 5SL 1937–9; VA 1939; 1CS, Home & Med Fleets; N cdr MENACE; 4SL 1941–3; C-in-C Levant & Adm 1943, later C-in-C Med; 1SL 1946–8; Adm of Fleet 1948; Chm, Iraq Petroleum Co 1948–58.

[2]*Primaguet*: 1926, 7250t, 8×6.1in, 12tt, 33k; beached Casablanca after action with USN Nov 1942.

65. *To his wife*

24 September 1940

. . . Now that it's public news I can talk about this Dakar business. When I was asked about it at the Admiralty I said emphatically that unless it was just a walk in it ought to be dropped. Well it wasn't a walk in and now there seems to be a proper old battle going on there. And we've just had our share of it because the French planes came over and bombed us in harbour this afternoon from 12.50 to 2.30 p.m. – an absolute plastering and it was just luck we weren't hit as some were very close. I knew it would happen and told the Admiralty yesterday that I intended to put to sea at 7 p.m. last night. But of course they knew best and said we were to remain in harbour and that was the result. Owing to the Levanter which put a curtain of cloud on top of the rock we couldn't see the damn Frenchies and had to shoot blind. They of course could see the rock quite clearly . . . I'd argued about this possibility and persuaded the soldiers to use a barrage but they don't use it at all intelligently . . .

And here we are driven from home and where to go I'm damned if I know. Most annoying because Jack Tovey[1] arrived on a flying visit in more senses than one as he's going home for a week to discuss things with the Admiralty and I particularly wanted to see him. . . . Just as we were going to sit down for lunch there was the swish of a bomb and the roar of an engine and a dive bomber had planted one not far from Dudley's house . . . These blasted French adventures fill me with the deepest gloom. They're always too precipitate. At Dakar, as at Oran, if only given more time we should probably get what we want. I noticed that one of the BBC bulletins said that the failure of de Gaulle to be received at Dakar was due to the arrival of six French warships. I suppose they'll try and put the blame on me if Dakar is a blob as it looks like being at present. Forts versus ships – I thought we'd learnt our lesson about that years ago but apparently we haven't. Anyhow I'm glad I wasn't put in charge of that party. DP[2] was quite apologetic about it when I was at the Admiralty and explained it was necessary for the Flag Officer in charge to be in close touch with de Gaulle and the British Government. I was only too pleased to be out of it though I've signalled that if required I shall be glad to work under the orders of J.H.D. Cunningham. . . .

---

[1] Then 2nd-in-Cmd, Med F and shortly to be C-in-C, Home F.
[2] Dudley Pound.

66.   *To his wife*

25 September 1940

. . . Here we are steaming about the ocean and supposed to pounce on any Frenchman going the wrong way though how I'm supposed to spot them with just this ship I don't know. Another affair in the Straits last night. Apparently 4 French destroyers passed through going east and opened fire on one of our patrol destroyers who returned the fire but no hits.[1] It's all a proper ghastly muddle and we simply don't know where we are or who we are supposed to be fighting. I envy ABC who has not got to deal with this ghastly French problem. I signalled my appreciation of the situation to the Admiralty which was that the Dakar business ought to be called off at once since if it isn't and the French continue to attack us at Gib, etc., it will be quite impossible for me to control the Western Med. How the Germans and Itis must be chuckling with joy. It simply maddens me that we could have been so stupid. It we'd withdrawn directly it was clear that de G would *not* be welcomed at Dakar no great harm would have been done. Gib has been off the air most of the afternoon and this evening we learnt that there had been an even heavier air raid than yesterday. Cheerful prospect for me and a damned awful worry having to hang about in one spot and try to arrange for the destroyers to be refuelled. . . .

67.   *To his wife*

26 September 1940

. . . Well they've called it off at last – but much too late. The question now is will the French go on attacking Gib? This affair has shown them so clearly how to get one back on us. . . . The BBC bulletin today said the Govt never had any intention of stopping those French cruisers from going to Dakar which is a pretty good bender. I wonder if they'll try and make me a scapegoat for this blob. I shall have something to say about it if they do. . . . Dudley's secretary was one of the few people killed in the last raid. . . . Poor D will be very upset because DS[2] was a first class fellow and such a nice chap. . . .

---

[1]*Hotspur.*
[2]Paymaster-Cdr J. E. D. Smith.

68. *Report of Proceedings, 20–28 September 1940* (cont.)

27 September

27.   I had intended to return to Gibraltar by 0730/28, but on receipt of Naval Attache, Madrid's 2256/26 which stated that M Laval[1] had asked Germany to release the whole Toulon fleet with the object of attacking us, I decided to remain at sea another day in order to await developments. ...

28 September

29.   Since no comment from the Admiralty on the Madrid report had been made and in view of the report from the Admiral Commanding, NAS, that three Italian submarines were expected to pass through the Straits between 27 and 29 September, I decided to return to Gibraltar ...
30.   At 1045 ... a submarine on the surface end on was sighted bearing 024° distance 10 miles from *Renown* ... At 1051 the submarine dived. *Wishart* was immediately detached from the screen to hunt the submarine and was seen to commence depth charge attack at 1125. Admiral Commanding, NAS, was asked to send aircraft to assist in the hunt and at 1355 one London flying boat had closed *Wishart* to assist in the hunt. At 1230 *Wishart* reported good contact, four patterns dropped. Large amount of oil on surface.[2]

69.   *To his wife*

28 September 1940

... Just as we were thinking of going back yesterday I got a charming message to say it was rumoured the whole of the Toulon fleet was coming out to have a scrap with us. Not wishing to have an Oran done on me I decided to stay out. However hearing that 3 Iti submarines were on the way here and since the Frogs show no sign of movement at present I've decided to go back this evening. We saw one of the Iti U-boats on the horizon this morning. Cooper – John's Term Officer[3] – was sent to hunt him and I have hopes has done so to good effect. Evidently a big stink is going on at home about Dakar because more people are being asked where they were on such and such dates, etc. ...

---

[1]Pierre Laval (1883–1945): lawyer, jnlst, business; Socst Dep; Minr 1920s; PM Jan 1931, June 1935–Jan 1936; For Minr 4 tms 1932–6; anti-Br, appeaser; principal Vichy minister; regarded as collaborator; ousted Dec 1940, reinstated April 1942; tried & exec 15 Oct 1945.
[2]The submarine was not sunk.
[3]Cdr E. T. Cooper: Cdr *Wishart* Aug 1939; LDD 1941; *Duke of York* 1943.

70.   *To his wife*

29 September 1940

... Can you beat it. After getting back at 7 p.m. last night here we are off again at 7 a.m. this morning and on the wettest sort of job that can possibly be imagined – looking for a certain ship that might have left a certain place and might be going somewhere. Two blind men in a large forest would have a better chance of finding one another. Destroyers being run off their legs and this ship too because she's been at continuous short notice for weeks now. I really can't imagine what possesses the Admiralty these days. ...

I went to see Dudley last night and had dinner with him. ... The second day's bombing was even heavier than the first. Jack Tovey came in for it. ... Apparently he and Andrew share exactly the views Dudley and I have about this French business and are furious about it all. Andrew B is not sick so I believe it may be that Andrew will relieve DP and Jack will take ABC's place. ... As we left this morning two French destroyers passed through the Straits going west. They cracked on to full speed directly they saw us and were evidently very nervous we were going to open fire. This afternoon a French aircraft has been shadowing us for a bit so as they know just where we are the chance of our intercepting any of their ships is nil. I've pointed this out to TLs[1] but expect they're all taking a nice Sunday off. ... I'm itching to get at the soldiers about the A/A and other matters.

71.   *To his wife*

30 September 1940

... Steaming west all day and the wind and sea have got up a bit. I'm wondering how the devil I'm going to get the destroyers oiled. It's always such a continual anxiety – this oiling of the destroyers. And then I have the other problem of where the Germans are likely to land[2] and how the devil to intercept them with the small force I have available. As usual I get no information from the Admiralty, no appreciation of the situation. Just left to grope in the dark. Geoffrey Blake is a good deal to blame for this as he's supposed to be looking after foreign operations. I've sent him several letters on the subject but they don't seem to have any effect. ...

---

[1]Their Lordships.
[2]In the Azores; no such expedition was ever launched but there were many false reports.

72. *To his wife*

1 October 1940

. . . Got a signal just after midnight to say that a battleship, 3 cruisers and 4 destroyers had been seen off Finisterre yesterday at noon steering SSW. Now who the hell can they be? Can't be *Richelieu* because she'd hardly have got there and I can't believe that Vichy is going to join up with the Huns.

Later: After 9 hours the Admiralty have signalled they were Spaniards so that's OK. Tried to oil the destroyers this morning but too much swell and had to give up after nearly having a crash. Wonder when I shall be able to give them a drink of oil It's a damnable anxiety and a lousy position to be in. . . . Signal from Andrew to the Admiralty which suggests he's not at all happy about the French situation. This coupled with news from the Admiralty that the French Navy is solidly pro-Vichy and against us suggests that I may have been right about Oran and that it was the biggest political blunder we could have made and handsomely seconded by Dakar. I believe we'd have had the French Navy on our side by now if it hadn't been for Oran. Is it likely that the French Navy will forget easily all the officers and men we killed there? I'm sure we shouldn't if the roles had been reversed.

73. *To his wife*

2 October 1940

. . . Had a ticklish job yesterday oiling the destroyers from us at sea. Still quite a nasty swell and with our great bulges and all the merest touch while they are alongside would do an immense amount of damage. . . . Problem now is what to do next. We can only last about another 24 hours out here and then we must have some oil. Can't get it from the oiler at sea unless it's an absolute flat calm which it never is in these parts. Can't anchor anywhere because we've got to keep out of sight so where do we go? I've had to break wireless silence and ask TLs what they'd like done about it. They've kept a most dignified silence the whole time. . . .

74.   *To his wife*

4 October 1940

... Just after Their Lordships spoke and said we were to go back to our base. I rather expected that would be the answer so before the boys left me the day before yesterday I told them where to meet me today and trust they will turn up. But it's dull, overcast and raining so we may have a job to find one another. ... By the time we get back we shall have been a fortnight at sea barring a break of 11 hours in harbour.

Later: The weather cleared and I collected all four of the boys and then went to see if we could spot our oiler and tell her go back to Gib. Sighted her on the horizon eventually but would the damn fool close us? No. Had to send a destroyer chasing after her to order her back to Gib. ... I shan't see my *Ark* yet awhile and am very lost without her. ...

75.   *To his wife*

5 October 1940

... At 2.30 a.m. they reported to me that there was a darkened ship right ahead and crossing our track. My damned destroyers never spotted her until we'd done so which was pretty thick and *Renown* was pretty slow in getting ready to deal with the situation so raspberries have been flying pretty freely as you can imagine. ...

76.   *Report of Proceedings, 29 September– 7 October 1940*

7 October 1940

29 September

3.   At 2011 a further signal was received from the Admiralty ordering *Renown* to proceed at 20 knots and patrol to intercept *Richelieu* if she was proceeding from Dakar to a Bay of Biscay port.
7.   I informed the Admiralty in my 0635/29 that I intended to proceed with *Renown* to Cape St Vincent and if the air reconnaissance off Casablanca was negative, to continue to the northward and establish a patrol in the vicinity of Cape Finisterre. Air reconnaissance from the UK to the west and south-west of Finisterre was requested for p.m. 29 and during 30 [September] and 1 October.
8.   At 0700 *Renown* screened by *Hotspur*, *Encounter* and *Gallant*

sailed from Gibraltar. Half an hour later *Firedrake* who had been on patrol also joined the screen.

9. On leaving harbour two French destroyers, *Epée* and *Frondeur*,[1] were sighted passing through the Straits to the westward. These destroyers increased speed to about 28 knots on sighting *Renown*. ...

12. ... In view, however, of the report that two German Merchant ships with troops on board had been reported in the south-east corner of the Bay of Biscay and that the Admiralty considered it possible that these vessels might be proceeding to capture the Azores, *Renown* was ordered to proceed to the vicinity of these islands. ...

30 September

15. At 0039 I received AM 2340/29 ordering *Richelieu* to be shadowed if she was met on passage to the Azores.

1 October

20. At 1800 destroyers were detached and ordered to patrol as follows:–

Encounter – northern approaches to Horta.
Hotspur – southern approaches to Horta.
Gallant – off Angra.
Firedrake – off Ponta Delgada,

subsequently rejoining *Renown* ... at 1300 on 2 October, for fuel, since they would have insufficient fuel remaining by the time *Orangeleaf*[2] arrived.

2 October

23. At 1912 AM 1835/2 was received ordering *Ark Royal* to carry out air reconnaissance between the Azores and Cape Finisterre with the object of identifying shipping approaching [the] Azores.

4 October

25. The Admiralty ... ordered *Renown* and destroyers to leave patrol at a.m. 4 October and return to Gibraltar.

7 October

39. *Attitude of the Portuguese.* Should it be necessary to re-establish

---

[1]*Epée*: 1938, 1772t, 6×5.1in, 7tt, 37k; scuttled Toulon Nov 1942. *Frondeur*: 1930, 1378t, 4×5.1in, 6tt, 33k; sunk Casablanca Nov 1942 by US forces.
[2]*Orangeleaf*: oiler, 1917, 12,370t, c. 5000t capacity, 14k.

the patrol off the Azores, information of the following points would be of assistance:–

(a) What is the attitude of the Portuguese towards attempted invasion?
(b) Have the Portuguese made any preparations to deal with invasion?
(c) Are the Portuguese prepared to co-operate with us in resisting inva-sion? If so, can local W/T and/or V/S alarm signal be arranged to indicate to our forces that an attack is being made?
(d) Observing that Fayal and San Miguel are 150 miles apart, would close watch on one to secure possession of a base for counter-attack be sufficient? If so, which is preferred? ...

77. *To the Admiralty*

7 October 1940

Be pleased to inform Their Lordships that on my return to Gibraltar this forenoon I was shown a copy of AM 0233 of 2 October by the Admiral Commanding, North Atlantic Station.

2. In view of the orders contained in AM 1724/28 June, para. (iv), I have hitherto assumed that responsibility for intercepting enemy war vessels attempting to break out of the Western Mediterranean rested with the Flag Officer Commanding Force H. I also assumed that these orders were to include French war vessels if the latter had to be inter-cepted.

3. My reasons for not intercepting the French Squadron referred to in AM 0233/2 October ... are contained in my *Report of Proceedings* of 17 September.[1]

I have nothing to add to these reasons, except that I discussed the situ-ation fully with the Admiral Commanding, North Atlantic Station. Rightly or wrongly we were both of the opinion that, in view of what appeared to be the ample warning Their Lordships had received of the intended movement and notification of the presence of these vessels approaching the Straits, it was not desired to interfere with this move-ment or to provoke any sort of incident.

4. If, however, the action taken is considered to have been incorrect, I wish to accept full responsibility, since at the time in question I acted in the full belief that responsibility for any action to be taken by Force H rested with me.

[1]See No. 62, paras. 6–8.

78.   *To his wife*

8 October 1940

... When I got ashore Dudley showed me a signal from the Admiralty saying he was to report in writing why *he* did not order Force H to sea when the French Squadron passed through here. I was damn well furious when I saw it because it is my responsibility. They argued if you please that we ought to have gone because in a signal made in *July* the Admiralty said they reserved the right to stop French War vessels going to *German occupied ports.* Can you beat that as a flimsy excuse to make Dudley and me the scapegoats? ... They won't keep us informed and in the picture, they keep us guessing and if we guess wrong then they want to have our blood. ... it looks to me as if they are trying to put the blame for this disastrous Dakar business on Dudley and me. Well, I have a mouthful to say on the subject. ...

79.   *To his wife*

9 October 1940

... So the story now is that through some oversight at the Admiralty Dudley Pound and the War Cabinet knew nothing about the passage of the French ships until it was too late! Well it is a bit difficult to swallow but in any case if at that time and not after the event they attached so much importance to stopping French ships why was the possibility [not?] considered and instructions given to me? So far as I know the whole idea was to avoid incidents. Personally I don't believe for one moment that the arrival of those ships made all the difference. Both Admiral Ollive at Casablanca and the Admiral at Dakar[1] were intensely anti-British as the result of Oran and I have no doubt they had the military completely under control and ready to obey their orders. To my mind it has all been quite clear – if de Gaulle had been received with no resistance or purely nominal resistance then it would have been all right but if the French showed that they meant to fight then the party ought to

[1]Adm E. L. H. Ollive (1882–1950): ent navy 1899; torpedo specialist; Lt de V 1911; naval artillery battery on W Front; CO *Fauconneau* 1918, *Téméraire* 1919; Capt de Frégate 1922; Capt *Algérien* & 2nd D Sqdn 1924; Capt de V 1927; N War Coll 1932; RA 1933; Inspr-Gen Northern Naval Forces; Commdt 1st Destroyer Sqdn 1935; 3rd Light Sqdn 1936; VA 1937; C-in-C Med Sqdn 1937; Préfet Maritime Toulon 1938; C-in-C Med F 1939, then S Atl & Africa; C-in-C & Préfet Maritime, 4th Region, Algeria July 1940–Oct 1942; Adm Nov 1940; i/c Med convoys to France; ret 1943.
C-in-C Dakar not known.

have been called off at once. I said so before it started and directly I heard that things were not going as expected. . . .

80. *From the Admiralty*

15 October 1940

With reference to your letter No. 69/102 of 7 October[1] concerning the passage of the French Force through the Straits, Their Lordships note that you considered that the responsibility for intercepting any ships passing through the Straits was yours.

It is obvious, however, that as you did not receive the Naval Attache, Madrid's signal 1800/10 September until 0800 on 11 September, you were unable to take action on that signal in time to intercept the ships.

This signal was received by the Flag Officer Commanding, North Atlantic, at 0008 on 11 September and it was his duty as Senior Officer to see that the necessary action was taken.

Their Lordships note that on receipt of *Hotspur*'s signal at about 0512 you took action at 0530 to bring *Renown* to one hour's notice for steam.

81. *Naval Attaché, Madrid, to Staff Officer (Intelligence), Gibraltar*[2]

Madrid,
1809, 10 September 1940

French Admiralty's to me begins – Please advise Naval Authorities Gibraltar departure from Toulon 9 September 3 cruisers type *Georges Leygues* and 3 French cruisers *le Fantasque* class which will pass Straits AM 11 September.[3]

National[?] fully painted ends. Probability not known.

82. *The Admiralty to Admiral North*

15 October 1940

6.   Their Lordships are of opinion that on receipt of Naval Attaché's signal at 0008, it was your duty to ensure that action was taken which would enable these ships to be intercepted, either on receipt of instruc-

[1]No. 77.
[2]Cdr G. H. Birley: Cdr Dec 1938; SO (I) *Cormorant* Jan 1939; NID 1942.
[3]*Georges Leygues, Gloire, Montcalm*: 1937, 7600t, 9×6in, 8×3.5in, 4tt, 34k.
Le Fantasque class: 1934, 2569t, 5×5.5in, 9tt, 37k.

tions from the Admiralty or without such instructions if the situation developed in such a manner as to need it.

7.   Their Lordships cannot retain full confidence in an officer who fails in an emergency to take all prudent precautions without waiting for Admiralty instructions. They have accordingly decided that you should be relieved of your present command at the first convenient opportunity.

83.   *To his wife*

25 October 1940

Dudley has just rung to say that he has received a letter from the Admiralty giving him the sack on account of the French cruisers getting through and that there is a personal letter for me from the Admiralty which he is sending round by orderly. It has just arrived and apparently whitewashes me because Dudley was the senior officer. I am absolutely furious. I have told the Admiralty that I considered it was my responsibility to take any action required and I purposely refrained because it seemed obvious to me that the Admiralty wished to avoid an incident.

Have seen Dudley and he is accused of not taking 'prudent precautions to deal with the situation'. That means of course that he did nothing – was in default as they say. Well at the most they can only accuse us of an error of judgement because we considered most carefully whether any action was desirable or not. Damn it all, the Admiralty must have envisaged the possibility of the French sending reinforcements to Dakar and if they really thought it was likely they ought to have told us to stop all French ships and use the guns of the fortress if necessary. I am excused on the grounds that I did not know in time to get to sea and intercept. But I thought I made it plain to them I never had any idea of creating an incident. Anyhow I am replying that whether I made it clear in my report or not it *was* my intention not to interfere and I wish to be perfectly frank about it and do not want to be exonerated on that score. It is the absolute bloody limit. I am sick to the teeth with all this damn French business out here and shall be quite pleased if they relieve me. Why, now we have been told to seize French ships in French territorial waters! I imagine this is bound to provoke the French into open hostilities with us and as they have very large superior surface, submarine and air forces a nice lot of fools we shall look. It all passes my comprehension and makes me feel so bitter at the pot mess they are trying to get us into. . . .

84.   *To the Admiralty*

25 October 1940

Be pleased to submit for the attention of Their Lordships that I have been informed by the Admiral Commanding, North Atlantic Station, that he has been held to blame for not ordering Force H to sea on the occasion of a French squadron passing through the Straits of Gibraltar on 11 September 1940.

I note, from Admiralty letter of 15 October,[1] that I am exonerated on the grounds that I did not receive sufficient warning of the impending movement to take action in time to intercept the ships in question.

I wish to be quite frank about this matter and to state that even if I had received sufficient notice to enable *Renown* and the one or two destroyers available to proceed to sea, I should have refrained from doing so for the reasons set forth in my *Report of Proceedings*, No. 60/8 of 17 September.[2]

I now consider that paragraphs 4 and 5 of my *Report* do not make this point sufficiently clear, and I should be most reluctant to feel that, if blame is to be attached to anyone in connection with the incident, I am to be exonerated because I failed to represent clearly and without any ambiguity my appreciation of the situation and my intentions consequent on that appreciation.

85.   *To his wife*

26 October 1940

. . . Did I tell you that Dudley North had asked the Admiralty to suspend action about him until he had had a chance to reply to the Admiralty letter. They signalled back that they would so he and I have been busy today drafting a reply which points out that we had no reason to assume that the Admiralty were not aware of the proposed movement of the French ships and our orders at the time were to avoid incidents with the French. . . .

---

[1]No. 80.
[2]No. 62, paras. 6–8.

86. *Memorandum by Admiral North*

HMS *Watchful*,
Great Yarmouth,
29 October 1943

*Passage of French Force through Straits of Gibraltar, 11 September
1940: Narrative of Events*

At 0008, 11 September, Naval Attaché. Madrid's 1809/10, addressed to the Staff Officer (Intelligence), Gibraltar (R) DNI was received. This signal was to the effect that the French Naval Attaché had told him officially that three French cruisers and three large destroyers had left Toulon on 9 September and would pass through the Straits a.m. 11 September. This information was passed to forces at sea at 0215. Further action was considered unnecessary, as definite instructions regarding the treatment of French warships was promulgated in AM 0241/12 July, and I was satisfied from my intelligence that the force was not bound for enemy ports.

At 0512 a signal was received from *Hotspur* reporting that the ships had been sighted and that she was shadowing, and I ordered her to cease shadowing and take no action. On receiving this confirmation of Naval Attaché, Madrid's report I consulted Flag Officer Commanding Force H and we were both of opinion that, as the Admiralty had received notice of the probable passage of these ships, it was evident they wished no action taken, in accordance with the declared policy of avoiding incidents as promulgated in AM 0241/12 July. As a safeguard, however, against any unexpected change of policy, Force H, then at two hours' notice for steam, was brought to one hour's notice. *Renown* could therefore have proceeded to sea at about 0715 if ordered out.

At 0617 I informed the Admiralty of *Hotspur*'s sighting report, adding the information that I had ordered her to take no action.

At 0711 I informed the Admiralty that I intended to keep in touch with this force by air and would report probable destination.

At about 0845 the French force passed through the Straits without incident.

At 1020 I approved Flag Officer Commanding Force H's request that Force H should revert to two hours' notice for steam.

At 1300 Admiralty's signal 1239/11 was received directing *Renown* and all destroyers to raise steam for full speed. . . .

87. *Memorandum by Admiral North*

29 October 1943

The Circumstances Attending my Removal from my Command at
Gibraltar by Their Lordships

. . . The date of the Admiralty telegram is very significant. The attack on Dakar failed on 23 September. The Admiralty sent off this enquiry on 27 September, when questions were being asked as to why these cruisers had not been stopped. It was not until then that the Admiralty began to enquire as to why the force had not been intercepted. . . .

As regards the actual ordering of HMS *Renown* to sea, I also pointed out that Admiralty instructions had made it quite clear that Force H constituted a detached squadron under the independent command of Admiral Somerville charged with certain special duties to be carried out subject to any instructions which might be given by the Admiralty, and that HMS *Renown*'s movements had always been ordered by the Admiralty or by the Flag Officer Commanding [Force H], and in no single instance by me. At the same time, in any emergency of which the Admiralty had no previous knowledge, I should not have hesitated to order HMS *Renown* to sea. In this case I had not considered it desirable as, had the Admiralty desired the force to go to sea there had been ample time to send orders to that effect. The Flag Officer Commanding Force H had brought his ships to short notice and had awaited instructions from the Admiralty as to action to be taken.

To this the Admiralty replied:

'Senior Officer, Force H, in his report states that he considers the responsibility for intercepting these ships was his, but however much this may be the case, the fact remains that the earliest information he received of the passage of these ships was at about 0512, which left insufficient time for *Renown* to proceed to sea to intercept them.'

This is totally untrue. Admiral Somerville's staff had been informed by telephone by 0512, [he] had brought his ships to short notice after consultation with me, and had it been decided that *Renown* should proceed to sea, Force H could have been outside in the Straits by 0715. The [French] ships did not pass until 0845 so there was ample time to spare. . . .

88.   *To his wife*

12 October 1940

. . . I passed a remark yesterday to someone that having had two quiet days I was sure a spasm would start and of course it did. We were supposed to be at 12 hours' notice making good defects and had discharged more than half our oil fuel to assist in repairing our bulge when at 6 p.m. last night we got orders to be at 4 hours' notice. I roused up everyone and got an oiler alongside and was able to report that we could leave at midnight with 1200 tons of fuel short but all engines and boilers ready or at 5 a.m. with all our fuel on board. TL selected 5 a.m. and made a signal to say that 'your performance bringing *Renown* to immediate notice is most creditable'. Perhaps that is just to soften the frightful raspberry about not stopping the French cruisers. I actually had to ask why we were going to sea as they had not told me and learnt in reply that it was to be clear of Gib in case the Frogs turned nasty again on account of some minor doings down south. Now isn't that just like them – during Dakar I appreciated the situation correctly and said I intended to put to sea and was stopped by TL and so got bombed and now it is not even left to my judgement. I should certainly not have gone had it been left to me, at least not until certain things boiled up. It is most annoying because Jack Tovey arrives this afternoon and leaves tonight and I most particularly wanted to see him and discuss a whole host of matters which affect us both. Also Sam Hoare arrives from Madrid on a short visit and I particularly wanted to see him too and discuss certain Spanish questions.

89.   *Report of Proceedings, 7–14 October 1940*

14 October 1940

7 October

8.   At 2115 I received AM 1635/7 stating that I might be required to take charge of an expedition whose object would be that laid down for operation ALLOY. I had no information or instructions concerning this operation but fortunately my Signal Officer[1] was able to inform me that it concerned a landing in the Azores. I subsequently found that the Admiral Commanding, NAS, had a copy of the orders for ALLOY which I obtained on loan. . . .

---

[1]Lt-Cdr Longden.

9 October

9.   At 2040 I received AM 1915/5 ordering HMS *Sheffield* to patrol in the vicinity of the Azores on parting company with Convoy WS3.

10 October

11.   HMAS *Australia*[1] arrived at Gibraltar and joined Force H in accordance with AM 1914/9.
14.   At about 1800 a French reconnaissance machine appeared over Gibraltar. Fire was opened by shore batteries, *Renown* and *Australia*, the latter ship being commendably quick in opening fire in marked contrast to the shore batteries. The machine made off in the direction of Tarifa.

11 October

16.   At 0804 AM 0108/11 was received giving a report that the French cruiser *Primaguet* had left Casablanca escorting a merchant ship loaded with munitions and bound for Dakar.
19.   At 1821 I received AM 1732 ordering *Barham* and 3 destroyers to intercept *Primaguet* and her convoy.

12 October

25.   At 1043 I received a signal from the Admiral Commanding, NAS, that SS *Starling* was being bombed and machine gunned off Cadiz by an Italian plane. An aircraft report was received at 1151 that *Starling* was hit and that the crew were in the boats 4 miles west of Cadiz. Five minutes later the aircraft reported that *Starling* required towage to Gibraltar.[2]
27.   At 1600 I received a signal stating that SS *Orao*,[3] on passage to Gibraltar under armed guard from *Hotspur*, was being fired at by a submarine and that the crew had taken to the boats . . . As there appeared to be a reasonable chance of attacking this submarine, I decided to send the whole of *Renown*'s screen to hunt this submarine. *Gallant* and *Griffin* were therefore ordered to proceed to the vicinity at full speed, *Wishart* and *Vidette* following at 25 knots. Meanwhile *Renown* increased to 24 knots and carried out a broad zig-zag, subsequently altering course at 1700 to 180°.

---

[1]*Australia*: 1928, 10,000t, 8×8in, 8×4in, 31.5k.
[2]*Starling*: 1930, 1320gt, Gen SN Co. She suffered severe damage and was abandoned temporarily. Repaired in Cadiz; wounded seamen taken to Spanish hospital. Towed to Gibraltar for full repairs. Later in the war she had further encounters with bombers and a U-boat but survived. See H. E. Hancock, *Semper Fidelis: the Saga of the 'Navvies' (1924–1948)* (London: GSNC, 1949), pp. 59–61.

30. . . . No contact had been obtained by midnight, at which time the destroyers left the area to rendezvous with *Renown* as previously arranged. A detailed report of the attack on *Orao* has not yet been received from the destroyers concerned but it is known that the submarine was of a large type mounting two guns. Before leaving, *Wishart* sank the *Orao* as she was still afloat and a danger to navigation.

13 October

34. At 1430, I received AM 1308/13 directing *Renown*, *Barham*, *Australia* and accompanying destroyers to return to Gibraltar if the *Primauguet* had not been sighted by 1800. . . .

90. *To Blake*

17 October 1940

. . . Now that the new dock is open, this place can be really useful and the only snag is that there aren't anything like enough dockyard maties.

Glad to see some dribs and drabs of Force H returning. Our hands have been very much tied for the last four weeks and without air we are singularly ineffective in the big, wide open spaces.

. . . The next east-going party won't be quite such an easy job as the last . . . These Itis seem a bit too handy with their torpedo aircraft at night and that's why I deprecated the job coming off anywhere near full moon. . . . You can't afford to dawdle within range of the shore-based aircraft.

Hope we shan't be stirring up the French again until the next job is over. When this harbour is packed with ships, there's not enough water left to catch the bricks. . . .

Everyone is in very good heart here, but we are longing to have a crack at the Iti's . . .

91. *To Blake*

22 October 1940

. . . If French ships are allowed to proceed to Casablanca, the chances of intercepting these subsequently are remote unless two carriers are available to maintain a continuous air patrol. Additional cruisers would also be required to maintain a standing interception force of the requisite strength. It seems to me, therefore, that instead of teasing or pin-pricking the French, we should try to arrive at some understanding.

Take for example the signal stating that it was HM Government's decision to stop French escorted convoys. Well, unless you're prepared to infringe territorial waters, and the message gives no authority to do that, the answer is obviously a lemon. The patrols might succeed in pouncing on perhaps one French ship before she could get inside territorial waters, but what use would that be? They'd give strict instructions in the future about keeping inside. Seems to me that if our patrols sight a vessel just outside, they should approach slowly and edge her inside rather than pouncing. Surely it's not worth creating an incident for one or two ships? We can pass the word, I presume, that all ships outside territorial waters, whether French or other neutrals, will be subjected to contraband control. . . .

We have been making some scale models of Italian ports with a view to bombarding, should opportunity occur. . . . If it's considered worth while, then I'm all for going ahead, but we've got to take a long view and the old *Ark* is a very valuable ship. I've been like a blind man without his dog whilst she's been away.

That was a good bit of work snaffling those two U-boats off Alboran. I hope those two young fellows who went down below in *Durbo* whilst she was sinking get an immediate award. *Wrestler* did very well in putting his ship alongside. In the case of the second one, Layman, in *Hotspur*, did well. He was in charge of the hunt and eventually rammed and sank the submarine after *Gallant* had brought her to the surface. 200 Group did a nice bit of co-operation.[1] . . .

I see Harwood is relieving you and I expect you are not sorry as you have had a pretty stiff time of it ever since you joined up. What's your new job? Something to your fancy, I hope.[2]

92. *Report of Proceedings, 14–20 October 1940*

24 October 1940

15 October

4. Transports *Etrick* and *Karanja*, escorted by *Wishart*, *Greyhound* and *Vidette* arrived. HMS *Barham*, in company with HMAS *Australia* and HM Ships *Fortune*, *Echo* and *Escapade*[3] arrived late in the forenoon.

---

[1]*Durbo*: 1938, 623/848t, 6tt, 1×3.9in, 14/8k; sunk 18 Oct by *Firedrake* & *Wrestler* assisted by 2 London flying boats of 202 Sqdn. Papers obtained from her disclosed the presence nearby of her sister *La Fole*, sunk 20 Oct by *Gallant*, *Griffin* & *Hotspur*.Cdr H. F. H. Layman: Cdr 1936; Capt *Hotspur* 1939; *Warspite* Jan 1941 as SO (P), Med F; SD May 1942; Actg Capt June 1943; Capt Dec 1943; SD (Y), DDSD (Y) Feb 1944.

[2]Blake became principal NLO with the US Navy in Europe.

[3]*Ettrick*: 1938, 11,279gt, P & O, serving as a troopship. *Karanja*: 1931, 9891gt, 16k, British India SN CO; an LS (L); wrecked by an explosion in Bombay harbour 1944. They were the core of a proposed expedition to seize the Azores or recapture them if the Germans got there first.

At 1115, Sir Samuel Hoare arrived and spoke to the Officers and Ship's Company [of *Renown*].

I discussed details of operation BRISK with Cdr Onslow and Captain J.W.A. Waller, RN, from HM Transport *Ettrick*.[1]

Single aircraft were reported in the vicinity five times during the day, but did not approach within range of the A/A defences.

16 October

8.   In the light of the discussions which had been taking place continuously during the past three days, I made my signal 1804 of 16 October to the Admiralty, giving my preliminary remarks on operation BRISK. These were to the effect that whilst the orders met requirements for the situation envisaged the most probable situation was that the Germans would arrive at the Azores first and consequently detailed plans for an opposed landing should be prepared.

17 October

10.   At 0109 I received AM 2319/16 stating that ships might revert to normal notice for steam if by 1400 on 17 October no French ships other than those reported by the Naval Attaché, Madrid, had been sighted and at 0303 received AM 2333/16 ordering *Australia, Echo, Escapade* and transports *Karanja* and *Ettrick* to sail for Clyde p.m. on 17th., ...[2]

14.   At 2003 AM 1921 was received ordering *Australia* and convoy to return to Gibraltar. This was followed three minutes later by Admiralty's 1926 ordering *Renown* to come to short notice and a patrol to be established to eastward.

AM 1856 giving the reason for these instructions, i.e., that *Strasbourg* and 20 units of the French fleet were reported to be leaving Toulon, was received at 2026. *Australia* and convoy returned to Gibraltar at 2200.

AM 2207 was received at 2301, giving the procedure to be adopted should *Strasbourg* and/or a force of 4 or more destroyers or a cruiser approach the Straits.

---

[1]Capt John W. A. Waller: N Asst to 1SL May 1941; Capt *Malaya* March 1942; RA July 1943; RA Red S & Suez C Area Oct 1943; *Saker* (BAD) British Admy Matériel & Supply Rep, Washington June 1944–5.

Cdr (later Adm Sir) Richard C. Onslow (1904–75): ent RN 1918; destroyer specialist; Cdr *Gypsy* 1938; OD 1938–40; *Ashanti* 1941; Arctic & Med; Capt (D), Eastern F 1944 & Pacific F 1945; IDC 1946; NOIC Londonderry; Dir Jt A/S Sch; DTSD; *Devonshire* 1951; RA 1952; Naval Sec to FL; FO (Flotillas) & 2nd-in-C, Home F 1955–6; VA 1956; Res F 1956–7; Adm & C-in-C Portsmouth 1958; Ret List 1960, having refused Med F on health grounds; scion of a famous naval family.

[2]Four S/M, an escort vessel & an oiler.

18 October

17. The situation regarding the French battlecruiser *Strasbourg* and the other French units, reported to have sailed from Toulon, was still obscure. In view of the effects the execution of my instructions would have on naval operations in the Western Mediterranean and since the prospects of effecting interception south of Casablanca were problematical, I forwarded my appreciation of the local situation in my 1441. I fully realise that there are many factors affecting the situation of which I am not aware. Nevertheless, I feel it is necessary to draw attention to the very serious effect which would result if the French air and surface forces engage in active operations against us in the Western Mediterranean.

18. At 1746 I received Admiralty's 1706, ordering *Australia*, transports and destroyers to be sailed; this signal referred also to the Naval Attaché, Madrid's 1210 (which I later received). The latter reported that the French Naval Attaché had stated that he knew nothing of any movement, but that *Strasbourg* was now repaired and that all warships at Toulon frequently go out for exercises. Admiralty, in their 1707, stated that the signal (AM 1926/17) ordering *Renown* to short notice was to remain in force for the present.

20. Although it had been desired for some time to carry out A/S sweeps in this vicinity, it had not been possible, up to this time, to spare the destroyers. The posting of the patrol to the eastward for reporting of *Strasbourg*, however, fortuitously provided the opportunity, with gratifying results.

At 1750/18, *Firedrake*, on patrol to the east of Gibraltar, saw two Londons[1] returning to base from reconnaissance. One of these machines was observed to turn, dive and release bombs. *Firedrake* and *Wrestler*, who had also observed this from the adjacent patrol line, both closed the position where the aircraft had bombed some oil bubbles. Contact was obtained and attacks carried out by both destroyers. Finally the submarine came to the surface and *Wrestler* placed his ship alongside and boarded. *Firedrake* also sent a boarding party by boat. Great courage and resource was shown by the officers and ratings concerned. Since the destroyers were operating under the orders of the Admiral Commanding, NAS, the detailed report and recommendations for awards are being forwarded by him.

The submarine proved to be the *Durbo* of the *Perla* class and she sank shortly after being abandoned.

---

[1]Saro London: flying boat, 1934, 155mph; an obsolete type, about to go out of service.

19 October

22.   *Faulknor*, with Captain (D), 8th DF, *Forester*, *Fury* and *Foresight* arrived at 0700 from Freetown.

20 October

26.   AM 2327/19, addressed to the Admiral Commanding North Atlantic, as repeated to C-in-C, Mediterranean, and myself, was received overnight. This gave HM Government's new policy in connection with French escorted convoys passing through the Straits, and stated that convoyed French ships were to be taken into Gibraltar, that their escorts were to be allowed to proceed, but to be compelled by force, if necessary, to desist from defensive action. The fact that such convoys proceeding through the Straits made use of Spanish territorial waters appeared to have been overlooked, though this has been represented on more than one occasion by Admiral Commanding North Atlantic and by me in my preceding letter of proceedings dated 14 October. I discussed this matter with Admiral Commanding North Atlantic and a signal expressing our views was despatched in which we pointed out that interception in the Straits must involve entry into French territorial waters. We suggested that in view of possible retaliation by the French on Gibraltar, everything should be done to avoid incidents with the French until after the completion of operation UNIFORM and until *Barham* was undocked.

29.   Books and papers extracted from the submarine *Durbo* disclosed the fact that her sister ship *La Fole* was operating south of Alboran Island and a search was at once organised. Six destroyers were detailed and a contact was first obtained at 1213/20; immediately afterwards a torpedo track was seen approaching. Attacks were promptly carried out by *Forester* and *Fury* and continued at intervals till 1545 when after attack by *Gallant*, *Griffin* and *Hotspur*, *La Fole* came to the surface ahead of *Hotspur* who rammed her at 1700. . . .

30.   A meeting was held by Admiral Commanding North Atlantic to discuss the manner in which our surface vessels could be used to the best advantage in maintaining a patrol of the Straits and reconnaissance east and west of the Straits.

It was agreed that a standing patrol either east or west at a distance to give sufficient warning to enable ships of Force H to leave harbour and intercept approaching high speed war vessels could not be maintained in view of other urgent commitments, e.g., A/S patrols, escorts. In view of this it was decided that an extended surface patrol should only be established when there was good reason to believe that a 'break in, or out' of the Mediterranean was probable. . . .

93. *Report of Proceedings, 22 October–7 November 1940*

HMS *Ark Royal*,
10 November 1940

23 October

3.   At 0837 I received AM 0056, made in reply to the Admiral Commanding, NAS's 1320/20 concerning the interception of French escorted convoys. This stated while Spanish territorial waters were to be respected, French territorial waters might be entered in order to intercept French convoys. No action was to be taken until *Barham* had been undocked, but after this the first favourable opportunity should be taken to bring in a convoy, using destroyers only and provided they were in overwhelming strength.

In my message 1517, I gave it as my opinion that the full support of Force H should be available in case attempts were made by superior French surface or air forces to release a captured convoy before it reached Gibraltar. I recommended that action should be deferred until four days after the undocking of *Barham* to enable her to complete with ammunition and provisions. In view of the probable retaliation of the French, which might well lead to action between surface forces, I felt it inadvisable for *Barham* to commence embarkation of additional ammunition ordered in AM 1628/22, until the situation had clarified. . . .

4.   I must confess I viewed this proposed violation of French territory with grave concern. Our experience up to date has been that the French resist with all their force any violation of their territory. To resistance they added retaliation after Dakar. The French air, surface, and submarine forces are superior to the British forces normally available in the Western Mediterranean. It seemed to me, therefore, that after intercepting the first one or two French convoys we might well be compelled to desist from further interference and at the same time [be] subjected to further air attacks on our only base in the Western Mediterranean. I prepared an appreciation on the situation for despatch to Their Lordships by the first opportunity.

6.   In my 1546/23, I asked that ASV Type 286 [radar] should be sent for fitting in *Renown* and two destroyers. The value of RDF has been so clearly demonstrated and even short range RDF sets will be of great service during operations in the Western Mediterranean.

7.   Lt-Cdr A.D. Clark, US Navy,[1] joined HMS *Renown* as US Naval Observer in Force H.

---

[1]Lt-Cdr A. Dayton Clark, US Navy: in 1944 a Cdr & USNLO, Eastern F; Capt, Navy Dept, Nov 1944.

25 October

12.   At 1937 I received Admiralty's 1835 to the Admiral Commanding, NAS, stating that the operation for interception of French ships was to be called RATION and that although preparations were to be made for it to be carried out on 29 October, in view of the French internal situation, it was not to be put into force until further orders.

27 October

18.   At 1656 *Sheffield* was ordered by AM 1615 to sail forthwith to carry out Azores patrol with the object of intercepting German troop transports from Biscay ports should they be attempting invasion of the islands. *Sheffield* sailed accordingly at 1930.

30 October

27.   A heavy explosion occurred in the north entrance to the harbour, about 40 yards north of the torpedo baffle. An anti-submarine search was immediately ordered by the Admiral Commanding, NAS, and motor boats of Force H were ordered to embark depth charges. At the moment it appears that one or possibly two 'one man submarines' were engaged in the venture but evidence on this point is not at present definite.

31 October

33.   Consul-General, Tangier's 1900/30 was received overnight. He stated that it was rumoured in Casablanca that the French ships there might sail at any time and that rush orders had been given for their refuelling and storing. In view of this and a report from *Griffin* that at 0610 she was shadowing 5 French destroyers in position 70° Almina Point, 70 miles, course 270°, I decided to put to sea.

34.   *Renown, Barham, Fortune, Firedrake, Fury* and *Greyhound* were accordingly sailed at 0830 and proceeded to the westward. The destroyers on the eastward patrol were ordered to return and join Force H to westward, with the exception of *Griffin* who was ordered to shadow the French force.

35.   By 1600 it was clear that the French destroyers were proceeding to Casablanca and air reconnaissance revealed no outward movement from that port. Opportunity was taken to carry out long range full calibre 15" throw off firing by *Renown* and *Barham* and at dusk 4.7" throw off firing by destroyers in company.

1 November

39.   *Renown, Barham, Fortune, Fury, Firedrake, Encounter, Greyhound, Gallant, Wishart* and *Forester* returned to Gibraltar at 1000.

Examination of area in which explosion occurred on 30 October resulted in the recovery of portions of what appears to be a torpedo or mine carrying machine controlled by personnel wearing shallow diving dresses. It is not clear, however, whether this machine was explosive itself or merely acted as a carrier.[1] . . .

3 November

52.   At 0634, AM 0404 was received, giving the information that the French battleships *Jean Bart* and *Richelieu* might shortly endeavour to proceed to Toulon, but that it was the intention of HM Government that these ships should not be allowed to go into the Mediterranean or into German occupied ports. The Vichy Government were being so informed and should information of such a movement be received Force H was to proceed to the eastward to prevent them from proceeding into the Mediterranean, by force if necessary. Patrols were to be instituted to give warning of such a movement, subject to the operations already arranged for Force H not being prejudiced.

5 November

73.   AM 2022 reporting that *Admiral Scheer*[2] was operating in the North Atlantic was received at 2127. At 2235 a message was received ordering *Renown*, *Barham* and destroyer screen to raise steam. . . .

6 November

76.   At 0126 AM 0018, ordering me to transfer my Flag to *Ark Royal* or *Sheffield* and *Renown* to proceed with despatch towards 37° 30'N, 20° 00'W, was received. Since it was not known for how long *Renown* was to be detached, I decided to move the whole of my Staff and office. The complete organisation had left *Renown* by 0340 and the latter sailed immediately. I hoisted my Flag in *Barham* temporarily, transferring to *Ark Royal* on her arrival.

77.   HMS *Sheffield* arrived at 0600 from Azores patrol. *Ark Royal* arrived at 1315, *Berwick* and *Glasgow* at 1430 and *Duncan*, in company with *Isis*, *Foxhound* and HT *Pasteur*, at 1630.[3]

---

[1]The Italians had equipped some of their submarines to carry submersible two-man chariots, from which explosive charges could be fitted to ships in harbour. They enjoyed success later at Gibraltar (see No. 184) and, most famously, at Alexandria, where *Queen Elizabeth* and *Valiant* were severely damaged in Dec 1941; see Cunningham, *A Sailor's Odyssey*, pp. 433–5.

[2]*Admiral Scheer*: 1934, 12,000t+, 6×11in, 8×5.9in, 6×4.1in, 8tt, 26k; sunk by RAF, Kiel, 1945.

[3]*Berwick*: 1928, 10,000t, 8×8in, 8×4in, 31.5k. *Glasgow*: 1937, 9100t, 12×6in, 8×4in, 6tt, 32k. *Duncan*: L, 1933, 1400t, 4×4.7in, 8tt, 36k. *Isis*: 1937, 1370t, 4×4.7in, 10tt, 36k; sunk off Normandy 1944. *Pasteur*: 1938, 30000t, Sud-Atlantique Cie de Nav.

94. *Report of Proceedings, 7–11 November 1940*

HMS *Renown*,
12 November 1940

7 November

2.   At 1800, Force H and the reinforcements for the Eastern Mediterranean sailed from Gibraltar to carry out operation COAT.

Force H consisted of *Ark Royal* (flying my Flag), *Sheffield, Faulknor, Fortune, Fury, Foxhound, Forester, Firedrake, Duncan* and *Isis*, whilst the reinforcements comprised *Berwick, Barham, Glasgow, Greyhound, Gallant* and *Griffin*. Of the Force H destroyers, three (*Faulknor, Fortune* and *Fury*) were required to accompany the reinforcements to Malta.

3.   Troops were embarked in all ships proceeding to Malta, to the following approximate numbers:–

Berwick	750
Barham	700
Glasgow	400
6 destroyers	50 each
Total	2150

5.   A report was also received at this time that a reconnaissance aircraft had been unable to locate the two Italian U-boats which had entered Tangier harbour. Arrangements had been made for the Consul-General at Tangier to make an immediate signal if they sailed, but no such signal was received and it was assumed that the submarines were still at Tangier.

8 November

8.   A/S air patrols were flown off at dawn and were maintained throughout the day. The bad weather that had been hoped for did not materialise; on the contrary, the day was fine and the visibility extreme.

9.   At 0716 I received AM 0106 containing the route for *Despatch*[1] and *Argus* and ordering *Renown* to join *Despatch* and proceed in company to Gibraltar for operation WHITE.

10.   About 0900, two London flying boats were sighted astern of the Fleet. Their co-operation had been requested in the hope of catching a U-boat surfacing to make an enemy report astern of the Fleet.

12.   As the weather was fine and the visibility good, and since weather reports indicated no drastic change, I considered the Force would almost certainly be sighted on passage and be attacked by bombers. I therefore

[1]*Despatch*: 1922, 4850t, 6×6in, 3×4in, 12tt, 29k.

decided at 1530 to proceed ahead with *Ark Royal, Glasgow, Sheffield* and 6 destroyers and carry out the pre-arranged bombing attack on Cagliari aerodrome.

Speed was increased to 26½ knots, whilst *Berwick, Barham* and the remaining 5 destroyers continued on their course at 18 knots.

13.   . . . [At 1745] RDF picked up a plane distant 16 miles. Shortly afterwards *Ark Royal* sighted this aircraft, a Savoia 79, and opened fire with 4.5" guns to indicate the position to the fighters.

The latter gave chase and at 1830 the enemy was shot down and crashed into the sea . . . with no sign of any survivors.

9 November

17.   At 0233 I received Admiralty's 2348/8 (addressed to Admiral Commanding, NAS) stating that during the absence of Force H from Gibraltar every endeavour was to be made by submarine patrols to prevent *Richelieu* or *Jean Bart* passing through the Straits. They should, if possible, be warned by a surface vessel of some kind to return to Casablanca, but as a last resort might be torpedoed without warning.

19.   Course was altered to 320° without signal at 0430, the screen maintaining compass bearing. A striking force of nine Swordfish was then flown off to bomb Cagliari aerodrome with direct and delay action bombs. On completion of flying off, course was altered to 160° for flying on position and speed increased to 20 knots.

20.   At 0745 a fighter section, A/S patrol and the Fulmar section for Malta were flown off and all Swordfish of the striking force landed on. The fighter section landed at Malta at 1020.[1]

21.   The raid on Cagliari appeared to have been quite successful. Five aircraft attacked the aerodrome and hits were observed on two hangars and adjacent buildings; two fires were seen to break out and one heavy explosion occurred. One aircraft attacked a group of seaplanes moored off the jetty. Another attacked some factories near the power station and obtained a direct hit with a 250 lb bomb and incendiaries. The remaining two aircraft were unable to locate the target and attacked A/A batteries; two fires were seen to start but the batteries continued firing. Little opposition was encountered and no casualties were incurred. No enemy aircraft were observed on the ground, but about 20 floatplanes were moored at the seaplane base.

22.   The weather on this day could hardly have been less favourable for evasion. There was extreme visibility, calm sea and wind of about force 3 from the northwest.

---

[1]Three Fulmars for *Illustrious*.

23.　On completion of flying on, course was altered to rendezvous with *Berwick*'s force, which was sighted at 0910. Twenty-five minutes later the whole force was formed up in Cruising Disposition No. 5 on an easterly course at 18 knots.

24.　At 0930 a shadower was picked up by RDF distant 29 miles. After working round the Fleet in a clockwise direction, the aircraft was sighted by the *Barham* and subsequently by the Fulmar section on patrol. This aircraft was a large Cant floatplane and was shot down by the Fulmars 20 miles on the starboard beam of the Fleet at 1005.

26.　At 1048 a large formation of enemy aircraft was located by RDF 50 miles ahead of the Fleet and closing. Five minutes later, another section of Skuas was flown off.

27.　A section of Fulmars intercepted the enemy formation as they were working round to the sun and forced them to turn away but about 10 minutes later, the enemy again approached. The formation adopted was three flights (each of 5 aircraft in 'V' formation) in line astern with one flight of 5 aircraft on the port beam of the leading flight.

28.　The Fleet at this time was in two columns disposed abeam, distance between columns 10 cables, ships in open order and staggered; wind – force 4, broad on the port bow.

29.　The attack was of short duration, and consisted of one continuous stick of bombs dropped right across the Fleet from a height of 13,000 feet. The first bombs fell outside the destroyer screen to starboard, then across the starboard column, straddling *Barham*, then between the columns and across the port column, straddling *Ark Royal*. Several bombs were jettisoned on the horizon after the attack. *Barham*, *Ark Royal* and *Duncan* had near misses, but no damage or casualties were incurred in any ship.

30.　Though conditions were good, A/A fire was disappointing. Fighter aircraft reported that the bursts formed a level carpet about 2000 feet below the target.

31.　All three sections of fighters (one of Fulmars, two of Skuas) reported having obtained hits on the enemy but were unable to make them break formation. One aircraft of the leading formation is believed to have crashed as it was observed by *Glasgow* and one of our fighters to dive steeply towards the sea. A white splash on the horizon may have been caused by this aircraft crashing.

32.　. . . From 10 November, all destroyers would be away on escort duty and watch on Tangier would have to be reduced to one trawler, which, with an armed yacht, would have to carry out the duty of warning *Richelieu* and *Jean Bart* not to proceed further into the Mediterranean.

37.　At 1915, half-an-hour after dark, *Ark Royal*, *Sheffield*, *Duncan*,

Isis, Foxhound, Forester and *Firedrake* turned away to the westward at 26 knots. *Berwick, Barham, Glasgow, Faulknor, Fortune, Fury, Greyhound, Gallant* and *Griffin* continued to Malta under the orders of *Berwick.*

10 November

41. The return passage to Gibraltar was entirely uneventful. Throughout Sunday, 10th., the wind, force 4 from the SW, was very favourable for flying, as only slight alterations from the main line of advance were required.

In addition to maintaining continuous fighter and A/S patrols, new pilots were exercised in deck landing. Fighter patrols also carried out several approaches, representing high level bombing attacks, to exercise look-outs and control procedure.

46. C-in-C, Mediterranean's 1215, reporting that movements of convoys had been carried out according to plan and that *Barham, Berwick* and *Glasgow* and three destroyers had joined the Fleet, was received at 1930.

11 November

47. At 0710 course was altered to enter Gibraltar Bay and *Ark Royal* entered harbour at 0810.

Remarks

48. The outstanding points of this operation were:–

(a) The inability of the fighters to break up the enemy bombers' formation.

(b) The consistent and considerable burst-short of the A/A armament.

(c) The immunity from enemy interference after completion of his high-level bombing attack.

49. With regard to the above,

(a) The margin of speed enjoyed by the fighters, and especially the Skuas, is so small that they are severely handicapped in carrying out effective attacks on Savoias. Many of the pilots have had very little experience, and the form of attack adopted, viz., beam attack, was probably not well judged. Fulmar observers felt the need of a rear gun. Trials are being carried out with a sawn-off Lewis gun, to see if this can be used out of the side windows from the rear seat.

(b) Calibration trials, with theodolite measurements, have been carried out at Gibraltar. A report as to the conclusions drawn and certain recommendations are being furnished separately.

(c) Subsequent photographic reconnaissance established the absence of land bombers at St Elmas aerodrome. It seems probable, therefore, that the attack was launched from Alghero, and possibly the greater distance involved deterred the enemy from further attacks. It is possible that the time bombs dropped on St Elmas prevented it being used as a refuelling and rearming base.

It is difficult to explain the absence of any attempt by submarine or surface forces to dispute the passage of reinforcements. Possibly the precautions taken at Gibraltar to conceal the destination of the Force proved successful.

50. I was much impressed by the speeding-up of flying-on which has resulted from the new crash barrier in *Ark Royal*. Not only does this permit of a higher speed of advance if the direction of the wind is unfavourable, but it also reduces substantially the time during which the carrier and the Force covering her have to remain on a fixed course, possibly during an impending bombing attack.

51. I wish to bring to the attention of Their Lordships the names of the following officers and ratings of HMS *Ark Royal* –

Recommended for immediate awards –

Lt-Cdr Mervyn Johnstone (Pilot and striking force Commander)
Lieut Terence Waters Brown Shaw (Observer).

These officers led the striking force against Elmas aerodrome on the night 8/9 November, in a successful attack. They illuminated the target with accuracy enabling their own and the following aircraft to carry out their attack without delay and to drop bombs on hangars and buildings on the aerodrome.

This is the fourth attack carried out by these officers on Cagliari and the third which they have led. They were recommended by me previously in connection with operation HATS.

52. I also desire to refer to the valuable assistance given to me by my Staff, and in particular to the services of:

Captain Eric Gordon Jeffery, my Chief of Staff, and
Cdr Anthony Wass Buzzard, DSO, my Staff Officer (Operations).

On these two officers has fallen the principal work of preparing plans and operation orders and I attribute the success of this and previous operations very largely to the excellent work, and attention to detail, of these two officers whose services, I consider, merit award in due course.[1]

95. *To his wife*

10 November 1940

We are just completing another little job of sending a lot of reinforcements through to Andrew and it seems to have gone off all right much to my relief because I did not have *Renown* and nothing like the formidable party I had last time. However we planned the whole thing very carefully but did not deceive the Itis all together because we came in for a good bombing yesterday which did no harm I am glad to say. A shadow[er] spotted us on the second day and our fighters shot him down. Yesterday we got another shadower but the weather was clear and the visibility maximum so he could hardly miss us. They came in one big wave – four sections of five bombers each. Our fighters engaged them as they came in but could not make any visible impression on them. A lot of the pilots were changed whilst *Ark* was at home and the new lot are still pretty green. Our A/A fire as they came over was damned bad and I was very angry. Of course this is just an odd collection of ships that have never worked together so what can you expect. My ships are always being changed so I never get a chance to work them up. I think we brought down one of the bombers because he was seen diving steeply towards the sea but we did not actually see him crash in. What with bombs falling all around you can't watch individual incidents very closely and I have to keep my wits about me to see that the fleet is on the right course to bring all guns to bear and that we keep as much as possible under our destroyer screen so that no U-boats will get a shot in. I forgot to say that early that morning we delivered a bombing attack on Cagliari. It is a weird sight seeing the Swordfish all lined up in the pitch dark. As they start up their engines they give out beastly sparks and flashes which you feel sure will be spotted by some Iti surface craft or U-boat, and one is on tenterhooks until the whole party is off. Having seen and talked to the pilots and observers before they took off one waits anxiously for their return and it is a joyous feeling when you have counted them back. Then comes the ticklish job of flying them on. You have to keep an eye cocked all the time for fear that the enemy may come and attack when you are stuck to one course, i.e., straight in the wind's eye and therefore have no freedom of manoeuvring. However although I say it but shouldn't, I am getting quite good at it now and I am sure that old *Ark* is much better covered now than when old Nutty [Wells] was in her. By the way – to my surprise I have heard that Mark[1] is here as an observer. He is in a

---

[1] Lieut Mark Somerville.

flight of fighters and his section leader seems to think the world of him. The boys are very amused when I roar him up in the pilots' and observers' room and ask why the hell he hasn't brought his uncle back any Savoias or Capronis. He was in the party when they attacked the bombers and had a very good bird's eye view of the bombing. . . . We parted from Andrew after dark and then came racing back west as quickly as possible so as to avoid more bombing today. We ought to be in by daylight tomorrow and I hope in a few days to be back in *Renown.*

96.   *Report of Proceedings, 11–19 November 1940*

HMS *Renown,*
19 November 1940

11 November

3.   . . . In a further signal to Malta, timed 1005, I requested that adequate reconnaissance might be provided during operation WHITE on 14 and 15 November and to cover *Newcastle*'s[1] eastward passage on 16 November, and mentioned that bombing of West Sicilian aerodromes on the night 15/16 November would assist the operation.

12 November

8.   HMS *Renown* returned to Gibraltar at 1515 on completion of operations concerned with protection of convoys from attack by *Admiral Scheer.* . . .

13 November

9.   At 0800, I transferred my Flag from *Ark Royal* to *Renown.* A conference of Commanding Officers was called at 1430, to discuss the plans for operation WHITE.

11.   In my 1435 to the Admiralty, I requested confirmation that the four corvettes which were to take part in operation COLLAR (*Peony, Salvia, Gloxinia* and *Hyacinth*) were fitted with asdics and asked for any information concerning their ability to maintain speed in adverse weather[2].

12.   At 1835, I received the Admiral Commanding, NAS's 1620/12, addressed to Admiralty, concerning the situation in Gibraltar Dockyard. He observed that the facilities which were provided for the maintenance of a few small ships were inadequate to cope with the large and varied

---

[1]*Newcastle*: 1937, 9100, 12×6in, 8×4in, 6tt, 32k.

[2]'Flower' class corvettes: numerous vessels, of slightly differing designs, built 1940–2, based on a whaler design; 925t, 1×3in or 1×4in, 16k; *Salvia* sunk E Med Dec 1941, *U568.*

Force now based on Gibraltar and urged that the situation be reviewed with a view to increasing the establishment of personnel and material.

14.   The NOIC, Malta's[1] message 2155, received at 2358, confirmed that air reconnaissance revealed no bombers at Elmas aerodrome or elsewhere in Sardinia, except at Alghero, where there were 20 Savoia 81 bombers.

14 November

20.   At 1743, I received AM 1254 in reply to my signal 1435/13, confirming that all corvettes were fitted with asdics and giving details as to their performance in rough weather. It appears that unless favoured with a leading wind the prospect of these ships being able to maintain station on a 14-knot convoy is somewhat remote.

21.   HMS *Argus* arrived at 2100 and anchored in the Bay. She was fuelled and unloaded mails and stores into the oiler, in order to avoid any contact with the shore which might disclose the object of operation WHITE.

15 November

26.   At 0400, Force H, comprising *Renown* (flying my Flag), *Ark Royal, Argus, Sheffield, Despatch, Faulknor, Fury, Fortune, Forester, Firedrake, Foxhound, Duncan* and *Wishart*, sailed in bright moonlight for operation WHITE.

Cruising Disposition No. 20 was formed and course shaped at 16 knots to pass south of Alboran Island.

27.   A/S patrols were flown off at dawn and the Fleet assumed Cruising Disposition No. 6.

28.   The wind remained westerly, force 4, throughout the day, necessitating course being reversed for flying, the carrier operating in the line. Opportunity was taken to carry out deck-landing training and dummy torpedo attacks whilst the Force steamed on a westerly course for 1½ hours to avoid being too far to the eastward.

16 November

34.   After dawn, course was altered to the south-eastward and shortly afterwards, fighter and A/S patrols were flown off. The westerly wind had increased to force 6 and remained at that strength throughout the day.

35.   By noon, the sea had increased and the conditions for operating aircraft had become severe. As visibility from the air was low and as the

[1]Adm Ford.

RDF screen remained clear, I decided to cancel flying operations and maintain a fighter section at readiness in the carrier.

36. As there appeared to be every chance of avoiding detection and since bad weather conditions appeared likely to persist, I decided at 1430 not to carry out the bombing attack on Alghero aerodrome.

37. A summary of reports received from FOIC, Malta, indicated that a battleship, 7 cruisers (of which 3 were 8") and a number of destroyers were apparently concentrated to the south of Naples. The whereabouts of the other battleships and cruisers formerly at Taranto and Brindisi did not appear to have been established. It appeared to me that:–

(a) The Italians were probably aware of our departure from Gibraltar to the eastward.

(b) They might well consider the possibility of engaging Force H with superior forces in the hope of balancing to some degree their losses at Taranto.

38. In view of this I decided to fly off the Hurricanes from a position as far to the westward as weather conditions would admit. In reply to an enquiry *Argus* informed me that, with the wind as at present Hurricanes could be flown off from longitude 6° 40'E. . . .

Since all available meteorological information indicated a continuation of westerly winds and no suggestion of easterly winds, I decided to accept this as the flying off position.

39 At 1600 the course of the Fleet was therefore reversed for an hour to reduce the chances of detection before dark in order to maintain a speed of not less than 16 knots during the night.

17 November

41. By 0200 the strong westerly wind had backed slightly and dropped considerably. Visibility had improved and was maximum at dawn.

42. At 0545, the Force split into two groups – *Argus, Despatch* and three destroyers to fly off Hurricanes for Malta, as ordered by the Commanding Officer, HMS *Argus; Renown, Ark Royal, Sheffield* and five destroyers to fly off A/S patrols, a fighter section and a reconnaissance to the eastward.

43. At the time of flying off, the wind at 2000 feet in the flying off position was 200°, 20 knots, and the latest forecast received from Malta, which was timed 1130/16, reported the wind in the Malta channel as southwest. As no further report was received it was presumed there was no change.

44. The first flight took off at 0615 in position 37° 29'N, 6° 43'E and the second flight at 0715 in position 37° 24'N, 6° 52'E.

45.   Arrangements had been made for a Sunderland to meet the first flight 5 miles to the NW of Galita Island, and for a Glenn Martin[1] to meet the second flight in the same position. From signals intercepted it was apparent that the Sunderland had effected a rendezvous but that the Glenn Martin had failed to do so.

48.   I was deeply concerned to learn from subsequent signals that only 1 Skua and 4 Hurricanes succeeded in reaching Malta.

49.   So far as I can judge at the moment it would appear that the aircraft met with an unexpected easterly wind of considerable force and that in addition a marked reduction of visibility in the vicinity of Malta, coupled with the failure of the Skua leading the second flight to receive D/F bearings, accounted for the tragic loss of so many pilots and their aircraft.

50.   Had I entertained any suspicions that weather conditions were liable to prove adverse, I should not have hesitated to proceed further east in order to make certain of achieving the object of the operation.

51.   From the information available I felt satisfied that a reasonable margin of safety existed since the range of the Hurricanes in still air had been given as 521 and the distance to be flown was 400.

56.   Admiral Commanding NAS's 1252 was also received reporting *Newcastle*'s departure at 1230 and giving her expected time of arrival at Malta as 0930 (Zone 2), 19 November. At 1749 I informed C-in-C, Mediterranean, that there was no evidence to suggest that operation WHITE had been observed by the enemy, and that the westerly gale then blowing should afford good cover for *Newcastle*.

58.   Shortly afterwards, AM 1800 was received stating that reports had been received pointing to the *Admiral Scheer* being in the vicinity of the Azores and ordering *Renown, Ark Royal* and other units at my discretion to proceed to Gibraltar at maximum speed, refuel and proceed thence to the Azores. Withdrawal of support for *Newcastle* was accepted, and operation COLLAR would be deferred if necessary. In reply I stated that by proceeding without a destroyer screen *Renown* and *Ark Royal* could proceed at a somewhat higher speed, provided the situation justified the additional submarine risks.

59.   Speed was increased to 12 knots at 2006 and to 13 knots at 2035. At 2100 I received Admiralty's 2025/17 ordering me to retain the destroyers.

---

[1]Glen L. Martin Maryland (USA): medium bomber/reconnaissance, intended for France.

18 November

61. AM 0135 addressed to the NOIC, Malta, was received at 0220 stating that long distance reconnaissance must be concentrated on preventing the interception of *Newcastle* by superior forces.

19 November

68. At 0230, as the Fleet was about to enter Gibraltar Bay, AM 0140 was received cancelling the previous instructions for ships to proceed to the Azores. . . .

97. *To his wife*

15 November 1940

We are off again on a party to the East to fly a lot of Hurricanes in *Argus* into Malta – a repetition of the job we did before, but then I had *Valiant* with me. However after the knock the Itis have had[1] we ought not to have much trouble except it is a full moon which is the worst possible time for these adventures. Douglas-Pennant came in yesterday on a smallish boat[2] and had lunch with me. I had letters from Andrew B., Bill Ford and Geoffrey Blake who are all most indignant at Dudley North being made a scapegoat. Geoffrey said he had had been doing his damnedest to get the people outside the Admiralty to drop this stupid French policy and hoped I would continue to air my views on the subject. This I don't fail to do – by signal when the matter is urgent and invariably in my letters of proceedings. . . . Unfortunately that blasted Spanish Mail plane passed astern of us this afternoon and I bet the blighter has reported us. What with French and Spanish aircraft mucking about over this narrow gut it is practically impossible to keep one's movements hidden. If they spot and bomb us tomorrow afternoon that may bring those cruisers along[3]. Nothing I would like better if only I hadn't got that old pantechnicon of an *Argus* to look after. She has got no aircraft – except the Hurricanes for Malta – and once they are flown off they can't land back on her again and she has only got two small guns sticking out of her very plain black behind. No I can't say I am very attached to *Argus*. Incidentally she can only do about 18 knots. . . .

---

[1] The severe damage done to three battleships at Taranto by the FAA on 11–12 Nov.
[2] Cdre C. E. Douglas-Pennant: Capt 1935; *Effingham* 1939; CSO, *Pyramus*, Kirkwall 1940; *Despatch* June 1940 & Cdre, W Indies; N SO to C-in-C Home Forces April 1942; RA 1944; NEPTUNE; CNSO, SAC, SEAC Nov 1944.
[3] Several cruisers had recently moved to Palermo and Messina.

98. *To his wife*

17 November 1940

At last my luck was out – damnably so! Of 2 Skuas and 12 Hurricanes that we flew off to Malta only 1 Skua and 4 Hurricanes have arrived. The rest either couldn't find Malta or ran out of fuel and have come down in the sea and I fear the chance of their pilots being picked up is very small. It's a damnable business. In view of the presence of those Italian ships I asked *Argus* last night what was the furthest distance from Malta she could fly off the Hurricanes. Actually we were some 10 miles further towards Malta than the position she gave. So they either experienced some quite unexpected headwinds or it was thick weather there and they could not find it. Whatever it was the expedition has been a frightful failure and not only cost the lives of so many pilots but deprived Malta of a much needed reinforcement. I have just asked *Argus* if she can account for the disaster and she has replied that all machines should have had ample fuel to reach Malta. Well it is a setback and no mistake and just when everything seemed to be going so well. Apparently the Itis never spotted the operation at all so at least we have had no shadows or bombers and by now we ought to be almost out of range of the latter. That's a small account! The object was to get 2 Skuas and 12 Hurricanes to Malta and in that we have failed.

99. *To his wife*

20 November 1940

You can imagine my *fury* when I got a signal to say that we were to start intercepting French merchant ships next day! We are on the point of starting the most important and complicated operation, my destroyer chaps are worn out and sadly battered by the gale and in fact it was an absolute outrage to suggest such a thing. Both Dudley and I sent signals on the subject asking to have it postponed. I went so far as to say that I considered everything possible should be done to avoid adding to the difficulties of those responsible for executing the most complicated operation. Well last night the reply came that HM Government was determined etc. and it was to be done tomorrow but was not to delay the main operation. That was a nice thing to add. Whatever happens I am bound to be wrong. It makes me quite sick of the whole business and the sooner I retire along with Dudley the better. . . . I went over to *Argus* and saw Rushbrooke[1] who told me he couldn't understand the failure of the

[1]Capt E. G. N. Rushbrooke: Capt 1936; *Guardian* 1939; *Argus* 1940; *Eagle* April 1941; Cdre & DNI Nov 1942; Actg RA July 1945.

Hurricanes. He never had the slightest doubt [that] the position we flew off from was quite satisfactory and wind measurement gave a westerly wind of 20 knots at 2000 feet. He believes the fighter pilots did not know how to run their engines economically and that consequently the figures given by the Air Ministry were entirely wrong. Apparently the Observer in the second Skua, the party who failed to find Malta at all, was a sub-lieut RNVR doing his first operational flight. That I consider a positive scandal. I shall send in a pretty hot report about this and suggest that if it is to be repeated then the Navy must take over the machines and assume all responsibility. At present we take them to the spot and they are supposed to do the rest.

About Dakar – Dudley North has now heard from the Admiralty to say that TL see no reason to change their decision and he is to be relieved. To me they merely replied that the contents of my letter had been noted. That was the one in which I said I wished to make it perfectly clear that it was never my intention to interfere with the French ships and I entirely agreed with the views expressed by Dudley North[1]. He and I are both furious about it and the dirty trick of making us naval officers responsible for a damn bad political blunder. Dudley and I passed that on to Anthony Eden too[2]. Thank heavens I have no axe to grind and I will never be a blasted yes man but continue to say what I think and if they sling me out of it it won't break my heart because I have had a very good run for my money. . . . However there appears to be no sign of it at present except the arrival of Fat Fred[3] in his boat but apparently he comes under my orders. . . .

Later.

Just heard from Andrew that the party arrived safely so that's alright and one feels slightly rewarded for all the labour and anxiety. The Admiralty always seem to take these expeditions more or less for granted and quite ignore the fact that we do them with a collection of strange bodies hastily collected and without any previous training. If I only had a standing party of ships and little boats that I really knew and who knew me I should fear nothing at all but it is having to deal with strangers all the time that makes things so difficult. . . . It is rather odd the number of things one has to attend to in this job. An intercepted reply from the

[1]Nos. 77, 80, 84.
[2]R. Anthony Eden (later Earl of Avon, 1898–1977): double 1st Oxford; journalist, art collector; King's Royal Rifle Corps 1915–18 & youngest brig-maj 1918; MP Warwick & Leamington 1923; junior appts 1920s; Ld Privy Seal 1933; extensive experience in disarmament talks; Minr for League of Nations 1935; FS 1935–8; Sec State for Dominions 1939; Sec State for War 1940; FS 1940–5, 1951–5; PM 1955–7; earldom 1961.
[3]Vice Adm Edward-Collins.

Admiralty to Andrew B. suggests that the latter has been protesting about these French adventures. I though the Admiralty reply was distinctly weak. Apparently I have got to tackle the *Jean Bart* and *Richelieu* should they come into the Med and that mark you between a number of important operations now in hand which hardly gives me any breathing space.

100. *Report of Proceedings, 19–29 November 1940*

5 December 1940

19 November

3.   Soon after arrival, I received AM 0150/19, instructing the Admiral Commanding, NAS, to be prepared to carry out the interception of a French convoy on 20 November, but not to act without further instructions. Until such orders were received, Force H could be placed at four hours' notice for steam and *Royal Sovereign*[1] was to be maintained in a condition to proceed to sea if necessary.

4.   In view of the extreme importance attached to the successful accomplishment of operation COLLAR by all authorities, an importance which had doubly increased since the breaking out of hostilities between Italy and Greece, both the Admiral Commanding, NAS, and myself felt it imperative that nothing be done which was likely to prejudice the execution of this operation. The destroyers of the 8th and 13th Flotillas had not only taken part in both operations COAT and WHITE during the preceding month, besides carrying out routine patrols and escort duties, but had also a severe dusting during WHITE and sustained damage. It appeared to us both that a period for rest and repairs was important for these ships, both from the point of view of the efficiency of the personnel and of the fighting efficiency of the ships.

5.   I was anxious that the vigilance and fighting efficiency of the Force should be at its highest since I considered it more than probable that the Italian Fleet might attempt to compensate themselves for the heavy losses sustained at Taranto by the interception of Force H by superior forces during operation COLLAR.

6.   It was also my intention that the M/T ships and corvettes passing through to the Eastern Mediterranean should be routed partly along the North African coast in order better to conceal their destination and character. An incident with the French at this stage might well provoke retaliation which would not only necessitate a strong escort for the convoy

[1]*Royal Sovereign*: 1916, 29,150t, 8×15in, 12×6in, 8×4in, *c*. 20k.

but might also result in the bombing of Gibraltar harbour at a time when it was congested with ships.

7.   These points were represented to the Admiralty, who replied that in consequence of a decision of HM Government, interception was to be carried out at once, on 21 November, or if there was no convoy passing, on 22 November, and left it to the   discretion of the Admiral Commanding, NAS, what forces he employed, providing that operation COLLAR was not delayed.

20 November

13.   Owing to the presence of U-boats in the vicinity of Freetown, the Admiral Commanding, NAS, was directed to sail two destroyers to meet *Furious* and escort her to Freetown and Takoradi[1]. *Foxhound* and *Fortune* were accordingly detailed for this duty.

Kelvin and Jaguar[2] were sailed from England to take their places in operation COLLAR.

14.   Information having been received on the previous day through the Consul-General, Tangier, that a visit from Italian bombers might be expected, steps were taken to prepare a suitable reception. No raid materialised, however, and the only result was that the daily French reconnaissance machine received a much warmer welcome than was his due. A/A gunnery from ships was again disappointing, the bursts being as usual low and behind.

15.   The information available at this time regarding the disposition of Italian surface ships was scanty. Of the three remaining undamaged battleships, one had been reported at Spezia 7 days ago; the other two had not been located for even longer. There were indications, but no definite information, that the number of cruisers in the Western basin had been increased.

15a.   In the light of the Taranto episode, it appeared to me that the obvious strategy for the Italians to adopt was to reinforce the Western basin, where they could achieve a considerable superiority over Force B & F, which would be forced to stand and fight owing to the presence of the slow MT ships. For this reason I requested Admiralty approval for *Royal Sovereign* to take part in the operation.

I also proposed to the Admiralty that *Despatch* should be included in this operation. This latter proposal was approved.

---

[1]*Furious*: 1917–18, initially as light battlecruiser, converted to carrier, finally completed 1925, 22,450t, 33 aircraft, 12×4in, 31k.
[2]*Kelvin, Jaguar* (sunk E Med 1942 *U652*): 1939, 1690t, 6×4.7in, 10tt, 36k.

21 November

19.　Since the opposition which might be expected from surface forces appeared to be greater than from bombing attacks, I decided to abandon the attack I had intended to carry out on Alghero aerodrome in order to conserve the TSR aircraft for reconnaissance and torpedo-bomber striking forces should the need arise. The bombing of the south and west Italian air bases by the RAF was reported to be impracticable on account of scarcity of aircraft.

20.　*Manchester* (flying the Flag of Vice Admiral L.E. Holland, CB, VAC 18th Cruiser Squadron) and HT *Franconia*, escorted by *Forester* arrived at Gibraltar at 1830[1].

In order to preserve the secrecy of the operation, always a particularly difficult problem in Gibraltar, I gave instructions that not more than 200 men were to be seen on deck on *Franconia* at one time during daylight hours, from the time of passing Tarifa until they had transferred to *Manchester* and *Southampton*[2] for onward passage. I arranged that this transfer should take place after dark on 24 November. No leave was given and no inter-ship or shore communication was allowed except for those on duty. Special arrangements were made for the supply of fresh provisions, collection of mails, etc.

22 November

21.　... Admiralty stated that *Royal Sovereign* was urgently required to join the N. Atlantic escort force and it was not desired to employ her in COLLAR unless this was considered essential. The message added that with the exception of an additional battleship, the concentration of Italian surface forces in the Western basin did not appear to be unusual.

I replied to this message that it appeared the Italians could concentrate 3 battleships, 5 to 7 8-inch cruisers and other light forces in the Western basin between the time Force H left Gibraltar and the critical period during the passage south of Sardinia. This force could join action either with Force H, consisting of *Renown,* three modern and one old 6-inch cruisers, who would be saddled with a 15-knot convoy and an aircraft carrier to protect, or else with *Ramillies, Newcastle* and *Coventry* proceeding to join Force H at mid-day. The presence of *Royal Sovereign* would allow Force H to support *Ramillies*'s force should it be threatened before concentration was effected. I therefore considered the inclusion of *Royal*

---

[1]Vice Adm Lancelot E. Holland: Capt 1926; RA Jan 1938; RA, 2BS, 1939; VA & joint head, Admy-Air Min staff cttee Dec 1939; VA 18CS April 1940; C-in-C, Battlecruiser Force May 1941; lost in *Hood. Franconia*: 1923, 20,175gt, 17k, Cunard White Star Line.
[2]*Southampton*: 1937, 9100t, 12×6in, 8×4in, 6tt, 32k; sunk C Med Jan 1941, Ger a/c.

Sovereign in this operation essential unless the possibility of Italian concentration of forces could definitely be excluded.

The C-in-C, Mediterranean, considered my appreciation unduly pessimistic and the chance of any concentration against Force H more remote now than in any previous operation since HATS. He added that three Mediterranean Fleet battleships would be within range. This I interpreted as moral rather than material support.

Admiralty approval of my proposal was received but further examination of *Royal Sovereign*'s boilers showed she could not be ready for sea in time to take part in the operation.

22. A favourable opportunity for interception of a French merchant ship being presented, *Despatch* (flying the Broad Pendant of Commodore C.E. Douglas-Pennant, DSC), *Faulknor* and *Forester* proceeded to sea at 1020 to carry out this operation.

Manchester was brought to short notice for steam from 0100/23 in case she should be required to support *Despatch*.

The operation was carried out without incident, however, and the force returned to Gibraltar with the French merchant ship *Charles Plumier*[1] in company, at 0730/23.

23 November

24. . . . Vice Admiral Holland . . . said that he was most strongly of the opinion that *Manchester* and *Southampton* should not be included in Force F for the following reasons:–

(a) Extreme importance was attached to the safe and timely arrival of the RAF personnel at Alexandria. The best way to ensure this was for the cruisers to proceed independently and rely on their high speed and mobility for the achievement of their object.

(b) With so many men on board, the ships were not in a fit condition to fight. If obliged to engage casualties might be heavy and the object of this part of the operation compromised.

24a. I informed Admiral Holland that I fully agreed his ships would not be in a satisfactory state for action and that the achievement of one of our objects, namely the safe passage of personnel, was more certain to succeed if the cruisers proceeded independently. On the other hand, I considered it was essential for the achievement of both objects, viz., the passage of personnel, and convoy with corvettes, that we should make a show of force, since this was more likely than anything else to deter the Italians from attempting to interfere with the operation.

[1]*Charles Plumier*: 1938, 4504gt, CG d'Armements Maritimes, Havre.

24b.   At Admiral Holland's request I sent the following signal to the C-in-C, Mediterranean, repeated to Admiralty and NOIC, Malta:–

> CS18 asks to be informed whether safe passage of MT ships or safe passage of air personnel embarked in cruisers should receive priority should circumstances arise which make a decision necessary after Force F has parted company for passage of Narrows.

– to which the latter replied 'Personnel'.

A further instruction on this point was received from the Admiralty which read as follows:–

> The decision given in your 1415/23 is concurred with, subject to over-riding consideration that if Italian surface forces are in sight, action taken by warships carrying Army or RAF personnel must be the same as if personnel were not on board.

25 November

26.   Following the appearance of the *Admiral Scheer* in the N. Atlantic and in view of the probable existence of 5 enemy armed raiders elsewhere, the Admiralty announced that a redistribution of forces would be made in order to provide hunting groups and escort forces for the greater security of communications. It was noted that Force H was little affected by the changes, the alteration being that *Enterprise* (temporarily detached for service in the S. Atlantic during the absence of *Hawkins*[1]) would not return to the Force and that *Ark Royal* would be relieved by *Formidable* when that ship had completed working-up.

27.   *Duncan* (Captain (D), 13th. Flotilla), *Hotspur* and corvettes *Peony, Salvia, Gloxinia* and *Hyacinth* sailed at 0001 to rendezvous at 0800 . . . with *Velox, Wrestler* and *Vidette,* escorting the MT ships *New Zealand Star, Clan Forbes* and *Clan Fraser*[2]. These MT ships, taking part in operation COLLAR, proceeded eastward through the Straits without calling at Gibraltar, passing Europa Point at 0200. After effecting a rendezvous *Velox* and *Wrestler* returned to Gibraltar.

28.   Transfer of personnel from *Franconia* to *Manchester* and *Southampton* commenced at 0400 and proceeded according to plan. Approximately 660 were embarked in *Manchester* and 760 in *Southampton.*

29.   The remainder of Force H, comprising *Renown, Manchester,*

---

[1]*Hawkins*: 1919, 9800t, 7×7.5in, 4×4in, 4tt, 29.5k.
[2]Capt (D), 13DF was Capt G. F. Stevens-Guille: Capt Dec 1939; Capt (D) March 1940; *Victory* 1941; *Cardiff* 1942; *Durban* 1943; Capt of F, Med F *Hannibal* Dec 1943. *New Zealand Star*: 1935, 10740gt, Blue Star Line. *Clan Forbes* (1938), *Clan Fraser* (1939): 7529gt, 17k, Clan Line.

Despatch, Ark Royal, Southampton, Sheffield, Faulknor, Fury,
Firedrake, Forester, Kelvin, Jaguar, Encounter and *Wishart* sailed at
0700 to carry out operation COLLAR, . . .

26 November

34.   A/S patrols and a reconnaissance to locate the MT convoy were
flown off at dawn. Shortly afterwards *Despatch* was detached to escort
the convoy whilst on passage off the N. African coast.

39.   Course was altered to the southward at 1450 to cover the convoy,
and at 1710 *Manchester, Wishart, Encounter* and *Fury* were detached to
join the latter. . . .

40.   At dusk, course was altered to 085°, speed 15½ knots, with the
object of maintaining a position approximately 25 miles on the port bow
of the convoy. As far as was known, neither of the two forces had been
observed by shadowing aircraft during the day.

27 November

46.   Nine Swordfish were flown off at 0745 to cover an area of maximum depth to the eastward, up to 100 miles to the northward, and 50
miles to the westward. A/S and fighter patrols were also flown off, after
which course was altered to the westward to gain touch with the convoy.
At this time the wind was from 120°, force 3, visibility good, blue sky
but considerable cloud.

48.   The M/T convoy was sighted at 0940 bearing 250°, 15 miles.
Southampton and *Firedrake* were then detached to join the convoy
escort. It was learned that the four corvettes had been detached at 1800
the previous day, having been unable to make good the speed of the convoy.

At 1005 a report of 5 cruisers and 5 destroyers . . . was received by V/S
from *Ark Royal.* This position was 60 miles 045° from *Renown.* It was
not clear whether this was an enemy report, and *Ark Royal* was asked to
confirm. It appeared more probable that the report referred to Force D,
which consisted of 1 battleship, 3 cruisers and 4 destroyers. Nevertheless
all ships were at once ordered to have steam for full speed.

49.   Ten minutes later a further report of 2 battleships, 7 destroyers,
course 225°, 10 miles to the north-eastward of the original report, was
received from *Ark Royal.* . . .

50.   I at once ordered *Despatch* and *Duncan* and *Hotspur* to proceed to
the south-eastward with the Convoy at full speed. *Ark Royal* was ordered
to prepare a striking force and act independently, with *Kelvin* and *Jaguar*
as a screen. All remaining units were ordered to join me and proceed at
maximum available speed to concentrate with Force D. My position,

course and speed was communicated to *Ramillies* with instructions to join me, reporting position, course and speed. *Ramillies* was also ordered to detach *Coventry* to join the Convoy.

51.   At this stage my intention was to concentrate as rapidly as possible and then endeavour to bring the enemy battle fleet to action. Cruisers and destroyers were stationed on a bearing 050° 5 and 3 miles respectively from *Renown*, i.e., on the assumed bearing of the enemy battlefleet.

52.   At 1025 a further report was received of 6 cruisers, 8 destroyers, course 250°. It was by no means clear whether this referred to one of the enemy forces previously reported, or to an additional force.

53.   At 1050 I ordered *Ark Royal* to fly off the striking force and attack. A few minutes later a Sunderland flying boat was seen approaching. In reply to a signal, she reported that *Ramillies* then bore 070° 34 miles from *Renown*. The Sunderland was then ordered to shadow and report the composition of the enemy. By this time *Renown* was proceeding at 28 knots.

54.   At 1115, since concentration with Force D was assured, speed was reduced to 24 knots in order to maintain a position between the enemy and the convoy until concentration had been effected. Light forces were also re-disposed on a bearing of 010°.

55.   At 1125 an air report was received that the course of one enemy battleship, one cruiser and 6 destroyers was 075°, and at 1125[?] another air report gave the course of 2 enemy battleships, 3 cruisers and 4 destroyers as 020°. These reports did nothing to clarify the position, either as to the composition or the movements of the enemy force. It still appeared quite possible that I was opposed by three enemy battleships in addition to a considerable force of cruisers and destroyers.

56.   Three minutes later the masts of Force D were sighted from *Renown*, . . . As the enemy had apparently altered course to the eastward, speed was again increased to 28 knots and course altered to 050°. I also ordered *Ramillies,* who had been steering towards *Renown*, to steer 045° in order that she should not lose ground in the chase that appeared likely to develop. Cruisers and destroyers were re-disposed on a bearing of 040°.

57.   At 1140 I ordered the VAC, 18th CS, to take all the cruisers (less *Despatch* and *Coventry*) under his orders. Four minutes later a report was received that *Duncan,* escorting the MT convoy, had lost water in all boilers and was stopped. As there was no vessel with A/S gear in company with the convoy, I ordered *Wishart,* who was finding difficulty in maintaining the speed of the force and was also short of fuel, to proceed to join the convoy.

59.   The nearest reported position of the enemy battleships was such

that at 1152, I deemed it advisable to order *Ramillies* who was several miles ahead and steering a parallel course to *Renown* to join me since a turn towards by the enemy might have brought her under concentrated fire and unable, owing to the limited range of her guns, to reply.

60. At this time the prospects of bringing the enemy to action appeared favourable:–

(a) We had effected our concentration, of which the enemy appeared to be unaware, since no shadowers had been sighted or reported by RDF, and his speed had been reported as 14 to 18 knots, which suggested he was still awaiting the reports of reconnaissance.

(b) The sun was immediately astern and would thus give us the advantage of light.

(c) As the TSR striking force had just been sighted on passage to the enemy, there seemed every possibility of a synchronised surface and T/B attack provided the enemy did not retire at once.

61. At 1205 smoke was sighted from *Renown* bearing 006°, and I at once altered course to the northward. Three minutes later masts were sighted on the same bearing. These were shortly reported by *Berwick* as three *Zara* class cruisers[1].

62. Simultaneously I was informed that *Renown* had a bearing overheating on one shaft and that in consequence the speed on this shaft had to be reduced. The net effect of this reduction, coupled with paravanes being streamed and the ship being seven months out of dock, was to limit *Renown*'s speed to a little over 27 knots.

63. An air report was received that the enemy battleships bore 015° from *Berwick*, 54, 000 yards. By this time it was known that they consisted of one *Littorio* and one *Cavour*[2]. *Renown* was now ahead of *Ramillies* and rapidly increasing distance.

64. Fire was opened by the enemy 8" cruisers at 1221, followed one minute later by our own cruisers and another minute later by *Renown* at a range of approximately 27,000 yards.

65. Almost immediately after opening fire the enemy cruisers and destroyers commenced to emit dense smoke and retired behind it. Conditions for gunfire became extremely difficult.

66. At 1244 H/A bursts were observed in the sky on the starboard bow and it appeared probable that the T/B striking force was making its attack.

---

[1]*Zara, Fiume, Pola, Gorizia*: 1931–2, 11,500–11,900t, 8×8in, 12×3.9in, 32k; first 3 sunk 27 March 1941 off Cape Matapan; *Gorizia* scuttled Sept 1943.

[2]In fact *Vittorio Veneto*: and *Giulio Cesare*.

67. At 1250 two enemy battleships were reported in sight from *Renown*. As these appeared to be on a closing course I decided to concentrate with *Ramillies* and informed her accordingly. Immediately afterwards, however, when it was evident that the enemy's battleships were turning away, I negatived this movement and *Renown* continued on her course at maximum speed in an endeavour to close the enemy. *Ramillies* at this time was making good a very creditable 20.7 knots.

68. At this time the VAC, 18th CS, was forced by the fire of the enemy battleships to haul off slightly to starboard, but a few minutes later resumed the chase. Ranging rounds were fired by *Renown* but fell far short.

69. At 1310 the situation was as follows:–

(a) Firing had ceased owing to the enemy drawing out of range.

(b) The heavy smoke made by the enemy prevented accurate fire during the chase, and as far as could be ascertained, no damage had been inflicted.

(c) In reply to a signal from me to the VAC, 18th. CS, at 1308 – 'Is there any hope of catching cruiser?' – I was informed 'No'. (In a later message the VAC, 18th CS, estimated the enemy had 3 knots excess speed.)

(d) It was known that the T/B striking force had attacked. No reports of the results had been received, but it was evident that the speed of the enemy had not been materially reduced. Consequently it was presumed that the attack had been unsuccessful, which was not unexpected.

70. In view of our rapid approach to the enemy coast, now 30 miles distant, I had to decide whether a continuation of the chase was justified and likely to be profitable. . . .

71. . . . I was being led towards a dense smokescreen in close proximity to his air, submarine and light forces base at Cagliari; the possibility of this being a premeditated move to draw my ships into a dangerous area could not be disregarded. Should any of my ships be damaged, the support of my whole force would undoubtedly be required to effect their extrication, and this could only be provided by neglecting my main object, and allowing the convoy to proceed unescorted through the Narrows. Further, the cruisers and destroyers reported to the NW might already be working round towards the Convoy and *Ark Royal*.

72. As the enemy was outside gun range the sole remaining method of reducing his speed was by air attack. I estimated that the second T/B attack could not take place until 1530 or 1600, by which time the enemy fleet could be under cover of the shore defences of Cagliari.

73. I therefore decided that my correct action was to discontinue the chase and make contact with the convoy before dark; only thus could the necessary protection against T/B aircraft attack at dusk and the essential escort for the passage of the Narrows be provided. I consequently ordered all units to withdraw on a course of 130°.

75. After proceeding on the withdrawal course for 20 minutes, an air report was received at 1335 of a damaged cruiser stopped 10 miles from the enemy coast. I considered the desirability of detaching cruisers to search for and attack this cruiser. Whatever force was sent for this purpose, it would be necessary for the main force to remain in a position to support that force and prevent them being cut off by enemy forces; this could only be done at the expense of jeopardising the security of the convoy. Further, isolated ships in such close proximity to the enemy coast would be singled out for air attack, and if seriously damaged would have involved all my forces to effect their extrication.

76. There was no evidence that the damaged ship would remain stopped; (in fact subsequent air reconnaissance showed her stoppage was only temporary).

77. I therefore decided that the detachment of a small force was unjustifiable. I instructed *Ark Royal*, however, to endeavour to sink her if this was considered feasible.

78. At 1345 I ordered the VAC, 18th CS, to proceed with *Manchester* and *Southampton* to join the convoy and provide surface and A/A protection.

79. All ships reported no damage with the exception of *Berwick*, who had received two 8" hits aft, one of which passed through the training space of 'Y' turret, putting the turret out of action. Casualties were 1 officer and 6 ratings killed, 2 ratings seriously and 7 ratings slightly wounded.

81. At 1405 RDF reports indicated that a bombing attack was imminent. Simultaneously *Greyhound* observed an aircraft fall into the water astern of the Fleet and proceeded to investigate. . . .

82. The raid developed at 1435 when 10 aircraft attacked at a height of about 13,000 feet. A number of bombs were jettisoned a long distance from the Fleet as a result of interception by our fighters, but the latter were unable to break up or disturb the enemy formation. Bomb aiming on this occasion was most inaccurate, the bombs falling in one long stick from a position about 3 miles on the port bow to 3000 yards on the port beam, where the last few bombs narrowly missed a destroyer on the screen. A/A fire was ineffective, but contrary to normal practice some of the bursts were undoubtedly over owing to the use of arbitrary height corrections and cross-prediction. One Fulmar was lost during this attack.

83.   Shortly after this a report was received from *Ark Royal* that a second T/B striking force of 9 Swordfish had been sent at 1410 to attack the enemy battleships, and that a force of 7 Skuas would take off at about 1500 to dive bomb the damaged enemy cruiser.

85.   Owing to the necessity of diverting the convoy to the southward of the route intended, and also to the slower speed made good than had been anticipated, it was now evident that the rendezvous with the 1st Division, 1st Battle Squadron, could not be reached at the appointed hour. There was also a possibility that the enemy might endeavour to attack the convoy while rounding the northern end of the Skerki Bank. I therefore asked the VAC, 18th CS, if in the circumstances he would prefer to make the passage through the Skerki Channel while I provided cover to the northward. He replied in the affirmative. I therefore informed the C-in-C, Mediterranean, accordingly.

86.   Indications of approaching air raids continued intermittently from 1530 until 1635, when three groups were reported closing. Three minutes later several bomb splashes were observed some 8 or 10 miles away, presumably in consequence of attack by our fighters.

87.   The attack was carried out in three waves, each of five aircraft, at about 14,000 feet, and was concentrated on *Ark Royal*. Bombing accuracy on this occasion was good and there were several near misses among the 30 bombs that fell around *Ark Royal*, but she emerged untouched with all guns firing. A/A fire was again ineffective.

88.   A report was received from Ark Royal at 1705 that the second T/B striking force had attacked a group of three cruisers and had obtained one hit[1].

89.   At 1710 all units were ordered to join up with their respective forces for passage to Malta or return to Gibraltar. Force F then proceeded under the orders of the VAC, 18th CS, Force B remaining in company. No further enemy air activity occurred. . . .

90.   A further report was received from *Ark Royal* at 1810 that the Skua striking force had failed to locate the damaged enemy cruiser but had attacked three cruisers of the *Condottieri* class[2], obtaining two very near misses, and that an RO 43 float plane[3] was shot down on the return passage.

91.   At dusk Force B altered course to the north-eastward and an hour later to the westward, speed being increased to 19 knots. By this time it was clear that the enemy battle fleet was retiring to the northward up the E. Coast of Sardinia.

---

[1]No hit was obtained.
[2]Light cruisers, several types.
[3]Meridionali Ro43: seaplane, usually carried on cruisers and battleships.

92. After sunset *Berwick* held a funeral service and buried at sea the officer and six ratings killed in the action.

29 November

97. At 0900 *Renown, Berwick, Sheffield, Faulknor, Fury, Forester* and *Firedrake* increased speed to 24 knots and proceeded ahead. *Ramillies, Ark Royal, Despatch, Newcastle, Duncan, Wishart, Encounter, Kelvin* and *Jaguar* continued at 18 knots.

99. The leading group entered harbour at 1430, followed an hour later by the remaining units. . . .

101. *To his wife*

25 November 1940

Well here we are off on a much more ambitious operation than we have attempted hitherto and with rather less than the usual force with which to achieve our object. Passing more ships and men and this time transports from west to east. All a bit tricky as it's a slow speed job and if the Itis like to concentrate they would of course bring a greatly superior force, be able to get at us before Andrew could possibly come to our assistance. But they have shown no initiative so far and I trust they will continue as usual. The worst of the job I have to do is that it is always our object to avoid meeting them if possible – we want nothing to interrupt the safe passage of whatever we have to pass through. It will be a welcome relief if we could go out with a high speed force and just look for the toads and it would do us all a lot of good. . . .

102. *To his wife*

28 November 1940

Well well, we did have a day of it yesterday. And what do you think – the old Bo[1] and I in action together against the Iti fleet and *Defender* nipping across our stern or round our bows and the Old Bo and I waving to one another like mad. I could see his old red face grinning away on the bridge and it did me a world of good. . . .

All was quiet until 10.20 yesterday 27th., when we got a report from *Ark Royal* that there were two battleships, one *Littorio* and one *Cavour* class, six cruisers and a number of destroyers about 40 miles to the N of us. There was I still 90 miles away from *Ramillies, Berwick, Newcastle,*

[1] Lieut John Somerville, his son.

Coventry and five destroyers including *Defender* who were coming to meet us from Malta. What I had foretold had come to pass and there was I in a pretty sticky position. A *Littorio* is equivalent to a *Nelson* and *Cavour* is about the same age as *Renown* and like her reconstructed and modernised. So even if I succeeded in concentrating with *Ramillies*, I was outmatched and I had this appalling slow convoy to protect! I told the latter to steer SE with *Despatch* and two destroyers. I ordered *Coventry* to join the convoy and then steamed at full speed with the rest of my party to join *Ramillies*. I was very relieved when she came in sight . . . And I knew that at any rate we could not be mopped up in penny numbers. . . .

We stood to the S until about 2.45 p.m. when the Iti bombers came over and delivered a rather rotten attack, all the bombs fell a long way clear except some near our destroyers on one side. *Defender* luckily was the other side but the next attack about an hour later was a stinker. They picked out *Ark Royal* as principal target and she had a very lucky escape. She was entirely obliterated by enormous columns of water from which she would emerge with her guns blazing furiously. Also our A/A fire was bum, all short again and I certainly don't know what to do about it to get it better. About 5.30 p.m. we managed to my great relief to connect again with the convoy and after dark we separated sending them in charge of Lancelot [Holland] whilst I turned back for Gib. A very dark smooth night and we were lucky to escape the attentions of E-boats, submarines and torpedo aircraft. In fact we were damn lucky throughout the day if you ask me. I had one bad moment during the afternoon just before the second air attack came in and I had to decide which course to turn to bring all guns to bear. Well the best one put *Defender* on the side the attack was coming from and I felt rather unhappy and then kicked myself for allowing any such consideration to enter my mind. After all just before the action started in the morning I nipped down to my sea cabin for a few seconds to say a good prayer for you, the Bo and myself, so the whole matter was in better hands than mine. It is a strange sensation when you are in a situation such as I was and had to make decisions which if wrong or right for that matter might have a decisive effect on the war. If the Italians had succeeded in sinking *Renown* and *Ark Royal* just think how that would have buoyed them up. As it was they ran like stags in spite of their superiority . . . And then when I get back to Gib I have this board of enquiry[1]. Well this last little affair will show that I am amply justified in assuming the Italians *could* effect a concentration in the western Med. It was damn lucky they didn't do it while I only had

---

[1] Into the loss of the Hurricanes flown off *Argus* for Malta.

Renown, Sheffield and *Despatch* with *Ark Royal* and *Argus* to look after. We might have been badly had. . . .

In addition to the above we shot down two and possibly three Iti aircraft and a bloody Frenchman. Our fighters saw the latter apparently shadowing *Renown,* swooped down on him and shot him up. . . . The Admiralty as usual appears to be critical. Why did not the second flight of torpedo bombers attack the battleships? When did I first learn that a *Littorio* had been struck by a torpedo and so forth? Well the answer is quite simple – the second flight was sent off to attack the battleships but it was decided that they were too heavily screened so attacked the cruisers instead. I don't know the details yet but I imagine he[1] was quite justified in as much as I know that he has a lot of very green pilots and they have had no practice for weeks in doing these attacks. Unless they are continually practiced you never get good results. As regards the second question the signal we had reporting the result of the first attack was corrupt and appeared to refer only to the composition of the enemy battle fleet. As we had information that they were retiring at high speed I assumed that the first torpedo attack was ineffective. As it happened I should not have taken any different action as it was not possible for *Renown* to engage two battleships with any chance of success and *Ramillies* would have been some 30 or 40 miles away or more before we could catch up. But I shouldn't be surprised if some [people?] at the Admiralty don't argue that I should have continued the chase. Well supposing *Renown*'s speed had been reduced by a lucky hit, torpedo or bomb, the Italians could then have turned and polished us off easily and think how that would have cheered them up. Well it will all be plotted and argued over and produced in histories of the war and provided I can sit quietly with the trees and the dickies I shan't worry . . . I have no ambition as you know and unlike Nelson don't crave for glory. All I want to do is the best I can to help the country as *I* see it. I have an urge to throw caution to the wind and take a chance on things but I stifle it when I feel that to do so would not be the right or best service I could do the country. I don't suggest by any means that my judgement is infallible but where that judgement leads me I go and don't think of personal consequences . . . Occasionally I get a bun from TL but usually it is carping criticism and I feel that if they don't feel that I am the right one for this job then they had better get rid of me.

---

[1] The CO of the second flight.

103.   *To his wife*

30 November 1940

Apparently TL do not approve of my actions in Wednesday's engagement because Cork and Orrery and George Lyon[1] are arriving here by a destroyer on Tuesday to hold a Court of Enquiry on the action and in particular why it was broken off and why the second torpedo bomber flight did not attack the battleships. So that's that. I seem to be entirely surrounded by Boards of Enquiry and I imagine the net result must be that I shall be seeing you before long. So that is something cheerful anyway. Mind you I am not prejudging myself but knowing old Cork I imagine he will take the view that I ought to have gone haring after the Itis whatever the disproportion in forces and possible consequences to the achievement of my object. I had a brief conference this morning with the Commanding Officers of ships who were present and asked them to say quite frankly whether they considered we could have continued the action with advantage and they all said no. I have drafted out a summary of my views of the situation and concluded it by saying that I had to resist the temptation of attempting to score a small advantage by sinking an Iti ship at the expense of achieving my object which was to pass the convoy, corvettes and personnel through to the eastern Med. This I accomplished and have had signals of thanks and congratulations from the Governor of Malta[2] and old Ma Ford. It is odd to think that as we came into harbour yesterday the ships and destroyers all cheered and I had all sorts of congratulatory signals and now comes this lovely cold douche. . . .

I spent all today attending the enquiry about the loss of those Hurricanes. The air people at Malta are now trying to make out that a very badly worded message from the Air Ministry indicated they did not agree with the proposed position for flying off. Actually in evidence today it appeared that the pilots of the Hurricanes had no idea what was the economic speed for their machines. They had never been told! Only one knew apparently, and he arrived with plenty of petrol to spare.

Old Dudley North and my staff are simply livid about the whole business. But all the same if it leads me to obscurity along with you I don't really mind for myself.

[1]Vice Adm (later Adm) Sir George H. D'Oyly Lyon: Capt 1922; RA 1934; VA 1938 & C-in-C Africa (Freetown) Sept 1938–41; C-in-C Nore March 1941–July 1943; Adm June 1942; Ret List Aug 1943.

[2]Lt-Gen Sir Frank Dobbie RE: 2Lt 1899; S Africa 1901–2; Capt 1908; W Front 1914–18; SO, WO 1919–20, Aldershot 1920–4; Col 1926; Brig, Egypt 1928–32; Maj-Gen 1932; Cmdt Sch of Mil Engineering 1933–5; GOC Malaya 1935; Govr & C-in-C Malta 1940–2.

104.   *Report of Proceedings, 29 November – 14 December 1940*

19 December 1940

30 November

8.   A signal from the C-in-C, Mediterranean, to the Admiralty, . . . strongly represented the grave dangers of continuing operations in the Mediterranean on our present scale when the air reconnaissance was so far below the acceptable minimum. He observed that as a result, operation COLLAR was carried out with insufficient information and battleships which had remained unlocated for 15 days after their departure from Taranto until met by Force H, were again unlocated after their retreat.

There is no doubt that had adequate air reconnaissance been available prior to COLLAR, more weight might have been given to my appreciation of the possible Italian concentration in the Western Mediterranean.

1 December

10.   Work of preparing material for the Board of Inquiry into COLLAR fully occupied the attention of my staff and myself to the detriment of considering plans for future contemplated operations, in view of the short time which elapsed between the return of Force H to harbour and the expected time of arrival of HMS *Jersey*[1], bringing the principal members of the Board. . . .

3 December

13.   The Board of Inquiry into operation COLLAR opened at 1500, and continued daily until 7 December.

I should like to record my appreciation on the manner in which this Inquiry was conducted, observing that I was present on all occasions when witnesses were under interrogation.

105.   *To his wife*

4 December 1940

This is the second day of the blasted enquiry and I have been asked innumerable questions as you can imagine. I am sticking to my points namely that 1) my principal object was to ensure the safe passage of convoy, personnel and corvettes; 2) when faced with a superior enemy force I attacked them at once, drove them off and only ceased chasing them

[1]*Jersey*: 1939, 1690t, 6×4.7in, 10tt, 36k; mined off Malta 1941.

when I considered that to continue further would not produce any results and would expose my convoy; 3) after ceasing the chase I received a report of a damaged enemy cruiser 10 miles off the coast and decided not to go back as that would have jeopardised the safety of my convoy.

During the enquiry it has been pretty definitely established that the hit on the *Littorio* battleship did not reduce her speed below 25 knots so *Ramillies* could never have caught up. And the damaged cruiser was eventually able to steam at 20 knots so we had little chance of catching her.

George Lyon told Simeon[1] last night that he thought James had put up a damn fine show. Simeon could not finish his talk with him but wants him to know how absolutely livid all the captains are at this being put on me. Whether I did right or wrong the people who were there all seemed to agree that what I did was absolutely right and very well judged. But I am not so sure about old Cork. He suggested some wild things to me: 'Why didn't you ask C-in-C Med to take over the convoy whilst you continued chase?' Reply: 'Because those units were so far away they couldn't possibly have reached the convoy before dark'. And a lot of other equally pointless suggestions . . . I got a reply from DP to my personal signal which merely said 'I appreciate your feelings but in war it is not always possible to follow peacetime procedure'[2]. I don't think much of that for a reply.

106. *To his wife*

6 December 1940

The enquiry drags on. What is abundantly clear is that old Cork is much too old for the job. His mind wanders and he gets confused and mixes up things hopelessly. What I think emerges clearly is that 1) when I broke off the action I had no reason to think that the enemy had been damaged; 2) the enemy had drawn out of range and were increasing their distance from us; 3) there was a body of enemy cruisers to the NW and unaccounted for which might well have threatened my convoy and therefore entirely justified my returning to it without delay.

That's how it strikes me and I imagine it must strike the Board the same way. Lancelot Holland came in this morning and it will be interesting to hear what he has got to say about it. . . .

---

[1]Capt C. E. B. Simeon: Capt 1930; *Renown* 1939; RA Jan 1941; Dep Cntrlr & Dir N Eqpmt April 1941; VA on Ret List 1944.
[2]This refers to a message dated 1 Dec, expressing Somerville's surprise and concern at the summoning of a Board of Enquiry before a full report was received by the Admiralty; see Somerville to Pound, 1 Dec 1940, in SMVL 7/21. A fuller version is given in No. 108.

I have just been on board *Ark Royal* to see Hooky [Holland] and to tell him that I asked to be recalled by the Board so that I could tell them that his actions and those of the leaders of the second striking force had my complete approval and were entirely in accordance with my express wishes.

107. *To his wife*

7 December 1940

I have finished my seance with the Board yesterday afternoon when they asked me if I wished to make any further statement. I said yes but I would like the shorthand writer to leave. I then said that I had sat there day after day and it might be inferred that I felt no special concern in appearing before this Board of Enquiry. That was very far from being the truth. I was highly indignant at this outrage that had been put upon me and so are my captains. Cork stopped me and said that they could not possibly listen to what was a direct attack on the Admiralty. I said I fully appreciated that and would not continue except to say that I had sent a letter to TL in the strongest possible language. That evening George Lyon told me that I had placed Cork in an awkward position. I said that I did not care a damn and then George said 'But the point is that we think just the same about it as you do'! I gather that in their report there will be something to the effect that if B of E are ordered immediately after an action and before any details are known the confidence of the Service will be ruined. So apparently they at any rate do not consider that I acted wrongly on this occasion. But I shouldn't be a bit surprised if the Admiralty in order to justify their action in ordering a B of E will say that I did. I have shown my letter to Dudley [North] and have asked him to show it to George Lyon. Dudley reckons it is absolutely red hot and not a word could be improved upon. I decided finally to cut out the paras about publishing an account and my being relieved because it seemed a bit out of place. As the letter stands it refers only to the outraged feelings that everyone felt. And I really think it will make them sit up a bit. As a rule if an action had been a flop we get some undercurrents of criticisms from officers who are present, sort of 'pity we didn't do this or that'. But in this action so I am told there has not been a whisper. Merely horrified indignation at what the Admiralty has done.

108. *To the Admiralty*

6 December 1940

2. The information available to Their Lordships concerning my actions in this engagement was limited to that contained in my messages 1318/27 and 1530 of 28 November.

These messages, transmitted while at sea, quite obviously could not and did not purport to give all the circumstances and considerations which governed my actions on this occasion.

But the bare facts which emerged were that I had fought an action with a superior enemy force and driven him off to the very approaches to his defended base. Being satisfied that his main forces could no longer threaten the safety of my convoy, and incidentally, that I had no reasonable chance of bringing his battleships to action, I had returned to the convoy as soon as possible in order to ensure the achievement of what the Fighting Instructions describe as the only object in convoy defence, namely the safe and timely arrival of the convoy at its destination.

3. I had every reason to believe that I had performed my duty successfully under somewhat difficult circumstances. That officers and men under my command shared this view is evidenced by the fact that on return to harbour *Renown* was greeted with cheers and bands playing.

4. . . . But without waiting for essential information on which to base a considered opinion on my actions, Their Lordships have seen fit to order an immediate inquiry, thereby suggesting a lack of confidence in my leadership and doubts concerning my fitness to command Force H.

5. My Captains were indignant when I informed them they would be required to give evidence before the Board of Inquiry and it is to this indignation on their part that I wish to address myself particularly to Their Lordships.

6. It is quite clear that my Captains have not lost their confidence in me, but I have serious apprehensions that their confidence in other respects has been rudely shaken. I have not, of course, discussed this matter with them, but I know, as every Flag Officer should know, what passes in the minds of my Captains. To them it is apparently inconceivable that without awaiting any proper report of the action, it should have been decided that its conduct was open to serious criticism.

7. . . . The fact that a Board of Inquiry is being held on this action is, of course, common knowledge throughout Gibraltar . . . This knowledge will certainly not be confined to Gibraltar. I anticipate that very shortly the Spanish Press will publish this information and embellish it with articles on the 'Inquiry into a British reverse'.

Officers and men ask with some bitterness, how it is that an action in which they took part and in which they succeeded in driving off and inflicting damage on a superior force of the enemy, is now regarded as almost a defeat rather than a victory. It is when they ask themselves this question that I fear their criticism will be directed, not towards me, but elsewhere.

9. The effect on myself of this Board of Inquiry I consider of no account. I have not, and never have had, any personal ambition, and am content to serve the Country in any capacity for which my experience and ability may fit me. But I do take, and always have taken, great account of the good of the Service.

Their Lordships may well have failed to appreciate the full consequences of this action on their part, and I conceive it to be my duty to draw their attention to a matter which I, and others, judge to be of the gravest importance.

109. *From the Secretary of the Admiralty*[1]

10 January 1941

I have received and laid before My Lords Commissioners of the Admiralty your letter of 6 December containing your observations on their decision to convene a Board of Inquiry to investigate the action which took place on 27 November last between the forces under your command and a portion of the Italian Fleet.

2. Their Lordships note that you comment on a Board of Inquiry having been ordered without Their Lordships having received a written report from you, on the grounds that without such a report Their Lordships could not be in possession of essential information.

The main point at issue was the discontinuance of the chase of the enemy at 1310 and, in the opinion of Their Lordships at the time, your messages 1318 of 27 November and 1530 of 28 November contained all the information which was necessary to enable them to arrive at a decision to order a Board of Inquiry.

Subsequent perusal of the full documents has not caused Their Lordships to change this opinion.

3. With regard to your remarks in the letter under reply on the conduct of the action itself, Their Lordships refer you to Admiralty letter NL 14593/40 of 20 December 1940, which contains the report of the Board of Inquiry and the Board [of Admiralty's] views thereon.[2]

---

[1]Sir Henry V. Markham.
[2]No. 115.

110.   *From Admiral of the Fleet the Earl of Cork and Orrery*

7 December 1940

I hope after what passed yesterday that you do not feel I have not sympathised with you in the position in which you have been placed after
your successful action of last week. I have very much.

It is possible however that you take rather too harsh a view of the
Admy. action for the following reasons.

There are always critics ready to raise their voices and suggest what
might have been done although they are quite ignorant of what really
happened or of the prevailing conditions.

These people, impatient for results, exist both in and out of Admy.,
and in high quarters (I speak from personal experience), and no doubt
have raised their voices on this occasion and the most expeditious way of
silencing them has in this case been adopted.

As a result I do not think you need anticipate hearing anything further,
this is as far as I can judge and sincerely hope.

All best wishes for the future to you personally, and to your fine command.

111.   *To his wife*

8 December 1940

. . . I wrote in reply to Cork thanking him very much but saying that I
looked to my brother flag officers at home to protect and champion me
until it was established that I had done wrong and then and only then was
I content to be judged by them. I now hear that all the wardrooms were
seething with indignation and in fact the whole force is savage at this
monstrous insult to which they and I as their leader have been subjected.

112.   *To his wife*

11 December 1940

I must confess that I am somewhat disturbed by some of the things I
found waiting for me. I am all for not rating the Itis higher than they need
to be rated but to hold out too tempting a bait is asking for trouble. We
want to go on hitting them and if we give them too easy a chance to hit us
they may take it and that might well put them on their feet again. I can't

quite understand what is going on because in one message the Admiralty say that you must be sure that we have at least equal forces with which to meet the Itis and then they proceed as if this was of no account and tell me I needn't expect anything additional. So I have had to send off another of my appreciations which states the cold hard facts and make it quite clear that I at any rate go into this matter with my eyes open – as I did when we started the operation which led to our battle on the 27th. Talking about that I have seen the findings of the B of E though I'm not supposed to of course. . . .

113. *To Cunningham*

8 January 1941

The enclosed [report of the Board of Inquiry] will interest you. I suppose the Board [of Admiralty] had to find *some* reason for ordering a Board of Inquiry but I can hardly take their comments seriously. However some chaps seem to think you can take control of a tactical situation from an office in the Admiralty.

In spite of my protests this bloody stupid [notion?] continues. I hoped Fred Collins[1] would throw some light on the matter but he says everyone is dead against it in the Admiralty and no one really knew the object. Apparently Winston is now the complete dictator with master RK at his elbow repeating continually that he – RK – is the only real leader the Navy has got and that what the Navy suffers from is lack of guts! The idea of putting that [–] in command of WORKSHOP[2] is fantastic. I hear DP is livid about it. If that's right then he ought to do something drastic.

There seems to be some Jonah about EXCESS. First our bulge and then this gale which swept these chaps ashore.[3] You and I have warned them of the hazards but I'll bet you that if we *do* strike it unlucky there'll be a bloody fine howl and poor old Mr Justice Cork sent out on circuit again.

FC[ollins] tells me that a host of Flag Officers (including himself) asked to be considered as reliefs for me! Just shows how a bad smell suggests that something is dead. I rather gather that Winston (who now

---

[1] Adm Edward-Collins, fresh from UK.
[2] Adm of the Fleet Sir Roger Keyes, Director of Combined Operations. WORKSHOP was an operation designed to seize the Italian island of Pantellaria, off the N African coast. Cunningham condemned it bluntly; see *A Sailor's Odyssey*, pp. 290–1. The island was eventually taken in 1943.
[3] *Renown*'s starboard bulge had torn away at the forward end. A gale had blown a transport ashore in Gibraltar harbour; see para. 17 of No. 133.

makes the appointments) is anxious to heave me out but fears the public might not like it and start asking questions. AVA[lexander] is apparently rather disturbed over the DN[orth] business and says the situation here is 'very difficult'. I reckon it's time the old Navy was purged of politics and honest men left to ply their trade without interference. Anyhow I hope to goodness they'll have more sense than to interfere with you. Let's start winning the war somewhere.

114. *Finding of the Board of Inquiry*

December 1940

(a)   The original orders for the operation issued by the Flag Officer Commanding Force H were clear and concise. The situation envisaged . . . actually arose on the forenoon of 27 November.

(b)   The conduct of the action that ensued was correct and spirited and its success ensured the attainment of what had been selected as the primary object of the operation, viz.:–

The safe and timely arrival of the convoy at its destination.
(*Fighting Instructions*, Section XX, 625),

and this in the face of a superior force.

(c)   In order to maintain this object and to conform to the *Fighting Instructions* . . . a decision had to be come to as regards discontinuing a chase which was causing the main force to become widely separated from the convoy.

(d)   . . . We consider that the correct decision was taken. We are of the opinion that on principle a chase should be continued to the last possible moment, and it may appear that the time chosen was slightly early in view of:–

(1)   *Manchester*'s enemy report of battleships timed 1303, which would have afforded an opportunity of ascertaining whether any reduction of speed had been achieved.

(2)   No report of the first T/B attack having been received. But bearing in mind all the other considerations, we consider that the decision was correct.

The danger to a convoy at the hands of an enemy who had shown little sign of initiative may, perhaps, appear exaggerated, but this was a point which had to be taken carefully into account.

(e)   As regards the second T/B attack, the attacking force did not leave the carrier until after the chase had been discontinued.

The officer in command was given discretionary power as to selection of target should attack on the battleships not prove feasible. This he considered to be the case, and in view of his knowledge that the chase had been discontinued, and the relative position of the forces, we do not consider his decision to have been a wrong one.

(f)   All behaved as might confidently have been expected.

115.   Conclusion of the Board of Admiralty

c. 20 December 1940

The Board of Admiralty are in general agreement with the finding of the Board of Inquiry that the operation was well planned and its conduct up to 1310 correct and spirited. The conduct of the operation ensured the attainment of what had been selected as the immediate object, namely, the safe and timely arrival of the convoy at its destination.

The Board of Admiralty, however, do not feel able to accept the view implied in the report that when the immediate object of an operation is the safe and timely arrival of a convoy it should necessarily prevent the exploitation of a possible opportunity for the pursuit and destruction of important units of the enemy's fleet. . . .

The Board of Admiralty consider that in breaking off the chase at 1310 the Flag Officer Commanding Force H was over-influenced by his anxiety for the security of his convoy, but they realise that the emphasis which had been laid on the need for the safe arrival of the convoy in Admiralty messages may have contributed to this. In their view, however, he could have continued the pursuit until it was clear beyond doubt that no possibility of the destruction of any of the enemy units remained.

Failure to 'fix' any of the enemy vessels resulted in an indecisive action on this occasion; but the Board of Admiralty note with satisfaction that this engagement has once again demonstrated the moral superiority which our Naval Forces have established in the Mediterranean.

The Board of Admiralty cannot emphasise too strongly that in all cases, especially when dealing with an enemy who is reluctant to engage in close action, no opportunity must be allowed to pass of attaining what is in fact the ultimate object of the Royal Navy – the destruction of the main enemy force when and wherever encountered. Only thus can control of sea communications be properly secured.

116. *To the Admiralty*

2 January 1941

2. In the last paragraph of their Conclusion, Their Lordships state that 'in all cases . . . no opportunity must be allowed to pass of attaining what is in fact the ultimate object of the Royal Navy – the destruction of the main enemy forces when and wherever encountered'.

This suggests that the 'Object' in Convoy Defence, as defined and heavily emphasised in Clause 625 of the *Fighting Instructions*, no longer holds good and that, whether the opportunity offered is favourable or unfavourable, the safety of the convoy becomes a matter of secondary importance. If this inference is correct, I consider the *Fighting Instructions* should be amended accordingly.

3. In the third paragraph of their Conclusion, Their Lordships state that in their view I 'could have continued the pursuit until it was clear beyond doubt that no possibility of the destruction of any of the enemy units remained'. If construed literally, this suggests that pursuit should have been continued until dusk and regardless of the proximity of enemy surface, air or submarine bases or the safety of the convoy, with the destruction of perhaps one enemy destroyer as the immediate object. I feel that action of this character, so contrary to the accepted practice of naval warfare, can hardly be intended and that possibly the drafting of the paragraph in question has failed to convey clearly Their Lordships' view.

117. *Somerville's Observations on the Action off Cape Spartivento*

18 December 1940

Results obtained by air striking force torpedo bomber attacks

20. The results obtained by torpedo bomber attacks on high speed targets during the present war have fallen far short of the estimates based on peacetime practices adjusted for 'opposition'.

So far as *Ark Royal* is concerned, this is attributed entirely to lack of initial training and subsequent runner practice. Skilful, unobserved approaches were made in each case and the attacks pressed home with courage and resolution, but the results obtained were disappointing. A suggestion has been made that the Duplex pistol is open to suspicion, but on this I am unable to remark.[1]

---

[1] The Duplex pistol was a magnetic one, as opposed to the conventional contact pistol. See No. 161, paras. 22, 24, 32. The Germans also had problems with magnetic pistols.

Delay in reporting result of first striking force attack

21. It is not always appreciated that sustained observation on enemy ships by the crews of aircraft in the striking force is impracticable. Observation of 'own drop', even in peacetime practices, is very difficult, and under action conditions, quite fortuitous. Succeeding attackers may, or may not, be able to observe hits from previous attacks, but in general the only definite evidence, especially with Duplex pistols, is the subsequent behaviour of the target. On this occasion it was not until the return of the striking force to *Ark Royal* had afforded opportunity for the interrogation of all aircraft crews, that the probability of one hit on the *Littorio* class was established. Subsequent observation of the target indicated that her speed had not been reduced to an extent which prevented her keeping in company with the *Cavour* class, at about 25 knots, but does not disprove the estimate that one hit was obtained.[1]

Shadowing or action observation aircraft are probably in the best position to report results of air striking force attacks, based on subsequent behaviour of the target. This is rarely observed by the striking force, since the latter retire at a low altitude to avoid A/A fire and fighter interception.

Enemy's Gunnery

26. The attention of Their Lordships is invited to the remarks of the Vice Admiral Commanding, 18th. Cruiser Squadron, in paragraph 37 of his report. Both in this war and the last, action reports have frequently remarked on the accuracy of the initial enemy salvoes and on the inadequacy of the Barr and Stroud coincidence rangefinders.

I am aware that comparative trials with stereoscopic rangefinders have been carried out on several occasions during the last 20 years. Nevertheless, I believe that the British Navy is the only Navy in the world that still relies on the coincidence type of rangefinder. It seems possible that in past trials the stereoscopic rangefinders employed have not been of the same efficiency as those used by other nations. In any event, I am of the opinion that the stereoscopic rangefinder has been too lightly discarded – both for low angle and high angle purposes – and I suggest that further efforts be made to obtain a satisfactory rangefinder of this type, possibly by purchase from America in the first instance.

Operation of carrier borne aircraft

35. Providing the Commanding Officer of the carrier is fully aware of the Admiral's views on how his aircraft are to be employed, it is most

[1]No hit was obtained.

desirable that the carrier should act independently. Signalled instructions concerning striking forces, reconnaissance, etc., add to wireless congestion and may be impracticable to execute precisely without dislocating the intricate flying on and off programme.

Special circumstances may arise which call for special instructions, but the policy should be for the Commanding Officer of the carrier to act in accordance with the general situation and with what he knows to be the Admiral's views.

118. *Somerville on the Functions of Force H*

December 1940

The functions originally allotted to Force H were as follows:–

(i)   To control the Western exit of the Mediterranean.
(ii)   To carry out offensive operations against the coast of Italy.

2.   In connection with (ii), in July I received certain proposals from the Admiralty and C-in-C, Mediterranean, which envisaged operations against shore targets in the Tyrrhenian Sea and elsewhere, in close proximity to the enemy coast and at distances of over 800 miles from Gibraltar.

I represented that these operations appeared to involve risks to *Ark Royal* and *Renown* out of all proportion to the result likely to be achieved. C-in-C, Mediterranean, accepted this view, and when I visited the Admiralty in August, I was informed verbally that it was agreed the proposed operations were not justifiable unless for some special reason, such as breaking down Italian morale at a critical period.

3.   To the functions originally allotted to Force H the following have since been added:–

(a)   The passage of reinforcements to the Eastern Mediterranean.
(b)   Control of the movements of all major units of the French Fleet.
(c)   The hunting of the *Scheer* and other raiders in the Atlantic.
(d)   Offensive operations against the Spanish Fleet and harbours in the event of war with Spain.
(e)   The capture of the Azores in certain circumstances.
(f)   The control of the Indian Ocean in certain other circumstances.

4.   To replace *Renown* in the performance of the majority of these functions we have, at present, no other powerful ship with the necessary speed and endurance. Nor is there any substitute available for *Ark Royal* without detracting from other vital requirements.

5. Quite apart from the considerations affecting the objects to be achieved in operation COLLAR, the acceptance of additional risk to *Ark Royal* or *Renown*, over and above that necessary to achieve the object in view, must form the subject of continual consideration and must not be undertaken lightly unless there is a reasonable prospect of achieving some profitable, counterbalancing aim.

The Relative Importance of Ensuring the Passage of Reinforcements as Compared with the Destruction of Enemy Naval Forces

The crux of the future strategical and political situation in the Central and Eastern Mediterranean lies in the relative strength of military and air forces.

2. This in turn depends to a considerable extent on our control of sea communications within the Mediterranean. Although this control is not being disputed seriously by the Italian *surface* forces, the destruction of these forces is always desirable since this allows our own surface forces to be released for service elsewhere.

But providing we can continue to exercise our present degree of control over sea communications within the Mediterranean, it is clearly the military and air situation that must, for the present, at any rate, receive prior consideration.

3. Both in operation COLLAR and in previous operations this priority exercised a distinct influence on the relative importance to be attached to the conflicting requirements of protecting the convoy and destroying the enemy. It is on this account that it has always been the policy to conceal the movements and intentions of Force H so far as practicable, since on no occasion have sufficient forces been available to ensure the safe passage of reinforcements and at the same time engage the enemy's main forces.

119. *From Vice Admiral G.C. Royle*[1]

The Admiralty,
28 December 1940

Let me wish you all the best in the New Year and then add my heartiest congratulations for the way you have carried out quite the toughest

---

[1]Vice Adm (later Adm Sir) Guy C. C. Royle (1885–1954): ent RN 1900; Lt 1906; gun splist; Grand F, Jutland; Cdr 1916; Flag Cdr to Madden, C-in-C Grand F 1917–19; FGO Atl F 1919–20; EO *Iron Duke* Med F 1920–2; N Ordance Dept 1923; Capt 1923; NA Tokyo 1924–7; *Canterbury* 1927–9; *Excellent* 1929–31; *Glorious* 1932–4; N Sec to 1st Ld 1934–7; RA 1935; RA (A) 1937–9; N Sec 1st Ld Sept 1939; 5SL Nov 1939; VA 1939; 1st N Mem,Commonwealth N Bd, Australia, 1941–5; Adm Oct 1942.

and most difficult and tricky job any FO could ever have had. You have been magnificent and a little thing like a Board of Inquiry is meant just 'to keep you humble'.

I think I must have felt and many others much the same as you when it happened with those terms of reference and you would have smiled to see us sitting round and talking about your action and whether there was the remotest possibility of doing anything more. Whether you should have held on any longer with your very inadequate force, etc., etc. I think most chaps were fed up with the whole business and reckoned you and the FAA had done magnificently not only in your lap at the enemy but also in getting the convoy safely to its destination.

. . . I quite agree it would be an excellent thing if more senior officers had had practical experience of the work of the chaps in FAA. I am sure you and Cedric Holland in *Ark Royal* make a very good and happy combination.

Operation WHITE was unfortunate but there again I reckon the whole party was let down by the infn. given by A[ir] M[inistry]. People at home are feeling very confident and *think* that we have seen the worst the Hun can do in the bombing line and that gradually we shall be able to reduce its effect. . . .

We miss you on the wireless.

We reckon the serious business is going to be fought out in the NW Approaches and if you can eliminate the party in the Med. we shall be grateful for reinforcements. I have been unable to trace a *Littorio* class in dock except the one damaged at Taranto and yet those 5 observers in *Ark Royal* couldn't very well be mistaken – the explosion may have taken place just ahead or astern. It was a gallant attack against a high speed well screened target.

I am sorry Dudley North is being relieved from Gib. I reckon he has done very well.

These d----d politicians who know nothing of the real difficulties are responsible for most of these *stunts*. . . .

I am so pleased the FAA have had a chance of showing what they can do in spite of the rotten aircraft they find themselves with. It takes a hell of a time to get a new type. We shall have some good American single seat fighters early in the New Year.[1]

---

[1] The Grumman Martlet.

120. *From Cunningham*

30 December 1940

I can understand very well your feelings about the B of I. It was scandalous I think.

I had a letter from DP telling me it had to be for what I thought were damned poor reasons and I am going to tell him quite straight what I think about it. I don't believe he's at the bottom of it but he allows himself to be talked into these things by WC[hurchill] and others.

I am also going to tell him what I think about Force H. A force with two objects will very naturally be able to do neither adequately, and that is what appears to be happening to you.

I feel they would be better to have two battleships however slow and an A/C and tie them down to doing things in the Western Med. If running a convoy stay with the convoy. And let *Renown* go off into the blue after raiders. You can't imagine the dislocation that takes place this end when a day's delay takes place in any operation. This time it's chaos. I had hung up various Greek convoys and told the army the dates I could give them support and the whole thing has gone west. You see we work on such a small margin.

I don't think you should complain about *Malaya*. *Barham* is much the same. *Malaya* has been in much the same state the last six months without giving trouble so there is no reason she shouldn't do another two or three. She wants docking badly and our own dock can't at the moment lift a capital ship.

Where you gain is that *Malaya* is a very highly trained unit and in great fighting trim which *Barham* is not. It was the docking that decided it.[1]

121. *Report of Proceedings, 29 November–14 December 1940* [cont.]

19 December 1940

3 December

14.   In reply to a signal from C-in-C, Mediterranean, asking whether consideration had been given to the bombing of Leghorn by the RAF, since it was believed that tankers for Libya loaded from large stocks there, the Admiralty stated that this target was beyond the range of the

---

[1]*Barham* had recently joined the Mediterranean Fleet and the decimation of the Italian battle fleet at Taranto allowed Cunningham to part with *Ramillies*, sailed west in November, and now *Malaya*.

existing heavy bombers operating from the United Kingdom. It was further stated that it would be within the range of the new types of bombers coming into service in the New Year, but that if earlier attack was considered desirable, then bombardment of the refineries and storage tanks by Force H should be considered.

C-in-C, Mediterranean, asked for my remarks on this suggestion, and in reply I gave my general proposals for such an operation.

I added, however, that the risk to which *Ark Royal* and *Renown* would be exposed was considerable, and in any case the operation must be governed by weather conditions. I was naturally not in a position to express an opinion on whether the urgency of the operation (which, in any case, could be carried out more effectively by shore-based aircraft in January) was sufficient to justify the risks involved.

6 December

18.   Information was received from the C-in-C, Mediterranean, that he intended to pass *Malaya* through to the Western Mediterranean, making the passage of the Narrows about 21 December, and was considering the return of the three MT ships ex-operation COLLAR at the same time. He asked if Force H could co-operate about this date.

Later in the day I was informed by the Admiralty that it was the intention to pass MT ships, leaving the UK on 18 December, through to the Eastern Mediterranean. In order to provide essential air reconnaissance in the Mediterranean[1] . . . 18 boxed Swordfish were being sent to the Middle East in these ships and 6 more in flying condition would be sent in *Argus* with their crews, to be flown off for Malta from *Ark Royal* during the operation.

In remarking on these operations subsequently to the C-in-C, Mediterranean, I felt that recent experiences in COLLAR had accentuated, rather than relieved, the problem of becoming engaged with superior enemy forces in restricted waters with a convoy in company, and in view of the lack of shore based air reconnaissance.

I suggested that the passage of MT ships either way should not be attempted until Force H (now consisting of *Renown, Ark Royal, Sheffield* and about 10 destroyers) had been reinforced by *Malaya* and the temporary addition of more cruisers.

7 December

20.   In considering plans for the safe passage of the MT ships through the Mediterranean, it was of importance to know whether French reac-

[1]The comparative lack of shore-based air reconnaissance was one of both Somerville's and especially Cunningham's regular complaints.

tion to interception of their convoys was likely to provoke them to such measures as would make routeing of convoys close to their coast undesirable or make it necessary to strengthen the escort force. This depended on the extent to which RATION was likely to be repeated and, incidentally, on whether one of the objects of the exercise was to provoke an incident with the French.

8 December

25.   It has never been clear to either the Admiral Commanding, North Atlantic, or myself, what is in fact the ultimate object of RATION, but we are both naturally very much alive to the possible adverse reactions which this operation may exercise on subsequent operations by our forces in the Western Mediterranean basin. Representations to this effect have been made from time to time, but since it appeared possible that these had not been expressed adequately, opportunity was taken to inform Admiral of the Fleet the Earl of Cork and Orrery of our views, which he stated he would represent on his return to the United Kingdom.

29.   At 2300 I embarked in *Ark Royal* in order to proceed to sea on the following morning to witness flying training.

My purpose was two-fold, namely, to renew and refresh my flying experience, and, by climbing to high altitudes, to rid my system of poison which recent events might have engendered. Both objects were fully achieved. I took part in torpedo runner exercises, dive-bombing practices, and fighter interception and encounters.

I am convinced that when opportunity serves, it is most desirable that Senior Officers should take part in such practices in order that they may acquire a full appreciation of the problems which face the FAA pilots and observers.

11 December

36.   Consideration of the forthcoming operations in the Western Mediterranean and the forces it was proposed to employ for these operations, led to me signalling my appreciation of the situation.

This was, in effect, that if we continued to offer the Italians an opportunity to score a success, they might well summon initiative to seize it as a set-off against their recent reverses. Recent changes in the Italian Naval High Command suggested this purpose might well be in mind.

For the above reason I considered that the forces to be employed in forthcoming operations should be at least comparable to the Italian forces. If this was accepted, the issue of any encounter would not be in doubt.

If no additional cruisers are available, the addition of *Rodney*[1] to Force H would undoubtedly exercise a moral effect out of all proportion to her material value.

If, however, no reinforcement was possible and if it was decided to accept the risk of our forces being engaged by greatly superior enemy forces backed by a shore-based air force, I suggested

(a)   a maximum concentration of submarines suitably disposed in the Western basin,

(b)   operation of air striking force from Malta against the Italian Fleet on critical days,

(c)   a feint movement of heavy forces from the Eastern Mediterranean towards the Narrows on the afternoon and night before the most critical day.

13 December

40.   The two Italian submarines which had taken refuge in Tangier in a damaged condition in November, were reported to have sailed at 0430.

A/S trawlers and destroyers were sent to patrol the vicinity, and to hunt to the west of Cape Spartel. The force available for this was much reduced by four destroyers being involved in operation RATION.

41.   At 0956 *Forester* boarded the French ship *Avant Garde*[2] in position 266° Cape Trés Forcas 6 miles, in pursuance of operation RATION. *Faulknor*, *Fury* and *Isis* remained within reach, but their support was not required. The French vessel was brought into Gibraltar without incident. Interception did not take place until the escort had parted company with the convoy.

14 December

42.   At 0237, Force H was ordered to proceed to sea as early as convenient and proceed towards the Azores. Operation RATION was suspended until further orders. Orders were issued accordingly and destroyers were recalled from patrol.

Force H, comprising *Renown*, *Ark Royal*, *Faulknor*, *Fury*, *Forester*, *Isis*, *Encounter* and *Duncan*, sailed at 1030.

---

[1]*Rodney*: 1927, 33,950t, 9×16in, 12×6in, 8×4in, 2tt, 23k.
[2]*Avant Garde*: steam trawler, 1920, 780t. A sledgehammer to crack a nut.

122. *From Lieutenant Mark Somerville*

HMS *Ark Royal,*
12 December 1940

I am very glad that I was able to see so much of you whilst you were on board but I'm sorry that you weren't able to have a proper run in a Fulmar.[1] . . .

The signal which the Captain made to you represents the view of the entire ship's company but there is a lot more to it than that. Your visit made a tremendous impression on everybody and acted as a real tonic to all of us. The general view that I have heard expressed by FAA Officers is that the ship is now operating under a Flag Officer who not only understands the general aspect of naval aviation but who had also taken the trouble to investigate the practical and personal side of it, and thus understands the small difficulties which sometimes appear so trivial and yet which are, in reality, so important. Most of us have suffered at one time or another under Flag and Commanding Officers who were abysmally ignorant of what an Observer or Pilot really did when he stepped into an aeroplane, and life is so much more pleasant now working under somebody who really understands.

If the Officers are pleased with your visit, the Air Gunners are more than delighted, and I have heard expressions of unbounded astonishment and admiration on all sides. You have shamed quite a few of my own Air Gunners who after a year of flying experience, consistently fail to establish W/T with their ship or other aircraft! The Engine-Room Department too are extremely pleased that you managed to find time to have a look round down below and the remarks which you apparently made about the cleanliness were very much appreciated.

Perhaps I shouldn't write all this, but I am doing so because I have never before seen or heard of so much genuine enthusiasm aroused amongst all sections of the Ship's Company and I must find an outlet for my own enthusiasm and admiration.

I have always been inordinately proud of being your nephew, but I have never been prouder than I am now.

---

[1]Owing to a damaged propeller on his machine.

123.   *Report of Proceedings, 14–19 December 1940*

20 December 1940

14 December

3.   At 1330 I received Vice Admiral, Submarines, 1026/14, stating that *Upholder*, *Usk* and *Unique*[1] had been diverted to patrol in the Bay of Biscay. From this it appeared that a German move from French ports was anticipated.

5.   At 1730 I was informed by Admiralty that the sailing of Force H was a precautionary move, and that further information would be passed later.

15 December

7.   During the night information was received that it had been decided to postpone operations EXCESS and WORKSHOP until the moonless period in January.

10.   At 0730 I received Admiralty's 0216/15 directing the Admiral Commanding, North Atlantic, to sail *Orangeleaf* to join Force H and at 0945 I received Admiralty's 0200/15 instructing me to establish a patrol off the Azores to prevent any enemy attempt to capture the Islands.

11.   At the same time a further signal was received from the Admiralty stating that secret information indicated the Germans might attempt to capture the Islands, either by a sea-borne expedition or by transport aircraft – if the former, by embarking at Bordeaux or Gijon, and if the latter from Bordeaux or Laon.

15.   At 1745 . . . the A/S patrol sighted a raft 15 miles to the starboard of *Renown*. *Fury* was detached to investigate and located the raft, which was found to belong to SS *Gwalia* of Gothenburg.[2] There were no survivors, but three life-belts, four blankets and four oilskins were recovered from the raft. It is believed that SS *Gwalia* was torpedoed when in convoy OG 46 bound for Lisbon.

17 December

22.   At 0100 on receipt of Admiralty's 0125/17, instructing the Force to return to Gibraltar at best convenient speed, course was altered to 095°, and speed increased to 18 knots.

[1]*Upholder, Usk, Unique*: 1940, 545/740t, 6tt (*Usk* 4), 1×3in, 13/10k; all lost 1941–2, Med.
[2]*Gwalia*: 1907, 1258gt, 9k, Svenska Lloyd.

18 December

31.   At dawn 12 TSRs were flown off to carry out an extensive search with the object of locating the German ship *Baden*,[1] which had been reported as having sailed from Tenerife on the night 15/16 December.
35.   Information was received at 1800 pointing to the presence of the German pocket battleship *Admiral Scheer* in the vicinity of 00° 57'N, 22° 42'W. A much mutilated message had been received from SS *Duquesa* reporting that she was being shelled in this position.[2]

124.   *Report of Proceedings, 19–24 December 1940*

28 December 1940

19 December

2.   Force H . . . returned to Gibraltar at 0800. *Sheffield* was already in harbour, having returned from Azores patrol on 16 December.
3.   Ships were refuelled ready for departure on the following day for operation HIDE . . .
4.   My instructions for the westbound Force F (*Malaya, Hyperion, Ilex, Hero, Hasty, Hereward, Clan Forbes* and *Clan Fraser*) in the event of enemy forces being located in the vicinity of the rendezvous, were as follows:–

(a)   MT ships to proceed close along the Algerian coast unescorted and prepared to display French ensigns.
(b)   Forces F and H to concentrate with a view to early attack, destroyers to seize any favourable opportunity for attack before daylight.

20 December

7.   With the object of economising fuel in a proportion of the destroyers and thus enable a destroyer search to be carried out ahead of Force H before dawn on 22 December to cover the passage of Force F from the Skerki Channel to the rendezvous, *Duncan* (Captain (D), 13th Flotilla), *Encounter, Isis, Wishart* and *Jaguar* (known as Group 2) sailed to the eastward at economical speed at 0930, carrying out an A/S sweep *en route*.
12.   Force H (less the 5 destroyers who had sailed earlier), comprising *Renown, Ark Royal, Sheffield, Faulknor, Forester, Fury, Firedrake, Fortune* and *Foxhound* (known as Group 1), sailed at 1800 in daylight,

[1]*Baden*: 1922, 8204gt, 12.5k. Hamburg-Amerika Line; see No. 127, para. 20.
[2]*Duquesa*: 1918, 8651gt, 14.5k, Furness-Holder Argentine Lines; captured by *Scheer* 18 Dec 1941, sunk 20 Dec 1941.

and shaped course to the westward at 18 knots. An hour and a half later, when it was completely dark, course was reversed and the Force proceeded eastward at 23 knots.

The strategical situation at the commencement of the operation was very similar to that which obtained during COLLAR. . . .

21 December

14.   As dawn broke the five destroyers of Group 2 were sighted on the starboard bow and were ordered to join Force H. . . .

15.   A/S patrols were maintained ahead of the Force and one section of fighters kept at readiness on deck throughout the day . . .

16.   At 1800, Group 2 (less *Wishart*) proceeded ahead at 26 knots to carry out the moonlight and dawn search (operation SEEK). Group 1 . . . proceeded at 20 knots until 1930, subsequently at 22½ knots.

22 December

17.   The moon rose at 0135 and thereafter visibility was high. A torpedo bomber striking force was kept available from 0200.

19.   Air reconnaissance from Malta indicated that on 21 December the main units of the Italian Fleet were disposed between Spezia and Naples, one battleship and four cruisers being observed at Spezia and two battleships and four cruisers at Naples.

20.   At 0400 a signal was intercepted from *Malaya* to Captain (D), 14th DF, stating that *Hyperion* (one of *Malaya*'s screen) had been mined . . . Captain (D) was ordered by the C-in-C, Mediterranean, to detach a destroyer to sink *Hyperion* (unless she was able to steam)[1] and then join the FOC, Force H. . . .

21.   At 0834 I intercepted Captain (D), 14th DF's 0800 reporting that *Hyperion* had sunk and that he was returning to Malta with Force D and *Ilex*, . . .

22.   Shortly before dawn, 8 TSRs were flown off to carry out reconnaissance to maximum depth to the eastward, and to a limited extent to the northward and westward.

23.   No enemy surface craft were sighted by either the air reconnaissance or the destroyer search. One Cant 506b seaplane was, however, sighted by a Swordfish at about 0930 SW of Sardinia; the Cant immediately beat a hasty retreat. *Jaguar* also sighted an aircraft in the dark at 0716 at a height of 6000 feet, on an easterly course, and opened fire with pom-poms.

---

[1]*Hyperion*: 1936, 1340t, 4×4.7in, 8tt, 36k; originally thought mined off C Bon but probably torpedoed by Italian S/M *Serpente*.

Captain (D), 13th DF, in charge of the destroyer search, reported on rejoining that he had detached *Jaguar* and *Encounter* to join Force F.
25.   By 0940, Forces H and F had joined; . . . course [was] shaped to the westward at 15 knots. A fighter patrol was flown off at 1020 and a section maintained in the air throughout the rest of the day.
27.   At 1245 three TSRs were flown off to maintain a security patrol to a depth of 40 miles between W and N, and to a depth of 20 miles between N and E. This patrol was maintained until sunset.
28.   Shortly afterwards, . . . an aircraft was detected by RDF. *Ark Royal* subsequently reported that the Skua patrol had driven off a shadowing Cant at this time. It it thought that this Cant did not sight our forces.

23 December

30.   A security patrol was maintained from dawn to 1330, as on the previous day.
34.   At 1700, the fleet split into two groups. Group 1, consisting of *Renown, Ark Royal* and *Malaya*, screened by 9 destroyers, proceeded ahead at 18 knots. Group 2, consisting of *Sheffield, Clan Fraser* and *Clan Forbes* and 5 destroyers, following at about 13 knots.
37.   All ships of Group 1 had entered harbour by 1000 and were followed at 1400 by those of Group 2.
38.   I consider it is quite possible that owing to the initial movement to the westward when sailing from Gibraltar, and the subsequent high speed approach to the eastward, the operation was not detected by the enemy. The weather on 22 December, whilst our forces were south of Sardinia, was unfavourable for air reconnaissance or operations owing to low visibility.

125.   *To his wife*

22 December 1940

Here we are in the middle of another damn difficult operation. . . . It was not until we were almost on the front door so to speak that I learnt that one battleship and some cruisers were at Spezia, two battleships and some cruisers at Naples and other chaps could have got to me before I met *Malaya* and the transports coming from the eastern Med. We have just met thank goodness but as the transports can only do 14 knots we are waddling along about 60 miles off the Sardinia coast and I shan't be able to feel at all easy until dark tonight. Luckily it is overcast and the visibility is not too good so I hope we may escape being spotted. . . . It is all devilish tricky and what infuriates me is that TL just sit back and say no reinforcements are available and never a damn word that they fully realise that I have got a damn tricky job to do and it is fully appreciated. Just something to show that they can put themselves in my position but they just sit back in their armchairs and treat it all as a matter of course. I must be in very bad odour with them at present and they evidently don't intend to give me a civil word of any sort. . . .

126. *To his wife*

23 December 1940

All quiet last night and with this strong westerly wind I don't expect the Iti air will trouble us today but the head sea is keeping us back and we are not making more than 12 knots. . . . as it will be Christmas Eve I would like to get in before dark if possible so that the sailors can get the mess ready for their bit of fun on Christmas Day. But even on that day we shall have to be ready to slip out at short notice in case they try and catch us napping . . . Just heard a long blast on the syren so rushed up on to the bridge thinking it was a submarine contact to port. However it was only a signal lanyard that had fouled the syren lanyard so I at once hoisted in flags PARDON. Must give the boys a simple laugh now and then.

I notice that in reply to some even more ambitious proposals from the Admiralty ABC has more or less repeated what I said only not so plain spoken. I believe in calling a spade a spade and if I consider you want three battleships for a job I say so. If the Admiralty wish to do a job with less then it's their affair but I consider it to be my business as the bloke in charge of the cart to say how many horses are required to drag it if you want to be reasonably assured of a safe arrival. I am sure they will seize on this last operation as an excuse to say I over estimate. They'll over-look the fact that before we started I was watching the weather like a cat and was able to carry out an evasive movement which probably threw the Itis right off the scent. And I had to take a chance doing it because if I forecast the weather wrong and we had been late at the rendezvous there would have been a fine to-do. It seems to me that we chaps have to stand all the rubs and get all the kicks and none of the halfpence. Not that I want the latter for myself but my disodour reacts on those under me.

127.   *Report of Proceedings, 24–30 December 1940*

1 January 1941

24 December

[-]   Instructions were received by the Admiral Commanding, NAS, that operation RATION was to be carried out on 26, 27 and 28 December, as opportunity offered and force available permitted. It was to be carried out as on previous occasions, since it appeared probable that after one or two such interceptions, the escort would accompany convoys beyond Spanish territorial waters and thus afford an opportunity to intercept the convoy in the presence of the escort. This would provide the test case required by the Admiralty.

25 December

4.   At 1020 an enemy report (TOO 0642) of a pocket battleship (subsequently corrected to an 8" cruiser)[1] . . . was received from *Berwick*. I immediately ordered Force H (less *Malaya*) to come to one hour's notice for full speed. . . .

5.   Ships commenced to leave harbour at 1315 and by 1430 *Renown*, *Ark Royal*, *Sheffield*, *Faulknor*, *Fortune*, *Firedrake*, *Foxhound*, *Duncan*, *Wishart*, *Hero* and *Hereward* were clear of the harbour and on a westerly course.

I was gratified to observe the fine spirit in which the order to proceed to sea on Christmas Day was carried out. Ships remaining in harbour cheered those that were leaving and these cheers were returned with great heartiness. On clearing the entrances the order to close up to action stations was obeyed with even greater alacrity then usual.

6.   The Rear Admiral Commanding, 15th CS,[2] and the Senior Officer, Force K,[3] had been ordered by the Admiralty to 'close enemy'. *Furious* and *Argus* were also hunting for the enemy. I therefore shaped course for position 37°N, 16°W, as being the best position from which to either cover the convoy or assist in the hunt for the raider. . . .

---

[1] The *Hipper*, which was damaged and returned to Brest.

[2] 10CS, cmded by Rear Adm (later Adm Sir) Harold M Burrough: M/sman 1904; Capt 1928; gunnery specialist & Capt *Excellent* 1937; RA & ACNS (Trade) 1939–40; 10CS Sept 1940; Vaagso raid, Malta convoys 1941–2; VA Oct 1942; FO Gibraltar & Med Approaches Sept 1943; Actg Adm & ANCXF, NW Europe Jan 1945.

[3] SO Force K was Rear Adm (later Adm Sir) William F. Wake Walker (1888–1945): *Britannia* 1903; torpedo specialist; Lt-Cdr 1916; Cdr 1920; RNC, Admy & Tactical Sch 1921–5; *Castor* 1928–30; DD, DTSD; *Dragon* 1932–5; *Revenge* 1938–9; RA 12CS 1938–9; RA (M) 1939; Dunkirk 1940; 1 M/L Sqdn 1940; Force K & 1CS 1940–2; shadowed *Bismarck* May 1941; VA, 3SL & Controller 1942–5; Adm 1945; appointed C-in-C Med F 1945 but died before taking it up.

26 December

20. A report from *Bonaventure*,[1] received at 1630, indicated that she had intercepted the German ship *Baden* . . . and had not yet made contact with the *Empire Trooper*.[2] The crew of the *Baden* had abandoned and set fire to their ship. The weather being unsuitable for boarding, *Bonaventure* had torpedoed her and set course for Gibraltar.

21. The situation at 1700 was as follows. The approximate position of all HM Ships in the area (other than corvettes) was known. *Cyclamen*, with her W/T out of action, was believed to be standing by *Empire Trooper*, and it appeared probable that the three remaining corvettes (*Jonquil*, *Clematis* and *Geranium*) had proceeded to Ponta Delgada to fuel. Only one merchant ship had been located, viz., the *City of Canterbury*, in company with *Dunedin*.[3] Whilst the situation of *Empire Trooper* caused some anxiety my major preoccupation was to assist in rounding up and covering the remainder of the convoy which might be making for position 37°N, 16°W by these routes.

22. My intentions were therefore communicated at 1720 to all units, who were instructed to act as follows:–

(a) Force H to maintain position between the northern and southern approaches to position 37°, 16°W.

(b) Senior Officer, Force K, to continue search for ships passing through position 39° 08'N, 21° 38'W.

(c) *Furious* to arrive in position 37°N, 16°W, at 1400/27, searching to N and E for ships proceeding direct to Gibraltar.

(d) *Berwick* to search to N and W of 37°N, 16°W, during the forenoon 27th, rendezvousing with me in that position at 1400/27.

(e) *Dunedin* to rendezvous as for *Berwick*.

All ships were directed to report at 2200/26 and 1200/27 the number of merchant ships in company.

23. The 2200 reports indicated that only three merchant ships had been located, two by the SO, Force K, and one by *Dunedin*. SO, Force K, also reported that *Norfolk*'s speed would be limited to 12 knots after reaching the rendezvous at 0800/28. *Dunedin*'s fuel was also getting low. At the same time *Berwick* informed Admiralty that it would be necessary for

[1]*Bonaventure*: 1940, 5450t, 8×5.25in, 6tt, 33k; sunk S of Crete 1941, Italian S/M *Ambra*.
[2]*Empire Trooper*: ex-German *Cap Norte*, 1922, 13,994gt, MWT.
[3]*Cyclamen, Jonquil, Clematis, Geranium*: 'Flower' class. *City of Canterbury*: 1923, 8331gt, 13.5k, City Line. *Dunedin*: 1919, 4850t, 6×6in, 3×4in, 12t, 29k; sunk C Atlantic 1941 *U124*.

her to proceed to Gibraltar to make good underwater damage, to free 'X' turret, and to fuel.

27 December

31. Reports from all units indicated that a total of four merchant ships had been located by 1200. SO, Force K, at this time ordered *Furious*, *Argus*, *Dunedin* and the five EXCESS MT ships, when collected, to proceed to Gibraltar with the necessary destroyers; *Berwick*, *Sheffield* and the remaining destroyers to remain at the rendezvous until Force K arrived.

36. At 1700 a report was intercepted from *Cyclamen* (TOO 1015/27) that she was standing by *Empire Trooper* who had been holed in Nos. 1 and 4 hatches and whose situation was serious. . . .

39. At 2300 Admiralty instructions to all concerned regarding *Empire Trooper* were received. *Kenya*,[1] *Berwick*, *Cyclamen*, *Clematis*, *Jonquil* and *Geranium* were to join *Empire Trooper* and escort her to Ponta Delgada. If it was found *Berwick* could remain with *Empire Trooper*, *Bonaventure* was to be released for operation EXCESS as soon as *Berwick* relieved us; otherwise *Bonaventure* was to remain with *Empire Trooper*.[2] . . .

128.   *To his wife*

25 December 1940

Whilst I was in the midst of the mess deck rounds a signal comes ordering us to sea with all despatch – a German 8" cruiser has been sighted west of the Azores so here we are now preparing for sea and off at 1.30 p.m. instead of sitting down to our Christmas dinner as we had hoped. I feel so sorry for the men because they do enjoy their bit of fun on Christmas Day and because they don't get much fun these days.

Turned out at 6.30 a.m. so as to attend Communion at 7 a.m. and whilst I was in my bath the band started playing Christmas carols outside. It made me blub in my bath and all, when I thought of all the happy Christmases we have had together and now this should be such a lousy one.

---

[1] *Kenya*: 1940, 8525t, 12×6in, 8×4in, 6tt, 33k.
[2] Burrough was placed in command of the remaining operations.

129. *To his wife*

26 December 1940

Well that was a nice Christmas Day for all of us I must say. After Breakfast I had been on board each ship in turn and wished them a Happy Christmas and say how glad I was we were in harbour on such a filthy day – it was blowing hard and raining in torrents and then just as we were starting the mess deck rounds on *Renown* I get the signal from *Berwick* to say that she had sighted a German 8-in cruiser. Had to continue the rounds drawing aside every now and then to dictate signals. . . . The situation appeared to be very involved because about 5 p.m. we heard that *Berwick* had been in action with a cruiser and suffered a little damage and that owing to low visibility the cruiser had disappeared to the west. Later still we learned that the convoy had scattered and various other ships were ordered to the spot to try and round them up. It appeared to be a pretty good old pot mess and at 4 a.m. this morning I was ordered to take charge of the situation and clear it up. Not so easy as you can imagine. I don't know at present where any of the ruddy ships are or what they are doing and in spite of my request for information most of them are preserving a dignified silence. We have been roaring along at 26 knots ever since we left and luckily the wind and sea are astern. It is going to be a hell of a job to sweep up this mess. *9 p.m.* – we have had no luck so far and I'm damned if I know where this blasted convoy can be. They scattered and the visibility has been very poor so neither *Formidable* nor *Furious* have been able to use their aircraft. We did a good air search this afternoon which found nothing at all. So now we have got to wait until tomorrow morning and see what luck we have then. And of course all this time boats are getting short of fuel and will have to turn back tomorrow whatever happens. . . . The Christmas present that Dudley and I got from the Admiralty was that operation 'RASH', i.e., seizing French ships, was to be carried out on 26/27/28th. Can you beat it? Just when we are about to do some tricky stuff and it's *all-important* not to provoke any French retaliation. However I spitchered that all right by taking all the destroyers to sea with me so it damn well can't be done. I bet that bloody Winston is a bit mad but I was well within my rights.

130.   *To his wife*

27 December 1940

The situation gets more and more involved. At 1 a.m. I get a signal from the Admiralty to say that one of the transports with 2500 troops on board is in trouble and can I do something to help them. Well, I had already sent an armed merchant cruiser and *Bonaventure* to look for her but without aircraft it is damn hard to find a ship when you don't know just where she is. So the only thing to do was to go off in *Renown* and *Ark Royal* full belt, leaving *Sheffield* and the destroyers behind to round up the convoy until Wake Walker in *Formidable* took charge down there. We have got about 600 miles to go . . . *6 p.m.* – the transport has at last made her position. She is in a badish way and can only make 5 knots. I have called up the AMC and *Bonaventure* to proceed to her assistance and ordered two destroyers as well if they have enough fuel whilst we and *Ark* have also turned NW so as to try and locate her at dawn tomorrow and what then? This part is pretty lousy with submarines so we can't afford to stop and take the troops off. In fact having once found her we'll have to shin off out of it. . . . And all the time I've go this job hung up and everyone asking when it can start. I expect it will end up with my having to do the job with even fewer ships than usual.

131.   *To his wife*

28 December 1940

We plugged along all night towards where we reckon the transport might be but the weather got thicker and thicker and at dawn it was quite clear that air operations were out of the question. On top of all that we found that our starboard bulge had torn away for about 30 feet at the fore end, was bent right back and was beating the ship's side. Water was coming in fast on the mess deck and in certain of the store rooms and the ship's side working in an ominous manner. So that decided me and I signalled to Harold Burrough to take charge of operations in connection with the transport whilst I returned to Gib with the convoy. Further south it appears that Wake Walker has managed to round up most of the convoy so it looks as if we are getting things straightened out at last. But the air has been blue with wireless and every U-boat must have been collecting like a vulture. Hope by tomorrow I may be able to pick up a couple of destroyers as a screen. We can't do more than 18 or 19 knots now with this loose piece of skin. Trouble is we are due for another job immediately and I don't know how we shall get old *Renown* moderately seaworthy in time. Every day it is postponed, the moon gets higher and makes the job stickier . . .

132.   *To his wife*

31 December 1940

We got back at 8.30 a.m. yesterday and went straight into dry dock. There was a huge piece of our bulge torn away and bent back against the ship's side. It has been cut off but it will take a week to make good the damage. The harbour is absolutely bunged full of ships. I don't altogether like it and on top of it all came orders from the Admiralty to pursue the French business harder than ever. Fat Fred Collins, who takes over tomorrow, says he simply can't understand what they are driving at. It is just Winston and apparently Alexander is completely in his pocket and says 'OK Chief' to everything. I am fed up with the whole party. DP ought to damn well resign if he doesn't agree with the policy now being carried out. According to Fred RK[eyes] is an absolute menace. He came into Harwood's room the other day and said what the Navy lacked nowadays was guts. Harwood nearly blew up but RK is another of Winston's pets. He has no responsibility and only thinks of glorifying the name of RK. He doesn't take any long view as to what our policy should be until we are in a position to strike really hard. If I had just been a yes man and followed blindly the suggestions or even instructions I have had from time to time both *Renown* and the *Ark* would have been out of it by this time with nothing to show for it.

133.   *Report of Proceedings, 30 December 1940–6 January 1941*

11 January 1941

30 December 1940

4.   A new statement of the functions of Force H was issued by the Admiralty, cancelling the previous statement issued in AM 1742 of 28 June 1940. This was as follows.

(a)   The Flag Officer Commanding, North Atlantic Station, is responsible for preventing the passage of the Straits of Gibraltar by all enemy vessels and by vessels of other nations as may be ordered by the Admiralty from time to time.

(b)   While Force H is based on Gibraltar, the FOC, NAS, is to call upon the Flag Officer, Force H, for such assistance as may be necessary. Except when directed to carry out specific tasks by the Admiralty, the FOC, Force H, is to comply with such requests so far as he is able, but if, owing to conflicting claims he is unable to do so, the Admiralty should be informed.

(c) Force H is available for operations in the Mediterranean as agreed to by the Admiralty and as mutually arranged by the C-in-C, Mediterranean Station, and the FOC, Force H. It will be lent temporarily to the Mediterranean Station when so employed.

(d) The FOC, Force H, remains responsible for the administration of Force H and for its tactical employment during operations, whether acting under the strategical control of the Admiralty or C-in-C, Mediterranean, or in compliance with a request from the FOC, NAS.

5. Orders were received to put operation RATION into force on 31 December and on subsequent days. No limit was placed to the number of interceptions to be made, but the results of each were to be reported as soon as possible. The object of the operation was given as follows, 'to prevent the French making a hole in our blockade' . . . This was the first intimation I had received concerning the object of operation RATION and it was still not clear to me how our policy of infringing territorial waters to enforce the blockade could be reconciled with the policy adopted in connection with other neutral countries. . . . I have asked to be furnished with further information on this and other points connected with the interception of French convoys.

. . . The VAC, North Atlantic, drew the attention of Their Lordships to the state of Gibraltar at this time, which rendered it particularly vulnerable to air attack. Almost every available berth was occupied, and the ships included three capital ships, two aircraft carriers and other warships, five large MT ships containing important and valuable cargoes, including a large number of mines, and more were expected shortly. I have had occasion to represent previously that operation RATION not only imposes a heavy strain on destroyers but limits very severely the activity of A/S patrols in this area and training practices of ships and carrier aircraft.

1 January 1941

13. *Bonaventure* was ordered to sea to support Captain (D),13th DF, in *Duncan*, who in company with *Jaguar*, *Foxhound*, *Firedrake* and *Hero*, had proceeded to carry out operation RATION. At 1200, a French convoy consisting of *Chantilly*, *Octane*, *Suroit* and *Sally Maersk* escorted by the French trawler *La Toulonaise* was intercepted . . . active obstruction of the armed party boarding *Chantilly* from *Jaguar* resulted in the latter firing a burst of machine gun fire into the water close to the merchant

ship; two passengers were killed and four wounded, it is presumed from richochets. The escorting vessel was permitted to proceed to Oran and the merchant ships were brought into Gibraltar without further incident,[1]
. . .
14.   . . . It appeared to me probable, in the event of a continuance of RATION before EXCESS took place, that the French would re-establish air reconnaissance of the areas east and west of the Straits, in which case the proposed action to cover the movements of the MT ships and Force H would be of little avail. . . . however, Admiralty orders were received that RATION was to be continued. Shortly after receipt of these instructions the first French reconnaissance aircraft for some considerable period appeared over Gibraltar.
17.   A heavy southwesterly gale during the night caused the MT *Northern Prince* to drive ashore in the vicinity of the destroyer trot north of the harbour. MT ship *Clan MacDonald*[2] parted her cable but was able to proceed out of harbour and anchor without sustaining damage.

2 January

21.   Colonel Donovan, US representative, accompanied by Colonel Dykes,[3] lunched with me on board *Renown*. In compliance with Colonel Donovan's request I informed him as fully as lay in my power of the general situation in the Western Mediterranean and the functions of Force H. . . . We also discussed the manner in which the American Navy could best be employed to assist the British Navy should the occasion arise. I gathered he had been informed previously that assistance in dealing with raiders, convoy protection, and A/S operations were required with a view to releasing British ships from other duties. With this suggestion I expressed general agreement.

3 January

22.   At 0930 a French reconnaissance aircraft was engaged by the shore batteries, the A/A fire on this occasion reaching a new low level of efficiency. It was, in fact, a deplorable exhibition. . . .

---

[1]*Chantilly*: 1922, 9986gt, 13.5k, Messageries Maritimes. *Octane*: 1939, 2020gt, Cie Nav des Petroles, Havre. *Suroit*: tanker, 1938, 554gt, Citerna Maritime, Rouen. *Sally Maersk*: 1923, 3252gt, A.P. Möller, Aalborg, Denmark.
[2]*Northern Prince*: 1929, 10,917gt, 16.5k, Prince Line; she eventually went to Suez via the Cape. *Clan MacDonald*: 1939, 7980gt, 17.5k, Clan Line.
[3]Col William J. Donovan, US Army: Republican politician but confidant of Roosevelt, who sent him on several information-gathering missions in Europe; he reported on British defences in July 1940; this particular trip was from London, Dec 1940, to the Middle E, Jan 1941. He became Chief of the Office of Strategic Services, a forerunner of the CIA and the equivalent of British units like SOE. Col. Vivian Dykes, British liaison officer.

134. *To his wife*

5 January 1941

. . . in the process of seizing a French convoy there was a shooting match and a harmless French passenger and a small girl were killed and several wounded. That is going to cause a hell of a row but it's just exactly what I foretold would happen. It seems to me that we are just as much a dictator country as either Germany or Italy and one day the Great British public will wake up to ask what we are fighting for.

135. *To his wife*

6 January 1941

. . . Incidentally, the Government has now come almost completely round as regards the French business. All sorts of restrictions as to when and how French ships may be stopped and a request I made that it should be called off so as to let me rest and repair the destroyers was approved at once. Formerly I got just a direct snub. HE[1] flew home last night to put his views on the French business before the Government. As he hasn't really got any views he asked for some ammunition which I was only too glad to give him.

136. *Report of Proceedings, 7–11 January 1941*

17 January 1941

7 January

2. Force H, comprising *Renown, Malaya, Ark Royal, Sheffield, Faulknor, Firedrake, Forester, Fury, Foxhound, Fortune* and *Jaguar*, left Gibraltar at 0805 for operation EXCESS. For the purposes of the operation this Force was known as Group 1 to distinguish it from the MT Ship convoy (Group 2, comprising *Bonaventure, Duncan, Hereward, Hasty* and *Hero,* SS *Clan MacDonald, Clan Cumming, Empire Song* and *Essex*[2]. Group 2 had feinted the previous evening to the westward and returned eastward through the Straits under cover of darkness.

3.   . . . A/S patrol was flown off from *Ark Royal* on leaving harbour and maintained throughout the day.

[1]The Governor of Gibraltar, Lord Dillon.
[2]*Hereward* (sunk off Crete May 1941), *Hasty* (sunk off N Africa 1942 E-boat): 1936, 1340t, 4×4.7in, 8tt, 36k. *Clan Cumming*: 1938, 7264gt, 17k, Clan Line. *Empire Song*: 1940, 9228gt; mined off Malta May 1941. *Essex*: 1936, 11,063gt, 17k, Federal SN Co.

9 January

15. Speed was increased to 20 knots at 0025 in order to reach the position for flying off the Swordfish aircraft of 821 [Squadron] 'X' Flight. . . . All the aircraft landed safely in Malta[1].

19. Force B[2] joined the convoy when the latter was proceeding at 5 knots and streaming paravanes. . . .

24. By 1320 the RDF indicated a raid bearing 110°, approximately at the maximum working range of *Sheffield*'s Type 79, closing at 43 miles. Fourteen minutes later 10 enemy aircraft were sighted passing down the starboard side of the fleet, on the opposite course, out of gun range. The height was reported by *Ark Royal* as 11,000 feet.

At 1346 the raid started to come in from 145°, the bearing of the sun and two minutes later *Renown* and *Ark Royal* opened fire. The aircraft were initially out of range and the bursts were in consequence well short. As the formation approached, it came under heavy fire, the accuracy of which showed a marked improvement on previous encounters. Ships of Force H were firing up ladders for range, the steps of the ladder being applied from the best predicted range of the moment.

32. All flying-on operations were completed by 1815, and at 1830 *Malaya*, *Duncan* and *Firedrake* rejoined Group 1, the Rear Admiral Commanding, 3rd Cruiser Squadron,[3] being instructed to act independently.

Force H parted company with the convoy and escort at 1920, . . .

11 January

39. . . . *Renown* and ships in company entered harbour at 1920, and the remainder of Force H, proceeding at *Malaya*'s best speed, arrived at 2020.

137. *To his wife*

10 January 1941

Well we got through our part of the show alright but it was an anxious and trying time for me as you can imagine. On the night of the 8/9, we, *Ark* and Charles L[arcom's] ship[4] pushed ahead at high speed and at 5

---

[1]Five aircraft flew; another was unserviceable.

[2]*Gloucester, Southampton, Ilex.*

[3]Rear Adm E. de F. Renouf: Capt 1928, *Sheffield* 1938; RA Jan 1940, Admy; 3 & 7CS, Med July 1940–March 1941; duty with ACNS (W) April 1942; VA on Ret List April 1943; N Asst to D1SL July 1945. 3CS was Force B.

[4]Capt Charles A. A. Larcom: Capt 1932; DNAD 1939; *Sheffield* Dec 1939; Cdre & NOIC, N Shore Base, Aden May 1942; Ret List July 1942; *Daedalus* (Lee-on-Solent) Nov 1944.

p.m. in the pitch dark flew off 5 Swordfish for Malta. As these were my aircraft I took damn good care that they were all properly tested and good crews and in particular their endurance was carefully tested. . . . We then went back and picked up the convoy . . . About 9.30 a.m. we found we were being shadowed but the fighters could not catch him in the clouds. I forgot to say about 8.45 one of our reconnaissance aircraft reported two enemy cruisers and two destroyers so it looked as though another party was going to start. The evening before I was told that there were three enemy battleships at Naples and an undetermined number of cruisers there and at Messina and Palermo so prospects were not too bright for me as you can imagine. However this report of enemy cruisers turned out to be a mistake . . . Our reconnaissance found no surface ships but I had no means of being sure that they might not turn up in the afternoon. One of the transports was making volumes of smoke in spite of repeated signals and of course giving away our position. At 1.20 p.m. there were signs of a bombing raid and they came in at 1.46, 10 Savoias. Our A/A fire was much better this time and evidently put the Itis off. *Malaya* and one of the cruisers had some near misses but we and the *Ark* had nothing really near us. The Fulmar of which Mark is observer shot down 2 Savoias single-handed. One came down not far from us – a thrilling sight. . . . After dark we broke away from the party having seen them to the front door of the next parish. Owing to the bright moon and smooth sea I expected E-boats and other attackers but none materialised. At about 2 a.m. I was able to have a nice lie down and I wanted it I can assure you. It is a pretty strenuous 48 hours doing these jobs and when I do get my clothes off and have a nice rinse the bath becomes extremely cloudy afterwards.

138. *Report of Proceedings, 12–20 January 1941*

22 January 1941

12 January

4. . . . Consequent on the damage sustained by *Gloucester* and the sinking of *Southampton* as the result of air attacks on 11 January,[1] the C-in-C, Mediterranean, was asked whether he preferred *Bonaventure* or *Sheffield* as a replacement for *Southampton*, and also whether a relief for *Gloucester* was required while that ship was being repaired.

---

[1]This marked the appearance of the Luftwaffe in the Mediterranean. *Illustrious* was so badly damaged that she had to proceed to the USA for repairs, which took a year to complete.

I represented that *Renown, Ark Royal* and *Sheffield* had been working together for some time with a resultant increase of fighting efficiency, especially as regards fighter control by RDF, and asked that this should receive due consideration. The C-in-C, Mediterranean, replied that under present conditions he preferred *Bonaventure* to *Sheffield*, since he required a small ship with up-to-date A/A equipment rather than a heavier but less modern type. He added that for the time being, and provided that the Italians showed no signs of more activity, a relief for *Gloucester* could be dispensed with.

5.   The damage to *Illustrious* made it necessary to change the plans for *Formidable* who, it had been intended, should relieve *Ark Royal* in Force H in the early part of the year. In the circumstances, it was necessary to order her to the Eastern Mediterranean, where it was anticipated that she would arrive about 10 February.

6.   Lt-Cdr Stedman-Teller, US Navy, joined *Ark Royal* as US naval observer, instead of proceeding to *Illustrious . . .*

7.   I informed the Admiralty that only four destroyers were now available at Gibraltar for Force H and all local duties, and one of these (*Fury*) had one gun out of action. Two more would be available in 7 days.[1] . . .

13 January

8.   In response to an enquiry whether I should prefer to retain No. 800 (Skua) Squadron or to exchange it with a Fulmar squadron, . . . I reported that Fulmars were preferred, in view of the added importance of maximum speed fighters since the advent of the Luftwaffe into the Mediterranean and the few opportunities of using Skuas for offensive operations in the Western basin.

14 January

14.   . . . With the limited destroyer force available, it is of the utmost importance that defects requiring dockyard assistance should be dealt with promptly. On many occasions Force H has been immobilised owing to lack of destroyers fit for sea. I consider that very early reinforcement of the Dockyard staff is an urgent requirement.[2]

---

[1] Four (*Vidette, Velox, Isis, Encounter*) were at Freetown, the last two due to return to Force H. *Foresight* and *Fearless* were in the UK. *Wishart* was re-tubing her condensers. *Fortune* was refitting.
[2] This reinforced a plea by FOCNA.

139.   *Report of Proceedings, 21–31 January 1941*

2 February 1941

22 January

8.   Captain R. R. McGrigor, appointed to relieve Rear-Admiral C.E.B. Simeon in command of *Renown*, had taken passage in *Foresight* and joined HMS *Renown*.

12.   In reply to my request for an opinion whether the results likely to be obtained from the projected attack on Genoa were such as to justify the risks involved to *Renown* and *Ark Royal*, the Admiralty stated that the operation was considered fully justified. The C-in-C, Mediterranean, said he considered the operation would be most valuable, particularly the attack on Genoa, which should place the Italian fleet in some doubt as to the direction from which the coast might be threatened and also to divert air forces from southern Italy.

13.   He stated that it would not be possible to provide any but a small scale diversion owing to the subjugation of all operations to the movement of *Illustrious* from Malta, and the fact that *Eagle* would be in dock during the period of the operation. The Fleet would be temporarily without fighter protection or fleet reconnaissance and its movements would be limited. Any action possible would be taken, however.

26 January

38.   *Jersey* and *Jupiter* arrived at noon from the UK to take part in operation RESULT.[1] . . .

29 January

59.   Information was received that the German aircraft in Sicily were probably being reinforced by a long-range bomber group of 40 aircraft, practised in minelaying. It was estimated that the number of German aircraft in the Mediterranean was 160 long-range bombers, 20 bomber-reconnaissance, 150 dive-bombers, 40 twin-engined fighters and 40 to 60 transports, of which the majority were probably in Sicily.[2]

---

[1]RESULT was to be the bombardment of Genoa; on the way PICKET, a bombing raid on the Tirso dam in Sardinia, was to be carried out. Somerville discussed these operations with his Captains and his staff; most of them opposed the plans. *Jupiter*: 1939, 1690t, 6×4.7in, 10tt, 36k; mined off Java March 1942.

[2]There were presumably also Me109 single-engined fighters. This force, *Fliegerkorps X*, was specially trained to attack shipping.

140.   *To his wife*

2 February 1941

Well we have had a damnably disappointing day. All last night we steamed at high speed towards Sardinia, to a point about half way up the west coast. The wind was steadily rising all the time. Our object was to fly off the Swordfish from the *Ark* to attack the dam of a big reservoir which supplies about a third of the power in the island. The Admiralty said that at the top of the dam there were only 3 feet of concrete and suggested we should use torpedoes. They also said that it was probably not at all well defended by A/A. Well when the Swordfish took off the weather looked pretty filthy, pitch dark of course as the attack was to be at dawn.

The wind having increased so much it was necessary for us to meet the Swordfish at the same spot as we flew them off which wasn't so good as it was uncomfortably close to the coast and aerodrome where the German dive-bombers live. We had an anxious time waiting for them to return and when they got back I learnt that they had had heavy A/A fire during the whole of their approach up the valley to the reservoir and most intense A/A fire at the reservoir. Only 3 out of 8 torpedoes hit the dam and owing to the intense A/A no results could be observed. Worst of all one machine failed to return[1] . . . After that I had another operation in mind[2] but by this time the wind had increased to a gale with very heavy sea. The result was that we had to ease right down and although I flogged away all day to windward and the poor destroyers were badly battered [I} had eventually to give it up as hopeless and we simply couldn't reach the spot we had to at the right time. . . . Now why was it that on a Sunday morning of all times the Itis should have been so alert? They know we are out of course but why should they have been ready for our attack on a place we have never touched before? It is all very odd.[3]

141.   *To his wife*

7 February 1941

Here we are off again to try and do what we weren't able to complete on our last trip. Hope to goodness it comes off this time but there are a hell of lot of ifs about it all. I had to put it pretty plainly to TL that I

[1]Crew taken prisoner.
[2]The bombardment of Genoa.
[3]There had been loose talk in Gibraltar.

assumed they were prepared to accept this and that risk as 'I felt there should be no misunderstanding on this point'. That's the worst of the situation in which I find myself placed. I feel all the time that there is no frankness and no real confidence between me and TL. Not a word to the effect that 'we leave it entirely to your judgement and are quite ready to accept your decision whatever it is'. On the contrary it is a case of 'go and do this' and unless things went badly amiss I feel positive they would turn round and say 'oh we never meant you to go as far as that, you should have used your judgement'. Or if I decide that something is not justified I feel positive they would say 'you ought to have appreciated the importance of the matter and been prepared to take considerable risks'. . . .

142. *To his wife*

8 February 1941

A quiet night but alas this morning it is as clear as a bell with tremendous visibility. Unfortunately we have been sighted by a civil aircraft flying from Majorca to Marseilles and I feel sure they are bound to report it. This is a damn ticklish job to be sure and I shall be glad when the next 48 hours are safely over. I shall be either very much in the papers or very much in the soup, neither of which I care about! Funny thing, I always said I hoped I would be retired in the next war so that I could enjoy it by having some small job on my own, e.g., an armed yacht or something like that and here I am retired all right and this ruddy load of responsibility on my shoulders. At times it seems very light and at others particularly heavy. . . . Wherever one is war is a bloody senseless business and the sooner mankind realise it the better. . . . I used to be able to air my views to dear old Knight-Adkin but he's gone home as you know. I think one of my troubles – with him and old Dudley away – I have no-one really I can heart to heart with. Hook Holland, McGrigor, Palliser[1] are all good chaps that I can talk to quite freely in a sense but not so freely in another sense because it wouldn't do for them to know how I feel about war. The leader must be out for blood all the time (which I am of course) but must not show how filthy it all is. . . . *4 p.m.* – a number of alarms this afternoon from aircraft. We have to dodge away every time we think we are going to be sighted so as not to disclose our real destination. It has all got to be so damn quick. As it turned out most of the aircraft turned out to be French. I hope things being as they are at Vichy the Frogs won't

---

[1]Palliser was Captain of *Malaya*.

report us. But this part of the business is a bit of a strain I must confess and I shall be very glad when the next 24 hours are over and done with. We have had no luck with our fighters today. One Skua made a bad landing and the under-carriage collapsed whilst a Fulmar had to force-land before *Ark* was properly headed into the wind. . . .

143.   *To his wife*

10 February 1941

. . . some time ago I suggested that given the right conditions the bombardment of Genoa appeared to be quite possible . . . I laid down three factors as necessary if we were to avoid undue hazards: 1) intention to be concealed; 2) approach to be undetected; 3) sufficient destroyers so that they could work in reliefs as the distance was too great for one boat to go at highest speed all the way.[1]

. . . About 6.45 a dull smudge ahead of us showed the high mountains behind Genoa but it was terribly hard to be sure that we had hit the right part of the coast. Our luck was in and Martin Evans[2] got a fix which showed we were just right. Not a sign from shore, not a ship except our own on the sea. We steamed up to the beginning of the run, i.e., about 10 miles off Genoa and then flash went the broadsides. Of Genoa itself we could see nothing. Our guns were laid by gyro and our aircraft over the town spotted us on to the various targets. The first salvoes fell almost exactly where we wanted them and *then* I felt content. The curtain was up and the tragedy was on. For half an hour we blazed away and I had to think of Senglea, Valetta, London and Bristol, etc., to harden my heart. But I was watching the map and the reports of the aircraft and I do believe that practically all of our salvoes fell on works, warehouses, shipping, docks, etc. Still it is no use pretending that some innocent people were [not?] killed. War is lousy. After half an hour we turned away and steamed south at full speed to meet *Ark* who had been doing her stuff, blocking up the entrance to Spezia and plastering an all-important refinery at Leghorn that the RAF had never managed to hit yet. We made contact all right and again I gave a sigh of relief as we were now able to meet the expected air attacks with the whole force concentrated. Shadowers appeared and two were promptly shot down by our fighters. Then a bombing formation of only two bombers arrived and tried to

---

[1]Refuelling at sea was still not well practised in the RN.

[2]Cdr Martin J. Evans: Lt-Cdr 1935; Navigating Officer, *Renown* 1939; Cdr Dec 1940; Malta May 1941; CO, Escort Group B3, *Keppel* April 1943; Actg Capt, *Philante* July 1945.

attack *Ark*. Our A/A was not good but their bombing aim was even worse. Luckily the haze continued and although other bombers were hovering around they seemed unable to find us. But the wind was wrong and each time we had to fly on or off we had to turn back towards the enemy air and surface bases. Quite maddening, especially if some young pilots made a bad approach and had to be waved round again, losing us another precious 3–4 miles. In the afternoon we sight a convoy of 6 merchant ships. Are they Italians? If so the destroyers have orders to give them 10 minutes to man the boats and then torpedo them. The weather is fine and we are not far from land, but they turn out to be 5 Frenchmen and one Turk, so we leave them alone. By sunset we are out of imminent danger and am I tired? I can't recall having felt so worn out before. It was not only a very anxious and trying time for me then but we had only 48 hours in after that previous operation which was also a pretty good strain on me as you can imagine. But I had a good sleep last night – 11 p.m. to 4 a.m. without a break and I feel as fresh as a daisy this morning. . . . To me it is quite unbelievable that we should have effected so complete a surprise. Mind you I had taken infinite trouble to *try* and disguise our movements and intentions but one would have thought that the Itis would have had some form of patrol on the approaches to Genoa. They will now of course and aircraft too – which is just what we want them to do. Everyone in Force H is very cock-a-hoop about it all. . . .

144.   *Report of Proceedings, 5–11 February 1941*

18 February 1941

6 February

10.   For this operation, . . . GROG . . . Force H was divided into three groups.

Group 2, consisting of *Fearless* (SO, 8th DF), *Foxhound*, *Foresight*, *Fury*, *Encounter* and *Jersey*, left harbour unobtrusively in units of one or two ships between 1200 and 1400 and proceeded to the eastward as though on patrol or exercising. When out of sight of land, Group 2 concentrated and proceeded to the eastward at economical speed to rendezvous with Groups 1 and 3, a.m., on D3, carrying out an A/S sweep on passage.

Group 1, comprising *Renown*, *Malaya*, *Ark Royal* and *Sheffield*, screened by Group 3, comprising *Duncan*, *Isis*, *Firedrake* and *Jupiter*, left harbour between 1600 and 1630.

8 February

18.   My policy for the day was to make ground to the NE, remaining undetected if possible. The A/S patrol and fighters were instructed to avoid being seen by merchant ships and to give warning of their approach so that the course could be altered in time to avoid detection. Whenever an aircraft was detected by RDF, course was immediately altered S of E in order to give the impression that the objective was a town in Sardinia.

9 February

21.   *Ark Royal*, screened by *Duncan, Isis* and *Encounter*, was detached at 0400 to act independently to carry out air attacks on Leghorn and Spezia.

    At 0505 . . . *Ark Royal* flew off a striking force of 14 Swordfish, followed by 4 Swordfish carrying magnetic mines and later by 3 standby spotting aircraft with an escorting section of fighters. . . .

28.   Tuning in of spotting aircraft furnished by *Sheffield, Malaya* and *Ark Royal* commenced at 0655. At 0711 *Renown*'s spotting aircraft reported no battleships were present. By 0714 when fire was opened all spotting aircraft were in position and tuned in. At this time, and subsequently during the bombardment, nothing could be seen of Genoa and the firing was carried out using indirect fire.

30.   The opening salvoes from *Renown* fell as anticipated S of Malo Principe and were quickly spotted on to the Ansaldo Works, Marshalling Yards and factories on both banks of the Torrente Polcevera. Numerous explosions and considerable fires were observed in this area. Target was then shifted to the vicinity of the commercial basin where a big fire was caused and a merchant ship was hit. A salvo in the vicinity of the Power Station caused a particularly violent explosion and an oil tank was observed to be on fire. The smoke from this tank and various warehouses prevented the spotting of several salvoes but a little later rounds were observed to fall in the area W of Ponte Daglio Asscreto and Ponte Carriciolo. The last salvoes fired in this area fell on the latter causing an explosion followed by a considerable fire. Target was again shifted, and the electrical works appeared to receive a direct hit. Fire was moved up the left bank of Torrente Polcevera and having crossed it salvoes were spotted directly on to Ansaldo Works, but smoke by then rendered observation difficult. The secondary armament engaged the area along the water front.

31.   *Malaya* engaged the dry docks and targets in their vicinity throughout. Big explosions were observed in the docks and among ware-

houses. Several salvoes could not be spotted owing to smoke, but the last four were seen to fall among houses just NE of the docks.

32.   *Sheffield*'s opening salvoes were placed short in the sea and were readily spotted. Having found range, rapid salvoes were ordered and fire was directed at the industrial installations of the left bank at the mouth of the Torrente Polcevera. Many fires and two big explosions were caused in this area. Later, as smoke was obscuring the sea, fire was shifted to a tanker under way off the port and although three salvoes straddled no actual hits were observed.[1]

36.   Whilst the main force was approaching Genoa, *Ark Royal*'s striking force of 14 Swordfish, each armed with 4 × 250lb GP bombs and 16 incendiaries, had proceeded to attack the Azienda Oil Refinery at Leghorn. Eleven aircraft dropped their bombs on the refinery but no clear estimate could be formed of the amount of damage inflicted except that one definite explosion was observed. Surprise was evidently achieved as only one or two HA guns opened fire when the attack started. About 6 minutes later, however, the HA fire became severe.

37.   Two of the striking force, having mistaken their landfall, attacked alternative targets, one attacking Pisa aerodrome and the other Pisa railway junction.

39.   Three of the minelaying aircraft made a gliding approach from over the town of Spezia, two laying in the western entrance of the harbour and one in the eastern entrance. The fourth aircraft approached from the opposite direction and laid in the western entrance. There was only a partial blackout of the town. Short range A/A weapons of the Bofors type engaged the aircraft during their final approach and there was also some A/A fire from guns around the town, but these appeared to be firing blind into the air.

41.   By 0848 all spotting, minelaying and striking force aircraft had landed on (with the exception of the one reported missing[2]) and *Ark Royal* proceeded to rendezvous with the rest of Force H . . . at 0900. By 0919 the whole force was steering 180° at 22 knots.

11 February

56.   Force H entered harbour between 1430 and 1615. . . .

---

[1]Owing to an error in signalling, the tanker was not pursued.
[2]Brought down over Leghorn; crew taken prisoner.

145.   *Report of Proceedings, 11–25 February 1941*

26 February 1941

12 February

6.   At 1210 a raider report from position 37° 12'N, 21° 20'W, was received. Measures were taken to prepare Force H for sea immediately, . . . At 1307 orders were received for Force H to proceed to the assistance of Convoy HG 53.

7.   . . . by 1830 *Renown, Ark Royal* and *Sheffield*, screened by *Wishart, Jersey, Foxhound, Firedrake* and *Fury* were clear of the harbour and proceeding to the westward. It was my intention to retain the destroyer escort only if the weather was suitable. Later in the evening I learned that Force H was to take over escort of Convoy WS6 from *Rodney* who had been ordered to join this Convoy pending the arrival of Force H.

8.   The AMCs *Camito, Corinthian, Cavina* and *Maron* were proceeding from their patrol areas . . . to search for survivors from Convoy SLS 64. It was later learnt that the raider which had attacked this convoy had been identified by survivors as a *Blücher* class cruiser.[1] . . .

13 February

11.   *Sheffield* parted company at 1130 and proceeded in execution of previous orders. . . . Her presence afforded some slight degree of A/S protection to *Renown* and *Ark Royal*, and her RDF might have provided an opportunity for fighters to intercept any Focke Wulf aircraft carrying out a long range reconnaissance.[2]

12.   *Ark Royal* flew off an A/S patrol at 0900 and a reconnaissance of 5 Swordfish at 1330 . . . with the object of locating raiders or the Italian SS *Capo Lena*[3] which had been reported leaving Vigo at 1300/12. These aircraft returned about 1700 having sighted nothing.

17 February

21.   At dawn course was altered to 186° parallel to the course of the convoy and air reconnaissance was prepared in *Ark Royal*. At 0840 smoke was sighted bearing 280° and this was identified 15 minutes later as coming from the convoy. *Ark Royal* flew off an A/S patrol of 3 aircraft

---

[1]*Camito*: ocean boarding vessel, 1915, 6833gt, 14k, Elders & Fyffes; later war loss. *Corinthian*: AMC, 1938, 3122gt, 13.5k, Ellerman & Papayanni Lines. *Cavina*: 1924, 6097gt, 14.5k, Elders & Fyffes. *Maron*: AMC, 1930, 6487gt, 14.5k, Alfred Holt/China Mutual SN.

The *Hipper* again; this convoy had been undefended and lost 7 ships.

[2]*Sheffield* was equipped with an Asdic dome.

[3]*Capo Lena*: 1921, 4820gt, Cia Genovese di Nav.

to cover the area and on each side and quarter of the convoy and also flew off 6 aircraft for an all-round reconnaissance.

22.   By 1100 *Renown* had formed up in the convoy . . ., whilst *Ark Royal* remained outside for flying. My intentions were to keep *Renown*, *Birmingham* and AMC *Cathay*[1] formed in the convoy by day and outside by night, whilst *Ark Royal* did the reverse as long as conditions were suitable for flying. The convoy was steering 184°, 10½ knots.

21 February

35.   At 1015, 3 aircraft were flown off as A/S patrol and 6 for reconnaissance. At this time *Malaya*'s foretop was sighted bearing 190°, 15 miles. . . . I turned the convoy over to her. *Renown* and *Ark Royal* proceeded at 20 knots on a course 074° to Gibraltar.

22 February

42.   At 1330 I learnt that there were signs that the *Hipper* class cruiser in Brest might be preparing to leave port. As there appeared to be a possibility of intercepting her if she left harbour that night I altered course to the NE and informed the Admiralty of my intentions. At the same time I requested that a dawn reconnaissance of Brest and search to the southwestward might be arranged. I also requested the VAC, NAS, to order the destroyer screen to wait in position 37° 00'N, 12° 00'W, pending further orders.

23 February

46.   At 1846 I received news that the *Hipper* cruiser was still in dry dock at Brest and as lack of fuel precluded waiting for her departure I set course for Gibraltar at 20 knots.

25 February

50.   During the passage of the Straits a range and inclination exercise was carried out for the benefit of the Rock defences. *Renown* entered harbour at 0930. *Ark Royal* was detached to carry out torpedo bombing attacks and entered harbour four hours later.[2]

---

[1]*Birmingham*: 1937, 9100t, 12×6in, 8×4in, 6tt, 32k. *Cathay*: 1925, 15,225gt, 16.25k, P & O Line.
[2]*Sheffield* had been ordered to assist convoy SLS64 and then HG53 and, after refuelling at Gibraltar, escort SL65N. A westerly gale had forced destroyers to return to Gibraltar on 12 Feb. *Renown* required more work on her bulges.

146. *Report of Proceedings, 25–28 February 1941*

1 March 1941

25 February

3. I was able to meet Rear Admiral A.L.St.G. Lyster,[1] who was on passage by air from the Eastern Mediterranean to the UK. The opportunity was taken of discussing experience gained in the Eastern Mediterranean, particularly as regards air attacks, and much valuable information was obtained.

4. The presence of the Naval Attaché, Madrid, in Gibraltar provided an excellent opportunity of discussing Spanish affairs.

26 February

5. It was my intention, on completion of repairs to *Renown*, to carry out a sweep in the Western basin with the object of containing enemy forces by a threat of further action against the Italian coast. I accordingly signalled this proposal to the Admiralty but was informed that it was intended to employ Force H on Atlantic trade routes in the near future and therefore it was not desired that commitments in the Western Mediterranean should be undertaken at this stage.

6. I requested immediate information of the departure of a *Hipper* class cruiser from Brest, where she was in dock, in order to carry out an operation to intercept with *Renown* and *Ark Royal*. This operation depended on receiving notice of her departure within a few hours, and on weather conditions being favourable for a high-speed approach to the area of search and subsequent flying operations.

28 February

7. The Military Governor of Algeciras, General Don Muñoz Grandes, visited Gibraltar with his diplomatic advisor, the Marques del Valle Cerrado, his Aide-de-Camp, Lt-Col Lombana, and Lt-Cdr A. Urziaz, commanding the MTB Flotilla at Algeciras. These officers lunched with me on board *Renown*, together with the senior Naval Officers present in Gibraltar. . . .

[1]Rear Adm (later Adm Sir) Arthur L StG Lyster (1888–1957): ent RN 1903; Instr *Excellent* 1912; Gun O *Glory* 1914; Dardanelles; *Cassandra* N Sea & Baltic 1917; Gun O *Renown* 1918; Capt 1928; *Danae*, *Despatch* 1931–2; 5DF 1933–5; Gun Sch 1935–6; DTSD; *Glorious* 1937–9; RA Aug 1939; Norway 1940; Home F 1939–40; RA(A), Med F Sept 1940–Feb 1941; organised Taranto attack; 5SL March 1941–July 1942; RA (A) Home F July 1942; VA Oct 1942; N African landings Nov 1942; Ret List 1943; FO Corvette Training & Adm-in-Cmd, Largs April 1943–4.

147. *Report of Proceedings, 1–8 March 1941*

11 March 1941

3 March

8.   I arranged for my SO (P), Cdr A.W. Buzzard, to proceed to the UK by Sunderland in order to explain in detail my views and proposals for the employment of Force H on trade routes and to obtain information concerning a number of technical and strategical matters.

9.   At 1330 I embarked in *Ark Royal* and proceeded to sea, screened by *Fearless, Fortune* and *Duncan*, to witness and take part in flying exercises. In particular, I wished to experience for myself the speeded-up take-off of ranged aircraft following the practice which Admiral Lyster informed me had been tried successfully in *Illustrious*.

A number of exercises were carried out, including night landings, a night controlled landing and a night navigation exercise.

7 March

18.   Cdr Buzzard . . . brought back with him information concerning the proposed operations on the trade routes, the Spanish and Far Eastern situations and a number of technical matters. Occasional visits of this nature are undoubtedly of great value.

8 March

20.   A conference was held on shore attended by the FOC, Force H, the VAC, NAS, Major General F.N. Mason-Macfarlane,[1] and Captain L.V. Morgan,[2] to discuss the Spanish situation. . . .

The retention of naval forces at Gibraltar must depend to a very large extent on our ability to counter the enemy air offensive.

I took this occasion to point out to the General that not only did the A/A defence of Gibraltar still leave much to be desired, but it did not appear that the fixed defences could engage targets effectively by indirect fire.

The General agreed that the state of affairs was unsatisfactory and

---

[1]Maj-Gen Frank N. Mason-Macfarlane RA (1889–1953): 2Lt 1909; W Front 1914–15, 1917–18; Capt 1915; Mesopotamia 1915–16; GSO, India 1919–30; Maj 1927; Mil Att, Budapest 1931–5; Col & Mil Att, Berlin 1937; Brig, RA; Maj-Gen Aug 1938; DMI, BEF 1940; C-in-C Gibraltar 1941; head Br Mil Missn to USSR 1941–2; Govr Gibraltar 1942–4; Chf Cmnr Allied Contr Cmn 1944; Ret List 1945; Lab MP 1945–6.
[2]Capt Llewelyn V. W. Morgan: Capt 1933; *Royal Sovereign* 1939; CSO, *Lynx* (Dover) Jan 1940; *Cormorant* (Gibraltar) Feb 1941; *Revenge* July 1941–Nov 1942; RA & RIN Jan 1943; DSD Nov 1943–5.

expressed the hope that the joint committee formed to deal with this matter might effect some improvement.

22.   In view of the C-in-C, Mediterranean's signal 1132/4 it appeared
to me that no opportunity should be lost of creating diversions in the
Western Mediterranean in order to relieve to some extent the pressure on
the Eastern Mediterranean.

. . . I proposed proceeding with *Renown, Repulse*,[1] *Ark Royal* and
Furious to the eastward on 12 March and returning after dark to the
westward, *Renown* and *Ark Royal* subsequently to carry out a sweep
along the trade routes should it be necessary for *Renown* to return to
refuel before proceeding to the UK to refit. . . .

23.   These proposals, however, fell through on receipt of *Malaya*'s
report that at 1600, whilst escorting SL 67, . . . an unknown enemy vessel
had been sighted. . . .

At 1745 *Malaya* reported definitely that two *Scharnhorst* class battlecruisers had been sighted and, 3 minutes later, that they were retiring to
the west. . . .

148.   *Report of Proceedings, 8–23 March 1941*

24 March 1941

8 March

2.   *Renown, Ark Royal* and *Arethusa* sailed from Gibraltar at 2115,
screened by *Velox* and *Wrestler*, and proceeded at 27 knots towards the
Canaries.

3.   *Repulse* and *Furious* had been placed under my orders but in view
of their limited endurance and fuel remaining I considered they could
not be employed effectively in connection with potential attacks by the
German battlecruisers on the trade routes. I therefore ordered *Repulse*
and *Furious* to proceed to Gibraltar at maximum speed practicable, leaving *Strathmore*[2] to rendezvous with the destroyers, sent as local escort,
as previously arranged.

5.   *Velox* and *Wrestler*, being unable to keep up owing to weather conditions, were detached at midnight and ordered to return to Gibraltar.

10 March

11.   A further reconnaissance of 6 aircraft was flown off at 1330 to
search . . . to a depth of 80 miles. The Convoy having been located by the
air search, course was altered to 160° and at 1720 *Renown* and *Ark Royal*

[1]*Repulse*: 1916, 32,000t, 6×15in, 15×4in, 8tt, 29k; sunk S China Sea 10 Dec 1941,
Japanese naval aircraft.
[2]*Strathmore*: 1935, 23,428gt, 21k, P & O.

joined the Convoy which was being escorted by *Malaya*, *Cilicia*,[1] *Faulknor* and *Forester* . . . At 1750 *Malaya* was detached to return to Freetown.

16 March

40.   I learnt that *Hipper* had left Brest at some time during the previous 24 hours. I considered deflecting the convoy to the eastward to place *Ark Royal* in a more suitable position for a reconnaissance to endeavour to locate the enemy in the morning. The data was insufficient, however, to justify the diversion of the convoy with subsequent dislocation of local escort arrangements, and the considerable amount of signalling by light that would have been necessary.

19 March

58.   The evening reconnaissance also reported the Norwegian tanker *Bianca* . . . 12 knots, half laden. . . . as she was evidently in ballast and steering for Bordeaux, I concluded she must have a German prize crew on board. I therefore decided to intercept *Bianca* in the morning before carrying out the search for the German *Antartkis*.[2]

20 March

61.   At 1147 an aircraft dropped a message on board *Renown* reporting that the tanker *San Casimiro* had been sighted . . . An hour later another aircraft reported that the tanker *Polykarp*[3] had been sighted . . . Both these tankers . . . were probably in charge of German prize crews. In consequence I decided to intercept *San Casimiro* after *Bianca*, and subsequently *Polykarp* with the aid of an air search the following morning.
62.   The *Bianca* was sighted at 1210 . . . *Renown* closed and sent a boarding party, *Ark Royal* operating independently for flying. The weather was perfect for boarding. When *Renown* was 6 miles from *Bianca* she was seen to be abandoning ship, and as the boats pulled clear scuttling charges exploded and fire broke out in the engine room and on the bridge. The boarding party proceeded on board and the launch rounded up the *Bianca*'s boats and ordered them to return to their ship.

---

[1]*Cilicia*: 1938, 11,136gt, 16k, Anchor Line.
[2]*Bianca*: 1926, 5688gt, Rederi A/S Mascot; seized by Germans 15 March 1941; scuttled on approach of *Renown* 20 March 1941.
Antarktis: tanker, 1939, 10,000gt, Erste Deutsche Walfang, Hamburg; reported sailed from Vigo 17 or 18 March.
[3]*San Casimiro*: 1936, 8046gt, 12k, Eagle Oil; captured by Germans 15 March; scuttled 20 March on approach of *Renown*.
Polykarp: 1931, 6405gt, A/S Kristiansands Tankrederi; captured by Germans 15 March; not followed up; renamed *Taifun*; sunk 3 May 1945 by aircraft in Great Belt.

The fires were extinguished but the ship was low in the water with a considerable list to port and down by the stern. . . . When it was clear that the boarding party and crew [could] do nothing to improve the prospect of the ship remaining afloat I gave orders that they were to be recalled. It was my intention to return to this position subsequently to observe if she was still afloat and examine possibilities of towage by tugs from Lisbon.
67.   *San Casimiro* was sighted at 1715 . . . Immediately afterwards she abandoned ship and scuttling charges were fired. . . .
70.   The tanker's boats were closing *Renown* and the boarding party were in the act of transferring some of *San Casimiro*'s officers from the boat to the launch in order to return and see if anything could be done to save the ship when an enemy report was received by V/S from a Fulmar at 1815 that two enemy battlecruisers had been sighted at 1730 . . . steering north at 20 knots. This position was 110 miles NW of *Renown*. . . .
77.   At 2110 I informed the Admiralty that night shadowing and attack was impracticable due to low visibility and that I intended a dawn search in the direction of convoy SL 67 and to the westward thereof. If nothing was sighted I intended to return to Gibraltar. . . .

149.   *Report of Proceedings, 24–31 March 1941*

31 March 1941

24 March

5.   Lt-Cdr Ring, US Navy, US Naval Observer, joined *Ark Royal*.
7.   I signalled my proposals for the interception of *Gneisenau* and *Scharnhorst* should they leave Brest. . . .
9.   *Renown* and *Ark Royal* were brought to one hour's notice at 1900 and sailed at 2250, shaping course to the eastward at 17 knots, screened by *Foresight*, *Forester* and *Fortune*. *Empire Trooper*, who had sailed at 1530 to join convoy HG 57, was ordered back to harbour as the number of passengers carried was considered to be excessive having regard to her low speed.

25 March

14.   . . . the Admiralty . . . stated that it was not considered shore-based air reconnaissance could be relied upon to detect the departure of the enemy in time for the action suggested. Submarine patrols were, however, being established and it was hoped that this information would be received from that source. It was therefore considered that Force H should operate generally in the vicinity of convoy routes between the latitudes of Ushant and Lisbon, outside the area of enemy shore-based reconnaissance.

26 March

20. As the whereabouts of the enemy battlecruisers had not been established I decided to operate in an area which would afford cover for both OG 56 and *Sheffield*'s convoy which were southbound in the vicinity of 41°N, 20°W.

28 March

25. I received instructions that Force H was to return to Gibraltar, for operation WINCH,[1] and that the Force would be relieved by *Hood* and two cruisers from the Home Fleet p.m. on 30 March.

26. At 1800 course was altered to 090° to keep clear of the convoy route and at 2000 again altered to 010° to reach at dawn a more favourable position for the interception of the enemy battlecruisers should a report of their departure be received from the submarines patrolling in the Bay of Biscay.

Information was received at 2130 that air reconnaissance had located *Scharnhorst* and *Gneisenau* in Brest.

30 March

35. An intercepted signal from *Sheffield* indicated that operation RATION had resulted in an incident. Their Lordships will be aware that in previous Letters of Proceedings I have expressed the opinion that seizure of French ships in French territorial waters will most probably lead to reprisals. Providing 'incidents' are avoidable it is possible for our forces at Gibraltar to exercise a small nuisance effect on French trade. But if any serious interference with French trade is intended we must face up to the fact that we have neither surface nor air forces available to put this into effect. The French will call our bluff if we depart from the recognised procedure of limiting visit or search to vessels on the high seas or in enemy waters.[2]

31 March

36. *Napier* (Captain (D), 7th DF),[3] *Nizam* and *Fortune* joined at 0845 . . . and course was shaped for Gibraltar. . . .

---

[1]A delivery of Hurricanes to Malta; see No. 150.

[2]The failure to seize an inshore convoy and an inconclusive duel with shore batteries blighted Larcom's career and Somerville and Edward-Collins were also criticised by the Admiralty; as Somerville pointed out, they were on a hiding to nothing.

[3]*Napier* (L), *Nizam*: 1941, 1760t, 6×4.7in, 1×4in, 5tt, 36k; transferred to RAN.

Capt (D): Capt S. H. T. Arliss: Capt 1937; NA S Am 1939; *Napier* 1941; Cdre (D) Eastern F June 1942.

150. *Report of Proceedings, 1–4 April 1941*

7 April 1941

2 April

6. . . . By 0330 *Renown* and *Ark Royal*, screened by *Faulknor*, *Fearless*, *Foresight*, *Fury* and *Fortune*, were proceeding on a course 082° at 17 knots. *Sheffield* was delayed in leaving harbour and did not join until daylight. Speed was increased to 24 knots at 0355.

3 April

11. At 0600 course was altered to 250° into a light breeze, and 12 Hurricanes and two Skuas were flown off for Malta . . . The Hurricanes took off easily and in most cases were airborne between the island and the bows of *Ark Royal*. Force H then withdrew to the westward at 24 knots.

21. Information was received that HM Government might decide to prevent . . . *Dunkerque* leaving Oran on the following day by torpedoing her without warning, and that two submarines[1] were being sailed to take up an intercepting position.

4 April

25. . . . It appeared that in any case, if *Dunkerque* was torpedoed, the French would assume at once that it had been done by a British submarine since there can be little doubt that they would have advised the Italians of the intended movement.

If *Dunkerque* was torpedoed, an immediate and heavy air attack on Gibraltar must be expected, and having regard to the low standard of A/A defence at this base, it was imperative that the harbour should be cleared of as many heavy ships as possible. . . .

26. I therefore increased speed to 24 knots, with the intention of refuelling and transferring FAA stores with all despatch and sailing from Gibraltar as soon as practicable, carrying out operation TENDER[2] after sailing to the westward.

27. *Ark Royal* was detached with three destroyers at 0700 to proceed ahead at her best speed and enter harbour. *Renown* entered harbour at 1145, half an hour after *Ark Royal*.

---

[1]*Dunkerque* did not sail. S/Ms were *Olympus* (mined off Malta 1942) & *Otus*: 1929, 1475/2030t, 8tt, 1×4in, 15/9k.
[2]Fighters all arrived safely.

151. *To North*

7 April 1941

... By the way I found out what was in that famous letter which had to be returned unopened. It was to inform me that Bobbie Harwood would be relieving me. Apparently *that* was decided last September! In due course the letter was sent and someone woke up to the fact that it would be associated with the 27 Nov. and in view of the B of I that would *not* do. So that's why it was recalled so hurriedly. I also hear that Tom P[hillips] is the one who is striving so desperately to get rid of me and understand he's sick as mud about Genoa i.e. that it was not someone else who did the job. Well as you know I don't care a raspberry and if they've got a better bloke for Force H, then send him out quick. ...

152. *Report of Proceedings, 4–16 April 1941*

17 April 1941

6 April

11.   Shortly after midnight I was informed that there were indications that the two German battlecruisers might leave Brest on the night of 6/7 April, and was instructed to proceed westwards as soon as ready.
12.   Having completed with fuel . . ., Force H, comprising *Renown*, *Ark Royal*, *Sheffield*, *Fiji*,[1] *Faulknor*, *Fearless* and *Foresight*, sailed from Gibraltar at 0300 and proceeded to the westward at 21 knots.

8 April

26.   At 2100 I received instructions that C-in-C, Home Fleet, in *King George V*,[2] was to return to Scapa, that *Repulse* was to proceed to Gibraltar and that I was to assume command of the remaining forces operating in the Bay area, issuing any instructions considered necessary.
    The position allocated to *Queen Elizabeth*[3] and to a less extent that allocated to *Hood* appeared to me to be too far to the westward to provide a reasonable prospect of making contact with the enemy before shadowing by shore-based aircraft ceased owing to darkness or distance from their base. I did not, however, consider that it was justifiable to break W/T silence at this stage.

---

[1]*Fiji*: 1940, 8525t, 12×6in, 8×4in, 33k; sunk off Crete May 1941, Ger a/c.
[2]*King George V*: 1940, 35,000t, 10×14in, 16×5.25in, 28k.
[3]*Queen Elizabeth*: 1915, extensive modernisation 1937–40, 32,700t, 8×15in, 20×4.5in, 24k.

11 April

44.　At 1700 information was received that both battlecruisers were still in Brest at 1400/11. This early receipt of the results of reconnaissance was of great value.

14 April

61.　. . . As nothing more was heard by 1800 course was altered to the westward for two hours and then to 150° to return to Gibraltar. It was estimated that *Repulse*, northbound to start her patrol, would cross the latitude of Force H, southbound, a.m. on the 16th. . . .

153.　*Report of Proceedings, 16–24 April, 1941*

24 April 1941

17 April

8.　In reply to a communication from C-in-C, Mediterranean, that Force H should provide a diversion in the Western basin for his intended bombardment of Tripoli on 21 April, I had regretfully to state that defects to ships in Force H had now reached a stage where they seriously affected the efficiency of the Force, and these could not be completed in time to sail on 19 April.

24 April

22.　*Argus* arrived at 0605 and work of transferring the Hurricanes commenced as soon as she had berthed.[1] . . .

24.　Information was received from the Captain on the Staff, Alexandria,[2] that such data as [was] available, though far from conclusive, indicated that the disposition of the Italian main units was as follows:–

Taranto	1	*Littorio* battleship
	2	8" cruisers
	2	6" cruisers
Messina	1	8" cruiser
Palermo	2	6" cruisers
Southern ports	2	6" cruisers
Upper Tyrrhenian Sea	3	*Cavour* class battleships

[1]22 Hurricanes for Malta.
[2]Probably Capt B. C. B. Brooke.

154. *Report of Proceedings, 24–28 April 1941*

1 May 1941

24 April

4. Force S, comprising *Dido* (Senior Officer), *Abdiel*, *Kelly* (Captain (D), 5th DF), *Kipling*, *Kelvin*, *Kashmir*, *Jersey* and *Jackal*,[1] sailed at 2200 and feinted to the westward before turning back and entering the Mediterranean under cover of darkness.

Force H, consisting of *Renown*, *Ark Royal*, *Sheffield*, *Faulknor*, *Fearless*, *Fury*, *Foresight* and *Fortune*, sailed at 2300 and proceeded direct to the eastward.

25 April

5. From intercepted signals received at 0231 I became aware of the impending evacuation of our forces from Greece. This emphasised the importance of incurring as little delay as possible in the passage of Force S. I feel it necessary to draw attention once more to my serious lack of information concerning events in the Eastern Mediterranean. Unless kept informed of the general situation, it is difficult for me to determine whether certain risks should be accepted and whether action on my part can assist the C-in-C, Mediterranean Fleet.

27 April

21. The Hurricanes were flown off in three flights, each led by a Fulmar. Flying off started at 0515 and was completed by 0613 . . . On completion of this operation one A/S patrol and a section of Fulmars were flown off and withdrawal was made on a course 300° at 27 knots.
25. The destroyers were overtaken at noon and formed screen. Speed was reduced to 18 knots in order to remain in a supporting position for Force S.[2] . . .

---

[1]*Dido*: 1940, 5450t, 10×5.25in, 6tt, 33k. *Abdiel*: fast minelayer, 1940, 4000t, 6×4.7in, 156 mines; mined Taranto Sept 1943. *Kelly* (L: sunk off Crete May 1941, Ger a/c), *Kipling* (sunk S of Crete 1942, Ger a/c), *Kashmir* (sunk off Crete May 1941, Ger a/c), *Jackal* (sunk S of Crete 1942, Ger a/c). Capt (D), 7DF was Lord Louis (later Adm of the Fleet Earl, of Burma) Mountbatten (1900–79): son of Adm of Fleet Prince Louis of Battenberg, 1SL 1914–15; related to British & other Royal families, ent RN 1913; *Lion* 1916; Royal tours 1920s, with Prince of Wales; signal specialist; senior radio appts; Cdr 1932; *Daring* 1934; Admy, FAA; Capt 1937; *Kelly* & Capt (D), 5DF 1939; *Illustrious* in US 1941; Chief Combined Ops, Actg VA & member COS 1942–3; Sup Allied Cmdr, SE Asia, 1943–6; Visct 1946; Viceroy & Gov-Gen India 1947–8; RA 1CS; VA 1949; 4SL 1950; C-in-C Med F 1952; Adm 1953; Sup Allied Cmdr Med 1953; 1SL 1954; Adm of Fleet 1956; Chief of Defence Staff 1959–65.
[2]Force S and all Hurricanes arrived safely at Malta.

155.   *Report of Proceeding, 28 April–12 May 1941*

12 May 1941

2 May

16.   In view of recent reports that much material for Tripoli is being shipped from Naples, the Admiralty considered that a bombardment of that port, even if only by a cruiser, as part of operation TIGER, might produce good results.

In reply I informed Their Lordships that the possibility of bombarding Naples had been under consideration recently. An operation such as TIGER provides valuable cover, and up to the present we have always achieved surprise. However, I was of the opinion on this occasion, that the chances of surprising the enemy were not good, since unless favoured by thick weather operation TIGER might be detected on D2 and would certainly be detected on D3. This would put the enemy on the *qui vive* and render the chances of carrying out the bombardment and escaping interception by superior forces remote. To employ both capital ships would necessitate leaving TIGER convoy about three hours before dark, prejudicing chances of surprise and depriving the convoy of considerable protection against air attack – the chief danger during the latter part of D3.

It did not appear justifiable to risk a valuable ship like *Ark Royal* in the Tyrrhenian Sea, and without fighter protection, air spotting was unlikely to prove of much service to bombarding ships. Taking all circumstances in consideration, I did not consider the results likely to be obtained would justify this operation, which entailed far greater hazards than those of a similar nature previously carried out.

3 May

26.   Fifteen Beaufighters[1] passed through Gibraltar en route for Malta, having been sent out in time to provide additional fighter protection for operation TIGER.

31.   The NOIC, Malta, reported that the AOC, Mediterranean,[2] was unable to undertake any action against Sardinian or Sicilian air bases from Malta.

4 May

37.   *Queen Elizabeth, Foresight, Fortune, Fearless* and *Velox* sailed at 1600 to rendezvous with TIGER convoy and escort . . . on 5 May, and

---

[1]Bristol Beaufighter: fighter/torpedo bomber, 1939, 4 cannon, 6mg, 1 torpedo, 320mph.
[2]Air Vice Marshal H. P. Lloyd.

thus allow *Repulse, Havelock, Harvester* and *Hesperus* to proceed ahead to Gibraltar to refuel.

Gloucester, Kashmir and *Kipling* arrived at 1800 and *Gloucester* proceeded direct to dock.[1]

5 May

39.   At 0850, *Kashmir* and *Kipling* left harbour and carried out A/S and S/A sweeps in the Bay prior to *Renown, Ark Royal, Fiji* and *Sheffield* proceeding. When S of Europa Point, *Ark Royal* landed on aircraft from the North Front, and by 1020 the Force was proceeding westward to rendezvous with *Queen Elizabeth*, escorting the convoy of 5 MT ships, consisting of *Clan Campbell, Clan Lamont, Clan Chattan, Empire Song* and *New Zealand Star*.[2]

6 May

45.   *Faulknor, Forester, Fury, Havelock, Hesperus* and *Harvester* sailed from Gibraltar eastward at 0330, followed at 0420, by *Gloucester*, who had been temporarily repaired after bomb and mine damage.

8 May

64.   At 1345, 8 aircraft were sighted approaching very low, fine on the starboard bow. . . .

65.   Of the 8 aircraft which attacked, one was brought down during the approach, probably by fire from the destroyers, and two others were seen to fall into the sea during their retirement. . . .

70.   The first high level bombing attack of the day developed at 1622, when three S79s approached from astern at about 5000 feet, i.e., just under cloud level. One diverted by gunfire, jettisoned his bombs and subsequently crashed astern of the Fleet. The other two dropped 12 bombs close ahead of *Ark Royal* and then escaped into cloud. It is probable that both of these were hit by the concentrated H/A fire with which they were met.

About 10 minutes later, a single aircraft approached from astern and, encountering heavy fire, turned across the stern of the Fleet, dropping bombs well astern.

71.   At 1710 another S79 shadower was shot down in flames on the port

---

[1]Entrances to Malta mined, so ordered by Cunningham to sail to Gibraltar to await TIGER.

[2]*Clan Campbell, Clan Chattan, Clan Lamont*: 1937–9, 7250–7500gt, 17k, Clan Line. RA 15CS was Rear Adm E. L. S. King: RA 1938 & COS, C-in-C Home F; Med F May–Oct 1941; ACNS (Trade) Oct 1941–Nov 1942; VA 1942. *Naiad*: 1940, 5450t, 10×5.25in, 6tt, 33k; sunk off Egypt 1942, *U565*.

quarter of the Fleet by a Fulmar piloted by Lieut. R.C. Hay.[1] Twenty minutes later S79s attacked the Fleet from S to N. Two broke formation under gunfire and the remainder delivered a poor attack, bombs falling near the screen. A similar attack by three S79s took place at 1800, when bombs were again dropped near the screen.

72.   The provision of adequate fighter protection for the Fleet was a difficult problem with the small number of fighters available. Aircraft returned to the carrier at various times with damage and failure of undercarriage, and every opportunity was taken, whenever the RDF screen cleared, to land on, refuel and rearm the Fulmars, sometimes singly and sometimes two or three at a time. There were occasions when no more than two fighters were in the air, but whenever an attack appeared to be impending every fighter that could be made serviceable was sent up.

73.   At 1910 raids were detected at about 70 miles approaching from Sicily. At this time only 7 Fulmars were still serviceable, of which 4 were on board. These were flown off.

The total number of hostile aircraft is uncertain, but Fulmars sighted three separate formations of 16 Ju87s, 12 Ju88s and 6 Me110s.[2] . . .

75.   During this attack, P3 4.5" mounting in *Renown* fired two rounds into the back of P2 mounting owing to the failure of the interceptor release gear.

I regret to report that the following casualties occurred:–

5 ratings killed.
5 ratings seriously wounded (one of whom has since died of wounds).
One Officer and 21 ratings wounded.

77.   As a result of the day's air attacks, 7 enemy aircraft were destroyed, 2 probably destroyed and at least 3, and probably more, damaged. Of the 7 destroyed, A/A fire accounted for 4 and fighters for 3. No hits, either by bomb or torpedo, were obtained on our ships, nor were there any casualties (other than those caused by the accident in *Renown*). Two Fulmars were lost, but the crew of one was saved.

Enemy CR 42 fighters were frequently encountered escorting bombing and T/B aircraft. These did not approach within gun range of the Fleet but waited in the vicinity to attack our fighters, who were no real match for these far more manoeuvrable aircraft.

[1]Lieut R. C. Hay RM: Lt 1937; FAA 1939; 801 Sqdn *Ark Royal*; Actg Capt & CO 761 Sqdn, *Heron* (Yeovilton) Jan 1942; Capt & Actg Maj Nov 1942; *Formidable* June 1943; RNASIO *Bherunda* Dec 1943; Ldr 47 Fighter Wing *Victorious* Sept 1944.
[2]Junkers Ju88: 1936, 3960lb of bombs, several mg, 273mph. Messerschmitt Me110: fighter/bomber, 1936, 2–4 cannon, 2 mg, 342mph.

The scale of attack was very much less than had been anticipated. There is no doubt that this was due to

(a)   the degree of surprise which weather conditions and evasive action had rendered possible,
(b)   cloud conditions which favoured the defence, and
(c)   the magnificent work of the small force of Fulmars, who intercepted and broke up incoming raids and formations. Seeking safety in the clouds, hostile aircraft lost touch with each other and either jettisoned their bombs or carried out an independent attack.

78.   The work of the Fulmars and of *Ark Royal* is deserving of the highest praise. *Ark Royal* started the day with a total of 12 fighters. After a very short time the number of serviceable aircraft had been reduced by combats to 5. It never exceeded 7. By rapid re-equipping and re-servicing, a permanent patrol was maintained, varying in number from two to the full number that remained serviceable.

9 May

86.   . . . A Fulmar was also flown off to carry out a reconnaissance of Oran. This aircraft took photographs and reported *Dunkerque* in her usual position at Mers-el-Kebir, surrounded by nets with lighters alongside and with a pontoon gangway to the shore. One large and two small destroyers were located at Oran and possibly 6 or 7 submarines.
87.   The six destroyers of the 8th DF which had taken part in operation TIGER sailed from Malta at 2000 on their return passage to Gibraltar. It was learnt later that *Foresight* had returned to Malta, having run a main pinion bearing. Force B[1] altered course to the eastward at 2200 so as to be within supporting distance of these destroyers during daylight the next day when passing S and W of Cagliari.

156.   *To his wife*

9 May 1941

. . . I got a signal from *Ark* that Mark and Tillard were missing after a gallant fight against a number of Italian fighters. I have always been on

---

[1]Effectively Force H. Somerville gave high praise to McGrigor and Maund for the skilful handling of their ships in avoiding bombs and torpedoes; aboard *Ark Royal*, 4 medals were earned and 8 men were mentioned in despatches. There were congratulations, too, for the CO, officers and men of *Fortune*, which suffered severe damage from 5 near-misses but struggled back to Gibraltar.

tenterhooks when a Fulmar is missing or shot down that it would be those two and now it has happened. I am very upset about Mark as the more I saw of him the more I liked him as a young fellow. We had become great friends and it was a friendship I really valued. He was an amazingly fine officer and consumed with zeal for the service which he put before everything else. Hook Holland gave him quite the best report of all his officers. He and Tillard were the backbone and mainstay of my fighter squadrons and their loss is a serious one. I feel so sorry for Harold and Vera.[1] . . . It all seems quite damnable. . . .

157. *To North*

14 May 1941

Here is an account of our last effort. It was repetition of EXCESS with five MT at 14 knots, *QE*, *Naiad*, *Fiji* and *Gloucester*. The last named got mined out of her usual abode and had to come here with a couple of 'K's'. But there was *this* difference. I had to send Tony de Salis and all six of his to Bill Ford for the passage of the Narrows.

Well we started off with an elaborate Westward blind & a proper jigsaw of destroyer exchanges and refuelling. The MT were ships that pass in the night & as the result of this & also most favourable weather I don't believe Itis had any idea until 5.30 on D3. There *must* have been a flap then but it was not until 1.45 that the first attack came in. Eight or nine wicked looking brutes just skimming above the sea. They attacked my column & dropped their torpedoes at about 3500 yards just outside or inside the screen. One was shot down before he dropped, two crashed after dropping. Then we had to comb the tracks. McGrigor did this damn well but as we were combing one successfully the damn thing suddenly altered 90° to Port and came straight for our bow. Now we're for it I thought but, would you believe it, the damn thing had finished its run & I watched it sinking about 10 yards from the ship.

Six CR42 fighters had come in with the T/B aircraft and were most gallantly engaged by Tillard and one other fighter (we only had 12 serviceable altogether). In this fight Tillard and my nephew Mark were shot down and are missing & I fear must be considered dead. It was upsetting to get the news almost at once because I was very fond of Mark. But I had no time to think of my affairs because bombers started to come in & we had intermittent attacks all the afternoon. Luckily the cloud base was

[1]Lieut Mark Somerville was lost in action with a group of Fiat CR42s, along with his pilot, Lt-Cdr R. C. Tillard: Lt 1932; CO, 808 Sqdn, *Ark Royal* Oct 1940; Lt-Cdr 1941.

about 5000 feet and they *didn't* like it. We put up a hell of a fire and our Fulmars, at times reduced to two in the air, mixed it up magnificently. I can't say too much in praise of the wonderful show they put up. The result was that except for one stick just ahead of *Ark* the bombing was ineffective. At 6.30 p.m. we found some very large formations approaching from Sicily. Between 25 and 30 dive bombers with 8 or 10 Me100s escorting them. Up went all our six fighters (all we had left because another had crashed & others were shot up). They mixed it up so well that a lot of the Ju's dropped their bombs miles away. The whole party disappeared to the W and then returned to the E but carried on home and never attacked us. By this time we were right in the entrance to the Skerki Channel and I had to turn Force H West – time 8.15 p.m. – as the water was too narrow for the *Ark* to operate. We'd hardly finished turning when 3 T/B aircraft attacked from right ahead, i.e. from the W. The three destroyers on the screen (temporary boys – 'H's') never saw them until they dropped. We opened a hell of a fire and I saw bits coming off one aircraft as it roared past but I didn't see it crash. Again Mac combed most skilfully but it was the last attack we had. . . . The convoy and rest got through OK except for old Norman Pirie[1] who bought a mine and *QE* missed by torpedoes from aircraft.

We poled off W all that night and then jogged so as to wait for Tony de Salis's return in case we should have trouble. He started next night but at 10 a.m. was picked up by a shadower from Galita and at 1330 reported being bombed and Sinclair's ship[2] down to 7 knots! I was 120 [miles] off but went to meet him at full bat. It was blowing a Westerly gale and *Ark* only had four fighters serviceable so it was not (R) not a very nice prospect. Picked him up at 5.30 p.m. and found the little boat with the seas washing over the Q/D continually. It didn't look good as we still had 3½ hours of daylight and within easy bombing range. But they didn't come. Our fighter chaps reckon the enemy mistook our Fulmars for Hurricanes! Luckily the wind dropped during the night and the little chap was able to work up to 10 knots and later that evening to 12. But it was an anxious time for me as you may imagine. Well we got her in all right but the operation was an 8 days' job and a fairly exhausting one at that.

. . . Gort who has arrived and taken over[3] told me that WC[hurchill] was very nervous about this party and well he might have been. We

---

[1]Probably the Master of *Empire Song*, lost by mining; *New Zealand Star*, also mined, managed to reach Malta.

[2]Lt-Cdr E. N. Sinclair: Lt 1932; *Gallant* i/c 1939; Lt-Cdr Aug 1940; *Antelope* 1941; *Eskimo* Feb 1944.

[3]Gen Gort had become the new Govr-Gen of Gibraltar.

again had the luck of the gods [– ?] with the weather and all but it's wrong that I should have to start a show like that with only 12 instead of 24 Fulmars. I feel that Mark would still be alive if we'd had our proper complement. As it was it was always a case of 2 or 3 of ours against 6 or 9 of them and the Fulmar is *no* match for the CR42. Shore based fighters are bound to be superior. . . .

Ronald Hallifax[1] was through here on his way to Red Sea but I didn't see him. Fred tells me his [news?] was now that WC is getting tired of Tom P and the latter is looking for a berth at sea and looking most anxiously towards Force H. . . .

Truant[2] went and copped a Frog on her way here from E[ngland] right in the middle of our op. I got all sorts of signals to go and escort etc. *subject* to not prejudicing the job I was on. Needless to say Aunt Fanny Adams describes the action I took because I was *livid*. To muck about

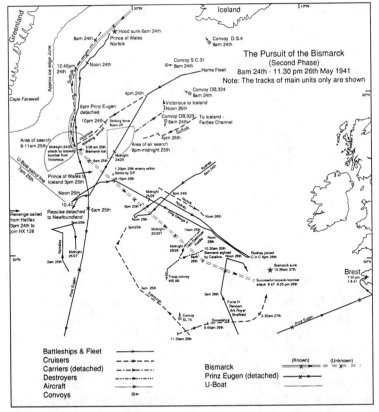

[1]Rear Adm Ronald H. C. Hallifax: Capt 1927; RA 1938; RA (D), Home F May 1939; SNO Suez Canal & Red Sea 1941; d 1943.
[2]*Truant*: 1939, 1090/1575, 10tt, 1×4in, 15.25/9k.

with Frogs inside the pond is just too stupid for words. Actually the Frogs sent two U-boats and 3 destroyers to retrieve the ship and did so. We just look BFs. Have sent a letter to TLs on the subject – one of my usuals – almost word for word with what we used to concoct. . . .

158. *To North*

23–28 May 1941

. . . Fat Fred tells me that he wrote to DP last week to say that a good many senior officers had passed through here and that all, without exception, had spoken very strongly about the way you had been treated and that if you were not to be given another appointment you ought to be granted an enquiry and he felt DP should know what was being said about the matter. Now I think that was rather decent of Fred as he's no particular friend of yours. . . . As to my application to be restored to the Active List TLs were 'loath to refuse my request but regretted they must adhere to established precedent'. I suppose . . . you must never admit you've made a mistake.

Alan Hillgarth who's just been home dined with me last night. He'd been at Chequers for the week-end. Asked Winston why a Board of Inquiry had been ordered on me and all Winston said was 'My boy mistakes are often made in war'. You can take that answer either way. After dinner I got a signal that *Bismarck* and *Hipper* [*sic*] were out . . . And by the time this reaches you the drama in the Denmark Strait will have been played out. My first Flagship in these parts! I knew only too well the soft spots and you may remember discussed them with you. But if she and *P of W* engaged Bismarck together then our luck must have been damnably out. Poor old Lancelot Holland – I was very fond of him . . .

159. *To his wife*

24–27 May 1941

Alan Hillgarth, who has just been here, dined with me last night and we had a long talk. . . . He says that Force H operating under their eyes month after month and apparently always doing what they set out to do has impressed the Spaniards tremendously.

. . . now the drama is developing – our ships closing in on *Bismarck*. Will they get her or will she find some patch of thick weather? . . . We are crashing along towards the party but have a long way to go and can hardly expect to be in the party unless she makes a dash for Brest or unless one of the battlecruisers comes out to try and make a diversion to help her. I wish they would so that we could have a go at them. . . . My chief concern at the moment is to get a reasonable amount of sleep tonight so as to be ready for what tomorrow may bring. I don't want much sleep as you know but unless I get a bare minimum I am not at my best during the day.

25 May

After doing the most admirable and classical piece of shadowing for over 24 hours *Suffolk* and *Norfolk*[1] lost touch with *Bismarck* at 3 a.m. this morning in the dark. . . . I am steering so as to cut them off if they come S which they may do in order to oil from the tanker somewhere in mid-Atlantic. On the other hand as she is damaged she may try and break back to Germany or else try and hide in a Greenland fiord. I am a bit anxious that we haven't heard yet [that] they've been picked up again as it is now 10 a.m. and I should have thought that the air search would have found them by now. . . . If she does come S and I can get in touch with her I am sure my lads in the *Ark* will get her speed down enough for me to be able to hang on to her until someone can come along and help me to finish her off. 9.30 p.m. – still no news of *Bismarck*'s whereabouts and the Admiralty now think she may be going to Brest. Well Force H is the only force in a position to intercept and we are therefore proceeding along those lines. but if my lads do find her tomorrow the problem is still a bit difficult. *Renown* is obviously no match for *Bismarck* so unless the boys in the *Ark* can reduce her speed very considerably I shall have to be pretty artful. A nice problem and on top of it all I have had no news at all of whether the two battlecruisers are still at Brest. Can't make out why the people at home so lack imagination. Surely they must realise that it is of *primary* importance I should know where they are. I might be in a very awkward position if I had those two as well as *Bismarck* to deal with. Well it is no good worrying and this is merely to give you some idea of the problems I have to deal with and how they develop.

26 May, 9.00 a.m.

Still no news of *Bismarck* and it is blowing hard from the NW with a filthy sea into which we are punching. I have just had to send off the air search under conditions which are tabled as 'extremely severe and entailing a great hazard to aircraft'. How I hate seeing them go off and wondering how many of those brave lads will return. It's on these occasions that I think they appreciate I know what conditions are as a result of going up with them occasionally. . . . Didn't get much sleep last night

---

[1]*Suffolk*: 1928, 10,000t, 8×8in, 6×4in, 31.5k.

as we had to keep easing down and altering course on account of the weather and recasting the search in consequence.

27 May

Well we have sunk the *Bismarck* and am I tired? Well you're asking me. Soon after I had finished writing to you yesterday morning a flying boat reported that she had sighted a battleship but soon afterwards reported that she had lost touch. However our air reconnaissance was up and within a very short time they had got her and held on to her. She was evidently making for Brest and doing about 22 knots. . . . my object was to try and launch a torpedo attack from my aircraft which would reduce her speed and allow Jack Tovey in *KGV* and *Rodney* to catch her. . . . It was a ticklish job as I couldn't afford to get too close for fear she would round on me whilst *Ark* was flying on aircraft – the weather was foul, blowing hard, *Ark* pitching like the Devil and the visibility very poor at times. At 2 p.m. I decided to detach Charles [Larcom, in *Sheffield*] to shadow. He is nimble and fast and could get away from her quickly if she tried to round on him. At 3.15 I sent off my brave old Stringbags with their torpedoes, my heart in my mouth as they left the heaving, pitching flying deck. Two hours later they returned and reported that in thick weather they had attacked Charles Larcom by mistake! Luckily no hits! What had happened was that the signal I had made to Charles had not been repeated to *Ark*. Well it was bad enough having attacked the wrong ship, it was worse still that the attack had been wasted. As soon as they were rested and re-armed they took off again and this time scored two hits, one amidships, the other on the starboard quarter. The latter must have damaged the steering gear as *Bismarck* made two complete circles and after that never appeared to be under proper control. I tried to get in a third attack but by this time it was getting too dark. However most opportunely Philip Vian[1] and four of his boys joined up. Just managed to spot one of them in the evening gloom and signalled the bearing and distance of the enemy. They did good work that night in shadowing and slipping two more torpedoes into her. But I had an anxious time as I could not make out just where Jack Tovey and *Rodney* were. I got explicit orders from the Admiralty that I was not to engage *Bismarck* unless *KGV*

---

[1]Capt (later Adm of the Fleet Sir) Philip L. Vian (1894–1968): Lt 1916; Jutland; gunnery specialist; Cdr 1929; Capt 1934; Res F DF; 1DF, Spain 1936; *Arethusa* 1937–9; convoy destroyer flotilla 1939–40; 4DF 1940; rescued Br POWs from *Altmark* Feb 1940; RA July 1941; liaison officer USSR; Force K, Spitzbergen expedition Aug 1941; actions off Norway; 15CS, Med F Oct 1941; Malta convoys; staff appt 1943; Sicily ops 1943; Eastern TF D-Day; cmd fleet carriers BPF Nov 1944; VA 1945; 5SL 1946–8; C-in-C Home F 1950–2; Adm 1952; Adm of Fleet 1952.

and *Rodney* were already fully engaged with her. Eventually Jack Tovey asked me if I would go S of *Bismarck* whilst he and *Rodney* remained in the N. All that night we manoeuvred with *Ark* to get round behind and to the S of her but it was difficult to know exactly where she was. Occasional flashes of gunfire on the horizon gave some indication and also wireless bearings. But I simply couldn't make out exactly where Jack T was. It was a horrid dawn, overcast, thick and blowing like the Devil from the W. I sent off one aircraft to try and locate Jack and was just sending off the torpedo boys again when *Ark* said that conditions were so bad she feared we might have a repetition of yesterday's affair with Charles L so I cancelled it for the time being. By this time I was getting distinctly anxious – and incidentally very weary as I had only half an hour's shut eye during the 24. No sign or news of Jack and doubtless a super U-boat and air reception being prepared for us, so I closed toward the place where I thought *Bismarck* was and closed a bit too much as I got within 16 miles of her. This decided me to send off the torpedo boys again and whilst they were being prepared we heard sounds of heavy gunfire and I concluded that Jack and *Rodney* had found *Bismarck* and were engaging her. I couldn't leave *Ark* alone so had to remain with her until I collected Charles Larcom. As soon as he arrived I started to move in towards the fray but by this time I had got a signal from Jack to say he was going N with the rest and another one from the Admiralty to say that very heavy air attacks might be expected. So I went back to my *Ark* like a bloody old Noah and wondered what the hell had happened. My torpedo chaps were in the air but had *Bismarck* been sunk or not? Not a word from Jack. Eventually I asked him 'Have you disposed of enemy?' to which he replied 'Unable to sink her by gunfire have got to go back short of fuel'. I thought it was all very odd and hoped that my torpedo boys would dispose of her but then got a signal from *Dorsetshire*[1] to say that she had torpedoed *Bismarck* and she was sinking rapidly and finally that he was attempting to pick up survivors. But in that very rough sea there seemed very little hope of collecting many, so I called the torpedo boys and started to get away to the west. Up came a lousy great Focke Wulf[2] and started shadowing us in and out of the clouds. He waited until *Ark* was landing on the torpedo flight and then dropped a stick of bombs which missed just astern of her, thank goodness. We gave him a good beating up with A/A and he made off. I quite expected a heavy air attack after this so did a bit of dodging and so far we have been left in peace.

---

[1]*Dorsetshire*: 1929, 9850t, 8×8in, 8×4in, 8tt, 32.25k; sunk SW of Ceylon 5 April 1942, Japanese carrier planes.
[2]Focke Wulf Fw 200C 'Condor': 1937, bomb load 3300lb, 1 cannon, 5mg, 240mph, range 3950mls.

Well it is good work that we got that blighter – the newest battleship on her first outing and it shows what a long arm the British Navy has. ... TL have got a bit crapulous with Jack Tovey this morning and asked what the hell he was doing going off and leaving her still afloat. Must confess I was rather surprised. It was old Wake Walker who told *Dorsetshire* to go in and torpedo her at close range. Well a very tiring and exacting 24 hours but the war seems made up of that. ...

160. *Report of Proceedings, 23–29 May 1941*

23 May

3. A message was received at 0323 to the effect that a *Bismarck* class battleship with four merchant vessels had been sighted ... and a *Hipper* class cruiser and one destroyer, with three merchant vessels and a number of minesweepers ... Information had previously been received that it was considered these two warships would be engaged in commerce raiding.

24 May

9. At 0109 instructions were received from the Admiralty to proceed to sea as soon as ready to join convoy WS8B after daylight 26 May.

Force H, comprising *Renown, Ark Royal, Sheffield, Faulknor, Foresight, Foxhound, Fury* and *Hesperus* sailed accordingly to the westward at 0200, and proceeded at 25 knots with the intention of rendezvousing with the convoy. ...

161. *To C-in-C, Home Fleet*

Destruction of the German battleship Bismarck *on 27 May 1941*

4 June 1941

25 May

2. At 0330 on Sunday, 25 May, Force H was in position 39° 35'N, 14° 10'W, steering 310° at 24 knots. At this time instructions were received to steer to intercept *Bismarck* from the southward. The enemy had last been located in position 56° 30'N, 36° 00'W, at 0306 when *Suffolk* lost touch. The existing course and speed was therefore maintained.

3. At 0400 instructions were received that destroyers should be sent back to Gibraltar before it became necessary to fuel them, as Force H might be required for extended operations. The three screening destroyers[1] were therefore detached at 0900 with instructions to transmit two signals when 150 miles clear, one informing the Admiralty of the posi-

[1]*Faulknor, Foresight & Hesperus*: 1940, 1340t, 3×4.7in, 8tt, 36k; acquired by RN 1939 while building for Brazil.

tion, course and speed of Force H at 0730, and the other requesting C-in-C, Plymouth[1], to keep me fully informed of the results of Brest reconnaissance.

4.   At 1100, . . . orders were received by Force H to act on the assumption that the enemy had turned towards Brest at 0300/25. Course was therefore altered to 360°.

5.   At 1215 Force H altered course to 345° to reach the initial position for an air search a.m. / 26 based on the assumption that the enemy's maximum speed of advance was not more than 25 knots. It was my intention to carry out, if necessary, three searches of the area across the Bay of Biscay allowing for the enemy making a substantial detour to the southward.The first search was designed to cover enemy speeds of 25 to 31 knots, the second 18 to 21 knots and the third 16 to 18 knots, Force H maintaining an intercepting position to the eastward throughout.

26 May

6.   During the night the north westerly wind and sea increased and speed had to be reduced . . . finally to 17 knots at 0112.

10.   10 Swordfish were flown off at 0835 . . . Two cross over patrols by Catalinas[2] . . . lay along the western edge of *Ark Royal*'s where wind [was] from 320° force 7, sea rough, sky overcast, visibility 10–12 miles. It had been hoped to increase the density of the search by the use of Fulmars, but weather conditions rendered this impracticable. The *Ark Royal*'s round down was rising and falling 56 feet at times . . . The handling of the aircraft on the flight deck was always difficult and several slid bodily across the deck which was wet with spray.

11.   At 0930 the A/S patrol was landed on; no relief was flown off in order that every available aircraft should be available for a torpedo striking force. Whilst the search was in progress Force H proceeded at 15 knots on a course of 015° to reach a position to windward so that the operation of aircraft would not be impeded by subsequent alterations of course of the *Bismarck*, should the latter be located.

12.   At 1030 a Catalina made a report of '1 BS 240° 5' steering 150° . . .' This report . . . placed the enemy 285° 112 miles from *Renown*. An amplifying report 5 minutes later gave the enemy's speed as 20 knots. I instructed *Ark Royal* to fly off two shadowers fitted with long range tanks to gain touch as I feared the Catalina's position might be somewhat inaccurate in view of the weather conditions and the distance from her base. . . .

[1]Adm Forbes.
[2]Consolidated Vultee Catalina: flying boat, 1935, depth charges, 5mg, 179mph, range 3100mls.

14.   At this time (1125) the Catalina lost touch and I instructed *Ark Royal* to send at least four aircraft. Before these could be flown off one of *Ark Royal*'s aircraft reported in touch (at 1114) . . . and gave the position of the enemy as 77 miles to the W of Force H. Seven minutes later a second aircraft of the reconnaissance gained touch and reported that the enemy was a battleship. . . .

20.   It was evident at this stage [noon] that unless aircraft from *Ark Royal* could reduce the enemy's speed he could not be overhauled by our battleships till well within range of bombing aircraft from the French coast the following day. It was also doubtful whether the C-in-C, Home Fleet, would have sufficient fuel to enable him to continue the chase until the following day.

21.   At 1315 I detached *Sheffield* with orders to close and shadow the enemy . . . The V/S signal ordering this movement was not repeated to *Ark Royal,* and as will be seen later this omission had serious consequences.

22.   . . . The torpedoes were fitted with duplex pistols. The striking force of 15 Swordfish took off at 1450 . . . One aircraft had to return and made a successful emergency landing with the torpedo in place just after the last of the striking force had left the deck. It had been intended to carry out a synchronised diversion by Fulmars, but this had to be abandoned owing to sea and cloud conditions.

23.   Weather and cloud conditions were particularly bad over the target area when the striking force took off. Reliance was therefore placed in the ASV set carried in one of the aircraft of the striking force. This aircraft located a ship 20 miles from the position given to the leader on taking off. This ship was *Sheffield* of whose presence near Bismarck the striking force were not aware. . . .

24.   At 1550 on reaching a position over the supposed target an attack through the cloud was ordered, and 11 torpedoes were dropped at *Sheffield.* The latter increased to full speed and took successful avoiding action. Of the 11 torpedoes dropped, two were observed by *Sheffield* to explode on hitting the water and three more exploded when crossing her wake. During this unfortunate incident it is satisfactory to record that not a single round was fired at the attacking aircraft by any gun in *Sheffield,* where the mistake had been immediately appreciated.

28.   The striking force returned to *Ark Royal* at 1720. Owing to the motion on the ship the three aircraft who had realised that the target was friendly and who had not fired their torpedoes were ordered to drop them before landing on. . . .

29.   On completion of landing on speed was increased to 29 knots to regain lost ground, and by reducing the distance from the enemy to assist the next striking force in gaining contact.

30.   At 1747 *Sheffield* gained touch with Bismarck and made her first enemy report. Being in some doubt regarding the C-in-C's intentions, I requested his position, course and speed and asked whether he wished me to leave the carrier and join him. I added that should no reply be received I would remain with the carrier. A second striking force of 15 aircraft was prepared with all possible speed. Owing to the limited number of serviceable aircraft, to provide this number it was necessary to refuel and rearm most of the aircraft that had just returned.

31.   At 1900 the Polish destroyer *Piorun*[1] was sighted 9 miles to the southward and the bearing and distance of the enemy was passed to her. The latter portion of the signal, instructing destroyers to shadow and attack as opportunity offered, was not passed owing to visibility closing down. Having sighted *Piorun* it appeared evident that the four destroyers which had been reported by the Catalina at 1208 as four UN and had also been sighted by the first striking force were Captain (D), 4th DF, in *Cossack,* with *Zulu, Maori* and *Sikh*[2] in company. To assist these destroyers and the striking force in making contact, *Sheffield* was ordered to make her call sign for D/F-ing purposes.

32.   The second striking force took off at 1915 . . . when the enemy bore 167°, 38 miles. In view of the failures with the duplex pistols in the preceding attack, contact pistols were employed on this occasion, torpedoes being set to run at 22 feet. The striking force had orders to make contact with *Sheffield* before launching the attack, both to ensure gaining contact with the enemy and to avoid any possibility of *Sheffield* being mistaken for the target. *Sheffield* was instructed to home the striking force by D/F.

34.   The aircraft approached *Sheffield* at 1955 below the clouds and then climbed to a height of 6000 feet. The weather conditions at this time appeared to be ideal for a synchronised torpedo attack, cloud 7/10 from 2000 to 5000 feet. During the climb contact was lost with *Sheffield* but regained at 2035 when a bearing and distance (110°, 12 miles) of *Bismarck* was passed by *Sheffield* by V/S. The force took departure for the target in sub-flights in line astern at 2040. On nearing the enemy a thick bank of cloud with base about 700 feet and top between 6000 and 10,000 feet was encountered and the force split up. At 2047, when it was calculated that the enemy would be in a suitable position for an attack down wind from astern, No. 1 sub-flight dived down through the cloud, but on reaching the base the enemy was seen down wind to the eastward. Position for an attack on the port beam was gained by approaching just in the clouds, and the final dive to attack was made at 2055. One aircraft

[1]*Piorun*: ex-*Nerissa*, 1940, 1760t, 6×4.7in, 1×4in, 5tt, 36k.
[2]*Cossack, Zulu, Maori, Sikh*: 'Tribal' class.

from No. 3 sub-flight followed closely and also attacked from the port beam. This aircraft observed a hit on Bismarck about two-thirds of her length from forward. All four aircraft came under intense and accurate fire from the first moment of sighting until out of range.

35.   No. 2 sub-flight, having climbed to 9000 feet, dived down on a bearing obtained by ASV and two aircraft attacked from the starboard beam under intense fire. The third aircraft having lost touch with his sub-flight in the clouds returned to *Sheffield* for a range and bearing on the target. Having obtained this he pressed home a lone and determined attack from the port bow in face of very heavy opposition, and his crew saw the torpedo strike *Bismarck* amidships port side.

36.   N. 4 sub-flight followed No. 3 sub-flight into the cloud and became iced up at 6000 feet. After 7 minutes the aircraft dived and found a clear patch at 2000 feet. *Bismarck* was sighted almost at once engaging No. 2 sub-flight to starboard. All four aircraft circled astern of the target and attacked simultaneously from port coming under heavy fire. One aircraft was hit many times and both pilot and air gunner were wounded, the observer being uninjured. 175 holes were counted in this aircraft which had to be written off as one of the longerons had been cut.

37   No. 5 sub-flight of two aircraft lost contact with the remainder and with each other in the cloud. Having started to ice up at 7000 feet they came down and while still in cloud at 3500 feet one was engaged by A/A fire. On coming out of the cloud the pilot saw the enemy ahead of him and down wind so retired into the cloud, being engaged continuously while gaining a more favourable position. He eventually came in low on the *Bismarck*'s starboard bow and dropped just outside 1000 yards. The other aircraft of this sub-flight made three attempts to come in but was so heavily engaged on each appearance that he finally jettisoned his torpedo and returned to *Ark Royal*.

38.   No. 6 sub-flight followed into the cloud and when at 6300 feet turned 40° to port and climbed clear at 7450 feet, waited for about 15 minutes and returned to *Sheffield* for another range and bearing of the enemy. These two aircraft then searched at sea level and attacked on the starboard beam. Intense fire prevented close approach and one dropped at about 4000 yards while the other returned to the carrier and jettisoned before landing on.

39.   The striking force attack took much longer than had been anticipated (2055 to 2125) owing to bad weather conditions around *Bismarck* who appeared to be under a cold front.

40.   At 2040 a signal was received from C-in-C, Home Fleet, giving his position, course and speed . . . 22 knots, with *Rodney* in company. He also stated that unless the enemy's speed was reduced he would have to

return in *King George V* at midnight to refuel, leaving *Rodney* to continue the chase. He recommended that *Renown* should remain with *Ark Royal*.

41. During and after the torpedo attack on *Bismarck* shadowing aircraft reported frequent alterations of course and that she was making smoke. On receipt of these reports *Renown* and *Ark Royal* altered course as requisite to maintain a position some 40 miles distant from the enemy in order that flying operations should not be unexpectedly hampered. It appeared possible that *Bismarck* was endeavouring to shake off shadowers before dark; on the other hand she might have suffered damage to shafts or steering gear as a result of the torpedo attacks.

42. Owing to the time taken to deliver the T/B attack insufficient light remained to carry out another attack before dark. Aircraft could have flown off but in failing light location of the target would have been difficult, friend might have been mistaken for foe and certainly many of the aircraft would have failed to regain the carrier. It was therefore decided to maintain shadowing aircraft as long as possible and concentrate on preparing all Swordfish for a strong striking force at dawn.

43. C-in-C, Home Fleet, requested that aircraft might give the destroyers a visual link with the enemy and *Ark Royal* was instructed to comply. The two shadowing aircraft were instructed to remain in touch as long as possible and establish this link before returning. They left the *Bismarck* at 2230 and, after making a detour in heavy rain, located the destroyers. By this time, however, they were not certain of their own position and were unable to assist the destroyers. These two aircraft were D/F'd back to *Ark Royal*, landing on at 2320 when it was practically dark.

44. At 2220 *Ark Royal* reported that one torpedo had definitely hit *Bismarck* amidships and C-in-C, Home Fleet, was informed accordingly at 2225. Later information was received from *Ark Royal* that a second hit had been most probably obtained aft, and C-in-C was again informed at 2240.

45. *Sheffield* made her last enemy report at 2140. At this time *Bismarck* turned and fired six accurate 15" salvoes at *Sheffield* at a range of 9 miles. The latter turned away at full speed and made smoke but suffered a few casualties and superficial damage from splinters. These casualties consisted of one killed, two dangerously wounded who have since died, two seriously and six slightly wounded. All were ratings. After this *Sheffield* lost touch but at 2142 sighted Captain (D), 4th DF, in *Cossack* with three other destroyers closing the enemy and signalled the last observed bearing and distance of *Bismarck*.

46. At 2251 *Zulu* made a contact and reported the enemy steering 110°. From this time onwards Captain (D), 4th DF, and his destroyers

maintained contact, reporting the enemy's course as 110°, 060°, 340° and finally by midnight 310° into the sea. RA, 18th CS, in *Edinburgh*[1] was sighted to the westward at 2315.

48.   At 2345 I informed C-in-C, Home Fleet, of my position . . ., that no further T/B attack was possible that evening and that I intended turning W for a short distance to keep clear of him. Shortly afterwards I received his intentions to engage from the westward at dawn and directions that *Renown* and *Ark Royal* were to keep not less than 20 miles to the southward of Bismark. . . .

27 May

49.   At 0036 *Ark Royal* reported that after being torpedoed, *Bismarck* made two complete circles and reduced speed. I informed C-in-C, Home Fleet, accordingly at 0046.

50.   It was evident that C-in-C, Home Fleet, was in some doubt regarding the position of *Bismarck*. I therefore reported to him at 0112 that the estimated bearing and distance of the enemy from me was 165°, 41 miles.

51.   The situation at the time was as follows. *Renown* and *Ark Royal* some 40 miles to the northward of *Bismarck*, working round to the W to reach a position to the southward; C-in-C, Home Fleet, proceeding southward to engage at dawn and RA, 1st CS,[2] working round to the NE. *Dorsetshire,* who had left SL74 . . ., was closing from the SW. *Sheffield'* s position was not known exactly but assumed to be in vicinity of *Bismarck* and to the westward of the latter.

52.   At 0115 a flash was seen bearing 152°, followed four minutes later by heavy gun flashes. Course was altered to 210° to keep to the westward. During the middle watch the destroyers carried out attacks, and signals were received between 0202 and 0210 stating that *Zulu, Maori* and *Cossack* had attacked, the last two claiming one hit each. *Maori* added that there was an extensive fire on the forecastle.

53.   At 0210, RA, 1st CS, reported his intention to keep to the northward and flank mark for *King George V* and *Rodney.* At 0301 *Dorsetshire* reported her position, course and speed which indicated she would cross some 10 to 15 miles ahead of *Renown.*

54.   The destroyers were instructed by C-in-C, Home Fleet, that after all attacks were completed they were to fire starshell every half hour to indicate the position of the enemy, whose course and speed were now reported as 310°, 8 knots.

---

[1]RA 18CS was Syfret. *Edinburgh*: 1939, 10,260t, 12×6in, 12×4in, 6tt, 32k; torpedoed by German destroyer, Barents Sea, May 1942.

[2]Rear Admiral Wake Walker, in *Norfolk.*

58.   At dawn visibility was low, and after consultation with *Ark Royal* I decided to delay flying off the striking force as there was a serious risk of mistaking friend for foe and as I was in considerable doubt as to the position of *King George V* and *Rodney*. Having informed C-in-C, Home Fleet, that the striking force would arrive at 0745, I later informed him that the attack was postponed on account of low visibility, and later still that I had cancelled the attack on account of the difficulty of identifying our own ships in the existing visibility. I was satisfied that until the situation clarified it was undesirable to fly off the striking force.

59.   While these signals were being passed the destroyers' reports of the position of *Bismarck* suggested she might be as much as 60 miles to the northward of *Renown*. Course was therefore altered to the northward, and at 0810 after *Ark Royal* had struck down her aircraft as it was impossible to keep them ranged, *Maori* was sighted to the northward. *Maori* reported the enemy as being 009° distant 11 miles from her and thereby only 17 miles from *Renown*. . . . As contact was now definitely established course was altered to 180° to range the striking force and aircraft were flown off at 0926 . . .

61.   After sighting *Maori* I considered detaching *Ark Royal* to the southward to range the striking force, keeping *Renown* in the vicinity of *Maori* ready to support *King George V* and *Rodney* if required. I decided however that the appearance of *Renown* on the scene before *King George V* established contact was undesirable in view of the low visibility and furthermore it was imperative to afford *Ark Royal* the maximum degree of protection should *King George V* fail to establish contact and thus leave the third striking force as the only means of dealing with *Bismarck*.

62.   Heavy gunfire was heard to the northward at 0855 but no report was received indicating what ship or ships were in action.

63.   At 0940 *Sheffield* appeared from the westward, and I ordered her to join *Ark Royal* . . . while *Renown* turned toward the scene of action to investigate. *Ark Royal* was instructed to fly off a spotting aircraft for *Renown*.

65.   The C-in-C's signal ordering the destroyers to close coupled with *Norfolk*'s signal that she had ceased flank marking and RA, 1st CS's signal ordering *Dorsetshire* to torpedo *Bismarck* at close range, led me to suppose that the action was successfully concluded so in view of the Admiralty signal which had just been received indicating that a heavy scale of air attack was to be expected I decided to rejoin *Ark Royal* to afford A/A protection. I informed C-in-C, Home Fleet, accordingly at 0955.

67.   The torpedo striking force from *Ark Royal* located the *Bismarck*

just in time to see the finish of the action. The enemy was down in the water, on fire and silenced. *Dorsetshire* was seen to be in close proximity to *Bismarck* and would have been endangered by a torpedo attack on the latter. The striking force therefore closed *King George V* for instructions but obtained no answer either by V/S or W/T. The striking force then returned to the vicinity of the *Bismarck* and were in time to see *Dorsetshire* sink her with torpedoes from close range

68.   Meanwhile at 0955 an enemy aircraft had been sighted by *Renown* and engaged. About this time *Cossack* and *Norfolk* both reported they were being bombed. *Sheffield's* RDF was not efficient owing to damage from splinters . . . Enemy aircraft were sighted from time to time and engaged whenever they came out of the clouds. Weather conditions prevented the use of fighters. There appeared to be both Focke Wulfs and Heinkels[1] present.

69.   The striking force returned about 1115 and were ordered to jettison their torpedoes before landing on as the motion on the ship was even greater than the previous day and to land on with torpedoes would have jeopardised the aircraft. Whilst landing on was in progress a Heinkel came out of the clouds and dropped a stick of two large and about five smaller bombs 600 yards astern and to port of *Ark Royal*. This was the last interference experienced by Force H. Landing on was completed by 1152, and from then on the air appeared clear of enemy aircraft and course was shaped to the southward at 24 knots.

162.   *Report of Proceedings, 29 May–7 June 1941*

11 June 1941

5 June

37.   . . . the Force, comprising *Renown, Furious* and *Ark Royal*, screened by *Faulknor, Foxhound, Foresight, Forester, Fearless* and *Fury*, . . . proceeded eastward to carry out operation ROCKET. . . .

6 June

43.   At 0930 the first Blenheim[2] was detected by RDF . . . *Ark Royal* at once started up her Hurricanes and worked up speed for flying off. . . .

47.   . . . withdrawal to the westward was made at 24 knots. Each carrier kept a section of fighters ranged.

51.   A signal was received from NOIC, Malta, at 1852, stating that 43 Hurricanes and 8 Blenheims had arrived safely at Malta.

---

[1]Heinkel He111: 1936, bomb load 5510lb, 1 cannon, 6mg, 258mph.
[2]Bristol Blenheim: 1936, bomb load 1000lb, 5mg, 266mph.

163.   *To North*

15 June 1941

... just at sunset I got one of the usual claims that *D[unkerque]* had left Oran. I at once sent off a dicky to examine and he returned at 11.30 to say, as usual, same place, same everything. This report reached me just as I got one from TLs to say that if *D* had gone I was to intercept and put [her] in Mr D.J.'s locker. I ask you! There was I with two plain vans, little boats out of fuel and only six at that. Luckily it didn't arise. That was quickly followed by one to say that certain action would be taken next day which would probably provoke a Frog Blitz on the happy home. Then I *did* [talk?] and pointed out there would be *four* yes *four* plain vans in, or in the immediate vicinity of, our home and that no more perfect target could be provided. I therefore asked that they should put their party off so as to give me time to oil and get clear W though as I pointed out a bevy of six U-boats was concentrated in that area. To my surprise SYRIA was postponed 24 hours. ...

164.   *Report of Proceedings, 7–15 June 1941*

18 June 1941

7 June

6.   ... at 2230, Force H ... sailed with *Furious* to the westward, in order to clear the harbour in the event of bombing attack by the French in retaliation for our forthcoming action in Syria. ...

10 June

25.   ... I found difficulty in making constructive proposals since the only information I had concerning the situation was based on the BBC broadcasts. On previous occasions I have experienced and represented the same difficulty. I am convinced that a brief Admiralty appreciation would prove of the greatest value to Senior Officers at sea and would once again urge the transmission of such appreciations.

13 June

43.   Force H, comprising *Renown, Ark Royal, Victorious*, screened by *Faulknor, Fearless, Foresight, Forester, Foxhound, Hesperus* and *Wishart,* sailed for operation TRACER at 1130, shaping course to the eastward ... at 21 knots.

14 June

50.

	Victorious	*Ark Royal*
1st Hurricane off	1045	1047
23rd Hurricane off	1134.30	
24th Hurricane off		1133.30

For a new ship not fully worked up *Victorious* made a good evolution of the flying off.

53.   . . . Further information received from VA, Malta, at 2100 showed that out of the 4 Hudsons[1] and 47 Hurricanes which had taken off, all had arrived safely with the exception of one which was seen to break formation and make for the N African coast, one which crashed into the sea, the pilot being saved, and two which crashed on landing, the pilot of one being killed.

165.   *To Cunningham*

11 June 1941

I wonder if you'll ever have a let up? No sooner do you finish one bloody awful job than you get landed with another. I hope the postponement did not upset matters unduly but on the night in question there was every prospect of having four carriers in harbour together, a proper nest of U-boats to the westward and no A/S escorts to deal with the situation. So I felt it was necessary to ask for a postponement though I didn't know at the time what 'action' was intended.

With regard to these Hurri[cane] jobs I feel very strongly that we must either use long distance escorts or no escorts at all. The squadron leaders are quite confident they can find their way without escort if necessary and unless we use the long range of the Hurris we are bound sooner or later to find ourselves in the position that the carriers, with their decks littered, can neither operate nor fire a gun. Seems to me it's much better to risk a few eggs rather than have the poor bloody old goose killed or knocked out.

Unfortunately the long range jobs do not afford the diversion that would assist you at your end. If only I could get a small spell clear of

---

[1]Lockheed Hudson USA: 1938, bomb load 1400lb, 5–7mg, 253 mph, range 2800 mls. These were destined for Freetown but used temporarily to navigate Hurricanes to Malta. One Hurricane unserviceable. Blenheims on passage to Middle E.

these delivery jobs I could stage something though my six destroyers are dropping to bits and have to be nursed. I'm always calculating on speeds which ships can't stand this or that on account of excessive vibrations. Of course they all differ.

I see that 'Head Office' shared your views about the lack of aircraft. Well it was pretty obvious what the answer would be but it's poor consolation for you who had to suffer so many losses on account of other people's lack of vision. It made me angry to learn from some of the Hurri pilots that they'd hardly seen a Hun for months past. There must have been loads of aircraft that could have been spared for your end.

Gort – the new Governor here – is giving this place a proper shake up and high time too. He's established a new priority:

(1)   Aerodrome to facilitate passage of aircraft east
(2)   Fixed and A/A defences to protect the naval base.
(3)   Fortress defence against assault.

. . . The Pongos are very angry with me for laying bare their deficiencies and lack of drive but Gort welcomes every criticism and suggestion.

. . . we watch with the very greatest interest and admiration your doings in the east. It will be a bloody fine chapter of Naval History and no mistake.

166.   *Report of Proceedings, 16–22 June 1941*

23 June 1941

18 June

25.   A very welcome signal was intercepted at 1130 stating that the five 'F' class destroyers returning to Gibraltar had sunk a German U-boat in position 36°N, 8°W.[1]

167.   *Report of Proceedings, 22 June–1 July 1941*

6 July 1941

22 June

3.   At 0900 the Ocean Boarding Vessel *Marsdale*[2] reported having sighted a suspicious vessel resembling the German *Alstertor*[3] . . . Two Catalina aircraft were sent to assist and the available ships of the 8th DF

[1]*U138.*
[2]*Marsdale*: 1940, 4890gt, Kaye, London.
[3]*Alstertor*: 1938, 3063gt.

ordered to raise steam with all despatch in readiness to proceed to intercept. . . . *Faulknor, Fearless, Foxhound, Forester* and *Fury* sailed westbound at 1430.

Subsequent reports from the Catalina aircraft throughout the day confirmed the ship was an enemy supply ship or raider. Bombing attacks were unsuccessful and the aircraft finally lost touch at 0030/23, but the prospect of interception by the 8th DF appeared to be good.

23 June

6. At 1442 *Fury* reported sighting the German merchant ship. Captain (D), 8th DF, ordered the remaining ships of the Flotilla to concentrate on *Fury*. At 1543 *Fury* reported that the ship had given her name as *Alstertor* and had signalled she had British prisoners aboard. She also stated she had a letter and requested a boat might be sent to collect it. At 1550 *Fury* was joined by *Fearless* and at 1610 *Fury* was ordered to go alongside and board. Whilst approaching the raider at 1633 scuttling charges were observed to explode amidships and *Fury* lay off as further charges were fired and *Alstertor* took a list to port; she sank finally at 1729. The survivors picked up comprised British, natives, German officers and German ratings.

26 June

12. *Renown* and *Ark Royal* left harbour in low visibility at 0400 and proceeded eastward at 20 knots screened by *Hermione, Faulknor, Forester, Fury, Lance* and *Legion*.[1] . . .

27 June

19. The first Hurricane took off at 0526. . . .
20. . . . the 22nd at 0623 . . .
22. . . . the force withdrew at 25 knots. A fighter patrol and A/S patrol were flown off and maintained throughout the day. . . .
27. Information was eventually received from VA, Malta, at 1510 that all aircraft had arrived safely at Malta, but that one had crashed on landing, the pilot being safe.

28 June

35. Force A, comprising *Furious* (carrying 16 Hurricanes Mark 11A) stowed in the hangar, *Hermione, Fearless, Foxhound* and *Legion* accordingly sailed to the westward at 1830.

[1]*Lance* (bombed Malta 1942): 1941, 1920t, 6×4.7in, 8tt, 36.5k.

29 June

39. . . . Force B, comprising *Renown, Ark Royal, Faulknor, Fury, Forester* and *Lance* passed Europa Point at 0215 steering 082° at 18 knots. Forces A and B joined company at 0700 . . .

30 June

46. . . . The first Hurricane was flown off *Ark Royal* at 0557 . . .

50. *Furious* having now reported flying completed, Groups I and II closed and withdrawal was made to the WSW at 25 knots. It was then ascertained that after the first Hurricane had taken off successfully from *Furious* the second swerved when halfway along the deck and hit the port navigating position. A long range tank was wrenched off and the aircraft crashed over the side. Burning petrol enveloped the port side of the bridge, the port navigating and signalling positions and the look out huts.[1]

51. As the bridge was burning furiously the ship was turned out of the wind and engines stopped. As soon as the fire was under control flying off was resumed and the first flight was airborne by 0525. The formation of 9 led by the Blenheim then proceeded to Malta.

54. The promptness with which the operation of flying off the first flight of Hurricanes was recommenced and successfully completed after the accident reflects credit on the ship and especially on Cdr M. Cursham (Commander Flying)[2] who was himself suffering from burns and shock.

58. At 1245 information was received that all 6 Blenheims and 35 Hurricanes had arrived safely at Malta.

168. *To Cunningham*

2 July 1941

Provided we can achieve surprise and don't meet too many mines I think there's a fair chance of a proportion of the convoy reaching Malta. I say this because with this Russian business on it seems to me that the strength of the enemy air in the Central Mediterranean must have been reduced to a considerable extent. The chief snag is that bombers will certainly have fighter escorts and so far our Fulmars have not proved too successful against the CR42.

---

[1]Nine dead, four injured.

[2]Cdr M. Cursham: Cdr 1937; Air Personnel Dept 1939; N Air Div 1940; Cdr (F) *Furious* Feb 1941; Actg Capt *Sparrowhawk* (Hatston, Orkney) May 1942; DD, N Air Ordnance Div May 1943; Actg Capt *Ringtail* 1945.

I must confess I'm a bit doubtful about getting the empties back as a convoy. It looks to me rather as if we may be risking too much by doing so and stand to lose more than we shall gain. I'm not sure it wouldn't be better to wait for a thick patch and slip them out singly routed close to the French [N. African] coast in the hope they may be mistaken for Frogs. . . .

We have just got three Sea Hurricanes but have not yet had a chance to operate them. Have you used this aircraft yet and if so, any special technique? Seems to me they ought to be held back until it's pretty certain that a party will be taking place within the next 15 minutes and then flown off. The snag about them is even if [parked?] just before the barrier in *Ark* they will probably be damaged by the blast of her guns. . . .

Later. You will have got my proposals about SUBSTANCE. I haven't asked Bill Ford yet what he can do in the way of air recco but it's important that *Ark* should be relieved as much as possible in order to concentrate on fighters and A/S. Always I think we should block the hole between Sardinia and Sicily with as many submarines as can be spared for the purpose. I imagine it would be a bit too hot (from A/S point of view) for them to operate successfully off Naples, Messina, Palermo, etc. The old *Nelson* won't be much help in catching anything or keeping off the bombers. But she may give the *Ark* a nice relief as the main target.

We were extra tickled at the pat the ER of the *Rodney* got for the distance they've steamed. *Renown* is now three-quarters of the way to the Moon and it looks as if we shall bump the bloody thing before she gets a refit. As for the 8th DF! – I hardly dare look the poor little sods in the hawse pipes. Run right off their poor little legs and [we] shall end up one day with the whole lot in tow.

I hope the stream of Wellingtons,[1] Blenheims, Beaufighters, etc., that pass through here reach you in due course. If they do then Gib is darn valuable as a stepping stone and I do trust the great ones won't stir up the Frogs at this end by doing something which brings us no return and merely lands us in the soup. . . .

169. *Statement on First Year of Force H's Operations*

9 July 1941

This Force completed one year's service on 28 June 1941, and the following information with regard to the various units up to that date may be of interest. . . .

[1]Vickers Wellington: 1936, bomb load 6000lb, 6mg, 255mph.

With regard to other units, since joining Force H, the 8th Flotilla have covered an aggregate of 500,000 miles (*Faulknor* 84,000 miles with 266 days at sea), and *Sheffield* over 75,000 miles with 240 days at sea.

The two main units, *Renown* and *Ark Royal* have steamed 74,164 miles, 232 days at sea, and 83,780 miles, 230 days at sea, since joining the Flag of Vice Admiral Sir James F. Somerville. . . .

170. *To North*

13 July 1941

. . . Syfret has joined me temporarily and from talks I've had with him it's abundantly clear that Winston was at the bottom of your affair and mine too! I told Syfret that what *we* objected to was the fact that our brother Admirals did not have the guts to stand up to W even when they knew that something quite unfair and improper was being done. . . .

171. *To Force H and SUBSTANCE Convoy*

20 July 1941

The main object of the operation on which we are now engaged is to pass a convoy of seven transports containing personnel and stores to Malta.

For over a year Malta has held out most gallantly against all assaults of the enemy. Until Crete fell we were able to supply Malta from both ends of the Mediterranean, but since the evacuation of Crete the situation has changed. For the present, Malta can only be supplied from the west and this is the task with which we have been entrusted.

To assist the achievement of our object every effort must be made to deny the enemy knowledge of our movements and intentions. This can be assured to a large degree if we

(a)   avoid making smoke, either from the boiler rooms or the galleys;
(b)   use the lowest brilliancy lights for signalling, especially at dawn and dusk;
(c)   take infinite care that no lights are visible at night;
(d)   keep a very special look-out for the low-flying snooper that appears and disappears just on the horizon.

If the enemy detect our presence and attack with high level bombers, keep a special look-out for the very low-flying torpedo aircraft that may be attacking at the same time.

During this operation there will be long periods of first or second degrees of readiness. Everyone must make a point of taking rest and sleeping when not closed up, so as to be fresh and ready for action when required.

We must all of us have uppermost in our minds this one thought – the convoy *must* reach Malta. And it *will* reach Malta if every officer and man accepts his personal responsibility in ensuring the success of the operation and realises it's TEAM-WORK which does the job. Everyone must go full out, must key himself up for the maximum effort and not relax until the word is passed to 'stand easy'.

If the enemy attempts to stop us by surface, air or submarine forces, it is my intention to attack him and keep attacking until he desists.

THE CONVOY MUST GO THROUGH!

172. *Report on Operation SUBSTANCE*

4 August 1941

Departure from Gibraltar [21 July]

27.   About 0320 the squalls decreased in intensity and the fog cleared sufficiently to allow *Manchester* to sail, followed by *Leinster. Renown,* preceded by *Ark Royal* and destroyers, slipped at 0426. . . .
31.   At 0915 information was received from VACNA that the personnel ship *Leinster* was ashore near Cape Tarifa. . . .
32.   I considered it impracticable to take any steps to transfer the personnel from *Leinster.* . . .

Torpedo Bomber and High Level Bombing Attack on Fleet, AM 23 July

47.   The first group of enemy aircraft was detected at 0910 . . . This developed into a well synchronised torpedo bomber and high level bombing attack . . . 6 torpedo planes attacked from ahead and concentrated on the convoy while 8 high level bombers crossed from S to N dropping their bombs amongst the convoy.

Loss of Fearless

49.   The two aircraft which attacked *Fearless* released their torpedoes from a height of 70 ft and at a range of about 1500 and 800 yards respectively. Avoiding action was taken and the first torpedo passed about 90 yards ahead. The torpedo from the second aircraft ran shallow. Course was shaped to comb the track but when abreast the stem on the port side, at a distance of about 30 ft, the torpedo broke surface, altered course to port, and hit the ship abreast the 3" gun.

50. Both engines were put out of action, the rudder was jammed hard-a-port, all electric power failed due to the switchboard being demolished and an extensive fuel fire was started aft. One officer and 34 ratings were killed outright or died later. *Fearless* reported that she was entirely disabled. As she was badly on fire and I did not consider the detachment of a second destroyer to attempt towing was justified under the circumstances, I ordered *Forester* to take off survivors and then sink the ship. . . .

Damage to, and detachment of, Manchester

51. Meanwhile, *Manchester* who was to starboard of the convoy sighted torpedoes approaching and turned to port to comb the tracks. Two torpedoes were seen to pass down the port side and another one passed astern from starboard. In order to avoid collision with *Port Chalmers*[1] a turn to starboard was then commenced. At this time another aircraft released a torpedo from a position between the first and second MT ships of the port column. Wheel was immediately reversed in an endeavour to avoid this torpedo, but it struck *Manchester* aft on the port side.

52. The immediate effects of the torpedo hit were to cause a list of 12° to port with large reduction of speed and steering gear out of action. Steering was changed over to the after position and a reasonable degree of control was obtained. Subsequently the steering motors failed and hand steering had to be used. The explosion had travelled upwards through the decks to the upper deck driving large quantities of fuel oil upwards into all the compartments affected. Water and oil fuel flooded the after engine room, after 4" magazine, main W/T office, X magazine and various other compartments between 179 and 209 bulkheads. Many ratings were overcome by fumes from the oil fuel but most of these recovered after treatment and were able to resume their duties. Only the starboard outer shaft remained serviceable. A speed of 8 knots was at first obtained which very gradually increased to 12 knots. Emergency leads were run to the steering motors and mechanical steering was again in use by 1315.

53. *Manchester*'s initial signal informed me that she could steam 8 knots so I ordered her to return to Gibraltar escorted by *Avon Vale*[2]. Her casualties were 3 naval officers, 5 military officers, 20 naval ratings and 7 other ranks killed, 3 naval ratings missing, and 1 military officer, 1 naval rating and 4 other ranks wounded.

---

[1] *Port Chalmers*: 1933, 8535gt, 15k, Port Line.
[2] *Avon Vale*: 'Hunt' class destroyer, 1940, 1050t, 6×4in, 27k.

54.   *Manchester* had approximately 750 military personnel on board but as the sea was calm I decided to limit her escort to one destroyer in the hope that a single cruiser and destroyer might either escape detection by enemy aircraft or else avoid attack in view of the better targets offered by the convoy and its escorts.

57.   In the first high level attack Fulmars shot down 2 S79s and 2 more probably failed to return. Three T/B aircraft (S79s) were shot down by gunfire, . . .

T/B attack on Manchester *and* Avon Vale, *PM 23 July (D3)*

59.   . . . At 1805 they were attacked by 3 torpedo bombers. These approached from astern and proceeded well inside territorial waters to reach a position up sun. *Avon Vale,* anticipating an attack from out of the sun, moved in that direction to a distance of about 2 miles from *Manchester.* The aircraft then approached low down on the starboard bow and were subjected to a heavy flanking fire from *Avon Vale* and to a barrage from A and B turrets backed up by the starboard 4" battery of *Manchester.* The enemy appeared so deterred by the volume of fire that they did not press home the attack. One torpedo was dropped at *Avon Vale* and the other two were dropped at such long range that *Manchester* had no difficulty in taking avoiding action. . . .

Abortive T/B attack on Fleet, PM 23 July (D3)

60.   At 1643 a group of aircraft was detected bearing 338°, 43 miles, closing the convoy. Fifteen minutes later 5 S79s led by a Cant were sighted low down on the port quarter. Fighters intercepted this group which consisted of torpedo planes and shot down 2 S79s and damaged the Cant. The remainder retired without attacking.

Detachment of Force X

61.   By 1713 the convoy and escort had reached the entrance to the Skerki Channel and *Hermione* was ordered to take *Manchester*'s place in Force X. Group 4 parted company and withdrew westward with the intention of covering *Manchester* and affording such protection to MG 1 on D4 as was practicable. A section of fighters remained with the convoy until 1830, when they were relieved by Beaufighters from Malta. . . .

Passage of Force X through the Narrows on the night of 23/24 July (D3/4)

62.   While Force H returned to the W, Force X and the convoy contin-ued through the Skerki Channel towards Malta, one destroyer with TSDS streamed and locked in the low speed setting being stationed

ahead of each column of the convoy. They were attacked at 1900 by 4 T/Bs which approached from the starboard beam and were heavily engaged. One aircraft was seen by *Farndale*[1] to crash. Avoiding action was taken but 2 torpedoes passed close to *Edinburgh* and 1 close to *Hermione*. The Beaufighters failed to intercept this raid.

HLB attack on Force H on 23 July (D3)

63. At 1945 a high level bombing attack developed from 12,000 ft. Two Beaufighters at 8000 failed to intercept. They had been instructed by R/T from *Edinburgh* to circle at 10,000 ft, 5 miles, 070° from the convoy in a position to intercept the incoming aircraft. They failed to do this and approached from the same direction as the enemy without identifying themselves and were engaged by the gunfire of the fleet. They then withdrew as the enemy approached, 3000 ft above them. About 20 heavy bombs fell and one either hit or very nearly missed *Firedrake* who was towing TSDS ahead of the port column. At the same time one torpedo passed astern of *Edinburgh* but as no T/B aircraft were seen this torpedo may have come from a U-boat.

Damage to, and withdrawal of, Firedrake

64. *Firedrake* was holed in No. 1 and 2 boiler rooms and temporarily immobilised, but suffered no serious casualties. *Eridge*[2] having been ordered by the RA, 18th CS, to stand by and escort her to Gibraltar, *Firedrake* reported that she hoped to have steam in one boiler shortly. In the meantime *Eridge* took her in tow . . . *Firedrake*'s steering gear being out of action, considerable difficulty was experienced in turning to the course for the Galita Channel, and equal difficulty in maintaining that course. Fortunately the steering gear was repaired by midnight, and no further difficulties arose; speed being slowly worked up to 10 knots. The hopes that had been raised regarding the possibility of steaming the one remaining boiler proved false, for this boiler primed so badly that *Firedrake* reported that she would be unable to steam for some considerable time.

67. At 0930/25 *Firedrake* slipped, after being in tow for 37 hours. *Eridge* then towed her alongside for 2 hours, during which 10½ tons of feedwater and 2 tons of drinking water were transferred. *Firedrake* then cast off and proceeded at 9 knots under her own power.

68. The damage to *Firedrake* was doubly unfortunate in that it deprived the port column of the convoy of TSDS protection. *Fearless*

---

[1]*Farndale*: 'Hunt', 1941.
[2]*Eridge*: 'Hunt', 1941; irreparably damaged E Med 1942.

and *Nestor* had been detailed as spare TSDS ships. . . . The delay which would have resulted while *Nestor*[1] streamed her sweep could not be accepted. Furthermore, in the absence of *Fearless*, *Firedrake*, *Avon Vale* and *Eridge*, the screen was already undesirably thin. The RA, 18th CS, therefore decided to accept the increased risk of damage by mines and to press on without further delay, . . .

E-boat attack on Force X, 0300, 24 July (D4)

74.   . . . three unidentified objects were detected by *Cossack*, . . . on her RDF.

75.   At 0250, short flashes of light followed by the sound of motor engines starting up indicated to *Cossack* and *Edinburgh* (leading the port column) the presence of E-boats. One was promptly illuminated by searchlight and heavily engaged by these two ships. *Manxman* found the target perfectly illuminated by cross searchlight beams and also opened fire. After firing torpedoes, one of which passed under the stern of *Cossack*, the E-boat retired at high speed but not before she had been repeatedly hit. Two torpedoes, either from the same or another E-boat, passed down the port side of *Edinburgh*.

76.   Shortly afterwards, *Arethusa*, the rear ship of the port column, sighted another E-boat, which had apparently passed down between the port column of the convoy and the destroyer screen. This boat was engaged by both *Arethusa* and *Farndale* (the rear ship of the port screen), and hits were observed. One officer in *Arethusa* was confident that the boat was stopped; there is no evidence, however, that she was sunk.

78.   At 0305 the noise of an E-boat was heard by *Edinburgh* on the port side and immediately afterwards its wake was seen. It was promptly illuminated, and raked with pom-pom, 0.5" and Oerlikon[2] fire at 1500–2000 yards range, the target appearing to be enveloped in a hail of tracers. The E-boat stopped out of control, and at this moment the main armament fired a broadside of 12 guns at fixed sight range. When the splashes subsided nothing was seen. *Edinburgh* reports that when the target was first brilliantly illuminated one North Country gunlayer so far forgot his Whale Island training as to report 'There's the bastard' instead of the more orthodox 'Gunlayer on'.

79.   Meanwhile, *Cossack* detected hydrophone effect by asdic in several positions ahead, and at 0315 sighted another E-boat on the port bow. Speed was increased and endeavour was made to ram, but the boat

[1]*Nestor* (RAN): 1941, 1760t, 6×47in, 1×4in, 5tt, 36k; sunk off N Africa 1942, Ger a/c.
[2]A Swiss designed 20mm A/A gun.

passed across *Cossack*'s bows too close for the searchlight to follow. Fire was opened and sounds like splintering of wood heard. A torpedo was fired by this boat, and it is estimated to have passed immediately under the stem of *Cossack*, who was only 100 yards from the enemy at the time.

Torpedoing and escorting of Sydney Star

84. *Nestor*, who at 0255 had observed one ship of the convoy dropping astern, proceeded to investigate, and on closing, it was seen that the ship, identified as SS *Sydney Star*,[1] was moving slowly through the water on an opposite course to that of the convoy. On closer approach it was observed that the starboard boats were being lowered; the ship however appeared undamaged, with no list and at normal trim.

85. . . . *Sydney Star* reported that she had been torpedoed in No. 3 hold, and that she had 30 ft of water in that hold and appeared to be sinking.

86. *Nestor* therefore decided to embark the troops, numbering 470, and proceeded alongside for this purpose. Planks were rigged from *Sydney Star*'s gunwhale to *Nestor*'s forecastle and jacobs ladders employed aft. Transfer occupied 50 minutes . . .

87. Throughout this operation both ships were lying stopped in a position 4 miles from Pantellaria. Three E-boats were observed whilst the transfer of troops was proceeding, but no attacks developed. On completion of the transfer, personnel on board *Nestor* numbered 774 (231 ship's company, 56 army passengers, 487 ex-*Sydney Star*).

88. Whilst alongside, *Nestor* formed the impression that the Master of the *Sydney Star* was unduly pessimistic concerning the state of his ship. *Nestor* impressed on the Master the absolute necessity of keeping his ship afloat and getting her under way again. At 0410 *Nestor* cast off and as the result of his salutary admonition had the satisfaction of seeing *Sydney Star* go ahead on her engines and follow at 12 knots.

89. At 0556, *Sydney Star* informed *Nestor* that the ship had 12 ft of water in No. 1 hold and 7 ft in No. 2 hold . . . It subsequently transpired that the ship had been holed by a projectile fired by one of the escort during the E-boat melee.

90. At 0615 two T/B aircraft were sighted by *Nestor* on the port quarter. Barrage fire was opened and the aircraft crossed astern making off in the general direction of the convoy. At 0650 two more T/Bs were sighted, this time on the port bow. Barrage fire was again opened and the aircraft crossed ahead and made off towards the convoy. Thinking that the *Sydney Star* was about to be attacked, *Nestor* made a 'Help' signal, in

[1]*Sydney Star*: 1936, 11,095gt, Blue Star Line.

consequence of which *Hermione* was detached by CS 18 at 0700 to join *Nestor* and *Sydney Star*.

Approach to and arrival at Malta, 24 July (D4)

94.   There appeared to be little likelihood of enemy surface forces making contact with the main convoy, a greater source of worry being the *Sydney Star*. At 0730 the situation appeared easier, and realising that any further delay might jeopardise the arrangements for getting the convoy into Grand Harbour and for sailing Force X to rejoin Force H, RA, 18 CS, with *Arethusa* and *Manxman*, parted company from the convoy and proceeded at 25 knots to Malta. . . .

95.   At 1000, *Sydney Star*, *Hermione* and *Nestor* were attacked by Ju87 dive bombers . . . and two high level bombers. The attacks were well synchronised, and in the case of the dive bombing attack, well pressed home. One bomb fell 20 yards to port, and another 20 yards to starboard of *Nestor*; others fell close to *Hermione* – but no ship was hit. One Ju87 was shot down by A/A fire. One Beaufighter was in company but failed to make an interception.

96.   *Edinburgh*, *Arethusa* and *Manxman* entered Grand Harbour at 1130 with ships' companies fallen in and bands playing. A great reception was accorded them by the people of Malta.

97.   *Hermione*, *Nestor* and *Sydney Star*, having taken the route N of Malta, arrived at 1400. The safe arrival of *Sydney Star* reflects great credit on the CO of *Nestor*, Cdr A. R. Rosenthal, RAN[1] who showed judgement, initiative and good seamanship in handling a delicate situation so close to the enemy's coast and in the presence of enemy E-boats. . . .

98.   The main convoy escorted by *Cossack*, *Maori*, *Sikh*, *Foxhound* and *Farndale* continued without incident and proceeding by the route S of Malta, entered harbour at 1530.

Movements of Force H, 24 July (D4)

100.   At 0816 a Cant was sighted 10 miles to the eastward and was shot down by the fighter patrol . . .

101.   The situation at 1000 was as follows. Force H . . . steering 290° at 18 knots. *Firedrake* and *Eridge* S of Galita making 8 knots to the westward, having been reported by a shadower at 0710. Convoy MG 1 in 3 Groups ranging between 40 miles W to 20 miles E of Galita with one ship, the *Svenor*,[2] just outside Malta. *Manchester* and *Avon Vale* about

---

[1]Cdr A. R. Rosenthal, RAN: Cdr 1937; *Nestor* 1941; *Torrens* 1945.
[2]*Svenör*: tanker, 1931, 7616gt, Norway.

65 miles to the westward of Force H proceeding at 11 knots and possibly reported by a reconnaissance aircraft at 0700.

102. I decided that Force H should continue to the westward till about 1330 by which time *Manchester* would be reasonably clear of enemy air attack, and would have 3 destroyers in company, VACNA having ordered *Vimy* and *Vidette* to rendezvous with her. About 1330 I intended to turn E in order to fly off 6 Swordfish for Malta during the night and then rendezvous with Force X in the vicinity of Galita Island about 0730.

103. During the day calls for help were received from all 3 groups of the MG convoy. The first came at 1230 from *Encounter*, who was escorting Group 2. She reported a threatening aircraft in the vicinity and later reported an attack by 4 T/Bs, but all torpedoes missed. The attack was followed about 20 minutes later by high level bombing when some 30 bombs fell between *Amerika* and *Thermopylae*.[1] ...

104. At 1342 Group 1 called for help ... A high level attack resulted in bombs dropping between *Talabot* and *Breconshire*[2] and half an hour later *Breconshire* was near missed by some small bombs from a Caproni. Group 3 called for help at 1711 ... and again at 1815.

105. *Encounter* left Group 2 at 1340 and proceeded ahead at 28 knots to join and escort Group 1. At 1740 she was attacked unsuccessfully by 3 high level bombers. ...

Despatch of Six Swordfish to Malta

108. At 0100 *Ark Royal* flew off 6 Swordfish fitted with long range tanks for Malta. ... These all arrived safely.

116. Force X joined Force H 26 miles NW of Galita Island at 0815 and course was shaped to the westward at *Nelson*'s best speed.

HLB attack on the Fleet, AM 25 July (D5)

120. At 1035 a large group of aircraft was detected ...

121. The Fulmars attacked with great dash and bombs could be seen being jettisoned far away on the port quarter of the Fleet between 1107 and 1110. Three S79 high level bombers were shot down for certain, one was probably destroyed and two others were damaged.

122. In this encounter we lost two Fulmars. One crew was recovered unhurt by *Nestor*. The other aircraft ... was seen by *Sikh* to crash vertically into the sea at high velocity. There were no survivors.[3]

---

[1]*Amerika*: 1930, 10,218gt, 15k, E Asiatic Co, Denmark. *Thermopylae*: 1930, 6655gt, 15k, W. Wilhelmsen, Norway.
[2]*Talabot*: 1936, 6798gt, W. Wilhelmsen, Norway. *Breconshire*: auxiliary supply ship, 1939, 9000t, *c*.18k, Glen Line.
[3]Second Fulmar crew lost that day.

Movements of Units, 26 July (D6)

127.   *Manchester* arrived at Gibraltar at 0239. . . .

129.   During the afternoon the Fleet was turned to the eastward for a few hours to avoid reaching harbour before daylight. At 1640 the fleet was manoeuvred to pass on opposite courses to *Firedrake* and her escort of *Avon Vale* and *Eridge* who were . . . 88 miles from Cap de Gata proceeding at 9 knots, and ships' companies cheered ship on passing.

Arrival at Gibraltar, 27 July (D7)

134.   At 0300 *Hermione* with *Manxman* and *Arethusa* proceeded ahead at 24 knots to enter harbour. *Ark Royal*, *Edinburgh* and 4 destroyers followed at 0600, whilst *Renown* and *Nelson* screened by 7 destroyers manoeuvred as requisite to act as a target for a long range throw off firing from the Rock. This shoot was deplorably bad and once more demonstrated the lamentable inefficiency of the Fortress long range artillery.

General

137.   Outstanding points in this operation were:–

(a)   *Effective work of Fulmars*
The Fulmars of *Ark Royal* contributed in no small measure to the safe arrival of the convoy at its destination.[1] . . .

173.   *To North*

30 July 1941

. . . that convoy job kept me fully employed. Must confess I never expected we'd get them all through or even more miraculous get the 7 empty ones back. And the latter were all damn good ships. The fun started as usual on D3 – a very well synchronised torpedo and high level attack. The party of T/Bs that came in on the Starboard bow were a really gallant lot & though they were all shot down eventually they hit *Fearless* and *Manchester*. Poor *Fearless*, badly on fire aft, engines disabled and large explosions. All I could do was to take off the chaps and sink her but it was sad to see the first of the 'F's' go west. *M* had 740 Pongos on board & when I saw her listing & not under control it was not so good. All I could do was to detail one destroyer to accompany her as she limped

---

[1]Following representations to AOC Med, Beaufighters did rather better on the return trip.

back at 8 knots & hope the [enemy] wouldn't spot her. They did as a matter of fact & attacked twice but failed to register. The HLBs did no harm but got some near misses. We had further doses of them but *Ark*'s boys got busy & shot down 4. In the afternoon another T/B party attacked but again the lads swooped down and shot up 2 and sent a Cant, who was with them, limping home. I had to turn back at the usual place & then go off W to cover *M*. Syfret took the party through the Narrows & had a hectic time. T/Bs, HLBs, E-boats, mines but the only casualty was one hit on an M/T which didn't stop her getting in and a near miss on Norris's little ship[1] which put her out for nearly 12 hours during which another little boat towed her gallantly back towards Gib until she was able to steam herself at 9 knots. Things looked a bit odd on D4. The damaged ships & empty M/T were strung along about 300 miles of coast & I had to be back the next morning at windy corner to meet Syfret and his boys returning. Throughout the day the [enemy] air boys attacked the empties but by shooting down any Cants that appeared we kept them off *Manchester*. However they scored no hits. That night . . . I did a successful Hurry with 6 Stringbags as a side show & buttered up with Syfret before the first attack came in. *Ark* went for them bald headed & they pulled off their bombs about 12 miles away. Our score was 12 certain, 4 probable & a number damaged. We had 6 F's down but the crews of 4 picked up unhurt. . . . The morning after the little boat came in I pulled my skiff into her boiler room & out again.

I'm now in *Nelson* with old Tom Troubridge as Flag Capt. He's good value. . . .

174. *Report of Proceedings, 27 July–4 August 1941*

HMS *Nelson*,
12 August 1941

27 July

7.   Ships of the 8th DF celebrated the millionth mile steamed by them since the outbreak of war. The manner in which these little ships have been kept running reflects the greatest credit on their Engine Room Departments.

28 July

13.   HE the Governor of Algeciras, Excme. Sr. General Don Fernando

---

[1]Lt-Cdr S. H. Norris: Lt-Cdr 1934; *Firedrake* 1938; Cdr June 1942; *President* 1942.

Barrón y Ortiz,[1] paid a call on HE the Governor and C-in-C, Gibraltar, . . . I did not attend the ceremony since the attitude of the new Governor towards us is not yet established. Until this has been determined HE the Governor considers it would be desirable to avoid furnishing an opportunity for a request being made to visit HM Ships.

30 July

30. . . . Force [H], comprising *Nelson* (Flag), *Renown, Ark Royal, Faulknor, Foresight, Fury, Foxhound, Cossack* (Captain (D), 4th DF), *Maori, Nestor, Encounter* and *Eridge* proceeded independently to the eastward owing to fog.

33. As a security measure, Force X, comprising *Hermione, Arethusa, Manxman, Lightning*[2] and *Sikh*, who had embarked stores during the night, were brought to one hour's notice for steam in order to stop all shore leave.

31 July

34. Force X sailed at 0100 with 70 officers and 1676 other ranks and proceeded to the eastward at 16 knots, altering course as necessary to avoid shipping.

1 August

43. At 0310, . . . *Ark Royal* flew off 9 Swordfish . . . for a bombing attack on Alghero aerodrome. On completion of flying off the fleet withdrew . . . at 20 knots. The standard arrangements used by Force H for such operations were employed, i.e., destroyers formed an all round screen, the course for flying off was passed by shaded light to ships in the line, the destroyer screen conforming to the movements of the heavy ships and preserving compass bearings.

46. Two direct hits were observed on the equipment shop where a fire broke out. The eastern and western hangars and the living quarters were also hit and fires were caused in the two latter targets.

2 August

60. At 0510 . . ., Lt. J. B. E. Wainwright, the Navigating Officer of *Hermione*, sighted a U-boat in surface trim and apparently stopped fairly broad on the port bow distant 3½ cables. He at once ordered port wheel and conned the ship to ram. When *Hermione* was about 2 cables distant

---

[1]Don Fernando Barrón y Ortiz: Nationalist Col, prominent in advance on Madrid; Mil Govr, Algeciras, July 1941.

[2]*Lightning*: 1941, 1920t, 6×4.7in 8tt, 36.5k; sunk off N Africa 1943, E-boat.

the U-boat started to crash dive but 2 ft of the conning tower was still visible above the surface as the U-boat disappeared from view below *Hermione*'s bull ring. *Hermione* with what the CO in his report describes as 'a lovely crunch' struck the U-boat beam on at 28 knots. Light diesel oil sprayed over the compass platform and small objects flew past the port pom-pom director platform. A portion of the U-boat, since identified as probably the exhaust manifold, remained wrapped around *Hermione*'s stem. *Lightning* was detached to search but having seen or heard nothing was ordered to rejoin. The U-boat appeared to be an Italian *Tembien* or possibly 'H' class. The damage to *Hermione* was slight[1] . . .

Force X arrived safely at Malta at 0900 and entered harbour with hands fallen in and bands and troops paraded. They were accorded an enthusiastic reception by the Maltese.

66.　. . . Force X sailed at 1600 augmented by *Farndale* who had remained at Malta during operation SUBSTANCE as the result of condenser trouble. The force proceeded at 24 knots, this being *Farndale*'s best speed. At 1730 when N of Gozo, *Farndale* reported she could not maintain a higher speed than 18 knots. She was ordered by *Hermione* to return to Malta since this low speed was unacceptable at this juncture. . . .

67.　Force X then increased to 26 knots and returned by the same route which they had followed successfully through Tunisian territorial waters. . . .

175.　*To North*

5–6 August 1941

5 August

All well so far. On the morning of the 1st we bombed Alghero aerodrome whilst *Cossack* and *Maori* went to P. Conte & Alghero to shoot up the seaplane base at the former & sink any ships at the latter – I told them not to bombard the town. We got the aerodrome buildings & hangars a good crack but found no ships at Alghero. However a starshell set fire to a large two storied building on the outskirts of the town. Had favourable weather for the getaway as it came on thick with tremendous thundering. This diversion seems to have drawn the Cagliari boys up N as the cruisers had a clear run to Malta. . . . The Itis have not attacked.

---

[1]Lieut J. B. E. Wainwright: Lt 1934; *Caradoc* 1939; *Hermione* 1941; Lt-Cdr Feb 1942; *President* 1942; staff C-in-C Med 1943; d Sept 1943; apptd DSO for sinking s/m.
It was *Tembien*: 1938, 680/860t, 6tt, 1×3.9in, 14/8k.

They had 6 bloody great cruisers sitting in Palermo. *Renown*'s Port bulge has torn off & folded back so we are down to 18 knots & she's making a hell of a wave. . . .

6 August

. . . The second part of a lousy job – the passing through the 1600 troops, who'd missed their passage owing to *Leinster* grounding & *Manchester* turning back,went off OK though it was a bloody ruse. I'd already transferred to *Nelson* but decided that *Renown* must come too as it seemed impossible the Itis would make no move. . . .

. . . at 0315 on D3 I flew off the striking force to bomb Alghero aerodrome. All this to draw the Itis up N away from the cruisers.

All went according to plan but alas as the 3rd Swordfish landed on, a 40lb [bomb] that had not released clear of the rack, came away & went off & the aircraft was at once a blazing furnace. 4 officers & 2 ratings killed & a hole 2 ft big in the flight deck. Took them an hour to get the deck ready to land the remainder what time they were flying round & round getting shorter & shorter of petrol. You can imagine my feelings! . . .

176. *Report of Proceedings, 5–14 August 1941*

17 August 1941

5 August

4. I met Cdr I.L. Fleming, RNVR, of the NID,[1] . . . and discussed with him and HE the Governor a number of matters concerning intelligence and 'Y' work at Gibraltar.

Visits of Admiralty officers such as this are undoubtedly of great value.

7 August

7. I reported to the Admiralty that the available destroyers in the 8th DF remaining to screen *Nelson* and *Ark Royal* were now limited to three.

As this number was obviously inadequate, and the 13th DF could only provide one Fleet destroyer on rare occasions, owing to the intense enemy U-boat activity in the vicinity, I requested that *Encounter* should remain until the return of one of the 'F' class destroyers from the UK.

---

[1]Actg Lt-Cdr Ian L. Fleming, RNVR: Lt July 1939; NID 1940; Lt (Special) & Actg Lt-Cdr June 1941; Actg Cdr 1944; journalist & author of 'James Bond' books; brother of explorer and writer Peter Fleming.

8 August

9.   At 0130, temporary repairs to her port bulge having been completed, *Renown* sailed for the UK to undergo refit, SS *Pasteur*, HM Ships *Cossack*, *Maori*, *Sikh* and *Lightning* in company.

The RA, 18th CS, sailed at 0900 in HMS *Edinburgh* for Atlantic convoy duty.

9 August

13.   The C-in-C, Mediterranean, was informed by the Admiralty that in view of the casualties to Force H destroyers and defects in *Faulknor*, it was necessary to retain *Nestor* and *Encounter* temporarily at Gibraltar. . . .

11 August

23.   *Furious* reported that experience in operation RAILWAY, when 22 Hurricanes were erected before arrival at Gibraltar, showed that such an arrangement made the ship unpleasantly top-heavy and it was, of course, impossible for *Furious* to operate her own aircraft with the Hurricanes erected on deck. As the ship had been shadowed by enemy aircraft on her last two passages to Gibraltar and bombed once, her CO had hoped on this occasion to operate Sea Hurricanes. This would allow 60 unerected Hurricanes, 9 Swordfish and 4 operational Sea Hurricanes to be carried, but would not permit any erection of aircraft.

12 August

25.   In reply to a suggestion which I had made verbally to the Admiralty through the CO, HMS *Manxman*, the C-in-C, Mediterranean, was informed that the Admiralty approved the use of HMS *Manxman* for a minelaying operation off the W coast of Italy, provided he concurred. *Manxman* could be ready to leave Milford [Haven] on 17 August with a mixed outfit of mines.

I informed the C-in-C, Mediterranean, that my proposal was to lay mines to intercept coastal shipping S of Leghorn, . . . The proposed programme was as follows.

D1   *Manxman* to arrive Gibraltar after dark and refuel.
D1   *Manxman* to sail before dawn, speed of advance 18 knots, route between Balearics and Spain.
D2   Increase to 37 knots at sunset, . . . and carry out minelaying, returning by same route and reducing speed about sunrise on D3.
D4   Arrive Gibraltar after dark and refuel.
D5   Sail for UK before dawn.

Force H to leave Gibraltar on D1 and operate in Western basin from D1 to D3.

The C-in-C, Mediterranean, informed me he fully concurred in the proposed operation.

177.   *To Cunningham*

10 August 1941

I've sent you a copy of my report on SUBSTANCE so that you can see what happened. I was amazed that we should allow the Itis to score two torpedo hits in a day attack . . . Pugsley the Captain of *Fearless* is a very good hand and I think his hit was pure mischance.[1] *Manchester*, I believe, was a shade too close to the convoy and was not searching [–?] at speed as she ought to have done. But here again if the torpedo was dropped the other side of the convoy to her it was not easy to spot or forecast the course of approach.

The RDF interception with fighters was good on the whole and the Fulmars did very well. But the pilots lack experience and that probably accounts for our having 6 shot down.

Syfret handled Force A and the convoy very well – I thought he might be a bit rusty after nearly two years ashore but he proved to be very much on the spot. . . .

The destroyers – we are now down to 3 'F's' and at the moment can't go to sea except with an entirely inadequate screen. It's a darn nuisance as I feel it's absolutely essential we should keep stirring up the Western Basin and not limit our sorties to specific operations. If we do, why even the Itis must get wise to it and manage some real dirt. It won't be too funny if we get ships disabled under the enemy's coast and 700 miles or more from Gibraltar.

I feel sure we could do quite a lot in the Western Basin if we had *Manxman* here for a bit to do more stuff with the independent company. . . .

Voelcker suggests that with another two 'T' class submarines here we might do a good deal to harass the convoys from Genoa and Naples. Every patrol we've had on the West Coast has seen a lot of shipping and they've bagged 2 tankers already in spite of the gunboats that have been operating. *Olympus* lost her chances but I believe it's about the first offensive patrol she's done.[2]

---

[1]Cdr A. F. Pugsley: Cdr 1936; *Javelin* 1939; *Fearless* Dec 1940; *Paladin* Sept 1941; Capt Dec 1942; *Jervis* Jan 1943; cmdg Force T, Naval forces assaulting Walcheren Oct 1944; Capt (D) 19DF *Trafalgar* July 1945.

[2]Capt G. A. W. Voelcker: Capt June 1939; *Elfin* (S/M & A/SW) 1940; Capt (S), 8 SF, *Maidstone*, Gibraltar, April 1941; *Charybdis* 1942; d Oct 1943.

178. *Report of Proceedings, 15–26 August 1941*

28 August 1941

21 August

32.   Force H, comprising *Nelson, Ark Royal, Hermione, Nestor* (SO, 8th DF), *Encounter, Foresight, Fury* and *Forester*, sailed for operation MINCEMEAT at 2200, shaping course to the E at 17 knots.

22 August

33.   *Manxman*, who had arrived in the Bay and berthed alongside *Brown Ranger*[1] at 2320/21, completed fuelling and sailed at 0210, being out of sight of land by daylight. . . .

179.   *Orders for Operation MINCEMEAT*

20 August 1941

Object

To make a diversion to cover operations taking place elsewhere. . . .

Asdic Contacts

15.   Asdic contacts are to be counter attacked until they are no longer a danger to ships being screened, when destroyers are to rejoin the screen.

If a submarine contact is obtained at night, the Fleet will be turned as necessary by fixed light manoeuvring signals or W/T.

Contact with Surface Forces at Night

16.   Heavy ships and the destroyer screen on the disengaged side will be turned away until the nature of the enemy force encountered has been determined.

Cruisers and destroyers on the side making contact should close and engage.

A similar policy will be adopted if surface vessels are detected at night by RDF. Searchlights are to be used in preference to star shell for illumination. . . .

Cessation of A/A fire during Fighter Attacks on Enemy Aircraft

18.   If our fighters are in hot pursuit of an enemy who is under fire from the fleet, or is about to come under fire from the fleet, *Ark Royal* may order 'Cease Fire' – followed by a bearing on the RDF reporting wave of

[1]*Brown Ranger*: RFA oiler, 1941, 3417gt, 14k.

1875 K/cs. On receipt of this signal, which is to remain operative for one minute, all ships are immediately to check fire on the bearing ordered. The order to cease fire is only to be given when there are good prospects of our fighters either destroying the enemy or preventing an attack on the fleet. It is <u>NOT</u> to be given when dive bombers are in the near vicinity of ships. . . .

Air Operations by Ark Royal

A/S Patrols
20.   One A/S patrol will be required daily from daylight to dusk, but may be dispensed with a.m., D3.
Fighters
21.

D2 AM   One section to be ranged on deck.
   PM   One section in the air and one section ranged on deck.

D3 AM   One section to be flown off when the TSRs have landed on. From 0800 two sections to be in the air and two sections ranged on deck; thereafter as required
D4   One section to be ranged on deck.

180.   *To North*

26 August 1941

. . . We left on the 21st to cover a minor but important operation elsewhere. My idea was to carry out an incendiary attack on the cork woods at the N end of Sardinia, early a.m. on the 23rd & get the Itis guessing that this was probably a feint to cover another convoy gong through to Malta & so concentrate all their forces S of Sardinia – where I wanted them. A couple of snoopers found us on the 22nd. The fighters made a good intercept but these blasted Cants now appear to be armoured because although they knocked bits off them & killed the rear gunners they could *not* bring them down.[1] . . . Early on the 23rd we flew off the striking force, a dark clear night and we were pretty close in. All the boys returned at dawn & reported the woods and a factory well alight. . . . During the forenoon I heard that the Iti Fleet had been sighted by an aircraft from Malta S of Cagliari patrolling at 12 knots. I waited for further reports but nothing came in so eventually I had to break W/T silence & ask . . . Bill Ford if he was keeping them under observation. I was about

---

[1]Fighters now needed cannon armament.

220 miles from them but hoped that I might possibly be able to reach a position from where the TSRs could do a dusk torpedo attack. But of course it was essential that I should know where they were. As at 4 p.m. I still had no news of any sort & since if the Iti Fleet had come W they might have been quite close to us I sent out a recco to see if I could get a trace & at the same time turned W so as to keep my distance. Not a word until 7 p.m. by which time it was much too late. I was certainly not going to send in the striking force blind & have them shot down by CR42s whilst looking for the Itis & incidentally losing a number through failure to find the ship in the dark. Incidentally my destroyers only had enough fuel for 3 or 4 hours' high speed steaming.

Well apparently the Its retired into the lower Tyrrhenian Sea for the night & came out again next morning hopefully thinking that we were still trying to pass a convoy through. Actually I went off Valencia yesterday & steamed by about 6 miles off with 15 Fulmars & 10 TSRs cruising overhead. Hillgarth had reported the Spaniards believed the Itis' stories that Force H was dead. . . .

181. *Report of Proceedings, 26 August–14 September 1941*

23 September 1941

28 August

7. . . . At 2000 I left Gibraltar in company with Lord Gort for England.

29 August

9. VACNA was ordered to sail *Nestor* and *Encounter* to join convoy WS 11 and proceed in company to Freetown, since it was not considered that their retention for operation STATUS was now necessary. Arrangements were made for them to proceed to join the Mediterranean Fleet via the Cape.

30 August

11. VACNA was instructed that until further orders the destroyers *Farndale*, *Heythrop* and *Croome*[1] should remain at Gibraltar, where they could be used for local escort.

14. Information was received from the Naval Attaché at Madrid that the demonstration made by Force H off Valencia was most successful. The Spanish appeared to be both impressed and pleased by the appearance of Force H and the naval aircraft off their waters.

---

[1]*Heythrop* (sunk off N Africa 1942, *U652*), *Croome*: 'Hunt' class. *Farndale*, detained in Malta with engine defect, had made an independent return.

3 September

18.   In a signal to the AOC, Mediterranean, the Air Ministry stressed the importance of providing adequate air reconnaissance for Force H, particularly before and during major operations, and stated that the Vice Admiral, Malta, should be consulted in respect of relative priorities, if necessary. Malta replied that priority was always given to Force H, but that serviceability of the Maryland reconnaissance aircraft was bad.

4 September

20.   I returned from the UK by Sunderland aircraft in company with HE the Governor at 1730.

7 September

27.   After dark, *Furious* was warped close up to *Ark Royal* and 26 Hurricanes and 1 Swordfish of 812 Squadron were transferred by means of the ramp.

8 September

30.   After flying off 1 Swordfish and 1 Fulmar to North Front, course was shaped to the eastward with *Gurkha*,[1] *Lively*, *Lance* and *Forester* acting as A/S screen and 1 Catalina as A/S patrol.

9 September

40.   At 0637 a second Blenheim was sighted to the southward. . . . Before the Blenheim had completed two circuits of the ship, the first flight of 14 Hurricanes had taken off and when formed on the Blenheim was given the order to proceed to Malta.
42.   The Hurricanes and their Blenheims arrived safely at Malta at 1115.

10 September

52.   *Ark Royal* entered harbour at 0915 and I returned to *Nelson*.
53.   Work of transferring 14 Hurricanes from *Furious* to *Ark Royal* was commenced at once and completed by 1330.
57.   Signals were received from Vice Admiral, Malta, concerning the route to be used in operation HALBERD and also the proposed disposition of submarines in this operation. In order that a sudden air offensive against Italian ports and aerodromes should not indicate that HALBERD was imminent or in progress, I requested Vice Admiral, Malta, to

---

[1]*Lively* (sunk S of Crete 1942, Ger a/c), *Gurkha*: 1941, 1920t, 6×4.7in, 8tt, 36.5k; ex-*Larne*, renamed after 'Tribal' *Gurkha* lost in 1940; herself lost off N Africa 1942, *U133*.

arrange a heavy scale bombing attack on some suitable target on the night 11/12 September, during operation STATUS II. This was done.
60.   *Furious* sailed at 1900 in company with *Legion*, *Foresight* and *Forester*, and shaped course to the W. The remainder of Force H, comprising *Nelson*, *Ark Royal*, *Hermione*, *Lively*, *Lance*, *Zulu* and *Gurkha*, sailed to the westward at 2150. . . .

12 September

72.   Speed was reduced to 17 knots at noon. At 1500 I learnt that the Force had been reported at 1010 as well as at 0930. There had been no indication of the presence of a shadowing aircraft at that time. Presumably the aircraft came in low below the RDF beam and was not sighted by look-outs. Again at 1655 an enemy report was intercepted without any sighting or RDF indication of shadowing aircraft.
82.   Immediately on completion of flying off [0706 to 0750] all ships formed on *Nelson* and course was shaped to the westward at 20 knots. At 0826 *Ark Royal* flew off an A/S patrol and a section of fighters. . . .
84.   It is clear that the enemy reconnaissance aircraft are taking full anti-RDF precautions. If the enemy aircraft do not attempt to gain height until out of RDF range they will enjoy a fair degree of immunity from fighter interception providing they restrict their observation to a short sighting and then withdraw below the horizon.

14 September

88.   The passage back to Gibraltar was uneventful and the day was devoted to various practices which included the following:–

Dawn ALT Attack.   Height Finding Exercise.
Fighter Training.   Destroyer A/S firing at smoke bombs.
Range and Inclination Exercises.   Dummy dive bombing attack. . . .

182.   *To Cunningham*

7 September 1941

As you may have heard I flew home with Gort on 28th in order to try and dispose of some of the wet ideas about Gib. that were in active circulation and emanating chiefly from Chequers.
   We achieved our object and made it clear that, with things as they are, any prospect of holding Gibraltar as a naval base after PILGRIM has started its stuff will be out of the question. Furthermore, the evacuation

of those not required for a siege will be limited to an untidy scramble spread over a few hours. . . .

The next SUBSTANCE was discussed at some length and it was agreed we must not take too great a chance on it – hence *Prince of Wales*.[1] But it seems to me the danger lies in that bit E of Skerki, though admittedly the Itis show no stomach for night fighting, and the final approach on D4. Provided we have adequate air striking forces at Malta, it may deter them though in theory they ought to be in a position to give us a good knock then.

In spite of all the reinforcements to Force H I feel that we must do all we can to profit by evasion and surprise so as to give them as little time as possible to concentrate their dirt in the Narrows. Will you be able to feint from the eastward and if so to what depth?

183. *To North*

8 September 1941

. . . Gort and I were summoned to Chequers to stay the night. . . . I gave him [Churchill] my views about Oran & Dakar & what really happened when the cruisers passed the Straits. Chapter & Verse, as you have it set out. He gave several disturbed grunts but wouldn't argue or discuss the matter at all. . . .

184. *Report of Proceedings, 14–24 September 1941*

26 September 1941

14 September

3. . . . The majority [of ships taking part in HALBERD] were to return to the UK as soon as possible, *Euryalus*, *Farndale* and *Heythrop* were to join the Mediterranean Fleet, and *Rodney*, *Ark Royal*, *Hermione*, *Cossack* (Captain (D), 4th DF), *Zulu*, *Gurkha*, *Lance*, *Lively* and *Isaac Sweers* were to form Force H.[2]

6. Arrangements were made for the bombing of Italian ports and aerodromes by aircraft of the Mediterranean Command to be maintained at as constant a level as practicable prior to and during the operation, in order to give no indication that this was being carried out as cover for sea operations. Bombing of Cagliari on the night D1/D2 was requested.

---

[1]*Prince of Wales*: 1941, 35,000t, 10×14in, 16×5.25in, 28k; sunk S China Sea 10 Dec 1941, Japanese naval aircraft.
[2]*Isaac Sweers*, R Neth N: compl 1940 in UK, 1628t, 5×4.7in, 8tt, 36k; lost off N Africa Nov 1942.

16 September

11. The C-in-C, Mediterranean, informed me of his intended disposition of submarines for operation HALBERD, i.e., one off Palermo, one N and W of San Vito, 2 N and 2 S of Messina; *Sokol* and *Trusty*[1] to extend the patrol line at intervals of 15 miles.

18 September

16. *Zulu, Gurkha* and *Lance* sailed at 1800 to rendezvous with Convoy WS 11X (HALBERD). *Furious*, screened by *Foresight, Forester, Fury* and *Legion*, sailed at 2230, *Furious* bound for the USA to refit. The destroyers were ordered to rendezvous with WS 11X on parting company with *Furious*.

20 September

19. At 0749 *Sheffield* reported an explosion amidships in RFA *Denbydale*,[2] lying at the Detached Mole. Ships in harbour were ordered to close all watertight doors and to raise steam. Motor launches were sent out by VACNA to sweep the head of the Bay, *Cossack* and *Heythrop* following, the former . . . being ordered to take charge of the A/S sweeping operations.

Motor boats, armed with depth charges, were sent to patrol inside the booms at both entrances.

A breathing apparatus, picked up in the Commercial anchorage, where an oil hulk, the *Fiona Shell* had been sunk and SS *Durham*[3] damaged, indicated that the probable cause was attack by two-men submarines.

20. A/S sweeps produced no result and *Sheffield*, who was due to sail in order to rendezvous with the HALBERD convoy, was ordered to proceed at 1045, being instructed to steam at high speed for a short period after leaving harbour. Ships in harbour were reverted to a half-hour's notice for steam and at 1230 returned to normal notice, viz., 4 hours, watertight doors being opened at the same time.

21. Wing-Cdr Harris and the OC the Beaufighter Squadron, Mediterranean Command, having arrived by Sunderland aircraft from Malta, came on board *Nelson* to discuss air co-operation during HALBERD. Careful consideration was given to the air reconnaissance

[1]*Sokol*: Polish N: 1941, 540/730t, 4tt, 1×3in, 11/9k; ex-*Urchin. Trusty*: 1941, 1090/1575t, 11tt, 1×4in, 15.25/9k.
[2]*Denbydale*: oiler, *c*.1941, 17,000t, 11.5k, 12,000t capacity; severely damaged & reduced to harbour hulk.
[3]*Fiona Shell*: 1892, 2444gt, Anglo-Saxon Petrol Co. *Durham*: 1934, 10,893gt, 16k, Federal SN Co.

required and with particular reference to early warnings of any attempt by enemy surface forces to attack the convoy on D4. It appeared to me that the striking force available to deal with such an attack was hardly adequate. It was agreed that the Beaufighters should be reserved for operating on D4, *Ark Royal* providing fighter protection on D3.

22.   HE the Military Governor of Algeciras . . . lunched with me unofficially on board HMS *Nelson*. His Excellency was shown around the ship and afterwards visited a submarine.

23.   Information was received that the merchant ship *Empire Guillemot*,[1] which had sailed unescorted from the Straits for Malta, had arrived safely. By making use of false colours and recognition signals she had passed several ships and been sighted by aircraft without being challenged.

22 September

28.   The C-in-C, Mediterranean, informed me that he intended to keep the Mediterranean Fleet at short notice during operation HALBERD, in order to proceed to sea and be sighted steaming westward as soon as it was apparent that our forces in the Western Basin had been sighted by the enemy. By this means he hoped do dissuade any westward movement of German air forces from Libya.

23 September

36.   . . . when the dim form of *Prince of Wales* was first sighted, hands on watch on the Admiral's bridge of *Nelson* exclaimed enthusiastically, 'Good old *Rodney*, here she is at last!' This was quickly changed to 'Gawd, she's one of them new bastards' and the *Nelson*s had to guess again.

24 September

37.   . . . I further informed the Admiralty that it was my intention to remain in close support of the convoy and not be drawn away from it by a speedier enemy, unless he should close the convoy or one of his capital ships be crippled by a substantial reduction in speed.

41.   At 1800 my flag was hoisted in *Rodney*, and at 1815 *Nelson* sailed, escorted by *Garland*,[2] *Piorun* and *Isaac Sweers*, shaping course to the west. The band played suitable 'home-going' airs on leaving harbour, and a farewell message was made, purporting to be addressed by me in *Rodney* to *Nelson*. . . .

---

[1]*Empire Guillemot*: 1919, 5720gt, MWT; ex-US; probably torpedoed by Italian aircraft en route Malta–Gibraltar *c*.20 October 1941.

[2]*Garland* now manned by Poles.

It appears from information received subsequently that this ruse was successful, for a time at least, and may have resulted in a certain amount of confusion in the minds of enemy observers in Algeciras. . . .

43. RFA *Brown Ranger*, escorted by *Fleur de Lys*,[1] sailed at 2000 to the eastward in order to rendezvous on D2 with destroyers of the HAL-BERD escort and refuel them.

44. After *Hermione* had embarked personnel and aircraft torpedoes, and *Foresight* had embarked RAF stores, all destined for Malta, *Rodney*, *Ark Royal*, *Hermione*, *Duncan*, *Foresight*, *Forester*, *Gurkha*, *Zulu*, *Lance*, *Legion* and *Lively* sailed at 2300 to the eastward to rendezvous with HALBERD convoy and escort.

185. *Report on Operation HALBERD, 24–30 September 1941*

HMS *Rodney*,
9 October 1941

Movements of Forces on the night 24/25 September (D-1/D1)

12. The forces then formed two groups, as follows:–

Group I
Nelson (FOC, Force H), *Ark Royal*, *Hermione*, *Cossack* (Captain (D), 4th DF), *Zulu*, *Foresight*, *Laforey* (Captain (D), 19th DF), and *Lightning*.[2]

Group II
Prince of Wales, *Rodney*, *Kenya*, *Edinburgh*, *Sheffield*, *Euryalus*, *Duncan* (Captain (D), 13th DF), *Gurkha*, *Legion*, *Lance*, *Lively*, *Oribi*, *Isaac Sweers*, *Piorun*, *Garland*, *Fury*, *Farndale*, and *Heythrop*, and the convoy, HMS *Breconshire*, *Clan MacDonald*, *Clan Ferguson*, *Ajax*, *Imperial Star*, *City of Lincoln*, *Rowallan Castle*, *Dunedin Star* and *City of Calcutta*.[3]

---

[1]*Fleur de Lys*: 1940, 'Flower' class corvette; sunk W of Gibraltar 14 Oct 1941, *U206*.
[2]*Laforey*: leader, 1941, 1935t, 6×4.7in, 8tt, 36.5k; sunk off Sicily 1944, *U223*. Capt (D), 19DF: Capt R. M. J. Hutton: Cdr 1932; Staff Coll 1939; Capt 1940; OD May 1940; *Laforey* 1941; Flag Capt & CSO to RA (D) Home F *Tyne* Dec 1943; Cdre 1 Cl, Home F DFs *Vindictive* July 1944.
[3]*Euryalus*: 1940, 5450t, 10×5.25in, 6tt, 33k. *Oribi*: 1941, 1540t, 4×4.7in, 1×4in, 4tt, 36k. *Clan Ferguson*: 1938, 7347gt, 17k, Clan Line. *Ajax* 1931, 7539gt, 16k, Alfred Holt. *Imperial Star*: 1935, 10,733gt, Blue Star Line. *City of Lincoln*: 1938, 8039gt, 16k, Ellerman & Bucknall SS Co. *Dunedin Star*: 1936, 11,168gt, Blue Star Line. *City of Calcutta*: 1940, 8063gt, Ellerman City Lines. Vice Adm A. T. B. Curteis, 2nd-in-C, Home F, flew his flag in *Prince of Wales*, Burrough was in *Kenya* and Syfret in *Edinburgh*. The forces sailed independently to deceive enemy shadowers and joined early on D3 (27 Sept).

Air Attacks on the Fleet, PM, 27 September (D3)

(a) First Attack (1255–1310)

39.   RDF reports at 1255 indicated that two formations were approaching the fleet, one from the N and one from the E, both 30 miles distant. These formations were reported as diving.

Fighters were vectored towards the formations, but as they made contact with the enemy, RDF plots became too confused to be used for fighter direction. One enemy T/B (probably Cant 1007) was shot down by Fulmars at 1300.[1]

40.   Six T/Bs (BR20)[2] approached from the port bow and beam and were engaged by the port wing of the screen and the ships on the port side of the fleet. Two T/B aircraft were shot down at 1302, probably by barrage fire from *Rodney* and *Prince of Wales*.

41.   An unknown number of torpedoes was dropped about 5000 yards on the port beam of the convoy, which altered course . . .

Three of the 6 attackers tried to approach over the port wing of the screen but unable to face the barrage put up by the destroyers, they dropped their torpedoes at the port wing ship, *Lance*, who had considerable difficulty in avoiding them, two torpedoes passing very close.

The torpedoes were released from about 300 ft height and appeared to take up their depth very quickly, the tracks showing up plainly. *Isaac Sweers*, next in the screen to *Lance*, reported one torpedo passed within 30 yards; *Rodney* was swung 60° to port to avoid a torpedo which passed 100 yards to starboard.

42.   One of these three aircraft was shot down by the destroyers, and crashed in flames close to *Lively*. Another T/B aircraft was shot down by fighters N of the fleet at about this time.

43.   . . . a Fulmar . . . was shot down by barrage fire from *Prince of Wales*, . . . through a phonetic misunderstanding . . . .[3]

(b) Second Attack (1327–1337)

47.   A group of aircraft splitting into two formations was reported by RDF closing from the eastward at 1327. Destroyers on the starboard wing of the screen opened fire at 1329, when 6 or 7 T/Bs (BR20) were seen approaching very low from the starboard bow and beam.

---

[1]Cant 1007: 1937, bomb load c.2500lb, 4mg, 255mph.
[2]Fiat BR20: 1936, bomb load 3520lb, 4mg, 255mph.
[3]Two Fulmars were shot down by our own ships; one crew was lost.

48.   Three of the aircraft pressed on through the barrage of the starboard wing destroyers, and carried out a most determined attack on *Nelson*, who was swinging to starboard to comb the tracks. One aircraft dropped its torpedo about 450 yards 20° on *Nelson*'s starboard bow, passing over the ship at about 200 ft height. This aircraft was almost certainly shot down astern of *Nelson* by *Sheffield* and *Prince of Wales*.

49.   The track of the torpedo was not seen until about 150 yards dead ahead of the ship, which had been steadied on a course which proved to be the exact reciprocal of the torpedo. No avoiding action was possible and a second or two after the bubbles disappeared from sight there was a large 'crump', the ship whipped considerably and a column of water rose approximately 15–20 ft high above the forecastle deck port side. The torpedo had hit on the port bow abreast 60 station, 10 ft below the water line. *Nelson*'s speed was reduced to 18 knots, pending a report on the damage sustained.

50.   A few seconds later another T/B of this formation dropped a torpedo from about 500 ft 1000 yards fine on the starboard bow of *Nelson*. This torpedo passed about 100 yards to starboard. The third enemy at this formation was shot down by destroyers just ahead of the screen of 1333. This aircraft was claimed by *Laforey*. *Forester* picked up the W/T operator, the only member of the crew alive. He had a badly broken leg.

51.   Meanwhile, 3 or 4 T/Bs who had split up from this group attacked from the starboard quarter without result.

52.   One enemy T/B was shot down by fighters, on the port quarter of the convoy at 1336.

A Fulmar was unfortunately shot down by *Rodney*'s pom-pom, but the crew was rescued by *Duncan*.

(c) Third Attack (1345–1405)

54.   Six minutes after the end of the second attack, RDF reported a group closing from the SE and diving. At 1345 a formation of 10 or 11 S79s were sighted very low about 10 miles to the southward. These split up into two groups when they came under fire from the escorting ships on the starboard side of the convoy, and 7 or 8 retired to the SW and disappeared.

Three others tried to work around the starboard bow, and the convoy was turned away 60° to port. These aircraft were turned away by the gunfire of the screening destroyers, having dropped their torpedoes well outside the screen. One torpedo narrowly missed *Lightning*, but they dropped at too great a range to be a danger to the convoy. One of these aircraft was shot down by fighters as it retired.

55.   Of the 7 or 8 aircraft who turned away when first fired at, 3 returned from astern of the convoy at 1354, two of which retired again

on being fired at. The third pressed on to attack *Ark Royal* but was shot down by the combined fire of that ship and *Nelson* while still 1000 yards away from *Ark Royal* and before he had dropped a torpedo.

56.   At 1358 one aircraft, seen right ahead of *Nelson*, dropped a torpedo outside the screen. *Cossack* was able to avoid this torpedo by the warning given by hydrophone effect in her A/S set.

57.   At this time (1359) one CR42 was seen to be diving on the starboard wing of the destroyers, and performing aerobatics over them, evidently to make a diversion for the T/Bs. In so far as the destroyers expended a large amount of ammunition he succeeded, but after 6 minutes was either shot down or failed to pull out from a dive. None of the destroyers reported being machine gunned.

58.   *Result of the Third Attack* – . . . It was most noticeable that this attack was not pressed home with the same determination as the first two attacks. Of the 10 or 11 S79s which originally approached, only 4 fired torpedoes, and these were dropped at too great a distance to endanger the convoy. . . .

59.   No further actual attacks developed before dark, though on several occasions RDF indicated that enemy aircraft were closing the fleet. Generally by the time they were within 15 miles of the fleet, RDF reported our fighters among them and they were driven off. . . .

General Remarks on Day Attacks

60.   So far as can be ascertained 30 T/B aircraft attempted to attack, but not more than 18 came within torpedo range.

Aircraft destroyed

6 T/Bs and 1 fighter certainly destroyed by gunfire.
4 T/Bs and 1 shadower certainly destroyed by fighters.
1 T/B probably destroyed (cause unknown).

62.   *Barrage Fire* from 6" [and] 4" guns was most effective and accounted for at least 4 aircraft.

The barrage was fired on two steps to burst at 4000 yards and at 1500 yards. A fairly high proportion of shells was seen to fall in the water before bursting, and though this may partly be accounted for by badly set fuses, it is chiefly due to insufficient elevation.

63.   *Close range weapons.* At least one aircraft fell to pom-poms, but there appeared to be a general tendency for close range weapons to be astern and low. *Prince of Wales* reported that Mark IV pom-pom directors were most valuable, as the pom-poms were often shrouded in smoke.

64. Nelson's *A/A Armament*. *Nelson*'s lack of A/A guns which will bear on fine bow bearings was possibly the cause of her being torpedoed; she has not a single A/A gun which will train across the bow at low elevation. When *Nelson* turned towards her attackers there would have been a good chance to shoot them down had guns been available to cover adequately the arc right ahead. . . .

66. *Effectiveness of screen against T/Bs*. On several occasions aircraft which tried to come in low over the destroyer screen were turned back and only 4 aircraft faced their fire and pressed on over the destroyers.

No aircraft were able to reach a good position to torpedo a ship of the convoy during day attacks. . . .

Attempt to intercept Enemy Battlefleet, PM 27 September (D3)

68. Reports of air reconnaissance from Malta carried out on D2 indicated the main units of the Italian Fleet were located as follows:–

Taranto	1	*Cavour* in Floating Dock
	2	*Littorios* and 1 *Cavour*
	6	Cruisers
	5	Destroyers
Naples	2	*Cavours*
	1	Cruiser
	12	Destroyers or Torpedo Boats
Messina		*Bolzano*
Palermo		nil.

69. When the third T/B attack was still in progress at 1404, an emergency report was received from aircraft 'B' (RAF, Malta) of 2 battleships and 8 destroyers . . . steering 190° at 20 knots at 1340.

70. . . . the enemy unit was therefore 74 miles 076° from *Nelson* assuming it had continued at the same course and speed. At this time *Nelson*, with gun armament unimpaired, was thought to be capable of 18 knots or possibly more.

71. My appreciation of the enemy's intentions was that either he did not realise that I had more than one battleship with the convoy and that he would attempt to intercept the convoy near the western entrance to the Skerki Channel, or that he would wish to draw away my escorting force to the north-eastwards, thus leaving the convoy open to attack by light surface forces in the Skerki Channel at dusk.

72. I therefore decided:–

(a) To proceed towards the enemy at best speed with *Nelson*, *Prince of Wales*, *Rodney* and 6 destroyers, leaving *Kenya*, *Edinburgh*,

Sheffield and 10 destroyers with the convoy; *Ark Royal* escorted by *Hermione, Euryalus, Piorun* and *Legion* to continue operating in the vicinity of the convoy.

(b) To fly off 2 Swordfish from *Ark Royal* to take over shadowing duties and keep the enemy under observation until the striking force could attack.

(c) To fuel, arm, range and fly off an air striking force as soon as possible.

73.   These dispositions would place the battleships between the enemy and the convoy and enable the enemy to be brought to action should he persist in attempting to intercept the convoy.

75.   . . . a signal was received (timed 1425) that the total enemy force consisted of 2 battleships, 4 cruisers and 16 destroyers.

77.   I . . . informed Vice Admiral, 2nd in Command, Home Fleet,[1] that *Nelson*'s speed was reduced to 15 knots and ordered him to proceed with *Prince of Wales, Rodney, Edinburgh, Sheffield* and 6 destroyers at best speed to close and drive off the enemy. . . .

78.   . . . a signal . . . reported that the enemy fleet had reversed course . . .

79.   It was now clear that the enemy intended to avoid contact. I still hoped, however, that the air striking force might be able to materially reduce his speed and allow the Vice Admiral . . . to overtake him before dark.

81.   . . . The striking force of 12 Swordfish escorted by 4 Fulmars took departure at 1540.

82.   Between 1620 and 1645, Fulmars drove off an attack threatening from the port side of the convoy, and at [a] later time another section of Fulmars shot down a shadower 10 miles astern.

84.   With the position of the enemy force in doubt and since available evidence suggested he was probably retiring at speed to the NE I signalled to [the] Vice Admiral . . . at 1658 to rejoin. My appreciation at this time was that even if the striking force succeeded in reducing the speed of the enemy radically it would not be possible for [the] Vice Admiral to make contact until after dark and consequently a successful issue was highly problematical. On the other hand it was essential for the cruisers to return to the convoy before dark and the destroyers were also required to furnish a screen for *Nelson* and *Ark Royal*. Any further reduction of Force X destroyers for this purpose was, in my opinion, unacceptable.

---

[1]Actg Vice Adm A. T. B. Curteis: Capt 1926; RA & Cdre RN Barracks, Devonport 1938; 2CS May 1940–May 1941; Actg VA & 2nd-in-C, Home F June 1941; VA Dec 1941; SBNO, W Atlantic, Bermuda Aug 1942; Ret List Dec 1944.

88.   The air striking force reported to *Ark Royal* at 1740 that they were unable to find the enemy . . .

Detachment of Force X

90.   Force A, consisting of the battleships and carrier, with destroyer screen, parted [company] from the convoy and Force X (cruisers and destroyers) at 1855 on reaching the entrance to the Skerki Channel.

Force A turned to 285°, while Force X and the convoy continued to the eastward under the command of the RA, 10th CS.[1]

Night Torpedo Bomber Attack on Force X and Convoy, 27 September (D3)

109.   Between 2000 and 2040, four T/B attacks were made from the port beam, 2 or 3 aircraft taking part in each attack.

(a) First Attack

110.   At 1955 . . . *Cossack* . . . detected aircraft [on] Type 286 [radar] and about 5 minutes later sighted an aircraft on the port side. . . .

111.   The RA, 10th CS, ordered an emergency turn of 40° to port together by rapid manoeuvring procedure. *Kenya* sounded two short blasts and turned, followed belatedly by the port column of the convoy.

This signal was incorrectly transmitted as 40° to starboard and *Edinburgh* and the starboard column turned to starboard.

(b) Second Attack

114.   Aircraft were reported bearing 090° 3 miles at 2010 and others were detected on the starboard bow. Both these formations crossed from starboard to port, and attacked from the port beam. . . .

(c) Third Attack

115.   Three T/Bs attacked from the port beam at 2022. *Hermione* saw a torpedo explode at the end of its run on the starboard quarter of the convoy. Aircraft were sighted and engaged by the port screen and convoy.

(d) Fourth Attack

117.   *Cossack* sighted aircraft on the port side at 2027. A torpedo was dropped on *Sheffield*'s port bow at 2029, and 5 minutes later she had to turn to starboard under full rudder to avoid another dropped on her port beam.

118.   At 2032 . . . *Imperial Star* was struck port side aft by a torpedo. . . .

119.   *Oribi* was attacked at 2036, a torpedo being dropped 800 yards just abaft her port beam, which she avoided by turning stern-on and increasing to full speed. This aircraft was shot down with pom-pom and Oerlikon guns by *Oribi*.

[1]Adm Burrough.

Remarks on Night T/B Attacks

121. *Enemy Tactics.* All attacks appear to have been made from the port beam, although this was not directly up-moon, which was on the starboard quarter.

Torpedoes were observed to be dropped from a greater height than in most of the day attacks.

122. *Gunfire.* On several occasions the cruisers leading the column were prevented from firing a barrage by the destroyers adjacent to them.

Gun flashes probably showed the convoy up to aircraft manoeuvring to attack. Flashless charges would be most useful for barrage fire at night. . . .

Loss of MV Imperial Star

124. When *Imperial Star* was torpedoed at 2032 it is probable that the explosion blew away both propellors and her rudder; in addition No. 6 hold and the after engine room were both flooded.

126. About 2045 *Euryalus* ordered *Oribi* to go to the assistance of *Imperial Star.* When *Oribi* closed, *Heythrop* was already standing by, and while *Heythrop* took off *Imperial Star*'s passengers, *Oribi* pro-ceeded close alongside to obtain reports from the Master and the NLO.

They were first insistent that an attempt should be made to tow the vessel back to Gibraltar, but the CO of *Oribi* (Lt-Cdr J. E. H. McBeath, DSO)[1] realised that the only chance of saving the ship was to tow her the 220 miles to Malta, and prepared to do so.

127. *Heythrop* parted company at 2200 to rejoin the convoy. By 2235 *Oribi* had *Imperial Star* in tow with 90 fathoms of special 5" wire hawser provided by *Imperial Star.*

128. For two hours the most determined attempts were made by *Oribi* to tow *Imperial Star* towards Malta. Although a speed of 8 knots through the water was made nothing would prevent her steering in circles.

Imperial Star's normal displacement was 17,000 tons; in her damaged condition she was drawing 38 ft aft, and it is possible that her damaged stern was acting as a rudder.

129. Eventually, at 0120, *Oribi* found herself being dragged stern first by her tow sheering off, and was forced to slip the tow.

. . . It was reluctantly decided that it was impracticable to tow the ship without tugs, which were not available at Malta, and that the remaining 141 persons aboard should be taken off by *Oribi* and the ship scut-tled. . . .

[1]Lt-Cdr J. E. H. McBeath: Lt 1931; 1st Lt *Garland* 1938; Lt-Cdr Oct 1939; *Venomous* Jan 1940; *Oribi* May 1941; Cdr Dec 1941; *Pembroke* May 1943.

Scuttling arrangements were not in place, and most of the flooding valves were jammed by the torpedo explosion. *Oribi* therefore placed 3 depth charges lashed together just below the waterline abreast a bulkhead, and these were fired by a safety fuse.

130.   *Oribi* cast off at 0340 and the charges fired 11 minutes later, starting a large fire aft. As this did not spread quickly, *Oribi* shelled *Imperial Star* with 4.7" SAP shell, and left her at 0452, heavily on fire fore and aft and listing badly.

Aircraft from Malta sent to search for *Imperial Star* the next day failed to find any trace, and there can be no doubt that she sank or blew up.

131.   *Oribi* proceeded along the convoy route at 32 knots, and came up with them off Malta at 1215, having passed unmolested within 7 miles of the Sicilian coast in daylight.

Passage of Force X and Convoy through the Narrows

132.   Meanwhile, Force X proceeded through the Narrows by the route previously arranged, i.e., along the S coast of Sicily. . . .

133.   *Hermione* parted company from the convoy at 2030 to carry out a bombardment of Pantellaria harbour. . . . this operation . . . was very skilfully planned and executed by *Hermione* (Captain G.N. Oliver)[1] . . . Rear Admiral [Syfret] reports that the bombardment caused a most spectacular diversion which was clearly visible from the convoy and escort, then distant 50 miles.

137.   Although several formations of enemy aircraft were detected between dawn and the arrival of the convoy at Malta, the excellent protection given by shore based fighters from Malta prevented any attack from developing.

Two Fulmars arrived over the convoy at 0615, followed at 0700 by 6 Beaufighters, and subsequently Hurricanes. Fighter direction was carried out by *Edinburgh* and the co-operation of the fighters left nothing to be desired.

138.   At 0800 a report that no enemy surface forces were to the northward or southward of the convoy's track was received from the Vice Admiral, Malta. [Syfret] consequently detached *Kenya*, *Sheffield*, *Euryalus* and *Hermione* to proceed ahead to Malta to fuel. . . . They were accorded a great welcome by the people of Malta.

---

[1]Capt (later Adm Sir) Geoffrey N. Oliver (1898–1980): ent RN 1915; gun splist; notable contributions to destroyer commands 1934–6; Capt 1939; SD 1939–40; *Hermione* 1940–2; Army Liaison, Med; N African Landing Craft; Sicily & Salerno; Cdre; D-Day; carriers off Greece 1944; E Indies F 1945; RA 1945; Adm (Air) 1946; ACNS 1946; Pres, RN Coll, Greenwich 1948; VA 1949; C-in-C E Indies 1950–2; Adm 1952; C-in-C Nore 1953–5.

139. The whole convoy, with the exception of *Imperial Star*, entered harbour undamaged early in the afternoon of 28 September (D4).

Movements of Force A from Dusk, 27 September (D3) to PM, 28 September (D4)

140. After landing on all aircraft Force A proceeded to the westward at 14 knots, this being *Nelson*'s best speed at the time. . . .

141. In view of the low speed of *Nelson* I did not consider that action to afford close support to the ships of MG 2 was justified since this would have involved an unacceptable reduction in the destroyer screen then available. I wished also to convey the impression that a general withdrawal of forces to the westwards was in progress and would be continued.

143. An enemy report made by an RAF aircraft received at 0958 indicated that 2 enemy battleships, 5 cruisers and 13 destroyers were 70 miles, 105° from Cagliari at 0940, steering 195°. These ships, which were not in a position to menace the convoy, manoeuvred in this area throughout the day.

144. *Nelson* sighted a Cant 506 very low down at 1025, and fighters were vectored. After a chase to the SE he was shot down 55 miles from the Fleet and only 200 yds from the Algerian shore, near Cape de Fer. This was a fine example of fighter control and relentless pursuit which reflects the greatest credit on those concerned. . . .

147. Speed was reduced to 12 knots at 2010 to reduce the strain on bulkheads and decks in the wake of flooded compartments in *Nelson*. At this time *Nelson* was approximately 8 feet down by the bows and it was estimated that 3500 tons of water had entered the ship.

148. At 2100, Group II of Force A, consisting of *Prince of Wales*, *Ark Royal* and 6 destroyers, were detached to proceed to the eastward and rendezvous with Force X a.m. on D5. Group I, consisting of *Nelson* and 3 destroyers continued towards Gibraltar.

149. By keeping the battleships concentrated until dark, I hoped to have concealed damage to *Nelson*, and that consequently enemy surface forces would keep clear while Force X made the passage westward from Malta.

Submarine Attacks on Force A, AM, 29 September (D5)

151. *Gurkha* obtained an A/S contact, classified as a submarine, . . . at 0810, two hours after the previous attack. The contact was nearly ahead and a deliberate attack with a 14-charge pattern was carried out at 0815. Six minutes later a heavy underwater explosion was heard and felt – this was similar to that felt after the successful attack on a U-boat next day.[1]

---

[1] No submarine sunk.

Westward Passage of Force X from Malta, 28/29 September (D4/5)

152.   After fuelling, *Farndale* and *Heythrop* sailed from the Grand Harbour at 1500, followed at 1615 by *Kenya, Edinburgh* and *Oribi*. The remainder of Force X sailed at 1830.

154.   Force X proceeded on a course to make the Tunisian Coast, and thence to Cape Bon, keeping close to the coast.

Passage of Nelson *to Gibraltar, 29/30 September (D5/6)*

156.   At 0700/29 I informed VACNA of *Nelson*'s position, course and speed, and requested additional A/S vessels and escort. This message was purposely delayed until this time in order to give no indication that *Nelson* was proceeding independently.

163.   At 1100/30 *Nelson* entered Gibraltar harbour. Tugs were used ahead and astern as the ship was sluggish under helm, especially at low speed.

Passages of Forces A and X to the Westward, 29 September (D5)

164.   After Force X had joined Force A at 1030/29, course was shaped to the westward, keeping 40 miles clear of the African coast.

165.   At 1645, *Lively* . . . sighted an object . . . distant about 1000 yards. *Lively* identified this as a submarine periscope and conning tower, . . . two torpedo tracks, course 010°, were sighted soon afterwards . . . a counter attacking 14-charge pattern set to shallow depth was fired at 1650. *Legion* . . . fired a 5-charge shallow pattern about a minute and a half earlier. Action to avoid the torpedoes was taken by the fleet. *Legion* then stationed *Lively* on her starboard beam and both ships hunted the submarine.
. . . Contact was lost at 400 yards and not regained. The hunt was abandoned at 1745 in order to rejoin the screen . . .

166.   *Prince of Wales, Kenya, Sheffield, Laforey, Lightning, Oribi, Foresight, Forester* and *Fury* parted company from the remainder of the Force at 1930 and proceeded ahead in order to arrive at Gibraltar p.m. 30 September.

Return of the Units under Rear Admiral [Burrough], 30 September/ 1 October

169.   At 0928/30 . . . *Gurkha* obtained an echo bearing 240° – 2000 yards, which was confirmed as a submarine. She immediately attacked, held contact up to 100 yards, and fired a 14-charge shallow pattern at 0935.
    A black circular buoy with electric cable attached came to the surface after the attack; at 0945 a loud underwater explosion was heard and felt, and oil started to come to the surface. *Gurkha* was unable to regain contact.

Legion, who was hunting with *Gurkha*, obtained contact, and attacked with a 14-charge pattern set to minimum depth at 0955, regaining contact at 1001, and attacking with another 14-charge pattern set deep at 1009.

During *Legion*'s second attack, wreckage and oil appeared close to where her first pattern was dropped.

Among the wreckage picked up were an Italian dictionary, a mattress, pillow, numerous pieces of wood, some with bright screws, and a piece of human scalp attached to a piece of wood by a splinter of metal. The interiors of the dictionary, pillow and mattress were dry.

There appears to be no reasonable cause to doubt that an Italian U-boat was destroyed by *Gurkha* and *Legion*.[1]

171.   The force entered harbour between 0700 and 0900/1.

Convoy MG2 – Passage from Malta to Gibraltar

172.   . . . SS *Melbourne Star* sailed from Malta at noon on 26 September (D2).

The remaining two ships, SS *Port Chalmers* and SS *City of Pretoria* left Malta at 1030 on 27 September (D3) escorted until 1930 by *Gloxinia*.[2]

173.   After an uneventful passage *Melbourne Star* arrived at Gibraltar at 0700 on 29 September (D5).

174.   *Port Chalmers* and *City of Pretoria* were reported by Italian aircraft at 1200/27, shortly after leaving Malta. No enemy surface craft or aircraft were seen until 2320, when what was believed to be an E-boat was sighted by *Port Chalmers*, who was following in the wake of *City of Pretoria*. The enemy craft when first sighted by *Port Chalmers* was lying stopped 300–400 yards on the port beam of *City of Pretoria*, who saw nothing except gunfire from her consort.

Port Chalmers sheered off to starboard, and 10 minutes after first sighting heard E-boat engines approaching from the port quarter; she turned to starboard to bring the enemy astern, and opened fire with her 4" gun at the enemy's bow wave.

The enemy opened fire at *Port Chalmers* with her machine gun, but scored no hits, and after Port Chalmers had fired 6 rounds of 4", the enemy crossed astern and made off. . . .

This action took place 15 miles SSW of Pantellaria.

175.   At 0535/28 the Commodore of the convoy ordered *Port Chalmers* to part company. The latter then proceeded at full speed, wearing French colours.

---

[1]*Adua*: 1936, *c*.680/860t, 6tt, 1×3.9in, 14/8k.
[2]*City of Pretoria*: 1937, 8046gt, 15.5k, Ellerman & Bucknall SS Co.

179. *City of Pretoria* was attacked at 1725/28 by 3 T/B aircraft. As these approached with obviously hostile intentions, British colours were hoisted and fire opened as the leader came in range. There is good reason to suppose the leading aircraft was damaged.

By skilful handling all 3 torpedoes were avoided. While one aircraft was machine gunning the ship at long range, a submarine periscope was reported on the starboard quarter by two independent look-outs.

Three smoke floats and a depth charge set to 150 feet were dropped and under cover of smoke *City of Pretoria* turned away.

180. As *City of Pretoria* was approaching Cape de Gata at 0200/30 (D6) an unidentified vessel, possibly a submarine, was seen to be following. Two or three rapid shots, followed by a dull explosion, were heard. *City of Pretoria* made smoke and dropped smoke floats and then made close in to Almeria Bay, into territorial waters, thus shaking off her pursuer.

181. *Port Chalmers* arrived at Gibraltar at 0900/30, followed during the afternoon by *City of Pretoria*.

182. The able and resolute handling of both *Port Chalmers* and *City of Pretoria* in successfully driving off enemy attacks deserves high praise.

Both Masters showed excellent restraint in withholding fire at enemy aircraft while there was a chance of their false colours being effective, and also in keeping W/T silence when attacked . . .

General Remarks

190. *Enemy T/B Attacks.* The rough handling which the enemy T/B aircraft received while passing over the destroyer screen may have accounted for the tendency of the attacks to be delivered from abaft the beam. Should this direction be adopted it will be necessary to station additional destroyers on after bearings at the expense of A/S protection.

Deliberate attacks by T/B aircraft against destroyers on the screen may force the latter to take drastic avoiding action. This will have the effect of disturbing gunfire and distracting attention, thereby opening a gap in the screen through which successive attackers could pass. Destroyers on the screen adjacent to the vessel attacked and close escorts on the threatened bearing, must maintain a careful watch in order to frustrate such manoeuvres.

191. *Failure to locate enemy battle fleet.* The operation orders stated clearly that the primary object of the operation was the safe arrival of the convoy at its destination, and any action taken to deal with enemy surface forces in the vicinity must be related to the achievement of this object.

At no time did the enemy surface forces constitute a serious threat. On the other hand enemy air forces remained a potential and serious threat throughout the day and after moonset. Under these circumstances the maintenance of fighter patrols assumed an importance which could not be ignored. Light variable winds added to the difficulties with which *Ark Royal* was confronted and I consider that her CO[1] acted throughout with great judgement and a well balanced appreciation of the situation.

Had the shadowing aircraft from Malta been able to maintain observation on the enemy battlefleet for a longer period the two reconnaissance Swordfish should have experienced no serious difficulty in making contact. Unfortunately, communications, due to atmospherics and congestion, were difficult. Congestion was due in part to the damage sustained by *Nelson* involving a last minute alteration of the pre-arranged plan to deal with the situation. With a force occupying a front of 12 miles the delay caused by W/T communication was unacceptable.

Failure of Malta and HM Ships to receive the all important signal timed 1515[2] . . . undoubtedly contributed largely to the failure of the striking force to locate. It appears now that whilst the enemy was at pains to withdraw as quickly as possible he was presumably concerned to keep under a CR42 umbrella furnished from Cagliari.

192.   *Added hazards due to the operation taking place during moonlight.* It cannot be emphasised too strongly that if operations of this character are carried out during the moonlight the hazards are increased to a very considerable extent. Had the enemy concentrated his T/B aircraft in attacking from dusk onwards he might well have succeeded in torpedoing a large part of the convoy.

193.   *U-boat activity.* Once the nature of the operation was disclosed the enemy took vigorous action to station submarines on the expected courses of the fleet; not a difficult matter in view of the relatively narrow waters of the Western Mediterranean. . . .

194.   *RAF Co-operation.* I wish to place on record my high appreciation of the excellent co-operation furnished by the RAF throughout this operation.

The bombing and machine gunning of enemy aerodromes in Sicily and Sardinia undoubtedly reduced to a considerable extent the scale of air attack which the enemy intended to launch. Apart from the circumstances attending the sighting and reporting of the enemy battlefleet which may well have been due to circumstances beyond the control of the aircraft in question, the reconnaissance of enemy bases and in particular of the approaches to Malta on D4 were adequate and most valuable. . . .

195.   I attribute the immunity from attack experienced by Force X and

[1]Capt Maund.
[2]A signal from an aircraft, not received at Malta or by the force, which stated that the enemy fleet had altered course to the N.

the convoy after passing Skerki Channel to the route proposed by the Vice Admiral, Malta. This well-judged move coupled with *Hermione*'s bombardment appears to have deceived the enemy completely. . . .

186. *To his wife*

27 September 1941

. . . As regards the torpedo attack we took our toll of them. There were some indescribable scenes. I saw one burst into the most enormous sheet of flame as she was hit and brought down by one of our destroyers. The one that hit us flashed by with tracer bullets going into him and disappeared with smoke coming from an engine, whilst another that flashed by was hit by one of our pom-poms and burst into 3 pieces in the air. About the same time a CR42 fighter that was machine-gunning one of the destroyers was brought down and crashed into the sea whilst a Fulmar sent an escaping aircraft spiralling down in flames. A most hectic afternoon, believe me. Countless other alarms and attacks coming in which our Fulmars broke up but no bombers anywhere near the fleet.

I had to leave the convoy at 7 p.m. as she approached the narrow channel and am now limping back to the westward with the other battleships as support. Alas we can't turn E again tomorrow evening to meet the returning cruisers so I shall have to send *P of W*, *Rodney* and *Ark* back to do that and limp on home to Gib. It's so damn annoying as it was just one chance in a thousand that that torpedo should have hit us.

187. *To Cunningham*

4 October 1941

. . . That Far East party! Tom Phillips, Stuart Bonham-Carter and Jock Tait,[1] no one with sea experience in this war. . . .

[1]Actg Adm Phillips, formerly VCNS, now C-in-C, Eastern Fleet (Force Z). Rear Adm Stuart S. Bonham-Carter: Capt 1927; RA & N Sec to 1st Lord Jan 1939; RA, Halifax, NS, Jan 1940; apptd as RA 3BS, Eastern F, under Phillips Oct 1941, but did not serve; 18CS Jan 1942; Arctic convoys; VA June 1942; VA Malta Dec 1942–Sept 1943; Ret List Dec 1943; Cdre 2nd Cl, RNR, *Eaglet* (Liverpool), for convoy duties, May 1944. Vice Adm W. E. Campbell Tait (1886–1946): *Britannia* 1902; Lt 1909; Jutland; Lt-Cdr 1917; Cdr 1921; *Victoria & Albert*; China Sta; Chatham 1924–6; Capt 1926; *Dragon, Capetown, Delhi, Despatch*, all on NA & WI Sta; DDNID; China Sta 1933–4; *Shropshire* 1934–7; Cdre, Portsmouth Barracks 1937; RA 1938; DPS, 1940–1; VA Oct 1941; selected as 2nd-in-C to first Phillips & then Somerville; became C-in-C S Atlantic instead, Feb 1942; Ret List Dec 1944 & Govr-Gen S Rhodesia; Adm 1945; known as 'Jock' or 'Tufty', possessor of largest eyebrows of any FO.

Hope to goodness I can get *Renown* back here as *Malaya* is quite useless to me for anything out to the W and not particularly good for anything to the E. If we have not got good legs in this force we can't do our stuff properly. *Prince of Wales* going eastward is a great mistake to my mind. Apparently the PM and Anthony Eden insist though what it had to do with the latter I don't know and can't imagine.[1]

188. *To Cunningham*

6 October 1941

I think we got off cheap on the whole during HALBERD but it was a nuisance *Nelson* getting pipped. The drop was only 400 yards fine on the starboard bow and we swung towards and steadied. The chances of a hit seemed remote until the bloody bubbles appeared about 120 yards ahead and coming straight for us. Possibly helm hard over, or keeping her swinging to starboard *might* have let us take it on the bulge but I doubt it. Anyhow there was always the danger of a hit right aft which would have been worse. The 6000-yard screen seemed to work pretty well on the whole and destroyers' barrage made a lot drop outside. But short range weapons as usual shot below and behind. . . .

It looks now as if they are going to try and get at us with U-boats in the Western Mediterranean. A/S conditions are still pretty poor so I reckon full main expeditions ought to be off unless they're urgent. *Nelson* has got a bloody great hole and does she stink! 19 tons of rotting beef and *all* my cold stores still in process of being removed. I've got no destroyers at the moment otherwise I'd have a dummy run out to the W so as to get the Itis guessing.

189. *Report of Proceedings, 30 September–16 October 1941*

HMS *Rodney*,
20 October 1941

2 October

13.   At 1100 *Nelson* was docked without difficulty and pumping out commenced at 1315. When the damage was exposed, it was found that the hole was . . . approximately 38 feet by 15 feet, with cracks in the bot-

---

[1]Churchill and Eden thought that Force Z would exercise a considerable deterrent effect on the Japanese; see C. Thorne, *Allies of a Kind: The United States, Britain and the War Against Japan, 1941–1945* (Oxford: Oxford U Pr, 1979), pp. 4, 56.

tom plating running down to the keel. It was apparent the damage was far more serious than had been anticipated. . . .

4 October

21.   In reply to a suggestion that *Ark Royal*'s aircraft should be used to protect OG and HG convoys in certain areas where attacks had been persistent, I informed the Admiralty that the endurance of Force H destroyers would restrict such operations to one day unless destroyers were refuelled. Prospects of refuelling in the areas under consideration were not good and *Ark Royal* was only suitable for fuelling destroyers in good weather. *Hermione*, who would be required as escort for *Ark Royal*, also has poor endurance and would require to be refuelled at sea.

Summing up the pros and cons, it appeared to me that the results likely to be achieved did not justify in any way the risks involved to *Ark Royal*.
22.   Major Bentley, the US Air Attaché from Tangier, whom I met on board *Nelson* and who has recently been in Italy, informed me that bombardment by submarines of objectives on the Italian coast produced a moral effect out of all proportion to the results achieved. This information was passed by me to VACNA and Captain (S), 8th Submarine Flotilla,[1] with a view to appropriate action being taken.

8 October

31.   *Argus*, in company with *Cossack*, *Zulu* and *Sikh*, arrived at 1400 . . .

13 October

50.   Information having been received that a number of U-boats were believed to be shadowing convoy OG 75, I ordered *Ark Royal* to fly off a squadron of Swordfish to attack. At this time, however, 816 Squadron was in the air carrying out a shadowing exercise, whilst 812 Squadron was returning to North Front after completing their ALT practice; this left only 4 serviceable Swordfish on board, which were armed with depth charges and flown off at 1212. Enemy aircraft also having been reported near the convoy, a fighter escort of 4 Fulmars was flown off. The A/S patrol was maintained over the convoy until 1745, while the fighter escort was withdrawn at 1600. . . .

The convoy arrived in harbour unharmed.

16 October

58.   Information was received that it was intended to relieve *Rodney* in

[1]Adm Edward-Collins and Capt Voelcker.

Force H by *Malaya*. In view of the speed, lack of endurance and paucity of anti-aircraft armament of this ship, I expressed the hope that her allocation to this Force is very temporary.

190.   *Report of Proceedings, 16–19 October 1941*

HMS *Malaya*,
8 November 1941

2.   The object of this operation [CALLBOY] was twofold:–

(a)   the passage of 12 Albacores and 2 Swordfish aircraft to Malta; . . .
(b)   the passage of Force K, consisting of *Aurora, Penelope*,[1] *Lance* and *Lively* to Malta.

16 October (D1)

3.   Force H, consisting of *Rodney, Ark Royal, Hermione, Cossack, Zulu, Sikh, Legion, Foresight, Forester* and *Fury*, sailed from Gibraltar at 1100.
5.   Force H shaped course to the eastward, zig-zagging at a speed of 18 knots. Outer and inner A/S patrols by 2 Swordfish aircraft were maintained during daylight.

17 October

17.   A low flying enemy aircraft (Cant 506), which had not been detected by RDF, was sighted from *Ark Royal* at 1350, and one section of fighters was vectored towards it.
     The enemy aircraft was shot down after a chase of 20 miles at sea level; the only return fire experienced was from a side window of the fuselage.

18 October

24.   11 Albacores and 2 Swordfish aircraft were flown off between 0135 and 0145.[2]
28.   A signal reporting the arrival at Malta of 11 Albacores was received at 0849, and later a further signal announced that one Swordfish had arrived. No news of the second Swordfish was received. . . .
29.   An aircraft was sighted from *Sikh* SW of the fleet at 0958, and fighters sighted an Italian BR 20 soon after they were vectored. After a

[1]*Aurora* (1937), *Penelope* (1936; sunk NW of Naples 1944, *U410*): 5250t, 6×6in, 8×4in, 6tt, 32.25k. This was to raid Italian convoy routes to Libya, which it did with conspicuous success.
[2]Another Albacore was unserviceable.

chase of 45 miles to the SE, the enemy was shot down about 10 miles from Cape Bengut. The pilot concerned was Sub-Lt (A) J. F. Underwood, RNVR.[1] ...

19 October

41.   The fleet entered Gibraltar Bay at 1617 ...
Passage of Force K from Gibraltar
42.   *Aurora* and *Penelope* arrived in Gibraltar Bay at 2200/D3, and oiled from *San Claudio* and *Viscol*.[2]
    While oiling each ship embarked:–

17 18" torpedoes
200 rounds 4" Mk XVI SAP ammunition (reserve for *Lively* and *Lance*)
1 Oerlikon gun and 2400 rounds of ammunition ex *Rodney* and *Hermione*.

43.   *Lively* and *Lance* each embarked 2 18" torpedoes and 200 rounds 4" SAP ammunition in addition to their outfit and sailed for full calibre firings at 1715/D3. They remained to the eastward of the Rock during the night, and joined *Aurora* and *Penelope* ... at 0800/D4. ...

191.   *To Cunningham*

20 October 1941

... We haven't met any Germans yet really but when we do I shall remember *Greyhound* and the others.[3] God how I hate the Germans. ...
    As you may know I've been ordered home for 5 days for a conference on some project in which I am to be naval commander. Wonder what the hell it is and if I am likely to see eye to eye! If I don't I shan't hesitate to say so. ...
    So far as bombing Cagliari is concerned I feel that *effective* bombing can be done better from Malta. On the other hand if the Swordfish disclose themselves sufficiently it will make the Itis appreciate that Force H is in the vicinity. The whole idea must be to concentrate the effort in a useless spot, i.e., the Itis' effort.
    An alternative would be to suggest some major operation further N – Genoa way. but I feel that is more likely to be looked on as a mere double

---

[1]Actg Sub-Lt (A) J. F. Underwood RNVR: *Ark Royal* 1941; 778 Sqdn *Condor* (Arbroath) 1942; S-Lt (A) 1942; *Jackdaw* 1943; *Daedalus* 1945.
[2]*San Claudio*: RFA, 1928, 2712gt, 10k, Eagle Oil Co. *Viscol*: oiler, 1916, 2410gt, 9.5k.
[3]*Greyhound* was sunk by German aircraft off Crete in May 1941.

crossing and that simulation of a convoy passage will probably be the most effective and keep their minds on a single track.

I still feel that if we can 'dissipate' the convoy on D3 it will give them a lot to think about. If Force H can also disappear into thin air on D3 so much the better but that all depends on visibility. In November the weather should be pretty foul towards the Gulf [of Genoa].

I shudder to think of the Pocket Napoleon[1] and his party. All the tricks to learn and no solid sea experience to fall back on. They ought to have someone who knows his stuff and can train up that party properly on the way out . . .

192. *Report of Proceedings, 19–31 October 1941*

HMS *Malaya*
9 November 1941

21 October

4.   At 0630 I took off in a Sunderland aircraft . . . for the UK, with the object of visiting the Admiralty to discuss future operations.

22 October

8.   *Malaya* was ordered to be sailed to Gibraltar to relieve *Rodney* in Force H, exchanging A/S escorts with *Argus* and *Eagle en route.* . . .

9.   Two merchant ships ex-HALBERD, *City of Lincoln* and *Dunedin Star,* and *Empire Guillemot* (who had proceeded to Malta independently) sailed from Malta, the first two together until reaching Cape Bon, and thence independently. *Dunedin Star* and *City of Lincoln* were attacked on passage by Italian torpedo bombers, but successfully avoided torpedoes and drove off the enemy by gunfire, inflicting some damage. *Empire Guillemot* was not so fortunate, and after some days without news of her it was learned that she had probably been sunk by Italian torpedo aircraft off Galita Island and that survivors had landed at Algiers.

23 October

10.   *Cossack* was torpedoed . . . whilst escorting convoy HG 75. The forepart of the ship, together with most of the bridge, was completely destroyed. *Legion,* who was standing by with *Carnation* and *Commandant Duboc,* reported that the after part of the ship was still afloat and fit to tow, and requested that air escort and a tug should be

---

[1]Adm Phillips, who was short of stature.

sent. *Legion* was ordered to return to the convoy at 0724, whilst *Carnation* who was standing by to take in tow, was ordered not to tow but to provide A/S protection; the tug *Thames* was sent at 0630 in company with *Jonquil* to bring *Cossack* into Gibraltar.

24 October

12.   *Clan Ferguson,* the third of the merchant vessels ex-HALBERD to be sailed from Malta independently, was sighted by enemy air reconnaissance and was therefore recalled to Malta.

25 October

13.   *Dunedin Star* and *City of Lincoln* arrived at Gibraltar from Malta.

14.   *Hermione* returned at 0730 after a fruitless search for a suspected enemy tanker and docked on arrival for bottom-cleaning and repairs to damage sustained in ramming an Italian submarine during operation SUBSTANCE.

15.   *Cossack* was reported as being in tow of tug *Thames* at a speed of 3 knots escorted by *Jonquil* and *Carnation.*

26 October

16.   Tug *Rollicker,* escorted by *Lord Hotham,* was sailed at 1828 to relieve *Thames*[1] and enable her to proceed to the assistance of AMC *Ariguani,*[2] also torpedoed and damaged in the stern.

17.   At 2110 *Jonquil* reported the situation regarding *Cossack* as critical, and stated that she had taken off the remainder of *Cossack*'s crew.

27 October

18.   At 1302 it was reported that *Cossack* had sunk. . . .

193.   *Report of Proceedings, 1–9 November 1941*

12 November 1941

5 November

15.   *Sikh* and *Duncan* were ordered to return with despatch to Gibraltar, and the course of *Argus* and *Athene,*[3] *en route* to Gibraltar, was changed

---

[1]*Carnation*: 'Flower' class corvette. *Commandant Duboc,* Free French: 1939, c.650t, 2×4in.
   Rollicker: 1919, 1400t, 14k. *Lord Hotham* was probably an armed trawler. *Thames*: 1938, 624t, Dutch.
   [2]*Ariguani*: AMC, 1926, 6746gt, 14k, Elders & Fyffes.
   [3]*Athene*: aux a/c transport, 1941, 10,700t, 40 a/c (crated), 2×4in, 17k; she was carrying Hurricanes for Malta but was delayed by engine trouble.

to bring them further E. This and other information available indicated the possibility that Force H might be required to put to sea, but at this time no A/S screen was available for immediate action to be taken.

6 November

16.   At 1000 I presided over a meeting of an Inter-Services RDF Committee held on board *Malaya,* which had as its object the raising of the general standard of RDF detection in the Fortress and the co-ordination of the work of the technical officers of all three Services to this end. . . .

18.   Ships of Force H were brought to 2 hours' notice for steam, following the arrival of *Sikh* and *Duncan*, and indications that a German naval unit might be putting to sea.[1]

20.   VACNA signalled a summary of the situation with regard to A/S escorts and ships available for patrol; his various commitments left him no destroyers, corvettes or A/S trawlers for additional escorts or for emergencies.

7 November

25.   *Argus,* screened by *Laforey* and *Lightning,* arrived at 2300. Work of unloading Hurricane aircraft was proceeded [with] during the night.

8 November

26.   HMS *Athene,* in company with *Gurkha, Zulu* and *Isaac Sweers,* arrived at 0600. . . .

194.   *Report of Proceedings, 10–13 November 1941*

24 November 1941

10 November

2.   Force H, consisting of *Malaya, Ark Royal, Argus, Hermione, Laforey, Lightning, Legion, Zulu, Gurkha, Sikh* and *Isaac Sweers,* sailed from Gibraltar at 0235, . . .

3.   *Hermione* and destroyers were formed on screening diagram No. 7A, and the Force was zig-zagging at a speed of 18 knots.

4.   *Argus* flew off one aircraft for A/S patrol at 0800, and a Catalina aircraft joined from Gibraltar at 0930. At 0932 I . . . enjoined a very careful watch for submarines and low flying shadowers.

---

[1]Probably one of the major German warships at Brest.

12 November

18.   Shortly after midnight a signal was received from No. 200 Group, informing me that as weather precluded a night take-off, it was intended that zero hour should be 1000.[1]

24.   ... by 1021, 13 Hurricanes had flown off *Ark Royal* (A Flight) and 6 from *Argus* (B Flight).

25.   Blenheims for C and D Flights ... were sighted at 1048, and 5 minutes later *Ark Royal* had flown off the first of her second range. Flight C ... consisted of 13 Hurricanes and 2 Blenheims.

26.   One engine of Flight D in *Argus* failed at first, but did not delay for more than 2 or 3 minutes the departure of this flight of 5 Hurricanes and 2 Blenheims ...

28.   Groups 1 and 2 were reformed at 1130 into single line in the order *Malaya, Ark Royal* and *Argus,* screening diagram No. 7A was taken up by *Hermione* and the 7 destroyers, and course 290° was set, the fleet zig-zagging at 16 knots.

This was the maximum speed which destroyers could maintain without damage in the short rising sea.

One Swordfish was flown off *Ark Royal* for A/S duties, and 4 Fulmars as fighter patrol. These patrols were maintained until dusk.

31.   . . . At 1625 the Vice Admiral, Malta, informed me that 7 Blenheims and 34 Hurricanes had arrived. No news was received of the missing Hurricanes.

13 November

35.   An underwater explosion observed by *Legion*, in her wake at 0413, was also heard by several ships. *Legion* at this time was the starboard destroyer. This was probably a torpedo exploding at the end of its run, but the occurrence was not reported to me until daylight.

36.   *Ark Royal* flew off 6 Swordfish at 0645 to carry out a dawn ASV search to a depth of 70 miles ... but nothing was sighted.

Outer and inner A/S patrols were established and maintained throughout the day. ...

37.   At 0817 I informed Force H that submarines had been reported in the vicinity and that great vigilance was necessary.

Until 0900 course had been shaped to give the impression that it was intended to pass S of Alboran Island, but at this time a sharp alteration was made to 305° to pass to the northward, subsequently turning to 270° and approaching Gibraltar directly from the eastward, through the centre of the area.

[1]Hurricanes were ranged on deck, thereby precluding normal reconnaissance and fighter cover.

On previous occasions Force H has usually returned to Gibraltar along either the Spanish or Moroccan coasts, making the final approach from the NE or SE.

This was probably known to the enemy and it was thought that in consequence any U-boats in the vicinity were more likely to be in positions near the shore.

38. At 0955, *Laforey* reported investigating a contact to starboard, and an emergency turn away 90° was made. *Laforey* dropped 2 depth charges, but contact was lost and the fleet turned back to 310° at 1008.

40. At 1157, *Lightning* reported contact to starboard, and an emergency turn of 90° to port was made. The contact was immediately negatived and the mean course of 270° was resumed at 1201.

41. *Ark Royal* requested freedom of manoeuvring to carry out deck landing training after 1515, and I replied approving this, provided *Ark Royal* kept well inside the A/S screen during flying operations.

45. *Ark Royal* informed me at 1418 that she had 14 aircraft to land on at 1515, and suggested she should do this from a position on *Malaya*'s disengaged (port) quarter, as *Malaya* was expected to be firing at that time.

I approved the proposal . . . – 'Your 1418 approved, but keep well under the screen'.

46. *Laforey* reported a contact to port at 1518, and an emergency turn was made to starboard.

47. *Ark Royal* altered course to 286° for flying at 1529, and flew off 6 Swordfish and 2 Fulmars. Five Swordfish were flown on, and at 1535 *Ark Royal* turned to port to regain her position in the line, altering course again to 286° at 1538 to fly on.

48. *Legion,* the starboard wing destroyer, turned to 250° at this time to cover *Ark Royal,* turning back to port when *Ark Royal* moved in to regain station. Just before turning to the course of the fleet hydrophone effect was reported on the starboard bow, but as this coincided with the approximate bearing of *Gurkha,* the next ahead, and faded out when *Legion* turned to the course of the fleet, it was disregarded and not reported by *Legion.* The S.D. operator subsequently stated that H/E on this occasion was louder than any he had heard previously. This suggests that the H/E heard was in fact that of the torpedo fired at *Ark Royal.*

49. At 1540, the remainder of the Force turned to 290° in accordance with zig-zag No. 11 which had been ordered. At this time I instructed the CO, *Malaya*[1] to keep clear to port of *Ark Royal,* who was 4 cables on

[1]Capt Cuthbert Coppinger: Capt 1933; Capt of DY, Dep Supt & King's Hbr Mr, Portsmouth DY 1939; *Malaya* May 1941; Med F HQ, Alexandria March 1942; Ret List July 1942; Alexandria DY June 1943; *King Alfred* (Hove) June 1945.

Malaya's starboard quarter, until she had completed flying on, as the courses of the two ships converged slightly.

50. At 1541, . . . *Ark Royal,* who was bearing 077° 4 cables from *Malaya,* was struck by a torpedo on the starboard side. . . .

Malaya altered course away to port, increased speed and eventually steadied on 240°. *Gurkha* and *Legion,* the rear destroyers on the starboard wing, at once turned outwards to search the area to the N and E of *Ark Royal,* i.e., the probable direction of the attack.

Captain (D), 19th DF, in *Laforey* ordered the remaining destroyers to form screening diagram No. 5 on *Malaya.*

51. At this time *Ark Royal* was still going ahead at considerable speed, listing to starboard and apparently under port wheel. A number of aircraft were still circling overhead.

52. At 1549 *Laforey* and *Lightning* were ordered to join *Ark Royal* who appeared to be easing down. Signals were made to VACNA to send tugs to assist *Ark Royal* and for the immediate despatch of all A/S craft and aircraft from North Front to patrol.

53. *Hermione,* some 6 miles distant was ordered to join *Ark Royal.* At 1552 the remaining 3 destroyers, viz., *Sikh, Zulu* and *Isaac Sweers,* were ordered to form screening diagram No. 3 on *Malaya.*

Situation at 1610

Ark Royal was apparently stopped and listing heavily to starboard, but reported she had steam on her port engine. *Laforey, Gurkha* and *Lightning* had closed and were circling *Ark Royal. Legion* was alongside *Ark Royal* and *Hermione* was closing. *Malaya,* now distant 4.5 miles from *Ark Royal,* was returning to Gibraltar at 18 knots, screened at first by 3 destroyers and subsequently by 2 destroyers, when at 1622 I despatched *Zulu* to join *Ark Royal. Argus* was some distance astern but overhauling *Malaya. Argus* flew off 2 Swordfish for A/S patrol at 1615.

56. . . . *Malaya* entered harbour at 1820 and before the ship was berthed I transferred to *Sikh* and left at 1845 to proceed to *Ark Royal* . . .

58. After boarding *Sikh,* course was shaped at 32 knots towards *Ark Royal*'s estimated position. The night was very dark, and on approaching this position it was necessary to ease down on account of MLs and other vessels in the vicinity also engaged in locating *Ark Royal.*

59. Eventually the outer circling pair of destroyers was reached and since these and the inner circling patrol of MLs were dropping depth charges at regular intervals, I deemed it inadvisable for *Sikh* to proceed and ordered her to establish a patrol to the westward until circumstances or light permitted an approach to *Ark Royal* without interfering with the patrols and hazarding *Sikh.* I also ordered *Wishart,* who was in the vicinity, to keep in company with *Sikh.*

Situation as it appeared at 2040

60.   *Thames* and *St Day* had arrived and *Ark Royal* was in tow proceeding at 2 knots, and hoped to have steam shortly. (*St Omer* failed to locate *Ark Royal* and returned to Gibraltar).[1] The chief danger appeared to be an attempt by enemy submarines to approach from up moon after moonrise at 0130. For this reason I had ordered *Sikh* to patrol to westward and *Isaac Sweers* and *Wishart* to take up 'B' and 'G' patrols respectively to guard against submarine reinforcements arriving from the westward. . . .

Situation as it appeared at 2224

61.   The Captain (D), 19th DF, reported that he had left *Ark Royal,* who had her own steam and power, that flooding was apparently under control and no more tugs were required until off harbour. At 2238 I informed *Rhododendron, Marigold* and *Pentstemon*[2] of the position, course and speed of *Ark Royal* at 2010 and ordered them to establish an A/S patrol 5 miles astern of *Ark Royal,* closing her at daylight.

14 November

62.   Captain (D), 19th DF's message timed 0221/14, that *Ark Royal* had lost steam and required powerful pump, and his signal 0242, that another tug was required, indicated that the situation in *Ark Royal* had deteriorated, and accordingly I instructed *Sikh* to close, and informed Captain (D) and *Zulu* that she was closing from the westward. Captain (D) had ordered *Pentstemon* with pump to close *Ark Royal* and I requested VACNA to send tug *Rollicker; St Omer,* then at the examination anchorage, was also ordered by VACNA to proceed to *Ark Royal.* On approaching *Laforey* who, with *St Day,* was alongside the port side of *Ark Royal,* Captain (D) signalled that I had better transfer to an ML.

This was done and I proceeded to *Laforey* at 0430 to find she was on the point of casting off from *Ark Royal* with Captain L. E. H. Maund and the last of the steaming party. *Ark Royal* now had a list of over 35° and was evidently listing still further judging by the straining and parting of the wires securing the ships alongside her. The situation was reported to the Admiralty at 0446.

63.   After getting clear I ordered *St Day* to go ahead of tug *Thames* but at 0600 the latter reported that she had cast off the tow as *Ark Royal* was sinking. *Ark Royal* did not finally turn over until 0613, when, after remaining bottom up for a few minutes, she disappeared from sight. This was reported to the Admiralty at 0623.

65.   I returned to Gibraltar in *Sikh* arriving at 0830.

---

[1]*St Day, St Omer*: tugs, 1919, 820t, 12k.
[2]*Rhododendron, Marigold* (sunk off N Africa 1942, Ger a/c), *Pentstemon*: 'Flower' class corvettes.

195. *To his wife*

14 November 1941

It was the blackest of days when I saw my poor *Ark* sink at 6 a.m. this morning. Just a blur in the dark as she lay on her side for some time and then slowly, slowly she turned over like a tired and wounded ship going to sleep. I knew there were U-boats about and had made a signal enjoining the greatest vigilance. We had successfully passed the narrow point by Alboran Island where I expected them to be and we were then 30 miles or so off Gib. I had a good destroyer screen out inside of which we were well tucked in. It was just before 4 p.m. whilst *Ark* was flying on some aircraft I suddenly saw an explosion on board her, it seemed to be just before the island. It was so heavy that the aircraft on the forepart of her deck jumped clear of the deck and down again once or twice. Almost immediately afterwards she started to list and started to ease down, black smoke pouring from her funnel. . . . *Malaya* entered harbour at 6.30 p.m. and before she berthed I was hoisted out in the barge and went straight off to *Sikh* . . . and back to the *Ark*. *Ark's* reports were encouraging as they had raised steam in one boiler room and had the flooding under control and the list was not so bad. I kept clear to the westward waiting for the moon to rise at 2.30 a.m. and hoped for the best as the tugs had *Ark* in tow. However at 4 a.m. I got a message saying more tugs were required and so I closed and found her with a terrible list. Apparently a fire had broken out in the boiler room so all pumps and electric power failed. I think some bulkheads must have burst too. By this time practically everyone was off the ship and as I got alongside Maund was the last to go. She was obviously doomed but for 2 hours the tugs tried to get her along but she fell over further and further whilst the edge of the flying deck was in the water. And finally she went. I am rather cut up about this because I was so proud and fond of my *Ark*. As I signalled to the Admiralty this gallant ship has paid a fine dividend during this war and her loss is deeply regretted. The strange thing is that our Asdics gave no warnings this time and no one saw the track of the torpedo. I can't understand how one torpedo should have caused the loss of this fine ship.

196. *To Cunningham*

18 November 1941

A sad business about the old *Ark* and many thanks for your kindly signal. I must confess that when we were within 30 odd miles of Gib. and returning via the middle, instead of the sides as we usually do, I felt it was very unlikely that we should be attacked. However I didn't relax any precautions except to send *Hermione* off the screen to act as throw-off target for *Malaya*. We have to do our firing on these occasions as we never have any destroyers at other times. We had 7 destroyers on the screen, and inner and outer A/S aircraft patrol and the sky filled with aircraft either flying off or landing on. *Ark* practically in station on *Malaya* and second in the line when hit. No sign of a contact but it now transpires that *Legion* the rear ship of the starboard wing heard H/E on the starboard box and thought it was her next ahead as she was under helm at the time. . . .

It was not until 0230 that I felt unduly concerned but after a signal asking for more tugs and a sloop with a portable pump to come alongside I decided to close at once. On getting alongside I found that owing to a fire in the boiler room, caused by flooding of the funnel uptakes, she had lost all steam and the list which had been slowly increasing was now over 30° and she had been abandoned though still in tow. It was obvious that the list was increasing every minute and though she hung for some time with the flight deck level with the water i.e. at about 45° she eventually turned over and sank.

A board of enquiry with Charles Forbes as President[1] is on its way to investigate so I won't express any definite opinion on what might or might not have been done. But what does stand out now is that certain arrangements in the carriers require revision. In Ark at any rate flooding can pass from one funnel uptake to the next if the ship is listing heavily and if the list is to starboard the funnel uptake can be sealed by water and so no steam can be raised. . . .

I estimate that the U-boat fired at maximum range and was possibly just outside the screen. Asdic conditions have been very bad but have been improving and seemed fairly good on the whole on the day in question. But with all that air about one would have thought a submarine at periscope depth for any length of time should have been spotted though with so many porpoises and blackfish a feather is not likely to be noticed.

I am so sorry that we were unable to carry out a diversion at our end to help you but with the circumstances I expect it was not wise to send *Nelson* and *Argus* up the Western Mediterranean as *Nelson* though protected is not of course 100% yet. *Malaya* unfortunately ran a plumier [-?] block bearing.

One has got to expect these knocks in war but it was too bad it should have been the old *Ark*.

---

[1]Adm of the Fleet Sir Charles Forbes, C-in-C Plymouth.

P.S. *Ark* as you know was badly shaken by two depth charges last spring that went off just forward of the torpedo hit. I'm afraid the temporary repairs must have failed under the shock.

197. *To his wife*

21 November 1941

Inquisitors have finished their enquiries and are off tonight so Charles Forbes takes this with him. Apparently they had no criticism or remarks to make on my conduct of the operation, or the steps I took to deal with possible U-boat attacks. So far as what happened where the *Ark* is concerned, I feel that possibly what occurred there may be open to some criticism. Maund thought about 20 minutes after *Ark* had been torpedoed that she might capsize very shortly and therefore ordered everyone up from below. But when you see that enormous great flying deck canted over at an angle of 20°, you certainly do get the impression that the ship must be going right over and with over 1700 people on board and the difficulty of getting on deck in a Carrier, I for one don't blame him for his decision. Actually I doubt if it would have made any difference even if the steaming watch had remained below. The torpedo got her in her very worst spot.

I think that I was rather misinformed by the *Ark* – I mean they were too optimistic about the ship until 2 a.m. But here again I doubt very much if there was anything I could do to help her at that stage. Unless she had steam herself it was almost impossible to deal with the flooding on board. I think the Enquiry was conducted very loosely and that Charles will get a pretty good raspberry from TLs. I have been trying to keep them in the line though of course it's no business of mine. . . .

198. *To Cunningham*

25 November 1941

. . . It was quite the worst inquiry I have ever attended. . . . Forbes appeared to be convinced it was poor asdic conditions. I don't agree as I think the shot was fired just outside the A/S range. *Legion* . . . heard H/E but did not report it . . . Had she reported it I think we could have turned in time to make it miss ahead. . . .

The bad thing is that one torpedo should have caused so much damage. An M/L only 50 yards off when she capsized had an Aldis [lamp] on her and reported the hole as being 120–150 feet long and 30 wide mid-

way between the starboard bilge keel and the centre line of the ship.
. . . It now appears that the damage must have been far more extensive
than it appeared to be at first.

Sturges, Servaes and two staff officers have been here about TRUN-
CHEON.[1] I've given it in my opinion as an entire gamble. If there
is opposition and especially air we shall probably mess up the place but
it will be an expensive job and not worth the price we should have to
pay.

DP asked me if I thought *Argus* alone would be enough [for] the
job. She can carry 12 fighters and to fly them off takes at least 40 minutes.
Can you beat it! I replied she would be quite useless and only a commitment.

With Tom Phillips's circus on tour we have no spares left so we can't
afford to expend what we have left on enterprises where the odds are too
heavy against us. A point I have rubbed in is that the mixed party for the
job will never have worked together before and consequently their fighting efficiency will be low. . . .

I am not at all happy about the A/S situation here. . . . Fred splutters
and splurges but the fact remains the U-boats just pass in and out as they
like. Joubert[2] has just paid a visit and I've suggested he should send out
one of his best chaps to look into the organisation of the air patrols and to
suggest the best means of conducting the surface patrols. The Straits
patrols appear to be quite useless.

I'm quite convinced we've made a hash of our French policy during
the last 6–8 months. Tough one week and all smarmy the next.

199.   *Report of Proceedings, 14 November–8 December 1941*

14 December 1941

16 November

9.   HMS *Argus* proceeded to sea at 1400, escorted by *Zulu, Sikh,*

---

[1]Actg Maj-Gen (later Lt-Gen Sir Robert) R. G. Sturges RM: Col 2nd Cdt, Deal 1939;
Actg Col Cdt & Temp Brig 1940; Actg Maj-Gen RM Div 1941; HQ Spl Services 1943; Lt-
Gen June 1945. Capt R.M. Servaes: Capt 1935; DD Local Defence Div 1938; DLD Oct
1939; *London* Oct 1940; RA & ACNS (F) 1943–5; RA 2CS, BPF June 1945. Probably a
descent on Sicily; not carried out.

[2]Air Marshal (later Air Chief Marshal) Sir Philip Joubert de la Ferté (1887–1965): RA
1907; transf to RFC 1913, already a pilot; Capt 1914; sqdn cmdr 1915; Egypt 1916–17;
cmded RFC in Italy; Wing-Cdr & cmdr 2 Group 1918; Staff Coll 1920; DD Personnel; Grp
Capt 1922; IDC 1926–9; Air Cdre 1929; Comdt RAF Staff Coll 1929–32; Air VM 1933;
Fighter Cmd 1934; Air M & AOC, Coastal Cmd, 1936; AOC, India 1937; Asst CAS
1939–41; Air CM & AOC Coastal Cmd 1941; Inspr-Gen RAF 1942–3; Dep COS to SAC,
SE Asia 1943; Ret List 1945.

Gurkha and *Lightning*, to fly on 8 Swordfish and 2 Fulmars from North Front, returning to harbour on completion.

10. At 1830 a dummy convoy, comprising *Brown Ranger, Blair Atholl, Baron Newlands, Shuna, Cisneros* and *Ottinge*,[1] escorted by *Deptford* (SO), *Wild Swan, Pentstemon, Convolvulus, Rhododendron, Samphire* and *Marigold*,[2] sailed to the E as a diversion (operation CHIEFTAIN). Merchant vessels were to break from the convoy at intervals, returning to Gibraltar independently, the same night, while the escorts were to carry out an A/S sweep between Gibraltar and 1° 30'E, returning to Gibraltar on the night of 19/20 November.

11. *Nelson, Argus, Hermione, Laforey, Zulu, Sikh, Gurkha, Legion, Isaac Sweers* and *Lightning* sailed to the westward at 2300. . . . *Nelson*, screened by *Zulu, Sikh* and *Gurkha*, proceeded to the UK.

12. At 2316 *Marigold*, who had been delayed by engine defects and was proceeding to join up with the escort of CHIEFTAIN convoy, attacked a U-boat . . . The submarine was first detected on the surface by Type 271 [radar] and dived as *Marigold* was attempting to ram. Depth charges were dropped and contact was lost but subsequently regained and at 0013 *Marigold* reported the U-boat sunk and that she was picking up survivors, who proved to be German.[3]

25 November

39. In view of the reported presence of U-boats in the western approaches to Gibraltar, I informed the Admiralty of my intention that available Force H destroyers should proceed on an A/S sweep, returning on 1 December. These destroyers could be recalled and available to act as a screen for Force H, if required, within 24 hours. . . .

28 November

51. HNM Submarine *0–21* returned to harbour at 0928 having sunk a German U-boat[4] . . . Twelve survivors were picked up and landed.

29 November

55. Captain G. E. Creasey, DASD, accompanied by Professor

---

[1]*Blair Atholl*: 1925, 3318gt, G Nisbet & Co. *Baron Newlands*: 1928, 3386gt, 10.75k, H. Hogarth & Sons. *Shuna*: 1937, 1575gt, 10k, Glen & Co. *Cisneros*: 1926, 188gt, 9.75k, MacAndrews & Co. *Ottinge*: 1940, 2870gt, Constants, Cardiff.

[2]*Deptford*: 1935, 990t, 2×4in, 1×3in, 16.5k. *Wild Swan*: 1919, 1500t, 4×4in, 3tt, 28k (sunk N Atlantic 1942, Ger a/c). *Convolvulus, Samphire* (sunk 1943 off N Africa, Ital S/M *Platino*): 'Flower' class corvettes.

[3]*U433*.

[4]*U95*.

Blackett,[1] who were visiting Gibraltar for the purpose of inspecting A/S arrangements, visited me aboard HMS *Malaya*.

30 November

56.   Destroyers of the 19th Flotilla on A/S patrol were ordered to divide into two forces during daylight, sweeping N and S respectively of a line 270° from Cape Spartel, on an arc between 20 miles and 30 miles from Spartel. A Catalina was allocated to each force, to sweep over an arc 35 to 45 miles from Spartel, N and S respectively of a line bearing 270° from Spartel. At dusk both parts of this group were to meet and operate as previously ordered. . . .

200.   *To Cunningham*

5 December 1941

. . . It's a pity we can't do something at this end to draw off some of the stuff from your end but I can't move until destroyers are available and with things as they are it's difficult to see when we can get a screen of any sort. So many odd ships to be escorted apart from the present intensive U-boat patrol. It's disappointing that we've got no positive asdic result these last four days. The ASV in the Swordfish has done well and there have been at least two promising attacks, but no scalps and without scalps you can't call it a death. I have no idea what casualties you had in B[*arham*] but trust they were not serious.[2] . . .

---

[1]Capt (later Adm of the Fleet Sir) George E. Creasey: ent RN 1908; torpedo splist; N Sea 1914–18; Cdr 1930; Tactical Sch; SO (O) Med F; Capt 1935; ADP; Capt (D), 1DF 1938–40; Dunkirk; Pers Asst to 1SL; DASD Sept 1940–2; *Duke of York*, Home F 1942; RA 1943; COS to ANCXF (Ramsay); FO (S) 1944–5; FO (Air), Far E 1947; VA 1948; 5SL & DCNS, VCNS 1949–51; Adm 1951; C-in-C Home F 1952; C-in-C Portsmouth 1954; Adm of Fleet 1955.
Prof (later Lord) Patrick M. S. Blackett (1897–1974): ent RN 1910; Falklands & Jutland; Lt 1918; sent to Cambridge by Admy & resigned to read maths & physics; Fellow, King's Coll; Prof Physics, Birkbeck Coll 1933; FRS 1933; Prof Physics, Manchester U 1937; Air Defence Cttee 1935, esp radar & bomb sights; Sci Advisor, A/A Cmd 1940; Op Research A/A & Coastal Cmds; Dir, Naval Op Research 1942; atomic bomb development; Nobel Prize 1948; Imperial Coll 1953; Sci Advisor to Govt 1964; Pres R Soc 1965; baron 1969.
[2]*Barham*'s casualties were 56 officers & 806 men killed.

201.   *To his wife*

11 December 1941

Of course I have no details – all I know is that I questioned at the time the use of sending just two ships like that. I assumed that appropriate reinforcements from the US Navy would join up with them before they attempted any operations but it doesn't appear that this occurred. As you know I always express my doubts about the advisability of sending out someone who had no personal experience of the war at sea. Tom P has always been an advocate of pushing on regardless of the consequences and I imagine that on this occasion he hoped to catch the Japanese party landing in N Malaya. But it was obvious they would be covered with shore based air from Thailand and I should think it was very doubtful indeed if we could provide shore based fighter support to those two ships. I personally would not have dreamt of taking up two Battleships like that without adequate air and surface support. In any case *Repulse* was a most unsuitable ship – I refused to have her in the Western Med because she had not been modernised and lacked proper A/A equipment. Altogether a deplorable and tragic business.

202   *To North*

11 December 1941

. . . Alas our forecasts about Tom P were only too true. I felt in my bones all the time that he would have to pay sooner or later for his lack of practical war experience & his lack of sea sense but I did not imagine it would have to be at such a price. . . . I assumed that in the event of war with Japan they would either be reinforced forthwith by an American squadron or else withdraw to Trinco[malee] until the Americans were ready to reinforce. Battleships by themselves are quite useless whilst co-operation with shore based aircraft requires a lot of practice *and* experience. It's all very lamentable and should not have happened.

What the next move will be I can't say but if I'm to be marooned here for long I'd sooner pop home and take a spell of leave. . . .

203.   *To his wife*

15 December 1941

Have just had a strictly personal signal from the Admiralty to say that I may be required to take command of the Far East Fleet. Consequently

Syfret is being sent out to relieve me and I am to return home to study the situation and also have 'some well earned leave'. Well that's that. I shall of course do whatever I am asked to do. Apart from J. H. D. Cunningham there is no-one on the Vice Admiral's list who seems specially suitable and I imagine they want someone with enough seniority to hold his own with the Yanks. . . .

204. *To Cunningham*

16 December 1941

. . . Syfret, in my opinion, is a very sound chap and [if] I'd been asked to make a selection I should have chosen him. . . . I think the time has come when Force H should be made part of the N Atlantic command and when one officer should have the responsibility of deciding how the available forces – especially destroyers – should be employed. Whether the Senior Officer should be ashore or afloat is a matter of opinion but I think he should be ashore. But I believe you want a really good fellow here as FOCNA with a really good staff. When Force H is augmented to carry out some specific operation it should be possible to augment the staff afloat, temporarily, from the staff ashore. I have made a point of offering my staff to Fred during the recent intensive U-boat hunts but he seems reluctant to use them. Very much afraid of my 'butting in' I think. This [is] all wrong as we ought to get all our heads together to deal with these problems.

I am convinced, as you appear to be, that a Straits patrol is unable to prevent U-boats passing into the Mediterranean. We must try and get them either in the western or eastern approaches. So far the organised destroyer and corvette hunts have been ineffective so far as 'kills' are concerned. The latter have all been obtained by more or less fortuitous encounters.

Bad luck about *Galatea*[1] – we have had an easy time with the Iti U-boats but these Huns are a different proposition. We've got 4 of them since Ark was sunk but I feel we ought to have had more. Lack of A/S training is one of the principal snags and here again there should be one authority to decide whether A/S craft are to be taken off patrols, etc. in order to do A/S exercises and whether submarines are to be used for training. A nice balance must be kept but it is no use assuming that because a ship has asdics she's an effective A/S unit.

I shall be sorry to leave Force H though I must admit that in its present

---

[1]*Galatea* was sunk off Alexandria by *U557* on 15 Dec 1941.

state of immobility I get exceedingly restive. It seems that I can do nothing effective to ease the pressure on you and yet at this stage it's obviously important to keep the Itis occupied in the W. We have fitted up old *Argus* as an operational carrier but all her Stringbags are hunting U-boats and until we get them back she's not really fit for operations. . . .

205. *Report of Proceedings, 9–19 December 1941*

29 December 1941

10 December

10. Information was received from the Admiralty that owing to the lack of sufficient capital ship reinforcements it would not be possible to pass a convoy through to Malta from westwards during the January dark period, nor would it be possible for Force H to create a diversion in the Western Mediterranean whilst tankers were passed from Alexandria to Malta.

11 December

18. *Sikh*, *Maori*, *Legion* and *Isaac Sweers* sailed at 0530 for Malta to join the Eastern Mediterranean fleet. Their orders instructed them to simulate carrying out an A/S sweep until reaching long. 3° 30'E after which the Force was to close up and proceed at high speed practising evasion.
22. . . . Information was received that *Indomitable*[1] which it was understood would relieve *Ark Royal* in Force H, had been ordered to proceed to the Cape.

13 December

29. Information was received that Group I had sighted an Italian force of 2 cruisers and 2 torpedo boats steering to southward ahead of them near Cape Bon. Action was joined with the result that one cruiser and one torpedo boat were sunk and a cruiser left on fire. The latter apparently sank later. No damage or casualties were sustained by our destroyers.[2]
36. In reply to a suggestion by the C-in-C, Mediterranean, that the present time might be a suitable one for sending merchant ships W from Malta, the Vice Admiral, Malta, stated that Group I destroyers had been

---

[1]For ferrying Hurricanes to the Far E.
[2]The cruisers were *Alberto di Giussano* & *Alberico da Barbiano*: 1931, 5200t, 8×6in, 6×3.9in, 4tt, 37k.

shadowed during the day prior to their arrival in Malta, and he considered this in conjunction with the presence of many U-boats in the Western Mediterranean, made it inadvisable to send these ships for the present.

15 December

44.   At 1042 *Nestor,* on passage to Gibraltar in company with *Gurkha, Foxhound* and *Croome,* sighted a submarine at 15,000 yards and turned towards to attack. At 1114 contact was obtained on a bearing 230°, range 1600 yards; the ship turned towards and commenced attack at a range of 900 yards. A pattern of 5 charges was fired on the target at 1118. *Foxhound* obtained contact on completion of *Nestor*'s attack, but on the run in contact was lost and charges were not fired. On passing over the position where *Nestor* had fired, *Foxhound* heard and felt a heavy explosion directly underneath. *Nestor,* who was by this time about 2000 yards from *Foxhound,* also heard this explosion. About 5 minutes after the explosion, *Croome* closed the position where *Nestor*'s charges had been dropped, and having obtained a firm contact, fired a pattern of 5 charges, though contact on this occasion was fair only. The results of the search were at first negative, but subsequently a large oil patch was seen in the position of *Nestor*'s first attack, in which there was a large quantity of wreckage in very small pieces. The wreckage included pieces of human flesh, clothing marked with German names, gratings, etc.

I consider that the destruction of the U-boat was achieved as a result of *Nestor*'s attack[1].

17 December

48.   . . . At 0918 A/S patrol from *Audacity* reported sighting a U-boat 22 miles on the port beam of Convoy HG 76. *Stork, Blankney, Exmoor, Stanley* and *Pentstemon* were detached to attack, and after a doubtful contact had been investigated the U-boat was sighted from *Stanley,* and fire was opened from 7 miles range by *Blankney, Exmoor, Stanley* and *Stork. Audacity*'s aircraft, whilst carrying out an attack on the submarine, was shot down, the pilot being killed.[2]

The U-boat returned the fire of the ships and did not attempt to submerge; she finally sank . . . 55 prisoners were taken.

51.   At 1306, . . . *Stork* sighted a U-boat bearing 60° 10 miles distant, . . . *Stork* closed, obtained a good contact and succeeded in sinking the submarine *(U-131)* at 1339.[3]

---

[1]*Croome*: 'Hunt' class. *U127.*
[2]*Stork*: 1936, 1190t, 6×4in, 18.75k. *Blankney, Exmoor*: 'Hunt' class. *Stanley*: ex-US destroyer *McCalla,* 1919, 1190t, 1×4in, 3tt, 30k; sunk 19 Dec 1941, *U574.*
[3]Paras 48 & 51 relate to the same sinking *(U131).*

18 December

53.   Whilst escorting Convoy HG76, . . . at 0651, *Stanley* sighted a U-boat on the surface bearing 190° distant 6 miles. *Blankney* and *Stanley* proceeded to attack and the submarine dived immediately. Contact was gained at 0929 and a pattern of 6 charges was fired by *Blankney* at 0934. *Stanley*'s A/S was out of action, but she fired a 14-charge pattern as directed by *Blankney*. The latter, proceeding at slow speed, had closed to 600 yards by the time all *Stanley*'s charges had fired, and decided to attack again at once, before the U-boat commander had had time to recover from the effect of *Stanley*'s attack. *Blankney* accordingly steered straight for the contact and dropped a pattern of 6 charges. The submarine surfaced at 0948, about 2000 yards distant; *Blankney* increased to full speed to ram and opened fire with No. 1 gun. The enemy commenced to abandon ship, with the exception of the 1st Lieut. who continued to fire at the ship until *Blankney* struck the submarine a glancing blow. In a few minutes the submarine blew up. Survivors of this submarine stated she was *U-434*.

19 December

58.   A U-boat having been sighted . . . on the port beam of Convoy HG 76 at dusk the previous evening, *Stanley, Convolvulus* and *Pentstemon* were left searching for her. At 0415 *Stanley* was torpedoed and sunk. A/S contact was obtained by *Stork* and two attacks carried out, after which the submarine surfaced and attempted to escape. Fire was opened from Lewis guns, and *Stork* then rammed and fired a 10-charge pattern, sinking the submarine and completing her hat-trick. Survivors of the boat stated she was *U-574*.[1]

59.   At 1030 *Malaya,* screened by *Laforey, Foxhound, Hesperus, Whitehall, Nestor, Fortune, Arrow, Campbeltown, Zulu* and *Gurkha*, sailed to the westward for practice firings.[2]

---

[1]The same U-boat that had sunk *Stanley*. The escort was commanded by Cmdr F. J. Walker in *Stork*: the greatest escort group commander; Cdr 1931; Exprmtl Dept, A/S Est *Osprey* (Portland) 1937; SO (O & A/S) *Lynx* Nov 1939; *Stork* Oct 1941; Capt June 1942; *Starling* 1943; d 1944. *U567* was destroyed by *Deptford* & *Samphire* of the group on 21 Dec but *Audacity* was torpedoed on the same day by *U751*.

[2]*Whitehall*: 1924, 1120t, 4×4.7in, 3tt, 31k. *Arrow*: 1930, 1350t, 4×4.7in, 8tt, 35k; irreparably damaged in explosion, Algiers 1943. *Campbeltown*: ex-US destroyer *Buchanan*, 1919, 1090t, 1×4in, 3tt, 30k; used to ram and blow up dock gates at St Nazaire 28 March 1942.

206. *To Cunningham*

21 December 1941

. . . The *Prince of Wales* and *Repulse* affair seems to have been a thoroughly bad show. No air support, but in any case fancy relying on quite untried shore based air for cover! Why the hell didn't they send *someone* out there who has been through the mill and knew his stuff. I'm completely in the dark as to what is now proposed but have written to DP to say that if it is seriously intended I should go out E I don't want any leave but want to get my hand on the party as soon as possible to wake them up. . . .

207. *Report of Proceedings 20–31 December 1941*

1 January 1942

20 December

2.   At 0900, *Argus*, *Hermione*, *Laforey*, *Zulu*, *Gurkha*, *Nestor*, *Arrow*, *Foxhound*, *Whitehall*, *Hesperus* and *Fortune*, sailed to the E of Gibraltar for exercises, returning at 1800. . . .

3.   I reported to the Admiralty and C-in-C, Mediterranean, the situation regarding destroyers available for screening at Gibraltar. Advantage had been taken of the presence of Group II destroyers to exercise *Malaya* and *Argus* for one day each, but after Group II had left, escort commitments would reduce the number available for Force H or patrols to 5 or 6, depending on the numbers boiler-cleaning or defective. The same number would be available should Force H be required to put to sea in an emergency.

Apart from these considerations, the present U-boat dispositions in the vicinity of the Straits precluded the possibility of carrying out further practices until about 7 January.

21 December

8.   At 0320 a Swordfish, after obtaining an ASV contact, sighted a U-boat on the surface in position Cape Spartel, 13 miles. Complete surprise was achieved and the submarine made no attempt to dive or reduce speed. Attack was carried out with 3 depth charges which straddled the submarine's course, the centre charge exploding directly under her. By the light of flares the aircraft observed a large patch of oil, and the submarine had disappeared. Flare floats were dropped to indicate the posi-

tion to patrol vessel *Myosotis*, who subsequently picked up the only survivor, Oberleutnant Hohler. The submarine was *U-451*.[1]

22 December

14.   At 0530 HMS *Dido*[2] and Group II destroyers, comprising *Gurkha, Zulu, Nestor, Foxhound and Arrow*, sailed for Malta. . . .

25 December

36.   Christmas Day was observed in the traditional manner in so far as this could be done without impairing the readiness of all ships for immediate action. I visited all ships under my command during the forenoon.

The air-raid alert was sounded at 1430, and all forces stood to. This and a subsequent alert at 2130 served to remind everyone that no relaxation was permitted on account of Christmas Day.

28 December

37.   At 1830 I received information that photographic reconnaissance of Brest had failed. The Admiralty observed that the possibility could not be ignored that *Gneisenau* might attempt to make the passage of the Straits.

Ships of Force H and all available destroyers were brought to two hours' notice for steam, and patrols were warned accordingly. Torpedoes were transferred from *Argus* to the North Front for the arming of a Swordfish striking force if required.

Clyde[3] was sailed by VACNA to carry out a patrol within 3 miles of position 154° Europa Point, 10 miles.

30 December

43.   I requested the Admiralty for any further information concerning the possibility that *Gneisenau* might attempt the passage of the Straits, or for an assessment of the probability of this happening, since the measures taken to counter such a movement considerably restricted the scale of A/S action by local air and surface forces.[4]

---

[1]*Myosotis*: 'Flower' class corvette. Swordfish from 812 Sqdn.
[2]Rear Admiral H. E. Diesen (1882–1953), head of the Royal Norwegian Navy, sailed aboard *Dido*: RA 1938; Ret List 1941; head of Naval District West 1945–7.
[3]*Clyde*: 1935, 1850/2723t, 6tt, 1×4in, 22.5/10k.
[4]The attempt was not made.

208.   *Pocket diary, 1942*

3 January

My last day in Force H so busy packing. To *Argus* to say goodbye to officers and men and then to *Laforey* and *Malaya* where I also visited the wardroom. To Tower for Type 271 conference. . . . On board *Hermione* at 6.30. Fred[1] there to say goodbye. We slipped at 7 p.m. and proceeded. And so goodbye to Gib. and Force H.

---

[1] Adm Edward-Collins.

PART III

THE EASTERN FLEET

January 1942–August 1944

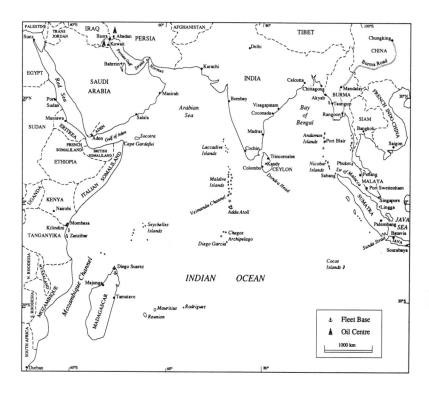

The Indian Ocean, 1942–1944

INTRODUCTION

For the United States the most traumatic event in the Pacific war was the attack on Pearl Harbor on 7 December 1941; for the British it was the sinking of the *Prince of Wales* and *Repulse* on 10 December. This is not the place to discuss the issues of whether Force Z should have been sent to the Far East, whether it should have been stationed at Singapore and whether Admiral Phillips should have acted as he did; these questions have been debated fully elsewhere.[1] However, the fate of Force Z did have major implications for Somerville's career and he expressed, both before Phillips went east and after his tragic death, strong views on the whole sorry adventure.

As early as October 1941, when the command structure and purpose of Force Z became known, Somerville had written to Cunningham full of a sense of foreboding [187, 191]. He criticised both the decision to send the two capital ships to the east, believing correctly that it was an entirely political decision,[2] and the selection of its high command, on the sound professional grounds that none of the three flag officers, Acting Admiral Tom Phillips, Vice Admiral W. E. C. Tait and Rear Admiral Stuart Bonham-Carter, had sea-going experience in this war and in particular were ignorant of the awesome power of massed air attacks. It is true that Somerville had little regard for Phillips, holding him responsible, along with Churchill, for most of the wild schemes proposed for the Mediterranean and for the hasty and inexcusable board of inquiry into the Cape Spartivento action and other attempts to relieve him from Force H. When news of the disaster filtered through to Force H, Somerville was in a position to say 'I told you so' [201, 202, 206, 208]. He condemned the despatch of a token force, unless it could have formed part of a formidable Anglo-American fleet, which before 7 December was diplomatically, and afterwards militarily, impossible. His own experience in the western Mediterranean and the Royal Navy's hard-earned knowledge off Norway, Dunkirk, Crete and elsewhere demonstrated the

---

[1]On the whole sorry business of Force Z, see A.J. Marder, *Old Friends, New Enemies:The Royal Navy and the Imperial Japanese Navy*, vol.1, *Strategic Illusions* (Oxford: Oxford U Pr, 1981), *passim*, and C. Barnett, *Engage the Enemy More Closely*, pp. 376–422.

[2]See S. W. Roskill, *Churchill and the Admirals*, pp. 196–203.

inability of ships to operate within reach of shore-based bombers without adequate fighter cover, a basic rule apparently ignored by Phillips. Like many senior officers, Somerville seems to have felt that Singapore was indefensible and that any force sent out should have been based either on Australia or Ceylon. He was equally insistent on constant training for all eventualities and guessed that little had been done to bring Force Z up to the standard of fighting efficiency considered necessary in Force H.

Of vastly greater importance was the consequence for Somerville of Phillip's demise. Within two or three days of the catastrophe, the Admiralty had begun to organise a new and more substantial fleet for the Far East and had sounded out Somerville as its prospective commander [202]. It is not clear why Somerville was chosen. It may have been because of his successful experience against great odds, his deservedly high reputation as a fleet trainer and handler, his grasp of air power, both seaborne and land-based, or his seniority. His qualities of leadership and his ability to foster high morale in difficult circumstances would be of immense value in the desperate situation created in the Far East by the early Japanese triumphs. Furthermore, he was known to be kicking his heels at Gibraltar, having difficulties with Edward-Collins and in need of a sea change. However, after spending most of January 1942 at the Admiralty briefing his successor, Vice Admiral Syfret, and discussing with the naval staff the situation in the Far East, he was appointed to command the new Eastern Fleet, the advance elements of which were scheduled to leave the Clyde in mid-February [203, 206, 208].

Somerville's preparations for his new post revealed clearly both the fruits of his wartime experience and his general approach to the business of high command. He began by insisting on flag and staff officers who had recent sea-going experience and in particular men who had undergone frequent and heavy air attacks. He required, too, men who were as quick of mind and as dynamic as himself. When he arrived at the Admiralty early in January, he found that Vice Admiral Tait, who had not been with Phillips in the debacle, was nevertheless expected to remain as second-in-command and he at once protested vigorously at this assumption. He objected to Tait simply on the grounds of lack of 'personal experience of active sea conditions at sea during the present war' [210]. One would have thought, after Phillips's lamentable last voyage, that the Admiralty would have drawn the same conclusion and reassigned Tait but, despite Somerville's adamant stand, Alexander and Pound sought several times to reverse their earlier acquiescence to his firm demand and the issue was in doubt until the day of Somerville's departure from London [209, 211]. Somerville's obduracy was based on his determination to avoid a further disaster and his perceptive grasp of the strategic situation, his likely naval resources, their role and the training required to raise them to an acceptable standard. His successful insistence on the right appointments displays his fundamental clarity of purpose, foresight and uncompromising professionalism. Few officers of his rank matched him in these qualities; that the Admiralty appreciated his services, abilities and the scale of his forthcoming task was indicated by his promotion to the rank of Admiral, though still on the Retired List.

Somerville left the Clyde in the modern carrier *Formidable* on 17 February [211, 212] and arrived in Colombo some six weeks later, hoisting his flag in command of the Eastern Fleet on 28 March. During the long voyage to the Indian Ocean, several tasks occupied him. The constantly deteriorating situation in the Far East led to several exchanges with the Admiralty further defining the role of the Eastern Fleet, its relations with other parts of the naval establishment in the east and with the other services, and the ships that were to join it, both in the short term and in due course [214–26]. On the face of it, Somerville would have a powerful fleet but most of the ships suffered from one or more major deficiencies: lack of modernisation, the need for a refit, little recent war experience, and unfamiliarity with fleet work. Given these shortcomings, Somerville would have to stand on the defensive until he had welded his heterogenous command into a fleet approaching Force H's legendary efficiency. He quickly put into practice what he had preached at the time of Phillips's departure, a comprehensive training programme, starting from the most basic exercises and driving his ships and aircraft hard all the way from Biscay to Capetown. Confirmation of the dire need for this rigorous schedule came almost on departure from the Clyde. His temporary flagship *Formidable*, severely damaged off Crete in May 1941, had spent the rest of the year in dockyard hands in the USA where her crew had experienced the lavish and overwhelming hospitality characteristic of the Americans and extended to an increasing number of British warships. Somerville felt that this made ships' companies soft, complacent and slack. Apart from her need to shed the effects of peacetime luxury, *Formidable* had also to cope with air squadrons for the most part straight from flying school. Since everyone around him was either green or ignorant of the situation and the urgent need to improve performance, Somerville had to shoulder the full direction of his force's remedial education. As naval air power was likely to be the crucial factor in future operations, and as he was well versed in its handling, his immediate task was to drill the carrier's airmen and flight deck party in everything from the ability to take off and land safely and quickly, to accurate navigation, and to carry out fighter interception and torpedo launching as well as informative reconnaissance operations. The lamentable state of affairs he found on arrival is amply documented in his letters, diary and reports on the outward voyage. Constant practice did improve performance but not to combat standard; several weeks' further exercising in company with the assembled Eastern Fleet would be required before operations were possible.

What, then, was to be the new fleet's role? Both imperial geography and enemy pressures decreed that it should be an Indian Ocean fleet. That vast sea was a crucial strategic area for the British Empire, especially as convoys could not then pass through the Mediterranean; in early 1942, all men and material for the defence of Egypt had to be sent through the Indian Ocean. A considerable proportion of its territory, communications, bases and resources lay around it. The Cape and Suez routes to Asia and Australasia crossed it, as did the line to the Persian Gulf oilfields, the principal source of the Empire's oil. From its shores came many vital raw materials and it was termed 'a pivotal area of global strategy'.[1] Britain had dominated the area for two hundred years yet by this time the Indian Ocean was a weak link in the imperial chain. It lacked an industrial base; manufactured goods had to be brought thousands of miles. There were no first class bases between Suez and Singapore and such bases as existed lacked adequate defences, equipment, skilled labour and local support structures. India, supposedly the jewel in the imperial crown, was in reality a gross liability, increasingly restless under the British yoke. South Africa, Egypt, Iraq and Iran were unreliable associates. Nature was distinctly unhelpful – vast distances, deserts and jungles, the world's highest mountains, monsoons and an enervating climate, and overpopulation in many lands. There was no concrete pre-war strategy for the region. The only guiding principle was the entirely negative (and complacent) one that the region was unlikely to be threatened, cushioned as it was by substantial forces in the Middle East and at Singapore. However, by late 1941 there was a dawning realisation that the area could not be protected against a determined and co-ordinated Axis attack. The imperial bluff was about to be called, overstretch was about to lead to overbalancing. Between December 1941 and June 1942, the Axis threat was at its most dire and came simultaneously from three directions. The German thrust into the Crimea

---

[1]H. P. Willmott, *The Barrier and the Javelin: Japanese and Allied Pacific Strategies, February to June 1942* (Annapolis, Md: Naval Inst Pr, 1983), pp. 47–50.

might very easily turn south to the Gulf oilfields, while Rommel might seize the Suez Canal; in the east, the Japanese rampaged northwards from Singapore, through Burma, to the gates of India.

Should the Axis succeed in co-ordinating their strategy, there was little to prevent their overwhelming and rapid triumph. Both the Eighth Army and the Russians were in headlong retreat and the once-formidable Mediterranean Fleet was reduced to a handful of cruisers and destroyers, while the Luftwaffe ruled the skies above it. In the east, the RAF, never prominent, had virtually ceased to exist, while the Army, streaming dazedly from Burma into India, was demoralised by its own inept leadership, inadequate training, deficient equipment and dismal inability to cope with either the jungle or the troops of a nation dismissed contemptuously by British leaders a few weeks earlier. Such territory as the British still held remained vulnerable to both external attack and internal rebellion, for the triumph of the Asiatic Japanese had destroyed for ever the myth of Western superiority.

Despite the desperate plight of this vital area, Churchill could offer it little assistance in the foreseeable future. It is little wonder that the Chiefs of Staff confessed in April 1942 that 'we are in real danger of losing our Indian Empire'. The Prime Minister, whose strategic vision veered wildly between the patently absurd and the stunningly brilliant, was in his more perceptive mode when he told Roosevelt on 15 April:

> Until we are able to fight a fleet action there is no reason why the Japanese should not become the dominating factor in the Western Indian Ocean. This would result in the collapse of our whole position in the Middle East, not only because of the interruption of our convoys to the Middle East and India, but also because of the interruption to the oil supplies from Abadan, without which we cannot maintain our position either at sea or on land in the Indian Ocean Area. Supplies to Russia via the Persian Gulf would also be cut. With so much of the weight of Japan thrown upon us we have more than we can bear.[1]

Given these strategic verities in the Indian Ocean and the inability of their principal Allies to assist them, what could the British do? General

---

[1] J. R. M. Butler, *Grand Strategy*, vol 3, pt 2, June 1941–August 1942, p. 484; M. Howard, vol 4, August 1942–September 1943, pp. 51–5 (London: HMSO, 1964 & 1972); Marder et al., *Old Friends, New Enemies*, vol 2, *The Pacific War* (1990), pp. 3–80, 96–8; W. Kimball, *Churchill and Roosevelt: The Complete Correspondence* (Princeton, NJ: Princeton UP, 1984, 3 vols), vol 1, pp. 298–301, 381, 411–12, 418, 438–9, esp. 452–4.

Alexander,[1] having extracted the Army from Burma with some skill, set about reorganising it for the defence of India. The RAF scraped up aircraft from elsewhere for the defence of Indian ports, Ceylon, the trade routes and the airlift to China. However, for the first half of 1942, the principal threat was likely to come upon the sea and the Eastern Fleet therefore assumed prime importance in British strategy. Should our enemies sever the lines of communication between the home islands, Egypt, the Gulf and Australia, they would have taken a giant stride towards ultimate victory. On the other hand, the restoration of historic British dominance in the region would contribute only indirectly to the defeat of the Axis. In a nutshell, the war could not be won in the Indian Ocean but it might very well be lost there.

The strategic situation as Somerville set sail was that Ceylon was being developed as our principal base, Vice Admiral Layton[2] being given dictatorial powers as Commander-in-Chief there [219, 222, 228]. Though Japanese intentions following their conquest of Burma were unclear, most senior officers expected attacks against Ceylon and our sea lanes. Somerville, supported by his new second-in-command, Vice Admiral Willis,[3] whom he met at Capetown, and Layton, rejected Admiralty suggestions that Ceylon should be defended principally by naval forces; the likely scale of Japanese attack would overwhelm them and the proper defence of Ceylon was by adequate shore-based air power [215, 216, 217, 220, 221, 224, 225]. Somerville, relieved to find that Willis thought along the same lines, proposed to keep his fleet 'in being', avoid attrition, defend the sea lanes and train it thoroughly so that when substantial reinforcements of modern ships and aircraft became available he could use it offensively as a fast carrier task force, a form of

[1]Gen (later Field Marshal Earl, of Tunisia) Harold R. L. G. Alexander (1891–1969): Irish Gds 1911; France 1914–19; Capt 1915; Maj 1915; Lt-Col 1917; Actg Brig-Gen 1918; E Europe after war; CO, Irish Gds, Constantinople 1922; Staff Coll 1926–7; IDC; SO 1931–4; NW Frontier 1934; Maj-Gen 1937; 1st Div 1938; I Corps, Dunkirk 1940; Lt-Gen 1940; S Cmd; Burma Feb 1942; C-in-C, Middle E Aug 1942; Dep C-in-C to Eisenhower, 1943; 15 Army Group, Sicily; FM 1944; SAC Med 1944–5; Visct 1946; Gov-Gen, Canada 1946-52; Earl 1952; Minr Defence 1952–4.

[2]Vice Adm (later Adm) Sir Geoffrey L. Layton: Capt 1922; RA 1935; VA 1938; VA, 1BS & 2nd-in-C, Med F Aug 1939; VA, 18CS Home F Nov 1939; C-in-C China Sta July 1940; C-in-C Eastern F Dec 1941–March 1942; C-in-C Ceylon March 1942–Aug 1944; C-in-C Portsmouth Aug 1944.

[3]Vice Adm (later Adm of the Fleet Sir) Algernon U. Willis (1889–1976): *Britannia* 1903; Lt 1909; torpedo splist; Grand F 1916–18; Cdr 1922; Capt 1929; N War Coll 1930–2; *Kent* China Sta 1933–4; *Nelson*, Home F 1934–5; *Vernon* i/c 1935–8; *Barham*, Med F 1938; Cdre & COS to C-in-C Med (Pound & Cunningham) 1939–March 1941; RA 1940; Actg VA & C-in-C S Atl Sept 1941–2; VA, 3BS & 2nd-in-C Eastern F March 1942; Force H i/c 1943; C-in-C Levant 1943; 2SL 1944–6; Adm 1945; C-in-C Med 1946–8; C-in–C Portsmouth 1948–50; Adm of Fleet 1949.

naval warfare to which he was already giving some thought and which was well suited to that vast ocean [217, 221, 222, 225, 228].

When Somerville arrived in Ceylon in the last week of March he found a confused situation and uncertainty over the enemy's next move, compounded by a lack of intelligence and reconnaissance, panic and gloom in much of the high command, and inter-service ignorance about each other's functions and forces [227, 228].[1] The dynamic and stout-hearted Layton was beginning to make an impression on Ceylon but Somerville had no chance to visit most of his new command before reports of an imminent Japanese attack on Ceylon forced him to put to sea at once to avoid an eastern 'Pearl Harbor'. In characteristic manner, Somerville sandwiched what training he could between collecting and organising his fleet and disposing it for possible action [229]. Now began the most testing time of his flag career; the first two weeks of his new command were a long drawn out nightmare.

Intelligence sources indicated a strike against Ceylon on about 1 April, though the date was uncertain and nothing was known of the purpose, nature, scale or duration of the attack. The likelihood was that it would be a tip-and-run raid but full scale landings could not be ruled out and there was almost certain to be a campaign by aircraft, surface raiders and submarines against our trade routes. It was likely that the Japanese would seek also to destroy Ceylon's port facilities and defences, destabilise India by terrorising the coast, and force the cessation of air supplies to China. In addition they might make a gesture towards Axis strategic co-operation by co-ordinating their operations with the German drives in Egypt and the Caucasus. Aware that a sizeable British fleet was being formed they would endeavour to whittle it down or perhaps seek a major fleet engagement; certainly they would want to impress Somerville with their might and overawe him.[2]

With his hastily gathered, untrained and ill-assorted fleet, which he divided into Force A (the more modern ships) and Force B (the older vessels, under Willis), Somerville could do little but patrol to the south of Ceylon until definite reports of the enemy's strength and line and speed of advance had been received from RAF long range reconnaissance. Were the Japanese force to be a cruiser and destroyer raiding party, he would be expected to engage it but if it contained carriers and battleships he would have to avoid action during daylight hours and rely on his exclusive possession of ASV radar to launch a night air attack. In the meantime he drilled his raw recruits – staff, airmen and ships –

---

[1]Marder, vol. 2, pp. 104–15; H. P. Willmott, *Empires in the Balance; Japanese and Allied Pacific Strategies to April 1942* (Annapolis, Md: Naval Inst Pr, 1982), pp. 435–40.
[2]Marder, vol. 2, pp. 81–94.

remorselessly, though he recognised it would take several weeks before they were properly combat-ready [229, 230]. When the 1 April deadline passed, Somerville was left with several problems. In the first place, his older vessels were short of water and oil and would require replenishment almost at once. Some of his ships were required urgently elsewhere – the old light carrier *Hermes* to train for the forthcoming landings in Madagascar, the heavy cruiser *Cornwall*[1] to escort a troop convoy from Ceylon to Australia, and her sister ship *Dorsetshire* to complete her interrupted refit at Colombo. It was still possible that the enemy would appear unexpectedly and in strength and catch him refuelling and with some important units in Ceylonese waters vulnerable to a 'Pearl Harbor' attack. Somerville had no choice but to leave his patrol area and refuel though, wisely, he avoided returning to Ceylon, steering instead for the remote atoll of Addu, then being developed as a secret emergency fleet base. However, though he thus guarded against being caught in Ceylon with his whole fleet, he had to accept the risks to *Hermes*, *Cornwall* and *Dorsetshire*; he could not unduly hold up other operations. Moreover, the information he had received about the enemy's intentions was extremely vague and might well be false; no enemy forces had been sighted.

Somerville arrived at the inhospitable Addu Atoll early on 4 April [230, 231] and commenced refuelling and watering. About half way through this lengthy process, he received an air sighting report of a substantial Japanese force, steaming north west and 350 miles south of Ceylon. He realised that he had no hope of catching the Japanese until the return leg of their assault on Colombo but hastened to complete refuelling in the hope of launching his projected night air attack. The strength of the Japanese force was still unclear and in fact Somerville seems never to have had an accurate report on its composition though he was aware that it included battleships and carriers. On hearing of the definite sighting, he exclaimed in typically earthy fashion 'Damn and *blast*, it looks as if I've been had' [230]. Though his initial reaction was one of disappointment at not being in a position to intercept the Japanese and perhaps prevent an attack on Ceylon, he was soon to learn that his enforced retirement to Addu Atoll was a true blessing in disguise. The Japanese had sent out their 'first eleven', Admiral Nagumo and five of his carriers fresh from their triumph at Pearl Harbor and embarking 350 aircraft, escorted by four fast battleships, three cruisers and 11 destroyers; in addition, Vice Admiral Ozawa led a commerce-raiding force con-

---

[1] *Cornwall*: 1928, 10,000t, 8×8in, 8×4in, 31.5k; sunk off Ceylon, 5 April 1942, Japanese carrier planes.

sisting of a light fleet carrier, six cruisers and 11 destroyers.[1] Neither qualitatively nor quantitatively was the Eastern Fleet a match for this armada; as Somerville's chief of staff confessed, 'they could polish us off in minutes'.[2]

When 127 Japanese carrier planes attacked Colombo on 5 April, they found the harbour virtually deserted, the alert Layton having sailed as many vessels as possible. However, *Cornwall* and *Dorsetshire*, ordered to rendezvous with Somerville, were sighted by Japanese reconnaissance aircraft and caught by over 50 dive bombers and sunk in fifteen minutes in an attack unparalleled in its clinical efficiency [238]. Somerville had felt 'no undue anxiety' over the cruisers, as they were 150 miles from Colombo and making 27 knots; this would have put them beyond the reach of British carrier aircraft – but evidently not the Japanese. Indeed, Somerville was fortunate not to share the same fate, as he was only 85 miles away at the time. He hoped to shadow Nagumo and launch his intended night attack but contact was lost. When daylight came on 6 April, he recognised that he had to remain well out of range of his awesome opponent. 'My appreciation was that the Japs would bomb Colombo and Trincomalee and then shin out of it as fast as they could to the east', he wrote; if he, too, stood to the east, the enemy, calculating that he would have turned westward, might be misled [230]. As with Nelson, the boldest course seemed likely to be the best one. In any case, he was determined to rescue the numerous survivors from the cruisers. His main force supported a high speed dash by a cruiser and two destroyers, returning with 1100 men, who had spent 30 hours in the sea [234, 238]. 'We knew Sir James would come back for us', survivors said and one of Somerville's staff remarked that it was 'one of the best reasons why sailors in his fleet worshipped him'.[3] It was nevertheless a mission fraught with great danger, for the Japanese were searching for him and at one point a plane was reported within 13 miles; Somerville's chief of staff, describing it as 'a very nasty situation', recalled that 'it was astonishing that they never found us'. [233]

The Japanese were, however, more intent on swinging round to the north east to attack Trincomalee, which they struck with 130 aircraft on 9 April, while another 90 planes despatched the fleeing *Hermes* and several other vessels [240]. During this time Ozawa's force 'have been roar-

---

[1]For information on Nagumo and Ozawa, see Marder, vol. 2, pp. 93–6. For respective naval strengths, see Kirby, vol. 2, App. IX, p. 448.
[2]Cdre Ralph Edwards, diary, 10 April 1942, REDW 2/7, Edwards Papers, Churchill A C.
[3]Vice Adm Sir W. Kaye Edden (a Cdr and SO (P) at the time) to Marder, 24 Feb 1977 (in possession of John Somerville). Marder, vol. 2, pp. 116–33.

ing up the Bay of Bengal and sinking merchant ships right and left'
[232]. It was, mercifully, the last blast of the east wind. The material and
psychological damage to the British Empire was substantial: one light
carrier, two heavy cruisers, two destroyers, a corvette, an armed merchant cruiser, 25 merchantmen and 39 aircraft, together with the destruction of port installations, and virtual elimination of air power in Ceylon,
the creation of panic in South India and the total disruption of the sub-
continent's sea communications, all for a handful of Japanese aircraft.[1]
The Japanese retired to Singapore and then, two months later, came
nemesis in the Coral Sea and off Midway. The Imperial Japanese Navy
was never again to be a serious threat in the Indian Ocean.

Somerville's hair-raising escapes alarmed Churchill. Recording that
'We had narrowly escaped a disastrous fleet action',[2] he ventured to the
First Sea Lord that Somerville had not explained satisfactorily 'the
imprudent dispersion of his forces'. To his credit, Pound defended the C-
in-C with vigour and Churchill, facing the Commons with yet another
bleak report, affirmed the Government's confidence in Somerville [242,
243, 245]. Nevertheless, the question must be asked: did Somerville
unduly hazard the Eastern Fleet?

The disasters at Pearl Harbor, to Force Z and in the Java Sea had
induced in Somerville a healthy respect for Japanese prowess. He cannot
be blamed for underestimating the speed and range of Japanese ships
and aircraft; solid information was hard to obtain, and this was the first
occasion on which these advantages had become clear. He was entirely
justified in placing himself athwart the enemy's probable line of advance
until he had gauged the enemy's strength; had the Japanese force been
merely Ozawa's raiders, he could have engaged it with confidence. The
lack of endurance, common to most British ships, and the absence of a
fleet train forced him to refuel several hundred miles away when the
enemy at last appeared; indeed, his handicap turned out to be a stroke of
good fortune. RAF reconnaissance, patchy and inexperienced, served
him badly – but there were only six Catalinas available and two were
shot down while gallantly closing Nagumo's force to relay accurate
details [245]. 'The most dangerous moment' was his daring rescue of the
cruisers' survivors, a step taken against the advice of his staff and captains. 'He knew full well the risk he was running'[3] but apart from the dic-

---

[1]The Japanese lost 33 aircraft during the raids on Colombo and Trincomalee. Marder,
vol. 2, pp. 134–6
[2]Churchill, *The Second World War*, vol. 4, *The Hinge of Fate* (London: Cassell, 1951),
p. 158.
[3]Vice Adm Sir Kay Edden to John Somerville, 24 July 1990 (in John Somerville's
possession).

tates of humanity and the need to conserve scarce trained manpower, he was determined to establish high morale in his fleet. Had he lost more ships in the rescue attempt, he would have been condemned – but what would have been said had he left 1100 men to drown? Moreover, he had to remain within Nagumo's consciousness to induce some measure of caution in the enemy and he was justified in believing that ASV gave him a chance of inflicting substantial damage on the Japanese in a night attack [241]. Willis believed that Somerville had hazarded the fleet unnecessarily[1] but he had snatched his men from under the enemy's noses and had made sure that his force was concentrated or in a position to support detached units; he flew extensive reconnaissances and he had radar warning of approaching aircraft. Moreover, once the cruiser survivors had been rescued, he made an elaborate detour on his return to Addu. He had clarity of purpose, iron resolve and accepted personal responsibility for the consequences of his actions. High command in war involves the constant calculation of risk and agonising decisions as to its acceptability in given circumstances. Along with judgment and experience must go an element of boldness and the willingness to do the unexpected. Somerville, surmising that the enemy must soon turn east and then north to attack Trincomalee, judged correctly, if with little margin, that he could probably carry out the rescue safely; he also took every possible precaution against being caught unawares and with his fleet scattered in penny packets. It is clear, however, from his letters to his wife, that he was under greater stress than ever before and that the experiences of 5 to 9 April 1942 shook him more than any other in his flag career [232, 234, 238].

Any sighs of relief that the fleet was largely intact, that Ceylon was still in our hands and that the damage there was not irreparable were tempered by the knowledge that the Japanese might return, that Axis submarines were likely to pose the biggest threat to our communications, that the enemy still had sizeable and well-trained shore-based air forces at hand, and that our strategic problems were no easier and their solution even more distant. Somerville wasted no time in analysing his situation in the light of 'black week'. Force B, the core of which was the four unmodernised 'R' class battleships, more of a liability than an asset, was despatched, with Admiralty blessing, to Kilindini in Kenya, while Somerville took Force A to the safe anchorage of Bombay. Addu, virtually undefended, made Somerville nervous and Ceylon was ruled out of bounds by the Admiralty, though Somerville needed no reminder that it

[1] Adm of the Fleet Sir Algernon Willis, 'General remarks on Gen. Kirby's History of the War against Japan, vol. 2', undated, WILLIS 5/5 Willis Papers, Churchill A C.

was likely to be unsafe for many months to come; while brief visits might be paid to both islands, a secure main base would have to be found elsewhere [235, 239, 247, 250].

Somerville's appreciation of the situation after Nagumo's sortie was that the Japanese had command of the eastern half of the ocean and that he could not challenge them until he had been substantially reinforced with modern ships and aircraft, with high speed and good endurance. He proposed to stay at sea as much as possible; not only was this safer than lengthy stays in harbour but it would keep the Japanese guessing as to the fleet's whereabouts and strength, forcing them to employ large forces in any future operations. Force B was to safeguard the vital communications with the Middle East and the Persian Gulf and Force A was to act as a fleet in being, taking care to avoid an engagement with both shore-based bombers and any substantial Japanese fleet [235]. Meanwhile, Somerville intended to get to know his staff, commanding officers and ships and to continue his high pressure training programme [238, 248]. His most pressing need was for up-to-date carrier aircraft reinforcements, planes capable of matching those of the Japanese [236, 240]. The respite afforded by Nagumo's withdrawal allowed Somerville to meet Wavell[1] and inform him about the limitations imposed on the Eastern Fleet [249–51]. It took Somerville several months to get Wavell to understand the naval situation [252] but Churchill and the Admiralty also needed to be convinced of the fleet's desperate position. Somerville drew the firm conclusion that Japanese air strength precluded daylight attacks by the British and that our own fleet's air defence depended on adequate numbers of high performance fighters, depressing news which was unpalatable to the authorities in London, who were slow to appreciate the sharp lessons taught by Nagumo's fliers [251, 254, 255, 256].[2]

The British still feared a co-ordinated Axis drive against their position in and around the Indian Ocean; in particular, they were concerned that the Vichy French who held Madagascar, situated close to our principal sea lanes, would follow the lead of Vichy Indo-China and permit the Japanese to occupy the island or use its harbours and airfields. Accordingly, early in May, British forces seized Diego Suarez;

[1]Gen (later Field Marshal Earl) Sir Archibald Wavell (1883–1950): from a mil family; Sandhurst 1990; Staff Coll 1911; W Front, Russia, Palestine 1914–18; WO & staff posts; Palestine i/c 1937; S Cmd 1938; C-in-C Middle E July 1939; C-in-C India July 1941; Sup Cmdr, ABDA 1942; Viceroy 1943–7; a scholar in several fields.

[2]The Japanese Navy O fighter (the Mitsubishi 'Zero' or 'Zeke') was superior to most Allied fighters of 1941–3: 1939, 2 cannon, 2 mg, 351 mph. See Cdre Edwards's diary for April 1942, REDW 2/7 and the exchange of messages between Churchill and Roosevelt, in Kimball, vol. 1, pp. 450, 452–6, 461, 464, 468–9.

Somerville supplied many of the escorting warships and with the remainder provided distant cover [259], though further operations were required in September 1942 to pacify the remainder of the island [286, 287]. It is now known that the Japanese had no designs on Madagascar but more importantly the nightmare of an octopus-like squeeze from several Axis tentacles never materialised. Though the enemy powers divided their strategic responsibilities along longitude 70°E, their co-operation in the Indian Ocean theatre was even worse than that of the Allies. Our opponents remained indifferent to each other's possibilities, ambitions and requirements and pursued their own aims without reference to their partners. For the Japanese, the Indian Ocean was good teasing ground but strategically beyond their capacity to conquer or dominate except close to the shores they held already. By June 1942, after their crippling losses in the Coral Sea and at Midway, they were at full stretch; the Indian Ocean was a sea too far. If the British fought a five-ocean war with a two-ocean navy, the Japanese fought a two-ocean war with a one-ocean navy. Thus the British, bereft of the means to resist further encroachments, were let off the hook.[1]

The destruction of Japan's offensive capability, the climax of the developing crisis in the eastern Mediterranean in the summer of 1942, the development of a loosely integrated Axis submarine campaign in the Indian Ocean and later the TORCH operations in the western Mediterranean led to the whittling down of Somerville's fleet. Indeed, between the summer of 1942 and the spring of 1944, it was a fleet in name only, consisting chiefly of a handful of cruisers, destroyers and escort vessels engaged on convoy operations. No offensive operations were possible, other than occasional feints to the east. In an operational sense Somerville was becalmed in the doldrums but as busy as ever, training his forces, liaising with statesmen and commanders in India, Ceylon and South Africa, supervising the development of base facilities all round the shores of the Indian Ocean and all the time dreaming of a reconstituted battle fleet and carrier task force to enable him to take revenge on the Japanese, preferably in a fleet engagement.

Somerville's first requirement was a secure base and, after considering several possibilities, he decided on Kilindini. It was relatively undeveloped, had an awkward entrance and was rather cramped when the whole fleet was there but it was safe and ideally situated for the fleet's main role, the defence of the convoy routes. Somerville set up his headquarters at Government House, though he spent little time there, his

---

[1]Willmott, *Barrier and Javelin, passim*; Marder, vol. 2, pp. 137–51, 155–6; S. W. Kirby, *The War Against Japan*, vol. 2, *India's Most Dangerous Hour* (London: HMSO, 1958), pp. 127–31.

Chief of Staff ashore, Vice Admiral Danckwerts,[1] being chiefly responsible for the local organisation and the convoys [260, 262, 263, 264, 266, 270, 273]. In the meantime, energetic steps were taken to improve the air defences and port facilities of Colombo and Trincomalee, preparatory to the eventual return there of the Eastern Fleet, which took place in September 1943 [302, 312, 313].

During his sojourn at Kilindini, Somerville found that his fleet became virtually a floating reserve for operations elsewhere, especially in the Mediterranean. Within a few months of his arrival in the east, he had lost his carriers and battleships and had to voyage between his various bases by cruiser. Even when he had capital ships available, his shortage of destroyers often prevented him going to sea [262, 263, 264, 277, 283, 284, 286, 288, 290, 291, 292, 297, 299, 300, 303, 315]. The supply of modern carrier aircraft and the availability of long range shore based reconnaissance planes presented continuing problems [261, 273, 274, 278, 282, 297, 312]. Despite pressure from London and Washington for offensive operations [265, 268, 269, 273, 275, 276], Somerville was able to undertake only deception schemes [298, 302] and brief feints into the Bay of Bengal, studiously avoiding coming within range of the formidable Japanese land-based bombers [264, 265, 272, 279, 281, 282, 283, 300]. These caused an occasional flurry of air and radio activity on the part of the Japanese but their main purpose, distracting Japanese attention from forthcoming American offensives in the Pacific, does not seem to have been achieved. Otherwise, Somerville's forces were stretched to the extreme in the bid to defend the sea lanes against surface raiders, fortunately a rare threat, and submarines, both German and Japanese, which on occasion inflicted severe losses. Somerville moved his scarce air and naval resources to threatened areas but had insufficient escort craft to convoy all mechantmen. The defence of trade became his main preoccupation – and headache – during his stay in East Africa [267, 277–80, 290, 293, 294, 299, 301, 303, 305, 306, 312, 317].[2] With the constant departure of ships to tasks elsewhere and the frantic attempt to plug holes in trade defence, training in fleet operations had to be fitted in on voyages undertaken for other purposes [273, 285, 312].

Somerville spent as much time at sea as he could, for not only did he

---

[1] Actg Vice Adm Victor H. Danckwerts: Capt 1930; DP 1938–Jan 1940; Admy 1940–1; Ret List June 1941; COS (Shore), Eastern F, March 1942; d 1 March 1944.

[2] On IRONCLAD, the operation against Diego Suarez, see Kirby, vol. 2, pp 133–44. On the Fleet's operations in the period spring 1942–end 1943, see C. Barnett, *Engage the Enemy More Closely*, pp. 862–8; S. W. Roskill, *The War at Sea*, vol. 2 (London: HMSO, 1956), pp. 185–92, 236–8; vol. 3, pt. 1 (London: HMSO, 1960), pp. 219–21; Marder, vol. 2, pp. 137–219.

believe that the fleet commander should be sea-going but also he was by nature a deck rather than a desk sailor. Nevertheless, as time went on, it became necessary for him to go ashore more frequently and for lengthy spells. It was necessary for him to inspect his scattered bases and to liaise with the authorities in the countries for whose defence he was in part responsible. He enjoyed his visits to South Africa, where he made firm friends with the Prime Minister, Smuts [295, 306] but he was less happy in the enervating and bureaucratic atmosphere of Delhi. It was necessary, however, to consult with the Viceroy,[1] the C-in-C, India (Wavell) and his own naval colleagues [273, 278, 297, 298, 301] from time to time, increasingly about proposed combined operations in Burma and islands to the south [273, 302–04, 307, 310–13], all abortive exercises since the necessary forces could not be spared from the Mediterranean and Pacific. He found Wavell rather inclined to act as if he was a Supreme Commander, a notion to which Somerville was opposed [285, 301] and at times his close friend Geoffrey Layton took a rather proprietorial attitude to the Eastern Fleet, a tendency of which Somerville was quick to disabuse him [278, 282, 308]. With his own staff, especially Willis, Danckwerts and Tennant and those who served on board ship with him, he had excellent relations [273, 288].

On two occasions Somerville was summoned home to discuss future operations, including proposed landings in Burma or the East Indies islands. The first occasion was in November 1942 but following talks in London again in May 1943, Churchill whisked Somerville and his fellow commanders from the Indian theatre off to Washington [296, 297, 307, 310, 311]. Somerville seems to have got on well with the redoubtable Admiral King, the US Chief of Naval Operations,[2] though he had often complained about the lack of information about American naval operations in the Pacific, which hampered his own operational planning [270,

---

[1]The Marquis of Linlithgow (Victor A. J. Hope, 1887–1952): succ 1908; Col, TA 1914–18; Civil Ld, Admy 1922–4; Pres, Navy League 1924–31; Chm, Med Rsch Cncl; int in sci & agric; Chm, Jt Sel Cttee on Indian constnl rfm 1933–4; Viceroy 1936–Oct 1943; Chm Midland Bank 1944–52; pub svc in Scotland.

Field Marshal Jan Christian Smuts (1870–1950): Boer cdr 1899–1902; lawyer & poln; Minr Defence, Un of S Af 1910–19; as field cdr, evicted German forces from SW Af 1914–17; PM 1919–29, 1939–48; War Cab 1917–19.

[2]Adm (later Fleet Adm) Ernest J. King (1878–1956): US N Acad 1897–1901; Lt 1906; instr, staff & engineering appts; Lt-Cdr 1913; CO *Terry*, *Cassin* 1914; staff of Adm Mayo, C-in-C Atl Fleet Dec 1915–April 1919; Cdr 1917; N Acad 1919–22; S/M Div 11 1922–6; Capt & CO *Wright* 1926; qualified as pilot 1927; Bur Aeronautics & other aviation cmds; *Lexington* 1930–2; N War Coll 1932; RA & Chief, Bur Aeronautics 1933–6; further aviation commands; Cdr Patrol Force Atl Dec 1940; Adm & C-in-C Atl F Feb 1941; COM-INCH Dec 1941; CNO March 1942–Dec 1945; Fleet Adm Dec 1944; legendary figure, so tough he was reputed to shave with a blowlamp; see T. B. Buell, *Master of Sea Power* (Boston: Little, Brown, 1980).

288, 291, 295]. He was anxious to foster closer co-operation with the Americans in the South West Pacific theatre, though little was achieved before the spring of 1944 [273, 281, 285, 289, 294, 309–11].[1]

His visit to Washington in the spring of 1943 was, however, the prelude to two important events in the early autumn, the fleet's return to Ceylon and the establishment of the South East Asia Command, with Acting Admiral Lord Louis Mountbatten as Supreme Allied Commander [307, 310, 313, 314, 317]. Mountbatten's appointment came as a surprise to everyone, not least to Mountbatten himself but what lay behind it was Churchill's impatience with the inability of British forces to recover lost imperial territory and his increasing sensitivity to American jibes that the British in India would not and could not fight. From the spring of 1943, when the Allies began to consider how they might take the offensive, the Prime Minister had talked of a young fighting leader with drive, imagination, optimism and new ideas, capable of welding together the Chinese, American and Imperial forces on land and sea and in the air. Opinion in the Anglo-American high command was hardening towards a supreme command for South East Asia, though partly, one suspects, because every other theatre had one. Whatever the reason, the Churchill–Roosevelt summit at Quebec in August 1943 set up South East Asia Command, covering the eastern and central Indian Ocean, Burma, Ceylon, Malaya, Sumatra and sundry smaller islands (but not India, which, though it played host to most of SEAC's forces, remained a purely local, solely British command). Mountbatten, aged 43 and in substantive rank only a Captain, was an engaging, brave, resourceful, technically accomplished officer, on the fringes of the Royal family, and already spoken of as a future First Sea Lord. Elevated to the Directorship of Combined Operations in 1941 and made an Acting Vice Admiral, he had thus sat with the Chiefs of Staff and had met all of the American leaders. Not only did he seem to have all of the qualities for which the Premier was seeking, he had managed also to charm that prince of charmers, Franklin Roosevelt.[2]

[1] See Layton to Admy, 6 March 1942: 'I am in complete ignorance of what the [US] Pacific and Asiatic Fleets are doing', quoted in Butler, p. 484, who states (pp. 501–2) that 'co-operation amounted to hardly more than one admiral asking the other if he could take supporting action on some particular occasion'. See also Howard, pp 75–88, 95–107, 292–8.

[2] On Mountbatten generally, see P. Ziegler, *Mountbatten: the Official Biography* (London: Guild Publishing, 1985). On his appointment as SACSEA, see Thorne, *Allies of a Kind*, pp. 297–9; Howard, pp. 437–47. Churchill's *Directive* to Mountbatten of 21 October 1943 forms App 3 of S. W. Kirby, *The War Against Japan*, vol. 3 (London: HMSO, 1961) pp. 456–7. Also important is Churchill to Roosevelt, 13 June 1943, in Kimball, vol. 2, pp. 248–9; and Churchill to C. R. Attlee, 22 August 1943: 'There is no doubt of the need of a young and vigorous mind in this lethargic and stagnant Indian scene', in M. Gilbert, *Winston S. Churchill*, vol. 7, *The Road to Victory, 1941–1945* (London: Heinemann, 1986), p. 470.

Somerville, as surprised as everyone else by Mountbatten's appointment [313], nevertheless welcomed it warmly, feeling that Lord Louis would galvanise the high command in the region. He had a high regard for Mountbatten's abilities and had always been on good terms with him and therefore anticipated no difficulties. For his part, Mountbatten replied to Somerville's congratulatory wire with a degree of flattery and coyness and looked forward to working with a senior officer for whom he had immense respect and admiration. On the surface, therefore, the omens for a fruitful and friendly partnership were good. There were, however, straws in the wind which portended difficulties. Somerville was concerned that Mountbatten should not adopt a 'MacArthur set up'. In the South West Pacific theatre, General Douglas MacArthur[1] was in direct command of all air, sea and land forces and his naval chief was a definite subordinate who carried out plans drawn up by MacArthur's staff. Somerville believed that Mountbatten should adopt the 'Eisenhower model',[2] drawing upon the Mediterranean experience, in which Eisenhower had been merely the co-ordinating chairman of a committee of independent Commanders-in-Chief. Mountbatten seemed inclined to follow the Eisenhower pattern, though with substantially less bureaucracy, a promise quickly broken. He further promised to respect the fact that Somerville was operationally under the Admiralty's control and that his command covered also the western side of the ocean and the Persian Gulf, which lay beyond the bounds of the new supreme command but this was also to become a matter of contention. Mountbatten's directive gave him command of Somerville's forces only for combined operations; for all other aspects of sea warfare, Somerville retained full responsibility [318]. The Supreme Commander also courted controversy by appointing to his naval staff able but abrasive officers. Whatever hidden reservations Somerville harboured about the new command and commander, he did set out to co-operate with Mountbatten as amicably and fully as possible and to make available to the younger man his experience of the theatre and of high command. There was no lack of genuine friendship and goodwill in either party at the outset [319].

The undercurrent of doubt about the new man and his methods was

---

[1]Gen Douglas MacArthur (1880–1964): son of an inf capt; W Point 1899–1903; service in Philippines; engineer; Gen Staff, War Dept 1913–17; Col 1917; Brig-Gen, AEF 1917–18; outstanding combat record; Supt W Point 1919, reforming instn; Philippines 1922–30; Maj-Gen1925; corps cmd, USA; COS Nov 1930–Oct 1935; Mil Advisor to Philippines Govt Oct 1935; Gen & Cdr US Army in Far E July 1941; SAC, SW Pacific March 1942–April 1945; Gen of Army Dec 1944; Sup Cdr Allied Powers, Japan 1945–51; UN C-in-C, Korea July 1950; relieved of all commands by Pres Truman April 1951 following dispute over strategy & general policy; reputation as a general still matter of fierce debate but sizeable reputation as 'Viceroy' in postwar Japan.

[2]In which the Supreme Commander was in effect a chairman of the Cs-in-C committee.

present even from his arrival [321] and Somerville sensed that he would have to restrain both the energetic Supreme Commander and the less tactful members of his staff. Confusion over the roles of the Supreme Commander's staff and those of the Commanders-in-Chief was apparent from the beginning and though Mountbatten reiterated his desire to follow the Eisenhower pattern, the trend was clearly towards the MacArthur mode. Within a month of Lord Louis's arrival Somerville was struggling to hold the new establishment to its declared policy [325]. From that time until his departure from the station in August 1944, Somerville battled to uphold his prerogatives as a C-in-C and to get Mountbatten to commit himself finally to the Eisenhower prototype. The increasing differences between the two men overshadowed the remainder of Somerville's time in the Indian Ocean. It is not too much to say that at times be became obsessed with them and their constant repetition in his papers becomes tedious.

There were, however, important issues of command at stake for both men and their disagreements were frequently sharp and fundamental, dragging in Churchill and other senior military figures, including Americans. Nevertheless, they preserved an essential cordiality and their relationship resumed its previous warmth when Somerville moved to Washington, where he sought constantly to assist Mountbatten's operations and obtain for him due recognition of his achievements. There were several broad but related areas where their views clashed. The basic conflict was over the nature of the new command. Somerville was convinced that a supreme commander could not direct the operations of all the forces, organised in several commands, across this vast theatre and that he should concentrate on combined operations involving forces from several nations or from different services, though even then exercising no more than a presiding role over these activities to ensure harmony and integration with other aspects of theatre strategy. Mountbatten, though professing a personal preference for the Eisenhower model [314, 322, 327] insisted that Churchill, the Americans and our own Chiefs of Staff intended him to be more like MacArthur [326, 338]. Mountbatten distorted the truth; others present when he was appointed recalled no such instructions.[1] Somerville, by character and status the most independent of the three British Cs-in-C, set himself the task of warning Mountbatten of the impracticality and dangers of adopting a MacArthur model and stood his ground firmly, recognising that the Supreme Commander and his staff viewed him as a troublemaker [325, 339, 353, 388]. He advised Mountbatten that a centralised system would breed inefficiency and rancour and constantly

[1]See S.W. Roskill, *Churchill and the Admirals*, pp. 258–9.

urged him to adopt the Eisenhower system [331, 356]. In this endeavour
he had the support of the new First Sea Lord, Sir Andrew Cunningham,
who had recent experience of the Eisenhower style in the Mediterranean,
though Cunningham observed that the American tendency was towards
the MacArthur model [332, 352, 391]. Mountbatten, in turn, quoted
Churchill's verbal gloss on the written directive the Prime Minister had
given him and continually used his direct channel to 10 Downing Street
to get his way [368, 385, 387]. Though the two remained on good personal terms and Somerville frequently praised Mountbatten's abilities,
while Lord Louis paid tribute to Somerville's deserved reputation [331,
374, 392, 397], each expressed exasperation with the other. Matters
came to a head in the summer of 1944 and both referred their differences
to London [387, 388]. It was at this time that a mutual friend, Captain
Charles Lambe,[1] arrived in the Indian Ocean, to command the carrier
Illustrious. Somerville credited him with making Mountbatten see sense
and commit himself finally to the Eisenhower model [389] though he felt
also that consistent opposition by the three Cs-in-C had prevented the
disastrous adoption of a dictatorial and inefficient MacArthur pattern.[2]

Much of the division between the Supreme Commander and his three
British Cs-in-C, led by Somerville (the only one of them not directly
responsible to Mountbatten) arose over the planning arrangements for
the supreme command. Mountbatten, despite early promises to the contrary [314], acquired an enormous staff (totalling over 5000 men and
women) [336, 347, 353] and intended that his planners should devise
operations which the Cs-in-C should then carry out without question.
Somerville, Giffard and Peirse[3] objected to this; as they had the respon-

---

[1]Capt (later Adm of the Fleet Sir) Charles E. Lambe (1900–1960): ent RN 1914;
Mid/mn 1917; torpedo splist & pilot; Cdr 1933; staff of RA (D) (A. B Cunningham) Med
F 1934; *Vernon* i/c 1935; Capt 1937; *Dunedin* 1939–40; ADP, DDP & DP 1940–April
1944; *Illustrious* 1944–5; RA,ACNS (Air) & FO Flying Training 1947–9; RA 3rd Carrier
Sqdn 1949–51; VA 1950; FO (Air) Home 1951–3; C-in-C Far E 1953–5; 2SL 1955; C-in-
C Med 1957–9; 1SL May 1959–May 1960; Adm of Fleet 1960; resigned through ill health.

[2]On Lambe's successful peace mission, see O. Warner, *Admiral of the Fleet: the Life of
Sir Charles Lambe* (London: Sidgwick & Jackson, 1969), pp. 120–1. Ziegler, pp. 230–6,
says Lambe told Mountbatten that continued friction with the Naval C-in-C 'would
gravely damage his chances of becoming First Sea Lord'.

[3]Gen Sir George Giffard (1886–1964): Queen's R Regt 1906; E Africa, King's African
Rifles 1913–18; Actg Col 1917; Staff Coll 1919; SO 1920; IDC 1931–2; Lt-Col, 2 Bn,
Queen's R Regt 1932; SO; Maj-Gen, African Col Forces 1936; Mil Sec to Sec State for
War 1939–40; GOC Palestine 1940; C-in-C W Africa; Gen 1941; Eastern Army 1943; C-
in-C 11 Army Group; fell out with Mountbatten 1944; Ret List 1946.

Air Marshal Sir Richard E. C. Peirse (1892–1970): pilot 1913; S-Lt RNR; Belgian coast
ops; flt cdr 1915; sqdn cdr 1916; wing cdr Dover; Sqdn Ldr 1919; W-Cdr Staff Coll
1922–3; Air Min 1926–7; Mid E & Palestine; DDO 1 1931; AOC Palestine 1933–6; Air
VM 1936; DO & I & DCAS 1937; Actg AM 1939; VCAS April 1940; C-in-C Bomber
Cmd Oct 1940–Jan 1942; Actg Air Chf M & AOC-in-C India 1942–4.

sibility of executing the plans, they felt they should have a hand in preparing them [322, 325, 327, 331, 334]. Mountbatten claimed that the Chiefs of Staff and the Americans insisted on him having his own planning staff, though here, too, he clearly and probably wilfully misinterpreted what he was told [339]. In the face of Somerville's continued opposition to his intended mode of planning he modified his proposals and offered a division of labour [342]. Somerville rejected this and continued to insist upon a joint planning staff composed of the Supreme Commander's planners and those of the Cs-in-C [354], in his view a much more efficient arrangement. The Cs-in-C should act as the Supreme Commander's chief advisors [356]. Somerville's view was supported by the Admiralty and by General Ismay, Secretary to the Committee of Imperial Defence and Chief of Staff to the Minister of Defence (Churchill)[1] [332, 350, 358]. After several months of wrangling, Mountbatten accepted a neat formula put forward by Somerville which allowed the Supreme Commander, his planners, the three Cs-in-C and their respective staffs to participate in the planning process, making optimum use of their special interests and knowledge. Nevertheless, Mountbatten's planners, who included Americans wedded to the MacArthur system and British officers dedicated to enhancing the status of the Supreme Commander, resisted this proposal [384]. However, Mountbatten overruled his staff and set up a new body along the lines recommended by Somerville [390, 391, 392], though in doing so he offended his senior American advisors.

Equally contentious was the issue of command of the Eastern Fleet. Somerville was quite certain that his ships came under Mountbatten's control only when earmarked for combined operations [318]. For all other purposes and for those large areas of the Station which fell outside SEAC's boundaries, the Fleet was under Admiralty control. However, it soon became apparent to Somerville that Mountbatten aspired to control of the Fleet at all times [327]. The issue was referred to the First Sea Lord and the Prime Minister, who attempted to clarify the position, though little new was added to the original directive [328–33]. Though Somerville's original assumption was endorsed, the Admiralty advised him to avoid separating his command too rigidly and obviously from SEAC, as this would give the Americans the excuse to deny the Supreme

---

[1]Lt-Gen (later General Lord) Hasings L. Ismay (1887–1965): Indian Army 1905; E Africa 1914–20; Staff Coll Quetta; HQ Staff India; RAF Staff Coll 1924–5; Asst Sec CID 1925–30; Mil Sec India 1933; SO; Dep Sec CID 1936; Sec CID 1938; Maj-Gen 1939; link between PM & COS; Head of Mil Secretariat; Lt-Gen 1942; Gen 1944; Ret List 1946; baron 1946; served under Mountbatten 1947–8; Sec State Commonwealth Relations 1951; 1st Sec-Gen NATO 1952–7.

Commander any control over their forces [351, 352]. Nevertheless, Somerville remained convinced that Mountbatten was still intriguing to obtain command of the fleet [372–74, 385].

A further area of dispute was over Mountbatten's right to visit ships and establishments of the Eastern Fleet. Somerville was astounded to receive almost regal proposals for visits by the Supreme Commander [342]. Quite apart from the ritual laid down by the Supreme Commander, Somerville was concerned that ships' companies, many of them new to the Station, would get the impression that Mountbatten commanded the Fleet. Somerville proposed, therefore, that he should make the necessary arrangements and that he should accompany the Supreme Commander [348]. The Admiralty, asked to advise the C-in-C, upheld his position but suggested that he should invite the Supreme Commander to make appropriate visits [349, 351, 352]. Somerville duly extended invitations but complained that Mountbatten abused the privilege [385].

The final controversy was over public relations, specifically who should issue communiques and press statements about naval operations. The Navy locally seems to have been loth to allow SEAC any latitude in this matter [328, 330] and again the Admiralty counselled more flexibility [351], though Somerville felt that SEAC press releases on operations devised and carried out by the Fleet suggested that SEAC had masterminded them.

There were thus several related areas of dispute between Mountbatten and Somerville. Though they professed to remain on good personal terms and co-operated happily in some respects, inevitably they became exasperated with one another from time to time. Such controversy between two of the senior British figures in the Command can have done little for its cohesion, efficiency and morale, let alone inducing the Americans and Chinese to extend full co-operation to SEAC. Conflict was always likely, given lack of precision in Churchill's directive to Mountbatten and his alleged verbal gloss, which seems to have endowed the Supreme Commander with more authority than the Chiefs of Staff had intended. Furthermore, SEAC's area did not include most of the Eastern Fleet's station, the western half of the Indian Ocean, the Gulf region and East Africa. Mountbatten came into an already complex and well established set of command structures and had the well nigh impossible task of exerting influence, and at times authority, over them and welding them into a genuinely integrated offensive campaign. He lacked substantive flag rank and experience of high command in the field. The theatre was a backwater militarily speaking and never enjoyed first call on resources of shipping, landing craft and other essentials for the major amphibious operations which were intended to be its *raison d'être*. The Supreme Command Headquarters was therefore underemployed and, according to Somerville, inclined to interfere in matters which were not its concern. As Somerville recognised, Mountbatten himself had many of the necessary qualities for supreme command. He was charming, energetic, imaginative and quick to grasp new subjects. After an exciting two years as a destroyer leader, he had gained strategic experience as Director of Combined Operations and had developed a good understanding of the necessary relationships between the services. On the other hand, he seems to have lacked the necessary degree of tact, consistency and sound judgment for his new post. Somerville, though he doubted the necessity for a supreme command, was determined to make the new regime work and instructed his staff firmly that their warm co-operation was expected. He welcomed Mountbatten's appointment, judging that his dynamism, wide range of abilities and attractive personality would galvanise operations as the Allies moved from the defensive to the offensive in the theatre.

Somerville clearly had reservations from the outset. He obviously preferred the Eisenhower or chairman conception of a supreme commander to the authoritarian or MacArthur model. Somerville was right to insist upon a clear distinction between the Fleet's regular and purely naval duties and those integral to proposed combined operations; his geographical and operational responsibilities were much wider than those of SEAC. He was on equally firm ground in insisting that plans should be made jointly by the SEAC Headquarters staff and the Commanders-in-Chief and their planners, especially as the Cs-in-C had the responsibility of carrying out the subsequent operations; they had to have confidence in the plans they executed and to which many men and much matériel would be committed. Their own planners were experienced, knowledgeable and practical. The Supreme Commander's men, by contrast, were fresh from home, enthusiastic, fired by great strategic visions and ignorant of the often dire local conditions; Somerville clearly thought some were arrogant and convinced of their own rectitude. Differences of opinion between their principals were reflected in the two sets of staff members. Somerville was on less firm ground in his possessive attitude towards news and Lord Louis's visits to naval units; he failed to give enough weight to the awkward relations between Mountbatten and other forces in the theatre, particularly those of the United States. Mountbatten had a difficult balancing act to perform and Somerville should have been less assertive about his own prerogative, though Mountbatten should also have been less forceful and more subtle. The series of disputes absorbed much time which could have been devoted to more important issues. Had both Mountbatten and Somerville been engaged in more continuous and large scale military activity, they might have found less time for wrangling over matters, which, while some – the style of command, authority over the fleet and the structure of planning – were clearly important, others, such as publicity and visits, assumed importance largely because a dispute had already arisen over other issues. In sum, the episode did not present either man at his best.[1]

South East Asia Command was set up to prosecute amphibious operations against Japanese-held islands and coasts in the eastern and southern Indian Ocean, dovetailing these with strategic air operations and ground attacks by Imperial, Chinese and American forces on inland fronts. Much of Somerville's time from the autumn of 1943 was occupied with discussions about possible combined operations. Several operations were proposed, some more than once, but none took place. It proved difficult to co-ordinate thrusts by the many forces involved and even operations against single small islands seemed to require forces of enormous scale. Moreover, many of the proposed objects had little military value or were inconsequential to the defeat of Japan. Even if agreement could be reached between the medley of nations and services nominally under Mountbatten's control, the necessary forces were never forthcoming. On every occasion when forces began to be built up for a major operation, demands from the Mediterranean, the cross-Channel invasion, or the Pacific led to their assignment elsewhere. The underlying if harsh fact was that the Indian Ocean was not a crucial theatre in the offensive sense. It was essential that the Allies maintained their sea and air communications across the Indian Ocean; that they held on to their main bases in India and Ceylon; that they prevented a conjunction of the three Axis powers; and that they continued to derive vital resources – especially oil and metals – from the region. But all this implied a defensive strategy. The destruction of Nazi Germany, Fascist Italy and Imperial Japan had to be accomplished in their metropolitan centres and the Allies' land, sea and air resources had to be applied chiefly to those direct assaults. SEAC thus represented two years of continual frustration

---

[1]Ziegler's discussion of the differences (pp. 231–40) is generally fair to both men, though he is unjust to both in his assertion (p. 238) that 'It was inevitable that he [Somerville] would resent the incursions of this whipper-snapper, equally inevitable that Mountbatten should be on his guard against slights or patronage'. He is also incorrect in his characterisation of Somerville (p. 238) as 'irascible and with a strong sense of hierarchy'. Roskill, *Churchill and the Admirals,* pp. 257–60, is equally fair. Marder, vol. 2, pp. 311–29, has the fullest treatment, placing the issues within their strategic context. Vice Adm Sir Kaye Edden, 'Admiral of the Fleet Sir James Somerville', in *Yearbook of the Friends of the Royal Naval Museum, Portsmouth* (1990), p. 10, remarks that 'Sir James could have been more magnanimous and Mountbatten less tactless'.

for Mountbatten and the long-suffering forces in this forgotten theatre. As so often, Churchill summed up the situation accurately:

I give Dickie full marks; we gave him a lousy job, and we have given him absolutely no help ever since he has been there, in fact the reverse, but nevertheless he has kept the show running and always turns up smiling, whatever we do to him. We really must try and help him all we can in the future.[1]

But of course, they never did; it *was* a lousy job. Mutual distrust, national ambitions which diverged markedly, a legacy of failure and neglect which was almost impossible to shake off, prickly personalities like General 'Vinegar Joe' Stilwell,[2] lack of precision in directives, an awkward relationship with its host – India Command – and the continual seepage away or non-arrival of earmarked forces, led to virtually nothing being achieved until the last year or so of the war. It was left to Wingate and Merrill[3] and their dramatic (if dubiously effective) jungle commando raids, the Eastern Fleet's attacks on Japanese bases and shipping, the East Indies Fleet's harassment of the Burma coast, and finally Slim's Fourteenth Army to gain whatever glory Mountbatten and SEAC earned.[4] Most of these successes took place after Somerville left the station but for the last year of his command he had to go through the wearying process of discussing plans which were fated never to come to fruition [320, 334, 337, 340, 342, 347, 348, 354, 357, 385, 389, 391, 399].

Even when forces for substantial operations began to become available following the defeat of Italy in September 1943, the destruction of Germany's surface fleet and the Normandy landings of June 1944, SEAC failed to benefit. By the autumn of 1943, the Chiefs of Staff had concluded that the principal British contribution to the defeat of Japan should be a British Pacific Fleet centred round the battleships and fleet carriers which had come into service during the war. It would testify to

[1]Churchill, quoted in Ziegler, p. 283.
[2]Gen Joseph Stilwell, US Army: an old China hand; commanded Chinese & US army in Burma; stormy relationship with practically everyone, hence nickname of 'Vinegar Joe'; eventually fell foul of Chiang Kai-Shek, the Nationalist Generalissimo, once too often and dismissed in Oct 1944.
[3]Maj-Gen Orde C. Wingate (1903–1944); born in India; RA 1923; explorer, scholar; service in Sudan; artillery appts, England 1933–6; intelligence staff Palestine 1937; Brig-Maj, A/A 1939; guerilla organiser, Abyssinia 1941; Burma 1942; Long Range Penetration Group, Brig & ops Feb 1943; Maj-Gen 1943; killed in air crash March 1944; unorthodox, uneasy relationships with superiors, not surprisingly a protégé of Churchill. Merrill's Marauders were an American equivalent of Wingate's Chindits.
[4]Plans for SE Asia are discussed fully in Thorne, pp. 288–302, 333–9, 401–16, 450–5, 520–42, 586–92; Howard, pp. 398–404, 539–51; J. Ehrman, *Grand Strategy*, vol. 5, *August 1943–September 1944* (London: HMSO, 1956), pp. 124–53, 155–65, 183–93, 211–23.

our determination to fight the eastern war to the last, to our long term strategic interests in the Far East, our intention to share in the postwar settlement in the Pacific and our recognition that concentration of force against the enemy's heartland was the quickest and most effective means to victory. At the Quebec conference with Roosevelt in September 1944, Churchill offered this powerful and up-to-date force, to work under the United States command; 'No sooner offered than accepted', said the President.[1] Yet that brief exchange was the climax of a year-long struggle whose twists and turns, cliff top dramas and global repercussions were as epic in their way as the fight against enemies in the field. As Somerville recognised [343], the decision to send the main fleet further east effectively stymied any major operations envisaged by SEAC. The theatre nevertheless reverberated to the echoes of the contest between the Prime Minister and the Chiefs of Staff in London. Churchill, though apparently convinced by the Chiefs of Staff of the strategic, resource and political advantages of a predominantly Pacific thrust, none the less continued to instigate plans for significant operations in South East Asia, encouraging Mountbatten to explore and advocate them [346, 347, 348, 351, 360, 365, 367, 369]. By the time this cataclysmic dispute, which led to the Chiefs of Staff threatening resignation, was brought to an end, Somerville had handed over to Admiral Sir Bruce Fraser, who would take the bulk of the reconstituted Eastern Fleet into the Pacific.[2] Somerville himself was not convinced that the Pacific strategy was the correct one, though he accepted the Chiefs of Staff's decision with utter loyalty; he felt that it would be difficult to sustain a much greater effort in the Pacific and that a solely British attack on Malaya and Singapore would return strategic and political dividends [345, 362].

The principal advocate of a British Pacific Fleet had been Admiral Sir Andrew Cunningham, who became First Sea Lord in October 1943. He

---

[1] See *A Sailor's Odyssey*, p. 611.

[2] Adm (later Adm of the Fleet Lord, of North Cape) Sir Bruce Fraser (1888–1981): entered RN 1902; Mdshpmn 1904; Lt, *Excellent* 1911; *Minerva* July 1914; Indian O & E Med 1914–15; instr, *Excellent* 1916; Gun O *Resolution* 1916–19; imprisoned by Bolsheviks, S Russia 1920; Cdr (G) *Excellent* 1921–2; Admy 1922–4; FGO, Med F 1925–6; Capt & AD Tac Div 1926–9; *Effingham* E Indies 1929-32; DNO 1933–5; *Glorious* 1935–7; RA Jan 1938 & COS to C-in-C Med (Pound); 3SL & Cntrlr March 1939–June 1942; VA 1940; VA & 2nd-in-C Home F June 1942–May 1943; C-in-C Home F May 1943–June 1944; Adm 1943; C-in-C Eastern F & BPF June 1944–June 1946; C-in-C Portsmouth May 1947; 1SL & Adm of Fleet Sept 1948–April 1952. See R. Humble, *Fraser of North Cape* (London: Routledge, 1983).

The deep disagreement between the Prime Minister and the Chiefs of Staff is well covered in Thorne, pp. 410–15; he describes it as 'perhaps the most serious disagreement of the war'. See also Ehrman, pp. 421–533; the fundamental positions of both parties are well dealt with on pp. 441–9 and App. IX (pp. 566–8) is Ismay's attempt to resolve the differences.

was one of Somerville's oldest and closest friends but Somerville did not expect an automatic continuation of their good-humoured partnership in the Mediterranean. Cunningham, always a hard man, at least on the surface, seemed to become more short-tempered with age; his obduracy, so evident in his dealings with Churchill,[1] caused Somerville some concern, as did Cunningham's disdain for staff work [319, 325] and his long delay in replying to Somerville's letters. However, the First Sea Lord gave Somerville firm support in his dispute with Mountbatten, and resumed his former close association with him.

The Eastern Fleet, which had been rapidly scaled down after the initial Japanese thrust in 1942, was nevertheless kept at full stretch with a variety of operations. Chief among these was the defence of the sea lanes. Though there were occasional forays by Japanese surface raiders, the main threat arose from both German and Japanese U-boats, mostly operating out of Penang. They ranged over the whole Indian Ocean, supported in the case of the Germans by tankers. To meet this threat, Somerville had totally inadequate air and sea escort and patrol forces and was often unable to form convoys; when he did so, the escort was likely to consist of no more than an old cruiser and two destroyers, frigates or smaller vessels. Either because of circumstances or conviction, Somerville also favoured the formation of hunting groups, though again he rarely had sufficient ships to enable him to do this; many officers clearly remained convinced that hunting was a waste of scarce resources and that convoy, a live bait which attracted submarines, was the only effective form of both trade defence and of counter-attack. Anti-submarine efficiency was much lower than in the Atlantic, partly because of the heterogenous collection of ships, ever-changing and required for a multiplicity of duties. The struggle against the U-boats was therefore a see-saw, in which a report of a kill of an underwater enemy was generally balanced by an account of the loss of a merchantman. Reinforcements were hard to come by as the U-boats extended their operations outwards from their North Atlantic hunting grounds and also developed advanced submarines which put Allied counter-measures under great strain in the later months of the war. However, Somerville's forces, using Ultra decrypts, sank two supply tankers off Madagascar [316, 324, 334, 335, 341, 342, 348, 355, 357, 359, 361, 365, 367, 369, 373, 386, 389, 399].[2]

Somerville had, until the autumn of 1943, few submarines of his own.

---

[1]M. A. Simpson, 'Viscount Cunningham' in M. H. Murfett, ed., *The First Sea Lords: From Fisher to Mountbatten:* (Westport, Conn., & London: Praeger, 1995), pp. 201–2).

[2]See F. H. Hinsley et al., *British Intelligence in the Second World War: Its Influence on Strategy and Operations*, vol. 3, pt. 1 (London: HMSO, 1984), pp. 229–30; pt. 2 (1988), pp. 487–8.

Until that time, they were employed chiefly on SOE operations [320]; there were in any case few Japanese targets at sea. As the Mediterranean naval war wound down, more submarines and their depot ships went east and this substantial accession of strength allowed Somerville to use them offensively [334, 343, 350]. Clandestine operations, together with inshore bombardments, were thereafter carried out mostly by light coastal forces, which did excellent work [367, 375, 384]. Despite the general unsuitability of British submarines for tropical service, they performed extremely well, seeking out elusive Japanese mercantile and warship targets, landing agents, carrying out bombardments and regulating the junk trade [346, 348, 359, 363, 365, 367, 369, 386, 389, 393, 399].

Much of Somerville's time was spent on visiting ships and shore establishments throughout his vast domain. He explained,

> The great distances covered by this station, coupled with the climatic conditions which invariably produce lassitude, makes it very necessary for the C-in-C to pay occasional visits to Naval bases and units in order to ensure that officers and men are on their toes, and to judge for himself whether preparations now going forward, are proceeding as rapidly and effectively as possible.[322]

Ships, especially those new to the station, were visited and problems of equipment and adjustment to tropical service were discussed. Frequent conferences were held with flag and commanding officers and considerable thought went into the choice of flag officers to represent Somerville's interests in Delhi and Ceylon [322, 323, 343, 359, 361, 364, 365, 367, 369, 381, 389, 393, 399].

From the beginning of 1944, the Eastern Fleet began to benefit from the defeat of Italy, the sinking of the *Scharnhorst* and the crippling of the *Tirpitz*;[1] capital ships, carriers, cruisers, destroyers and other vessels began to assemble in Ceylon and once again Somerville could look forward to having a battle fleet and an air striking force. However, the ships arrived in dribs and drabs, they often required modifications to fit them for tropical service and they needed training in fleet work. Most of their crews were young and green, while the fliers were often just out of flying school. It would be the spring of 1944 before Somerville had a fleet of the size and standard necessary for offensive operations against either Japanese surface forces or land-based aircraft and their ports and airfields [321, 322, 326, 334, 348]. As he was about to receive several carri-

---

[1]*Tirpitz*: 1942, 42,000t, 8×15in, 12×5.9in, 16×4.1in, *c*.30k; sunk in Tromsö fiord, 12 Nov 1944, by RAF.

ers [357], he began to consider how several of them could be operated simultaneously, a problem which had not faced a British Admiral hitherto. However, before he could assemble and train his fleet, the Japanese caused a brief but desperate alarm by sending the bulk of their surface fleet, including several carriers, to Singapore in February 1944 [361]. It followed the strengthening of shore-based naval aviation in the East Indies [323, 334] in the autumn. There were no clear indications of the purpose of the move; it was considered generally to be defensive, removing the Japanese fleet from the reach of the American juggernaut in the Pacific, but Somerville and his colleagues could not rule out a foray into the Indian Ocean and the Bay of Bengal of a strength comparable to Nagumo's raid in April 1942. Should that occur, Somerville proposed to take no risks at all and to place his fleet well beyond reach of the Japanese, to the west of the Maldive Islands [361]. He was well aware of the juicy targets on the still largely unprotected trade routes and galled to find that he was no better able to defend against a raid in force than he had been two years earlier [362]. Contingency plans were laid for increased fighter defence in Ceylon, for land-based torpedo bomber reinforcements and for deceptions; ships were hurried out from home – the cruiser *Nigeria*[1] arriving still in Arctic condition. Intelligence sources were combed for indications of the Japanese intentions. More significantly, a request made by the Admiralty for the loan of an American fleet carrier produced the veteran *Saratoga*.[2]

Intelligence predictions were correct; the Japanese move to Singapore was defensive. They were protecting their dwindling fleet from the Americans and had no thoughts of sortieing in the Indian Ocean; moreover, their shore-based air power, once so feared, was now in steep decline both qualitatively and in strength [369]. Japanese ships began to leave Singapore in the early spring of 1944 and Somerville's dawning realisation that his adversary was in fact weaker than the Allies at sea and in the air, together with the acquisition of a large and experienced US air group, opened up possibilities of offensive operations. The crisis had passed, indeed it had been grossly over-dramatised; nevertheless, it is testimony to the traumatic shock to British sea power administered by the sinking of the *Prince of Wales* and *Repulse*, the débâcle in the Java Sea and Nagumo's cheap victory in the vicinity of Ceylon that for fully two years our naval and air forces should retain at least a healthy respect, if not a fear, of Japanese capabilities. It is now clear that at least from the

---

[1]*Nigeria*: 1940, 8525t, 12×6in, 8×4in, 6tt, 33k.
[2]*Saratoga*: 1927, 33,000t, 90 aircraft, 20×5in, 34k; rebuilt as a carrier from battlecruiser hull; veteran of Pacific war, torpedoed twice & hit by a suicide bomber; intended as a training carrier after duty with Eastern F but recalled to front line to carry night fighters.

autumn of 1943, the Japanese in the East Indies resembled a fireless dragon.

Somerville was thrilled by the presence of *Saratoga*, not only because of the vast accession of strength which she represented and the opportunity of offensive action which she afforded but also because he had appealed constantly for more intimate co-operation with the Americans. Though both nations were fighting the same enemy in the east, it seemed to Somerville that they were really running two distinct wars. He complained that the Americans ignored his requests for information from the Pacific, which he required in order to better plan his own efforts. He sent his US Liaison Officer and various British officers to obtain information. He dutifully made feints with his grossly inadequate forces, at American request, to coincide with their operations in the Pacific and to distract and possibly divert the Japanese. When he met American senior commanders, he got on well with them – even the formidable Admiral King. The Eastern Fleet's brief association with *Saratoga* and her three destroyers, however, represented Anglo-American naval co-operation at its best; it was nothing short of a love feast.

News of *Saratoga*'s secondment was received at the end of February 1944 and Somerville began at once to consider how to integrate her into his multi-national fleet and in particular to operate her aircraft in conjunction with those from his own carrier *Illustrious* [363]. At first his proposals were modest – merely another feint [366] but he soon began to see more aggressive possibilities [367]; Vice Admiral Power,[1] the second-in-command, took the fleet to meet the Americans, who had sailed from Australia. Following her arrival, Somerville at once struck up an excellent relationship with *Saratoga*'s commanding officer, Captain John Cassady, US Navy.[2] It was decided to deliver a carrier air attack on the island base of Sabang, just off the coast of Sumatra; fear of Japanese land-based air power prompted Somerville to forego a surface bombardment. Elaborate plans were made for refuelling at sea and long range air

---

[1]Vice Adm (later Adm) Sir Arthur J. Power (1889–1960): *Britannia* 1904; Lt 1910; gunnery specialist; Dardanelles & Grand F; Cdr 1922; Staff Coll & Nav O 1920s; Capt 1929; *Dorsetshire* 1931–3; IDC 1933–5; *Excellent* 1935–7; *Ark Royal* 1938–9; ACNS (H) & RA May 1940; 15CS, Med F Aug 1942; FO Malta & Actg VA May 1943; 2nd-in-C Med F; 2nd-in-C Eastern F & VA 1BS Jan 1944; C-in-C E Indies Nov 1944–6; 2SL 1946–8; Adm 1946; C-in-C Med F 1948–50; C-in-C Portsmouth 1950–2; Adm of Fleet 1952.

[2]Capt (later Adm) John H. Cassady, US Navy (1896–): US N Acad 1915–18; Temp Lt (jg) 1918; served in European & Med waters & Puerto Rico 1918; pilot's wings Dec 1928, foll by increasingly important aviation appts, inc sqdn cmd, staff, training, Air O, to 1943; Ass NA, Rome 1937–9; *Saratoga* i/c Aug 1943–July 1944; RA & Dir Aviation Planning Div & ADCNO (Air) July 1944–Oct 1945; cmded carrier divs & air stas 1945–8; ACNO (Air) June 1948–July 1949; Cdr Fleet (Air), Jacksonville; VA & DCNO (Air) Jan 1950–May 1952; Cdr 6th F May 1952–March 1954; Adm & C-in-C, N Forces, E. Atlantic March 1954–April 1956; Ret List May 1956.

reconnaissance while Somerville, true to form, used the inward and outward voyages to exercise his still inadequately prepared fleet. As in the Mediterranean, Somerville sent his carriers ahead and on 19 April 1944, the Eastern Fleet at last struck a true offensive blow against the Japanese. Complete surprise was achieved, the port and airfield were hit heavily, resistance was feeble and the Allied force suffered no casualties. The raiders made a safe and uneventful return. It was a meticulously planned operation, in which Somerville exercised his usual firm control of the fleet. However, Sabang, though a worthwhile target, was not of first-rate significance and the damage, though severe, was not crippling. Nevertheless, the operation boosted Eastern Fleet morale after 18 months in the doldrums, gave ships and planes operational experience, offered valuable practice in fleet drill, refuelling, gunnery and air exercises and made it clear that the Admiral had not lost his skill in handling a large fleet [369, 370].

No sooner had the fleet returned to Ceylon than Somerville, Cassady and their staffs were planning a further operation which would make use of *Saratoga* on her return voyage to Australia. Admiral King had requested a strike at Sourabaya, a major oil refining centre and an important port [369]. Even more elaborate planning was called for this time, as the fleet had to refuel in Exmouth Bay, on the western coast of Australia, before carrying out the attack. As usual, constant exercises took place during the approach. Once again surprise was achieved and virtually no opposition materialised. Though substantial damage was claimed, it was in fact much less than the smoke and flames at the time suggested. When Somerville heard that the harbour was quite crowded with ships, he regretted that his defensive course following the attack placed him too far away to repeat it. The fleet again refuelled in Exmouth Gulf, after which *Saratoga* and her three destroyers took leave of the Eastern Fleet. Thus ended not only a successful operation but a brief and entirely satisfying association of Allied navies [373, 375–84]. Further training was carried out on the return voyage.

The Eastern Fleet now had high morale, substantial experience in fleet operations and a taste of action, so far without casualties. Churchill, King, Nimitz[1] and others pressed for yet more attacks on Japanese bases [381, 384]. A further feint followed and then Power led a one-carrier strike against Port Blair in the Andamans, another successful assault with again no casualties [386]. Somerville then led one final attack

---

[1]Adm (later Fleet Adm) Chester W. Nimitz (1885–1966): US N Acad 1901–5; Lt i/c *Decatur*; s/m splist; Atl F staff, 1917–18; Cdr 1921; Capt 1927; N War Coll; ONO & other Navy Dept appts; *Augusta* 1934–5; RA, BatDiv1 1938–9; Chief Bur Nav 1939–41; C-in-C Pacific 1941–5; Fleet Adm 1944; CNO Dec 1945–7; worked for UN following retirement.

against Sabang (25 July 1944), accompanying the air strike with a heavy bombardment from four capital ships and several cruisers, while a daring inshore squadron shot up port installations at virtually point blank range; at last Somerville had two carriers again, *Victorious* having recently arrived to join *Illustrious*. The operation dealt severe damage to Sabang and, as before, enemy reaction was feeble, the force suffering only a handful of casualties [392–95, 397, 398]. It was Somerville's last operation at sea but his fleet carried on in the same vein, accumulating experience of crucial value when it came to serve alongside the highly practised US Pacific Fleet in the spring and summer of 1945.[1]

By that time the fleet was under Somerville's successor, Admiral Sir Bruce Fraser, who had previously commanded the Home Fleet and was celebrated for sinking the *Scharnhorst*. Somerville welcomed the appointment [374] and handed over to his successor on 23 August 1944, leaving for home by air on 25 August [399], having well earned the Board of Admiralty's warm tribute, though characteristically he insisted that the credit for the fleet's success in defending the sea lanes of the Indian Ocean and latterly hitting the enemy in his bases should go to the whole team of Flag and Commanding Officers and his own devoted and capable staff [400, 401].

Thus ended Somerville's sea-going career and over two and a half years of strenuous service in an enervating climate, managing several hundred ships and a dozen or more shore stations scattered around the shores of the Indian Ocean. In addition to that he had liaised with other senior officers and statesmen like Smuts, attended meetings in London and Washington and brought successfully under his command men and ships from Australia, India, New Zealand, South Africa, France, the Netherlands, Italy, Greece and the United States. He had weathered the storm of the early Japanese fury, with the aid of good fortune as well as boldness. For 18 months thereafter he had directed operations from East Africa, keeping the vital seaborne traffic moving and hunting down the hidden enemies. His return to Ceylon in September 1943 coincided with the setting up of South East Asia Command and his relations with Mountbatten, though fruitful and friendly on occasion, were punctuated by wrangles, some inevitable, others certainly avoidable. It was fitting that having kept the seas open during the long defensive phase, though only by the greatest exertions and by the intelligent distribution of his emasculated force, Somerville should crown his long sojourn in such a demanding post by being able at last to carry the fight to the enemy and give him a succession of bloody noses in recompense for the damage the

[1]Marder, vol. 2, pp. 304 –11; Kirby, vol. 3, pp. 381–4.

Japanese had done in April 1942. If, overall, his command of Force H was personally more satisfying, his leadership of the Eastern Fleet was more difficult and taxing. Moreover, his role in the Indian Ocean was more crucial in terms of the Empire's survival and the Allies' ultimate triumph.[1]

[1]Marder, vol. 2, p. 329, pays just tribute to Somerville's command of the Eastern Fleet.

209. *To North*

The Admiralty,
January 1942

. . . Have had a hell of a battle over Tait's appt. but have at last got my point. Wake Walker relieves him[1] . . . DP nearly ratted on me three times. I finally told him another *P of W* affair would not do anyone any good & I should certainly have to leave on record my views if they refused to make a change. He's certainly getting quite worn out and slower than ever.

210. *To Pound*

12 February 1942

Before taking up my appointment as C-in-C, Eastern Fleet, I wish to make the following representations concerning the appointment of Vice Admiral W. E. C. Tait as Vice Admiral, 3rd Battle Squadron.

I was surprised and concerned when I learnt of the appointment of the late Admiral Sir Tom Phillips as C-in-C, Far East, of Vice Admiral Tait as second-in-command and of Rear Admiral S. S. Bonham Carter as Rear Admiral 3rd Battle Squadron, since none of these officers had personal experience of active service conditions at sea during the present war.

The surprise and concern that I felt appeared to be shared by a number of other Flag Officers . . . It appeared to many of us that the combination of these three Flag Officers was ill advised and might well lead to unfortunate incidents while they were in the practice of obtaining practical experience. I must point out that these opinions were expressed before the arrival of *Prince of Wales* and *Repulse* at Singapore. . . .

. . . the following points arise:–

(a) With the rapid and adverse development of the situation in the Far East a possible Japanese concentration directed either against our lines of communication or with a view to securing bases for operations against us in this area cannot be excluded.

---

[1]Wake Walker succeeded Fraser as 3SL and Controller.

(b) Until *Valiant* and *Queen Elizabeth* are available,[1] we shall have to depend largely on the 3rd Battle Squadron to provide a force to meet these activities. It follows from this that very special efforts are required to ensure that the 3rd Battle Squadron will be as efficient as it is possible to make them.

(c) The 'R' class battleships are old ships of relatively low fighting value and have in consequence been relegated mainly to convoy escort duty, a duty which provides small opportunity to promote fighting efficiency.

(d) In order to secure a satisfactory degree of fighting efficiency I consider the Flag Officer in command should be one who has had experience at sea, and especially experience of air attack. He should also be an officer keenly interested in gunnery efficiency and well informed on gunnery matters. In this connection it has been my experience that an officer who can talk from personal experience carries far more weight and provides a much greater incentive than one who can merely repeat what he has read in reports or what he has been told by other people.

Apart from the training of the ships in his squadron, the Flag Officer, 3rd Battle Squadron, may be called upon at any time to act for me if I am absent or incapacitated.

... What I require, and what I feel I should have, is a Flag Officer who can teach, not one who has to learn, and who, by visiting each ship in turn will raise the standard of fighting efficiency by personal attention and advice and above all, by constant recapitulation of the lessons which he has learnt by hard and bitter experience in other theatres of the war.

I therefore submit that the appointment of Vice Admiral Tait may be reconsidered.

211. *Pocket diary, 1942*

13 February

Papers indignant at escape of BCs.[2] Lunched at Junior and said goodbye to darling Pop and Rach[el]. To Downing St and had 1 hour and 10 minutes with Winston. Said I had complete confidence of Govt. and Admiralty. Saw DP and AVA. Have got Willis instead of Tait and Danckwerts coming as COS ashore. Dined at club and caught 9.15 [to Glasgow].

---

[1] They had been severely damaged by Italian limpet mines in Alexandria harbour in December 1941.

[2] *Scharnhorst, Gneisenau* and the heavy cruiser *Prinz Eugen*, which made a dash up Channel from Brest.

16 February

Bill Tennant arrived and came on board [*Formidable*] to see me. Went back with him to *Newcastle* and saw Wallop[1] and Figaro.[2] Latter knew me this time. To *Hermione* and had one in the wardroom. Sent off final letter and felt very homesick and miserable. How I hate this business. Heaven knows what losses and prisoners in Singapore. Rommel advancing in Libya. Not a gleam anywhere. Turned in in the sea cabin which is not bad but noisy.[3]

17 February

Very cold and foggy. Weighed and proceeded soon after midnight with *Malaya*, *Eagle*[4] and *Hermione* in company. Turned in again when we got clear. Vis[ibility] only about 2 miles when we got to convoy rendezvous. Had to [–?] a lot before we got tucked up into bed alongside old Crabbe.[5] Visibility remained poor all day so I decided not to fly off any aircraft.

212. *To his wife*

HMS *Formidable*,
at sea,
17–25 February 1942

17 February

Here we are off at last and am I elated at 'being bound on this high adventure'? Not a bit of it. Homesick as hell and feeling damnably mouldy. It was foggy and dark as we threaded our way out and at dawn we had the heck of a job to sort ourselves out with the convoy. Everyone groping about for their right place, a strange bridge, strange officers and everything twice as slow as I am accustomed to. ... On thinking matters over it seems to me that the idea of trying to wrest back from the Japs what we've lost by means of large sea-borne expeditions is wrong. It's like trying to stamp rather feebly on a man's feet instead of kicking him

---

[1]Capt P.R..B.W. William-Powlett: Capt 1938; PSD, DDPS (Manning) 1939; *Fiji* Dec 1940; *Newcastle* Feb 1942; *Rodney* & Capt of Fleet, Home F July 1944; RA (D) 1951.

[2]Sir James's cat.

[3]This was one of the lowest points of the war for Britain; Singapore had just fallen and the German Gen Erwin Rommel (1890–1944) was leading the Axis forces on their drive to Egypt.

[4]*Eagle*: 1923–4, 22,600t, 21 aircraft, 9×6in, 5×4in, 24k; ex-liner; sunk W Med on Malta convoy 11 Aug 1942, *U73*.

[5]Cdre L. G. E. Crabbe: Capt 1922; RA 1934; SNO Yangtze 1935; VA on Ret List 1937; FOIC, *Eaglet*, Liverpool Aug 1939; convoy Cdre 1942–5.

in the fork. That would double him up much quicker. So we ought to aim at striking the Japs amidships, through China, Vladivostok and the Pacific, and be content to hold his feet rather than overcome him by attacking his feet. However, that's only my vague idea at the moment. . . . This ship has had a pretty easy war on the whole. She arrived in the E Med in March, was knocked out in May and spent August to December in the USA so they have not had to sweat much.

22 February

Yesterday was not our lucky day. One of our aircraft failed to return from a reconnaissance, apparently his wireless broke down and he lost himself and we were therefore unable to home him back. I hate losing aircraft crews this way and somehow feel it would not have happened in the *Ark*. This ship is not properly worked up yet or at least not worked up to the standard I'm accustomed to. I shall have to get busy on her as soon as the weather improves a bit. . . . The Admiralty as usual are very constipated about giving me any information, so I have to rely mainly on the BBC and the Natels. *Later.* Our luck is still out. We crashed another aircraft on landing – a complete write-off and another one ran into the barrier but I hope can be repaired. Am seriously disturbed at the lack of skill and experience of the pilots in this ship. She evidently wants a proper training programme which I hope to give her when the weather becomes at all reasonable.

23 February

My two destroyers[1] have not turned up and a very limited air search this morning failed to find them. I daren't send out a proper search as I find the observers and pilots are terribly green and inexperienced. Arthur B[isset][2] quite hurt and surprised when I remark on this and it is quite clear to me that our standard in the *Ark* was well above anything they have here. They certainly want a good shake up. Managed to collect one of my destroyers with an air search, but the other one is still adrift so I had to make a wireless signal to tell her to report where she is. What is more annoying is that another Albacore[3] crashed on landing and is a complete write-off. I'm beginning to be seriously disturbed by the lack of skill and pep in this party here. They are all quite complacent and think they are the cat's whiskers and in my opinion they are quite bum.

[1]*Paladin, Panther* (sunk Aegean 1943, Ger a/c): 1942, 1540t, 4×4in, 8tt, 34k.
[2]Capt Arthur W. La T. Bisset: Capt 1932; *Shropshire* 1939; *Formidable* Aug 1940; RA July 1942; Admy; *Royalist*, RA Force H 1943; RA CVEs, Oct 1943 RA (A), Home F March 1944; attack on *Tirpitz* April 1944; Ret List Jan 1945, ill health.
[3]Fairy Albacore: 1938, bomb load 2000lb, 3mg, 161mph; intended as replacement for Swordfish.

24 February

In the face of some opposition from Arthur Bissett I insisted on the Albacore pilots doing deck landing training which they evidently needed sorely. I think that he and his Cdr (F) view with great dislike the fact that I know too much about operating aircraft and refuse to accept blindly any stuff they like to hand out. By the time we reach our destination, I hope I shall have them in proper shape. As an example I found that aircraft due to fly off at a certain time were always 10 minutes or more late. Arthur said 'I can't make these Fleet Air Arm fellows punctual'. My answer to that was 'Well if you can't I certainly can so you'd better think twice about it'. They've been absolutely punctual all day! . . .

25 February

Busy all day giving the pilots of the Albacores and the Martlets deck landing training and they are at last showing a great improvement. It's obvious that was wanted and the people in this ship ought to have seen that.

213.   *Pocket diary, 1942*

27 February

Full flying programme including several ALT, fighter R/T, etc., also sleeve target practice. *Formidable* made fairly good runs. One Albacore crashed into barrier but not much damage. Another taxied into island. C-in-C SA now Tait and signals Willis already left Freetown in *Reso[lution]* but says I meet him in S A[frica].

28 February

On an easterly course most of the day turning into Sierra Leone. Full day's flying. ALT, Martlets, long range RDF tests and the sleeve up for *Newcastle* and the destroyers to shoot at. . . .

214.   *To his wife*

Freetown,
Sierra Leone,
1 March 1942

I must admit that the situation grows more and more confusing and perplexing. Should imagine that Geoffrey Layton will be thankful to hand this thankless task on to someone else. If only Danckwerts gets out by the time I arrive at Colombo I shall be glad to leave the strategy to him and get on with the stuff I know which is handling the Fleet at sea. I'm told the Japs are afraid of the dark so I must try and specialise in night attacks.[1]

215. *From the Admiralty*

1 March 1942

D.   Future Japanese intentions as regards Indian Ocean still obscure, growing activity hitherto confined to operations by submarines in Bay of Bengal. No reports of any sinkings by these recently. Attacks on Ceylon relative to Pearl Harbor type or full scale invasion considered possible.
E.   Immediate steps being taken to provide two Fulmar Squadrons from Middle East. *Indomitable* will ferry further 3 Hurricane Squadrons from Middle East and these will probably go to Ceylon but decision as between Ceylon and Java not yet taken. C-in-C Eastern Fleet[2] has been instructed to keep 2 'R' class in Ceylon to operate against possible invasion and to retain *Hermes* until *Indomitable* is operational.[3]
K.   Following state of reinforcements for Eastern Fleet.

1.   Time of arrival of *Warspite* at Fremantle 5 March.
2.   *Illustrious* and *Adamant* leave UK 21 March.
3.   *Birmingham* joins EF after 1 month's refit at Simonstown.
4.   *Dauntless* leaves UK 5 March.
5.   *Devonshire* refit USA completes mid-March.
6.   *Gambia* ready for service in UK early April.
7.   *Frobisher* refit UK. Taken in hand end of March.
8.   *Hawkins* refit UK completes early June.
9.   Following destroyers ex-Mediterranean of 2nd DF have been transferred to EF:–

> *Griffin, Hotspur, Fortune, Arrow, Decoy, Foxhound.*
> These now on passage to Colombo except *Foxhound* leaves Alexandria 12 March.
> *Pakenham* and *Penn* accompany *Illustrious*.[4]

---

[1]This, like much so-called information about the Japanese, was a dangerous myth, as the battles in the Java Sea and off Savo Island were to prove.
[2]Adm Layton.
[3]*Indomitable* was still ferrying Hurricanes to the Far E.
[4]*Adamant*: 1942, 12,500t, 8×4.5in, 17k; depot ship for 4SF, Colombo Oct 1943. *Dauntless* 1918, 4850t, 6×6in, 3×4in, 12tt, 29K. *Devonshire*: 1929, 9850t, 8×8in, 8×4in, 8tt, 32.25k. *Gambia*: 1942, 8525t, 12x6in, 8x4in, 6tt, 33k: RNZN 1943. *Frobisher*: 1924, 9860t, 5×7.5in, 5×4in, 4tt, 30.5k. *Decoy*: 1933, 1375t, 4×4.7in, 8tt, 36k; RCN *Kootenay* 1943. *Pakenham* (L) (lost C Med 1943, Ital surface forces). *Penn*: 1942, 1540t, 4×4in, 8tt, 34k.

L.   *Air Reconnaissance for Indian Ocean.* US have agreed to turn over 18 Flying Boats to us and this will enable us to provide 3 Catalina Squadrons for Indian Ocean. 4 Catalinas have already left.

M.   Report has been received of 3 Japanese ships at Diego Suarez. This is now known to be not (R) not true.

N.   Decided to move HQ of C-in-C S Atlantic to Cape. FO S American division will become FOIC Freetown.[1]

O.   Question of command in Indian Ocean still under discussion as C-in-C EF reports confusion arising owing to presence of two Cs-in-C at Colombo.

216.   *To Pound*

HMS *Formidable*,
Freetown,
2 March 1942

3.   As regards *Formidable*, I was much concerned to find that her Squadrons were as green as grass. After we had crashed 3 Albacores and lost one on a very moderate recco I realised we had to start from scratch and therefore ordered a series of deck landing and other elementary practices, which were continued daily during our passage here. I don't think anyone on board here quite realised how bad they were, it was not only the flying but D/F, W/T, RDF, in fact everything as rusty as it could be. I hope that by the time we get to Colombo the ship will be in proper order, but she's a long way to go yet.

4.   These long sojourns in the States undoubtedly do harm. Officers and men are given too good a time and told continuously what fine chaps they are. The result is that everyone becomes soft and self satisfied. I noticed it in ships passing through Gibraltar.

5.   On arrival here I got Layton's 12432/16 February and your reply 0149A/19 February. They were of value in helping to put me into the picture but I am very much in the dark on other matters, e.g.,

(a)   What air and military reinforcements are being sent to deal with the Burma situation? Do we expect to stabilise that situation and if so on what lines?

(b)   To deal with heavily escorted convoys to Rangoon do we have sufficient air to counter enemy's air cover and thus give our surface forces a reasonable chance to operate successfully?

---

[1]This appears to have been Rear Adm F. H. Pegram, who died in March 1944.

(c)   How is it considered that 2 'R' class in Ceylon under fighter cover
      can repel a landing?
      It seems to me that unless we have a balanced force available we
      may get a repetition of *Prince of Wales* and *Repulse.*
(d)   To prevent a 'Pearl Harbor' at Trincomalee and Colombo we must
      have an adequate scale of defence. A few Hurricanes and 2 Fulmar
      squadrons are inadequate. Until a proper state of defence has been
      reached, and this must include sufficient A/A guns, long distance
      reconnaissance and a shore based striking force, I consider our
      forces will prove a better deterrent if kept at sea.
(e)   Are the Americans piling up air in Australia? Is it any good and can
      they co-operate properly with surface forces?
(f)   What is the proposed employment of the [US] Pacific Fleet? Are
      dates for completion of repairs to battleships likely to be extended?

217.   *To Pound*

2 March 1942

2.   The stationing of 2 'R' class battleships in Ceylon appears to afford
a vulnerable target rather than an effective deterrent in view of what
must be the very limited fighter protection available.
3.   Outstanding requirement appears to be air reconnaissance in depth
coupled with effective shore based T/B striking force. If fleet remains at
sea and if possible unlocated it should prove a far more effective deterrent.
4.   I appreciate that until we have sufficient force available we must act
on defensive but with the arrival of *Formidable* it may well prove that
our defensive dispositions will also afford opportunity to strike at the
enemy.
5.   If it is true that American submarines are unable to operate effectively in NEI[1] suggest every effort be made to obtain some for operations
in the western approach to Malacca Straits and in Sunda Straits.

218.   *Pocket diary, 1942*

3 March

Unable to do any sleeve target practice but carried out a big programme of W/T and ALT, also had the fighters up. Message from
Ad[miralty] giving general appreciation of Far East. *Indom[itable]* is to

[1]Netherlands E Indies.

fetch more Hurricanes from Aden for Colombo and Trinco[malee] but Ad still seems inclined to collect 'R' class there. Crashed yet another Albacore landing on but may not be a write-off. Crossed the line at 1800. Did a plotting exercise and after dark a night encounter which was spoilt by a very heavy rain squall.

4 March

ALT and sleeve target practice before breakfast. At 8.30 I went up with Gardiner[1] for an ALT. Martlets intercepted very well. We made quite a good attack and then I landed on at 9.15.

7 March

Another full day's flying exercises. One Martlet made a good landing but hook missed all wires and she had some damage. Sleeve firing in forenoon. RIX and destroyers' throw-off in afternoon. I went up for ALT in afternoon. W/T beacon and ASV all unsatisfactory but quite a good attack. 11 Albacores took off at 2030 for ALT. Had a job getting them back. One missing so sent destroyers on and turned back with a view to air search at daylight.[2] . . .

219. *To his wife*

8 March 1942

Geoffrey Layton has been made C-in-C Ceylon. . . . I think it's a good plan as I certainly cannot tackle the defence of Ceylon and the Fleet. So that means that I shall not have to go ashore at Colombo but will remain afloat and try and get my mixed bag into some sort of shape. Geoffrey has very rightly objected to certain wet ideas which I feel must have emanated from WC. Expect both he and I will be very much out of favour before long. . . . Don't think I shall be at Colombo more than 24 hours and after that up and down the high seas anchoring in some deserted coral atoll for fuel.

---

[1]Sub-Lt (A) J. R. N. Gardiner: Sub-Lt (A), 820 Sqdn, *Formidable*, Aug 1940; Lt, Oct 1942; 778 Sqdn, *Jackdaw* (Crail) Dec 1943; *Pretoria Castle* (CVE) 1945.
[2]This was piloted by Sub-Lt (A) Michael Lithgow, later a famous test pilot: Mid (A) 1939; *Raven* (Eastleigh), 759 Sqdn, April 1940; Actg Sub-Lt (A), 820 Sqdn, *Ark Royal* July 1940; Sub-Lt (A) Aug 1941; 820 Sqdn, *Formidable* Feb 1942; Lt (A) Jan 1943; *Daedalus* (Lee-on-Solent) Oct 1942; Actg Lt-Cdr *Saker* (BAD) Jan 1945. He and his crew were recovered.

220.   *Pocket diary, 1942*

9 March

Flew off Albacores for dawn ALT attack which was well carried out. Type 281 working well but 286 not so good at present. Sig[nal] from DP to say they were prepared to expend 2 'R's' in defence of Ceylon providing expenditure effective. Seems a bit wet. Carried out night exercise with destroyers which went much better. Some more of this and *Formidable* may become quite effective.

10 March

Sighted bright lights of Capetown at 0615. . . . *Resolution* arrived soon after. Budgen[1] and Willis on board to see me. At 10 we all went off to see Lord Harlech[2] and afterwards Field Marshal Smuts. A great little man and feels strongly we must not throw away EF. . . .

221.   *To the Admiralty*

Capetown,
10 March 1942

I have had an opportunity to discuss the situation with Admiral Willis and find that quite independently we had arrived at same conclusions which are as follows:–

2.   Before Japanese attempt capture of Ceylon they will specifically

(a) Reduce Eastern Fleet by attrition or
(b) Support attack with greater part of their fleet.

3.   The stationing of 2 'R' class in Ceylon would provide good opportunity for 2(a) with small probability of achieving any useful results, more especially as ships are not yet experienced in fighter direction. Until further reinforcements arrive we are not in a position to offer effective opposition to 2(b).

---

[1]Rear Adm (Ret) D.A. Budgen: Capt 1930; DLDD 1939; RA (Ret List) June 1941; SNO Simonstown; Naval Asst, STD 1942–3.
[2]Lord Harlech (Ormsby-Gore, 1885–1964): 4th baron; Con MP Denbigh 1910–18, Stafford 1918–38; Shrops Yeo, Egypt 1914–17; PPS to Milner 1917; Lia O, Zionist Mission, Palestine 1918; dip service; PPS Col Off 1922–4, 1925–9; PMG 1931; 1st Cmnr of Works 1931; Col Sec 1936–8; succ 1938; High Cmnr S Africa 1941–4; banker, philanthropist, scholar, art patron.

222. *To Pound*

Capetown,
11 March 1942

... [Willis and I] agreed that the loss of Ceylon would be a most serious matter, but felt that if the Japanese attempted the capture with practically the whole of their Fleet we should obviously be unable to deal with this scale of attack.

Providing the Americans adopt a more forward policy – even if it is for the moment confined to feinting or quite light scales of attack – we feel it is unlikely the Japanese would denude their lines of communication or protection in the Pacific.

If they attempt a lesser scale of attack on Ceylon the best deterrent, and the best counter, too, is to keep our Eastern Fleet in being and avoid losses by attrition. This can best be achieved by keeping the Fleet at sea as much as possible with feints east of Ceylon from time to time.

The maintenance of the Fleet at Trincomalee is undesirable as it is, or soon will be, within range of Japanese shore based reconnaissance and can in consequence be fixed too easily.

The main difficulty will be the maintenance of ships and it may well be necessary for individual ships to use other isolated anchorages in the islands west of Ceylon and accept temporary lack of A/S protection.

I feel however that we must avoid having our Fleet destroyed in penny numbers by undertaking operations which do not give reasonable prospects of success.

If the Japanese get Ceylon it will be extremely difficult but not necessarily impossible to maintain our communications to the Middle East. But if the Japanese capture Ceylon and destroy the greater part of the Eastern Fleet then I admit the situation becomes really desperate.

Willis has got a very clear head and sound judgment and is fully alive to all that must be done to get the Fleet into fighting trim. ...

In spite of continued exercises *Formidable* has still a long way to go before I can regard her as operationally fit. Fighter interception is still in its infancy and I find that in regard to this and other matters I have to take a hand personally in order to get a move on.

I shall get Denis Boyd[1] to shift his Flag into her as soon as he's satisfied with *Indomitable*. Incidentally the carriers will want intensive training in co-ordinated air operations.

I am glad that Geoffrey Layton has been put in charge of Ceylon.

---

[1]Actg Rear Adm Denis Boyd.

From what I saw of the soldiers and Governor[1] I'm convinced that they want a good driving hand on them all the time. I shall only stay at Colombo long enough to discuss matters with him and Arbuthnot[2] and then get off to my Fleet as soon as possible, hoisting my Flag in *Warspite*. I shall of course take Ralph Edwards with me but Danckwerts will be of great value ashore to size up all available information and put forward appreciations based on that information. I can go to Colombo by air or other means from time to time in order to discuss matters with the people there.

I was much impressed with Smuts. . . . He is fully alive to the danger of Madagascar but is against precipitating matters unless there is unmistakable evidence of the situation deteriorating. Consider SIRCE[3] is too optimistic about being able to take the place with a handful of Free French. If such a party *was* staged the air support could be furnished by Navy [carrier aircraft?] flown from the East Coast if it was desired to keep British naval forces out of the picture. . . .

Am sending Cdr Clark, USN,[4] to Australia to try to get the Americans to give us more news and to explain fully how essential it is to have co-ordinated action.

223. *To his wife*

14 March 1942

I hear a lot of blah about how everything now depends on our maintaining control of the Indian Ocean. That's poor bloody me and I wonder how the devil it's to be accomplished. My old battle boats are in various states of disrepair and there's not a ship at present that approaches what I would call a proper standard of fighting efficiency.

224. *Pocket diary, 1942*

19 March

Long signal from Admiralty in reply to my appreciation. They agree that EF must not be sacrificed to save Ceylon. Apologia for 2 'R' class in

---

[1]Sir Andrew Caldecott (1884–1951): Malayan CS 1907; Chief Sec, Fed Malay States 1931; Col Sec Straits Settlements 1933; Gov-Gen Hong Kong 1935; Gove-Gen Ceylon 1937.

[2]Vice Adm Sir Geoffrey S. Arbuthnot ('Buffy'): Capt 1926; RA 1936; 4SL 1937–41; VA May 1940; C-in-C E Indies May 1941–2; Admy Oct 1942; Adm, Ret List Feb 1944.

[3]Unidentified.

[4]Cdr A. Dayton Clark, US Navy: as Lt-Cdr US Observer, Force H, Oct 1940; later Capt, Navy Dept Nov 1944.

Ceylon rather weak. G. Arbuthnot suggests we use Colombo and Trinco as bases. G. Layton disagrees but says he would like to discuss with me. Admiralty message cuts across this by pointing out impossible to split Fleet between Colombo and Trinco. I entirely agree. Later message from Admiralty orders some 'R's', *Warspite*, etc., to R/V with us S of Addu. GL and night look-out exercise against destroyers.

225. *The Chiefs of Staff to Wavell*

19 March 1942

1. ... Following ships will be concentrated in Ceylon area by end of March. *Warspite, Revenge, Resolution, Royal Sovereign, Formidable, Indomitable* with 11 cruisers in Indian Ocean area and 14 destroyers. *Illustrious* joins in April and *Valiant* in June.[1]
2. Function of this Fleet will be to maintain control of the sea communications in the Indian Ocean. Both the Middle East and India depend on these. Such control would at the best be precarious if Japan obtained and we were denied bases in Ceylon. The security of our Fleet Base at Addu Atoll would then be threatened. We agree that the Fleet will be unable to prevent coastwise movement of the enemy up the Burmese mainland. Nor will shore based air support be sufficient for some time to enable it to maintain control in the Bay of Bengal if faced by superior Japanese Fleet.
3. Nevertheless so long as our Fleet remains in being, Japanese would have to provide permanent cover to the lines of communication of any direct sea borne attack on the coast of India or Ceylon with her fleet. They are unlikely to accept such a commitment particularly if pressure is applied by the US Pacific Fleet as it recovers from Pearl Harbor.
4. Therefore policy of our Fleet will be to act as a Fleet in being, avoiding unnecessary risks, crippling losses and attrition. While it does so we agree that the most likely courses of action for the Japanese are coastwise movement via Burma and raids of the Pearl Harbor type on Ceylon. It is to prevent risks of loss to the Fleet by the latter that strong Fighter Forces in Ceylon are necessary even at the expense of NE India about whose need we fully agree with you.
5. We fully realise that the defence of Ceylon is essentially an air and naval problem. Land forces now there are intended as a deterrent to attempts at occupation by the Japanese until air forces in Ceylon and naval forces in the Indian Ocean are built up. It is not (R) not certain that the 2nd E African Brigade will become available and you will realise 13 and 17 Australian Brigades are only temporary garrison.

[1]*Revenge* 1916, 29,150t, 8×15in, 12×6in, *c.*20k.

6. Admiral Somerville arrives in Ceylon area towards the end of March to take over the command of the Eastern Fleet. If you could arrange a meeting with him he would be able to give you fuller naval appreciation. We are hoping to arrange better co-operation with the US Naval Forces in the Pacific than exists at present.

7. Need for increased air forces fully realised and agreed here. This matter is under further immediate consideration by us. Urgent representations for American operational aircraft also being made. You will be notified of the outcome as early as possible.[1]

226.   *To his wife*

20 March 1942

An appreciation by the COS Committee and addressed to Wavell and repeated to me is practically word for word what I sent home from the Cape and uses the same expressions. And then I get a thing from the Admiralty full of windy generalisations which I can see was drafted by old Bobby Harwood. I'll send him back a nice bunch of unpleasant facts which cannot be ignored or glossed over. Think I shall be at Colombo a bit longer than I expected because there is so much to discuss with the two Geoffreys and also Wavell has been advised to come and see me there. I shan't stop longer than I can help as I must get busy and train my boats. TLs seem to think that a couple of days will put us all on the top line. It will take weeks and not days. Wish some of the senior ones at the Admiralty took a more realistic view of things.

227.   *Pocket diary, 1942*

28 March

Took over as C-in-C EF at 0800, and now my troubles begin. On board *Express*, *Arrow* and *Enterprise*[2] to speak to the hands. Lunched with the Arbuthnots, he full of moans and grievances. Helfrich[3] to see me in the afternoon and we discussed Fleet tactics and what happened in the Java Sea. Agar[4] also to call.

---

[1]This message was repeated to Somerville.
[2]*Express* 1934, 1375t, 4×4.7in, 8tt, 36k.
[3]Adm C. E. L. Helfrich, R Neth N: Dutch N C-in-C, E Indies; Actg N C-in-C, ABDA 1942; i/c all Dutch forces in SE Asia 1942.
[4]Capt Augustus W. S. Agar, VC: VC, Russia, with CMBs, 1918–19; Capt Dec 1933; *Emerald* Sept 1939; CSO, Portland Nov 1940; *Dorsetshire* 1941; *Unicorn* Nov 1942; Ret List Jan 1943; RN Coll, Greenwich May 1943; autobiography *Footprints in the Sea*.

228.   *To his wife*

Colombo,
26–28 March 1942

26 March

Drove to the Secretariat where Geoffrey was presiding at a meeting as C-in-C Ceylon. There was little doubt as to who was master in *that* house and I was much impressed. He's very drastic but that is what is needed here. . . .

28 March

Found India shouting on account of the Japanese attack on Akyab and both Wavell and Admiralty asking me what I was going to do about it. Replied I could do nothing until Fleet was trained and that I was not prepared to use it offensively until I was satisfied it was in a proper state. Damned if I'm going to fritter it away in penny numbers. . . . the trouble is they've been telling Wavell we have so many this and so many that out here just as if they were all ready for action now. I've had to signal Wavell to put him wise as to the situation. . . . A number of my Staff officers were in *Prince of Wales* and most had no war experience before joining her. It was all the most amateur party I ever heard of.

229.   *Pocket diary, 1942*

29–31 March 1942

29 March

To office early and had a series of conferences all forenoon over possible Jap carrier attack. Decided land-based striking force practically useless as Blenheims no experience and Swordfish have not got the range. So all depends on the carriers. *Hermes* cannot fly off T/B unless good breeze.[1] Lunched with Geoffrey. Back to office for further discussions and signals and then to Queen's House for talk with Governor and Lady C[aldecot]. Former most indignant at telegrams from Colonial Office saying Ceylon not doing its stuff.

30 March

. . . Weighed and proceeded at 2, with *Formidable, Enterprise, Cornwall, Dragon* and *Caledon*[2] and 6 destroyers. Executed man-

---

[1] Aircraft needed a good wind over the deck for take off, difficult to obtain with slow carriers in light wind belts.

[2] *Dragon*: 1918, 4850t, 6x6in, 3x4in, 12tt, 29k; Polish N 1943; sunk as part of Mulberry breakwater June 1944. *Caledon*: 1917, 4120t, 5x6in, 2x3in, 8tt, 29k.

oeuvres when clear of swept channel. Bit rusty but not so bad. Shaped course to S and E for the night. . . .

31 March

Information during night of Jap submarines to SE of Ceylon. Busy sending out tactical and other orders. *Warspite* did 6" throw-off and all ships tried out short range. Joined by *Hermes, Emerald, Heemskerck* and *Vampire*[1] at 1400 and later sighted Willis with all the 'R's' and remaining destroyers. Tremendous volley of signals in both directions and some pretty good pot messes going on. This party is damnably rusty and in no state really to engage, but we must do best we can. Reformed Force A – *Warspite*, 2 carriers, *Cornwall*, 2 'E's' and 6 destroyers and Force B the remainder. Proceeded to NE during first part of the night.

230.   *To his wife*

HMS *Warspite*
1–3 April 1942

1 April

Gosh but I've had a couple of [–?] strenuous days. A flat calm and a sun that scorches the skin off you and no shade under wartime conditions. My face and arms like raw beetroot. We've had no luck so far in sighting any enemy forces and I've tried to improve the shining hour by trying to polish up my party. The trouble is that the Fleet I now have is much bigger than anything anyone has had to handle before during this war. On top of that most of my staff are pretty green so I have to supervise almost everything myself. It will all improve as time goes on. But it certainly is the devil of a job at present. When this ship left the E Med she was gutted of all the things she ought to have as a Flagship.

2 April

The short bit I write each day shows how little time I spend in my sea cabin! I have to be on the bridge almost continuously because my staff are so untrained and so are my boats and I have to watch every damn thing. . . . Still no news of the enemy. I fear they have taken fright which is a pity because if I could have given them a good crack now it would have been very timely. Unfortunately I can't hang about indefinitely waiting for them.

---

[1]*Emerald*: 1926, 7550t, 7×6in, 3×4in, 16tt, 32k. *Heemskerck* R Neth N: completed in UK 1940, 4150t, 10×4in, 32.5k. *Vampire*, RAN: 1917, 1188t, 4×4in, 6tt, 34k; sunk off Ceylon 9 April 1942, Japanese carrier planes.

3 April

... Now I'm off to one of my ruddy Atolls which I understand is quite the last word in beastliness. However I must get the boys together for a nice talk as there's so much to discuss and arrange. I must say that as a result of these days at sea together the boys are beginning to shape up nicely and given the chance to continue these exercises I hope to have them in some sort of trim before very long. Have handed out a good many raspberries I must admit, but I believe it's essential to force the pace like blazes if you want to get a real move on. ...

231.   *From Commodore Edwards's diary*

4 April 1942

We sighted Addu Atoll at 0815, being followed by Force B at 2.30, and entered harbour. Addu Atoll is I think the most horrible place I have ever visited. The heat is intolerable; it consists of a series of small coral islands which form a ring. The ring, however, is not complete and we have had to put down various boom defences and indicator nets to make it reasonably anti-submarine proof. Even so, a submarine could sit outside and fire torpedoes into the fleet anchorage.

232.   *To his wife*

Addu Atoll,
4–6 April 1942

4 April

... Damn and *blast* it looks as if I've been had because a Catalina has just reported a large enemy force 350 miles SE of Ceylon – evidently the party I've been waiting for and here I am miles away and unable to strike. However I couldn't have stayed any longer as my miserable old battleboats were running out of water and short of fuel. But it's maddening to think they've slipped me this time. Of course there's a chance they might be coming to beat me up here so I'm off again tonight, but it's a pretty thin chance. Expect the India people not to mention those in Whitehall will want to know what the EF was doing. Crocks can't play centre court tennis and that's the answer. Also the proper way to defend Ceylon is *shore*-based aircraft and not the Fleet.

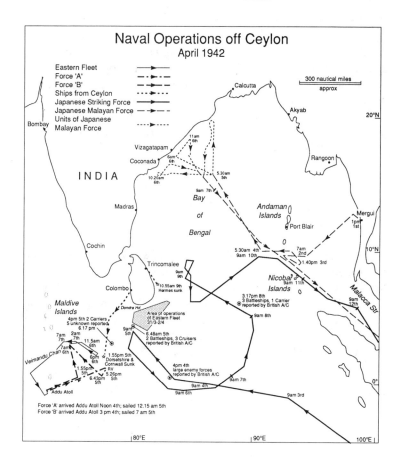

Naval Operations off Ceylon
April 1942

6 April (at sea)

I hope I shan't have to pass another Easter day like yesterday. It certainly was a black one. In my last letter I said we'd arrived at our Atoll. ... Algy Willis and Denis Boyd on board to see me, but we'd hardly got down to our talks when we got a signal to say that a large Japanese force had been sighted 350 miles SE of Ceylon and heading NW. The party we'd been out waiting for and here we were out of oil and water. In the blistering heat we set to and by midnight I was ready to leave with the carriers and some destroyers and cruisers, leaving the *Warspite* to come on later with the rest. *Dorsetshire* and *Cornwall* were at Colombo and had been ordered by Buffy [Arbuthnot] to go to the Atoll. I amended the order so that they could meet me at p.m. the next day. My appreciation was that the Japs would bomb Colombo and possibly Trinco and then shin out of it as fast as they could to the E and my only hope was that the Blenheims at Colombo might cripple one of their ships and I might be able to get at her with my own aircraft. I expected the attack on Colombo to take place at dawn or even earlier in the moonlight. Here I was wrong as the Japs did not attack until 8 a.m. All forenoon I waited anxiously for news of the enemy force but it was not until 1020 I had a report of enemy battleships about 320 miles NW of me. They seemed to be marking time and I appreciated that probably they were waiting for the carriers – which had not been located – to recover their aircraft. *Dorsetshire* and *Cornwall* by this time should have been S of the enemy about 150 miles and opening the range all the time so I felt no undue anxiety. We had no further news of the enemy until about 1.30 p.m. when a mutilated signal was received about a shadower. It was not until after 2 p.m. that it was identified as coming from *Dorsetshire*. That was the last we heard of her or *Cornwall*. An aircraft at 3.30 p.m. reported a lot of wreckage and some survivors and I sent off a destroyer to search but had to recall her after a short time as enemy forces including battleships and carriers were reported about 100 miles to the N of us, steering SW so I had to turn about to try and keep touch with them so as to attack after dark. Unfortunately my shadower was driven off by fighters and it was not until too late that I learnt that the enemy had altered course to the NW. By this time it was clear that I was greatly outnumbered by the enemy forces in the vicinity so all I could do was to retire W and join up with Willis at daylight. A black day – Colombo had been bombed and I had lost two 8" cruisers and nothing to show for it except 25 enemy aircraft shot down at Colombo but we lost a number of Hurricanes and two Catalinas.[1] Today I've been steaming back to where the two cruisers were sunk so as to try and pick up survivors and have sent a fast cruiser and two destroyers on ahead. But I've come to the conclusion that *until* I get a proper fleet out here I will simply have to hide, more or less. Nice prospect isn't it? Today the Japs have been roaring up the Bay of Bengal and sinking merchant ships right and left but I can do nothing. I haven't even a secure base to go to. . . . This is the biggest problem I've ever had to face and I look back with longing to what now appears to be the care-free days I had in Force H. Yes, anybody can have this job though at the moment I believe no one could do anything. The Jap ships have tremen-dous endurance whilst my old battleboats and destroyers have none. Well I can but do my best and hope that God won't be too hard on me if I try and do it. . . . Geoffrey Layton realises the fix I'm in and has sent a pretty strong telegram home which we intercepted today.

[1]The Japanese actually lost 7 planes; the British 25, including shore-based Fulmars and Swordfish.

233. *Extract from Commodore Edwards's diary*

6 April 1942

We rendezvoused with Force B at 0630 and steered to the Eastward to return to the area where the cruisers were last seen.

During the previous 24 hours and at this time there were continual tracks of reconnaissance aircraft being abroad and it was astonishing that the enemy never found us. We appreciated that the enemy would expect us to move W away from his main forces. We had furthermore some 1500 men in the water 100 miles to the E of us. We reckoned that probably the best way of dodging the enemy – which had by this time become the C-in-C's chief object – would be to move to the Eastward which would be the last direction in which the Japanese would expect us to proceed. This would not only (we hoped) fox them but also enable us to pick up our 1500 survivors. The C-in-C himself felt that the enemy would probably by now be moving E and would not be hanging about.

C-in-C Ceylon made a signal in which he said he considered a strong Japanese force was looking for the Eastern Fleet and was a very serious threat to the Eastern Fleet. In fact the signal contained the words: 'The Eastern Fleet now faces immediate annihilation'. The C-in-C decided to go and look for his survivors. Later on, two further signals suggested the enemy might still be looking for us and it was a very nasty situation.

234. *To his wife*

7 April 1942

Enterprise and the destroyers I sent off yesterday returned this afternoon with nearly 1200 survivors including both Captains of the 8" cruisers. That reduces the casualties to between 2 and 300 which is something to be thankful for. Apparently they were attacked by some 40–60 dive bombers and sank in about 15 minutes. Well it just shows that the Japs must have had a hell of a party out. It's just as well that they did not find me – and now I find I was only about 90 miles away from the cruisers – because I don't think we could have competed with that crowd of dive bombers. Any fighters that I could have sent over the cruisers would have been quite useless in the face of such an attack. In view of the fact that enemy forces appeared to be still in the vicinity I did not feel too happy about *Enterprise* and her destroyers until darkness fell when we turned W again. During the night my aircraft spotted 2 U-boats to the S of us so it looks as if the Japs had everything laid on to try and do me down. Now I'm in the unpleasant situation that I have to get oil and water and there is no guarantee that I shan't get roared up when I'm doing it as the place I have to use is quite unprotected. Well we've got to revise all our ideas and that's a fact. Until I can get reinforced I shall have to lie low in one sense but be pretty active in another – Keep the old tarts out of the picture and roar about with the others.

235. *To the Admiralty*

HMS *Warspite*,
8 April 1942

1. Enemy has complete command of Bay of Bengal and can, at his selected moment, obtain local command of the waters S and SW of Ceylon.
2. Our present naval forces and land-based air forces are quite inadequate to dispute this command. The Battlefleet is slow, out-gunned and of short endurance. Its available carrier-borne air protection would be of little use against repeated air attack on the scale used against the 8" cruisers. There is little security against air or surface attack at our naval bases in Ceylon and none at Addu.
3. It is not for me to say what balance must be struck between the Far East and other requirements, but unless naval and air reinforcements arrive or America does something to relieve the pressure in this area, there seems little to prevent the enemy establishing himself on the East Coast of India and eventually occupying Ceylon.
4. My intentions are as follows:

(a) To send Force B, consisting of 'R' class battleships, 'C' and 'D' cruisers and 6 destroyers to E African ports, where they can protect Middle East and Persian Gulf communications, and do some collective training. They are only a liability in this area at present.
(b) Force A, consisting of *Warspite*, large carriers, large 6" and 'E' class cruisers, to continue operating in Indian Ocean using Colombo, Addu, Bombay, Seychelles, Mauritius and occasionally E African ports as fuelling bases. Bombay and Durban to be maintenance bases.

5. Object of Force A is to deter enemy from attacking our communications in Indian Ocean with light forces and make it necessary for him to employ substantial forces for this purpose. Operations of Force A in Colombo–Addu area will be attended by some risks. This, I consider, must be accepted, but by constantly changing fuelling bases it should be difficult for the enemy to locate this force.

6.   Immediate intention for Force A to proceed to Colombo, carriers to replenish aircraft. *Formidable* now has only 6 serviceable fighters. Stay in harbour will be as short as possible, but essential I see Deputy C-in-C, EF.[1]

236.   *To the Admiralty*

8 April 1942

Experience of the last few days has shown the need for

(a)   More and first class fighters in carriers
(b)   A better performance aircraft than the Albacore for search and shadowing. Against Japanese aircraft these are not effective.

2.   State of fighter aircraft in Fleet now is: Martlet 6, Fulmar 8, Hurricane I 10, Hurricane II 1.
3.   Request immediate despatch more Fulmars as replacements.
4.   Can I be informed regarding

(a)   the extra fuel tank for Fulmars which is essential. It must not interfere with the work of the observer.
(b)   external long range tanks for Martlets and Hurricanes to allow them to act as escort fighters. An external jettisonable tank is an essential element of all carrier fighters.
(c)   when Martlet replacements will arrive.

5.   When these arrive intend to make the IE of Martlets 15 instead of 12 in *Illustrious* and *Formidable,* the extra aircraft to be stowed on outriggers, and to replace the 6 extra Fulmars in *Indomitable* with 8 or 9 Martlets depending on how many can be stowed.
6.   Request every endeavour may be made to make these intentions possible, and for Hurricane II's to replace Hurricane I's as soon as possible.
7.   When will Barracuda replace Albacore and Firefly the Fulmar?[2]

237.   *From Layton*

9 April 1942

1.   It is now quite clear that the Eastern Fleet will not be able to afford any appreciable protection to Ceylon or the East Coast of India for some

---

[1]Vice Adm Danckwerts.
[2]Fairey Barracuda: 1940, bomb load 1620lb, 2mg, 228mph; in service Sept 1943. Fairey Firefly: 1941, 4 cannon, bomb load 1000lb, 316mph; in service Oct 1943.

considerable time. It follows therefore that Ceylon requires a much more powerful Air Force than now exists.

2.   The FAA aircraft are proving more of an embarrassment than a help in comparison with land [-based aircraft] as they cannot operate by day in the presence of Japanese fighters and only tend to congest airfields. After today's operation our striking force consists of only 3 serviceable Blenheims which are of little [use?] against warships and extremely vulnerable to [Japanese] Navy 'O' fighters. What is required is a long range striking force. . . .

3.   The enemy must be expected to continue his attacks on Colombo and Trincomalee. Apart from the dislocation of work which is causing me grave anxiety I must emphasise the wasting effect on our fighter resources. At Trincomalee there are now 6 serviceable Hurricanes and in the Colombo area 16 [–?] which is in all 39 below our serviceable strength of a week ago. I regard with great concern the fact that the enemy is free to resume his attacks at any moment. Regard it as essential that our 3 Hurricane squadrons should be made up to strength immediately and one additional squadron[?] sent at once thus[?] making 4 out of the intended 6. Ample reserves of aircraft should be held at convenient aerodromes in India[?] ready to fly to Ceylon to make good waste directly it occurs. I suggest 100% would be appropriate.

238.   *To his wife*

9 April 1942

We got into our Atoll, refuelled and watered and have got out again without being roared up. Must say I was very relieved when we got clear. What a lousy position I'm in to be sure. TL's were kind enough to signal that they appreciated the very difficult 'game' I had to play! Know a lot better games I do than this one. Had the chance yesterday to get the boys on board and talk to them. Denis B[oyd] and Arthur B[isset] a little difficult. They both resent the fact that when it comes to carriers I know what I'm talking about. Algy Willis first class as usual. Am sorry to be parting from him and his chaps for the present, but it was the only thing to do. Believe the enemy have had U-boats watching my Atoll but rather think that I've hoodwinked them. Had a talk with Agar who was Captain of *Dorsetshire*. The Japs hit with their first bombs and it was all over in less than 15 minutes. The men behaved magnificently though they were in the water and on rafts for 30 hours before being picked up. Agar did very well and kept all the men together and their spirits up. One bright spot about this party. Now I'm in a fix because I simply must go to

Colombo with my staff to settle a whole mass of outstanding matters. *Later.* Trinco has been raided and damage caused in dockyard and an oil tank on fire. But, which is much worse, *Hermes*, a small carrier attached to me temporarily, which I sent back when the first attack failed to materialise as she was not much use to me, was apparently on her way round from Trinco to Colombo and was bombed and sunk. . . . We are having a hell of a time and no mistake – everything going against us at present and here I am quite unable to do anything at present to strike back. The situation is damned serious. If we only had a fraction of the hundreds of bombers that go from the UK to Germany every night out here it would alter the whole picture. *Later.* Just had news that 4 carriers, 9 heavy ships and destroyers have been sighted about 200 miles E of Ceylon steaming S at 25 knots. Well I'm going along the equator at present and shall turn N tonight. Apparently they sent off the Blenheims to attack the Japs – they got no hits and those that were not shot down are now unserviceable. What a party it is! No question of my going to Ceylon now so I shall go on up to Bombay as my ships simply must have a spell. . . . I am really perturbed now about the situation out here. The people at home don't seem to take any notice of the appreciations one sends them and it really looks as though we might lose India for the sake of a handful of aircraft and one or two decent ships. As for me going from pillar to post with no base –well it's just too lousy for words. *Later.* TL's have apparently woken up to our situation[1] . . . Glad they've woken up at last as I quite expected to get a message to say that I must take some offensive action against the Jap forces. However I'm quite clear in my mind what I ought to do.

239. *Pocket diary, 1942*

9 April

Third BS sailed for E African ports at 0300 which was later than I'd hoped. Force A left and I felt very much relieved when we got clear of Addu. Red warnings from Colombo and Trinco. Later we heard that Trinco had been bombed. *Erebus,*[2] Dockyard and China Bay aerodrome hit. Worst of all, *Hermes*, on her way from Trinco to Colombo, bombed and sunk and it looks as if *Vampire* and *Hollyhock*[3] also lost as no reply to signals. . . .

---

[1]Somerville was ordered to keep well away from Ceylon.
[2]*Erebus*: monitor, 1916, 7200t, 2×15in, 8×4, 12k.
[3]*Hollyhock*: 'Flower' class corvette; sunk S of Ceylon while escorting a tanker 9 April 1942. *Vampire* was sunk while escorting *Hermes*.

240. *To North*

10 April 1942

. . . I still can't make out what the hell the poor *Hermes* was doing 70 miles S of Trinco at 1100 when an air attack was expected. She ought to have been sailed the night before of course. . . . These Jap bombers certainly are the devil & we've got to revise all our ideas. You see we've never been up against carrier borne aircraft before . . . It's a damned unpleasant lesson we have to learn. My poor Albacores, Swordfish & Fulmars are useless against the Japs unless we can catch them at night.

241. *To the Admiralty*

11 April 1942

2. My appreciation of the scale of attack, based on information available, was two carriers with cruiser and destroyer escort, but allowance had to be made also for battleship covering force. Attack would be a hit-and-run raid with normal carrier aircraft, i.e., similar generally to Albacores.

3. On conclusion phase 1, when it became necessary for 'R' class to return and water, I decided against keeping Force A at sea as this was contrary to agreed policy.

4. Since no news of enemy received by a.m. 3rd it appeared enemy's intentions quite possibly misjudged or operation postponed. *Dorsetshire* had not completed repairs, *Cornwall* was required as an escort for Australian troop convoy, *Hermes* to prepare for special operation. These ships I accordingly despatched.

5. On receipt of information enemy at sea p.m. 4th I still adhered to my appreciation as in para. 2, and decided risk of Force A proceeding ahead of Force B could be accepted, provided the distance between the forces was not such that the enemy could interpose.

6. I was surprised at the attack on Colombo being delivered in daylight but considered this might be accounted for by lack of night flying experience. Apart from this, attack appeared to be on lines of appreciation though somewhat heavier than anticipated.

7. It was not until after 1700 when I was seriously concerned about *Dorsetshire* and *Cornwall* and when enemy force, including carriers, was sighted far S of estimated position, I realised my appreciation in para. 2 was incorrect and that the enemy had considerable carrier forces in the vicinity and was probably anxious to encounter my Fleet.

8.   The novel aspect of attack, viz, using, fighter dive-bombers,[1] was not appreciated until p.m. 6th on return of *Enterprise* with survivors.

9.   I then realised that, with very limited number of high-performance fighters I had available and vulnerability of 'R' class to this form of attack, it would be necessary to avoid an encounter until we were better equipped.

10.   It must be appreciated that my Fleet had had little or no gunnery training and the carriers are not yet up to normal standard of operating efficiency.

242.   *Pound to Alexander*

6 June 1942

. . . the Prime Minister has stated:–

No satisfactory explanation has been given by this Officer of the imprudent dispersion of his forces in the early days of April, resulting in the loss of *Cornwall, Dorsetshire* and *Hermes*. . . .

I do not think this can be allowed to go unchallenged and I accordingly suggest you should send a Memorandum to the Prime Minister on the lines of the attached draft.

243.   *Alexander to Churchill*

10 June 1942

I undertook to set out for you the true facts of the case, which are as follows:–

1.   Special intelligence showed the possibility of the Japanese carrying out operations against Ceylon, but the indications were vague and the date and scale of the attack were not known with any certainty.

2.   Admiral Somerville's appreciation of the scale of attack, based on information available, was two carriers with cruiser and destroyer escort, but he also made allowance for a battleship covering force. He assumed that the attack would be a hit and run raid with normal carrier aircraft.

3.   You will remember that Admiral Somerville put to sea on 30 March with the whole of his Fleet, including the 'R' class battleships.

---

[1]They were in fact the standard Japanese carrier dive bombers, Aichi D3A ('Val'): 1937, bomb load 816lb, 2mg, 266mph.

4. After a period at sea with no report of enemy forces, Admiral Somerville assumed that the enemy operations had been postponed or that enemy intentions had possibly been misjudged. The time had also come when it was necessary for the 'R' class battleships to return and water.

5. It was necessary to provide carrier protection for the 'R' class battleships during their return passage and hence the greater part of the Fleet had to return to Port T.[1]

6. As regards *Hermes, Cornwall* and *Dorsetshire* the C-in-C had to decide whether to take them to Port T and maintain his concentration or to disperse them. There were following reasons in favour of dispersion:-

Dorsetshire to complete repairs which she was carrying out when ordered to sea on 30 March.
Cornwall to escort an Australian troop convoy.
Hermes to prepare for operation IRONCLAD.

7. As no further indication had been received regarding the enemy's intentions and as several days had passed since the supposed date on which some unknown operation was to take place, Admiral Somerville decided to detach *Hermes, Cornwall* and *Dorsetshire* for the reasons just mentioned. The Admiralty saw no reason to dissent from this action.

8. C-in-C, E Indies, ordered *Dorsetshire* and *Cornwall* to prepare for sea on receipt of the enemy report early on 4 April and these ships were sunk the next day on their way to rendezvous with the Eastern Fleet.

244.　*Pocket Diary, 1942*

11 April

Formidable reported teeth stripped in gearbox. What a mess we are in to be sure. Signal from Buffy to say he sees no reason why Staff should leave and that Japs got a good knock! Looks to me like entirely false appreciation. Sent *Scout*[2] into Cochin with signals and orders to remain there. GL signalled that as Jap Fleet had returned to Singapore was it necessary for a Catalina to be sent to Bombay! First I've heard of the Jap Fleet going back. *Formidable* eased down to 8 knots to uncouple shaft. Remainder carried out A/A practice.

---

[1] Addu Atoll.
[2] *Scout*: 1918, 905t, 2×4in, 1×3in, 31k.

245.   *To his wife*

Bombay,
15 April 1942

It was perhaps unfortunate that the announcement of my appointment to the Eastern Fleet should have come at a time when the PM had to say that in spite of serious losses in the operations off Ceylon, the Government had not lost confidence in me! . . . I took great exception to the suggestion made by some members that there was a lack of co-operation between the RAF and Navy on this occasion. The trouble was that the RAF had nothing suitable or sufficiently trained to co-operate with. What little they had they did their best with. I sent a signal to say that so far as I am concerned there's no truth in the suggestion and the RAF did al they could[?] to help. I added that TL no doubt appreciated the loss of these ships was due in part to a wrong appreciation on my part . . .

246.   *To the Admiralty*

16 April 1942

If Fleet is to remain in Indian Ocean as I consider it should the part I may have to play against the enemy fleet will not necessarily be of my own selection. Unless my carriers are properly equipped my task of avoiding action with superior forces becomes increasingly difficult and the opportunity to strike back effectively should occasion offer becomes less.

2.   I have no information concerning spare aircraft at Kilindini or Aden but in any case consider concentration of Eastern Fleet not engaged on escort duties is now most desirable and cannot be unduly deferred.

An early decision is necessary.

247.   *From the Chiefs of Staff*

16 April 1942

1.   It is confirmed that it remains our policy to defend Ceylon. Should alternative arise of losing Ceylon or risking the destruction of Eastern Fleet, the former must be accepted as lesser evil.

2.   Colombo will be main base for fleet and both A/A defences and fighter protection should be given highest priority. A revised scale for defence of Colombo will be promulgated.

3.   Until such time as (a) adequate shore based reconnaissance is avail-

able (b) the air and A/A defences are available at Colombo (c) the Eastern Fleet is of sufficient strength and adequately trained, it will not be possible to use Colombo as main base and Kilindini is to be used as such temporarily. The question of providing fighter defence and A/A defence is under urgent consideration. The highest priority is to be given for all other defences. . . .

248. *Pocket diary, 1942*

17–21 April 1942

17 April

Still unable to get any news as to whether Cats really did see one B/S and one C/A off Ceylon. Hastened Buffy, Denis and Bill T[ennant] on board at 1045 for discussion of COS appreciation on 9-carrier striking force proposed by US. Too much about a balanced Fleet. Shall be relieved when this next phase is over.[1]

16 April

. . . signal from PM to Roosevelt[2] to ask him to send reinforcements here, and saying *Renown, Nelson* and *Rodney* all coming out here etc. So it looks as if they have really woken up.

19 April

Meeting of COs and FOs at 1045 and discussed situation and future movements. Admiralty have agreed to no further work on Addu at present. Wavell, Holland-Martin and Coats ADC[3] on board at 6.30 to embark for trip to Colombo. So far as I can make out coast clear, but Japs have told Germans they intend to attack W Indian Ocean. Shall be glad when my reinforcements arrive.

21 April

Flew off ALT attack at 0530 for dawn attack and during day carried out a number of air exercises, A/A barrage etc. Signals to show that

---

[1]Somerville was about to lose several major units to IRONCLAD; as Adm King disliked combining US forces with those of other navies, especially if command was to be exercised by a foreign officer, the super carrier task force came to nothing.
[2]Churchill to Roosevelt, 15 April 1942, in Kimball, vol. 1, pp. 452–4.
[3]Cdr D. E Holland-Martin: Lt-Cdr 1937; EO, *Tartar*, 2DF, Home F 1938; *Holderness* May 1940; Cdr Dec 1940; Admy Jan 1941; *Lanka*, Ceylon Jan 1942; *Nubian* June 1942; *Victory* June 1944; N Asst, 2SL June 1945. Actg Capt P. D. Coats: R Sig (TA); 2Lt Aug 1939; Lt March 1941; ADC to Wavell Aug 1941.

Renown is being sent right away to join me and that *Duke of York*[1] will follow in due course. Nothing further re *Nelson* and *Rodney*. . . . Long message about IRONCLAD, that it was not[?] fixed that I must support and call it off if necessary. No signs of any Jap move towards Ceylon. Laird and [?] convinced next move is in direction Australia.[2]

249.   *From Wavell*

HQ, C-in-C India,
Delhi,
20 April 1942

1.   Can you give me yet a forecast of the strength and disposition of your fleet

at the beginning of May,
at the middle of May,
at the end of May,

and what action you could take in the event of an invasion of India or Ceylon by those dates?
2.   Can you say at all by what date the preparation of Addu Atoll as a defensive base could probably recommence?

This will help me a great deal in the distribution of A/A, artillery and other troops.

I imagine that you would like all possible reconnaissance and preparation made so that, when the decision to recommence is taken, work can proceed as quickly as possible.

250.   *To Wavell*

21 April 1942

Strength of Fleet

The forecasted strength of the Eastern Fleet is as follows:

Beginning of May. Warspite, 4 'R' class, 3 carriers, 5 cruisers, 12 destroyers.

Late May.   By the end of May, *Valiant* and *Renown* and possibly one other capital ship, 2 destroyers and minor reinforcements may have joined.

[1]*Duke of York*: 1941, 35,000t, 10×14in, 16×5.25in, 28k. Neither she nor *Renown* materialised at this time.
[2]Actg Cdr (Ret) H. R. M. Laird: SO (1), Eastern F, 1942; Actg Capt, DNI, Eastern F & i/c OIC Feb 1944; Actg Capt *Saker* (BAD) 1945.

Disposition of Fleet

2.   The main body of the Fleet will be disposed, until at all events, late in May, on the western side of the Indian Ocean. From this main body there will be detachments of capital ships and cruisers as escorts to convoys, and one battleship may be refitting.

3.   It is not expected that reinforcements of sufficient strength will reach me before June to enable me to operate against enemy forces attacking India or Ceylon. If the Japanese employ a major Fleet concentration, my available forces would be insufficient.

4.   Until such time as my carrier-borne aircraft are adequate in numbers and of first class performance I shall not be able to operate my fleet against a concentration of enemy aircraft carriers or in waters which are within operating range of land based aircraft attack. This applies in particular to waters covered by long range shore-based fighters.

My Intentions

5.   My intentions are to remain at sea as much as possible and use unfrequented anchorages in order to make the Japanese uncertain of my movements. It is hoped thereby to deter them from attempting any interference with our Middle East and Indian communications, except with a heavy Fleet concentration. It should make them chary of sending raiding forces into the western Indian Ocean.

Addu Atoll

6.   A well defended, well equipped and easily maintained base in the Central Indian Ocean would be invaluable, but it would be of no use to prepare such a base until I am in a position to dispute effectively any Japanese attempt to seize the base.

7.   Until the situation in this respect becomes stabilised I consider no further development of Addu should proceed except the installation of, say, 4 heavy and 4 light A/A guns with which to engage enemy reconnaissance aircraft and convey the impression that the base is defended. No date can be given at present when work on Addu should commence as this must depend entirely on the situation.

251.   *To his wife*

at sea,
22 April 1942

Archie Wavell and two of his staff came on board to take passage to Colombo. . . . It's given me a good chance to have a real good talk to him and for him to see how the fleet does its stuff at sea and how the air works. We have floods of messages from Winston telling us what a lot of aircraft and ships we have, or are going to have and how vital it is for this, that and the other to be done. WC's arithmetic must be his weak point because his figures never correspond to ours. So far as I can judge the Japs don't meditate another strike at Ceylon just yet so with luck I ought to get in and away without running into a superior force. . . . WC has sent FDR a pretty good stinker pointing out our situation and asking him to reinforce me and do something but I don't flatter myself it will have any effect. . . .

252. *To his wife*

25 April 1942

In spite of Wavell and GL telling the COS Committee they couldn't possibly agree to my having any Cats they have been over-ruled. The COS say they agree with my appreciation and I am to have them.[1] . . .

253. *Pocket diary, 1942*

27–28 April 1942

27 April

. . . Signal from Syfret which says he and Smuts agree to extension of IRONCLAD. Oiling at Seychelles presents a bit of a problem as there is no protection against U-boats. Cruisers carried out a night attack. Type 271 made it all too easy to counter.

28 April

ALT attack before dawn but did not go off very well. ASV not doing its stuff. Destroyers and cruisers doing throw-off shoots. Had a good tactical exercise against cruisers. In the afternoon *Warspite* oiled *Decoy*. Latter made a proper mess of it and finally carried away hose and knocked a man overboard. Some of the signals we landed at Colombo do not appear to have been transmitted. What a mess it is out here. Did flare trials on cruisers after dark. Not at all successful.

---

[1]Somerville was to control all Catalinas in Indian Ocean; they were vital for longe range reconnaissance.

254.   *To the Admiralty*

29 April 1942

As stated in my 0306/10[1] use of Albacore or Swordfish striking force against Japanese carriers must be restricted to night or good cloud cover.
2.   Against Navy Zero fighters, Fulmars have inadequate performance. Range of Martlet or Hurricane when escorting Albacores or Swordfish is restricted to a short strike.
3.   In order to provide Eastern Fleet with an effective day striking force, however limited, request 880 squadron may be lent or re-equipped immediately with 14 Hurricane II with bomb racks.
4.   The performance of Hurricane II's is superior to Japanese fighter and in support of distant operations it is considered we may have good prospects of achieving success in a day strike.[2]

255.   *From Pound*

1 May 1942

Your policy to remain on the defensive if contact is made during clear weather thus leaving initiative to Japanese is as unattractive to us as I am sure it is to you, as unless your fighters can eliminate Japanese, some must get past your fighter defences.

You would thus be open to grave risk of carriers' decks being damaged and still be confronted with an undamaged enemy. Request you will signal more fully reasons supporting your policy.

256.   *To Pound*

2 May 1942

The unattractive policy you refer to is forced on me by the very unattractive aircraft with which my carriers are equipped.
2.   The situation is comparable to that at home, where low performance bombers are no longer used for daylight operations in clear weather.
3.   It is no use disguising the fact that for day striking we are outclassed by the Japanese, whose dual purpose fighter-dive bombers can be switched from attack to defence whilst in the air.[3]

---

[1]Not reprinted but the gist is in No. 236 & para. 4 of No. 250.
[2]This was at the very least highly debatable.
[3]Vals had successfully fought Fulmars.

4. I may be forced to make a day strike, but I shall avoid if possible subjecting my slow Albacores and Swordfish to so unequal a combat. It would be my endeavour to force on the enemy a long range day strike and to keep my fighters fresh and concentrated to break up the attack before it can get home. The alternative of a weak strike and weak defence does not appeal to me nor to my Flag Officers with whom this matter has been discussed.

5. At night or in low cloud the position is reversed and, thanks to ASV, we have the advantage both in shadowing and striking.

6. I regret that my 0306/10 did not make all this clear but I thought by now it would be appreciated that our FAA, suffering as it does from arrested development for so many years, would not be able to compete on all round terms with an FAA which has devoted itself to producing aircraft fit for sailors to fly in.

257.   *Pocket diary, 1942*

3 May

Reached first air search position at 0900 and sent off air recco to E to a depth of 195 miles. Sighted nothing. Oiled *Nestor*. Very bad at first and nearly came into us 3 or 4 times. Rosenthal not at his best! *Norman* after lunch was very much better[1] and *Warspite* quite good at it now. Japs have entered Mandalay and Akyab being evacuated . . . Signal from Admiralty to say extension of IRONCLAD to Tamatave and Majunga is not to be carried out. Seems a mistake.

258.   *To his wife*

3 May 1942

Lost one of my precious Martlets yesterday. . . . Another Martlet crashed into the barrier and lost its prop. Damn nuisance as they're as precious as gold and the only decent fighters I have. I'm getting a bit fussed about my ships as they all seem to be developing complaints as the result of this continuous sea time. I simply must try to get them a week in harbour though that will be barely enough. My Dutchman[2] has trouble with his rudder and I've had to send him to dock. Can't afford really to do without any of the force I have and so many of them are proper bits of old Ming.

[1]Cdr A. R. Rosenthal, RAN
Norman (L), RAN: 1941, 1760t, 6×4.7in, 1×4in, 5tt, 36k.
[2]HNMS *Heemskerck.*

259.   *Pocket diary, 1942*

5–7 May 1942

5 May

Sent off long distance air recco at 0700 and then steamed about 150 miles off NE coast of Madagascar. Intercepted a French signal to say they were being attacked and would fight to the last and refused to surrender Madagascar. Later reports that aerodrome bombed by us, hangars and all aircraft destroyed. Syfret reports operation proceeding according to plan and not much opposition. All Albacores returned safely from search in spite of v. bad weather. Turned NE at 1430.

6 May

Turned to NW again at 0130. Syfret giving very little information. Sent off air search at 1000 when weather cleared a bit. Situation report shows that resistance stiffening and do not expect to have harbour open until tomorrow. Sent *Resolution* and Force B with the two 'E's' back to Kilindini as short of fuel and water. Ultra[1] that 3 French submarines proceeding to Diego. Later report says that attack on naval base failed and 17 Brigade suffered 25% casualties and 50% tanks out of action. Night attack to be made and *Anthony*[2] to enter harbour and land 50 Marines as diversion. Trust this attack succeeds. Arrangements to bombard fort at entrance tomorrow morning and assault Orangia[?} peninsula.

7 May

Anthony got in and out with no damage or casualties. Assault on naval base successful. *Genista* got U-boat contact off [–?] Bay and later heard U-boat sunk and survivors picked up.[3] Ships took up position to bombard forts at entrance but SOF ordered bombardment to be postponed and it appeared later that French had decided to surrender. Carried out air search a.m. and p.m. and at 1700 turned to NW to shape course to Kilindini. Glad we've got Diego without too much trouble.

---

[1]Ultra, the code name for decrypts made from the Enigma machine at Bletchley Park, enabling Allied HQ to read enemy signals.
[2]*Anthony*: 1930, 1350t, 4×4.7in, 8tt, 35k.
[3]*Genista*: 'Flower' class corvette. The French submarine *Le Héros* was sunk off the coast but by a Swordfish.

260. *To the Admiralty*

9 May 1942

Colombo

2.   Colombo cannot accommodate whole Fleet until additional deep water berths have been dredged. In SW monsoon conditions entry of ships drawing 35 feet would not be practicable on occasions, sand in harbour at this period is also an adverse factor.

3.   Until such time as the approaches to Ceylon are so well covered with long distance air reconnaissance as to eliminate possibility of surprise, the concentration of Eastern Fleet in this relatively small congested harbour would be most inadvisable. During the SW monsoon and at other periods of low visibility possibility of surprise must always exist.

4.   Until an allied advance has removed Colombo from its front line position where it is under reconnaissance by enemy shore-based aircraft I consider it can only be regarded as an operational base at which part (R) part of fleet can refuel in favourable conditions and where one or two ships at a time can be sent for rest and refit.

5.   To meet above requirements I agree that every effort must be made to bring the defences of Ceylon, including long distance air reconnaissance, fighter protection and air striking force to the scale which its importance merits.

Kilindini and Diego Suarez

6.   Until the allies can advance to the eastward, Kilindini and its associated anchorages must remain the main base. Diego Suarez can only be accepted as a temporary occupational base until such time as whole island is in our hands. Occupation of island appears essential since otherwise necessity to forestall Japanese entry if French invite them will be an additional commitment for the Eastern Fleet.

Other Bases

7.   Seychelles is important as a fuelling base for detached units, but proximity to Diego Suarez renders it of less importance than hitherto.

8.   Mauritius is important as a fuelling base and should be given priority for scale of defence to meet this requirement.

9.   Addu Atoll – When Eastern Fleet is in a position to deny Japanese occupation in force, which, from the whittling down of proposed reinforcements, does not appear to be an immediate possibility, aerodromes and other defence measures should proceed with all despatch. This is the only suitably placed harbour which can accommodate the whole Eastern

Fleet, and probably the only one from which our movements will not be communicated direct to the enemy.

10.   Salala is required to deal with the possibility of Ceylon falling into enemy hands and as a base to deal with enemy raiding force in Arabian Sea.

11.   Diego Garcia is useful as a refuelling base for ships other than capital ships and as an operating base for flying boats.

261.   *Alexander to Churchill*

15 May 1942

. . . the Eastern Fleet now have available 43 Martlets including reserve aircraft in E Africa. There are 29 *en route* from the USA all of which should arrive at Mombasa this month. 36 more should have arrived by 7 July, then 21 in each of the 3 succeeding months followed by 33 which should reach Mombasa by 7 November. Altogether these numbers total over 200. As regards Sea Hurricanes Admiral Somerville should by now have 31 either in his Carriers or in E Africa. As you know production of this type has now ceased and they are due to be replaced by adapted Spitfires which will be called Seafires I and II.[1] The estimated production of Seafire II's is 6 this month, 20 next and 24 in July with completion of the whole order for 250 by the end of this year. It is our aim to send sufficient of this aircraft to meet the C-in-C Eastern Fleet's requirements. We are working to ship 20 Seafire I's in June and 10 in July as a start.

While we are therefore doing all we can to build up a substantial fighter strength for the Eastern Fleet we remain gravely concerned at the lack of up to date aircraft with which to strike at the enemy when the chance occurs. We accordingly attach the utmost importance to getting Barracudas at the earliest possible moment to re-equip our striking squadrons. Meanwhile the best we can do is to supply *Indomitable* with Hurricane II's fitted to carry bombs. Action to this end is in hand. Unfortunately *Indomitable* is the only modern carrier whose lifts will take this type.

262.   *To his wife*

18 May 1942

. . . I had to move into Government House as there was so much required my attention ashore I couldn't spare the time to take the boats

[1]Supermarine Seafire: 1942, 2 cannon, 4mg, 352mph.

out for exercises so left Algy Willis to do that and very well he did it. He's absolutely first class as my second in command and I couldn't have a better one. The rather wet project which I was asked to remark on and which was obviously a pet of WC's is now off.[1] As usual I gave my very candid opinion which they can take or leave as they like. This time they appeared to have accepted my views. However I've had to send a lot of little chaps and some others to . . . Bobbie Harwood who I trust will remain ashore in Alex as he's not had any practice in driving a team afloat. . . . No one can understand why we had to utter a word about the Free French in Madagascar. All it did was to make the whole population hostile and what the next move is I'm damned if I know. . . . The task of creating a first class base out of nothing is proving the hell of a job. My staff have to work all hours but we are slowly getting our heads above water.

263. *Pocket diary, 1942*

20–23 May 1942

20 May

. . . Admiralty now saying we must decide whether Diego or Kilindini should be main base. They plump for former whilst I prefer latter on grounds that any improvements will remain British and not much to choose strategically. USA wants us to send a carrier to SW Pacific. Quite useless.[2] Also Admiralty proposal to send 3 'R's' to Australia for anti-invasion. . . . Admiralty now saying any demonstration by Force A towards Sumatra etc. would have no effect on Japs. Don't believe this myself. . . .

23 May

. . . Admiralty say we have to send *Newcastle* and *Birmingham* for JULIUS.[3] Damned nuisance. Late message to say Yanks want Force A to go to Colombo. All the 5 crocks of destroyers left are laid up! . . .

---

[1]Churchill had suggested that Eastern Fleet should sail through the Suez Canal, fight a convoy through to Malta and entice the Italian Fleet into a major action.

[2]Adm King requested a British carrier to strengthen his depleted air power in the Pacific, in anticipation of the Japanese attack on Midway; even if the US had given us early, full and accurate intelligence, it would have been impossible for the RN to furnish a carrier in time.

[3]Presumably in the Mediterranean.

264. *To North*

27 May 1942

... Every time I try & get things going with my Fleet something inter-venes. Madagascar was the first. Some of my chaps were with Syfret & with the rest I had to act as long stop. A dull but necessary business. ...

No sooner was that party over than I've had to send all my boats for a proper SUBSTANCE.[1] Tremendous argument as to whether my own boat & 3 aerodromes should take part. Winnie evidently all for it. Alfred[2] against. I said it was the sort of party I liked but I reckoned the odds of 1320 dickies against 120 was such that the prospect of the aero-dromes being usable afterwards was remote. The arguments waxed hot but eventually they accepted my opinion.

Now I have tiresome requests that I should put 4 pints in a pint bottle at Geoffrey L's abode of love & take the chance of rude boys throwing stones & breaking the bottle. The big idea being to stop [the Japanese] from using the Bay of Bengal as their own pitch. The proper answer of course is a well balanced, trained &experienced air force on the E Coast of India. I keep on saying this ...

Well I'm now in the state that I have practically no trousers, so to speak, but must go over to see Geoffrey in order to attract attention & then disappear in the big wide spaces & see if I can get in a strike some-where.

The problem of starting a Scapa from nothing is terrific. It irks me to know that all the other ships[3] have lots of facilities & no boats whereas my case is just the reverse. Still I have some darn good chaps to help me. Algy Willis absolutely first class but looks like death always. Danckwerts my deputy as clever as they make them, Bill Tennant a charming and capable chap, Dennis Boyd capable but contentious, Read relieving Buffy at Colombo. Old Stuart (retd) as FOIC here.[4] ...

... As I've told TL's the Japs pulled a fast one on me & I was lucky to get off with that – I refer to the two 8". If I'd had any idea of the sort of party they had ready to hand out I should have acted quite differently. But when your long range recco is reduced to a very few Catalinas that

<hr>

[1]The Malta convoy of June 1942, HARPOON.
[2]Pound.
[3]A slip for stations.
[4]Rear Adm A. D. Read: Capt 1932; *Liverpool* 1938; *Ramillies* Nov 1940; RA & FO Ceylon May 1942; RA, 4CS, Eastern F Oct 1943; VA, Ret List June 1945; FOIC, Cardiff July 1945.
    Rear Adm C. G. Stuart: Capt 1928; Ret List; *Flora* (Invergordon) May 1940; *Bacchante* (Aberdeen) 1941; *Tana* (Kilindini) 1942; *Drake* (Devonport) Dec 1944.

get shot down as soon as they sight you don't get much news. Lack of a land based air striking force is yet another major handicap. But I accept full responsibility for the two 8" & can only say that we bought our experience somewhat cheaply on the whole.

Still you can imagine how I itch to get one back on those bastards.

I too was rather surprised at Tiny Little's appt. to Portsmouth as he's had a pretty good run already & they might well have kept it for others who have been prosecuting the war afloat.[1] We got the buzz out here that Winnie said if DP went Dickie Mount B should be the next FSL. I've a great admiration for his drive & brains but I think he's more of a nuts & bolts chap & doubt his ability to deal with the bigger questions. There would be much tooth sucking among the Flag Officers if such an appt. was made. Most plump as I do for Bruce Fraser.[2]

265.   *To his wife*

28 May 1942

Am having some terrific arguments with TL's these days. I think really it is Winnie who is insisting on certain things being suggested. I keep on saying these are quite unsound but I get rather tired at going on and on at the same subject. I shall eventually ask 'don't you read my bloody signals?' Well when I get off in the blue I shan't be able to answer at any rate. Expect to be with GL in about 8 or 9 days and after that wander about like a homeless dog seeing if I can pick up anything and taking care not to be picked up myself. All rather tricky but I hope it will pan out all right. . . . I know little cf how the war proceeds. The Japs seem to have moved E – that's one reason why I follow them so as to create a diversion. Wish I could catch some of them on the hop somewhere.

266.   *From the Admiralty*

2 June 1942

Colombo.   Operational base for Force A. The defence and berthing facilities already approved to be completed as soon as possible. It is

---

[1]Adm Sir Charles Little had been Head of BAD, Washington, being succeeded by Adm Sir Andrew Cunningham; he was to become C-in-C Portsmouth.

[2]See Roskill, *Churchill and the Admirals*, p. 143. It is curious that Somerville should opt for Fraser rather than Cunningham as Pound's successor, and moreover state that it was majority opinion among FOs. When Pound resigned in 1943, Fraser was Churchill's first choice; see Simpson, 'Cunningham', in Murfett, ed., *From Fisher to Mountbatten*, forthcoming.

anticipated that Force A will consist of 4 capital ships, 3 carriers, 2 cruisers, 2 destroyer flotillas.

Trincomalee. To be developed with highest priority as main Fleet base capable of berthing up to 10 capital ships and carriers, 10 cruisers, 24 destroyers, 3 depot ships, 10 submarines, 16 Fleet minesweepers . . .

Kilindini. To continue with arrangements already approved for using Kilindini and associated anchorages as a Fleet Base. . . .

The size of force which will make use of Kilindini at any one time is not expected to exceed 5 capital ships/carriers, 3 large cruisers, 3 'C' or 'D' cruisers, 3 destroyer flotillas (in addition to 2 depot ships and local forces). . . .

267. *Pocket diary, 1942*

31 May–11 June 1942

31 May

At 1 a.m. signal from Syfret to say that *Ramillies* had been torpedoed in Diego Suarez and later that a tanker had also been hit. Told *Duncan* and *Active* to leave us and go to Diego. Danks ordered the *Jan van Galen* to go there. Told the 'L's' to come on so as to R/V with us.[1]

6 June

Signal from C-in-C SA shows that there are two Jap raiders off Durban to eastward. 20 knot ships well armed.[2] What I've been expecting. Danks has taken all necessary steps. Told him to use *Indomitable* if necessary. . . .

7 June

. . . At least 4 U-boats operating in Mozambique channel. Danks has established a cruiser patrol off N end. told him I thought this was undesirable.[3]

9 June

U-boats still active in Mozambique [channel] and problem of *Queen Mary*[4] escort difficult. Told Danks to send *Devonshire* to escort and use

[1]By 2 midget submarines launched from the patrol s/m *I-10*; tanker sunk, *Ramillies* severely damaged. *Jan Van Galen*, R Neth N: ex-*Noble*, 1941, 1760t, 6x4.7in, 1x4in, 5tt, 36k. 'L's' were destroyers.
[2]Adm Tait. Probably *Hokoku Maru* and *Aikoku Maru;* they accomplished little.
[3]Presumably because of the presence of U-boats.
[4]*Queen Mary*: 1936, 80,774gt, 29.5k, Cunard White Star Line.

Gambia also. No sign of raiders. . . . Ashore to Naval offices and had a blow up with Buffy about security.

11 June

Danks evidently thinks raiders may be N of Seychelles and has *Indomitable* etc. disposed to catch them. I don't believe they have gone N. . . .

268. *Churchill to Pound*

10 June 1942

The loss of these four aircraft carriers etc[1] sensibly improves our position in the Indian Ocean and Bay of Bengal. For instance, Addu Atoll which can only be attacked by seaborne aircraft becomes pretty secure and is worthy of more attention. There still remain shore-based aircraft at the Andamans, but these are not very numerous and the distance is great from there to Colombo or Trincomalee. It seems to me that severe restraint is imposed upon the Japanese by their need to husband their large naval units. Perhaps you will consider what further instructions should be given to Admiral Somerville. . . .

269. *Pound to Churchill*

10 June 1942

1.   Our position in the Indian Ocean is improved inasmuch as the Japanese are less likely to stick their head out into it.
2.   . . . *Note.* It is true the Japanese Carriers attacked both Colombo and Trincomalee without suffering damage because we had no striking force of any value.
4.   I am of the opinion that the correct thing for Admiral Somerville to do is to get his Carrier force properly trained so that if the Japanese stick their heads out into the Indian Ocean we shall give them a knock. *Formidable* and *illustrious* should be efficient by now but what with the ferrying trips she did and the time she has spent in harbour putting her steam joints right the *Indomitable* will not be efficient for some little time.
5.   Whilst working up his carriers he should endeavour to destroy the Japanese surface raiders which are becoming active in the Indian Ocean.

[1] The four Japanese carriers sunk in the Battle of Midway earlier in the month.

7. I would propose to instruct Admiral Somerville in the sense of paras. 4 & 5, adding that it is not desired that he should expose his carriers to attack by shore based aircraft. . . .

270.   *To his wife*

at sea,
13 June 1942

Having sent off messages for the last month to the C-in-C Pacific Fleet, Admiralty and Washington, asking if I might be given some details of the Coral Sea action, I got it eventually from the BBC this morning. It really is the damn limit and I shall send a snorter to all concerned. All sorts of technical information I want which would be of the utmost value to me and I can't get it. Blast all Allies says I. . . . Over the argument that rages as to whether I should use my old parish as my main base I said that I didn't put much faith in the RAF there to look after me. GL took great exception to this, said they were all on the top line in a signal to the Admiralty. However on leaving we did some tests with them and I fear poor GL will have to eat his words as the tests showed I was perfectly right. After all it's the sort of stuff I do know something about. . . . What would do us all more good than anything else at the moment is to have some sort of crack at those ruddy Japs and do a bit of shooting at something. Fellows get stale and lose their edge if you don't have a mix-up at reasonably frequent intervals.

271.   *Pocket diary, 1942*

21 June

Signal from Admiralty that *Indomitable* is to fill up with Sea Hurricanes and to be at Freetown by 29 July. *Nelson* and *Rodney* to remain there also. Looks like another W Med convoy.[1] . . .

272.   *To Joan Bright Astley*

23 June 1942

. . . The Japs are attending to their sores at the moment but should not be surprised if they stage a face saving raid in these waters. I must therefore keep them guessing as to what I've got & where I've got it. I must

[1]PEDESTAL, the August convoy to Malta.

also give Danckwerts a hand for a bit as he's had to hold the baby over-much of late.[1] ...

273. *To Pound*

29 June 1942

BASES

Addu Atoll. The effect of the monsoon on the net defences has been much worse than expected and it will be necessary to alter the A/S scheme of defence radically. Stileman's[2] visit confirms that only one aerodrome can be made, i.e., that on Gan. ... Apart from its superior strategical situation *vis à vis* Colombo and Trincomalee and freedom from land based air attack, Addu has the great advantage that it is isolated and the enemy should be obliged to use direct observation to find out if the fleet is present. None of the other bases, Seychelles excepted, enjoys this security at present. I shall be sending you further views about the development of Addu after I have had a chance to discuss this with my 'defended base' experts now at Kilindini.

Colombo. As you will have gathered from my signals the air force and warning system in Ceylon at present is far from being sufficiently effective to provide reasonable protection to the fleet against heavy scale air attack by the Japanese. At the moment the Japs have not the forces required in the Malaya area but given a sufficiently tempting target, and by that I mean the full Force A marshalled like sardines in a tin in that small harbour, I feel sure they would feel it was well worth their while to plan a special operation and concentrate forces for that purpose. With 'special intelligence' in its present state and the PRU still inadequate we might well receive little or no warning that an attack was meditated. But I think a *sine que non* from the Jap point of view, would be that we were using the harbour for extended periods. ... By using Colombo for odd periods, i.e., in for 24 hours and out for a week and vice versa, I think the Japs would consider the target not sufficiently static to justify locking up any considerable force for a possible attack. As our recco., striking force and warning system, coupled with fighter direction, improve, we can afford to take more chances. But even so with ships packed so close together, a land based night bombing raid might do a lot of damage.

---

[1] Adm Danckwerts ran operations from Kilindini, including the heavy convoy traffic to and from Suez, the Persian Gulf and India.
[2] Cdr L. H. Stileman: Lt-Cdr Jan 1938; FTO, 8DF, Home F, *Faulkner* June 1939; Sqdn TO, *Renown* Dec 1941; Cdr June 1942; PD Aug 1942–4.

Trincomalee   The same remarks apply except that:–

1.   Ships are not packed so tightly.
2.   It has better intelligence security than a port like Colombo.
3.   More open to surprise by low approach land based air attack.
4.   Deep water approach favours U-boat operations, including two-man submarines.

When we can strike back at enemy air concentrations at Sabang and Port Blair, the situation will improve though aircraft dispersed in the jungle surrounding aerodromes in these parts are not easy to locate.

Diego Suarez.   The dock will be invaluable when it is able to operate and will relieve congestion at Durban, Colombo, etc. But until we have the whole of the island I shall never feel that our position is too secure.

Seychelles.   This is so important as a fuelling base that I feel it is essential to afford it some degree of protection. The harbour does not lend itself to fixed A/S protection and I feel that after blocking certain of the approaches we shall have to rely on A/S patrols to keep U-boats away from the tankers.

The new siting of the 6" guns should help to deter raiders from shaking the place up at close range. I was able to meet Col Lukis of the MNBDO and visit the new sites. He is a first class fellow[1] . . .

Mauritius and Diego Garcia.   These are being given a reasonable degree of A/S protection for use as fuelling bases but I fear the latter will never be suitable for battleships unless extensive deepening of the shoal patches is undertaken.

Kilindini.   I feel the decision to make this a principal base where ships can be at extended notice has been fully justified. Its position, on the E African line of communication, makes it most suitable for trade protection and it was necessary to have a place where the 'Y' organisation and the shore based staff could work undisturbed. Having no 'Singapore' in these parts is a serious handicap and makes it important that for the present ships should not be sent out here that are likely to require undue upkeep.

TRAINING

In odd snatches we have been able to put in a good deal of training but far more is required. I think the A/A fire shows the best advance so far but fighter interception still leaves a good deal to be desired. As I have so

---

[1]Col W. B. F. Lukis, RM: Lt-Col 1939; MNBDO 1940; Col 2nd Cdt May 1943; Actg Maj-Gen, MNBDO (1); Actg Brig & Col Cdt, Plymouth May 1944; Col Cdt & Actg Maj-Gen, RM Engrs June 1944.

frequently reported the IFF and poor R/T communication are the chief trouble, but there is also a sad lack of imagination on occasions.

AIRCRAFT

The Martlets, except for certain technical defects, are undoubtedly good and very robust. Fulmars are now relegated to fighter reconnaissance as they are no match for Jap Zero fighters. Both Albacores and Swordfish are too slow for day strikes in clear weather and except for relatively short distance strikes cannot be escorted by Martlets or Hurricanes owing to the wide discrepancy in cruising speed and endurance. If our fighters can have additional detachable fuel tanks, this will make all the difference.

The operation of aircraft from carriers is steadily improving and landing on times of about 30 seconds per aircraft for large flights are often achieved.

W/T communication in this area is always difficult and recent tests indicate that far too high a percentage of recco reports may fail to get through.

The best method of operating carriers at night is being continually reviewed but I have not yet had an opportunity to determine the extent to which 3 carriers can operate throughout the night and yet receive sufficient protection from the main body. Night strikes are being continually practised and should prove most effective. I believe we have the advantage here over the Japanese and that we should develop our tactics and techniques to this end. Good night recco is of course essential.

RDF

We are still having difficulty with the Type 281 and its failure to detect high raiders. I hope the experts from the Signal School will be able to help us.

The Type 285 – HA detection – sets are *most* disappointing and rarely give any results. The Type 284 – Main Armament Ranging – set unfortunately fails over 20,000 yards but may prove invaluable at night.

OFFENSIVE OPERATIONS

The outstanding need at the moment is action of some sort. A few ships had a mild blooding at Diego Suarez but apart from that we suffer badly from not being able to loose off our guns at something. I have considered a carrier attack on Port Blair and Sabang but to be quite honest I do not believe that any results we are likely to achieve would justify risking sending the carriers in except on the grounds that it would certainly be a good tonic to the fleet. My information shows that there are only flying boats at Port Blair and against them we should use fighters, but that means taking the carriers in to within say 70 miles. Helfrich says that the dispersal at Sabang is so good and easy it would be difficult to spot where it is and here again I rather doubt if a Swordfish-Albacore attack would produce sufficiently good results.

Nevertheless I am keeping this continually in mind and as soon as I can scratch up two long endurance cruisers to accompany the party, circumstances may justify one or both of these operations being carried out.

MINELAYING

It was quite obvious if anything was to come of Wavell's scheme for an attack on Rangoon we must not foul the approaches, so I've called off *Manxman*'s intended operation for the present. The monsoon does not permit laying off the coast between Rangoon and Akyab so I've told *Manxman* that after trying out her camouflage at Addu, she is to visit Madras, Vizagapatam and Calcutta so as to study conditions and facilities in order to be all ready for a quick lay from those ports if a favourable situation arises.

FUTURE OPERATIONS

During my discussions with Wavell on the proposed Rangoon operation, I found that in spite of previous discussions he was inclined to believe that carrier operated fighters could afford the protection required against land based air forces. I think he realises now that this is only the case when land based air forces are negligible and when we can establish our own land based air forces very shortly after the initial landing has taken place.

A glance at the map suggests that a successful attack on Rangoon would produce a far larger return than any bites at other points on the Japanese perimeter. The whole Japanese position in Burma would be threatened and we might be able to re-establish ourselves in the Andamans and exert control over the western exit of the Malacca Straits.

AUSTRALIAN VISIT

We must certainly seize the chance to establish closer inter-fleet relations with the Americans. Things would be so much easier if only we had more information about their tactics. I find that all Americans generalise so much, e.g., 'Guess you want as deep a recco as you can make it'. Yes but how far does your recco go? – 'Well that's just according to circumstances' and so on. You never get a hard-boiled answer. So if I can go myself I shall certainly do so, but I don't altogether like leaving the area for so long if things go even worse in the Middle East and the

Japanese are persuaded by the Germans to make a really heavy scale attack on the Middle East communications in this area. . . .

PERSONALITIES

Wavell. We get on very well when we meet, but I understand his staff are all rather frightened of him. He has no small talk as you know but by plying him with arrack and ginger ale mixed, Geoffrey Layton and I had him spinning stories – pretty good chestnuts but still quite an achievement. He has a slight tendency to regard the Indian Ocean as an ABDA area with India the one and only pre-occupation but at each meeting this point of view receives correction and I feel sure Palliser[1] will keep him straight on that point.

Layton. Takes complete charge of Ceylon and stands no nonsense from anyone. Sometimes tries to take charge of the Eastern Fleet also but fails. We are the best of friends . . .

Willis. A tower of strength in every way and an immense capacity for work. One has to watch him to see that he does not do too much. As soon as Force A gets together I want to give him every opportunity to handle it tactically so that whether he or I are in charge, there is no change of method.

Tennant. Full of ideas and enthusiasms and keen to get every cruiser right on fleet work, even if they are for the dockyard; to train officers and men and spread the doctrine.

Boyd. Knows his stuff but finds it difficult to believe that anyone except Boyd can really know much about carrier operation. Has not a great deal of imagination, is rather touchy and has to be carefully handled.

Danckwerts. I could not wish for a better deputy. He suffers fools more gladly than he used to. I think he's just the man for the job. . . .

P.S. It was so sad about *Hermione*. She was one of the best ships I've ever had the good fortune to have under me. G. N. Oliver is a first class and most determined leader and I'd welcome [him] out here in any capacity.[2]

---

[1] Rear Adm Palliser was Dep N Cdr, ABDA, and naval advisor to Wavell.
[2] *Hermione* was torpedoed by *U205* S of Crete on 16 June; Capt Oliver was an outstanding officer, highly regarded by Cunningham and others, and he stayed in Med & Channel.

274.   *Pound to Churchill*

11 July 1942

A.   *DISPOSITIONS OF ADMIRAL SOMERVILLE'S FLEET*

Warspite	
Illustrious	At Kilindini
Formidable	
Valiant	At Durban. Ready for service in mid August.
Royal Sovereign	
Resolution	At Kilindini.
Devonshire	Escorting *Orizaba* till 11 July. Joining WS 19L 15 July to relieve *Mauritius*.
Birmingham	At Kilindini.
Gambia	At Colombo. To escort *Schooner* to Australia.
Mauritius	Escorting WS 19L till 15 July, then to Kilindini, arriving 16 July.
Frobisher	Due Kilindini.
Enterprise	Escort duties Aden to Kilindini.
Dragon	Completing refit at Simonstown.
Dauntless	Guardship at Diego Suarez.
Caledon	At Kilindini.
Ceres	In Persian Gulf.

9 destroyers available.

Nelson, *Rodney* and *Indomitable* detached for special operation.[1]

B.   *ADMIRAL SOMERVILLE'S IMMEDIATE INTENTIONS*

On 3 July the C-in-C, Eastern Fleet's intentions were to remain at Kilindini in order to:–

(1)   Carry out exercises when destroyers are available.
(2)   Conduct sweeps for raiders if they re-appear within striking distance.

His movements will now depend on the possibility of co-operative action with the US Forces.

---

[1] *Mauritius*: 1940, 8525t, 12×6in, 8×4in, 6tt, 33k. *Ceres*: 1917, 4190t, 5×6in, 2×3in, 8tt, 29k. *Orizaba*: 1939, 4354gt, 15k, Hamburg-Amerika Line; presumably a German prize. *Schooner* unidentified.

C. *AIRCRAFT IN EASTERN FLEET CARRIERS*

Formidable	12 Martlets
	12 Fulmars
	16 Albacores
Illustrious	16 Martlets
	6 Fulmars
	18 Swordfish

D. *PROGRAMME OF HMS* QUEEN ELIZABETH

Queen Elizabeth is at Port Sudan and should be ready to leave soon. She has been instructed to submit a programme for passage to USA. . . .

275. *Churchill to Pound*

c. 12 July 1942

2. I feel anxiety about the negative attitude we are adopting towards Admiral King and the American operations in the Pacific. I promised we would assist by making diversions in any way possible but of course I did not commit us to any particular operation. We must now show a helpful attitude. I understand you have sent a telegram to Admiral Somerville asking him what he can do. . . . He has two first-class carriers and the *Warspite*. He has been doing nothing for several months and we really cannot keep his fleet idle indefinitely.

276. *Alexander to Churchill*

14 July 1942

INDIAN OCEAN

11. Although the Eastern Fleet is at present on the defensive it does not follow that it is not performing an important role. We cannot afford to reduce our naval forces in the Indian Ocean by sending them either to the Pacific or the Mediterranean until we have built up our land and air forces in key positions such as Ceylon to a far greater extent than we have at the present time. Before doing so, we must also be certain that these shore based air forces are efficient in operations over the sea.

12. As a matter of fact a large part of the Eastern Fleet is employed on a special operation. The transfer of heavy ships from the Indian Ocean to the Mediterranean would be known to the Axis at once and indeed one of the objects of such a move would be the publicity it would receive. This would at once tell the Japanese that they could now venture into the

Indian Ocean in comparatively small force and inflict serious damage on our trade routes practically without risk to themselves. Japan is quiet at the moment, but without the Eastern Fleet the whole East Coast of India lies open to a renewed Japanese threat.

THE PACIFIC

13. The Chiefs of Staff have under consideration the joint Anglo-American strategy for the eventual defeat of Japan. For this to start in 1943, the US Pacific Fleet will probably require the support of a major part of our Eastern Fleet. The loss or damage to important units of the Fleet when employed on operations in the Mediterranean would preclude this. . . .

277. *To Joan Bright Astley*

12 July 1942

. . . At the moment when so much depends upon our holding our position in Egypt I feel it's essential to protect the Middle East communications. . . . I don't feel it's right for me to gamble at the moment – much as I'd love to . . .

278. *To Pound*

15 July 1942

. . . I've just sent a signal about control of the Catalinas. It is of course ludicrous that these mobile aircraft should be apportioned to this area regardless of the situation at the moment. Owing to the various vested interests concerned, i.e., C-in-C India, C-in-C Ceylon, C-in-C EF, some basic allocation of the squadrons was necessary, but I have always emphasised to the other two that the Catalinas should be operated as necessary to deal with the situation.

I think that the other two are both inclined to take too parochial a view and insist on their pound of flesh even if they are not hungry – just in case they might feel hungry! Unless the Catalinas are used to the best advantage our cover against raiders and U-boats becomes exceedingly thin. There is a danger of getting into queer street through over insurance of interests not really threatened.

I shall be very glad when sufficient long range land machines are available to allow the Catalinas being used in their proper role, i.e., in those areas where land machines can't operate effectively.

With regard to Wavell there was certainly an initial tendency on his part to assume he would invariably be consulted, as opposed to informed, about the operation of the Eastern Fleet. I made it quite clear to both him and Layton at our last meeting that the Eastern Fleet operated under the general direction of the Admiralty and that whereas their responsibilities were limited to defence of certain territories the Eastern Fleet was charged in addition with lines of communication extending from the Cape to Australia and north to Aden and the Persian Gulf.

Furthermore the Eastern Fleet was an important force to be used in the ultimate operations of ejecting the enemy from Malaya and the Dutch East Indies, consequently both the Admiralty and myself had to take a long view of all proposals concerning its employment.

G. Layton and I are really as thick as thieves, but the old devil loves to try a bounce every now and then. He's got everyone under his thumb at Ceylon and tries to get me there too. I ought not to have teased him so much but shall take back a Nairobi ham with me and all will be well. He's doing first class work at Colombo.

Yes – the carrier striking force at present is a very poor thing I'm afraid. Much as I dislike to hold off at all I do feel very strongly that we must try to exploit our *night* striking to the utmost. . . .

An analysis of U-boat movements in the Mozambique Channel strongly supports the possibility of a supply ship somewhere south of Madagascar. If Force A had not been required to make this diversion I should have sent the two carriers down to make a sweep and see if we could nab her. Two carriers are far more effective than just twice one but of course it would entail destroyer escorts since to get the supply ship you must carry out the search at or about the time the U-boats are likely to be fuelling.

We have diverted some of the independently routed ships outside Madagascar but I feel we cannot overdo this as otherwise convoys who use that route will be the target and we have no A/S escorts for them. Directly I can scratch up a few more A/S escorts I shall try and do some group sailings from Durban and see how that works. The Jap U-boats seem shy of A/S escort.

279. *Pocket diary, 1942*

15–22 July 1942

15 July

Discussions with Danks and Bill T about employment of EF. They want to use B/S as escorts to release cruisers. Bill wants the carriers to operate separately to hunt raiders. Feel both are wrong.

16 July

Admiralty signalled requirements for diversion by Force A. Apparently has to synchronise with USA op. and contain enemy air.

18 July

Admiralty suggest sending one carrier to look for U-boat supply ship. Said I did not agree. Anyhow with only 5 destroyers out of the question.

19 July

Signal from Admiralty to say that Admiral King now in London says USA operation may start as early as 1 August, so I hope I can get going in time. Told them I would leave Tuesday a.m. Later message says they agree with my proposed diversion.

22 July

Irritating signal from Admiralty about group sailings in Mozambique Channel. Have already told them we have no escorts.

280.   *Pound to Churchill*

18 July 1942

2.   It would require at least 30 escort vessels to institute convoy. These are not available without robbing other areas which are already short and only a small proportion could be made available in the future as far as can be foreseen. We are however investigating where escorts would have to be taken from should the menace increase.

3.   Reinforcements to escort vessels in sight are:–

(a)   7 whalers fitting out in S African ports . . .
(b)   11 *Bathursts* completing in Australia, which are destined for the Eastern Fleet. . . .
(c)   3 *Bangor* class.[1] . . .

4.   For the present we shall have to continue the policy of diversion.
5.   Air patrols are only possible in the northern half of the Mozambique Channel. This is due to lack of airfields in Madagascar other than Diego Suarez. The area to be covered is nearly 1000 miles long and up to 500 miles wide; to cover this area adequately requires far more aircraft than will be available for a long time.

[1]*Bathurst* class: minesweepers/corvettes, 1940–43, 650–790t, 1×4in or 1×3in 15k.
Bangor class: minesweepers, 1940+, 590t, 1×3in, 16k.

6.   With regard to C-in-C, Eastern Fleet's proposals, on the evidence available we are agreed that the Japanese may very likely be using supply ships to the S or Southeastward of Madagascar. A signal has been sent to him suggesting that:–

(a)   he carries out the diversion in the Andamans area in conjunction with the Americans with *Warspite* and one carrier early in August;
(b)   he uses the other carrier to search for the supply ship.

7.   In view of the size of the Channel the proposal to send a force of destroyers to operate there is unlikely to produce any result. War experience has shown that A/S Hunting Forces produce very small results.

The demands on Eastern Fleet destroyers are considerable. They are required for escorting personnel ships, for the Fleet when exercising and for such work, as at present, in escorting *Warspite* and *Queen Elizabeth*.
8.   If Admiral Somerville's cycle theory proves later to be correct we may be able to take advantage of it by withholding sailings as far as possible during enemy submarine operating periods and increasing sailings during the time when the submarines are away refuelling.

281.   *To North*

20 July 1942

. . . In accordance with Uncle Sam's expressed desire I've been over to G Layton's abode, searched the ocean all round to the SE, found Miss Fanny Adams, returned there & am now nearly back to the land of elephants and giraffes. . . .

I do want to get to grips with the Yanks so that we can really get together when the occasion arises. . . . Feel sure that both sides would profit a great deal if we got together & discussed tactical aspects of these operations. I'm out to pick up any tips that I can.[1] . . .

282.   *To his wife*

31 July–3 August 1942

31 July

We left harbour in a hurry . . . because I got news that two Jap 8" cruisers and 4 destroyers had been sighted at the N end of the Malacca Straits

---

[1]Somerville sought in vain for effective co-operation with the Americans and for information about the Pacific war.

apparently heading for the Bay of Bengal. Rather odd because I'd arranged a diversion in these parts and it was not clear if this was an unexpected response much earlier than it should be, or just a coincidence. Anyway I bounced off hopefully with the boys on the off-chance of getting a contact but have had no further news. We may be lucky and meet them or else they may get wind I'm on the war-path and sugar off back inside the Andamans where I can't get at them. Found old GL quite friendly but 'must talk this out' sort of attitude which we did. Actually the Admiralty message giving me control of all Catalinas *and* long-ranged aircraft based in Ceylon had rather shaken old GL. . . . He took it very well on the whole and harmony was quite re-established.

1 August

No sign of our quarry so far but we spotted an odd air formation coming in from the eastward. They turned at 35 miles and may well have been the Sabang bastards. They were the party that got *P of W* and *Repulse*. . . .

3 August

Had rather a hectic time of it these last two days as we've been mucking about in a bit of water E of where we used to live and trailing our coat. The Jap cruisers did not put in an appearance but a good few of their aircraft have been on the move. Two of our little Martlets caught one of their big 4-engined flying boats napping yesterday about 30 miles from the Fleet and shot him down in flames before he knew what was happening.

283.   *To Joan Bright Astley*

11 August 1942

. . . You know of course all about our recent diversion in the Bay. I think it was rather successful because the Japs got all worked up & sent reinforcements to the W end of the Malayan barrier which was just what the doctor ordered. I rather hoped we might run into some of their surface ships but the Japs knew which side the butter is all right & sat tight under cover of land based air forces so it was obviously no go. Incidentally until I get more Martlets & until I get Barracudas instead of Swordfish & Albacores, my carriers are equal to about half a Jap carrier. I notice that DP has woken up to this.

. . . All these side shows keep taking my ships away or else employing them so I never get my proper Force A together. . . .

284. *Pocket diary, 1942*

5–31 August 1942

5 August

COS have told Wavell that landing craft and personnel are to be sent to Kilindini but refuse to allow any delay to assault ships, which seems a pity. . . . Report from Tokyo of presence of *Warspite* and 2 carriers etc. in Bay of Bengal. Diversion seems to have been quite good.

19 August

Signal from Admiralty to say that as *Illustrious* knocked out I must lend another carrier for TORCH! Decide it must be *Formidable.*[1]

31 August

Signal from DP to ask me to release 6 destroyers for TORCH! Told him I could let 4 go but STREAMLINE would be pretty thin.[2]

285. *To Pound*

1 September 1942

Many thanks for your letter of 14 August. I was very interested in your remarks on PEDESTAL, but I am still somewhat in the dark as to what exactly happened, especially with regard to the cruising dispositions, operation of aircraft, etc. You mention that the carriers had 3 days' drilling before the operation. In my opinion 3 weeks would be really all too short a time in which to develop the full offensive and defensive power of 3 carriers operating together.[3]

Many of us have had experience of operating a single carrier, and some of us two carriers, but as the number of carriers increases, so does the complexity of the technique which is required to obtain full results. I feel very strongly that this must be continually borne in mind, and that when my carrier force is brought up to full strength, I must have time for collective training before they are used for offensive operations. A well trained carrier force has immense potential powers for offence and defence, but this can only be secured when the Admiral in charge, fighter direction personnel, RDF ships and the squadron leaders have had a

---

[1]TORCH was the Allied assault on French N Africa, Nov 1942.

[2]The operation to occupy the southern part of Madagascar.

[3]There was almost no experience in the RN at that time of operating 3 carriers together.

really good dose of practice in mass manoeuvres and massed operation of aircraft.

With regard to the 5th Sea Lord, I agree that we have not yet had the right man. F.C. D[reyer][1] undoubtedly gets things done, and everyone will agree that the improvement he effected in merchant ship gunnery was outstanding. This, however, is his own special line, and my only doubt is whether at his age he can switch his great brain, nimble as it was and may be still, to so different a problem. With good supporters it may work all right as he will certainly provide the drive and energy, but I imagine that in the Service at large there may be some tooth-sucking over this appointment. . . .

I am sure that the visit of King and Marshall[2] came at just the right time, and that with close personal contact between you and the American leaders, our co-operation should become really effective very shortly. You may have seen the signal of mine which asked for visits by technical officers. . . .

Referring back to your letter, we all welcome the appointment of K.P. because he has a really fine brain, is extremely quick and can grasp details with amazing speed and accuracy.[3] It is right and proper that someone else should have the Fleet laid on a plate for you to use, and that you should not be bothered with details of training, etc. It is for very much the same reason that I want Algy Willis as my trainer in Force A when it is in full strength. As things have turned out I have hitherto done more than half the training myself, but I am giving Algy every opportunity to take parties out and put them through their paces so that it will make no difference to the Fleet who is at the helm, and so that we both adopt the same doctrine. We see eye to eye very closely, and I am old and ugly enough, thank God, to realise when I am wrong and take his advice. . . .

[1]Adm Sir Frederick C. Dreyer (1878–1956): *Britannia* 1891; gun splist; Lt 1898; GO, *Exmouth, Dreadnought* 1903–7; Cdr 1907; Flag Cdr to Jellicoe, Atlantic F 1913; Capt 1913; *Amphion, Orion*; Flag Capt, *Iron Duke*, Grand F 1915–16; Jutland; DNO 1916–19; Cdre & COS to Jellicoe's Empire mission; D Gun Div 1920–2; *Repulse* 1922–3; RA 1923; ACNS 1924; BCS 1927; VA 1929; DCNS 1930; Adm 1932; C-in-C China Sta 1933–6; Ret List 1939; convoy cdre 1939–40; Inspr merchant ship gunnery 1941; 5SL 1942; D Chief N Air Equipt 1943.

[2]Gen George C. Marshall, US Army (1880–1959): Va Mil Acad 1897–1901; Philippines & staff posts 1902–16; Capt 1916; AEF staff 1917–18; Aide to Gen Pershing 1919–24; China 1924–7; Inf Sch 1927–32; Brig-Gen, 5 Inf Bde; Chief, War Plans Div 1938; DCOS 1939; Maj-Gen & COS Sept 1939; Gen of Army Dec 1945 & Ret List; China mediation mission 1946; Sec State 1947–9; Sec Defence 1950–1; Nobel Prize for Peace 1953; dignity, devotion, duty, & distinction of highest calibre.

[3]Adm Sir Charles E. Kennedy-Purvis: Capt 1921; RA 1933; VA 1937; Pres, RN Coll, Greenwich 1938; Asst to DCNS (Cunningham) when 1SL (Backhouse) ill 1938; C-in-C NA &WI April 1940; D1SL 1942; died May 1946.

I have just received your signal about a supreme command, which I consider would be most inadvisable on this station. I am giving you my reasons by signal . . . .[1]

286.   *Pocket diary, 1942*

3–10 September 1942

3 September

To my disgust Admiralty say I must be responsible for Caspian.[2] Drafted signal to C-in-C Med[3] and Admiralty asking former if he can supply any A/S vessels for G of Aden.

4 September

More departures in connection with STREAMLINE. . . . M/V sunk by U-boat in entrance to G of Aden, which is a damn nuisance as I have nothing to send up there at all. . . .

6 September

No further news of U-boats in G of Aden. Hope they don't come down to Madagascar. C-in-C Med has sent 2 destroyers to Aden and I've sent 3 Catalinas.

7 September

Admiralty now asking if they can have *Hecla*![4] Shall have nothing left at this rate.

10 September

Signal from Bill [Tennant] to say operation started at 0330. . . . Brief message during forenoon show all OK and ships not required to bombard. Few casualties and Majunga occupied. . . . Spent most of the afternoon trying to ginger Bill up about news.

---

[1]See later papers (from No. 313) for Somerville's response to supreme command in SE Asia.
[2]This was a weird imposition, to say the least, but fortunately quickly rescinded.
[3]Now Adm Harwood.
[4]*Hecla*: destroyer depot ship, 1940, 11,000t, 8×4.5in, 17k; sunk W of Gibraltar Nov 1942, *U505*.

287. *To his wife*

Kilindini,
10 September 1942

I can now discuss what has been occupying my attention so much of late i.e. the further operations in Madagascar which started at 1 a.m. this morning and appear to be going quite successfully. . . . Ever since we got back here G[overnment] H[ouse] has been swamped out with soldiers and NOs all busy working out the plans and we have had endless conferences. As cover we staged some big combined exercises and did a landing which was to all intents a replica of what would happen at Majunga. Platt[1] and I are the two responsible Cs-in-C but much as I would like to have the done the job myself, it was obviously one in which I should stand back and continue to direct the general situation, leaving a junior flag officer to do the actual job. . . . the most elaborate precautions were taken and we were all lying like tooth-drawers for about a week before the show started. Reports up to date suggest very little opposition and that surprise was almost complete. . . . I've been pressing for this operation ever since Diego Suarez as I never liked the idea of leaving the rest of Madagascar open to a Jap assault and also I want all the aerodromes and harbours on the W side to assist in dealing with U-boats in the Mozambique Channel.

288. *To his wife*

25 September 1942

It looks as if the Japs are going to have a shot at trying to get the Yanks out of the Solomons. Wish I knew more of what the Yanks' strategical plan is but they have security on the brain. I long for the time when we can get busy and take a hand in the business ourselves, it's most irritating having to wait and wait. Incidentally I want to get to sea again as I don't like these protracted spells on shore. One gets too involved in some of the administrative details which should be left to others. If I'm on the spot I have to be consulted but if I'm not – well Danks and others have to do what seems best. Also being ashore one is not in such close touch with the boats. But whilst we are here it would be impossible to effect

[1]Lt-Gen Sir William Platt (1885–1975): Nthbld Fus 1905; NW Frontier; France 1914–18; Staff Coll 1919; Lt-Col, India & Egypt 1920–7; WO 1927–30; CO 2Bn Wilts Regt 1930; 7 Inf Bde 1933; Maj-Gen, Sudan Defence Force 1938; skilful E African campaign 1940–1; Lt-Gen 1941; GOC E Africa 1941–2; Madagascar 1942; Gen 1943; Ret List 1945.

proper control on board the ship as the bulk of my large staff has to be ashore. I find that with Fleet auxiliaries and all I have nearly 300 ships under my orders.

289. *Pocket diary, 1942*

26 September

DP says Yanks want *Heemskerck* and 2 Dutch destroyers in SW Pacific and says I must be ready to send them. Agreed but pointed out that we were taking a hell of a chance and training will be affected.[1]

290. *To North*

27 September 1942

. . . My chief preoccupation of late has been to try and keep my small ration of butter evenly spread over the very large hunk of bread which is my portion. No small job I can assure you & not made any easier by temporary withdrawals for other purposes.

. . . Jap U-boats have been a bit of a nuisance but on the whole show remarkably little initiative & persistence which is all to the good since at the moment I have not got the wherewithal to deal with them.

291. *To Cunningham*

9 October 1942

I am sending this by the hand of Boyd[2] who will give you all the latest news about the Eastern Fleet and what we want to get out of the Americans if possible. I have given Boyd a directive and also a copy of the questionnaire which we supplied to Cdr Clark, USN, my liaison officer who preceded Boyd to Washington. . . .

It is a great pity that the Americans will not realise how much is gained by keeping us more fully in the picture. This applies especially to the SW Pacific area at the moment, where the Americans are obviously having a difficult time[3] and where it might be possible for me to stage diversions in this area which would help to relieve the pressure.

---

[1]These were based on the west coast of Australia, for convoy work.

[2]Cunningham was Head of BAD in Washington and Boyd visited the US to learn more about American naval aviation developments.

[3] In and around New Guinea and Guadalcanal.

As you are of course aware, the Madagascar operations and TORCH have left me very thin for the moment, but I have reason to believe that the movements of Force A coupled with well organised W/T diversions have kept the enemy guessing in the past, and may well do so in the future, but to make this really effective, one must have some idea of projected operations in the Pacific. At the moment I am quite ignorant as to the strategical plan or the tactical means by which it is hoped to execute this plan. . . .

P.S. Clark, always known as 'The Senator', is a damn good one so if you meet him be nice to him.

292. *Pocket diary, 1942*

11 October

Admiralty have asked if I can send destroyers to Cape. Have replied this can only be done if Force A completely immobilised and continuation of this state of affairs most undesirable. . . . looks as if at least 11 ships have been torpedoed off the Cape so situation is serious but hard to see what we can do.

293. *To his wife*

11 October 1942

The blasted U-boats have appeared *en masse* off the Cape and TL's are shouting for me to send little boats down there.[1] They seem to have forgotten how to count or else they would have known that I have practically none in the bag. It's going to be a very difficult problem indeed but it's one which I felt sure would arise sooner or later. . . .

294. *Pocket diary, 1942*

13 October–11 November 1942

13 October

Admiralty say Cabinet approve of Force A being immobilised to release destroyers for the Cape. Sent signal to Archie Wavell to say

---

[1]Somerville's destroyers had been reduced so much by the demands of other theatres, repairs and refits that barely sufficient remained for a heavy ship screen; if others went to the Cape, the capital ships would be immobilised. However, 11 ships had been lost off the Cape, including the Orient liner *Orcades*: 1937, 23,456t, 22k.

unlikely Naval forces available for CANNIBAL[?] until late December or January.

1 November

Long signal from Admiralty about USA asking for immediate help Solomons where *Hornet* has now been sunk in addition to *Wasp*. Ask me what would be effect if EF reduced to 'R' class and cruisers with possibly *Unicorn*[1] as carrier!

3 November

Sent off my reply to Admiralty on policy re EF and told DP if he wanted to consult me mid-November would be appropriate time.

11 November

Signal to Admiralty that I am to proceed to UK after seeing Wavell.[2]

295.   *To Pound*

7 November 1942

I have not yet received any further communication from you with respect to the sending of reinforcements to the SW Pacific. I presume you are still awaiting the information asked for in your very pertinent signal to the Americans. It certainly is amazing that they should continue to keep us so badly informed of the situation. As you are aware I have tried by means of personal letters, personal messages and signals to get the Americans to put me in the picture, but so far without result.

I quite appreciate that for political reasons our hand may be forced, but I am still strongly of opinion that, to get full value out of any reinforcements, it is most desirable that they should be of such a character that they can operate together tactically without having to acquire the intimate knowledge of American methods, which is essential for really close tactical co-operation.

My visit to South Africa was certainly of very good value, because it gave me an opportunity to see all the leading Ministers, Military and Air

[1]USS *Hornet*: 1941, 20,000t, 100 a/c, 8×5in, 34k; sunk 27 Oct 1942. USS *Wasp*: 1940, 14700t, 84 a/c, 8×5in sunk 15 Sept 1942. *Unicorn*: a/c repair ship, 1943, 14,750t, 35 a/c, 8×4.5in, 22k; she could operate as a conventional carrier if required.
[2]After months of moving between Colombo, Trincomalee, Kilindini, Durban, Bombay and Diego Suarez, Somerville flew home on 18 Nov, arriving on 23 Nov.

Authorities (with the exception of Smuts), and put them in the picture with regard to what the Navy is doing and has done in the Indian Ocean. . . .

. . . They appeared to accept fully my explanation that the best defence of South Africa lay with the Eastern Fleet . . .

The development of Durban as a repair base has been quite remarkable. . . . We owe a great deal to Sturock[1] for this, and, of course, to Smuts for approving what has been done.

. . . the wonderful organisation at Durban to give the sailors a spell has been of the greatest benefit, and the ships come back from there really refreshed and ready for the next job. . . .

The 29th Brigade really know their stuff and Festing[2] is a first class leader. I believe if circumstances will admit, our best contribution to the problem of the SW Pacific will be Force A up to strength, acting in cooperation with the 29th Brigade as the spearhead of an attacking force. . . .

296. *To North*

London,
24 November 1942

. . . Am not over impressed by what I see here. DP more somnolent than ever. Fred Dreyer in a voluble and windy dotage, WC ruling the roost completely etc. However it does not stop me speaking my mind & saying what I think & they can take it or leave it.

It's typical that I should have to attend a meeting at No. 10 at 10.30 p.m. on Monday. Why must all these decisions be made at night?[3] . . .

---

[1]John D. Sturock: Engr Capt 1932; Cdre, 1st Cl (Ret); Minr of Railways & Ports, S Africa.

[2]Brig F. W. Festing: 2Lt 1921; Lt 1923; ADC, S Cmd 1926–30; Capt 1935; Air Lia O 1936–8; Maj 1938; GSO, WO Feb 1938; Brig 29 Bde, Madagascar Nov 1942.

[3]Somerville thought Pound was getting worn out, as well as worn down by Churchill. The Prime Minister really came alive late at night, hence the meeting at a time when others were already dog tired; perhaps their opposition to Churchill's ideas was thus much reduced.

297. *Pocket diary, 1942*

27 November–21 December 1942

27 November (Admiralty)

Long talk with FCD[reyer] and Renwick about FAA and then to see Jock Whitworth. Back to Admiralty and saw K[ennedy-]P[urvis] and Bridges[1] about new FAA aircraft.

28 November

With Ralph [Edwards] to Cabinet offices and saw Col Bevan about deception also Tony Buzzard[2] about SW Pacific policy. After what he said believe we shall have to release carriers for USA to use and that at least 3 will be required at home.

29 November

Conference with FSL at 1400 re despatch of carriers to SW Pacific. Decision that 2 should go and we must make shift with *Unicorn* and one auxiliary.[3]

2 December

At 1215 to see Admiral Stark[4] and gave him my views on US tactics. At 1.30 p.m. to No. 10 and lunched with PM and Sir Stafford Cripps.[5] Long talk about everything and got away at 1545.

3 December

To see Lord Leathers of MWT[6] and discuss situation of shipping in

[1]Actg Capt G. F. Bridges: Cdr 1936; *Rochester* 1939; China Sta; Actg Capt & DD Air Matériel Div April 1941; Capt Dec 1942; Dir Airfield & Carrier Rqrmts March 1943; *Howe* July 1945.

Vice Adm Sir William J ('Jock') Whitworth: Capt 1925; Capt of F, *Resolution*, Med F 1935; RA 1936; BCS, *Hood*, Home F 1939; VA 1940; 2nd Battle of Narvik April 1940; 2 SL 1941– 4; Adm Dec 1943; C-in-C Rosyth Feb 1944.

[2]Capt Buzzard was then in Plans Div. Bevan unidentified.

[3]In the event, *Victorious* alone went to Pacific.

[4]Adm (later Fleet Adm) Harold R. Stark, US Navy (1880–1972): destroyer & staff service, Med & UK 1917–18; N War Coll; Navy Dept; battleship cmd; Chief, Bur Ordnance; cruiser cmd; CNO 1 Aug 1939–26 March 1942; C-in-C, US N Forces in Eur Waters 1942–5: Fleet Adm; Ret List 1946.

[5]Sir Stafford Cripps (1889–1952): barrister; Lab MP; Solr-Gen 1929–31; Amb to USSR 1940–2; Ld Privy Seal & Ldr, Ho of Commons 1942; Minr a/c Prodn 1942–5; mission to India 1942; Pres, BOT 1945–7; C Ex 1947–50; left wing, extremely able but uncomfortable bedfellow in political world.

[6]Lord (Frederick J.) Leathers (1883–1965): self-made coal & shipowner; known to Churchill pre-war; advisor on shipping in both wars; baron & Minr War Transport May 1941; Sec State Transport, Fuel & Power 1951–3; visct 1954.

Indian Ocean. Very good value on the whole. To Buckingham Palace at 1215 and talked to HM until 1310.

4 December

Saw DP who said USA not so anxious now to have carriers. Lyster had already been proposed. I suggested Tom Troubridge. Claude Barry to see me also G. Blake who told me he was responsible for famous letter two years ago being cancelled. I told DP about opinions held re FCD and he was not best pleased. Thomas Binney says they are recommending retention of 'R' class in commission.[1]

21 December (Delhi)

Saw Peirse about lack of fighter direction for NIBBLE[2] and he promised to look into it. At 7 to see Viceroy. Said he felt he must accept Godfrey so I told him I still felt he was unsuitable.[3]

298. *To Pound*

28 December 1942

15.   We took off at 0630 on 17th in the *Corsair* flying boat and had a slow, uneventful passage to Basra where we arrived at 1630. Had a meeting with Ford Hammill[4] and discussed a number of local matters. I told him to let me have proposals for going through the motions of laying, and subsequently promulgating, a dummy minefield on the N side of the Straits of Hormuz in order to force the U-boats to come within range of RDF, etc., on the S side. This to be followed by a dummy SOS from a

---

[1]Actg Rear Adm Claude B. Barry: Capt 1933; N Asst 2SL 1939; Capt *Queen Elizabeth* & CSO to VA Pridham-Wippell Oct 1940; Actg RA & FO (S) Nov 1942; RA Jan 1943; planned X-craft attack on *Tirpitz*; N Sec to 1st Lord Feb 1945.

Adm Sir Thomas H. Binney: Capt 1922; RA 1934; VA Jan 1938; Cdt, IDC 1939; head of cttee on exchange of Sci & Tech info with US Navy Sept 1939–July 1940; FOIC Orkney Dec 1939; Adm April 1942; Ret List Dec 1943; FOIC Cardiff Feb 1944– July 1945.

Dreyer was not thought to have been a success as 5SL.

[2]Somerville left UK on 12 Dec, arriving Delhi 19 Dec. NIBBLE was probably a proposed combined operation in the E Indian Ocean.

[3]Vice Adm Godfrey, DNI since 1939, had been proposed as FO Cmdg R Indian Navy. An extremely able man, he was nevertheless rather abrasive and had become *persona non grata* to other members of the Joint Intelligence Cttee. However, as Somerville pointed out to Pound, the Viceroy and others, diplomacy, above all, was required in dealing with the rather delicate situation in the RIN. He opposed Godfrey's appointment on that ground. The then FOCRIN was Vice Admiral Sir Herbert Fitzherbert: Capt 1924; RA 1936; VA 1939; FOCRIN 1937–43; Adm on Ret List June 1943; SNO Persian Gulf, Basra April 1944. Godfrey remained FOCRIN until 1946 and got on amicably with Somerville.

[4]Cdre C. Ford Hammill: Capt 1933; *Cornwall* & CSO, 5CS, China 1939; MNBDO (2)1941; Cdre & SNO, Persian Gulf Feb 1942; Ret List Jan 1943; Cdre Durban April 1943.

ship getting mined, etc. If this comes off I shall get the Deception party to start the buzz. . . .

17. The shipping and store situation at Karachi has eased considerably of late, and I was told the capacity of the port was equal to demands at present made on it. There are no A/S defences installed, but it's not an easy approach and I doubt if the Japs think it worth a midget attack.

20. Whilst at New Delhi the following were discussed:

General Stilwell, the American – known as Vinegar Joe – attended one of the meetings. Looks just like an old tortoise and rarely opens his mouth but hits the bull when he does. He seemed more optimistic than Wavell about the land advance to occupy Upper Burma. The Generalissimo[1] has once more raised the question of the control of the sea route to Rangoon from Penang. I explained that the present situation did not admit of this being done by naval forces.

FOCRIN's Relief

I informed both the Viceroy and Wavell that, in spite of my views on the matter, the Admiralty still considered G was suitable. In these circumstances I recommended the retention of F[itzherbert] for the present as I'd heard from many quarters regrets that he should be leaving now. . . . if G does come out I shall of course help him in every way I can, but I still have serious doubts about his ability to deal effectively with the very difficult people he is up against. . . .

Flag Changes

21. . . . I think Algy Willis will do very well in Force H and, after seeing him on our arrival at Kilindini, I hope to arrange for him to proceed to Gib forthwith and possibly for Morgan[2] to go home for a bit of leave before relieving Palliser.

299. *Pocket diary, 1943*

7 January–17 February 1943

7 January

Signal from Admiralty to say *Illustrious* was to go home forthwith. Sent reply asking to delay until Force A had done its trip to Ceylon to cover Australian convoy. Seems odd after the PM was so emphatic we must not denude EF entirely.

[1]Chiang Kai-Shek, head of the Chinese Nationalist Govt since 1924.
[2]Rear Adm Morgan was to become naval representative at Wavell's HQ in Delhi.

8 January

At office found signal from Admiralty to say all points I'd raised had been considered and *Illustrious* must go. Capsizes all my programme.

9 January

Working out alternative programme for Force A with no carrier. Miller tells me he does not think Y here doing much good.

16 January

SI suggest a lot of U-boats are now on their way to the Cape area. Sent signal to Admiralty asking for decision about whether destroyers are to be sent. Arranged for Cat[alina]s to be sent from Ceylon.

9 February

Signal from Admiralty they can't give any forecast of EF reinforcements for ANAKIM so everything now in the air. . . . Cape U-boat campaign not yet started but believe U-boats have refuelled.

14 February

Held large conference to discuss development of Addu and move of EF to Trinco. Devil of a lot of work involved.

17 February

Not clear what Japs are up to. Some suggestion of landing men from U-boats on Indian Coast. Staged a wireless diversion to suggest Fleet in Bay of Bengal.

300.   *To North*

22 February 1943

. . . I'd been robbed of my last aerodrome & then had to cover the passage of the Diggers from Alex's place to their native shores. Not at all nice & all had to be done on bluff.[1] My old 'R' ladies pant like hell if you ask for more than 16. Still we did it & what's more worked a bloody good leg haul on [the Japanese] which worked a fair treat & has got them all guessing. But you can't play that sort of game indefinitely. Read – the FO – has done damn well & I was very pleased on the whole. . . .

Reverting to H[arwood] and P[alliser] I pointed out that P had war

---

[1]Somerville now had no carrier but had to escort an Australian troop convoy from Suez to Australia, hoping that the Japanese would not realise how weak his forces were.

experience of Fleet work in the E Med & Force H whereas H had not. The victor of the Plate has never been to sea with a carrier & when I saw him at Cairo it was clear that he was much more interested in the political situation in Turkey than how to sink Axis ships going across to Tripoli & Tunisia.[1] . . .

301. *To his wife*

on passage to Bombay,
23 February 1943

I've had to spend all my time working on the plans I have to discuss with Archie. Anticipate some hellish arguments with him since he wants to be Generalissimo. As I told you in my last letter both DP and I agree it is quite unnecessary and most undesirable. . . . The U-boats in Tufty's parish are a bit of a nuisance and although it's not my business I lend him little boats and flying boats so I like to keep an eye on how they are used.

302. *To Pound*

11 March 1943

Addu Atoll

7. In view of the immense effort which is required to construct works and maintain personnel at this place, I feel sure the right policy is to reduce our requirements to the barest limit. The place can never be made 100% submarine proof, and owing to the lowness of the land, a submarine at periscope depth can obtain a very nice view from outside of anything that is inside. Gan, the only practicable site for the aerodrome and other works, presents a very congested target. I feel it is undesirable to cram too much into this small pint pot. Nevertheless, as a temporary fuelling base, or a 'hide out' for the Fleet for a few days, it has great advantages and can be used successfully providing no call is made on the shore for water in large quantities or other maintenance facilities.

Ceylon

9. I spent a day at Trincomalee and was impressed by the progress made in all directions. In particular the Royal Marine engineering com-

[1]Harwood, then C-in-C Med, had been put forward as 2nd-in-C, Eastern F. Somerville was evidently critical of his abilities & performance. Harwood was to be ousted after complaints from Montgomery, somewhat unjustified, about the Navy's slowness in clearing former enemy ports. See Roskill, *Churchill and the Admirals*, pp. 211–14.

panies have done some very good work and shown their value in accommodating themselves to situations where initiative and resource are the primary requirements. I think that by the end of September everything should be ready to accommodate any Fleet likely to be available in these parts at that time, though the full requirements will not be met, so far as berthing is concerned, until the end of the year. I presume it will not be the intention to move the Eastern Fleet to Ceylon until it is of such strength that it does not provide an easy target for a detachment from the Japanese Main Fleet. Naturally the situation in the Pacific will govern this to a large extent.

11.   The FAA aerodrome at Katakarunda is now practically completed, and is a model of how an aerodrome should be laid out. From the air it was practically impossible to detect the dispersal points for the aircraft, or the hangars and workshops hidden in the jungle.

Delhi

16.   . . . the only discussions I have had with Wavell on ANAKIM all centred round the fact that

(a)   providing the Japanese were fully occupied elsewhere
(b)   we were assured of air superiority before, during and after the landing

it would be a feasible operation provided sufficient Naval and Military forces were available.

17.   By the time Dill and Arnold[1] had arrived at Delhi, the situation was very different. It was clear by that time we had no earthly chance of getting Akyab before the monsoon. Apart from this the Japanese have extended their aerodromes to the E and S in Burma and now have a chain from which they can hold aircraft in readiness out of range of our long range bombers from Burma, and also at a selected moment reinforce on the spot, and with such unlimited facilities for dispersal, that any attempt at effective reduction by preliminary bombing would fail . . .

[1]Field Marshal Sir John G. Dill (1881–1944): Leinster Regt; S Af War; Capt 1911; France 1914–18; Maj 1916; Actg Brig-Gen 1918; Staff Coll 1919; Col 1920; India 1929; Maj-Gen 1930; Cdt Staff Coll 1931; DMO & I 1934–6; Lt-Gen 1936; Middle E 1936–7; I Corps, BEF; Gen; VCIGS April 1940; CIGS 25 May 1940; FM Nov 1941; Govr-designate Bombay but went with PM to Washington Dec 1941 & stayed as head of UK Mil Mission; exceptionally close friendship with Gen Marshall & distinguished service; died there 4 Nov 1944.

Gen Henry H. ('Hap') Arnold, US Army AF (1886–1950):W Point 1903; Philippines 1907–9; flying sch 1911; 1st Lt 1913, Philippines; Capt, Aviation Secn 1916; Air Div, War Dept 1917; AD Mil Aeron & Actg Col May 1918; Cmd & Gen Staff Sch 1928–9; Lt-Col 1931; training & dev appts; 1st Fighter Wing 1933; Actg Brig-Gen, 1st Wing 1935; Actg Chf, AAC Jan 1936; Maj-Gen & Chf AAC Sept 1938; Chf AAF 1941; Ret List March 1946; Gen of AF May 1949.

23.   I found the Deception Section, under Brig. Hutton, and in which Peter Fleming is the moving spirit, was most helpful and full of ideas.[1] As you may have heard, we worked quite a nice little deception on the Japanese by means of wireless ruses which included a Catalina making a self evident sighting report of one battleship, 2 carriers, cruisers, destroyers, etc., in the middle of the Bay of Bengal, and then being told a quarter of an hour later not to be a bloody fool as she was reporting our own forces. This seems to have worked a fair treat, as the Jap wireless buzzed for hours afterwards like a lot of angry bees and one or two movements took place which may well have been associated with this deception. The trouble is that one cannot go on pulling the Jap's leg indefinitely without showing some evident piece of meat from time to time. This unfortunately I cannot do until *Unicorn* arrives, or something that looks like a carrier.

PPS. If no major operations are likely to take place in this area this winter and if you are short of Flag Officers, I hope you won't hesitate to use me in any rank or capacity if you feel I shall be better employed elsewhere.

As a retired officer I can serve in any rank and if you thought my sea cum carrier experience would be useful I shall be only too glad to serve anywhere and under anyone.

On the other hand if we are to have a show out here next dry season, it will probably be better for me to continue preparing the springboard, unless it was for only a short period.

303.   *Pocket diary 1943*

26 February–8 March 1943

26 February

To GHQ and saw Archie and Vinegar Joe Stilwell. Gave them my general views on ANAKIM. S thought CKS would not hold out if ANAKIM postponed. Conference to discuss plan in general terms.

---

[1]Lt-Gen T. J. Hutton RA: 2Lt 1909; W Front 1914–15, 1916–18; Capt 1915; Salonika 1919–20; WO 1923–4; E Cmd 1924–6; Maj 1927; WO 1927–30; Col 1930; WO 1933–6; Palestine 1936–8; Maj-Gen, Cdr W (Indpdt) Dist, Quetta; 1938; Actg Lt-Gen July 1940; Lt-Gen Dec 1942; Ret List 1945.
Col Peter Fleming (1907–71): explorer & author; Gren Gds; staff & guerilla ops Norway 1940; Greece deception ops; deception organiser SE Asia; he made the passage out with Somerville on board *Formidable*; they delighted in each other's witty company.

Argued with W about probable state of defences in R[angoon?] River. Darvall[1] pointed out that air cover very doubtful initially.

5 March

Admiralty say *Warspite* required for HUSKY[2] and must be in the UK by mid-May. Shall have no fleet left before long.

6 March

Admiralty now say they want a cruiser as well for HUSKY, so we shall have nothing left. Present U-boat campaign at Cape has got 12 ships altogether.

8 March

C-in-C SA has asked for more destroyers. Danks replied that he had to keep some for training. Admiralty . . . said training must take second place in view of U-boats.

304.   *To Joan Bright Astley*

7 March 1943

[On ANAKIM, Peirse said] that from the air point of view it was not so good a party especially since the operations on the Arakan coast have proved so abortive.

I told A[rchie Wavell] that I fully agreed with this & that it went far further than taking a bit of a chance. I was rather surprised to find A arguing on the lines that perhaps the Japs might have no air, no defences[?] etc. It all seemed so much wishful thinking on which to plan a major operation. . . . I felt it necessary to be absolutely frank about the matter. I cannot believe we should be justified in taking up all the shipping etc. & directing so much military effort to what may be just a gamble with all the odds against us. We [should] look round for something better.

---

[1]ANAKIM: proposed seaborne assault on Rangoon. Air Cdre L. Darvall: Grp Capt Dec 1940; Air Cdre Jan 1943; COS to AOC-in-C India (Peirse), who was ill at this time.
[2]HUSKY: landings in Sicily July 1943.

305. *To North*

8 March 1943

. . . U-boats have been very active again down in Tufty's parish. I've stripped myself to the bone to help him but am not at all sure that he has been too clever. It is difficult for me to butt in so I think I shall have to send a signal to DP suggesting that Admiralty orders a conference at the Cape between the two of us & our staffs so as to consider 'joint measures' or some evasive expression like that. The only snag is that this continued hopping about in cruisers with reduced staff makes it difficult to keep in touch with all the signals and papers. . . .

306. *Report of Proceedings, 18 March–7 April*

11 April 1943

2.   I left Kilindini in HMS *Mauritius* mid-day on 18 March, and arrived at Durban p.m. 21st, after an uneventful passage.

22 March

5.   I subsequently went on board and inspected HMS *Canton*, and was very impressed by the alterations which had been carried out, and as a result of which this ship has now a reasonable prospect of meeting German or Japanese armed merchant cruisers on equal terms. I also visited HMS *Wayland*[1] and addressed her ship's company. . . .

23 March

6.   . . . the aircraft crews employed on A/S work are, to a large extent, composed of those who are resting from the Middle East. These crews have neither the experience or the interest which is necessary for this work. This, coupled with the unsuitable nature of the aircraft employed, namely Venturas,[2] results in a low standard of the air protection afforded by the SAAF. Fortunately, the Catalinas also employed on A/S work are efficient, and the enemy so far does not appear to have appreciated the lack of efficiency of the shorter-range patrols.

24 March

8.   . . . After arrival at Capetown I proceeded to Naval HQ and com-

---

[1]*Canton*: AMC, 1938 15,784gt, 20k, P & O. *Wayland*: ex-*Antonia* (Cunard), 1922, acquired 1942, depot ship, 13,887gt, 4×4in, 15.5k.
[2]Lockheed Ventura: 1940, bomb load 3500lb, 6mg, 315mph, range 1100 mls.

menced discussions with Vice Admiral Sir Campbell Tait on the U-boat campaign. In view of certain information forwarded by the Admiralty, I signalled a proposal that HMS *Trusty* should be employed whilst on passage from Colombo to Durban to intercept, if possible, enemy U-boats to the S of Madagascar. I appreciated fully that there would be objections in the employment of air and surface forces for this purpose, but hoped that by means of a diving patrol by day it would be possible for *Trusty* to escape detection. I appreciated that the prospects of obtaining an interception were not good, and I feel Their Lordships' decision that the operation must not be carried out does not necessarily remove a good chance of inflicting loss on the enemy. . . .

25 March

9.   In the forenoon I called on Mr Sturock, and subsequently on the Prime Minister. I informed the Prime Minister of the reason for my visit to Capetown, which he said he welcomed and that he was most anxious to do all in his power to assist development of anti-U-boat measures. He said he would be glad to back up any recommendations made by the C-in-C, S Atlantic, and myself, and, if necessary, address a personal note on the subject to the home authorities. . . .

26 March

11.   I spent the day at Naval HQ investigating A/S measures, and the general organisation for dealing with U-boat attacks, and subsequently took up my residence at Groote Schuur.[1] . . .

30 March

16.   . . . the C-in-C, S. Atlantic, and myself had a conference with CGS[2] on the subject of air co-operation in connection with the U-boat campaign. The following points were made:–

(a)   Need for more highly trained crews.
(b)   Unsuitability of Ventura aircraft for A/S work.
(c)   The need for weatherproof runways on S. African air fields.

4 April

23.   HMS *Mauritius* slipped and proceeded at 0930, carrying out exercises with the local fighter and bomber squadrons after her departure.

---

[1]Official residence of S African PM.
[2]Adm Tait and the Chief of the S African General Staff.

7 April

24.   HMS *Mauritius* arrived in Kilindini at 1730 after carrying out a full day's exercises with aircraft and destroyers during her approach.

Appendix A
Summary of Conversation with Field Marshal Smuts

ANAKIM

Discussing ANAKIM, the Prime Minister considered that unless adequate air cover was available, the operation appeared to be one in which the risks were hardly acceptable. . . . He was firmly of opinion that no effort should be diverted from the W against Japan at present, beyond that required to hold the Japanese . . . he did not feel that American forces now operating in the Pacific should be diverted elsewhere, since the Japanese must be contained.

Indian Ocean

Turning to the Indian Ocean, the Prime Minister viewed with some concern the reduction of naval strength in eastern waters but agreed that the possibility of Japanese attack directed against India or Ceylon was now remote unless the US suffered a major naval reverse. He asked what action was possible, with the forces at present available, against minor raids by the Japanese surface ships or sea-borne aircraft in the Indian Ocean and was informed that until the Eastern Fleet had been reinforced, the prospects of bringing such forces to action were by no means good. Reliance had to be placed for the time being on as wide diversions of shipping routes as possible coupled with the maintaining of a maximum degree of secrecy in regard to the strength and disposition of Allied naval forces in this area, and the exercise of deception to suggest the strength of the forces present was considerably in excess of those actually available. . . .

307.   *Pocket diary, 1943*

8 April–5 July 1943

8 April

. . . signal from DP to say re my offer to serve elsewhere that they were considering appointing me as ACNS for U-boat warfare, in place of

Edelsten[1] in rank of VA, but this depended on whether ANAKIM was on or off. Not at all what I'd hoped for or want.

9 April

Sent signal to DP to say I'd go where wanted but did not feel suited for this job and further felt it should be much more independent and not under VCNS.

10 April

Signal from Admiralty to say I must be home before Wavell if possible. Asked W when he would be home and he replied 19th. Hell of a flap trying to get air passages. The whole thing a damn nuisance as I do want to stay put for a bit.

11 April

Have a feeling I shan't come back to the EF and feel depressed.

19 April (London)

Saw First Lord who discussed various matters including proposed U-boat appointment. Told him it was not my line of country at all.

20 April

Tony Buzzard told me JPS fully agreed with my view of ANAKIM. Saw Edelsten and discussed U-boat campaign. The more I hear of it the less I like the prospect of a job there. . . . Danks making a lot of signals with 'I' in them so told him to knock off.

22 April

To No. 10 at 3 p.m. for meeting. PM a bit vague about ANAKIM, what was the good of Burma anyway, etc. Archie said he was told to make plan for Burma so had done so. PM said we were to consider alternatives.

23 April

At 1130 attended COS meeting. ANAKIM paper worked[?] off. Modified land ANAKIM discussed together with alternative of air support only on the islands. Good deal of confused argument. DP very

---

[1]Rear Adm (later Adm Sir) John H. Edelsten: Capt 1933; DDPD 1937–9; *Shropshire* 1940; Cdre & COS, Med F March 1941; RA Feb 1942; ACNS (Trade, later U-boat Warfare & Trade) Dec 1942–4; RA (D), BPF 1945.

somnolent. .... Saw Harry Moore[1] who says I'm the only possible for the U-boat job. Feel very depressed.

27 April

Charles Lambe to see me about a reduced ANAKIM followed by Geoffrey Blake who strongly advised me against ACNS (U).

28 April

To COS meeting at 11 where a full discussion was had and paper agreed to. Re main policy v. Japan DP argued for Philippines with which I fully agreed. .... DP again raised ACNS (U) question but dropped it pro tem.

3 May

DP told me the U job must be considered off as otherwise the US will say we are packing up in Indian Ocean. Entirely agree. .... Col Wilkinson[2] on MacArthur's staff to see me. Latter wants EF on W side of Australia to support his operations against M[anila?]. Say quite out of the question at present.

10 May (RMS Queen Mary, *N Atlantic)*[3]

COS meeting with PM in the chair. Went over the new ANAKIM in detail. V. anxious to stage it early 1944. Alan Brooke[4] v.g. at these meetings.

12 May

COS at 9.30. Dill, Noble[5] there as well. D. gave a good review of US

[1]Vice Adm Sir Henry R. Moore: *Britannia* 1902; Capt 1926; RA 1938; 3 CS, Med F 1939; ACNS (Trade) 1940–1; VA & VCNS Oct 1941–2; 2nd–in-C, Home F 1943–4; C-in-C Home F June 1944–5; Adm 1944; Head of BAD Dec 1945.

[2]Lt-Col Theodore Wilkinson: British Liaison Officer on Gen MacArthur's staff.

[3]Churchill had decided at short notice to make a full-scale pilgrimage to Washington, with the COS and the SE Asia commanders in tow, to discuss future operations in that theatre.

[4]Gen Sir Alan F. Brooke (later Field Marshal Viscount Alanbrooke, 1883–1963): service in Ireland & India pre-1914; RHA, W Front rising from Lt to Lt-Col 1914–18; Staff Coll 1919; Instr 1923–6; IDC 1927; Brig, Arty Sch 1929–32; Inf Bde 1934; Inspectg Maj-Gen RA 1935; D Mil Training; Mob Div 1937; Lt-Gen, A/A Cmd 1938–9; C-in-C, S Cmd 1939; II Corps, BEF; C-in-C Home Forces 1940; CIGS Dec 1941 & Chm, COS Cttee; FM 1944.

[5]Adm Sir Percy L. H. Noble (1880–1955): *Britannia* 1894; *Ribble* i/c 1907–8; signal splist; Cdr 1913; Grand F 1914–18; Capt 1918; *Calliope, Calcutta* 1919; *Barham* 1922; *Ganges* (TS) & *St Vincent* 1925–7; DOD 1928–9; RA 1929; DN Eqpt 1931; 2CS, Home F 1932; VA & 4SL 1935; C-in-C China Sta 1937–40; Adm 1939; C-in-C W Apps 1941; BAD Oct 1942–June 1944; Ret List 1945.

outlook. V. anxious I should get on well with E. King. Lunch by US COS to us. Sat next King and we got on very well together.

14 May

Dr Evatt[1] to see me and was very rude! Cs-in-C attended joint COS to discuss ANAKIM. Admiral Leahy[2] presided. Archie again said it was a reasonable operation and was very long winded. Peirse and I not asked to speak. Lunch with COS and then to White House for session with President and PM on ANAKIM. Archie again made statement but when President asked me my views I said it was no good. Richard [Peirse] did as well. Vinegar J. for it, but PM said he would not countenance a silly operation of silly[?] people.

15 May

Looks now as if US will agree finally that ANAKIM is off.

21 May

COS meeting at 9.30 followed by combined COS at which Ernie King gave an account of past and present operations in the Pacific. Some interesting facts re sub patrols.[3]

22 May

To Navy Dept. where I had . . . long discussions with US Captains on deception, carrier tactics, A/A cruising orders etc.

25 May

Saw Percy Noble about tackling Ernie King over letting us have an ECM at K[ilindini]. . . . Saw Ernie K with Percy and he agreed to let us have ECM.

31 May (London)

Long screed from DP about position of Admiral in the Fleet, i.e. car-

---

[1]Dr Herbert V. Evatt (1894–1965), Australia: barrister; Lab politics 1925; Judge of Australian High Court 1930–40; MP 1940; Att-Gen 1941; Minr External Affs 1941–9; Leader, Labour Party 1951–60; Chief J, NSW Sup Ct 1960–2.

[2]Adm (later Fleet Adm) William D. Leahy, US Navy (1875–1959): US N Acad 1893–7; Cuba 1898; Boxer Rebn 1900; Philippine insurrection 1900–2; service on cruisers & battleships; Instr, US N Acad; *Dolphin* (Pres yacht & despatch vessel) i/c 1914; N Overseas Transport Service 1917–18; *St Louis, New Mexico*; gun splist; RA & Chief, Bur Ordnance 1927; Chief Bur Nav 1933; battleship sqdns; CNO 1937–9; Govr Puerto Rico 1939–41; Amb to Vichy 1941–spring 1942; COS to Pres & Chm, JCS July 1942; 1st Fleet Adm 1944; Ret List 1949.

[3]US submarines in the Pacific were carrying on the most effective *guerre de course* in history, decimating the Japanese merchant marine.

rier or battleship. I plunk for latter. Met Oliver Lyttelton[1] after lunch and had talk about command in India.

8 June

Denis Boyd to see me and long story about fight he has for FAA. Says he gets very little support from the Board and FSL and that PM feels that FAA have done nothing of late.

25 June

Denis Boyd in to discuss carriers, supply of US aircraft etc. Situation improving but still unsatisfactory. DP told me Americans have turned down Sholto Douglas at first and have asked for further names. DP has put me in as a candidate for Supreme Commander if an Admiral is wanted. Tedder[2] if airman. Said I did not like either idea.

28 June

Had further talk with DP about Far E command and Naval set-up. Miles[3] ordered to Delhi forthwith. Saw KP about carriers and had a talk about forthcoming promotions to Flag rank. I feel they are too old and not enough discrimination. . . .

1 July

General Denning to see me and described his visit to MacArthur. Not quite so down on him as Laird, Jolly[4] and others but agrees he is very difficult. . . . Had a long talk with DP about the Eastern set-up. FDR says

---

[1]Oliver Lyttleton (later Viscount Chandos, 1893–1972): Gren Gds, W Front 1914–18; businessman; Con MP; Pres BOT 1940; MP Aldershot 1940–54; Minr State Middle E & War Cab 1941; Minr Prodn 1942–5; Col Sec 1951–4; Visct 1954.

[2]Air Chief Marshal Sir William Sholto Douglas (later Lord Douglas of Kirtleside, 1893–1969): RFA 1914; RFC 1915; commanded fighter sqdns W Front; Maj 1918; civil pilot; rejoined RAF as Sqdn-Ldr 1920; Flying Sch, staff, IDC Sudan 1920–36; AVM, Air Min 1938; A & DCAS; AM & C-in-C Fighter Cmd Nov 1940; ACM & AOC Middle E 1942; Coastal Cmd 1944; C-in-C British AF of Occupation, Germany July 1945; Marshal of RAF 1946; C-in-C British Forces in Germany; Ret List 1947; Chm, BEA 1949–64.

Air Chief Marshal Sir Arthur W. (later Lord) Tedder (1890–1967): Col Service 1914; RFC, France, 70 Sqdn i/c 1917–18; Sqdn-Ldr 1919; training specialist; IDC; Staff Coll 1929–31; Grp Capt 1931; Cdt Air Armt Sch; Dir Training 1934–6; AOC Far E 1936–8; AVM 1937; DG R & D 1938; DAOC Middle E 1940; AOC June 1941; AM 1941; ACM 1942; C-in-C Med Air Cmd; Dep Sup Cdr, D-Day; Marshal of RAF 1945; CAS & baron 1946; Ret List 1949; Chm British Jt Staff Mission 1950–1.

[3]Rear Adm Geoffrey J. A. Miles: Capt 1931; Flag Capt *Nelson* Home F 1939; RA Aug 1941; head of N Mission Moscow Jan 1942; Comb Ops HQ June 1942; N Rep, India HQ, Delhi June 1943; VA March 1944; FO W Med July 1944; VA & FOCRIN 1946.

[4]Gen R. F. S. Denning: Beds & Herts Regt; W Front 1915–18; 2 Lt 1916; Adjt 1922–5; Capt 1925; staff appts E Cmd, Ireland, India; DAAG India 1933–5; DAAG N Cmd 1936–7; DAQMG N Cmd 1937; Maj 1938; Lt-Col Sept 1939; Col May 1941; Temp Brig Nov 1941; Temp Maj-Gen 1943. Cdr Laird, the SO (I). Jolly unidentified.

ABC would be very welcome and Tedder would be acceptable. Expounded my views that S[upreme] C[ommander] should act as a good Chairman.

5 July

Long talk about Supreme Command. PM won't spare Andrew or Tedder and [–?] about Leese.[1] DP and COS think latter has insufficient background and has only commanded a Division before.

308. *To the Admiralty*

3 July 1943

2. I quite agree that any of the duties of Flag Officer Ceylon that are concerned with the defence of Ceylon must be subjected to direction by C-in-C Ceylon. On the other hand such duties as maintenance of a shipping plot for the E Indies Station, defence of Addu Atoll and Diego Garcia, control, administration and operation of escort groups working on the E and W coasts of India and the collection of Naval intelligence for the Eastern Fleet are not primarily concerned with the defence of Ceylon and should therefore be under my direction[2] . . .

309. *From Admiral Sir Guy Royle*

Navy Office,
Melbourne,
25 May 1943

. . . I should have been glad to know of the Naval impressions you picked up in Washington, but if my reading of the picture is correct, there is no urgent desire on their part for the Eastern Fleet to participate in the Pacific Area and perhaps steal some of their thunder, whilst, on the other hand, they would probably be very glad if you could exert pressure from the Indian Ocean on the western flank of the Japanese occupied possessions.

I also think that MacArthur would be glad to be relieved of the respon-

[1]Actg Lt-Gen Sir Oliver W. H. Leese (1894–1978): Coldstream Gds Aug 1914; wounded several times in WW1; Staff Coll 1927–8; GSO & Adjt posts; CO 1Bn, C Gds 1936; Staff Coll Quetta 1938; BEF staff; Maj-Gen; Guards Arm Div 1941; Actg Lt-Gen XXX Corps Sept 1942; Sicily 1943; 8th Army i/c Italy Dec 1943; C-in-C Allied Land Forces, SE Asia Oct 1944; sacked by Mountbatten in circumstances still unclear 1945; GOC E Cmd; Ret List 1946.

[2]There had been occasional disputes between Layton and Somerville over who commanded what but they were essentially, as Somerville said, 'as thick as thieves'.

sibility for the Naval protection of the west coast of Australia and that he might welcome the movement of our dividing line from 110°E to 120°E. Such a suggestion would have to come from the highest quarter.

The bearer of this letter, Cdr Buchanan,[1] is joining your fleet as a Captain of one of your destroyers (the *Norman*). He is a very capable and hardworking young gentleman and has a complete knowledge of all our base facilities which have been prepared throughout Australia for the operation of the British Fleet including carriers. I strongly recommend him to your notice and you will find after a short talk with him that he has all the knowledge of this part of the world which would be required if you were ever intending a move in this direction. ...

310. *To Royle*

17 July 1943

Wavell, Peirse and I were ordered home because, whilst Wavell supported the proposed ANAKIM operation, Peirse and I did not agree, and I had informed the Admiralty I was unable to accept the plan proposed.

On our arrival in the UK, conferences were held and it then appeared that the joint planners were also very dubious about the plan, and the PM definitely turned it down. At this stage, we, i.e the three Cs-in-C, received an invitation from the American Chiefs of Staff that we should take advantage of being over in the UK to pay a visit to Washington and hold discussions with them concerning strategy in the Pacific. The PM, whilst agreeing that it was desirable for us to visit Washington, said it would be quite impossible for us to go by ourselves, and consequently at very short notice it was arranged that a large delegation should visit Washington.

The situation on our arrival was that, so far as the Americans were aware, ANAKIM was being actively planned and would be executed. They were naturally upset when they found out the plan was no longer acceptable, and pointed out this would have an adverse effect on the Chinese and their Generalissimo, who had apparently been informed that the re-opening of the Burma Road was only a matter of time.

After considerable discussions, the Americans agreed that the original plan was no longer workable, and accepted in lieu a modified ANAKIM, now called BULLFROG, which envisages an advance in Upper Burma, coupled with a seaborne assault on Akyab and Ramree by what approximates roughly to two divisions. ...

---

[1]Cdr Alfred E. Buchanan, RAN: Cdr Jun 1938; *Diomede* Aug 1939; *Valentine* 1940; Comb Ops HQ 1942; *Norman* June 1942; *Arunta* Aug 1943–5.

The strategy to be pursued in the Pacific and elsewhere with a view to the ultimate defeat of Japan was also discussed, but not in any very great detail. The American joint planners produced a skeleton plan on which they and our joint planners are now working in London. When this has been put into shape it is probable that a further combined conference will be held in order that the plan may be finally approved and form the basis of current and future operations in the Pacific, Bay of Bengal, etc.

Whilst at Washington I had an interview with Dr Evatt. . . . [He] raised the question of the Eastern Fleet being stationed on the west coast of Australia. I pointed out to him that the position of the Eastern Fleet must be governed by the interests it had to protect and by the particular danger to which those interests were exposed. At the beginning of '42 it might well have been thought that the western seaboard of Australia was liable to Japanese invasion, but at that time the Eastern Fleet had not been formed and when it was formed it was quite inadequate to deal with the scale of attack to which it might have been subjected if left in such close proximity to Japanese Naval bases; in fact for this reason the Fleet had to be withdrawn to Kilindini. I told Dr Evatt that in my opinion the chance of any Japanese invasion of the west coast of Australia was at the present moment remote and although the needs of Australia were carefully considered in conjunction with others, it was quite clear that as soon as the Eastern Fleet was re-formed the proper place for it was in Ceylon, which flanks or covers all vital lines of communication to the Middle East, India and Australia. The positioning of a Fleet at the terminal end of a line of communication is unsound and ineffective.

Dr Evatt then stated that the British Government had broken their agreement with the Australian Government that they would maintain a force of 5 battleships and 3 carriers in the Indian Ocean. I replied that I never heard of such an agreement and that in my opinion it would have been a most improper agreement, since it would have been contrary to the Casablanca decisions, which approved the policy that the defeat of the Axis in Europe should have first priority. To secure this defeat capital ships and carriers are required in the Western hemisphere. I had every reason to believe that as soon as the situation in the Mediterranean was stabilised we should look forward to substantial reinforcements being sent to the Eastern Fleet. We ended up finally on a friendly note. . . .

Harking back to grand strategy, I found that Admiral King was averse to the British and American Fleets being required to operate together tactically unless it was shown that this was absolutely essential. He considered that when the final strategical plan was worked out it would show that our object could best be achieved by simultaneous operations in the Pacific and on the western limits of the Malayan Barrier. If this proves to be the case, it would appear more suitable for the British to employ their forces in the Malayan Barrier rather than to have mixed forces operating either in both areas or elsewhere. With this point of view I am inclined to agree. Whilst it is quite possible the Eastern Fleet may have to use Western Australian bases at some period during the operations, initially Ceylon would be a more suitable base. I don't want to suggest from this that there should be any slowing down of preparations of Western Australian bases, but I wish to make it clear that the defence of Western Australia is best achieved by keeping the Japanese fully engaged in defending what they now hold.

I was interested to find that MacArthur is no one's friend at Washington; if it wasn't for, what I am told, is his expressed intention to run for President, I believe he would be recalled. . . . As American forces, e.g., air, Chinese forces under Stilwell, and possibly some Naval units, will be taking part in BULLFROG, it was necessary for us to agree to a Supreme Commander. The choice of the latter had not been made when I left England, but it will certainly be British, and possibly an Air Officer. I urged most strongly that this Supreme Command should be on the Eisenhower model rather than MacArthur . . . It seems probable that the Naval C-in-C will have to act more or less as Cunningham does, i.e. remain ashore, with another Flag Officer in command of the Fleet at sea.

The Supreme Commander's responsibility will, of course, be limited to the [combined] operations directed against the Japanese, and the Naval C-in-C will continue to act independently in regard to protection of communications, bases, etc., in the Indian Ocean. . . .

I am getting a little anxious about the Dutch destroyers on the west coast who are getting no Fleet training, and whose morale is inclined to suffer if left detached for too long a time. I may therefore suggest that two of my Australian destroyers should be sent to relieve them; and will be glad to have your reactions to this proposal.

I suggested to the PM it might be a good thing if I paid a visit to MacArthur. He quite agreed, and said when the time was ripe he would send MacArthur a signal suggesting this. I can't at the moment make any proposals for a date, because I have to go to Ceylon and India in the near future, return to Mombasa to clear up things here, and finally move over to Ceylon when we shift our HQ about early September. . . .

311. *Pocket diary, 1943*

8 July–23 August 1943

8 July (London)

Meeting in Cabinet office with Tony B[uzzard] to discuss grand strategy for Pacific. Looks like separate tasks for British and US.

25 July

The Auk[1] has asked for considerable additions for BULLFROG. . . . Ernie King says Dutch destroyers and *Tromp*[2] can return to EF if latter based Ceylon.

27 July

Struggling with a mass of detail over BULLFROG. Miles appointed Force commander but no other appointments yet.

23 August

Signal from Admiralty that no escort carrier until completion Med operation which begins middle of Sept.[3] Appear to be about 6 U-boats on their way out to the Cape.

312. *Report of Proceedings, 24 July–26 August 1943*

c.26 August 1943

2.   Accompanied by my Chief of Staff and a small staff I sailed from Kilindini in HMS *Sussex*[4] at 1500 on 24 July.
5.   On 30 July on approaching Ceylon, torpedo bombing, dive bombing and high level bombing exercise attacks were carried out against HMS *Sussex* by shore based RAF aircraft from Ceylon.
6.   Whilst at Ceylon I held several conferences with authorities concerned and settled a considerable number of matters mostly concerned with the forthcoming move to Ceylon of my shore HQ and the Eastern Fleet.

---

[1]Gen (later Field Marshal) Sir Claude Auchinleck (1884–1981): most of career in Indian Army; GOC, N Norway April 1940; S Cmd 1940; C-in-C Middle E 1941–2; C-in-C India 1941 & 1943–7; FM 1946.
[2]*Tromp* R Neth N: 1938, 4150t, 6×5.9in, 32.5k.
[3]The invasion of mainland Italy.
[4]*Sussex* 1929, 9830t, 8x8in, 8×4, 8tt, 32.25k.

Air Defence of Trincomalee and Colombo

The heavy and light air defences of Ceylon are at present largely concentrated at Trincomalee and Colombo as follows:

Trincomalee   48 HAA   44 LAA
Colombo   40 HAA   38 LAA

In addition there are 40 Army A/A searchlights available in Ceylon distributed between the two above ports, with the majority at Trincomalee.

10.   At 0900 on 5 August I embarked in HMS *Sussex* and sailed for Bombay. After leaving harbour, squadron T/B and dive bombing exercises were carried out by RAF aircraft from Ceylon. . .

12.   Whilst at Delhi a series of conferences were held. The following are the more important matters which were discussed:–

Operation BULLFROG

13.   The force Commanders' outline plan was examined in detail by the C-in-C, India and myself, together with the Chiefs of Staff, India.

The Force Commanders were instructed to investigate and elaborate certain items in their plan, and they were also directed to prepare two plans:–

Plan One – Based on the assumption that the additional assault ships and
            craft requested by them would be available and
Plan Two – That only the forces proposed by CCS would be available.

It was agreed that with the forces likely to be available operation LYNCHPIN[1] could not be carried out simultaneously with BULLFROG. The Force Commanders were directed to give consideration to staggering the two operations.

15.   One immediate effect of the dislocation of rail transport in Bengal due to the above floods is the military requirement to move 80,000 men from Madras and 6000 vehicles from Vizgapatam by sea to Chittagong. The military authorities wish to commence this operation in September and, due to the limited unloading capacity at Chittagong, it will be necessary to carry it out in a series of small convoys (2 personnel and 2 MT ships each) sailing at approximately 3 day intervals. The operation therefore will not be completed before December.

16.   Arrangements have been made to provide A/S escorts but owing to the small number of A/S escort ships now available on the E Indies Station, these escorts can only be provided by still further depleting the

[1]One of the many abortive plans made in the theatre.

already thin A/S escort provided for convoys in the Arabian Sea. I represented this matter to Their Lordships by signal on 12 August in which I requested that favourable consideration might be given to the early return to the E Indies Station of the 12 A/S escort ships loaned to the Mediterranean in the later spring for operations in that theatre and to the early provision of an escort carrier.

Air Situation in the Bay of Bengal

17.   In consultation with the AOC-in-C, India, a review was made of the air situation in the Bay of Bengal as regards protection of shipping and bases. This may be summarised as follows:

(a)   As long as the possibility of carrier borne aircraft attack on Ceylon remains, it is necessary to retain in Ceylon an air striking force.

(b)   For the present the following air striking force will suffice:

1 Liberator bomber squadron (less the aircraft allocated for PRU).
1 Beaufort T/B squadron.

(c)   the undermentioned additional squadrons now in Ceylon will be moved as follows:

1 Vengeance D/B squadron to be moved to Bengal where it is required for operation.
1 Beaufort T/B squadron to be moved during the autumn where it will be better placed to act as an air striking force in the northern part of the Bay of Bengal during forthcoming operations.[1]

20.   Although the present threat of enemy air attack against our shipping is small, the enemy may become more active, especially if information reaches them of movements of troop ships between Madras [and] Chittagong during the period September to December.

21.   The diversion of resources and labour which would be involved in building up the fighter protection has to be weighed against the possible enemy air threat. As this diversion could only be made at the expense of projects already in hand for long term and offensive operations, I agreed that the present fighter protection arrangements, although unsatisfactory, must be accepted.

22.   In these circumstances the availability of an escort carrier to provide fighter protection in addition to A/S protection for important troop convoys in the Bay of Bengal is considered a minimum insurance.

---

[1]Consolidated Vultee Liberator (US): 1939, bomb load 5000lb+, 10mg, 300mph, range 2100mls. Bristol Beaufort: 1938, bomb load 2000lb, 4mg, 265mph. Consolidated Vultee Vengeance (US): dive bomber, 1941, bomb load 2000lb, 5mg, 273mph.

Air Reconnaissance and Air A/S protection for shipping in the Bay of Bengal

23.   There are requirements for:–

(a)   Air reconnaissance to the eastward of the coastal shipping route to provide warning of the possible approach of enemy surface ships.
(b)   Air A/S escort for shipping and particularly for the troopship convoys necessitated by the dislocation of the railways caused by recent floods in Bengal.

At present the only aircraft available are as follows:–

(a)   *Catalinas* 1 squadron to operate from Madras for the northern portion of the route, 4 squadrons from Ceylon for the southern portion.
      The number of Catalinas available is however limited by the large detachment from Ceylon made to the Western Indian Ocean and to South Africa to combat U-boats in those areas.
(b)   *Liberators* In addition to the one G/R squadron in Ceylon, one squadron of G/R aircraft is now forming in Cuttack area but will not be fully operational before November.
(c)   No medium range G/R aircraft are available as the Wellington squadrons previously available in Bengal were moved to the Middle East earlier in the year.
      The only M/R G/R aircraft that can now be made available locally to reinforce the Catalinas is the Beaufort squadron due to be moved from Ceylon to Bengal. The employment of Beauforts on A/S protection must necessarily cause a reduction in their efficiency as a T/B squadron.

25.   Air HQ, India agreed to request the Air Ministry to return to Bengal at an early date at least one Wellington squadron.

Night fighters for Ceylon

26.   It was agreed that sufficient night fighters should be stationed in Ceylon to prevent the enemy carrying out with comparative impunity prolonged night reconnaissance, or night bombing, of important targets in the island.

AOC-in-C represented to the Air Ministry that one squadron of Beaufighters should be allocated to Ceylon, and has just informed me by signal that this has been approved. Pending the arrival of this squadron he intends to loan to Ceylon until November two Beaufighters out of the only flight now in Bengal.

SOE and the SIS Organisation

32.   At a conference with representatives of SOE and SIS organisations, it was agreed that:–

(a)   Fairmiles (D)[1] were not suitable for operations in the Mergui Archipelago or on the S coast of Sumatra and that, when available, submarines should be used in lieu.

(b)   The 3 SOE Fairmiles required to operate on the Arakan coast should be attached to the light coastal forces to be established on that coast and operate under cover of movements of these forces.

36.   I also visited the RIN Coastal Craft base at Bombay, and inspected the RIN MTB flotilla manned by RN officers and men. Provisional arrangements were made with the FOC, RIN, for pooling the future RN and RIN coastal craft resources in order to provide the coastal craft which will be required for operation BULLFROG (2 flotillas of HDML's, 3 flotillas ML's, 2 flotillas MTB's) and also for operations on the Arakan coast.

It was agreed that final details of the most practical way of combining RN and RIN resources should be discussed and formulated between the Officers Commanding RIN coastal craft and Captain A. G. V. Hubback, RN, now on his way to Ceylon to take command of the RN coastal craft allocated to the Eastern Fleet.[2]

39.   I sailed from Bombay in HMS *Sussex* at 1500 on 20 August and proceeded to Kilindini where I arrived at 1645 on 25 August.

During the approach to Kilindini interception exercises were carried out against *Sussex* by *Kenya* and *Emerald* under RA, 4th CS, and two Catalinas from Kilindini.

313.   *To Pound*

Kilindini,
27 August 1943

A/A Defences at Trincomalee and Colombo

4.   Although the RAF estimate of possible scale of air attack is based chiefly on what long range aircraft the Japanese are likely to be able to operate from the Andamans and Sumatra, I feel that if the target in the

---

[1]Motor torpedo boats: 105t, 4tt, 30k.
[2]Capt A. G. V. Hubback: Cdr 1936; PD 1938; French NLO April 1940; SO (O) Force H June 1940; *Galatea* Jan 1941; Actg Capt, *Nile* April 1942; Capt June 1942; Capt Cmdg Coastal Forces, Med March 1943; Cmdg Coastal Forces, Eastern F Aug 1943; ADP (SPS) July 1944.

harbours is sufficiently attractive, the enemy may well be tempted to carry out a sea-borne air attack. For this reason I am averse to any reduction in the scale of A/A defences in these places for the present.

Bombay Dockyard

7. This most inefficient establishment is making Ross Turner's hair turn greyer than it was before.[1] Labour troubles are incessant and it is with the greatest difficulty that any sort of output can be maintained. One has to remember that in India we are dealing with a foreign and to a large extent hostile population, and it is quite useless to expect whole-hearted co-operation in the War effort. So far as I can judge Turner is doing all that is possible, but as I have pointed out in signals to the Admiralty is greatly handicapped by lack of foremen, etc. This lack of supervision over the workmen further reduces their miserable output.

BULLFROG

10. This plan was carefully examined while we were at Delhi, and I am satisfied that if we want to make sure that the operation will succeed without doubt, we shall require the additional landing craft which the Force Commanders have requested. I referred to this in my signal to you in which I said that two plans were being worked out, but I feel that if the second plan, i.e., with reduced landing craft, is executed, we might well take a toss unless the scale and effectiveness of the Japanese defence is well below that we have estimated. I am not quite happy about the air situation since it appeared to me that the difficulty of controlling fighters in this particular area is not being fully appreciated. Compared with other recent combined operations the fighter cover we can give is pretty thin and since it will be composed of British and American shore-based and sea-borne aircraft there will be undoubted complications. I think the difficulties can be overcome providing the RAF fully realise the need for the most intensive training and exercises directly the aircraft are available for this purpose.

General

17. Dickie Mountbatten's appointment as Supreme Commander came as a bit of a surprise, but we all feel that his imagination and drive will be of the greatest value and may possibly put some life into the slow moving Indian machinery. I still feel, however, that the Supreme Commander should not be too individualistic and that at all costs anything of a MacArthur set up should be avoided. So far as the Naval side

[1]Vice Adm (Ret) Ross R. Turner: Capt 1923; RA, Adm Supt Portsmouth DY Sept 1935; VA (ret) May 1939; Adm Supt Bombay DY May 1943; SBNO Greece Feb 1945.

is concerned, I feel quite confident that this will not arise, since in all my past dealings with Dickie, I have found that we see very much eye to eye on most matters.

18. Tait informs me that Smuts would like to see me before I leave finally for Ceylon. I am, therefore, going down to Pretoria next week, and on to the Cape afterwards to see how the U-boat campaign is getting on. I shall go by air, and shall be back here about 10 September, and in Ceylon about the 20th.

314. *From Acting Vice Admiral Lord Louis Mountbatten*

Combined Operations HQ,
1A Richmond Terrace,
Whitehall, SW1
2 September 1943

Quite the most terrifying part of the task which has been so unexpectedly and undeservedly allotted to me was the prospect of having a great Naval C-in-C within the South East Asia Command.

Your typically thoughtful, charming and helpful telegram did more than anything else to reassure me and make me feel that after all the Naval aspect of my task was going to be made pleasant and easy for me.

. . . there is no real senior Naval Officer of my acquaintance who I feel would be so ready to play with an Officer whose naval experience is so very immature by comparison. . . .

. . . I have . . . expressed the hope that the three Cs-in-C will find it possible to set up their HQ in the same locality as my own and the Chiefs of Staff Committee informed me that it was their desire that this wish should be implemented. How soon and to what extent you may find it possible to establish an HQ in . . . New Delhi, I do not know, but in the meanwhile it has occurred to me that you may like to appoint a suitable senior officer from your staff to represent you in New Delhi. I gather Bill Morgan is carrying out this function for you at present and if you care to select him I shall be very glad as he happens to be an old personal friend.

I feel sure you will approve of my choice of Inter-Service Signal Officer-in-Chief, since I . . . am taking your late Signal Officer Micky Hodges[1] . . . He has been doing it for the last two years at COHQ with really great success.

---

[1]Actg Capt Michael Hodges: Cdr 1939; Sig Sch. The Nore; SD June 1941; Actg Capt, Comb Ops HQ Nov 1942; Inter-Service Sig O-in-Chief, SEAC; Actg Capt, *Duke of York* Dec 1944.

My one desire has been to keep my staff as small as possible. Eisenhower has got no less than 1500 officers at his HQ, not including the typists, clerks and orderlies. I hope to do with less than a tenth of that number.

Furthermore, I do not intend to make the mistake of setting up a separate and independent Naval Staff who would very likely end up by running counter to your wishes and annoying you.

I therefore trust that you will feel it possible to place in my HQ a small number of trustworthy officers for the operational and administrative planning and also for the signal planning inseparable from combined operations of the type which I have been instructed to carry out. . . .

I fully understand your direct responsibility to the Admiralty for sea communications and I hope I am a good enough sailor at heart to feel that this is absolutely right. I feel sure that you will make the necessary arrangements to keep me informed of the movements of your Fleet to comply with this part of your directive. During any combined operation when the Army and Air Force and our American Allies have a stake in your movements I hope that you will not mind that the Supreme Commander (who only happens to be Dickie Mountbatten by accident) will have a considerable say.

Although I have met your Military and Air colleagues I naturally do not know them nearly as well as you and hope you will not mind my leaning rather heavily on you personally for advice, not only about the Navy but about the SE Asia Command as a whole.

I have an uneasy feeling that this very unexpected and un-sought for job may have a disastrous effect on my Naval career and to that extent I am truly worried. I hope therefore that you will allow me to keep in touch with the Naval side sufficiently to enable me to go back into my original niche in the Navy after the Japanese have been licked. I am hoping perhaps when other things are quiet that you may be able to find a spare cabin to take me to sea as a passenger in order that I may keep in touch with the only profession I have ever really known or care about.

The First Sea Lord . . . told me that one of the reasons that made him vote for my appointment was the fact that you would be the Naval C-in-C with whom I should have to work, since he knew you to be one of those rare men who would be prepared to work in with an officer so many years your junior in his own profession.

Having unburdened all my secret trepidations to you in this letter I promise not to worry you again when I get out as I know I must put on a bold face and not flinch from the responsibilities which have been put upon me. It will be a great thrill to be associated with your great Command and I am so looking forward to seeing you again.

315. *Pocket diary, 1943*

16 September

Signal from Admiralty giving lists of ships to come here from Med but looks as if heavy ships not available [for] some months. Extra A/S to be at Aden by 1 October. . . . Am still concerned about U-boat situation here and feel I ought to have got destroyers N before.

316. *Eastern Fleet War Diary*

September 1943

Redisposition of Escort Forces

2. By the middle of September there were clear indications that an increase in U-boat activity in the Arabian Sea was to be expected.

3. To meet this threat it was decided to put as much shipping as possible into convoy and to cover such shipping as still had to proceed independently by the establishment of approach positions outside focal areas, air patrols being provided to cover the routes between the approved position and the port.

4. This policy necessitated the institution of regular convoys between Durban, Kilindini (DKA, AKD); Aden, Bombay direct (BA, AB) and Colombo, Bombay (BM, MB) and the provision of A/S escorts for these convoys. It was also necessary to allow for the increase of escorts for the convoys into and out of the Persian Gulf (PA, AP, PB, BP).

5. Arrangements had earlier been made for the institution of convoys on the Durban–Kilindini route, and the first of these sailed from Durban on 17 September; since the threat on the Mozambique Channel was now reduced it was possible for some of the escorts allocated for these convoys to be made available for work with the Kilindini–Aden portion. In addition, C-in-C, S Atlantic loaned 8 escort vessels for work on the Aden–Bombay route. Further reinforcements were available by the return of 3 sloops and 5 *Bathursts* from the Mediterranean. These were allocated as follows – the 5 *Bathursts* to reinforce the Persian Gulf convoys, the 2 AA sloops to troop convoys in the Bay of Bengal to relieve 2 *Bangors,* these two *Bangors* with the third sloop to be used for the Bombay–Colombo convoys.

6. The four coastguard cutters to come from the UK were earmarked for Kilindini. four destroyers were allocated to the Aden–Bombay escort force and *Falmouth* to Kilindini–Aden force so that the escort forces are now established as follows:–

Aden Escort Force

Quadrant	Tay	Thyme
Quickmatch	Derg	Nigella
Roebuck	Jasmine	
Relentless	Rockrose	

Kilindini Escort Force – for escort on Kilindini–Aden Route

Falmouth	Scriven	
Maid Marion	Lulworth	
Virginia	Landguard	on arrival
Tulip	Banff	
Fritillary		
Freesia		

ABC Escort Force – reinforcements

Cessnock
Cairns
Wollongong   to reinforce Persian Gulf convoys on arrival.
Lismore
Geraldton[1]

7.   It is intended that the new routine convoys should start early in October working on an eight day cycle with the exception of the DKA and AKD which will work on an alternate 10 and 11 day cycle. The convoys will include ships of speeds from 9 to 13 knots, ships outside these speeds proceeding independently making use of the approach positions mentioned above. . . .

Anti-Submarine

18.   The beginning of September saw the arrival of a group of German U-boats, estimated up to six in number, in the area SE of Madagascar. It was considered a refuelling operation was intended in this area prior to depredations against shipping in the focal areas around ports, and in the shipping lanes, of the North Indian Ocean and the Gulf of Aden.

---

[1]*Bangor* class fleet minesweepers: 1940–41; *c*.650t; 1×3in; 16k. *Cairns, Cessnock, Geraldton, Lismore, Wollongong*: all RAN *Bathurst* class fleet minesweepers: 1940–3; 650–790t; 1×4in; 15k. *Falmouth*: sloop; 1932; 1060t; 2×4in; 16k. *Quadrant, Quickmatch, Relentless, Roebuck*: 1942–3; 1705t; 4×4.7in, 8tt; 34–36k. *Derg, Tay*: 1942–3; 1370t; 2×4in; 19k. *Scriven, Maid Marion*: unidentified. *Lulworth, Landguard, Banff*: ex-US Coastguard cutters: 1928–30; 1546t; 1×5in; 16k. Remainder were 'Flower' class corvettes: *c*.900t; 1×4in; 16k.

Disposition of A/S escorts and air A/S forces was made accordingly, and the system of convoys reorganised to meet this impending threat.

19.   On 4 September the Admiralty estimated that 4 or 5 German and 1 Italian U-boat were within 200 miles of 34°S, 47°E bound E or ENE, and on 10 September that 6 German and 1 Italian were unfixed in the SW Indian Ocean possibly within 400 miles of 30°S, 57°E. The northward trend of the German U-boats now began to show and on 13 September a German U-boat was plotted by poor D/F fix to be about 300 miles to the S of Mauritius, probably northbound.

20.   Meanwhile a Japanese U-boat had entered the Indian Ocean and on 7 September fired torpedoes at the SS *Lyman Stuart* (US) in a position 350 miles to the SW of Colombo. On 9 September the SS *Larchbank* was torpedoed and sunk by a Japanese U-boat in an approximate position 7° 38'N, 73° 12'E. A second Japanese U-boat was plotted by D/F fix to be within 250 miles of 04°S, 85°E on 19 September. This position was to the SE of Ceylon.

21.   On 21 September the SS *Banffshire* (British) was torpedoed in position 009° 27'N, 071° 05'E by a German U-boat and it is considered that this U-boat appeared to be proceeding towards Bombay and may operate off there and off Karachi. The SS *Sandown Castle* (British) reported sighting an enemy submarine on the same day in the position 11° 40'N, 45° 31'E (Gulf of Aden).

23.   On 30 September a report of a periscope sighting was made by the SS *York* in position 1° 20'N, 77° 07'E. This may have been another German U-boat which was proceeding towards Ceylon.[1]

Attacks On U-boats–Reports

26.   On 23 September *Roebuck* attacked a submarine contact near the position 02° 08'N,50° 20'E. No further details have been received. . . .

317.   To Pound

19 September 1943

21.   On arrival at Mombasa I was able to make a further appreciation of where the U-boats would operate. The situation was not so good owing to the withdrawal of so many of our A/S vessels to the Mediterranean, and I am afraid our A/S protection will be somewhat meagre until I can get these A/S vessels back and the destroyers repositioned. . . .

[1]*Lyman Stuart, York*: unidentified. *Larchbank*: Andrew Weir, London: 1925; 5151gt; 11k. *Banffshire*: Houston Line, London: 1912; 6479gt; 13k. *Sandown Castle*: Union Castle Line: 1921; 7607gt; 10.5k.

22. My intention is to proceed to Delhi to meet Mountbatten after spending 3 or 4 days at Colombo. I must confess that I view the prospect of any prolonged stay at Delhi with considerable concern, since I feel it is essential for the C-in-C to keep in personal touch with his Flag and Commanding Officers and also with the men. . . .

318. *To his wife*

Colombo,
30 September 1943

You ask what Dickie has to do with EF? Well all that happens is that certain ships are placed under his orders for specific operations but he has nothing to do with operations to protect our communications or operations against enemy surface forces. For those I am responsible to the Admiralty. Unless he tries to do the MacArthur, which I trust he won't, I think Dickie ought to do quite well. Anyhow I shall do my best to help him over any difficult stiles where possibly my experience may be of value.

319. *To his wife*

Delhi,
5 October 1943

I wonder how old Andrew will make out.[1] Everyone seems to remark on how irascible he is these days. I've heard too that he has a special hate against Dickie so I must take care that there is no sign of disagreement between Dickie and myself, otherwise the fat will be in the fire. Not that I think there will be but with DP I always felt I did not have to pick and choose my words whereas Andrew is so inclined to fly off the handle.

320. *Desk diary, 1943*

6 October

A conference was held with Admiral Miles, Admiral Morgan and Staff officers in connection with operation CULVERIN,[2] and also the organisation of the SEAC HQ as far as this could be deduced from signals on the subject.

---

[1] Adm of the Fleet Sir Andrew Cunningham who had just succeeded Pound as 1SL.
[2] Operations planned against N Sumatra; a Prime Ministerial favourite.

2.   ... a conference, presided over by General Auchinleck, was held to review CULVERIN and other plans that had been prepared, and also to discuss the requirements of SOE and SIS in connection with the landing and re-embarkation of agents in Sumatra, Malaya, etc. SOE were pressing strongly for Catalinas to be employed to carry agents to certain islands in the Mergui Archipelago. Both the AOC and myself objected to this on the grounds that there were insufficient Catalinas to meet the requirements for protection of trade in view of the submarine campaign now in progress, and furthermore that the installation of radar, together with fighters at the aerodromes at Car Nicobar and Sabang had added to the hazards of the operation. No final decision was arrived at, and the matter was to be reconsidered at a further date.

11 October

After discussion with the Supreme Commander it seemed quite clear that there was little prospect of forces being made available to carry out CULVERIN and that consequently some other objective would have to be selected. Although BULLFROG had not been definitely cancelled, the Supreme Commander gave it as his opinion that it was most unlikely the COS would agree to its execution.

2.   I had a visit during the forenoon from Col Colin Mackenzie,[1] who reported the return of a Malayan contact with most valuable information concerning the existing partisan organisation which he hoped might be of the greatest possible value in the future. In view of the widespread nature of this organisation I suggested immediate steps should be taken to get in touch with the partisan Chinese in the Junk Trade since the transfer of agents and stores by submarines to these Junks would solve a large number of problems with which we are at present faced. Col Mackenzie fully agreed and said this would receive special attention. He discussed the various SOE and SIS operations which had been projected and was informed by me that these would continue to receive priority in so far as the employment of submarines was concerned.

321.   *To Tennant*

23 October 1943

... Dickie, Mickey Hodges & Arthur Levison stepped out of the aeroplane on their arrival looking like complete film-stars in their uncreasable American khaki. Dickie seems to have a passion for putting

---

[1]Col Colin S. Mackenzie: R Scots; 2Lt 1931; Lt 1934; Palestine 1936; SOE, SE Asia 1943.

his party in a different uniform & for setting up a little bit different from the rest. I shall do my best to dissuade him as it only leads to tooth-sucking in the end.

Planning is very much in the air because instead of suggesting a job, and providing us with the wherewithal to achieve it, the great ones at home have started the other way round, and asked what we can do with a certain amount of wherewithal; . . . I think Dickie is pretty sound and his experience on the COS Committee undoubtedly stands him in good stead; he is, however, somewhat ebullient . . . Giffard I consider a good sound fellow without any fireworks; Richard Peirse I think you know already. With regard to the Americans, I am very much impressed with General Wheeler, who is the (Q) King, also with General Wedemeyer,[1] who is one of Dickie's numerous Asst Chiefs of Staff. Henry Pownall[2] is, of course, absolutely sound. . . .

. . . The thing we shall have to tackle at once, when the Escort Carriers arrive, is how to operate them in quantity, and how to make sure that the fighter interception is really first-class. I have been talking to the Fighter Direction Officer from *Bulolo*,[3] a first-class fellow in the RAF, who came out specially to the *Ark Royal* to give them some tips, and he tells me that throughout the Mediterranean operations Fighter Direction was a flop, owing to lack of proper equipment and lack of practice. All they could do was maintain an umbrella, and hope that our enormous air superiority would keep the skies clear . . .

322. *To Cunningham*

Delhi,
27 October 1943

. . . Unfortunately, one or two of D's [Mountbatten's] staff started off on the tack that India, as usual, was all adrift, that India wanted waking up, and so on. This struck an extremely low note, and made a very poor opening chorus for the party. However, I was able to intervene at an early stage and get D to make a special point of thanking A[uchinleck?] for all that had been done . . .

---

[1]Gen Raymond ('Speck') Wheeler, US Army: Prin Admin O, SEAC; succeeded Wedemeyer as DCOS. Gen Albert Wedemeyer, US Army: DCOS; later US mil rep with Chiang Kai-Shek.

[2]Lt-Gen Sir Henry R. Pownall (1887–1961): RFA 1906; W Front 1914–19; Staff Coll 1926–9; NW Frontier 1931; CID 1933–6; Brig & Cdt Sch Arty 1936; DMO&I 1938; COS to Gort; Inspr-Gen, LDV; C-in-C N Ireland 1940–1; VCIGS 1941; COS, ABDA 1941–2; Lt-Gen & GOC Ceylon 1942–3; GOC Persia & Iraq; COS to SACSEA Oct 1943; Ret List 1945.

[3]*Bulolo*: HQ ship, 1938, 6267gt, 15k, Burns, Philp, Australia. The FDO is unidentified.

South East Asia Command Headquarters Organisation

. . . D explained . . . he had in mind the setting up of an organisation similar to that employed in the Eastern Med., in which the Minister acted as the Chairman of the Committee formed by the three Cs-in-C. (This is what I have always considered should be the right set-up for a Supreme Commander). With this in view he proposed bringing out a very small HQ staff, and relying on the Joint Planners of the Cs-in-C to carry out all planning.

D stated that this proposal was most vigorously opposed by the Americans and by our own Chiefs of Staff, who insisted that D must have his own fairly complete HQ staff. D stated that it was on account of this that he had brought out a much larger staff than originally intended, but that he hoped it would be possible for the HQs and Cs-in-C's staffs to work in parallel and close co-operation.

The first attempt to get this system going failed completely since at a meeting intended originally for Cs-in-C only, to discuss the amended BULLFROG, everyone put in his all, and there were so many cooks stirring the broth that it was only fit, finally, to be poured down the chute. We tackled D about this yesterday, and told him it was essential that the division of responsibility should be clearly indicated, and that the planners should be limited in numbers, and not have bright ideas thrust on them at every stage of the proceedings. Incidentally, the responsibility of those who have to execute the plan must be constantly borne in mind when the plan is being elaborated. I have every confidence that we shall get a working arrangement in due course, but it seems a bit odd, after all these years of war, that there is not [to] be now a cut and dried policy in the respect of these matters. . . .

Naval Staff at Delhi

. . . a single Naval C-in-C is required, but if he is to discharge his duties properly, I feel he must be adequately represented at the two centres of the station, e.g., Ceylon, and at the present moment, Delhi. The great distances covered by this station, coupled with the climatic conditions which invariably produce lassitude, makes it very necessary for the C-in-C to pay occasional visits to Naval bases and units in order to ensure that officers and men are on their toes, and to judge for himself whether preparations now going forward, are proceeding as rapidly and effectively as possible. During his absences on these visits, the C-in-C must feel satisfied that at either Delhi or Ceylon, he has representatives who can take decisions if necessary, and represent him fully on all occasions. . . .

Eventual location of SEAC HQ

. . . The whole atmosphere of this place both official and social, is wrong. Very slowly and very reluctantly, Delhi has been brought to realise that there is a war on, but the inertia and resistance to quick action seems fundamental in the place, and unlikely to be overcome by Dickie or anyone else. I was therefore not surprised when D informed us yesterday of his intention to move to Ceylon before the next hot weather.

Fleet Training

I hope very much that we shall get the Fleet here in sufficient time to carry out intensive training. It so often occurs that when ships arrive, especially after the rather long passage, they have defects to be made good . . . I feel that the Escort Carriers in particular will require intensive training, . . . In the operations we are likely to carry out, . . . it is most unlikely we shall have any land-based fighters available during the i nitial stages, and shall have to rely on the carrier fighters entirely. Furthermore, it is probable the enemy will use relatively large escorted strikes against us; under these circumstances, well controlled fighter interception may well spell the difference between success and failure. To achieve a really good standard of fighter interception under the special conditions we shall probably have to face, requires intensive practice, extending, I estimate, over at least a month.

323. *Desk diary, 1943*

29 October

At the Supreme Commander's meeting I referred to recent information which suggested Japanese activity in the Singapore and Malayan area. This activity comprised the transfer of troops to Singapore; the movement of aircraft carriers between Japan and Singapore apparently engaged in ferrying aircraft; the establishment ashore at Singapore of a Flag Officer of an Aircraft [Carrier?] Squadron; the reinforcement of air squadrons at Sabang and the Andamans together with the maintenance of fighters on Car Nicobar. The setting up of the SEAC would obviously suggest that offensive operations in this Theatre are envisaged, consequently movement of Japanese forces within the area might be purely of a defensive nature. On the other hand if the Japanese had a true appreciation of our present weakness in this area both in surface ships and air forces, they must realise that an attack on trade in Bengal or the East Coast ports of India and Ceylon could be carried out with small hazard to themselves and quite possibly give a very profitable return. Should the possibility of attacking suggest itself to the Japanese I considered that serious consideration should be given to what steps could be taken to meet this threat should intelligence and other information suggest it is imminent. So far as the Fleet was concerned I did not anticipate any heavy ship or fleet carrier reinforcements would reach me before the middle or end of December. The present naval forces we had available were barely sufficient to afford normal trade protection and were quite inadequate in numbers and composition to meet a Japanese force of, say, 1 battleship, 5 heavy and light cruisers, 2 carriers and an appropriate destroyer screen. I saw no reason why the Japanese should not be prepared to detach such a force for operations in the Bay of Bengal unless they had good reason to think that a heavy American attack directed against, say, their main base at Truk, was imminent. After discussion it was agreed that AOC-in-C should work out a scheme for the transfer of squadrons [of] both heavy and light bombers to the E Coast and Ceylon. I agreed that the Beaufort squadron from Ceylon at present employed on GR A/S duties in Bombay area should return to Ceylon immediately should circumstances render this necessary.

324. *Eastern Fleet War Diary*

October 1943

Anti-Submarine

21. During the month 5 German and 3 Japanese U-boats were operating on the station. Six ships totalling, 25,833 tons gross, were sunk, and 3 ships were damaged but reached port under their own power.

22. The U-boat activity slackened towards the end of the month when 3 German U-boats left the Station, Eastwards. One Japanese U-boat was still estimated to be in the Mozambique Channel and it was this U-boat which probably used its seaplane to make a reconnaissance of the Chagos Archipelago and Diego Suarez early in the month. One Japanese, after sinking a merchant vessel by gunfire in the vicinity of Addu Atoll, was estimated to be homeward bound and the third either still off the coast of SW India or homeward bound.

23. Of the two other German U-boats, one was probably sunk by aircraft in the Gulf of Oman on 16 October, and the second was estimated to be in the Indian Ocean still and possibly approaching the Malabar Coast from the NW.[1]

---

[1] *U-533*, sunk by an aircraft of 244 Squadron.

24.   Six attacks were made by surface vessels on U-boat contacts,
although in two cases only was the presence of a U-boat confirmed

Air

27.   A widespread search was carried out to the W of Addu Atoll in
order to locate and destroy a U-boat which was thought to be in the area
but with negative results.
28.   244 Squadron attacked and sank a German U-boat in the Gulf of
Oman on 16 October . . .
29.   A search was carried out on the 18th for a U-boat which attacked
the SS *Nizam*. Nil results.
30.   An A/S sweep was carried out by three Catalinas off the W coast of
India for a U-boat which sank [attacked?] the SS *British Purpose*. Nil
results.
31.   Catalinas searched for and found survivors of the SS *Congella*
which was shelled and sunk by a U-boat 140 miles NW of Addu
Atoll.[1] . . .

325.   *To his wife*

Delhi,
29 October 1943

I've spent most of my time trying to keep Dickie and his party on the
right lines. It's quite clear to me now that D is too much inclined to go
into detail and furthermore to try and centralise the conduct of operations in his own hands. I've told him that any attempt to set up a
MacArthur command is bound to end in failure and though he always
disclaims any such intention I'm not at all sure that he's not in fact aiming at it. Luckily – so far as I am involved – it does not concern me
greatly but so long as I'm associated with the party in any way I shall
continue to object to what I believe is a wrong set-up. both Peirse and
Giffard are in agreement with me on this. We had a long discussion
about planning this morning when Dickie broached the idea that we are
all just one big happy party all working together. I disagreed as I considered he had on his staff the 'crystal gazers' and the 'brains trust' whereas
we Cs-in-C were the practical chaps who had to evolve a practical plan
and consequently could not be interfered with constantly by his 'c.g,s'

[1]*British Purpose*: British Tanker Co. *Nizam*: Asiatic SN: 1914; 522gt; 12k. *Congella*:
Andrew Weir: 1914; 4532gt; 10.5k.

and 'b.t,s'. Max Langley and Michael Goodenough[1] are coming out on Dickie's staff and since both are always dead certain they must be right something had to be done about it. Dickie eventually agreed but the situation will have to be watched. . . . Have had no answer from Andrew [Cunningham] yet about Miles's appointment[2] and do hope he's not going to be obstinate. He always has an idea you can run everything yourself but apart from the huge distances out here he does not seem to realise that in the Med the constant criticism was the lack of a proper Naval staff. Time after time they were nearly in a mess on account of this, but being so close to the UK someone could always get out at short notice to save the day. You can't do that out here.

326. Desk Diary, 1943

31 October (Bombay)

At 9 a.m. I inspected the divisions on board *Battler*[3] and walked round the ship after addressing the ship's company. I was surprised to learn from the pilots that many of them preferred her flight deck to that of a fleet carrier. Apparently freedom from side obstructions was the advantage. I noted with interest the RP fittings on the Swordfish . . .

1 November

I spent the forenoon inspecting certain of the LSIs, and the HQ ship *Bulolo*, belonging to Force G, in company with Admiral Troubridge, commanding that force. Whilst in some cases the officers in the ships or in parties associated with these ships were of very good material, others, especially among the seniors, were obviously not well adapted in this role, ill-suited for active operations of this nature. I was interested to meet again Captain David Bone of the *Circassia*,[4] the well-known writer of sea stories, who is now 69 years of age, but still in very good heart and active for his age. Still, after all, he is 69 years old and one wonders whether this is a proper appointment for this fine old seaman at his time of life.

---

[1]Capt Gerald M. B. Langley: Capt 1936; DD N Air Div 1939; *Carlisle* Nov 1939; Dir Gunnery & A/A Warfare Div July 1941; Cdre, SACSEA staff Dec 1943; Cdre *Devonshire* Jan 1945.

Actg Capt Michael G. Goodenough: Lt-Cdr *Devonshire* 1939; RN Barracks, Chatham 1940; Cdr & PD June 1940; *Cumberland* April 1942; Actg Capt SACSEA staff Nov 1943; Capt June 1945; DOP (N) 1944.

[2]Representing him at SEAC HQ, then in Delhi.

[3]*Battler*: CVE, 1942, 10,200t, 15–20 a/c, 16k.

[4]Capt (later Sir) David Bone: one of a set of distinguished artistic brothers from Glasgow; Capt, Anchor Line.

2 November

3. In the afternoon I inspected the Landing Craft Repair Base and found the progress in developing this had been disappointingly slow. ... Whilst at this base I had an opportunity to take a trip in a DUKW, and was impressed by the performance of this vehicle.[1] It is quite clear that in this war we are turning quite a number of soldiers into very average sailors.

5 November

... Another point that has to be considered in planning of this nature is that practical aspects covering the tactical operation of a number of carriers are fully considered in the course of preparation of the plan. It is my experience that both Flag and Commanding Officers in carriers tend to become too single minded in regard to air operations, and give insufficient attention to such matters as A/S protection and the need for concentration, so far as possible, whilst flying operations are in progress. ...

6 November

BBC reports received on a naval action S of Bougainville. The Japanese claim to have sunk one large US carrier, besides damaging a number of other vessels, whilst the US claims to have sunk 2 Japanese cruisers and damaged 4 others.[2] It is very seldom that an accurate report is received here of actions in the Pacific until some time after they have taken place. Although claims on both sides are usually exaggerated, it seems important that the Supreme Commander in the SW Pacific should keep his next door neighbours informed of what has actually happened, since any alteration of balance in Naval forces must be of immediate concern. On every occasion of writing to MacArthur, I have stressed this point but without result, and I presume that it is Washington that imposes so rigid a censorship. ...

7 November

Inspected the ship's company of *Kenya* and divisions, attended Church and addressed the men afterwards. From there I proceeded to walk round my Flagship – *Tarantula*. Her enthusiastic CO, Captain Thelwell, RNR,[3] has been at great pains to fit this quite unseaworthy and very ancient river gunboat as a base ship for the Ceylon Escort Force,

---

[1]DUKW: amphibious landing craft.
[2]In fact the Americans lost no ships and the Japanese lost one cruiser and one destroyer.
[3]*Tarantula*: former China Rivers gunboat, 1916, 625t, 1×6in, 1×3in, 14k. Captain R. G. Thelwell, RNR: Cdr 1935; Chatham, misc duties 1939; Takoradi, Jan 1942; Capt June 1942; CO, Ceylon Escort Group Oct 1942; *Pleiades* Oct 1944.

and has succeeded admirably. He appears to have looted fittings and material from everywhere, and I had to ask him to spare my barge and private skiff.

11 November

3. I received a personal signal from the Supreme Commander in which he said he was drawing attention to the considerable discrepancies which appeared to exist between the telegraphed directive to him, the verbal instructions which he had received at Chequers, and the wording of the directive contained in COS (43) 496 (0). He had pointed out that if the principle of unity of command was not acceptable to the Navy, then he was sure General Stilwell would withdraw into his shell, and the one main object of appointing an Allied Commander would have been defeated.

327. *To Mountbatten*

13 November 1943

With regard to the question now under consideration at home on how the Eastern Fleet stands in relation to the SEAC, I would like to confirm that I have no personal views on the matter at all. On the other hand, I have certain general views which I will attempt to elaborate.

2. I believe that both you and I held the view originally that the functions of a Supreme Commander should be those of a Chairman of a committee, rather than those of a person exercising in himself a unified command.

3. In the Mediterranean it appears that the Supreme Commander rarely identifies himself personally with the allied organisation except on major matters. The HQ of the Allied command is always referred to as 'Allied HQ' as opposed to 'Eisenhower's'.

4. In the Pacific we see the reverse. Here MacArthur from the very commencement of taking over command made it clear that it is a 'MacArthur' rather than an 'Allied' set up. MacArthur's bombers, MacArthur's attacks, became so insistent at one time that it almost appeared as if the British were not concerned in these operations; this at times when the Australian and New Zealand troops were bearing the brunt of the fighting on shore. The bad feeling and lack of liaison in this area between the Navy, Army and Air, which certainly existed for a considerable time, was no doubt due primarily to personalities, but it is possible that the self-identification of MacArthur with every occurrence may have caused resentment.

5.   Another aspect of undue self-identification is that the HQ staff may tend to follow the lead of their commander and attempt to identify themselves with matters which are primarily the concern and responsibility of others. It must also lead to undue centralisation of headquarters.

6.   Please do not think I am having a dig at you personally because the papers have started referring to any activities of the SEAC as 'Mountbatten' rather than 'Allied'. I know that you would be the last person to encourage this sort of thing, but on the other hand I do feel that if this is not checked it will soon encourage a belief that the SEAC is to be a MacArthur model and controlled by a dictator rather than a chairman.

7.   It is, of course, arguable whether it is better for the Supreme Commander to be dictator rather than a Chairman. . . . If the Chairman rather than the dictator is preferred and if it is desired to avoid the suggestion of dictatorship and overcentralisation, I think the best way to achieve this is to have a well balanced system of decentralisation.

8.   It is at this point the position of the Eastern Fleet and certain of the air forces that co-operate with the Eastern Fleet come into the picture.

9.   The Fleet has certain specific functions to perform among which are:–

(a)   Protection of sea communications, and the conduct of operations directed against the enemy Fleet, or units of that Fleet outside the area of active amphibious operations.

(b)   Support of the Army and Air Force in the area of active amphibious operations.

10.   (a) has been under the direct control of the Admiralty hitherto, and I do not feel that any advantage would accrue if this responsibility was transferred to the SEAC, whether the latter exercised a nominal or an active control.

11.   (b) on the other hand directly concerns SEAC. Whatever units of the Fleet are placed at the disposal of the Supreme Commander for amphibious operations must be directly under his orders and entirely at his disposal until they are released.

12.   It seems to me as SEAC has, or will have in the future, more than enough to occupy its attention preparing for, and conducting, amphibious operations any decentralisation of activities not immediately concerned with such operations, i.e., outside the active theatre, should be welcomed. Apart from this such decentralisation would tend to remove any suggestion that a dictatorship has been established over SE Asia.

13.   I am fully alive to what can be argued on the other side, namely that proper control can only be exercised if one authority can do as he

pleases with any forces in the theatre however directly or indirectly these may be connected with amphibious operations. I do not feel that this is in fact the case, and in consequence I should welcome a more definite focusing of the SEAC HQ Staff on matters which are concerned primarily with present or projected amphibious operations in which two or more services are required to participate.

14. ... with your quick brain and lively imagination you must feel, and probably are, competent to grasp to an unusual extent the detailed technical aspects of Naval, land or air operations. If you are frank with yourself, you might perhaps agree when I say that you have a constant urge to see and find out for yourself. I think this urge must be resisted and restricted to such occasions as satisfying your self that what has been stated [as possible?] is in fact not possible, or increasing the standard of efficiency when it is clearly low and could be improved. At other times I feel it would be much better if you hardened your heart and left things not directly connected with your primary function to others, and thus free yourself and your staff of additional responsibilities which if discharged properly would overload you, but which if accepted but not properly discharged will certainly cause difficulties.

15. You have said in your letter to me that my suggestion to the effect that the Eastern Fleet is not at all times under your orders might have a prejudicial effect on the attitude of Joe Stilwell. I see your point and more especially as Joe Stilwell is Joe Stilwell, but on the other hand there would in fact be small grounds for his taking exception to the fact that Naval activities only remotely connected with combined active operations directed against the Japanese are decentralised as a matter of convenience and to avoid overloading.

16. ... Whatever is decided you may be quite certain that I will always do my best to meet your requirements in every possible way, and you can count on all my officers and men to follow my example.

17. It is a great pleasure and satisfaction to feel I can at any time write to you quite frankly like this and to know you will not, as they say in Tooting Bec, 'take umbrage'.

328. *Churchill to Cunningham and Ismay*

17 November 1943

1. My intention is set forth in para. 6 of my Directive and it is difficult to express it more clearly, but I will try:

'For all the purposes of the SE Asia Command the Naval C-in-C and all his forces are under the Supreme Commander. They therefore constitute a part of his Command and he may address them as such. When any of the three Cs-in-C sit in consultation with the Supreme Commander he has the power of over-riding decision and there is no question of a junta or a Committee.'

2. There must be no derogation from the integrity of the SE Asia Command within the sphere and for the purposes for which it is created. For instance, the Admiralty should not have withdrawn control over Naval correspondents and Public Relations matters from Air Marshal Joubert.[1] Within the limits and for the purposes of the SE Asia Command the Navy is on exactly the same footing as the Air and the Army; neither better nor worse.

3. All the above is without prejudice to the over-riding authority of the Admiralty over all ships and Commanders at sea in respect of all purposes not specifically delegated to the SE Asia Command. The Admiralty will be responsible to the War Cabinet for not issuing over-riding orders to the Eastern Fleet obstructive of the purposes of the Supreme Commander, SE Asia.

4. I cannot myself see that any difficulties should arise in practice, but if you would test the above by putting me a few hard cases I could immediately say what the answer should be.[2]

329. *Cunningham to Churchill*

20 November 1943

. . . it is not in my opinion possible to set out exactly rigid relations between and responsibilities of the three authorities concerned, i.e., the Admiralty, the Supreme Commander SE Asia Command and the C-in-C Eastern Fleet. They must be interpreted with elasticity and good will. Your para. 3 . . . brings out the fundamental difficulty in that there are no ships 'specifically delegated to the SE Asia Command'.[3] . . .

---

[1] Joubert was now DCOS for information & civil affairs.
[2] This seemed to change little.
[3] Lambe drafted a message for Cunningham to send to Mountbatten.

330.   *From Mountbatten*

Cairo,
24 November 1943

. . . I saw the First Sea Lord and got the knotty problem about the SE Asia Command and the Eastern Fleet settled. . . .

I am afraid I absolutely stuck out on the need for regarding the Naval Forces in the SE Asia Command as under the command of the Supreme Commander for all inter-service matters which are not governed by the strategic or operational considerations dealt with in para. 6 of the memorandum.[1] In particular I stressed that all general matters such as Public Relations must be dealt with by me and that I must be allowed to draft general instructions for the SE Asia Command and which would be obeyed by them.

I gave the First Sea Lord my assurance, which I repeat to you, that I would not do anything to interfere with the direct Admiralty control over the Eastern Fleet in matters reserved under para. 6.

This very helpful decision on the part of the First Sea Lord arrived at the right psychological moment for me to be able to get General Marshall to ensure that General Stilwell places his forces fully as much under my orders as the Fleet.

I am certain that the American forces will be guided in their acceptance of the SE Asia Command to a large extent by the arrangement with the Eastern Fleet, and I am therefore so glad that we have been able to make an arrangement which is satisfactory to the First Sea Lord and therefore I presume also satisfactory to you.

. . . I understand from Micky [Hodges?] that it was almost entirely due to your personal intervention that the C-in-C Ceylon was brought round to accept our move to Kandy. . . .

I am completely foxed over this question of the move of the Japanese aircraft carriers. I suppose you will have seen the Intelligence appreciation on this situation. It appears that Subhas Chandra Bose[2] has been announcing that he will carry out an enormous combined operation against India on 8 December and land all his jifs. We are watching the situation very closely in Delhi and Auchinleck, Peirse and I have reached a satisfactory agreement on the lines you wanted about moving air forces to meet this threat when it develops.

---

[1]This was Churchill's original *Directive.*
[2]He led the so-called Indian National Army under Japanese patronage; his plans came to nothing.

331. *To Cunningham*

4 December 1943

2. I am glad that a decision has been given in respect of the position of the Eastern Fleet *vis-à-vis* the SEAC since I am quite positive that the efforts now being made to centralise everything in the SEAC HQ will lead to tremendous overloading and consequent inefficiency. It is quite clear, however, that this decision has not been well received by Dickie; his objections that, unless the Eastern Fleet was regarded at all times as part of his force, the Americans would refuse to play are, I think, rather far fetched. So far as Stilwell is concerned I agree that he will probably always raise difficulties about everything and I cannot for the life of me understand why, when he had the chance to do so, Dickie did not get shot of him during his visit to Chungking.[1]

3. The organisation here is causing some concern to the three Cs-in-C, chiefly on the planning side and to a lesser extent on the administrative side. Dealing with the planning first, we are told that in this set up the Supreme Commander is in a totally different position to that occupied by Eisenhower. The argument put forward is that Eisenhower personally commands one of the Armies of the allied forces in N Africa, and that consequently he sits in with the naval and air Cs-in-C as one of them, and only incidentally, presides over the committee. In the SEAC set up we are told that Dickie is not identified with any particular force but commands all forces as Supreme Commander, and that for this reason he requires a planning staff of his own. We, the three Cs-in-C, feel that it is our planners who should do the planning whether forward or immediate, since they have roots which reach back to all sources of information, whereas the SAC's planners have no sources of their own so to speak and have to apply to the Cs-in-C's planners for all they want. These two teams of planners appear at present to be working in parallel; actually at the moment everything put up by the SAC planners has been shot down. So far as I can see the effect of this organisation is to duplicate every-thing and in consequence swell the staff at SEAC HQ to its present immense proportions. The number of bodies which complete this organ-isation, i.e., SEAC HQ, Navy, Army and Air Echelons, amounts to 4700 of which, it is interesting to note, the Navy's contribution is under 150, of which 101 are WRNS (i.e. my Naval HQ staff at SEAC).

4. The net result of this is that the SAC is fed with two sets of plans, one through the Cs-in-C who will be responsible for carrying out the opera-

---

[1] Chiang's wartime capital.

tions, and the other through their own planners who are not responsible for executing their plans. . . .

6. I have no doubt these things will adjust themselves in time but the impression I get now is of an immense, unwieldy and ineffective organisation which is growing bigger and bigger every day and in which no attempt whatever is being made to keep numbers and functions within reasonable limits. I think Dickie is obsessed with the idea that he must have absolute personal control over everything however remotely it may be connected with amphibious operations.

7. . . . Dickie is quite unable to resist the urge to have a finger in every pie and to discuss even the most minute details. . . . I do not think for a moment this indicates a lack of confidence in his Cs-in-C, but rather a continual urge to know everything all the time.

8. All the above criticisms might suggest that I feel thoroughly disturbed with the present set up, but that is not quite the case; what I do feel is that it tends to go the wrong way at present, but if only it could be directed into the right channels it might prove an outstanding success since Dickie's personality, drive and imagination are the most valuable assets we could have.

332. *From Cunningham*

19 December 1943

I hope the question of command which was vexing you and Mountbatten was satisfactorily settled by my signal from Cairo. I had a lot of trouble on the way to Cairo in discussing this question. The facts appear to me to be quite clear. Your forces working in the area of the SEA Command in operations arranged by the Supreme Commander are definitely under him and in so far as they are concerned, you are under him as well; but as C-in-C, Eastern Fleet, you are responsible to the Admiralty generally for the Eastern Fleet area. Mountbatten asked to have the whole Eastern Fleet area placed under him but I made him see that this was ridiculous.

. . . the British naval effort will be rather more in the S Pacific than in the SE Asia area, and towards the end of March a large slice of your fleet will go to the Pacific. I think it is likely that Power[1] will have to go with it and it appears that you will require another Admiral to take command at sea of the residue. . . .

I am sorry that Mountbatten has not taken the Mediterranean organi-

[1]Vice Adm Sir Arthur Power, new 2nd-in-C, Eastern F.

sation as his model. Out there, although several attempts were made to set up a separate planning staff for the Supreme Commander, the other three Cs-in-C always resisted it with success and the Supreme Commander's planning staff was composed of the planning staffs of the three Cs-in-C – an excellent arrangement which kept us all in touch and prevented the Supreme Commander going off at a tangent. . . .

333. *To his wife*

Delhi,
3 December 1943

Think I told you in my last letter that the powers that be have decided that the EF does *not* come under Dickie except for amphibious operations. Dickie said he'd had some difficulty getting the PM to agree to this! I ask you! What happened was that ABC naturally stuck his toes in . . . Evidently the PM agreed to the signal whilst refusing to alter the directive. . . .

334. *Desk diary, 1943*

20 November

2. My examination of the BULLFROG plan is proceeding. The weak points in this plan at present appear to be:–

(a) The dependence which must be placed on seaborne fighter cover and the adverse effect which light winds may have on carriers being able to perform their tasks adequately.

(b) The capture of the aerodrome and ability for our fighters to use it by D4 appears to be assumed. With the exception of the aerodrome at Guadalcanal it appears to me that a period of a week or longer has usually elapsed before we have been able to capture Japanese aerodromes after having approached quite close to the perimeter. The proportionate strength of the attacking force to the garrison does not suggest that the attack will necessarily be overwhelming.

(c) The plan states that the RAF will supply reconnaissance during approach and assault. It is by no means clear how effective this reconnaissance is likely to be and in any case the depth of this reconnaissance is not sufficient to cover the areas through which Japanese surface forces will approach with a view to contesting the landings.

(d) The plan envisages a covering force to include 5 battleships and 2 fleet carriers, but it will only consist of 3 elderly and 1 very elderly battleships and 1 fleet carrier, which is more of a token force than a force really capable of holding the ring against a small but well balanced Japanese task force operating under land based air. It is consequently essential that the Japanese Naval forces shall be fully occupied in the Pacific when the attack takes place.

(e) The proposal to attack Car Nicobar on D1 has little to recommend it. This attack must serve as pointer for the direction of the main attack and will certainly draw concentrated Japanese air attack and consequently may require a heavy force to achieve results. I appreciate that if surprise can be achieved the aerodrome may be captured by commandos, . . .

23 November

The latest indications are that the Japanese are putting the bulk of their naval aircraft ashore. A considerable force has already been collected at Singapore, and there are indications that these aircraft may be moved up into Sumatra and possibly the Andamans.

25 November

4.   I received the first report from the Base Censor on subject matter contained in letters from the Fleet. Points of interest were the general dislike expressed by the lower deck to regarding the Italians as allies;[1] the high praise given to the Services Welfare Organisation Committee (run by a voluntary ladies' organisation); some complaints about the messing at a dockside camp; the enjoyment apparently obtained by Australian ratings in teasing the unfortunate rickshaw men. . . .

28 November

3.   Captain Baker-Cresswell[2] handed in a most valuable report on the A/S situation out here. This report makes it quite clear that much has to be done if we are to reach anything like the standard of efficiency which obtains in the N Atlantic.

29 November

2.   With regard to the Kalantai FAA aerodrome RANASIO[3] pointed out that this would be essential in order to meet the Admiralty requirement of 50 FAA squadrons being based in Ceylon and Southern India by

---

[1]Italian ships served in the Indian Ocean after the collapse of the Fascist Govt.

[2]Capt A. J. Baker-Cresswell: Cdr 1937; *Warspite* 1939; Asst NA Ankara 1940; *Bulldog* Feb 1941; NID 1941; Capt Dec 1941; Capt ASW, Eastern F 1943; *Caradoc* April 1944; *Gorleston* 1945.

[3]Rear Adm Bisset.

the beginning of 1945. He understood the RAF contemplated extending existing runways and possibly building new aerodromes in the Island and felt that the priorities of the RAF and FAA over this matter must be referred to SEAC.

4.   In the afternoon Mr Putnam, an American, was brought to me by Captain Greene, USNLO. Mr Putnam described trials which had been carried out with DUKWs in the Ellis [Islands] Group under conditions which appeared to be quite extreme viz. a coral reef, breakers 8 ft. high, cross surf and variable wind. He stated the trials had been completed successfully and had proved that DUKWs could be used in circumstances that were not previously envisaged and provided a means of disembarkation which might radically alter preconceived notions of what is and is not possible. . . . he was mainly responsible for the design of the DUKW.

6.   I also had a visit from Cdr Miers[1] who had come over specially from Australia to discuss the question of British submarines operating in the S China seas and off Java. . . . on realising our position, i.e. that we shall have insufficient submarines for our own purposes until well on in 1944 he agreed that no action at the moment was possible. . . . He considered that the American submarines were far better suited than British submarines in almost every respect to the long distance operation which the war in the Pacific would require. In particular the American surface speed of 16 knots which they could maintain at all times, coupled with really good radar had revolutionised night attacks.[2]

7.   He suggested that for special operations on and within the Western Malayan Barrier, British 'U' [class] boats might meet requirements. He had been told there was little prospect of these boats being used operationally in any other theatre and would probably be relegated to A/S exercises and training.

30 November

3.   . . . The Generalissimo had stipulated that he would only advance providing an amphibious operation was carried out; there seemed to be no special connection between the two, but on the other hand he was quite adamant on this point, and also that a strong British fleet should operate in the Bay of Bengal.[3]

---

[1]Cdr Anthony C. C. Miers, VC: Lt-Cdr 1938; SO2 (O), Home F 1939; *Torbay*, Med, in which he made his reputation, Nov 1940; Cdr Nov 1941; BAD Nov 1942; Australia 1943; *Maidstone* May 1944.

[2]They had spent a great deal of time and effort in the inter-war years perfecting a good long range patrol submarine for Pacific operations.

[3]Chiang claimed that he had been promised a substantial British fleet would be available by early 1943; when it failed to materialise he charged the British with breach of promise; see Thorne, *Allies of a Kind*, pp. 225–6.

5. From the air point of view the story was very different; the original estimate of Japanese air strength viz. about 240 had now been considerably more than doubled as a result of special and other intelligence. With the seaborne fighters likely to be available viz. approximately 120 (excluding those in the fleet carriers) it did not seem a feasible proposition for us to hold the air ring against the air forces the enemy could collect. Any operation to neutralise Car Nicobar and the other two possible aerodromes in the Islands further S would require splitting up of available forces which probably could not be accepted. After discussion it was agreed that for the operation to be feasible from the air point of view we should require at least another 120 to 140 seaborne fighters and it would be necessary to ask the Americans if they could furnish these. The only alternative amphibious operation would be to return to the original BULLFROG which no one favoured and least of all the Prime Minister.

6. The Supreme Commander referred to the projected operations in the Eastern Mediterranean in the early spring[1] and said there had been some discussion at Cairo about switching forces from the Eastern Mediterranean to the Indian Ocean after completion of the operations in the Eastern Mediterranean. It was agreed by everybody that this was quite impracticable. I suggested that if we attempted to carry out operations simultaneously we might well find ourselves faced with a regrettable failure. If, as has been constantly stated, it was essential that the first operation in this Theatre should be a success then we would have to take very careful thought before embarking on an amphibious operation here which was not properly mounted and which we all felt was a very considerable gamble instead of a reasonable certainty. I believe this view was shared by most of those present, though obviously some of SEAC's staff viewed with grave concern the possibility of no operations being carried out next spring, since no doubt they felt their personal position might be somewhat ambiguous in these circumstances.

1 December

10 o'clock – Supreme Commander's meeting. A paper setting out the organisation for the planning in SEAC was discussed. The only point over which argument arose was in connection with one paragraph which stated that the Cs-in-C would examine and pass the Force Commander's plan before the latter was submitted to the Supreme Commander. The SC took exception to this and said he wished to be present when the plan was being examined by the Cs-in-C. I raised objections on the grounds that the Cs-in-C required this opportunity to decide matters of detail

[1] Possibly the Anzio landings.

apart from any main principles which should have been settled beforehand, and that overweighted meetings in connection with matters of
detail merely wasted time. My view was supported by the other two Cs-
in-C, and the SC finally decided to suspend issue of the paper whilst he
reconsidered this point.

6 December

3.   With regard to naval operations I gave it as my opinion that providing our naval forces included two fleet carriers, *Unicorn* and 3 escorts
this would enable us to carry out demonstrations in the Bay of Bengal
and N Coast of Sumatra which would certainly have the effect of containing both enemy air and surface forces.
4.   I suggested the possibility of a Doolittle raid on objectives in Java
using Mitchells flown off from carriers and landing subsequently in
Australia.[1] Cdre Langley did not agree that a force of this description
should be used to draw out land based air as he considered the risk to the
carriers would not [be] commensurate with the results likely to be
obtained. I pointed out that it would be impossible for us to sit back and
do nothing to contain the Japanese forces in this area and that the
Americans would most certainly raise objections if we did so. Provided
the operations were well planned and the force employed really well
trained, I felt that it was possible to make these demonstrations without
involving the carriers in undue risk. Furthermore we might initially be
able to score considerable success against any Japanese forces sent out.
Telegrams were sent off to the CCS putting up the above points of view
and also a personal one to General Wedemeyer pointing out that execution of BUCCANEER[2] was an essential preliminary to operations staged
against Rangoon or Bangkok, and was also essential if we were to obtain
a sufficient PRU for CULVERIN.

335.   *Eastern Fleet War Diary*

November 1943

Anti-Submarine

14.   Two Japanese U-boats are known to have been operating in the
Indian Ocean during the month. Another Japanese U-boat, returning

---

[1] A bombing raid by 25 US medium bombers, flown from USS *Hornet*, on Japanese
cities, led by Lt-Col James H. Doolittle, USAAF; they flew on to China after the raid, on 18
April 1942.
[2] A proposed descent on the Andaman Islands.

from Europe to the Far East, was on passage across the Indian Ocean during the second half of the month.

15.　One German U-boat was operating at the beginning of the month off Cochin, but after dark on 3 November it was attacked by a Catalina escort aircraft and probably damaged. This U-boat left the area for its Eastern base and as a result of searches and patrols was very probably attacked again on 8 November, but without result.

16.　Three ships totalling 21,896 tons were sunk during the month, these were all independents and no attacks on convoys were made.

17.　A number of attacks by surface vessels were made on suspected U-boat contacts during the month, but in attacks analysed to date the actual presence of a U-boat has not been confirmed.

Air

18.　Escorts were given to convoys during the month. One Catalina escorting convoy MB53 on 3 November attacked a submarine and reported probable hits. The submarine fired at the Catalina causing slight damage to the tailplane. Submarine dived and was not seen again although searches were laid on.

19.　On 9 November Liberator P/160 stated he was over a submarine and attacked, but depth charges failed to release. Searches were flown to find the submarine but were not successful.

20.　Japanese Navy. Four engined flying boats visited Madras, Trincomalee and Colombo on the night of the 12th and one was shot down off Colombo by a Beaufighter. Bodies and documents were picked up later in the day.

21.　SS *Scotia* was torpedoed 300 miles SW of Addu Atoll on the 27th. All the crew were located by Catalinas and *Okapi* was led to the scene and picked them up. Six of the crew had been shot including the Chief Engineer. The captain was taken prisoner. Catalina K/205 was responsible for this fine piece of rescue work. 205 Squadron now hold the record for lives saved, it being nearly 500.[1]

336.　*To his wife*

6 December 1943

At present it looks as if our bits and pieces may be wanted elsewhere, in which case we shall have this colossal staff doing nothing – it will be

---

[1]*Scotia*: Svenska Lloyd, Gothenburg: 1918; 1838gt; 9k. *Okapi*: unidentified.

the laughing stock of the East if it doesn't look out, all rather disturbing. The whole outfit seems so immature in many respects but perhaps it will grow up. One thing, though, and that is Dickie never questions my opinion on Naval matters.

337. Desk diary, 1943

8 December

4. Admiral Holland, who is taking up the duties of RA (Administration), arrived from Cairo. He said that BUCCANEER was now definitely off the map and that the resources for this would be used in supplementary operations connected with OVERLORD, in the Western Med and Levant. He also informed me of the Russian intentions with regard to the Japanese war[1] and brought with him the overall plan for the defeat of Japan prepared by the Combined Staff Planners before the Russian intentions were known. This plan has a different strategical conception to those previously prepared, and envisages a mere holding force in this theatre with the major weight of the British forces being applied in the Pacific in conjunction with the Americans. Should this plan materialise it is a matter for conjecture what will happen to the enormous SEAC HQ staff which continues to grow daily.
8. Admiral Troubridge arrived back from Cairo in the afternoon . . . He said it was quite obvious BUCCANEER did not appeal to the Chiefs of Staff . . . On the other hand the Americans were obviously most anxious that BUCCANEER should be carried out and Admiral King went so far as to promise the additional escort carriers we had asked for.
9. When it was finally decided to abandon BUCCANEER the Joint Planners and Force Commanders were instructed to make proposals for some alternative amphibious operation with whatever would be left over, and the conclusions they arrived at were almost identical with those signalled from here, i.e. there was no worthwhile amphibious operation; cut and run raids with Commandos were of no use whatsoever, and had a bad psychological effect. They agreed that the best way to exert pressure in the circumstances was by the employment of a carrier force, with suitable escorts, and that this force should be not less than 2 carriers and 3 or 4 escort carriers.

---

[1]Rear Adm Cecil Holland, formerly Capt of *Ark Royal*. The Levant operations were intended to capture Rhodes and encourage Turkey to enter the war, something the British Govt had been trying to bring about since 1939 and which was never a realistic hope. The Soviet Union had announced that it would enter the war against Japan three months after the defeat of Germany.

338. *To his wife*

8 December 1943

... He [Mountbatten] always brings up some mysterious instructions from the PM to the effect that he is in a different position to anywhere else in the world. These were verbal instructions so we have no means of testing the accuracy of his memory, which I think must be at fault. ... I told him that if he wanted to control everything himself it would be much better to have everyone on his staff and do away with Cs-in-C altogether, as they would be redundant. This rather took D aback and he said that was an extreme point of view and that we must have a compromise. I objected and said no compromise could be expected to work and the decision had to be whether to use the organisation which had been tried out and found the best elsewhere or adopt some entirely new plan. ...

339. *To his wife*

21 December 1943

I showed Henry Pownall – D's COS – a memorandum I proposed to send to the Admiralty giving an account of the discussions we've had about the staff at Delhi and said I should send D a copy. He was very upset and said D would not like this at all and rather suggested I was sneaking. I said that there were quite a number of Naval officers concerned and in my opinion it was high time that the Admiralty knew what was going on. If everything was as it should be then why should D have any objections to letting the people at home know! Of course the real answer is that they are in a proper mess and will not take advice or do anything to clear it up. General Holmes from the War Office[1] came to see me at Bombay and asked if I could throw some light on what was happening. When I told him how D had said the Chiefs of Staff insisted on his having a big staff he said it was absolute nonsense as he was at the meeting when it was discussed and there was *no* suggestion to that effect. It's very odd that either consciously or unconsciously D deceives himself and I find I can never quite believe what he says. If this very odd party continues in this very odd way I feel it's not altogether the party for me. My consistent oppositions to D butting in on things which the COS and Admiralty have made it quite clear have nothing to do with him must inevitably promote the idea that I'm an obstructionist so I shan't be surprised if D does not suggest a change.

[1]Probably Gen W. G. Holmes of the War Office & Min of War Transport.

340. *Desk diary, 1943*

31 December

... It is quite clear that we have not got the forces available for OVER-LORD, ANVIL and possible subsidiary operations in the Mediterranean if in addition amphibious operations are to be carried out in this theatre. Even if the LSTs in question had been retained, I consider the PIG-STICK[1] operation as planned has been mounted on far too small a margin, and that in particular its main object, i.e. the capture of Akyab, is likely to fail since we have not the numbers of small craft required for operating in this area which is so intersected by rivers and creeks. I fully appreciate, however, what a bad effect it must have on everyone in this theatre to find that once again the fine weather goes by without our being able to have an active part in the fighting against the Japanese. ...

341. *Desk diary, 1944*

2 January

2. Owing to a second ship having been torpedoed off Masirah I gave orders that ships between the Persian Gulf and Aden were to be put into convoy. I still feel that Cs-in-C are not sufficiently informed of the relative effect of sinkings versus hold up of trade, i.e. having regard to the volume of trade, and delays caused by convoy, what percentage of sinkings can be considered as balancing this in the sense that above a certain point sinkings take priority to hold ups.

342. *To Cunningham*

3 January 1944

11. ... Dickie said ... his present idea was that the officers on his staff ... should now be called his 'War Staff' and confine themselves to future planning, appreciations and preparation of directives. I said I felt it was wrong in principle to have two sets of planners ...
12. At the daily conference a review was made of the resources available after the bulk of Force G had been withdrawn, and it was decided that there would be enough left to lift one assault brigade and possibly the follow up of another, and this might be used for operations on the Arakan coast behind the Japanese lines, e.g., on the Mayu Peninsula.

---

[1]ANVIL was the proposed Allied invasion of S France. PIGSTICK was a proposed landing on the Burma coast but, as usual in SE Asia, an abortive plan.

Dickie expressed some confidence that CKS would still be prepared to co-operate with TARZAN.[1] I expressed great doubts and said I felt CKS would back out on the slightest excuse and that the abandoning of BULLFROG must certainly provide a good excuse. . . .

21. I received a rather extraordinary memorandum from Dickie in connection with the procedure to be followed on the occasion of his visits to HM ships. This was so royal in character and in certain respects so much a departure from ordinary customs in the Service that I returned the memorandum with certain suggestions couched as politely as possible. . . .

25. While I was at Bombay, the *Daisy Moller* was torpedoed N of Madras. This ship had made more false sighting reports than any other ship out here, and at first we concluded it was probably just another scare; unfortunately the wolf was there this time and what was worse her boats were rammed and machine gunned by the Japanese. . . . she had military supplies required for the front.[2]

26. . . . *Heemskerck* arrived from Australia and sailed again after two days to refit in the UK, but had to return on account of trouble with her manoeuvring valves. She is an exceptionally good ship with a fine spirit and burning to get into the war and their own back. I hope she may come back to these parts.

343. Desk diary, 1944

4 January

Received a signal from the Admiralty that *Renown, Illustrious, Victorious,* 4 cruisers, 12 fleets [destroyers], 10 frigates, *Woolwich, Unicorn* and *Resource*[3] are to form a British Naval Pacific Force and that they would leave for the Pacific towards the end of March. Any other reinforcements to the Eastern Fleet will also go to the Pacific. This information suggests almost conclusively that no major amphibious operations are to be staged in this Theatre and that our role will be to contain the Japanese forces and act as a stepping stone for reinforcements for the Pacific area.

[1]The land offensive in Burma.

[2]*Daisy Moller*: 1911, 4087gt, Moller Line, Shanghai; foolishly, she had been loaded with one year's supply of steamrollers (22) for the army.

[3]*Woolwich*: destroyer depot ship, 1935, 8750t, 4×4in, 15k. *Resource*: fleet repair ship, 1930, 12,300t, 4×4in, 15k.

8 January

At 9.30 [at Trincomalee] I held a Flag and Commanding Officers' conference on board *Newcastle* and subsequently walked round divisions, upper decks and mess decks in *Newcastle, Kenya, Suffolk* and *Sussex* and ended up on board the hospital ship *Tjitjalenka*[1] by which time I was sorely in need of medical comforts which were administered in her wardroom. After lunch on board *Newcastle* I visited the Naval Picket House, the old Canteen, new Canteen, Services Clubs, Dilkush Bungalow, Wrens' Sick Quarters, new jetty Cod Bay, Ceylon North Transmitting Station and the A/A Range. . . .

10 January

2.   Information received that a German tanker may proceed from the Sunda Straits to refuel U-boats in the S Indian Ocean. *Suffolk* and *Sussex* are the only ships with sufficient endurance to achieve interception to the eastward of 80° and *Battler* will not be available in time to proceed with them. It seems, therefore, that unless we establish a search in the vicinity of the estimated refuelling place a two ship search is unlikely to be productive.

12 January

Received a signal from the Admiralty stating it was important to intercept the tanker and that in consequence estimated R/Vs for refuelling could be approached within 100 miles and requested me to stage an operation. I ordered *Newcastle* and *Kenya* from Madras and *Suffolk* from Trincomalee to proceed to Colombo, and told the *Battler*, at present with an Aden–Bombay convoy, to proceed to the Seychelles with one frigate, refuel, and then go on to Mauritius. *Canton* and *Nepal*[2] from Durban were also ordered to Mauritius.

13 January

Plans for operation THWART, i.e. the interception of the tanker, are in hand and *Suffolk* arrived from Trincomalee. . . .
2.   The Dutch cruiser *Tromp* arrived and her Captain, Captain F. Stam, came to call on me. He said the ship was in good order and that he was very pleased to find himself with the Eastern Fleet though they had had a very good time, in fact too good a time, in Australia.
3.   I witnessed the take off of the first Hellcat erected at the Racecourse

[1]*Tjitjalenka*: 1939, 10,972gt, 15k, Java-China-Japan Line (Dutch).
[2]*Nepal*: 1942, 1760t, 6×4.7in, 1×4in, 5tt, 36k.

Aerodrome. A fine looking aircraft, but seems heavy for a fighter at 13,000 lbs all up.[1]

14 January

Samavati, on passage to Cocos with stores and reliefs, reports she encountered two U-boats about 600 miles SW of Achin Head and attacked one which she may have sunk. As she considered her visit to Cocos was compromised she had turned back and had subsequently counter-attacked another U-boat. They may have been ex-Italian blockade runners.[2]

18 January

4. As a result of representations by Captain S4[3] I sent a signal to SAC about clandestine operations; it is quite clear now that some of these are not justified and designed more to give the various MEW, SOE, etc., parties something to do. As this type of operation is invariably at the expense of patrols which are becoming more and more profitable I feel it right to protest and that my previous stipulations should have been properly enforced, i.e.:–

(a) these operations must be essential for implementing our strategy,
(b) they could only be carried out by a submarine.

344. *To his wife*

18 January 1944

D seems quite unable to accept the altered situation. I've had to write and tell him I feel it is up to us to implement and not question the Cairo decisions and that I do not wish to be associated in any telegrams home in which these decisions are questioned. I also sent a personal signal to ABC to say that it was essential the policy for this theatre should be stated definitely as D was planning all sorts of things which I felt were against the Cairo decisions. ABC replied I was right, that they were having difficulties at their end (with the PM presumably) but that he hoped the situation would be clear in a week or so . . .

[1]Grumman Hellcat, USA: 1942, 6mg, 376mph.
[2]*Samavati*: unidentified. No submarines were sunk.
[3]Captain S4: Capt H. M. C. Ionides: Cdr 1933; *Mackay* 1938; Capt June 1940; *Titania* 1940–1; *Forth* 1941–2; Capt S1 *Medway II* June 1943; Capt S4 *Adamant* Jan 1944.

345.   *To Mountbatten*

18 January 1944

. . . I have always advocated very strongly that the British effort in the Eastern Theatre should be directed towards breaching the Malayan Barrier since it seemed to me that, not only was it desirable to employ our mobility by striking in widely separated points, i.e. the Indian Ocean and Pacific, but furthermore the effective deployment and maintenance of a super Allied Amphibious Force in the Pacific appeared to present very great difficulty. It is of interest that when I discussed this matter with Admiral King at Washington he appeared to be also a strong advocate of this policy of a strike in both areas.

It seems obvious that at Cairo the policy for the defeat of Japan must have been very carefully reviewed, and though I am not aware of the reasons which led to the decision that the main strike should take place in the Pacific, I consider we must accept this and do all that we can to implement this decision.

If our primary object is to contain as many Japanese forces as possible, then I suggest the staff at Delhi should prepare as many deception plans as possible, e.g., submarines and aircraft for dummy COP parties; faked landings, or preparations for landings in as many areas as possible, including the Mayu River and Akyab; demonstrations by the Eastern Fleet towards Sumatra.

If we are not to carry out any major operations in this theatre during the 1944–45 season, it is imperative that we should cut down Naval personnel at bases, etc., to the absolute bare minimum required for minor operations and the mounting of, say, 4 Assault Brigades or whatever limit is imposed by the Chiefs of Staff. In E Africa and at all the Island Bases I am making drastic reductions on the grounds that, with an element of the Fleet stationed at Trincomalee, the possibility of the Japanese attempting any offensive operations W of Ceylon can be discounted. Furthermore, if the main Fleet is to be based in the Pacific, we should be able to reduce our ship repair requirements in Ceylon and at Kilindini.

. . . I assume the numbers required to move in PRELUDE will be reduced substantially. . . .

346.   *Desk diary, 1944*

19 January

Received *Tally-Ho*'s report on her patrol. After sighting a cruiser of *Kuma* class exercising outside the N entrance of Penang on the 9th, she remained in the vicinity until the 11th. That forenoon she saw aircraft coming out as if on patrol and finally sighted and attacked the cruiser after she left harbour. Seven torpedoes were fired at a range of 9000 yards of which two hit and the cruiser sank. On the afternoon of the 14th she saw an MV of 6000 tons entering the harbour of Car Nicobar. When this vessel left a little later *Tally-Ho* gave chase and eventually obtained one hit out of 6 torpedoes just after midnight and the ship sank.[1]

4. I received a signal from SAC in reply to mine about SEXTANT decisions[2] in which he stated that since the conference broke up he has received two signals from the Prime Minister urging him to press on with operation CULVERIN. This of course suggests either a divergence of views between the COS and the Prime Minister or alternatively that no firm decisions have yet been reached.

347. *To Tennant*

22 January 1944

. . . At the moment there is complete chaos in these parts because no one appears to know what the policy is to be. I get signals from ABC asking me to release personnel in view of our reduced commitments etc. & at the same time get proposals from D at Delhi in connection with operations on a considerable scale. When I tax D with these obvious conflictions of policy he tells me that he has received instructions direct from the PM. Now that the PM is at home I hope that he & the COS will have an agreed policy because otherwise life becomes very difficult.

The growth of D's staff proceeds apace; the grand total a month ago was 5500, but I have reason to believe it has expanded since then. I keep as clear of Delhi as I can, but twice a week an aircraft disgorges an immense pile of paper which has been produced by the staff, which I rarely look at since it contains nothing of any interest or importance. It seems a pity that what might have been a good show should become what I can only describe as a somewhat fantastic piece of tomfoolery with some very odd goings on all the time. Poor Geoffrey Miles has a difficult time of it, but once I know what the form is to be out here I shall get the Admiralty to withdraw him & most of the other Naval officers

---

[1] *Tally-Ho*: 1943, 1090/1575t, 11tt, 1×4in, 15.25/9k. The cruiser was *Kuma*: 1920, modernised 1934, 5100t, 7×5.5in, 8tt, 36k.

[2] SEXTANT was the Cairo conference of Roosevelt, Churchill and (for part of the time) Chiang. It marked the beginning of the long dispute between the Prime Minister and the COS over our Asian strategy.

now at Delhi. I should point out that out of a total of 5500 the naval contingent is only about 50 and will be a good deal less than that by the time I have finished with it. . . .

348. Desk diary, 1944

27 January

5. *Renown* entered harbour at 1450 looking very weatherbeaten and her drill for entering harbour distinctly poor. Admiral Power came ashore to call and had very little news. He said that the ships' companies of *Renown* and the two battleships[1] were all very green and they would require a lot of working up before they could be considered in any way efficient; he said the *Illustrious*'s aircraft also required a lot of training.

28 January

Templar reported she had got one hit on a Jap cruiser or destroyer; we believe it to be the former and a *Nitori*, but there is no confirmation that the ship sank.[2]
2. Two ships have been torpedoed E of Socotra and it seems likely that another ship overdue at Colombo was sunk in the 9° channel.

29 January

3. It seems quite clear now that operation THWART has failed, and I shall tell Colombo I consider CS4[3] and his party should return and refuel to await further news.

30 January

2. I examined the Junior CULVERIN plan and found it was in some respects a cheaper edition of the original CULVERIN plan in as much as it is now proposed to bypass Sabang and the Nicobars. The forces required include 5 divisions, and among other things 28 carriers and 86 destroyers. This seems so directly contrary to the global strategy which can be inferred from Admiralty signals that it does not seem to have a practical relation to the future situation.

31 January

3. I referred to correspondence I had had with the SAC about the question of his visiting HM ships at Colombo and Trincomalee; he had issued

---

[1] *Queen Elizabeth & Valiant.*
[2] It was *Kitakami*: 1921, 5100t, 7×5.5in, 8tt, 36k; severely damaged by attack.
[3] Rear Adm A. D. Read.

instructions concerning the procedure to be followed when visiting HM ships, and it appeared to me these were quite inappropriate in the case of ships which were not concerned with amphibious operations and therefore operated entirely under my orders as directed by the Admiralty. I informed him that I did not feel justified in being a party to the suggestion, which would obviously follow from such formal visits, that he was in Supreme Command of the Fleet at all times since this was contrary to the directive. I said I should be extremely pleased to accompany him on board any ships he wished to visit, and if he desired would arrange for him to address a ship's company upon request. In order that the matter might be cleared up I said I would send a personal letter to the First Sea Lord through him in order that he might add any comments.

349. *To Cunningham*

HQ, Eastern Fleet,
S. E. Asia Command,
New Delhi,
1 February 1944

I am asking . . . for guidance . . .
For example –

(a)   Should the SAC in his capacity as such visit officially HM Ships and Naval Establishments which are not actually allocated for or normally employed on amphibious operations?
(b)   Should press stories on patrol operations be considered as falling within the jurisdiction of the SEAC or solely Admiralty?

It is of course arguable in connection with (a) above that ships and establishments may at any time be required to take part in amphibious operations and consequently are under the command of the Supreme Commander.

I consider that the situation is clear in regard to inter-service matters, i.e. matters in which uniform action or practice is desirable or in which the action of one Service may impinge on other Services. But in other matters, such as are referred to above, I shall be glad if I might have guidance since the Admiralty may consider that the authority of the SAC does not extend to matters affecting the Naval service only, but is restricted to matters relating to amphibious operations or inter-service affairs.

350. *VCNS*[1] *to Cunningham*

Admiralty,
12 February 1944

I quite agree – as we always have done – with C-in-C's criticism of Mountbatten's super planning staff. It is easy to see that, with the present arrangement, there will be a growing tendency for Mountbatten to rely on the advice of his super staff rather than [that] of his Cs-in-C.

2.   I think, however, C-in-C is not on so good a wicket in his criticisms of Mountbatten's attempt to make a plan for the Autumn to fit the force he will have available. Admittedly this is wrong in principle but nevertheless it is virtually what the CCS have directed Mountbatten to do.

3.   Owing to the importance of obtaining intelligence, C-in-C has been giving clandestine operations priority over offensive operations. However, his submarine strength is growing rapidly making possible a much greater offensive effort. Now he has 13 submarines and in September he should have 29.

351. *VCNS to Cunningham*

Admiralty,
12 February 1944

All Naval forces and naval establishments are under the command of C-in-C EF.

Insofar as they are used for, or employed in, SEAC operations they come under the orders, or command, of SACSEA but this command must be exercised through C-in-C EF.

2.   If SACSEA was (a) superior in confirmed rank, (b) an Army or RAF officer, (c) an officer of an Allied nation, or (d) a wiser man, I don't suppose this difficulty would ever have arisen.

3.   It is very difficult, almost impossibly so, to define exactly the rights of each in the example referred to at (a).

4.   Tact and wisdom and understanding by one for the point of view and position of the other would have resulted eventually, I am sure, in a suggestion by C-in-C EF that Mountbatten might like to visit some of the ships and establishments of the naval command.

5.   Mountbatten would be well advised to wait for such an invitation. I am sure, if he did, his position in his command would be all the stronger.

[1]Vice Adm Syfret

6. As regards 'example (b)', I think official communiques should be issued from SEAC HQ or by Admiralty (consequent on C-in-C EF's reports) and that 'press stories' of operations might be left to C-in-C EF to release.

352. *From Cunningham*

10 March 1944

A. I find it difficult to answer your two questions but I think you must give the Supreme Commander a little rope in (a). Strictly speaking and in accordance with COS (43) 496(0) I suppose he has no right to visit any ships or naval establishments unless they are placed under his orders for amphibious operations but I think you must look at his difficulties. As you know well, the American conception of a Supreme Commander is very different from ours; in their view he is really a Commander and as such should directly command forces of all arms in his theatre. Mountbatten has many nasty problems of command *vis-à-vis* the Americans, e.g., General Stilwell, the Chinese Forces, the American [Army] Air Forces, Wingate's private American Air Force, etc., etc., and I think the Americans will only wholeheartedly recognise him if everybody plays likewise. If the US members of the SE Asia staffs once thought that the British Navy were regarding themselves as a race apart with a separate law unto themselves, the tendency would be for them to resist Mountbatten's control.

I feel, therefore, that you should extend an invitation to him to visit such ships or establishments as you think fit when you feel like it. Such a visit, of course, must not be an inspection and must take place under such rules as you lay down. I have told Mountbatten that I expect you will invite him to visit some ships or establishments. . . .

P.S: Life is not a bed of roses here. The COS and high ups are at complete loggerheads about the Pacific v. SEAC strategy.

The AXIOM team were accepted as heaven-sent by the PM and his chorus of yes men and there has been some pretty good tripe talked.[1] . . .

Our latest is that the Japs are more on the defensive than thinking of raiding you but I would not put it past them – they may want a cheap success to offset their American defeats in the eyes of the Jap people.

---

[1] A mission headed by Wedemeyer intended to persuade London and Washington to provide resources for major operations in SE Asia, notably CULVERIN; it was a hopeless last throw of the dice on Mountbatten's part.

353. *To his wife*

Delhi,
1 February 1944

... Dickie ... tried to convince me that his staff was really much too small and that he was only doing this and that because the PM insisted. I'm afraid I believed very little of what he said. ... I should certainly not refrain from criticising something which I and both the other Cs-in-C consider to be wrong. ... Henry Pownall ... says that Dickie considers I am the only one of the three Cs-in-C that raises objections. This is hardly correct because we have all together objected not once but on many occasions. I think that what he means is that when he [Mountbatten] gets George or Richard by themselves he can talk them round whereas it does not work with me.

354. *To Cunningham*

HQ, Eastern Fleet (SEAC),
New Delhi,
3 February 1944

I arrived here on 29 January and found great activity in connection with the despatch of what they have called the 'AXIOM Plan' party for CULVERIN.

... As always happens in these cases, the War Staff soon found that they had to apply to the Cs-in-C's planners ... before they could get enough information on which to base their Appreciation. I feel very strongly that an integrated planning staff would have provided the answer far more quickly and in much better shape.

... I pointed out that had this plan been prepared by a Joint Planning Staff this sort of situation would not arise since the Cs-in-C would be in the picture from the outset and not merely admitted after the plan had been worked out. Unfortunately Dickie's meetings are attended by an enormous mob including a host of Americans and he informed me subsequently that some Americans had taken exception to my remarks since they considered they were directed against them. I asked how this construction could possibly arise and he said that as they had adopted the American model for the staff any criticisms of this model gave offence to the Americans. ...

... I pointed out that ... our attitude ought to be that if a three pronged thrust is required, of which one prong would be directed against the

Malayan barrier, then CULVERIN appeared to afford the best solution as opposed to landings in Burma or elsewhere in this theatre. . . .

I have sent the Admiralty a signal about submarines and clandestine operations. Now that Lamplough and Garnons-Williams[1] have come out I shall be more satisfied that operations asked for are really worthwhile. . . . A number of targets escaped the attention they would have had if submarines had been available for offensive patrols exclusively. . . .

355. Desk diary, 1944

6 February

2.   I found that the second THWART operation to intercept *Charlotte Schliemann* had started, but as we have to depend on Catalinas from Mauritius with the *Newcastle* and *Relentless*[2] only assisting owing to *Battler* boiler cleaning, the prospects are not too good. Seven Catalinas are being assembled at Mauritius which is all that can be made available at the moment.

7 February

Consideration of the U-boat situation in the Gulf of Aden suggests that until sufficient escorts are available to put independent ships now arriving there into convoy from Colombo or Cochin, the only solution is to employ a hunting group. Unfortunately it is not at the moment possible to establish an effective hunting group owing to the lack of suitable vessels on the Station, but the situation should improve in due course. So far the air has not been at all successful in the Gulf of Aden in spite of the fact that aircraft are at present adequate in numbers; it seems probable that it is lack of training rather than lack of numbers which is the trouble.

8 February

It now appears that one German U-boat was responsible for the sinking of 5 ships in the approaches to the Gulf of Aden; it is unfortunate that no SOS or SS signals were received from any of these ships, and news of sinkings were not obtained until survivors were sighted by other ships. The Admiralty have asked what air and surface dispositions are being

---

[1]Gen C. R. W. Lamplough RM: 2Lt 1914; Lt 1915; Capt 1918; Maj 1933; head of SOE, SE Asia 1944. Actg Capt (Ret) G. A. Garnons-Williams: Cdr 1933; PD 1940; proposed blockings ops Zeebrugge & Ostend May 1940; blocking of Dieppe 10 June 1940; Actg Capt June 1941; Comb Ops Training Sch, Greenock, April 1942; SNO, Madagascar landings 1942; Ret List Jan 1943; SOE SE Asia 1944.
[2]*Charlotte Schliemann*: 1928, 7747gt, Schliemann & Meizell, Hamburg.
Relentless: 1942, 1705t, 4×4.7in, 8tt, 34k.

used to combat the U-boat threat in this area. I informed the Admiralty
[of] the present destroyer dispositions, and pointed out that only 5 were
available at present for training with the Fleet, and consequently the
Aden area could not be reinforced unless Fleet was immobilised. As a
temporary measure I intended that *Maidstone*[1] should proceed from
Suez to Massawa unescorted and that her 3 destroyers would be used for
a striking force in the Gulf of Aden.

356.   *To his wife*

8 February 1944

. . . I said that if D would only act less as a Supremo and more as a
Chairman of committee of his Cs-in-C all would be well. Matters had
come to a climax when I refused to agree to a plan they were sending
home with their special mission until I'd had an opportunity to study [it].
. . . they accepted all my amendments. I told D that all the wire-pulling
and manoeuvring left a very bad taste in my mouth and I would not be a
party to it. Richard P[eirse] was at home and George G[iffard] having
registered his protests felt he could not do more as he was directly under
D. I, of course, am not, but even if I was I should continue my protests.
Eventually D and HP[ownall] agreed to what I have pressed so consistently – namely that all the planning staffs should be in one party and that
the Cs-in-C should act as his advisors instead of his own staff. . . . I
know quite well events will show I'm right . . .

357.   *Desk diary, 1944*

9 February

Further signal from Admiralty about the carrier programme;
Victorious arrives late May and with *Illustrious* will leave for Pacific at
a date to be decided. *Formidable* arrives June, *Indomitable* and
Indefatigable[2] July. No assault escort carriers will be available until the
autumn, but there will be at least one fleet carrier always in the Eastern
Fleet from June onwards. Admiralty asked what are my intentions to
maintain pressure and force dispersions on the Japanese. I replied I
would discuss this with the VA and RAA[3] on my next visit to
Trincomalee. I had always hoped that an initial carrier operation in this

---

[1]*Maidstone*: 1938, 8900t, 8×4.5in, 17k; depot ship for 8SF, March 1944.
[2]*Implacable, Indefatigable*: 1944, 26,000t, 60–72 a/c, 16×4.5in, 32k.
[3]Power and Moody.

Theatre could be staged so as to draw the enemy striking force onto our fighters and give them a good knock. For this purpose I consider we should have 2 fleet carriers and 2 assault escort carriers.

3.   Received a signal from Giffard to ask if I could bombard Taungup Ramree in order to pin down the Japanese 54th Division as he thinks the Japanese penetration to Taung Besar indicates a possible general Japanese advance in the Arakan. . . .

10 February

. . . I received a signal from Miles to say that neither he nor Playfair[1] felt this bombardment could do much in so far as holding down the 54th. Division. I held a conference with the VA, RAA and senior staff officers, and there was general agreement that a bombardment under conditions prevailing was not a practicable proposition and that its effect at the best could only be temporary in view of the fact that Taungup had been bombarded at frequent intervals by the ML's. It would soon be clear to the Japanese that there was to be no follow up to this bombardment and it seems doubtful whether, in itself, it would have any effect on containing troops in this area.

2.   I decided better results would be obtained by sending *Renown*, *Illustrious*, *Tromp*, *Emerald* and 7 destroyers on a sweep towards Ramree, breaking wireless silence at selected times in order to give the impression that a force was approaching. To confirm the impression of an approach I asked the AOC, 222 Group for an aircraft to make a signal at 0830 on the 12th in self evident code 'nothing in sight 30 miles ahead of Fleet' in a position which would suggest that the force was still advancing towards Ramree. I also asked the Air C-in-C to lay on land-based air bombardment of the beaches at Ramree at dawn on the 13th, and on the previous evening to [simulate] by wireless the provision of fighter cover of a convoy proceeding from Chittagong. I felt that this plan was likely to be more effective than a bombardment by destroyers.

3.   Ships mentioned above left harbour at 1600 for this operation.

12 February

3.   At 0930 I took off by air [from Trincomalee] and arrived at Colombo at 1030. Found a signal from *Relentless* to say she had sunk a tanker and was now proceeding W at 20 knots. Unfortunately there are two British tankers which may possibly have not received the signal diverting them clear of the area so *Relentless* was told to amplify her sig-

[1]Maj-Gen I.S.O. Playfair RE: Maj-Gen 1941; later an official historian of the war in the Med & Middle E.

nal. I was much relieved to get a signal from *Relentless* at 3 p.m. to say that the tanker in question was the *Charlotte Schliemann* and she had picked up 41 survivors.

4. Indications received that there was a general alarm by the enemy on the Arakan coast last night as a result of a Calcutta–Chittagong convoy being sighted; so far no positive reactions to the sweep by the Fleet.

5. During the afternoon a signal was received from *Hawkins*, SO of a convoy consisting of 5 troopships conveying an E African Division from Kilindini to Colombo, to say that one ship of her convoy, the *Khedive Ismail*, had been torpedoed and sunk W of the 1½° channel. This was followed by signals from *Paladin* to say she was engaging the U-boat with gunfire and depth charges, and later that the U-boat, which was Japanese, had been blown up.[1]

A signal was received from Vizag[apatam] to say that the *Asphalion*[2] which had been torpedoed whilst in convoy to Colombo had been towed into Vizag. and that the latest reports from the escorts who had hunted the U-boat suggested the latter was sunk.

358. *From Ismay*

Offices of the War Cabinet,
Great George Street, SW1,
12 February 1944

. . . I told Wedemeyer frankly that SEAC were being much criticised for the inordinate size of their staff and that, apart from the terrible shortage of manpower, it would be a very good thing for Dickie's reputation if he would consent to drastic cuts, by making full use of the staffs of the Cs-in-C. . . .

. . . you say very truly that you have no clear statement of what was decided at Cairo in regard to the Far East. The fact of the matter is that the long term plan, which ABC told you about, was approved in rather a hurry 'as a basis for investigation and future planning'. Now that more thought has been given to it, objections are being raised in the highest quarters, and a definite ban has been put on communicating the plan to the Dominion Governments and SEAC. This state of uncertainty is very wearing and I am very much hoping that the talks with the Wedemeyer

---

[1]*Khedive Ismail*: 1922, 7290gt, Khedivial Mail Line, Egypt; she sank in 2 mins with very heavy loss of life (over 1000), esp WRNS bound for Ceylon. The submarine was *I–27*. *Petard*: 1942, 1540t, 4×4in, 8tt, 34k; supported *Paladin*.
[2]*Asphalion*: 1924, 6273gt, 13k, Alfred Holt/ China Mutual SN.

party will clear the air and enable either a decision to be taken, or, at least, a fresh view to be sent to Washington.

359. Desk diary, 1944

13 February

Signal received from *Petard* reporting that *Paladin* has sustained serious damage as a result of ramming the submarine, that her engine room, gear room and some after compartments were flooded and that she was being towed to Addu. I heard with regret that the *Khedive Ismail* had sunk in less than 2 minutes with very heavy loss of life. Apparently survivors did not number more than 200 out of a total of nearly 1500 on board.

4. In view of the *Khedive Ismail* sinking I informed the Admiralty I felt we were no longer justified in accepting, as we have had to hitherto, such light escorts for troop convoys, and that until troop movements at present envisaged were completed I must take destroyers from the Fleet for the purpose.

6. Signal received from *Stonehenge*[1] reporting she had sunk what appeared to be a seaplane carrier and one other ship.

14 February

Nothing has been heard of the U-boat that should have fuelled from the *Charlotte Schliemann* and CS4 thinks it unlikely that she did so; on the other hand one would have thought she would have kept company with the *Charlotte Schliemann* during the night but this seems improbable in view of the fact that she did not break wireless silence to report what has happened.

3. *Paladin* arrived at Addu in tow of *Petard* and reports her side was ripped open by the submarine's hydroplane. *Salviking*,[2] salvage ship, has been sent with an escort to assist in repairs. *Hawkins* and her convoy arrived at Colombo at 5 p.m. and from preliminary reports it appears that *Hawkins* and the 5 transports were in 3 columns 3 cables apart with *Paladin* and *Petard* 45° on each bow carrying out a broad zigzag; the U-boat periscope was sighted 800 yards on the quarter of the *Khedive Ismail* and from this position she fired a salvo of which 2 torpedoes hit the transport; the latter turned on her beam ends in 45 seconds and sank in less than 2 minutes. After *Paladin* had picked up survivors and after *Petard* had hunted the U-boat and lost contact, the latter surfaced a mile

---

[1]*Stonehenge*: 1943, 715/1000t, 7tt, 1×3in, 14.5/10k; lost off Sabang March 1944.
[2]*Salviking*: 1943, 1440t, 12k; sunk 14 Feb 1944.

away and a running fight ensued during which *Paladin* attempted to ram, was ordered not to by *Petard*, and in trying to avoid the submarine fouled the latter's hydroplanes. *Petard* eventually sank the submarine with the 7th torpedo she fired. From all accounts she appears to have been a singularly tough submarine.

15 February

Signal received from *Relentless* describing how she sank the *Charlotte Schliemann*. She appears to have carried out an extremely good curve of search and finally attacked and torpedoed the *Charlotte Schliemann* after making what appeared to be an unseen approach. . . . Prisoners report that 2 U-boats had already fuelled and one was just going to; also that 2 German and 2 ex-Italian blockade runner U-boats were on their way home.

2. *Fara*[1] reported that the salvage ship *Salviking* which she was escorting to Addu was torpedoed and sunk at 11 p.m. last night. Since it was dark at the time it seems an extraordinary mischance that so small and short a ship as the *Salviking*, proceeding at 13 knots, should have run across a submarine in this area. Incidentally before the sinking of the *Khedive Ismail* there were no indications of any submarines in the vicinity of the Maldives though it was thought that one might be operating in the vicinity of Ceylon.

5. Heavy rain prevented air sweeps being carried out to the S of Ceylon to locate the submarine which sank *Salviking*.

16 February

2. I visited the Netherlands destroyer *Van Galen* during the forenoon and addressed the ship's company who, as usual, were a good looking lot of men. Her Captain, Lt-Cdr Burghard, informed me they were delighted at finding themselves back with the Fleet and away from Australia where convoy duty had been their sole occupation.

4. It was decided to put the Persian Gulf–Bombay shipping into convoy since it seems probable that a U-boat will be operating in that area very soon; it is unfortunate that our escorts should be so weak and the best we can muster on many occasions is 2 corvettes for a convoy of 20 or 26 ships.

---

[1]*Fara*: trawler, 1941, 560t, 1×12pdr, 12k.

360. *From Mountbatten*

17 February 1944

[Enclosure]

Summary of AXIOM conversations up to 14 February, inclusive

AXIOM party arrived in London p.m. 11 February and were immediately confronted with most determined arguments for emphasis in the Pacific in the form of two thrusts from Central Pacific and SW Pacific.

2. At the first formal meeting with the Prime Minister and the Chiefs of Staff p.m. Monday 14 February, the First Sea Lord supported combining the Fleets in the Pacific, mainly because of the opportunity offered for active operations for the British Fleet.

3. CAS and CIGS supported the Pacific policy from a logistical point of view in that resources would not allow more than two Allied thrusts simultaneously.

4. It is still, however, not clear whether British participation in the Pacific is required and whether it can be supported logistically. Rear Admiral Cooke[1] has fortunately arrived in London this weekend and it is hoped it may be possible to obtain from him some indication of the US Chiefs of Staffs' views.

5. The Prime Minister is still strongly supporting CULVERIN, but has not committed himself with regard to post-CULVERIN strategy.

6. Detailed examination of CULVERIN is now being carried out by JPS and AXIOM planners with a view to an early report being put before the Prime Minister. The latter has called for smaller forces and a greater degree of improvisation than plan now allows for. November 1944 continues as target date.

7. Decision will probably turn on:–

(a) Whether British resources are absolutely necessary to two Pacific thrusts and whether they can be supported logistically.

(b) Diversionary effect of CULVERIN.

(c) Provision of resources for CULVERIN.

---

[1]Rear Adm (later Adm) Charles M. ('Savvy') Cooke, US Navy (1886–1919): US N Acad 1906–10; battleships 1910–14; s/m i/c 1915–20; engr, EO & gunnery appts 1920s; Bur Nav 1928–31; SubDiv 11 1931–3; NW Coll 1933–4; Cdt, Guantanamo Bay NB 1934–6; staff of C-in-C Fleet 1936–8; War PD, ONO, 1938–41; *Pennsylvania* i/c Feb 1941–April 1942; ACOS (P), C-in-C Fleet (King) April 1942–Oct 1943; DCOS Oct 1943–Oct 1944; COS Oct 1944–Aug 1945; DCNO(O) Oct–Dec 1945; Cdr 7th Fleet Dec 1945–Jan 1947; Cdr N Forces, W Pacific Jan 1947–Feb 1948; Ret List May 1948.

8. Complete agreement was reached on the Ledo Road, air transport, air offensive in China and limited extent of land and air operations in Burma.

361. *Desk diary, 1944*

21 February

I held a Flag and Commanding Officers' meeting at 1030 which was also attended by VAEF and RAA from Trincomalee. After discussing the general situation I held a conference with VAEF, RAA and CS4 to consider what action should be taken when the Germans appreciated that *Charlotte Schliemann* had disappeared. It seems probable that the *Brake* or another tanker will be sent from Singapore to take her place, and I decided that *Illustrious* and *Gambia* should sail from Trincomalee to cover an area SW of Cocos with a view to interception. I also decided that CS4 and *Newcastle* should sail so as to arrive in Mauritius in time to take charge of the hunt should the tanker proceed to one of the old refuelling positions SE of Mauritius. The *Tantivy* is off the Sunda Straits, and with *Illustrious* and *Gambia* SW off Cocos and CS4 with *Battler* and *Suffolk* plus 2 destroyers in the Mauritius area we should stand a good chance of catching anything that is sent out.[1]

2. Signal received from the Admiralty to say that they view with concern any idea of Fleet training and operations being limited by withdrawal of destroyers for escort duties, and that every economy must be exercised in areas where attack is not imminent. Unfortunately the distance factor on this Station prevents redisposition of escorts to meet new threats, and as we get no previous warning of the approach of Japanese submarines a degree of static disposition must be accepted. When the current rather heavy troop movements are completed the situation will improve, but the Admiralty state that apart from 2 frigates and 4 corvettes now on their way to join the EF, and 6 frigates and 2 sloops for the RIN which will be joining later, no further reinforcements can be expected.

22 February

Reports from American sources suggest that a considerable concentration of Japanese Fleet units may be taking place at Singapore, with a view to offensive sorties and air action in the Bay of Bengal in the near future. I think that these may well be connected with the drastic changes in the Japanese high command which were announced today.

[1]*Brake*: 1937, 9925gt, J van den Bergh, Hamburg.
Tantivy: 1943, 1090/1575t, 11tt, 1×4in, 15.25/9k.

2. In reply to a signal from SAC asking for my reactions to this information, I said there were good grounds to believe that 5 battleships, 2 aircraft carriers, 8 cruisers and 2 flotillas of destroyers were now at Singapore, and that a raid on the S coast of India or Ceylon, or a raid on shipping could not be excluded. The present EF was not only numerically inferior but was not yet fully trained, and it would be necessary for the Fleet to withdraw if the threat of a Japanese attack in force should appear likely to materialise. Until the Fleet is reinforced we have to rely on the air for defence. I intended to establish a submarine patrol off the Sunda Straits, and also reinforce the patrol in the Malacca Straits.

3. I saw the COs of *Launceston* and *Ipswich* in connection with their attack on the Japanese submarine off Vizag. and I feel quite certain now that it can be claimed as a kill.[1] . . .

23 February

Received a report that 3 ships in a convoy from Persian Gulf to Aden had been torpedoed; the convoy consisted of 19 ships with 2 *Bangors* as escort; this is generally speaking about the usual scale of protection we can afford to give these convoys.

Cdr Holmes, on my Intelligence staff,[2] who usually has a good appreciation of Japanese intentions considers it unlikely the Japanese will make a sally from Singapore. Discussing with the AOC and his staff the question of air recco. to give us warning of possible Japanese sorties it was agreed that an exit by the Sunda Straits was more likely than by the Malacca Straits in view of the known submarine activity in the latter area. At 2.15 I had conference with the VAEF, CS4, FOC, S4 and Staff Officers and discussed action to be taken should there be indications that the Japanese intended to make a sortie in force into the Bay of Bengal. I decided that the Fleet would go W of the Maldives if the Japanese moved towards the Bay of Bengal since it appeared to me to be undesirable that the Fleet should remain at Trincomalee to serve as a target for an air attack, and I considered it most unlikely they would attempt a sortie except in force. Under these circumstances *Unicorn* would move to Cochin. . . .

---

[1]*Launceston* RAN (CO Tempy Lt P. G. Collins RANR (S)); *Ipswich* RAN (CO Tempy Lt-Cdr J.S. McBryde, RANR (S)): both minesweeper/corvettes, *c.*1941, 733t, 1×3in, 16k.
[2]Actg Cdr Cecil H. Holmes: Lt-Cdr 1937; Sec to Noble, *Kent*, 1CS, China 1939; *Scout* Jan 1940; *Witch* May 1941; Actg Cdr & Japanese Interpreter, *Tana* Oct 1942; Cdr *Renown* June 1944; *Undine* Sept 1945.

362.   *To Mountbatten*

23 February 1944

... what strikes me so forcibly is that there seems to be no really hard and fast view as to whether the whole of the Allied forces available can be used effectively in the Pacific or whether they can be sustained there. ...

I trust very much, however, that the PM will not persuade the CCS to whittle down the present reduced CULVERIN. I feel sure if this were to happen we should find ourselves begging for every ship and landing craft and we should then have nothing in hand for replacement against unforeseen losses before the party starts.

With regard to the Japanese concentration at Singapore, ... it is very hard to determine whether it means business or not. For the last two years I have been at a loss to understand why the Japs did not raid our trade routes at least since we had nothing to stop them and they could have got away with it time after time. The change in High Command certainly suggests to me that a change in policy is likely and from the Japanese point of view I cannot imagine anything more fruitful than to attack our lines of communication or even E Indian ports.

As your people point out however, the make up of the Fleet is odd and is somewhat unbalanced for any excursions into the Bay of Bengal, though, taking into account the efficiency of what corresponds to our Coastal Command aircraft, I feel the Japs could quite well carry out even a bombardment and get away with it.

It is maddening for me that I should find myself in the same position now as I was two years ago, i.e. with a quite inadequate force which would be a gift for the Japanese if they came out in full strength. With another two fleet carriers out here I feel sure the Japanese would not show their noses outside the Malayan Barrier.

Even if this disposition is static it will prove a damned nuisance, since our Australian convoy routes will be subject to continual threat until we have enough carriers out here to make the Japanese shy of sending anything out.

The Admiralty appear to be quite firm in their determination not to increase materially the A/S escorts for this station, but I am sure this decision is based on a careful examination of all the factors involved. I am not prepared, however, to risk another troop transport with insufficient escort, and I cannot believe that the Admiralty wish me to do so.

Operation SLEUTH[1] which is now being laid on is at present a shot in the dark, but I feel in my bones the Germans must do something about the water-hogs who have lost their sow. If we could only catch the next one as well there might be quite a mess.

363.　Desk diary, 1944

24 February

The DNI[2] states he considers the chief factor governing the move of the Japanese to Singapore is to keep their Fleet clear of the Americans, but he does not exclude the possibility of an attack in the Bay of Bengal and along the trade routes. SAC on the other hand considers the Japanese still anticipate amphibious operations being staged in the near future and that the move is consequently defensive. SAC says that he concurs in withdrawing clandestine operations as a result of withdrawing the submarines for recco. purposes, and also empowers the AOC 222 Group to use the air forces at his disposal as requisite. I felt it necessary to point out to SAC that the movements of the submarines must be directed by me and that though, when circumstances admit it, I will give him previous warning of my intention to abandon clandestine operations, it must be clearly understood that he could not always be notified concerning the necessity to abandon clandestine operations. With regard to the air forces under AOC 222 Group, I pointed out that the AOC and myself were already empowered to use these forces against enemy surface forces and submarines as we thought fit.

25 February

The Admiralty . . . ask if the US can lend the EF a carrier to reinforce and say that if this can be done they on their side will reinforce the battleship strength. The Admiralty have signalled to me that 2 assault carriers are being sent out together with 4 squadrons of Barracudas and 4 squadrons of Corsairs or Hellcats[3] to reinforce the defence of Ceylon and India. They agree generally with my appreciation except they attach most weight to the Japanese endeavour to get clear of the American Fleet; they agree that the EF must not engage superior forces but say we must be ready to take advantage of any opportunities offered and deprecate a move from Trincomalee to the westward. They also ask about mining the Malacca Straits, and whether surface minelayers can be used.

[1] The attempt to catch the *Brake*.
[2] Actg Capt Laird.
[3] Chance Vought Corsair, USA: 1940, 6mg, bomb load 2000lb, 446mph.

3.   I sent a signal to the Admiralty to say that I did not favour keeping the Fleet at Trincomalee since I felt it was most unlikely the Japanese would make a sortie except in force and sufficient force too to cover retirement of any damaged units. I pointed out that our main weakness in this area was between Ceylon and 15°N; I felt it unlikely the Japanese would enter the northern part of the Bay of Bengal in view of our known bomber strength in Burma and in the Calcutta area.

4.   A signal from Delhi states that the Air C-in-C is sending a fighter squadron to Madras, and also considering reinforcement of this area with bomber squadrons. Admiralty have also sent a signal to say that 2 or 3 T/B squadrons from the Middle East may be sent out to Southern India.

26 February

Latest information suggests that some Japanese cruisers may be docking at Singapore and that one fleet carrier is going to Japan; if this is correct it suggests the movement of the Fleet to Singapore does not portend any immediate offensive operations.

2.   We received today a long appreciation by the JIC concerning the Japanese move to Singapore; this more or less conforms to my appreciation except that it gives more weight to Japanese fear of attack on the Andamans or Nicobars during this monsoon. It also points out that with the Fleet at Singapore the strain on tankers for their oil supply is decreased owing to close proximity to the oil fields.

3.   Information received that the Japanese are sending aircraft to recco. Cocos; this may be due to *K14*'s[1] activity off Christmas Islands.

4.   I discussed with the AOC the problem of how to suggest to the Japanese that we were maintaining a continual recco over the Bay of Bengal. We decided that a Liberator recco at night should be carried out with the object of being picked up by radar at Sabang and the Andamans. This would suggest to the enemy that we were well on our toes.

5.   We received information that an enemy torpedo boat in the Malacca Straits had rammed and sunk one of our submarines; this may be *Tally-Ho* but there is no definite evidence of sinking so far.

27 February

Narbada arrived wearing the flag of FOCRIN.[2] The latter discussed with me the future of the Indian Navy and said the Indians are most anxious to have what they consider a real Navy, and that this would include

[1]*K14*, R Neth N: 1932, 771/1008t, 8tt, 1×3.5in, 17/9k.
[2]*Narbada* RIN: 1943, 1340t, 6×4in, 18k. FOCRIN was now Vice Adm Godfrey.

3 cruisers on loan, 9 destroyers, 2 escort carriers and frigates in lieu of their older makeshift A/S vessels. It appeared to me that this programme was somewhat over ambitious and I suggested that the destroyers and escort carriers might be omitted with advantage since maintenance of these ships would present far greater difficulties than the others mentioned. . . .

28 February

Information received that the *Brake* is not due at Batavia until 29th. This unfortunately throws out the search by *Illustrious* as she will have to return before *Brake* can arrive in her area owing to shortage of fuel. I very much regret that we did not have the foresight to send a tanker to this area, but at the time the operation was launched it seemed quite certain that *Illustrious*'s endurance would cover amply the period during which *Brake* might be expected in this area. I ordered the *Sussex* to remain in the area to the S of the Cocos for as long as possible, but without air to help her, the chances of an interception are not good.

2.   I was relieved to receive a signal from *Tally-Ho* to say that while she had been damaged by the Japanese torpedo boat that rammed her, she was all right; she had sunk a submarine and a merchant ship.[1]

3.   VAEF and Captain S4 arrived for conference. Owing to the need to escort *Illustrious* on her return it will be necessary for the Fleet to remain in harbour on account of the destroyer situation, but I hope we shall be able to get the Fleet to sea about the 8th for a short spell.

29 February

Received a signal from the Admiralty to say the Americans are sending *Saratoga* with 3 destroyers to join the EF. My USNLO was laying 10 to 1 that this request of ours would not be met.

3.   Latest information suggests that the *Brake* may be making the passage through the Sunda Straits tonight. Am not too hopeful that *Tantivy* will intercept and it is most unfortunate that *Illustrious*'s search has had to be called off . . .

4.   The latest redistribution of the Japanese Fleet, in which the fast battleships form the First Fleet, some units of which appear to be going to Palau, does not suggest operations in the Bay of Bengal in the near future. It appears to me that this redistribution of the Japanese Fleet in the Singapore area may well have some effect on our general strategical plan. If amphibious reinforcements are sent by us to the Pacific, they

[1]The submarine was *U-It 23*, an ex-Italian boat, *Reginaldo Giuliani*: 1940, 955/1315t, 18/8.2k; converted to transport 1943; capt at Singapore after Italian surrender; sunk in Malacca Straits.

must presumably be accompanied by adequate naval forces; but if, owing to the presence of the Japanese Fleet at Singapore, we are compelled to maintain a Fleet of some size in this Theatre it may follow that the amphibious forces, which would be covered by this Fleet, will have to be employed in this Theatre. I imagine a good deal will depend on when the Japanese will consider it necessary to withdraw their Fleet to home waters.

364. *To Cunningham*

29 February 1944

The day before I left Delhi I had a long talk with Dickie and Henry Pownall about the set up of Delhi and told him I felt the time had come when he should decide definitely whether the Cs-in-C were to act as his principal advisors or his War Staff. I suggested when the first idea of an operation was mooted he should get the Cs-in-C together and ask them what they thought of it. If it was considered a good idea, then the planners, and by them I meant the proper Joint Planning Staff, would get busy and make out a plan. Throughout the planning stage the Cs-in-C would be in touch with progress so that when the plan was finally evolved it would represent their views. This appeared in every way preferable to the two stage planning which is at present taking place and which leads to so much confusion and difficulty. Both D and HP appeared to be impressed by this argument and D said an appropriate time to put this new organisation into effect would be when the move to Kandy took place. Unfortunately, neither Peirse nor Giffard are coming to Kandy for some months so I am not quite sure when the scheme, if adopted, will really take proper shape.

11. The following day [11 February] I visited *Queen Elizabeth*, *Valiant* and *Unicorn* to address the ships' companies and have a quick walk round. I was very much impressed by *Unicorn*. I spent the forenoon inspecting the MTB Flotilla, *Barracuda*,[1] Dockyard and other establishments. . . .

18.   We are going to find it difficult to accommodate the 8 squadrons of Barracudas, Corsairs, etc., and also leave space for disembarked carrier squadrons. The matter has been carefully examined with the RAF and I hope we shall get a satisfactory answer. The Barracuda range out here appears to be less than we had anticipated. The last figures I had from Moody suggest the radius may be as low as 180 miles. From what we

[1]Probably a depot ship for MTBs.

know of the Japanese it seems unlikely that they will come within this range unless they send any surface ships to attack coastal convoys. ...

365. *Desk diary, 1944*

1 March

4. From information received it appears that *Tantivy* was sighted and attacked by an aircraft whilst still 100 miles away from the Sunda Strait. This is most unfortunate as it precludes possibility of a surprise attack by her on the *Brake*.

2 March

I received a long personal signal from the First Sea Lord commenting on reasons given by me for moving the Fleet to the W of the Maldives. He did not agree that during an initial attack the efficiency of the air defences would be less than subsequently; he could not understand why the efficiency of the heavy ships was not up to standard and he felt that a withdrawal W of the Maldives would be bad for morale. He concluded, however, that I was in the best position to judge on the spot and whatever my decision he would support it.
3.   In reply I stated that the situation had now changed, e.g., Japanese appeared to be looking E rather than W; I though it was generally accepted that initial attack found defences in a less state of efficiency than subsequently and this had been my experience in the Western Mediterranean; it had never been my intention to remove the Fleet from Trincomalee entirely, but rather that their visits should be haphazard and occasional in order that the enemy should remain in doubt concerning movements and composition of the Fleet. I proposed, therefore, that the Fleet should go initially W of the Maldives to exercise oiling under way among the islands since this experience might prove useful subsequently. After that I proposed they should move S of the Line, in an area S of Ceylon in order to discourage possible Japanese attempts to interfere with the Australian shipping route. This I considered more probable now than an incursion in the Bay of Bengal.
6.   At 2042 a Catalina on patrol in the vicinity of which the *Palma*[1] was sunk, sighted a U-boat on the surface and straddled it with 5 depth charges as she was diving. Additional air patrol was ordered out and 2 of the destroyers returning to Trincomalee diverted to this area; 2 local patrols also sent.

---

[1]*Palma*: 6000t, 15k; sunk while sailing independently between Colombo and Madras.

3 March

Latest reports from the Catalina show that she straddled the U-boat with 6 depth charges and machine-gunned the conning tower as she dived. Depth charges spaced 45 feet apart and all detonated; a flare was dropped but no evidence could be seen of damage or destruction, only depth charge scum. The Captain of the Catalina is a very reliable and experienced officer, and it is difficult to believe that this submarine escaped damage even if she was not sunk.[1]

2.   Submarines are pretty active in this area at present. A German was fixed by D/F in the northern part of the Maldives, there are 2 Japanese submarines off the S and E coasts of Ceylon, another in this area probably returning to Penang, and one may be approaching the Seychelles en route for the Mozambique Channel. Another German submarine is in the Gulf of Aden, 4 are believed to be waiting for the *Brake* SE of Mauritius.

4 March

Report received that the survivors of the SS *Ascot*[2] have been picked up to the eastward of the Seychelles. . . . presumably this is the work of the Japanese submarine proceeding towards the Mozambique Channel.

2.   I sent a signal to the SAC in which I suggested that so long as the Japanese maintained their main naval force at Singapore it will be necessary for us to maintain a relatively large Fleet in this Theatre. If it was intended to send British amphibious forces to the Pacific, it appeared that in these circumstances, the Fleet component for this amphibious force would have to be divorced from it until such time as the Japanese Fleet were compelled to move away from Singapore. It seemed to me, therefore, that this was an argument in favour of a three-pronged attack, i.e., CULVERIN, as this would enable the amphibious force and its Fleet component to train and eventually operate together. Admittedly the mobility of the Fleet component was such that it could be switched quickly to the Pacific, but unless there was a sufficient interval for training it seems there would be a considerable advantage in a CULVERIN or similar operation, if this agrees more or less with the general strategy.

3.   An estimate of the extent to which the Japanese can raid the Australian shipping route indicates that the average spacing between ships is about 230 miles, and that a tip and run raid at 20 knots from the Sunda Straits might give a return of 2 or 3 ships sunk, If the raiding party, which it is assumed will include a carrier, made their arrival unde-

[1] No submarine was sunk.
[2] *Ascot*: 1942, 7005gt, Britain SS Co.

tected and could count on no interference for say 6 days they should be able to account for some 7 or 8 ships.

5 March

7.   I then visited *Adamant* and inspected *Taurus*[1] just prior to her proceeding on patrol. Her ship's company is in very good heart; her coxswain is only 21 years of age and has the DSM. . . .

8 March

2.   The US submarine on patrol in the Lombok Straits reports 2 or 3 large unidentified ships with an escort passed out to the S; this may indicate a break out by the Japanese, but the information is somewhat vague and might well be a normal passage of ships outside the Straits to escape the attention of US submarines which have been so active in the Java Sea. In this connection a signal was received from Captain Hillgarth to say that the Commander of Task Force 71 had informed him that with his 23 submarines, he sank 124,000 tons in January and 200,000 tons in February;[2] . . .

3.   I visited *Tally-ho* in dry dock, addressed the ship's company and inspected the damage caused by her being rammed by a Japanese torpedo boat; this is most spectacular and shows that the propellors of the torpedo boat ripped open practically the whole of her port tanks by means of a series of vertical gashes. . . .

5.   Reports from the *Truculent* and *Tactician* have been received; *Truculent* was machine gunned by a Mitsubishi on 11 February; missed an MV of 2000 tons entering Sabang on 14 February with 4 torpedoes; got one hit on a 7000 ton ship leaving Sabang on 15 February, but results were unobserved owing to counter attack. *Tactician* missed a Japanese 'I' class submarine with 5 torpedoes on the 20th, and on the 28th engaged with gunfire and finally sank by torpedo a 300 foot motor vessel laden with army motor transport.[3]

9 March

2.   . . . the COS and PM hold opposite views on CULVERIN. The for-

[1]*Taurus*: 1942, 1090/1575, 11tt, 1×4in, 15.25/9k.

[2]Now COIS. This was almost certainly TF51, commanded by Rear Admiral Ralph W. Christie, US Navy: b 1893; a submariner since 1917; Cdr *Ranger* 1934; Torpedo Secn, Bur Ordnance 1936; SubDiv 15 i/c, Hawaii 1939; SubDiv 20 Dec 1942; Capt i/c E Aust S/m Grp (TF42) 1942; RA Nov 1942; Inspr Ordnance, Torpedo Sta, Newport RI Dec 1942–Feb 1943; Cdr S/m SW Pac (TF51) & Cdr Allied N Forces W Aust March 1943; Bremerton NB Feb 1945–Jan 1948; US N Forces Philippines 1948–9; VA & Inspr Gen W Sea Frontier; Ret List Aug 1949.

[3]*Truculent* (sunk in collision with Swedish coaster, Thames, Jan 1950), *Tactician*: 'T' class, 1942.

mer consider that all possible forces are needed in the Pacific, and it seems unlikely that they will change their views except for some powerful political or non military reason. The PM is preparing a memorandum for the Defence Committee on the subject and it is believed a decision should be reached before very long.

In another signal the COS say there is ample room for the British Fleet to operate independently on the left flank of the main Pacific drive, and whilst the latest move of the Japanese Fleet will entail some delay in forces being sent to the Pacific, [and] the full strength will not be achieved until after Germany's defeat, they still feel that the Pacific policy is the right one.

4.   NOIC Addu Atoll reported that the tanker *British Loyalty*[1] was torpedoed this afternoon by a torpedo fired from a submarine through the Gan entrance.

10 March

4.   Signal received in the afternoon that the tanker *British Loyalty* had been abandoned and was in danger of sinking. I sent an immediate signal to NOIC ordering him to take steps at once to beach the ship.

5.   Received a signal from Admiralty that *Richelieu* might be sent out here as a reinforcement, until the *Howe*[2] was ready. It seems to me we shall have to erect a Tower of Babel as a PWSS Station.

11 March

. . . The cutting off of the oil supplies is a special task for the submarines this year, and [Cdr Miers] strongly urges that we should base a flotilla on the W coast of Australia in order to participate in these operations.

366.   *To Mountbatten*

11 March 1944

4.   As Miles will have told you, I hope to send the Fleet on a cruise on 20 March to meet *Saratoga* about half way to Australia; after her arrival and when I have found out what her form is, and also after the arrival of the two assault loaded carriers, we shall be in a position to go and tease

---

[1]NOIC Addu: unidentified. *British Loyalty*: 1928, 6993gt, 10k, British Tanker Co.
[2]*Howe*: 1942, 35,000t, 10×14in, 16×5.25in, 28k. *Richelieu* had been repaired, completed and manned by Free French following Allied conquest of French N & W Africa in 1942–3.

the Japanese, or at any rate trail our coats and give them something to think about. I believe very strongly that providing we can make a show of force in the area between Ceylon and Australia the Japanese are unlikely to attempt to raid. With the build up of air on the E coast of India I feel that raids in the Bay of Bengal are unlikely though of course they cannot be entirely excluded. It is very strange that the Japanese should show so little initiative and that they have failed to seize the golden chance of scoring a few points by attacking us before we were ready.

367. Desk diary, 1944

12 March

2. I inspected the divisions on board *Queen Elizabeth* at 0930 and was much struck by the extreme youth of the men; I understand the average age excluding POs, is 21½, and with the POs it is barely 23. From the appearance of the men and the appearance of the ship it was quite clear to me that they have some way to go before a proper standard is reached.

13 March

A very welcome signal received during the night from *Roebuck*[1] to say she had sunk the *Brake,* position about 100 miles SE of Mauritius. CS4's forces were ordered by me to return to Mauritius since any submarine hunt was clearly undesirable at this juncture and would probably be unprofitable.

3. There were some indications that a Japanese heavy unit might be proceeding to Port Blair; this received some confirmation by a report from *Storm,*[2] the southernmost submarine patrol in the Malacca Straits, who reported that in a heavy rain squall a force estimated to consist of one heavy unit and 5 destroyers passed her on a northwesterly course steaming at 16 knots. The *Taurus* is at present on patrol off Port Blair but has a mine leading in her tubes; the evidence is not yet sufficiently definite that this heavy unit proceeded to Port Blair, and Penang seems a more likely destination.

14 March

In view of movement reported by *Storm* yesterday, long range air patrols have been established to the eastward of Ceylon and Madras as a precaution against any incursion into the Bay of Bengal, though I think this is unlikely.

---

[1]*Roebuck*: 1943, 1705t, 4×4.7in, 8tt, 34k.
[2]*Storm*: 1944, 715/1000t, 7tt, 1×3in, 14.5/10k; cmded by Lt-Cdr E. Young, RNV(S)R, who wrote the classic *One of Our Submarines* (London: Hart-Davis 1952).

15 March

Latest information suggests that a U-boat has picked up survivors of *Brake* and will proceed with them to Batavia. *Tantivy* has been patrolling off the Sunda Straits and was relieved today by a US submarine. Information from C-in-C SA and other sources suggest that the supply U-boat proceeding from Europe to the East may have been sunk by Catalinas S of the Cape; a very large patch of oil has been sighted where the attack took place.[1]

I held a conference with VAEF, RAA and AOC to consider allocation of aerodromes for disembarked FA squadrons. It was decided that combined training of *Illustrious*'s and *Saratoga*'s fighters should have priority and that in consequence these should be disembarked at China Bay on completion of the forthcoming cruise by the EF.

3. It now appears that *Atheling* and *Begum*[2] have A/S squadrons and therefore will have to be equipped with fighters if they are to be used for offensive operations. A review of possible targets for carrier operations is not very encouraging; Palembang is a very attractive target but the distance that has to be flown over land, and the high intervening mountains suggest that the prospects of success are not good, and in consequence would not justify the risk involved to the carriers. Batavia is a little better in this respect, but the only readily approached target is Sabang. Since Sabang is within range of Liberators from Ceylon a seaborne attack would not of itself be justified; but if the main consideration of this attack is to draw the enemy strike and deal with it effectively by means of a largely superior fighter force, then the operation may well be worth while. It will not be possible, however, to arrive at any firm decision until after arrival of *Saratoga* and discussion with her CO as to what her squadrons can achieve.

4. RAA referred to the disappointing performance of the Barracudas which from the point of view of a strike with torpedoes will not have a radius of action in this climate exceeding 160 miles. Apart from this their cruising speed of 120 [mph] makes it very difficult to match them up with Corsairs and Hellcats. These aircraft, in fact, appear to be a thorough misfit.[3]

---

[1]This must have been *U-It22*: ex-Italian *Alpino Bagnolini* (1939, 1031/1484t, 18/8k): converted to transport 1943; capt by Germans, Bordeaux Sept 1943; sunk by SAAF.

[2]*Atheling, Begum*: US-built CVEs, 1943, 11420t, 20 a/c, 16k.

[3]This was a little unfair to the Barracuda, which, while it had deficiencies in range and handling, had performed well in northern waters, especially against the *Tirpitz*; it was also quite versatile.

16 March

Signal received from CS4 giving details of operation COVERT. The *Brake* was first sighted by *Battler*'s aircraft at 1000 on 12 March, steering W with 2 U-boats, one on each quarter, and another U-boat 18 miles astern with a good deal of oil round her. *Newcastle, Battler, Suffolk* and *Roebuck* were in company 38 miles SSE of the position where *Brake* was sighted. *Roebuck* was sent on ahead to attack, sighted at 1116 at 13 miles, opened fire at 1126 at 15,800 yards, and ceased fire at 1212. Apart from gunfire she obtained hits with 3 torpedoes and the tanker sank at 1215. *Newcastle* followed *Roebuck*, but did not close inside 23 miles, and CS4 thinks she could not have been sighted. However there is evidence that she must have been sighted by one of the submarines. After *Brake* had been sunk, *Battler* flew off 3 sorties of 2 aircraft to attack the U-boats; the first sortie was in daylight, and the others after the moon had risen. One U-boat was attacked by aircraft who claimed a possible sinking; information suggests the U-boat was damaged but not sunk.

17 March

2.   Report received from ACNB that a ship had arrived in Australia which intercepted a raider report from MV *Behar*[1] on 9 March. The *Behar* was due at Bombay tomorrow, and has not answered calls. Another ship is overdue by 5 days in Australia, and since both ships in question were in the same area to the SW of the Cocos on the 9th, it seems possible that the heavy ships reported by a US submarine to be leaving the Lombok Straits on 8 March indicates the Japanese launched a raid on the shipping route. Against this at present is that the ships must have proceeded at nearly 30 knots in order to have reached the *Behar* at the time she made her raider signal.

18 March

Further information now makes it quite clear that the *El Medina*[2] was torpedoed. I issued instructions that the Calcutta–Chittagong convoys were to restrict embarkation to 75% of life-saving capacity. These convoys were first started when the floods washed out the Calcutta railways, but have been continued in order to reduce the strain on the railways. The escorts available have never really been sufficient to afford proper protection, and at the moment cannot be immediately supplemented as a

---

[1]*Behar*: 1929, 6100gt, 14k, Hain SS Co; sunk by Japanese heavy cruiser *Tone* off W coast of India; many of crew massacred.

[2]*El Medina*: 1937, 3962gt, 15k, Scindia SN Co; there were 746 survivors out of a total of 1200+ on board.

number of the sloops are now refitting in order to be available for continual operation during the monsoon. The passage of the end sections of the
floating dock from Bombay to Trincomalee also absorbs a number of
escorts.

20 March

4. I discussed with RANASIO the need for training Avenger
squadrons so they will be capable of being carried alternatively to
Barracudas in *Illustrious;* he quite agreed this would be necessary for
carrier operations against land based targets and felt it might be possible
to get enough Swordfish to replace the Avenger squadrons in *Shah*[1] for
A/S duties.

5. Air Marshal Baker from Delhi paid me a visit . . . With reference to
Kantali aerodrome he said that in view of the high priority which had to
be accorded to operating B29s[2] from Ceylon it would be necessary to
defer work on the Kalantai aerodrome. I pointed out that in view of the
fact this would have an effect on carrier training and the readiness of the
Fleet at Trincomalee, the matter would have to be referred to the
Admiralty for decision by the COS. Apparently the B29s could reach
Palembang and therefore will have Linga and Singapore well within
range. Attacks on the two latter might well make the Japanese fleet move
off somewhere else.

21 March

I received a signal from the First Sea Lord asking what action we are
taking about the raiders and what is my appreciation of the situation; he
assumes I am furnishing *Saratoga* with an escort. . . . I referred to
Operation DIPLOMAT, i.e. the present movement of the Fleet along the
Australian shipping route, and stated that in my opinion recent raid . . .
was . . . a cut and run raid by one or more Japanese cruisers. Should the
Japanese venture out again while the Fleet is at sea there should be an
opportunity to intercept, but if no movement occurs wireless silence will
be broken to denote we are active on the shipping route.

3. Captain Yendell[3] of the *Shah* came to see me; he reports that his
speed is now down to 17 knots and that Avengers require at least 24

[1]Grumman Avenger USA: 1941, bomb load 2000lb, 5mg, 271mph. *Shah*: US-built
CVE, 1943, 11,420t, 20 a/c, 16k.
[2]Air Vice Marshal J. W. Baker: Snr Air SO Feb 1943. Boeing B29 Superfortress USA:
1942, bomb load 12,000lb, 1 cannon, 12mg, 357mph, range 3250mls; aircraft which
dropped atomic bombs; the first true strategic bomber.
[3]Actg Capt W. J. Yendell: Cdr 1937; staff course 1939; NID April 1940; lent to Greece
May 1940; *Nile* July 1941; Actg Capt *Shah* Oct 1943; Capt June 1945.

knots for taking off. The operation of the carriers in this area of light wind belts will certainly be difficult, though possibly good accelerator drill may help matters to some extent.

22 March

2.   Visited *Shah*, walked round and addressed the ship's company; the rise of the hangar deck both forward and aft makes it difficult to move heavy aircraft such as Corsairs. . . .

23 March

Report received that 2 U-boats that were on passage out to this Theatre have been sunk in the Atlantic by a US escort carrier;[1] this is most satisfactory as one of the U-boats was believed to be carrying a load of torpedoes for Penang. The U-boat that picked up the *Brake* survivors and was damaged by *Battler*'s Swordfish is not due at Batavia until 24th; this suggests that she has sustained more damage than was at first appreciated.

2.   The *Stonehenge* is now 3 days overdue and has to be reported as lost; this is the first submarine which we have lost in this Theatre. There is some indication that she was sighted and attacked off Sabang.[2]

24 March

3.   *Nigeria* arrived and Captain Paton, her CO,[3] came to see me. He said the ship was completely equipped with steam heaters for service in the Arctic, had no awnings, she had not been docked for 12 months and generally speaking she was hardly in a state to join the EF, though I appreciate she had been sent out at short notice to meet the emergency created by the Japanese concentration at Singapore.

4.   I ordered the Vice Admiral, who is now with the Battle Fleet approaching Cocos, to break wireless silence tomorrow in order to give the impression that carriers are working in his vicinity; I also arranged for W/T simulation at Trincomalee that a part of the Fleet was proceeding to sea and carrying out exercises in the vicinity; this I hope will tend to confuse the Japanese.

25 March

2.   . . . I saw an appreciation by the Director of Intelligence on SAC's staff, to the effect that a 1945 CULVERIN was unlikely to contain

---

[1]Probably *U801* & *U1059*, sunk on 16 & 19 March by USS *Block Island* & escort group.
[2]Definitely lost.
[3]Capt Sir Stuart H. Paton, bt: Lt-Cdr & Torpedo O *Rodney* 1930; Cdr 1932; *Vernon* April 1939; Capt Dec 1940; NID June 1941; *Nigeria* June 1942; DDPD (Q) Aug 1944.

Japanese forces. According to him it will not divert substantial Japanese forces from other areas, it may prevent the diversion of some 220 to 285 aircraft from S Sumatra and Malaya to other areas; it will not contain the Japanese naval forces whose movements will almost certainly be governed by the extent of the threat to communications by the Pacific operations.

26 March

4. The SAC said he had received a telegram from the PM stating the latter was still backing CULVERIN as hard as possible and that he was opposed to the operation of British forces in the Pacific. The SAC had also received a letter from Washington which suggested that Admiral King is equally averse to this, and had only agreed against his better judgment to the proposed despatch of British forces to the Pacific; there appear to be some extraordinary cross currents at work in connection with the general strategical policy for the East and I feel this must delay preparations for a well thought out final plan. Discussing the aerodrome situation in Ceylon the SAC agreed that the operation of VLR bombers would have the most important effect on the Naval situation since it might well persuade the Japanese to withdraw their Fleet from this area. He was, however, strongly in favour of pushing on with the construction of Naval aerodromes in order that these would be available for the mounting of CULVERIN; I judge that CULVERIN still has priority in the mind of the SAC and that this preference is perhaps influenced to a considerable degree by the feeling that he has collected a staff designed to plan amphibious operations and that he is most reluctant at the thought that these might have to be abandoned.

6.   Captain Rylands, CACF,[1] called on me; his MLs have done most excellent work on the Arakan coast but have had to be withdrawn owing to the increasing swell and general deterioration in the weather.

368.   *To his wife*

27 March 1944

D still very busy with his intrigues with the PM – it's a really extraordinary state of affairs and I shall be interested to learn in due course what ABC thinks of it all. The odd thing is that the Burma campaign has gone

[1]Actg Capt H. I. G. Rylands: Flo NO, 3DF, *Inglefield*, Med 1937; Lt-Cdr 1938; *Dryad* (Nav Sch, Portsmouth) Jan 1940; NO *Formidable* July 1940; Actg Cdr FNO, Med F *Hannibal* Jan 1943; Cdr Dec 1943; CACF, Burma 1944; Nav Br, Hydrographer's Dept Jan 1945.

a good deal better than anyone expected so everything seems to be in the melting pot again. . . . Philip Joubert has just been to see me with a priceless suggestion from D that I should send a memorandum home by J to be given to the COS apparently asking that I should have some more escort vessels. I told J that I was astonished at a suggestion that I should try and go behind the backs of the Admiralty and in any case did not agree since they were in a much better position than anyone to judge how escorts should be allocated and were fully informed of all losses in this and other Theatres. They really are an extraordinary lot and seem to think I'm tarred with the same brush.

369. Desk diary, 1944

31 March

3.   I hear with grave concern that shocking atrocities were committed by the Japanese submarine on the crew of the Dutch ship *Tjisalak*,[1] sunk on 26 March to the NE of Chagos; after the survivors had taken to the boats the latter were ordered alongside and the Captain and an American Red Cross nurse were ordered below and not seen again. The boats were then cast off and the crew ordered to fall in before and abaft the conning tower with strict instructions they were not to look toward the conning tower or they would be shot. The Japanese then began to tie the men together in pairs; on realising what this meant, one of the DEMS crew resisted and was promptly shot; this was a signal for a general massacre and the unfortunate crew were killed with tommy guns, axes, swords, crowbars and hammers. The mate, one Lascar and 2 other Europeans fell overboard wounded, . . . and after swimming 5 miles regained the boats from which they were subsequently picked up by *Emerald*.
4.   Information was received that a Japanese submarine may be proceeding S down the W side of the Maldives and subsequently E, S of Addu Atoll. Three destroyers and 4 Catalinas have been sent to carry out a hunt.

1 April

I sent a signal to the Admiralty giving a list of the atrocities which had been committed in this Theatre by the Japanese on the crews of torpedoed ships; in every case these were independently sailed ships and I expressed the view that when the news of these atrocities leaked out there might be a reluctance on the part of crews to sail in unescorted

[1]*Tjisalak*: 1917, 5787gt, 11.75k, Java-China-Japan Line. From time to time allegations have been made that some Allied submarines massacred survivors.

ships. A review of the additional escorts required to put all the ships into convoy showed that would require the following additional long range escorts:–

Australia to India and Ceylon	18
Colombo to Aden	10
South Africa to India	8

2. I pointed out that at present of the escort of carriers available, *Battler* was refitting and the squadron for *Shah* was still under training; in any case it appeared to me that escort carriers would be of little service unless they operated in conjunction with convoys.

2 April

There are signs that many units of the Japanese main fleet are moving E from Singapore and furthermore that as a result of the eastern movement of their forces there may be only some 50 aircraft in the Andamans–Nicobars–N Sumatra area, of which some 20 may be floatplanes. This suggested that the moment may be opportune to carry out an air and sea bombardment of Sabang. I therefore sent a signal . . . asking for the comments of SAC. I appreciate that the heavy ships have not yet done any bombardment practices, apart from harbour exercises, and that owing to lack of the necessary crystals it is not possible to operate the *Illustrious* and *Saratoga* fighters together. Nevertheless I feel that in a fortnight it should be possible to give these ships sufficient practice and an operation of this sort would undoubtedly have an extremely good effect on morale. As this may be my last chance to carry out an operation personally, I am debating whether or not I shall go with the party if it comes off.

2. The Admiralty have suggested we might amalgamate the Aden–Bombay–Persian Gulf convoys so as to economise on escorts; this proposal is being examined, but at first sight it seems doubtful if it will help us very much.

3 April

Took off in a Beechcraft[1] at 0830 and arrived at Trincomalee at 0930. Captain Cassady of the *Saratoga* came to call and expressed his pleasure and that of his officers and men at being with the Eastern Fleet, and was most grateful for all that had been done for him. I rather expected he would consider Trinco a proper one horse place in comparison with the

[1]This could have been a single engined Traveler or a twin engined Expediter, both US-built light communications planes.

naval bases they have been using and I was agreeably surprised to find that this was not the case. *Saratoga* has no boats at all. . . .

2. At the special request of VAEF I went afloat with my flag flying to return the call of Captain Cassady; I felt it a bit incongruous, however, with the bands playing 'Rule Britannia' when America has by far and away the largest fleet of any nation in the world. I was received by a guard and band on board *Saratoga* and then addressed the ship's company who were fallen in on the flight deck. . . .The conditions of the galleys, wash places, store rooms and living spaces on the deck immediately under the flight deck were extremely good, but I was not so impressed with the appearance of spaces below this deck. *Saratoga* has only one lift and thus is unable to strike down her fixed wing fighters with the result that the operation of aircraft is unduly slow and compares most unfavourably with that of *Illustrious*.[1]

3. I discussed the Sabang operation with Captain Cassady who expressed himself very much in favour of it and stated that *Saratoga* would be extremely disappointed if they were unable to take part in an operation with the British fleet after having come so far.

4. . . . Examination of the chart and available maps indicates that indirect fire will have to be employed which raises rather a problem since few if any of the observers have had any practice in spotting. I received here a signal from the SAC in which he stated that whilst he recognised the value of operation CRIMSON from the point of view of morale, he felt the results likely to be achieved would not justify the risk of valuable ships; possibly the Delhi estimate of enemy aircraft likely to be available differs from ours.

5. Received a long signal from the Admiralty concerning the policy under consideration for this Theatre; Admiral Daniel[2] and party had proceeded to Australia to examine possibilities of maintaining a large section of the British Fleet in the Pacific and in Australian bases. Although the signal suggested a slight bias in favour of carrying out CULVERIN it stated that no preparations for the latter were to interfere with the despatch of a Fleet to the Pacific should this be required.

7. Referring to the recent cruise by the EF to the SW of Cocos and back, the VAEF informed me that all ships had shown a great improvement in regard to Fleet manoeuvres and handling and that oiling at sea was on the whole quite satisfactory. The average rate using floating hose

---

[1] Perhaps the reason for *Saratoga*'s impending relegation to training duties, delayed by her use as a night fighter carrier.

[2] Rear Adm Charles S. Daniel: Capt 1934; Capt (D) 8DF, *Faulkner* 1938; DP 1940–1; Flag Capt & CSO, 2BS, *Renown* Aug 1941; RA Jan 1943; Comb Ops HQ June 1943; mission to Australia re logistics for BPF 1943–4; RA 1BS June 1945; Actg VA (Admin) BPF 1945; 3SL & Cntrlr Sept 1945.

appeared to be about 140 tons an hour, but destroyers using a double trough in some cases achieved 350 tons an hour; there is no doubt that when weather conditions permit the trough method is vastly superior but this cannot be used for heavy ships unless we have properly manned Fleet oilers.

4 April

Received a signal from the Admiralty quoting one from Admiral King which suggested we should carry out an operation similar to CRIMSON between 15 and 21 April, but as near the 15th as possible; this was to act as a diversion for intended American operations in New Guinea. ...

2. I held a conference with the Flag and Commanding Officers who will be concerned in Operation CRIMSON and discussed the general outline of the operation and my intentions which at present are to neutralise by air attack the enemy aerodromes at Sabang and Kota Raja immediately prior to a bombardment of all possible targets in Sabang by the heavy ships, cruisers and possibly some of the destroyers. This bombardment to be followed by an air attack after which the force would withdraw. I proposed the bombardment should take place as soon as the light was effective after dawn and that every effort should be made to achieve surprise. It would be necessary for the ships taking part in this operation to carry out bombardment exercises in the immediate future and to cover this I proposed sending a plain language signal to the VA suggesting that insufficient attention had been paid to this and requesting him to take necessary action. . . . I informed the conference that whilst we might hope to inflict considerable material damage on the harbour installations, barracks, etc., the main object of the operation was to create a diversion and also give as many ships as possible a chance of engaging targets since this would undoubtedly have a most beneficial effect on morale.

5 April

2. Captains Agnew of *Atheling* and Broome of *Begum* who arrived yesterday, in company with *Athene* and *Engadine*,[1] called upon me. These two escort carriers have brought out the 4 Barracuda squadrons and 4 fighter squadrons ex. Fleet Carriers, who join subsequently, and

[1]Capt R. I. Agnew, RCN: Cdr Jan 1930; RCN Barracks, Esquimalt, ic, Nov 1938; Capt July 1941; *Atheling* i/c June 1943; *Givenchy*, depot ship, Esquimalt, 1944.
Capt J.E. ('Jack') Broome: Cdr 1936; RAF Staff Coll 1939; SO (O), *Victorious* Dec 1940; Air Liaison O, *Eaglet* (Liverpool) Feb 1941; *Keppel* Sept 1941; Actg Capt *Avalon* (Newfoundland) Nov 1942; Actg Capt *Begum* i/c Aug 1943; *Vernon II* May 1945.
Engadine: a/c transport: 1941, 10,700t, 40 a/c, 2×4in, 17k.

are proceeding to Madras to discharge their aircraft. Broome was most anxious to get his squadron of Avengers to train as soon as possible so that he could commence A/S operations in this Theatre; he considered that providing he had 4 destroyers or frigates with him he might achieve success in areas where submarines were known to be operating. I pointed out that the provision of such escorts at the moment was quite out of the question and all we could do was use the escort carriers with convoys and thus make the frigates serve a double purpose of protecting the convoys and the escort carriers. Although not finally decided, it seems to me at the moment that it is better to arm the *Begum* with Avengers for trade protection and the *Atheling*, in the first instance, with fighters to supplement fighter protection of the Fleet if required.

3.   Cdr Ormsby of the *Spey*[1] also called and reported that he had a cracked LP cylinder; this will put the ship out of action for many weeks and until a new engine is received will reduce her speed to 13 knots. It appears that despite a fairly prolonged stay in Liverpool little was done to the machinery of the ship, and I am afraid this is another example of this Station being saddled with ships not fit on arrival to carry out the duties assigned to them.

4.   The FEO,[2] who has returned from a visit to Bombay, gave me a very gloomy account of the RIN dockyard organisation and everything connected with it; I told him to let me have a written report which I could forward to FOCRIN, but I feel that until the most drastic and complete reorganisation and substitution of real live Heads takes place it will make no substantial difference.

6 April

Admiral King sends complaint by US representative at Karachi that US tankers are not given proper protection between India and the Persian Gulf; this is not borne out by the facts since during the year ending 31 March only 2 tankers have been torpedoed between India and the Persian Gulf of which one was American, and only two between the Persian Gulf and Aden of which neither was American. I appreciate, however, that if the submarines show more initiative we shall certainly incur much heavier losses until further escorts are available.

2.   Staff officers from the Fleet came over from Trincomalee to discuss operation CRIMSON. The Vice Admiral suggests:–

---

[1] Cdr G. A. G. Ormsby: Lt-Cdr 1939; A/S O, Med F *Afridi*; Admy, spl & misc services April 1940; A/S O, Med F *Warspite* Jan 1941; A/SWD Feb 1942; *Vanquisher* Feb 1943; Cdr Dec 1943; *Spey* 1944; *Taff* May 1944. *Spey*: 1942, 1460t, 2×4in, 20k.

[2] Engr Capt L. C. S. Noake: Cdr (E) Dec 1931; Capt (E) 1939; Admy 1940–1; Eastern F April 1942; FEO Aug 1943.

(a)   that the air strike should precede the bombardment,

(b)   that *Renown* should remain with the carriers and

(c)   that the latter should be about 80 miles from Sabang when the bombardment commences.

I was unable to agree to these proposals since I consider:–

(a)   the air strike must come after the bombardment so that targets will not be obscured by smoke and dust.

(b)   *Renown* should certainly take part in the bombardment since the value of her main armament outweighs the support her long range A/A can give to the carriers,

(c)   80 miles is too great a distance even allowing for light easterly winds; I feel 45 miles is the maximum limit otherwise too much flying time is wasted by fighters in proceeding to and from the target area.

7 April

It now seems clear that the Japanese fleet is back at Singapore and includes 4 battleships, 2 fleet carriers and 10 heavy cruisers; return of the air forces to their stations on the Barrier is also becoming confirmed. In view of this I have sent a signal to the Admiralty to say that if these indications are confirmed operation CRIMSON would involve unacceptable risks. As an alternative we could either trail our coats so as to contain the Japanese or else keep the Fleet standing by to carry out CRIMSON at the first sign of another eastward move. I suggested we should ask Admiral King which he preferred.

2.   Staff busy at work making out plan for CRIMSON; I decided that unless we had fairly positive indications of the presence of submarines we must accept submarine risk during last stages of our approach; carriers must look after themselves during the bombardment and we could ignore risk of contact with enemy surface forces. The bombardment must be indirect and for all practical purposes would be an area shoot.

3.   RAA reports that *Shah* cannot obtain requisite wind over deck for landing training owing to the low airs at present experienced in these parts; he suggested she should be sent to the Cape but with this I cannot agree as it would take her off the Station far too long. *Saratoga* states they consider 30 knots over the deck is necessary for the training of Avengers in escort carriers and 28 knots is necessary for operations; if this is correct it would appear that during quite a considerable part of the year the escort carriers armed with Avengers would be unable to operate.

5.   The Admiralty . . . concerning the attack on *Tirpitz* state that this had achieved good results but must be repeated; this would hold up

Victorious and they ask that if *Saratoga* is not particularly required her stay with the EF may be extended after 1 May.

8 April

Latest indications concerning the Japanese fleet suggest they may be moving towards the Philippines about the 15th; the question now arises whether the air will go with them, but this seems doubtful unless they again believe that Palau and the Philippines are seriously threatened.

3.   Papers received from Delhi give the outline of the new CULVERIN plan which has apparently been prepared under the personal direction of the PM with an *ad hoc* team of planners. . . . The naval forces are to include 15 cruisers, 45 destroyers, 2 Fleet carriers, 12 escort carriers assault loaded; counter measures by the enemy fleet are to be disregarded.

9 April

Signal from the Admiralty confirms that the Japanese air has returned to the Malayan Barrier; as regards CRIMSON they say I must be the best judge of whether it is possible and they will accept my decision. They would prefer a demonstration to standing by to implement CRIMSON if air goes E again, but presume CRIMSON will take place during demonstration if circumstances are favourable. They do not consider it necessary to consult US authorities as to which course of action they prefer. In reply I said CRIMSON would certainly be carried out during demonstration if Japanese air is reduced to an acceptable degree, but that present count suggested over 270 aircraft in, or within 3 hours' flying of, Sabang and that this number was likely to increase to 400 by the end of the week. The effect of CRIMSON would be transitory when the Japanese appreciated there was no follow up and it was for this reason that I felt the US might like to call the hand in which case I would play whatever card they preferred.

2.   Actually since the object of the practice is to tie Japanese air to the Western Barrier, it is necessary that this should be kept in mind all the time; it seems to me that a threat is more likely to achieve this than an operation such as CRIMSON which might well disclose the fact that we had nothing further up our sleeve. . . .

10 April

Truculent returned from patrol and reported she had attacked a convoy of 3 ships in the Malacca Straits on 28 March and sunk one with a possible hit on another; on 1 April she sank a 200 ton steamer by gunfire.

5.   In reply to my signal to the Admiralty about the atrocities commit-

ted by the Japanese on the crews of torpedoed independent ships, they say that no more escorts are forthcoming and ask if we can use air from Diego Garcia or use escort carriers; insufficient Catalinas are available to maintain any sort of effective patrol from Diego Garcia, and with regard to the escort carriers the difficulty lies as usual in providing destroyers or frigates for them. The total number of ships sunk during March in the Indian Ocean is 13, all out of convoy with the exception of one. This compares with 10 sunk in February of which 4 were in convoy and 8 in January of which none were in convoy.

11 April

2.   At 1045 I proceeded on board *Richelieu* with my flag flying and after inspecting a guard of honour addressed the ship's company in English with a French officer translating for me. The men were clean, well shaved and well turned out and appeared to react to any mild witticisms and to welcome references to co-operation with the Eastern Fleet in ejecting the Japanese from colonial possessions. . . .

3.   After lunch I held a conference on board the *Renown* to discuss operation CRIMSON and alternative operations. After some discussion it was generally agreed that a strike of some sort would have more effect in containing the Japanese than a demonstration without a strike. RAA and Captain Cassady of *Saratoga* were both confident that even with the present disposition of Japanese air forces it should be possible to bring off a strike against Sabang and at the same time give the Fleet reasonable fighter cover during the withrawal.

12 April

3.   I sent a signal to the Admiralty giving the alternatives to operation CRIMSON, i.e, a bombardment of Sabang with air strike limited to what was required to neutralise aerodromes in order to afford maximum fighter cover for bombarding ships; a seaborne air strike against Sabang with the carriers supported by the Fleet; a demonstration to the SW of Sumatra; and demonstration to the W of the Andamans. I stated that of the foregoing I should probably carry out a seaborne air strike since I considered this would have more effect in containing Japanese forces than demonstrating without a strike.

4.   I discussed with the AOC the question of a Liberator strike on the Port Blair aerodrome just before the dawn of D-day; after discussion we came to the conclusion that this might offset surprise at Sabang and consequently we should do nothing to put the Japanese on the alert.

13 April

Information now indicates that Japanese carriers at Singapore are embarking their aircraft in preparation for carrier operations; I feel that these will be directed towards the E rather than the W.

4. Captain Hillgarth (DOIS) has handed in a very interesting and valuable report on his visit to Australia and the meetings he had there with various authorities. Admiral Kinkaid[1] considers that a strong British Navel force should be sent to the Pacific to act under his operational command; he considers future operations in the Pacific depend entirely on Naval carrier strength. General MacArthur considers that the development of a road to China through Upper Burma is nonsense and that our main effort should be to take Singapore from the S via Sumatra. . . . [He] says he would welcome a British squadron under his command and made it clear he would expect it to operate under his orders. Both Kinkaid and MacArthur agree with our appreciation concerning the motives which prompted the Japanese to move their fleet to Singapore. . . .

14 April

Received a long signal addressed by SAC to COS giving the former's general views on the strategic situation. SAC still considers the AXIOM proposals are the best, i.e., it is wrong to fight in Burma which favours the enemy [and] where our naval and air superiority cannot be exploited; help given to China by opening the Ledo Road will arrive too late and would be at the expense of the air ferry route; right strategy is to develop the air ferry route and carry out amphibious operations; since the AXIOM party left India Pacific programme has been speeded up, but progress of Burma operations does not suggest that we can maintain major forces in the forward positions during the monsoon. Proposed pipe line into China cannot contribute to Pacific operations due to be carried out in the spring of 1945, and cannot be secured against Japanese infiltration. Reconquest of Burma should not be attempted, but if it is to be attempted he considers the best means is by way of an air borne operation directed against Rangoon. I notice that except in his opening comment the SAC makes no specific reference to CULVERIN.

[1]Adm Thomas C. Kinkaid US Navy (1888–1972): battleships 1907–13; ordnance engr 1913–17; *Pennsylvania* June 1916; Lt att Admy 1917–18; GO *Arizona* Europe & ME 1918–19; Lt-Cdr & COS USNF E Med 1922–4; *Isherwood* 1924; N Gun Fac Washington 1925–7; FGO *Texas*; N War Coll 1929–30; EO *Colorado* 1933–4; Bur Nav; *Indianapolis* 1937–8; NA Rome 1938–March 1941; Des Sqdn 8 June–Nov 1941; RA Cru Div 6, Pac; Coral Sea, Midaway; Cdr TF16 *Enterprise*; Guadalcanal Aug–Nov 1942; Cdr N Pac Force Jan 1943; Aleutians; VA June 1943; Cdr Allied N Forces SW Pac & 7th F Nov 1943; Philippines 1944; Adm April 1945; E Sea Frontier Jan–June 1946; Atl Res F Jan 1947–May 1950; Ret List 1950.

15 April

I made my first landing in a Tiger Moth and only bounced three times.[1]

2.   Received a signal from Bombay to say that an ammunition ship had blown up in Victoria Docks, that these docks were wrecked and that several ships had been gutted and sunk including the *El Hind* and *Jalapadma*.[2] Apparently a large amount of landing craft stores and supplies have been destroyed.

16 April

2.   Latest intelligence reports suggest that the situation with regard to enemy air in Sumatra is more or less unchanged so I decided definitely to carry out operation COCKPIT providing the situation in respect of air does not deteriorate.[3] The two U-boats on their way to Penang appear to have been delayed and should now pass clear ahead of the track of the Fleet. Commencing at 1030 the Fleet started to leave harbour. . . . The Fleet was formed in two groups with the battleships and four 6" cruisers in one group, screened by 9 destroyers, and the *Renown* with two carriers and *London*[4] in the second group screened by 6 destroyers.

3.   Apart from the fact that ships were as usual using far too bright lights for signalling, the Fleet work was not bad though ships were obviously out of practice. The *ad hoc* staff organisation in the *Queen Elizabeth* and the *ad hoc* arrangements for this ship which is not fitted as a Fleet flagship worked fairly well on the whole but of course fell far short of what are usually considered to be minimum requirements.

17 April

2.   At 0930 speed of the Fleet was reduced to 12 knots and destroyers were refuelled from cruisers and *Renown*. Most destroyers took far too long to secure and start oiling, but *Napier* fuelled well from *Newcastle* at 16 knots without a breast or spring. Speed of the Fleet was increased to 16 knots at 1400.

3.   The Catalina patrols proved a distinct embarrassment since their IFF did not register on our radar. During the day ships were exercised in tak-

---

[1]De Havilland Tiger Moth: basic trainer, 109mph.

[2]The ammunition ship was *Fort Stikine*, 7142gt, MWT. *El Hind*: LSI (L), 1938, 5314gt, 12k, Scindia SN Co. *Jalapadma*: 1929, 3935gt, 10.5k, Scindia SN Co. Ten ships of 37,000gt were wrecked; thousands of people were killed or injured.

[3]The RN had a healthy respect, though unduly prolonged, for Japanese anti-ship bombers. There was some evidence of a recent build up from *c.*270 to *c.*400 planes.

[4]*London*: 1929, 9850t, 8×8in, 8×4in, 8tt, 32.25k; modernised later in 1944.

ing up cruising dispositions against air attack and also in blind barrage procedure; the latter did not go too well since some ships were firing much too high and others far too low; *Richelieu* slew off the mark in opening fire but her station keeping is quite good.

4. Signal from COMINCH in which he asked for *Saratoga* to leave not later than 10 May as she requires a refit.

18 April

Cloudy with occasional rain squalls and practically no wind. No flying is taking place from the carriers during the approach in order to avoid disclosing our presence. . . . I detached *Nigeria* and *Ceylon*[1] to join Force 70 (carrier force) in order to increase the A/A fire of that force. . . .

19 April

Cloudy at first but clearer later with maximum visibility; flat calm, practically no wind. At 0530 Force 70, which by then was approx. 20 miles eastward of Force 69 started to fly off. Force 69 was manoeuvred to make contact with Force 70 prior to flying on and came in sight at 0815 when flying on commenced; what little wind there was shifted to the NW and this was all in our favour. First reports indicated that the strike had been successful inasmuch as the oil tanks were set on fire, two medium sized merchant ships were hit with heavy bombs, two escort destroyers strafed and set on fire, warehouses, radio and radar stations hit by bombs, 21 aircraft destroyed on the ground at Sabang and 3 at Lho'nga. There was no fighter opposition but one American fighter was shot down by light A/A; the pilot was picked up by *Tactician*[2] who had been stationed there for the purpose. Later it was learnt that the rescue by *Tactician* was a fine piece of work inasmuch as she had to proceed to a position only 2 miles from a shore battery which was firing on her, and was also being approached by an escort destroyer which was finally driven off by attacks from our fighters.

2. The two Forces were able to remain in reasonably close support of one another whilst flying on was in progress and as soon as this was completed course was shaped to the westward. About 10 a.m. two enemy aircraft appeared on the radar screen approaching the Fleet to the eastward; in spite of cloud these were promptly intercepted by *Saratoga*'s fighters and shot down; both were Kates.[3] A similar fate

[1]*Ceylon*: 1943, 8875t, 9×6in, 8×4in, 6tt, 31.5k.
[2]*Tactician*: 'T' class s/m, 1942.
[3]Nakajima B5N 'Kate': 1937, 1 torpedo, 235mph.

befell a third Kate which approached shortly afterwards; weather had cleared by this time and the smoke of the burning Kate was clearly visible to the stern of the Fleet.

4.   During the afternoon *Saratoga* flew across some absolutely first class photographs taken by her wing leader of the bombing of Sabang. I made a signal to *Saratoga* thanking her for the photographs and asking if I was correct in assuming they were taken by 'Jumping Joe', the nickname of Wing Cdr Clifton. *Saratoga* replied that this was quite correct, but Joe could never be induced to open his mouth. One of these strong silent men I presume.[1]

20 April

2.   During the forenoon the heavy ships carried out a 15" throw-off blind shoot using radar against *Ceylon;* the shooting on the whole was very good and it is now clear that by shooting to radar range it should be possible to obtain straddles very early and, what is more important, hold the range. *Richelieu* was using coloured shell bursts which gave most impressive vertical splashes; I am not aware what progress has been made in producing bigger and better splashes to assist radar spotting forward shoot and feel this is a matter of great importance.

3.   As our information suggested it was most unlikely we should meet submarines I detached cruisers and destroyers to exercise independently during the day, and also seized the occasion to carry out manoeuvres with the battleships; *Richelieu* was very well handled during these exercises which included a number of equal speed manoeuvres. During the afternoon cruisers carried out blind radar torpedo attack on the battle fleet and the carriers carried out fighter interception and other exercises until 1730 when the Fleet was formed into three groups for the night preparatory to entering harbour. . . .

21 April

4.   At 1530 I held a conference of Flag and Commanding Officers to discuss the operation, lessons learnt, etc. The Captain of the *Saratoga* was most generous in the tributes he paid to *Tactician* for the rescue of their pilot and I feel sure this incident has been of the greatest value in promoting good feeling between the American Task Force and our-

[1]Cdr Joseph C. Clifton US Navy: b 1908; US N Acad 1926–30; Lt 1938; carrier flying appts; Flight Training O, Miami 1941; Lt-Cdr June 1942; CO Ftr Sqdn 12 *Saratoga*; Cdr Aug 1943; Cdr Air Grp 12; Capt (T) April 1946; EO & CO *Wasp* 1946; Air Warfare Div, ONO; Cdr Transport Sqdn 8 June 1949–Dec 1951; CO *Corson* Dec 1951; training & staff appts; RA 1958; Ret List 1963. Somerville had his leg pulled; it did not require copious helpings of spirits to induce 'Joe' to talk.

selves. I informed the Captain of the *Saratoga* privately that I had received instructions he was to leave the EF not later than 10 May, and it seemed to me it would be a pity for him to return to Australia without carrying out [another] operation; I had in mind that we might do an attack on Batavia and asked him to look into this matter from the point of view of distances, etc. Batavia seemed to me the best place to strike since it was out of range either of the VLRs from Ceylon or the Liberators from Australia; Sourabaya the alternative target had already been attacked three times from Australia and presumably the scale of defence was a good deal better than that of Batavia which has so far been immune. We had hardly finished discussing this matter when a signal was received from the 1st Sea Lord quoting a request from COMINCH that we should consider an attack on Sourabaya by *Saratoga* during her return passage; this attack should be supported by elements of the EF.

22 April

2.   . . . In order to make an undetected approach to Batavia it would be necessary to pass S and W of Cocos and possibly to the eastward of Christmas Island; the distance to be flown over land is in excess of that required for Sourabaya, and since the latter is undoubtedly a more important target as it includes the oil refinery, it was unanimously agreed that we should plunk for Sourabaya. I sent off telegrams to the 1st Sea Lord to this effect, and have also sent signals to the Commander, 7th Fleet asking if arrangements can be made for submarine patrols in the Lombok and Sunda Straits.[1] *Saratoga* suggested that *Renown* and *Richelieu* with some cruisers and destroyers would afford enough cover for the operation, but I feel myself that to leave the battleships behind would have an adverse effect on them and that as they are available there is no [reason] why we should not have the maximum insurance. In addition to this the most valuable opportunities for Fleet training would occur whilst the latter was on passage to and from the objective.

24 April

3.   I visited *Illustrious* at 1115 and addressed her ship's company, and afterwards had a talk with the pilots and observers who took part in the operation. There is no doubt that this operation has had a most stimulating effect on all the air crews. I took occasion to point out that owing to the lack of wind it was necessary to carry out deck landing training of the Avengers in *Illustrious* and for this purpose it would be necessary to replace Barracuda squadrons temporarily by Avengers; this of course is

[1]Adm Kinkaid.

in fact to prepare for TRANSOM. A signal was received from the Admiralty regarding the movements of major landing craft from the Mediterranean to the EF during the autumn which suggests that amphibious operations may be going to take place in this Theatre next spring; it is still most embarrassing to have no proper policy and in particular not to know what the requirements are likely to be in connection with landing craft bases, etc.

370.   *To Mountbatten*

24 April 1944

2.   It seems fairly clear now that the Japanese worked some deception on us that has led us to over-estimate considerably the probable air forces available in the Western Malayan Barrier; based on the estimate we had when the operation was launched I did not think we should be justified in committing ships to a bombardment but when on D-1 there were indications of an over-estimate of their air strength, we were already so far committed to the approach that it was not possible to change the operation.

7.   With regard to the next party, as it takes place outside SEAC I presume you are not directly interested, but I will keep you informed of course about dates, etc.

8.   ... I can say that so far as the air was concerned it would have been a particularly happy moment to have carried out CULVERIN; the Japanese are evidently hard pressed to the E and I doubt very much if they could have got together anything like the numbers to oppose us that were forecast in CULVERIN plan. ...

371.   *To Tennant*

25 April 1944

8.   Not having been to sea with the Fleet for some time I rather felt, when I embarked in *'Lizzy'*, I might be a bit adrift, more especially as she is not fitted as a Fleet flagship; however, all the old tricks came back in a flash, and to my great surprise my signalling was of quite high a standard; the party certainly did everyone a hell of a lot of good even if it was not a very important party, but the Yanks acted a bit too jealous and shot down the Bettys[1] with their fighters, before the boats had a chance to use their guns.

[1]There is some confusion here; No. 369, para. 2 states they were 'Kates'; the Mitsubishi 'Betty' was a twin engined bomber, as opposed to a single engined torpedo bomber.

372. *To his wife*

2 May 1944

The Kandy party are all twiddling their thumbs but so far have not interfered with me. Dickie on Saturday again raised the question that the EF should be under him etc. but I said that if I was at the Admiralty I should certainly not agree as neither he nor his Naval advisors know enough about Fleet work. Referring to the Press reports about Sabang[1] he said of course he had not passed it but his press advisor considered it was necessary to boost the SEAC and that he'd been told that if anything went wrong in Burma he would be blamed and not George Giffard. I told D that was his own fault because he always allowed his name to appear. In N. Africa Eisenhower's name was rarely mentioned and no one connected Eisenhower with any results achieved or mistakes made by Monty.[2] It's really just an intense form of egoism fostered by people like Micky Hodges, Gerald Langley and others.

373. *Desk diary, 1944*

2 May

2.   Aden reported a submarine had been damaged by aircraft to the S of Socotra; *Parrett, Raider* and *Falmouth*[3] have all been ordered to the spot to hunt.

4.   At 1100 I went on board the USS *Dunlap* and was taken round the ship by Captain Smith, COMDESDIV 12, and the Captain of *Dunlap*, Cdr Iversen.[4] These ships total about 2200 tons and are well laid out except that the top weight in some cases appears to be excessive and unnecessary; I understand this has been cut down in later classes. The plot is very well arranged in what used to be the charthouse on the foc'sle deck and there is a repeat PPI from the plot PPI on the bridge; the latter has all the disadvantages of being enclosed and was severely criticised by Captain Smith.

---

[1] A press release had suggested that Mountbatten had planned and staged the attack on Sabang.

[2] Gen (later Field Marshal Viscount, of Alamein) Sir Bernard L. Montgomery (1887–1976): R Warwks; Temp Capt 1914; seriously wded 1914; Brig Maj; Staff Coll 1920; Instr 1926; Lt Col Mid E & India 1929–32; Instr, Quetta 1934–7; 9 Bde 1937; 8 Inf Div Palestine 1938; 3 Div BEF 1939–40; V Corps 1940–2; 8 Army 1942; N Af, Sicily, Italy; cded D-Day landings; FM & 2nd Army Grp 1944; CIGS 1946; DSAC, NATO 1951.

[3] *Parrett*: 1943, 1460t, 2×4in, 20k. *Raider*: 1943, 1705t, 4×4.7in, 8tt, 34k. *Falmouth*: 1932, 1045t, 2×4in, 16k.

[4] USS *Dunlap, Fanning, Cummings*: 1936–7, 1465–1480t, 4×5in, 12tt, 36.5k; the destroyers escorting *Saratoga*; displacement given in text is fully loaded.

5. These destroyers have the usual bunk rooms and cafeteria system for messing; I am convinced this will never be popular with our men; the officers are very crowded, 17 being carried in lieu of the normal 8 in peace time. With regard to the armament I was impressed by the enclosed gun shields for A and B guns which seemed a very workman-like job and allowed the mountings themselves to remain in first class order.

3 May

Aden reports that a second aircraft has now attacked the submarine and the latter is unable to dive; . . .

4. At 1030 we received the welcome news from *Falmouth* that the German U-boat was close in shore 160 miles S of Guardafui, that she had blown herself up and her crew were escaping ashore; *Falmouth* was landing a party to round them up.[1]

5. I sent a signal to the Admiralty about my intentions for A/S protection of independent shipping; these are to form a hunting group of 2 escort carriers, 6 frigates and 3 sloops which should be ready to operate by the beginning of June. When the Fleet returns from TRANSOM a few Fleet destroyers may be available for a short period, but unless further frigates are forthcoming it will not be possible to operate 2 more escort carriers which will be available by then.

4 May

4. After lunch a series of meetings was held and a number of matters discussed; among these was the question of who should issue the communique about operation TRANSOM. SAC agreed to this being issued by General MacArthur and that I should give the latter the terms of the communique which I pointed out should be based on the following considerations:–

(a) The aircraft making the attack would be identified as British and American carrier borne aircraft.

(b) If the Fleet is not sighted it is desirable to leave the Japanese in doubt concerning the origin and identity of the force.

(c) If the Fleet is sighted and the identity of the ships probably established, the Japanese must be led to believe that only a part of the Eastern Fleet was engaged.

(d) No communique should be issued until it is reasonably certain that the Allied Fleet will not be intercepted by superior Japanese forces.

[1]*U852.*

5.   The SAC showed me a telegram he had prepared to send to the Admiralty in which he complained that he had not been informed about operation COCKPIT; I pointed out that this was quite incorrect. . . . I suggested the Admiralty were hardly concerned with the breakdown of his organisation and the signal was amended accordingly. Whilst I agree it is necessary SEAC should be kept fully informed of Fleet matters which may affect SEAC I feel there is a danger, especially when there is so little to do at Kandy, that attempts will be made to interfere with Fleet matters which have nothing to do with SEAC.

374.   *To Admiral Fraser*

6 May 1944

. . . I told ABC that no-one could wish for a better relief . . . I fully realise of course that after being so long in the saddle it is time for me to get off and give a younger chap the opportunity to ride a much better course. I am sure you will appreciate that I shall leave this appointment with great regret, more especially as it looks now as if things are likely to happen and keep on happening.

2.   In many respects it has been a most disappointing job up to date as we have not had the force available to take the offensive and have had to keep on the defensive with inadequate, and for long periods, merely skeleton forces. However, we have done our best to prepare the station as a springboard for future operations, though I have no doubt you will find plenty to criticise when you come out here, as this is most definitely a Ford, not a Rolls Royce outfit.

8.   With regard to SEAC HQ I fear I am in rather bad odour as I have had to disagree on so many occasions with the views which are held there concerning organisation and other matters. Dickie Mountbatten and I are on very good personal terms, but the one difficulty has been his obvious desire to have the Fleet under his orders. . . .

9.   Our liaison with the air in Ceylon has always been excellent and is even better now with the arrival of Durston.[1]

11.   Although I shall be very glad to see you again, Bruce old boy, it won't break my heart if your departure from the UK is delayed since the idea of the next job for which I am earmarked fills me with gloom and despondency. I would much sooner have command of a trawler.

---

[1]Air Vice Marshal A. Durston: formerly of Coastal Cmd; Snr Air SO, Ceylon Jan 1943.

375. *Desk diary, 1944*

6 May

I saw Cdr Ashby, RNVR,[1] who has been in charge of the ML's on the Arakan Coast; he said that both RIN and South African crews had done extremely well and that their active service operations put a fine finish on the flotilla. He was most anxious that these craft should be rearmed with 6 pdrs and 4" howitzers in lieu of 3 pdrs and 3" as the heavier armanent would prove much more effective and the boats are quite able to carry it. Although attacked by air on several occasions only one boat had been hit and in this case the bomb had gone straight through without exploding.

3.   I embarked in *Queen Elizabeth* with my staff at 4 p.m. and sailed shortly afterwards, *Saratoga* and *Illustrious* having preceded *Queen Elizabeth* out of harbour. *Cumberland*[2] and *Sussex* were arriving as we left, the former to dock and the latter to collect and exchange ratings before proceeding to the UK to refit.

4.   Course was shaped to pass round the S of Ceylon and meet the Trincomalee force at the R/V tomorrow noon.

7 May

2.   There were heavy rain squalls during the early part of the morning but weather cleared later on. The smoke of Force B, the Trincomalee force, was sighted when they were still some 28 miles away, only a few puffs, but quite enough to give their position away; they were picked up by surface warning radar set a long time before they came in sight. The force R/V'd at 1215 and were then sorted out into Force 65 consisting of the battleships and *Renown*, 2 cruisers and 9 destroyers as a screen; Force 66 consisting of the carriers, 2 cruisers and 6 destroyers. *Renown* was not placed with the carriers in order to economise her fuel and also since we should not be within any but very long range of enemy air during the passage; consequently her heavy A/A armament would not be required.

3.   The latest enemy intelligence still indicates the major concentration of the Japanese Fleet at Singapore and possibly an additional battleship and 5 carriers proceeding to Singapore from Japan; there are indications, however, that part of this force my be going to the Philippines.

---

[1]Tempy Actg Cdr R. R. W. Ashby RNVR: Lt Nov 1937; *Salsette* (Comb Ops) Nov 1943; SO Coastal Forces 1944.
[2]*Cumberland*: 1928, 10,000t, 8×8in, 8×4in, 31.5k.

8 May

2.   A signal received from the Admiralty says that *Victorious* should arrive mid-June, *Indomitable* mid-July and *Formidable* late July.

9 May

3.   Range and inclination exercises, exercises for taking up air attack dispositions and manoeuvring against air attack, and a rehearsal by *Illustrious* of her air strike with subsequent attack on Force 65 were carried out during the day. *Illustrious*'s flying off appears to be uncommonly slow at present but her Avenger squadrons are still somewhat green.

4.   Latest enemy intelligence suggest move of Japanese Fleet from Singapore, S of Borneo and towards the Philippines. Latest estimate of aircraft in Java is 40 of which the bulk are fighters.

5.   With the exception of one cruiser and 2 destroyers all ships with Force 65 have now got TBS which is certainly a most valuable addition providing its use is not abused when in the vicinity of the enemy. It is necessary to ensure, however, that other forms of signalling are not allowed to lapse merely because the TBS is so easy and efficient.

10 May

2.   *Saratoga* carried out rehearsal of her strike attacking Force 66; fighter umbrella stationed over Force 65 made a very good interception at 40 miles.

3.   At 0900 we commenced oiling destroyers under rather difficult weather conditions with the result that springs were being parted and hoses carried away. . . .

11 May

2.   *Saratoga* flew off her strike at 0615 and at 0730 attacked Force 65; this was an extremely good attack and far more finished in every respect than the previous one by *Illustrious*. I consider I was a bit slow in turning the Fleet to keep the A arcs open as the first flight came in but we were well placed for the subsequent attacks.

4.   Destroyers exercised separately throughout the day and carried out throw off shoots against Corsairs representing torpedo bombers making a high speed approach; the shooting was not good and we have a long way to go yet before we are up to standard.

5.   After dark destroyers carried out night attack on the battle fleet; this was done in 3 divisions rather than on the old fashioned plan before radar came into operation; it was quite clear to me that if these attacks are to

succeed it is necessary first of all for the destroyers to cover the Fleet on as broad a front as possible, and to operate properly, nothing larger than sub-divisions. It was quite easy for me to see what the destroyers were doing on the plot and for ships to open fire at 20,000 yards.

12 May

Overcast at first but clear and fine later with maximum visibility. The combined strike from *Saratoga* and *Illustrious* flew off for exercises at 0600. They seemed a long time in forming up and moving off; they went out to 100 miles and then returned to attack Forces 65 and 66 in two groups. The attack on Force 65 by *Saratoga* group was very well executed; the strike came in to about 6 miles and then remained in the cloud circling. Being inside the ground wave of the radar it was impossible to keep track of them and their dive through the cloud caught us slightly unprepared.

4. I received a report from the Commander[1] of the *Queen Elizabeth* in connection with a conversation he had with the Commander of the *Richelieu*. The latter made no bones about the fact that they took no interest in the Japanese war, and that their eyes were turned west towards the restoration of France. The men he stated were good, and the officers good technicians but the latter took no trouble about the men. De Gaulle was considered merely an English figurehead and if he came on board the *Richelieu* he would be thrown overboard.

13 May

2. Carried out heavy and throw off A/A firings in the forenoon whilst the destroyers exercised independently. The destroyers have benefited greatly by this opportunity to exercise divisional and sub-divisional formations, attacks, etc. which they had been greatly in need of but are unable to carry out normally owing to their continuous employment on the screen or for escorts.

14 May

4. Colombo now reports that there is again serious doubt about the position of the Japanese fleet; whilst some units may have moved to the Philippines there is no evidence that there has been a general movement from the Singapore area. I trust, therefore, the Japanese will not get wind of us during our approach.

[1]Cdr N. K. Tod: Lt 1932; *Ajax* 1938; Lt-Cdr Jan 1940; *Devonshire* 1941; *Norfolk* 1942; *Queen Elizabeth* 1943; Cdr June 1944.

15 May

2. To my great surprise Admirals Kinkaid and Christie with Cdre Pope, RAN,[1] came on board to see me [at Exmouth Gulf]; Kinkaid had flown all the way from Brisbane and the other two from Fremantle. Kinkaid informed me that the SW Pacific forces were making an attack on Wakde Island, W of Hollandia on the 17th, and that the Pacific fleet would be attacking Saipan about the same time. He said that surface forces and air cover in the SW Pacific operations were pretty thin but be thought they would chance it. He gave me the latest estimate of the positions of the Japanese fleet; these suggest they are pretty scattered between Singapore and the Philippines which is satisfactory.
6. At 1630 the Fleet proceeded; . . .

376. *To his wife*

16 May 1944

Our present party is a very long one and somewhat ambitious but so far all has gone well. Today is the critical day as we are making the approach and everything depends on our not being spotted before darkness sets in. Unfortunately it's absolutely gin clear with maximum visibility and I imagine that an aircraft would spot the fleet 100 miles away so we must just trade on our luck and hope for the best. Tomorrow we strike and after that I don't mind because we will have got in our blow and if they strike back we must look after ourselves. This long sea trip has done everyone good and the fleet is now shaping well and know their stuff – it's disappointing to think that this may be my last chance to use it but if it proves to be a good party I can't complain. You probably won't hear much about it in the press as we want to keep the Japs guessing who we are and where we come from – the press boys are all very disgruntled in consequences as they want to write up all and sundry. They always think that the object of operations is to provide them with stories! MacA will issue the communique as it's in his parish. . . . incidentally a little deception scheme we arranged before we left is now working and should make them believe that at this moment we are in the Bay of Bengal and apparently heading towards the Andamans.

[1]Cdre C.J. Pope RAN: Capt 1929; *Penguin* (depot ship, Sydney) 1939; *California* 1940; Cdre 2 Cl & NOIC Fremantle 1944.

377. *Desk diary, 1944*

17 May

... All quiet during the night and no sign that we have been spotted. At 0630 we arrived at the flying off position, some 90 miles offshore, and started flying off. The strike formed up and departed soon after 0715; Forces 65 and 66 were manoeuvred as requisite to keep in support of one another and to be in a position for recovering the strike on their return. *Illustrious* reported that 2 of her Avengers crashed on taking off but the crews were rescued. ... Sourabaya was alerted at 0830 which is just about the time the strike should be over their targets. About 0920 the radar showed the strike returning and the latter were in sight at 0950 in good formation and started to fly on at 1002 finishing at 1050. The wind was at 130° and about 10 knots which was satisfactory. *Illustrious* reported all her aircraft had returned, whilst *Saratoga* reported one of her Avengers, with Squadron Leader Rowbotham, had been shot down by flak, but the crew had been seen getting away in their dinghy and appeared to be making for a native boat not far off. Unfortunately the position was very close to the harbour and I very much fear the *Puffer*, stationed as air/sea rescue some 30 miles from Sourabaya, will be unable to make contact.[1] First reports show complete surprise was again effected, that there was no fighter opposition and that targets had all been covered satisfactorily; 10 merchant ships totalling 35,000 tons had been hit by bombs and one of these was seen to blow up; the oil refinery was completely destroyed, two floating docks hit by bombs; the naval base was well strafed and the Braak engineering works probably entirely destroyed; 2 enemy aircraft were shot down and 19 destroyed on the ground whilst others were damaged.
2.   After recovering the strike, course was shaped to the SW to avoid giving the impression to any shadowers that we were making for Exmouth Gulf. During the afternoon *Saratoga* dropped some extremely good photographs of the bombing taken by Group Leader Clifton ('Jumping Joe'); these suggested that there were at least 5 submarines in the harbour and that in view of the number of ships present it would probably have paid to have carried out a second strike, but by the time this was fully appreciated we were too far from the target; I feel we must make a reasonable distance to the SW from land before dark in view of the vulnerability of the Fleet to attack at dusk or at night. We require more practice still for our night barrages and of course have no night fighters to operate against such attacks.

[1]USS *Puffer*: 1942, 1525/2415t, 10tt, 1×5in, 20.5/10k. The aircrew were taken prisoner.

3. The enemy made no retaliation of any sort against our strike; this was very disappointing as I particularly wished the gun and fighter umbrella to have some practice. . . .

18 May

Sourabaya was alerted at midnight and remained alerted until 0300. This was obviously on account of the Liberator attack from Australia which was due about that time. There were no signs at all of any enemy aircraft during the night or that we had been shadowed. At daylight we took up A/A day cruising order as we are still within range of enemy aircraft, but shaped course to the S at 18 knots.
3. The association of the American Task Force with the Eastern Fleet has been of the happiest from the day they joined up until the day they left; I feel quite sure that when they return to the States they will have a good word to say for us and that their expressions of regret at leaving us were really genuine.

378. *To his wife*

18 May 1944

Our US friends left us today and we gave them a great send-off – the whole fleet in single line and as they passed down the line on opposite course they were cheered by all ships. It's interesting to note how formal the Yanks always are. Their men were all fallen in meticulously and dressed in white whereas ours were all massed on the foc'sles in shorts and no shirts. . . . The SO made some very nice signals to me to which I sent suitable replies. The problem now is to get back without the Japs realising that we are a bit shorn but my appreciation is that they are much too nervous to have a tilt at us. Just as well! . . . [I] have been busy today censoring some of the press stories so as to eliminate any suggestion that I or my fleet was present – these damn reporters do their best to suggest it in spite of my instructions on the subject. . . . I should think this is one of the longest 'strikes' in the war – first and last a matter of nearly 8000 miles.

379. *To General MacArthur*

c. 19 May 1944

Operation TRANSOM

Operation carried out according to plan and with complete success.

2.   I suggest a communique be issued on the following lines on receipt of this message.

'American and British aircraft carriers operating in conjunction with supporting Forces launched an air attack on the Japanese Naval Base at Sourabaya after dawn on Wednesday, 17 May. Complete surprise was achieved and considerable damage was caused by direct hits on shipping, naval base installations, oil refinery and aerodromes as follows:

(a)   Hits were scored on 10 ships in harbour, including a small tanker and possibly a destroyer. One ship was seen to blow up and others probably sank. A hospital ship close to the target area was carefully avoided.

(b)   Two floating docks were badly damaged by 5000 lbs of bombs.

(c)   The oil refinery at Wonokromo was completely destroyed. A direct hit demolished the power house. Storage tanks and stills were set on fire. Smoke rising to 5000 feet.

(d)   Direct hits caused considerable damage to Naval installations. The important Braak Naval engineering works were completely destroyed by 15,000 lbs of bombs.

(e)   Total of 21 enemy aircraft destroyed as follows: Two were shot down. At Tanjoeng Perak aerodrome 4 aircraft were destroyed on the ground. At Malang airfield a hangar was set on fire and 15 aircraft were destroyed on the ground. Many other aircraft were damaged at both aerodromes.

3.   Despite considerable light A/A fire only one of our aircraft failed to return. No other casualties nor damage were sustained by our forces.'

4.   For your personal information, strike consisted of 12 Avengers, 18 Dauntless,[1] 24 Hellcats from *Saratoga*, 18 Avengers, 16 Corsairs from *Illustrious*. Two Avengers from *Illustrious* crashed on taking off, crews rescued. One Avenger from *Saratoga* started but had to turn back . . .

5.   My general impression is that poor look-out was being maintained by the enemy and that his fighter defence was quite inadequate. No attempt appears to have been made to locate or shadow the Fleet after the attack although weather was clear and sighting was possible outside Radar range.

6.   This concludes a profitable and very happy association of Task Group 58.5 with the Eastern Fleet.

[1]Douglas Dauntless USA: 1939, bomb load 1000lb, 4mg, 252mph.

7. We all appreciate so much the opportunity you have given us to stage this small play in your Theatre.

8. I shall be grateful if you will convey to Admirals Kinkaid and Christie my sincere thanks for their most valuable co-operation and assistance throughout this operation.

380. *To his wife*

20 May 1944

I am so damned angry. After explaining most carefully to MacArthur that if we were not sighted it was most important not to give any indication of the identity of the supporting forces and after framing the communique so that nothing was disclosed, he goes and puts in a lot of blah about how the force was composed of units from Mountbatten's, MacArthur's and Nimitz's commands and included French and Dutch ships. This of course discloses that the EF took part . . . I suppose these damn Supreme Commanders feel they must have their names in the papers all the time. . . . we are busy doing day and night exercises all the time, – it's even more strenuous than the operation itself. We shall have had no fresh vegs for the best part of 3 weeks by the time we get back and the water has to be rationed pretty severely so it's not exactly yachting. . . .

381. *Desk diary, 1944*

20 May

. . . At 0700 I put the VA in charge of the Fleet since I intend to give him, the RA and the Com[modore] (D)[1] as much opportunity as possible to exercise independently whilst we are in waters free from submarines.

3. At 2030 we carried out a very good night attack exercise with the destroyers attacking the Fleet. The destroyers used the new technique of attacking on as wide a front as possible and carrying out final synchronised attacks. The night was pitch dark and thus furnished an excellent example of how radar revolutionises night attack procedure.

21 May

2. Throughout the passage a morning and evening search was carried out by Avengers since we cannot by any means exclude the possibility of

[1]Adms Power and Moody and Capt A. L. Poland: Capt *Black Swan* June 1939; *Nile* Feb 1941; *Jervis* Feb 1942; *St George* (I of Man) Feb 1943; Cdre (D) Eastern F *Woolwich* April 1944.

a sortie by the Japanese Fleet to cut us off on our return; in this connection MacArthur's disclosure in the communique is unfortunate.

3. Exercises of various sorts were carried out throughout the day including fighter direction; the very marked improvement which better radar and better communications has effected in fighter direction during the two years I have been out here is most noticeable.

5. I received a signal from the PM to say that he was studying our operations with great interest and would like a cabled report from me and considered operations suggested that the Japanese were not alert, and asked for results of submarine reccos in Sumatra and any information concerning the Sunda Straits, Java, etc. I intend to reply in due course through the First Sea Lord since I feel it is usually undesirable for Cs-in-C to engage in personal messages with the PM, and I have had experience of the unfortunate results which may accrue from such exchanges.

23 May

3. The Admiralty informed me that the arrival of the *Victorious* is delayed; this will involve deferring *Illustrious*'s refit as we must have at least one carrier out here. An urgent requirement is to give the squadrons of *Formidable* and *Indomitable* some deck landing training in order to have them ready by the time the carriers arrive; it looks to me as if we shall have to use *Unicorn* for this.

24 May

4. During the forenoon we carried out a blind radar approach and attack by destroyers on the Fleet to simulate night attack conditions and to enable the accuracy of plotting and blind laying of guns to be constantly checked. On the whole the radar results were very good and I feel that we now have good prospects of obtaining effective results with blind fire at 20,000 yards, though if circumstances admit it is still preferable to have a point of aim with starshell at 14,000 yards. The long range high speed torpedoes of the Japanese Fleet make it essential that, if circumstances admit, we should keep them abaft the beam and open fire at the longest range which is likely to produce results.[1]

382. *To his wife*

24 May 1944

There are indications of a nice concentration of U-boats waiting to give us a hearty cheer on our return. This I imagine is due to

---

[1]The fearsome 'Long Lance': 24in dia, fast, long range & high explosive power.

MacArthur's and the PM's indications about the EF being employed on this operation. It does annoy me having these extra hazards all for nothing. More especially as the weather has turned really sour, proper SW Monsoon stuff with rain and low visibility which may well make it impossible to operate our aircraft. Given clear weather and plenty of air, one can hope to keep the U-boats down but in thick weather it's another matter and I shall be glad when I have the fleet back safely tucked into bed. . . .

383.   *To his wife*

25 May 1944

The weather cleared again today and the sun returned to fry us like a lot of poached eggs, as the wind has been on the quarter. My problem now is to get the party back without giving these blasted U-boats a chance of getting at us and it's none too easy. I'm banking on the fact that they will expect me to expect an attack and that consequently I'll make an unusual approach. Hence I shall make a normal one and hope it comes off all right – we shall have plenty of air to cover us anyway.

384.   *Desk diary, 1944*

28 May

3.   I found on arrival a personal signal from the First Sea Lord to say that Admiral Nimitz would like a continuance of operations by the Eastern Fleet against the Malayan Barrier in order to assist the Pacific Fleet by maintaining pressure. It is unfortunate that for some time we shall only have one carrier as this must of necessity limit the scope of our operations.

30 May

3.   RAA and the Captain of the *Illustrious*[1] arrived to discuss future operations. After some discussion it was agreed that for *Illustrious* to operate singly against any target it would be necessary to reduce her strike to one squadron of Barracudas and to put an additional squadron of fighters in. At the moment there are no additional squadrons of fighters operationally fit and it will be some 3 weeks before their training can be completed. With regard to targets, the most suitable one for a single carrier attack appears to be Port Blair; this has been attacked on several

[1]Rear Adm Moody & Capt Lambe.

occasions by Liberators at night, but the bombing under these conditions is not very accurate, and it is believed that precision bombing by Barracudas on selected targets is likely to do more damage. *Victorious* should be available for operations by the end of June, and *Illustrious* must proceed to South Africa to refit during first part of July. *Indomitable* is not likely to be operationally ready until the latter part of July. When two carriers are available another strike on the aerodromes at Kota Raja may be considered together with the photographic reconnaissance required for some of the beaches in that area.

31 May

3.   I received a paper from Kandy on the subject of the organisation for planning. The War Staff and the Cs-in-C's planners are directed by the SAC to propose measures for better integration of planning; the paper they sent in points out that there is a fundamental difference of opinion between the War Staff and the Cs-in-C's planners which cannot be reconciled; it amounts in fact as to whether the Cs-in-C or the War Staff are to be considered as the SAC's principal advisors. The War Staff maintain it is their function to prepare plans and that whilst proposals from the Cs-in-C would be considered they would not necessarily be included, and that it is the main function of the Cs-in-C to execute plans which have been prepared by the War Staff and approved by the SAC.
4.   This is obviously an attempt to create finally an organisation similar to that at General MacArthur's HQ and directly contrary to that which obtains at Allied HQ in N Africa.

1 June

3.   . . . I discussed the proposed carrier strikes with members of the SAC's staff; after a wealth of talk I found they had no suggestions to make. I discussed clandestine operations with General Lamplough and Captain Garnons-Williams; on a recent occasion a COPP party landed from a submarine and whilst ashore caused an alarm. The party returned safely but with the second mission, to ascertain the possibility of an air strip, unexecuted. Returning to this area two days later the leader of the COPP party expressed the intention of landing again to complete the survey; the Captain of the submarine said that this was ill-advised, not so much on the score of danger to the submarine but that the alarm having once been raised it was unlikely that the party would succeed. However, the leader of the COPP party insisted he must go and was therefore landed with the result that after a short time heavy firing was heard including machine gun fire and the COPP party failed to return. After

discussion it was decided that in future the CO of the submarine would give the ruling as to whether the operation was to be carried out or not and that this decision was to be based not only on the question of endangering the submarine but also whether in the opinion of the CO the operation had a reasonable prospect of success. I find that dealings with General Lamplough and Captain Garnons-Williams are refreshingly simple and direct as compared with dealings with many members of SAC's staff.

5 June

In his report on the Sourabaya operation the RAA suggests it would have been profitable to have carried out a second strike in the afternoon. With this I am in full agreement but the Admiral can only decide such a matter if he has immediately available the results of the first strike together with a report on what targets were not covered and what new targets were discovered which had not been foreseen when launching the attack. To get this information quickly requires not only expert and rapid interrogation of aircrews on their return but also immediate development of photographs and again rapid interpretation of the latter. I am taking this matter up with RAA since I feel we are at present very much adrift in this respect.

6 June

2.   In spite of intensive efforts it seems unlikely that the two escort carriers and their escorts can be ready before the 15th to start operating. The frigates composing this escort have had so many machinery breakdowns that it has not been possible to give them the group training they require to be effective. All we can hope is that the submarine threat in the approaches to Aden does not develop before they reach the area.

385.   *To Cunningham*

12 June 1944

2.   I was not altogether surprised when I found that Henry Pownall was pressing for operations by the Eastern Fleet to be controlled by SEAC HQ. Matters have now come to a head at SEAC HQ, and I am quite convinced that both Dickie and his staff are determined to set up an organisation on the MacArthur model in order that he may be Supreme in every sense of the word. Since the interests of the Fleet are so closely involved, I felt it was necessary to inform him that I viewed this tendency with some concern, and I felt it was necessary to acquaint the Admiralty of

the situation. I have sent the Admiralty a copy of this memorandum together with a letter explaining briefly how this situation has arisen, and incidentally stating that if a MacArthur model is to be set up, then I think that a radical alteration in Naval representation at SEAC HQ is required. . . .

3.   The trouble is that at Kandy none of these fellows have enough to do, and therefore they have a most definite urge to butt in on other people's business. At almost every turn I find attempts are made to exercise the authority of SAC over the Fleet in matters which do not concern them. I have given him every opportunity to visit ships, and of these he has taken full advantage; in fact rather too much since on a recent visit to Trincomalee, when I was not present, he visited half a dozen ships and made a speech in each one. This was against my wishes, but Clem Moody, who took charge of the party, was, I think, bounced by Master Dickie.

4.   These squabbles all seem very trivial, but I feel there is a main principle at stake, and that is unless and until the Fleet is definitely allocated to a Theatre Commander for specific operations, the control of that Fleet should be exercised by the Admiralty. If the control is to be vested in a Theatre Commander then the latter must have really responsible and experienced Naval advisors and must be prepared to take their advice.

10.   I think that the limitations for maintaining a large Fleet, or for mounting a large expedition in this Theatre are by now fairly well appreciated, but I also feel that with the way the war is going in the Pacific it may not be necessary to mount a super expedition in order to effect an entry into the Malayan Barrier. The Japanese will undoubtedly fight hard at static defence, but I believe we shall find they lack mobility and will not have it in their power to concentrate really important air or surface forces to resist our attack. It is most unfortunate that in both our recent operations we were given no opportunity for a little gun practice, and only extremely limited opportunity to exercise our fighter interception which, from what I saw of it, is distinctly good. . . .

386.   *Desk diary, 1944*

12 June

2.   *Illustrious, Atheling, Phoebe*[1] and 6 destroyers proceeded to sea in connection with a feint attack on Sabang, backed up by wireless deception; this included a submarine 200 miles W of Sabang simulating an escort force commander ordering his party back to harbour.

[1]*Phoebe*: 1940, 5450t, 8×5.25in, 6tt, 33k.

13 June

4. *Stoic*,[1] who has been chasing a convoy in the Malacca Straits for the last 24 hours, reports she has now torpedoed one of them whilst at anchor at Phuket.

14 June

Although the estimated position of U-boats in the Indian Ocean is becoming somewhat more definite, it appears that the most definite quarry at the moment is a U-boat operating in the vicinity of the Maldives. This can be covered by land based air, but after discussion with Captain A/S I decided that Force 66 should take this on as a first task, since the probability of a kill will be greatly increased if we put on all the air possible and also have escort vessels in the vicinity available to assist.[2]

15 June

3. The latest appreciation from the Admiralty of the U-boat situation in this Theatre does not suggest that pack tactics against convoys are intended, but rather that efforts will be directed mainly against independent shipping on the route between the Maldives and Aden. It seems unlikely that the submarines will be able to operate effectively to the E of Socotra during the height of the SW Monsoon.

18 June

Received a signal to say that *Howe* was leaving with *Formidable* to join the EF on 11 July; it seems likely that Admiral Fraser will come out in her. . . .

19 June

Force 60, consisting of *Renown, Richelieu, Illustrious, Nigeria, Phoebe, Kenya, Ceylon* and 8 destroyers sailed for operation PEDAL, i.e. the air strike against Port Blair.

22 June

4. On my return from Trincomalee I received the reports from the VA which show that operation PEDAL was quite successful and carried out according to plan. 15 Barracudas were flown off of which 2 returned with engine trouble and 1 was lost over the target. The barracks, power house, MT yard, seaplane base and radar stations were bombed and

---

[1] *Stoic*: 'S' class s/m, 1944.
[2] An escort group with a CVE.

strafed. Only 2 aircraft were seen on the runway and both of these were set on fire. No enemy fighters were seen either on the ground or in the air. The Corsairs went in to strafe the aerodromes before the main strike and experienced intense light A/A and 5 were damaged; of these all landed on except one whose pilot had to bale out over the Fleet. The Barracudas experienced intense and fairly accurate heavy A/A fire on their approach to the target but this ceased before bomb release.

23 June

2.   57 aircraft were embarked in *Illustrious* for the operation and the range on deck for the strike was 39 of which the first 5 were accelerated. At one time there were 51 aircraft in the air and it was most fortunate that landing on was not delayed by a crash since otherwise some of the Barracudas would most certainly have had to land in the sea; tests of consumption once more indicated that the practical radius of the Barracuda is apparently not more than 125 miles.

26 June

2.   With regard to FAA matters on the Station, a point was made that unless *Atheling*, who is assault loaded, is likely to be employed during forthcoming operations it would be preferable for her fighters and pilots to be used in the Fleet Carriers. With this I agree since in certain of the operations envisaged it will be necessary to repeat the arming of the carriers as used at Port Blair, i.e. 3 fighter squadrons and 1 Barracuda squadron. The extra fighters will not be available unless we rob *Atheling*.
3.   The air searches we have sent out for submarines both E and W of the Maldives have so far met with no success. From information available in D/Fs it is quite clear there are some 2 or 3 submarines in the vicinity, but so far they have been unable to connect.

27 June

Lt-Cdr Brooke,[1] who has just returned from three months' visit to Australia as representative from SEAC HQ called on me today. . . .
4.   He said that he had discussed with General MacArthur the question of a British naval force operating in the SW Pacific and the General said that not only could he use them to great advantage, but he also considered it would be good for the Australians to have a detachment of the British fleet operating in their Fleet; he anticipated no logistic difficulties.

---

[1]Lt-Cdr R de L Brooke: Lt June 1934; *Anthony* Aug 1939; *Wheatland* i/c Oct 1941; Lt-Cdr June 1942; SEAC 1944.

6.   Referring to the RAN he [Brooke] said this was obviously mori-
bund, was used by the 7th Fleet for all the odd jobs and the financial
stranglehold kept over the Fleet and all to do with it by the Navy department was another factor which affected the efficiency adversely.
Officers stated freely they had no use for their Navy Board and furthermore it was completely out of touch with the US HQ at Brisbane. They
all wish for the arrival of part of the British Fleet with whom they can
work and they had also entertained great hopes that Mr Curtin would
succeed in getting more destroyers and an escort carrier transferred from
the RN to the RAN. They complain that the US ride roughshod over
them and obviously have a contempt for forces so singularly ill equipped
and maintained with such parsimony.[1]
7.   I understand that the Americans were very pleased at what they considered to be the prompt action of the EF in carrying out operations
against the Malayan Barrier at their request. To use their own expression, 'the EF kicked the ball directly it was at their feet'.

387.   *To his wife*

25 June 1944

. . . D said that his directive made him Supreme Commander in every
respect, that he was under no obligation to accept the advice of his Cs-in-
C and that I had no right as a subordinate to criticise him or his staff. He
ended up by requesting me not to communicate with the Admiralty on
such matters except through him and that I was not to exchange views
with the other Cs-in-C except through him. He enclosed a telegram he'd
sent to the Chiefs of Staff [in] which he said he regretted to report a difference of opinion had arisen between us on the interpretation of his
directive and that he'd found out that I'd sent a letter to the Admiralty
direct and not through him, and that in consequence he had informed me
of the proper interpretation of his directive. Can you beat it! Proper
Hitler-Mussolini stuff. I went from Trinco to Kandy on Friday afternoon
and on Saturday had an hour and a half with D. He regretted etc. but said
as my letter had come through his registry the Americans were aware of
it, that General Wedemeyer had sent a long signal to General Marshall to
say that I was attempting to undermine the position of the Supreme
Commander and a whole lot more! I told Dickie that as Naval C-in-C I

---

[1]John Curtin (1885–1945): journalist, TU leader; Lab MP 1928; leader 1935; PM of
Australia 1941–5. Australia had experienced very severe economic problems in the 1930s
and it is little wonder that RAN officers felt frustrated, especially after they saw the lavish
scale of American equipment.

was responsible for voicing not just my opinion but also that of the Admiralty and that whilst matters were under discussion I was at full liberty to obtain the views of the Admiralty in any way I liked. Furthermore I also considered I was at full liberty to convey my views on matters under discussion to my brother Cs-in-C. I would do so orally if they were present and if not by letter. As for his being criticised by a subordinate Commander I could not accept the suggestion that if I held different views to him whilst the matter was under discussion that this could be called criticism. Incidentally not a ship in the EF was under his orders at the moment or had been for many months. I told him finally that in my covering letter to the Admiralty I had said that if his staff were to advise him on naval matters he should have an officer with fleet experience. . . . D took all of this very well, said he realised he must make changes but wished it had not happened this way. That my immense prestige and the confidence the fleet had in me made it all the more difficult. I told him that on personal grounds I was equally sorry but this matter had been argued for months and months and in view of my approaching departure it was quite impossible for me to leave things in this sort of a mess without taking some action. Of course at the back of it all is the fact that D has asked that Giffard should be relieved[1] and now this bust-up with me must inevitably make people think that something rather odd is happening. He does not want a spot light on his party and he also does want if possible to establish himself as a sort of Hitler with everything under his personal control. . . .

388.   *To Cunningham*

27 June 1944

9.   . . . I do feel that as a result of my letter this tendency to swing towards a MacArthur model has been checked for the time being at any rate, . . .

10.   The SAC is most emphatic that should the Fleet be placed under his orders at any time he has the absolute right to over-ride any objections of the Naval C-in-C concerning its employment. Whilst I do not question that his directive may give him this right I feel that in any major matter it would be most inadvisable for him to take such action without informing the Chiefs of Staff beforehand in order that the First Sea Lord may intervene if necessary. With his present naval advisors it would certainly be essential to have some check over the employment of the Fleet if the latter was contrary to the views of the Naval C-in-C.

---

[1]Giffard, a stolid and capable but somewhat slow-moving soldier, had not enjoyed a happy relationship with Mountbatten.

11. Having a Naval officer as SAC, and a young one at that, my inclinations were all towards making the party a success, but on the other hand it was clear to me soon after the arrival of the SAC that it was essential someone should put on the brake and I appeared to be the only one willing and able to attempt this.

12. I considered of course that I should leave matters as they were until after Bruce Fraser had arrived, but I felt that the situation might develop too quickly at Kandy and that if anything I had perhaps been somewhat remiss in not representing the situation previously; in this connection I had been optimistic as a result of conversations I had before the party left Delhi that a more reasonable set up would be adopted after the move. In this I was disappointed. . . .

389. *Desk diary, 1944*

29 June

4. Having decided to put the East Coast shipping to Calcutta out of convoy we now receive information that a U-boat will probably be working off Colombo and to the S, and consequently the order has to be rescinded; it is a remarkable thing that on each occasion when we have tried to put this shipping out of convoy a ship has either been torpedoed or else we have almost immediate indications of the presence of a submarine.

1 July

I inspected the DEMS school and found it as usual in first class order. In conversation with Cdr Malden and Lt Clarke,[1] it appeared to me that these officers had a very good general knowledge of the state of efficiency of merchant ships visiting Colombo. I feel it is desirable that Naval authorities should have a line on these ships and know whether the Captains are good, what the officers are like, whether the ship generally is in good order, if the DEMS quarters are satisfactory and the ship's anti-sabotage organisation is up to the mark; I have therefore given instructions for rendering reports of all ships that are boarded so that this information may be filed with the ships' records in the Merchant Ship Plot.

[1]Cdr W. F. Malden, RNR (Ret): Lt Jan 1916; Ret List Oct 1929; *Fervent* Ramsgate Nov 1939; Cdr, DEMS Sept 1942; Chatham June 1941; i/c DEMS Sch, Colombo 1944; *President III*, Windsor April 1945. Lt W. Clarke (Ret): Lt July 1938; Chatham DY 1939; Ret List April 1940; *President III* Dec 1942; DEMS May 1943; Colombo 1944.

4 July

Stratagem reported that she had arrived at Car Nicobar with her party at 1730, that her reception was unfavourable and that she had 2 bow torpedoes left, so it looks as if her attack was unsuccessful. *Tradewind* reports her clandestine operation was successful and that she had bombarded the oil tanks at Sibolga until forced to dive by shore batteries; no definite damage observed though shells were bursting in the target area.
5.   In a later report *Stratagem* reported that she had obtained one hit on target with one of her two remaining torpedoes; the pertinacity of our submarines is most praiseworthy, but up to date the hits per torpedo fired are most disappointing.[1]

6 July

I drew the attention of the Admiralty to the fact that in the last communique issued about submarine patrols in the Malacca Straits, reference was made to two convoys being chased for a considerable period. This I consider regrettable since it gives the Japanese an indication of our methods and also enables them to make a better estimate of the number of submarines we have operating in this area at any one time.
2.   C-in-C SA[2] reports a successful Catalina attack on a U-boat to the W of Durban; *Pathfinder*[3] and other ships in the vicinity have been ordered to the spot.
3.   Boats have been sighted in the vicinity of Chagos who report they are from the *Nellore*,[4] apparently sunk on 28 June to the NE of Chagos. This is the first intimation we have had of the sinking, and is another indication of how often ships are sunk in this area without any SOS being received.

7 July

3.   *Victorious* and *Indomitable* arrive at 2.30 p.m.; Captain Lambe who is taking passage to relieve Cunliffe in *Illustrious* arrived by air from *Indomitable* . . . Discussing the planning organisation and general set up at Kandy, Lambe informed me that he had been at pains to impress on SAC the need to avoid the particular organisation which he was now set-

---

[1]*Stratagem*: 'S' class s/m, 1944; lost Dec 1944.

[2]Vice Adm Sir Robert L. Burnett: *Britannia* 1903; Lt 1910; i/c destroyers Grand F 1914–18; phys trng 1920s; Cdr 1923; Capt 1930; Capt (D) China Sta; Dir PT & Sports; S Af Sta; Cdre RN Barracks Chatham 1939; Actg RA, Home F M/L Sqdn; FO (D) Home F 1942; RA 10CS 1943–4; VA & C-in-C S Atlantic 1944; Adm 1946; C-in-C Plymouth 1947–50; Chm, White Fish Authy.

[3]*Pathfinder*: 1942, 1540t, 4×4in, 8tt, 34k. No s/m sunk.

[4]*Nellore*: 1913, 6942gt, Eastern & Australian SS Co; 156 survivors in 2 boats rescued by frigate *Lossie*.

ting up. It seems to me in fact that the advice which Lambe gave him was almost word for word what I gave him and since I know the SAC attaches great weight to Lambe's opinions, I feel a visit by him to Kandy would be profitable and may do some good.

4. Lambe told me he had constantly impressed on the SAC the need to curb the urge he always has to centralise and control everything himself; the same trouble occurred in Norfolk House[1] and as a result much of the SAC's real ability and efficiency is not put to the best purpose. He fully agreed that he should have had a Flag Officer of experience on his staff rather than a clever, prejudiced and over-confident staff officer.

10 July

Havfru[2] reports she is safe and proceeding on her voyage. The D/F obtained of a U-boat off Durban suggests either a second one is in the vicinity or that the attack on the one a few days' ago was not successful. 7 destroyers and escort vessels together with air are continuing to hunt for the U-boat attacked by *Racehorse* and *Raider* but so far without success.[3]

14 July

A report has been received from survivors of *Jean Nicolet* that they were subjected to even worse atrocities than usual by the Japanese submarine who attacked her; this is almost certainly *I-8*.[4] As before, survivors were either machine gunned in the water or else taken on board the submarine and massacred in the most brutal circumstances; the few survivors owe their lives to the fact that the presence of a Catalina caused the submarine to dive and thus leave those who were still in the water; one man had been able to conceal a knife with which he was able to release the hands of his shipmates and a small handfull together with a few who had not been killed in the boats or rafts, amounting to some 23 in all, have been picked up.

17 July

4. A large number of survivors from the *Tanda*[5] have been picked up and only about 21 are not accounted for and are probably missing as the ship sank in 6 minutes. The Wellington searching the area sighted a U-boat and carried out an attack which caused the U-boat to dive, and sub-

---

[1]Combined Operations HQ, London.
[2]*Havfru*: 1931, 7923gt, Norwegian; on passage Abadan–Melbourne.
[3]*Raider*: 1942, 1705t, 4×4.7in, 8tt, 34k. No s/m sunk.
[4]*Jean Nicolet*: 1943, 7176gt, US War Shipping Admin. *I–8*: 1938, 1950/2600t, 6tt, 2×5.5in, 17/9k.
[5]*Tanda*: 1914, 7160gt, Eastern & Australian SS Co.

sequently *Sutlej*[1] reported she had obtained a contact in the same vicinity and was attacking; no further reports received of any success and I fear the U-boat must have got away. Whilst the efficiency of our escorts and air is undoubtedly not so high as those employed in the Atlantic, yet on the other hand it is difficult to account for our lack of success in dealing with submarines. Captain Baker-Cresswell and other experienced officers in the Escort Groups are concerned at this and can give me no specific reason to account for our repeated failures to sink a U-boat.

5.   Captain Phillips and Cdr Davies on the staff of FO (S) who is sick at Alex., and also Captains S4 and S8 arrived for discussions on the future operations of submarines in this Theatre, and in particular the employment of X-craft and chariots.[2] It was agreed that in our present Theatre of operations opportunities to use X-craft or chariots were few and far between and that failure to keep the crews occupied inevitably resulted in some deterioration. I said that I should be unable to agree to the use of either of these craft against targets that were not really worth while unless the recovery of the crews are reasonably assured. The habit of the Japanese to torture prisoners in order to extract information makes it necessary that survivors should kill themselves rather than allow themselves to fall into the hands of these brutes.

18 July

Captain Willoughby,[3] Chief of Staff to RAA, visited NHQ and discussed the extent to which sea borne air can be used in support of Plan Z. It does not seem to me that we can count on the heavy units of the EF together with Fleet Carriers being present in this Theatre at the end of the year since there must be considerable objections to so powerful a fleet remaining inactive for so long a period. Whatever the difficulties are about the employment of the Fleet in the Pacific Theatre, I feel that even if used as an additional task force for a limited period, it would remove any suggestion or criticism that we had a powerful weapon lying idle which was not being used to assist in the early defeat of Japan. It is assumed, however, that escort carriers will be available in quantity and should further investigation show that wind conditions would allow

---

[1] *Sutlej*: 1940, 1300t, 6×4in,, 18k.

[2] FO (S) was Rear Adm C. Barry. Capt G. C. Phillips: Lt-Cdr 1935; *Ursula*; Cdr Dec 1939; *Usk* April 1940; SO (S/M) Portland Oct 1940; Actg Capt *Talbot* Dec 1941; Admin & Pers, *Dolphin* Jan 1942; *Talbot* 1943; Capt (S) 10SF, Malta 1943, Ceylon 1944; *Dolphin* 1945. Cdr G. P. S. Davies, who had been at Oran in 1940. X-craft were two-man s/m, used with some success against the *Tirpitz*; chariots were 2-man 'torpedoes'.

[3] Capt G. Willoughby: Cdr 1937; FAA 1939; NAD Feb 1940; Actg Capt *Activity* Sept 1942; Capt Dec 1943; CSO to RA (A) *Illustrious* June 1944; Air Warfare & Flying Training Div Jan 1945.

them to operate successfully at this time of the year in the Gulf of Martaban, it seems possible that we can provide the air cover which is required during the initial stages of the assault.

390. *To Cunningham*

18 July 1944

I have just received a paper from Kandy putting forward a new proposed organisation for planning which I think will go a long way towards removing previous objections we had and which is based more or less on the Mediterranean model. I hope, therefore, that matters are at last on the right lines and I attribute this largely to the fact that Charles Lambe paid a visit to Kandy. ...

The conferences of the Cs-in-C commence at Kandy on the 19th, and I shall bring it [the future of the Eastern Fleet] up at these conferences since it seems to me we must avoid being parochial and appreciate that however much we may want to have our share of operations in this Theatre, it would be wrong to tie up a powerful fleet if by using it elsewhere we could hasten the defeat of Japan. ...

391. *Desk diary, 1944*

19 July

2. ... The SAC then touched on three alternative plans for operations in N Burma; two of these, X and Y, are concerned with advances to the S from N Burma, Y being more ambitious than X. Plan Z was designed for an attack on Rangoon by means of 2 airborne divisions landed to the N of the town whilst a seaborne assault on the river was made by the 3rd Special Service Brigade and some elements of the leading follow up division, cover and support being given by the Navy. SAC said that the Americans obviously were very suspicious of Plan Z since in their view it did not comply with the directive and could be considered for having as its primary object the recapture of Burma rather than the opening up of communications with China. ...

20 July

At 1030 a conference was held to discuss Plans X, Y and Z ... Plan Z aimed at putting 2 airborne divisions in N of Rangoon and establishing airstrips within 24 hours from which fighters could operate with subsequent early extension of runways for medium bombers. On D+2 the seaborne assault would be made on Rangoon River and eventually

Rangoon would be attacked both from the N and from the river. This plan obviously requires air and amphibious forces from other Theatres if it is to be implemented. Although the difficulties which would be experienced in making good the advance up the river were too lightly glossed over, yet on the other hand there were possibilities in this plan and so far as the Navy is concerned it received full support on the grounds that Rangoon was, and always had been, the key to Burma. . . .

21 July

A signal was received from the Admiralty to say that 6 LSI (L) under Rear Admiral Talbot,[1] are being sailed to Australia via the Panama Canal to train US amphibian divisions to take part in operations in the SW Pacific. This hardly suggests that it is intended to send reinforcements of shipping to SEAC.

3.   Agreement was eventually reached to adopt the new planning organisation with one or two minor amendments, but Generals Wedemeyer and Sultan[2] asked that it should be recorded they did not agree and they considered that SAC should have his own staff who would be entirely responsible for preparing plans; in other words they advocated the MacArthur model.

392.   *From Mountbatten*

22 July 1944

This is such a tremendous occasion – the last time you hoist your flag in command of our biggest fleet at sea – that I feel I must write a line to tell you how much my thoughts and prayers will be with you.

In many ways it is a very sad occasion – certainly for the fleet and your many friends – but I feel it has certain romantic compensations because, after more than two years of waiting, you are about to open fire directly on the Japanese. I am glad that Bruce Fraser's arrival should have been postponed long enough to enable you to do this as your swan song.

I want to thank you also for your splendid support during these difficult meetings. I am so glad you are supporting the Z Plan and am delighted you are pleased with the new planning arrangements. Thank you for saying you will write to the First Sea Lord.

[1]Rear Adm Arthur G. Talbot: Capt 1934; Capt (D) 3DF *Inglefield* Med F 1937; DASD 1939–March 1940; *Furious* 1941; *Illustrious* Oct 1941; *Formidable* Aug 1942; RA July 1943; RA NEPTUNE 1944; RA LSI (L) *Lothian* July 1944.
[2]Lt-Gen D. L. Sultan US Army, i/c Chinese troops in N Burma.

Noel Coward[1] has a favour to ask – may he (if permitted) spend the night as Charles Lambe's guest on board *Illustrious* during his visit to Trinco?

393. *Desk diary, 1944*

22 July

2. The Fleet started to leave harbour at 1515, the carriers proceeding out first to fly on their aircraft. *Queen Elizabeth* left last at about 1700 and I found I had some reason to question the arrangements made by the VA for the departure of the Fleet since I found ships spread very widely outside Trincomalee and without adequate screens. I consider an enterprising submarine might well have had some easy shots.

23 July

3. Handling of units by Flag and Senior Officers is not all that I could wish; they are too slow in moving divisions when divisional movements are required and also in appreciating the value of a broad zigzag when it is required to drop bearing.

24 July

3. Colombo informed me that *I-8* (the butcher) and a U-boat coming from Batavia to Penang were outside Sumatra and might be in our area. It appears that after the sinking of the Japanese submarine off the one fathom bank by *Telemachus*,[2] they feel it safer to send the submarines outside Sumatra.

25 July

3. At 0600, the pre-arranged time, we could see gun flashes from A/A guns and later on shell bursts in the sky as the Corsairs flew overhead. At this time the heavy A/A fire, though fairly intense, did not appear to be very accurate. At 0615 a fire was visible on the aerodrome which showed that one or more aircraft had been set on fire. . . .
4. Exactly at the pre-arranged time at 0655 *Queen Elizabeth* opened fire with her 3 ranging salvoes and was followed on time by *Valiant*, then *Renown* and finally *Richelieu*. The cruisers had opened fire some 30 seconds earlier and it appeared to me that *Cumberland*'s second salvo fell on the wireless station – her target. Before the battleships opened fire the

---

[1]Noel (later Sir Noel) Coward (1899–1973): playwright, actor, composer, cabaret star; played Mountbatten the destroyer leader in wartime film *In Which We Serve* and a friend from 1930s.
[2]*Telemachus*: 'T' class s/m, 1943; sank *I–166*.

destroyer screen of 5 destroyers under Commodore (D) in *Relentless* had been detached to engage shore batteries and a radar station on the W side of the harbour entrance.

5.   From *Queen Elizabeth* the fire of the battleships seemed to be very effective; it is true there were a certain number of rounds falling in the harbour but as workshops, godowns etc. as targets present only a narrow strip, this was not altogether surprising. Heavy explosions, clouds of dust and a great deal of smoke soon made spotting difficult but the spotting aircraft – all Corsairs who did their work extremely well – reported that most salvoes appeared to be falling in the target areas.

7.   The Fleet withdrew to the westward initially at 15 knots to allow destroyers and cruisers to rejoin. I was glad to learn that the Inshore force had got off fairly lightly with 2 killed, 6 wounded and only minor damage to some of the ships; the *Quickmatch*,[1] the 3rd ship of the line, escaped scot free. *Nigeria* reported that a Corsair had force landed in the sea but the pilot had been recovered very much alive. . . .

8.   At 0937 an enemy aircraft which had been detected on the screen was intercepted and shot down by *Illustrious*'s Corsairs; this was a Sally.[2] At 1130 a long hunt in the clouds took place after another aircraft had been reported by radar; this one, a Zeke, was eventually shot down as a result of the fighter interception sandwiching the clouds with 2 above and 2 below and catching the Zeke as he came out.

10.   Very heavy rain occurred at 1715 and when this cleared RAA proposed to land on fighters in view of further bad weather ahead. To this I agreed, but just as carriers were turning into the wind to land on, an enemy formation was reported on the radar at 50 miles with first report of 12 plus. Umbrella was at once re-established and fighters also sent to intercept. Owing to cloud the interception was by no means easy, but the Corsairs eventually succeeded in shooting down 3 Zekes and damaging 2 others. It appears that this formation consisted of 8 Zekes led by a Sally or similar aircraft which obviously had good radar since at 25 miles it was clear that this aircraft was in contact with the Fleet and visibility at the time was certainly not more that 10 miles. By 1830 the screen was reported clear and aircraft were being landed on, the last being landed on as it was getting dark. I consider the Corsairs and the fighter interception officers did a very good job on this occasion, and the strength and composition of enemy air attack indicates very clearly the straits to which they have been reduced.

---

[1]*Quickmatch* RAN: 1942, 1705t, 4×4.7in, 8tt, 34k.
[2]Mitsubishi Ki21 'Sally': 1937, bomb load 2200lb, 6mg, 297mph.

27 July

3.   Captain Onslow[1] reported that at one time the Inshore Squadron was firing at ranges of 2600 yards and that their fire appeared to be most effective since shells could be seen entering warehouses etc. and bursts of flame subsequently coming out of the windows. Captain Stam of the *Tromp* was evidently delighted at having been able to engage the enemy at close range and said that this action had been of enormous benefit to his ship's company.

394.   *To his wife*

25 July 1944

My farewell party seems to have gone off with a swing so far. I've wanted to bombard Sabang for some time past but so far it has always seemed that the air the Japs had available was a bit too much for us to compete with. However after our first tap at Sabang and then Sourabaya and Port Blair it seemed that we had over-estimated the Jap air strength so I felt justified in going in this time. It was a very carefully planned operation with everything timed to take place to the tick and everything went exactly according to plan; we opened fire within one minute of the pre-arranged time. As usual the approach was a ticklish job since if we had been seen the day before we might well have found a nice bit of dirt waiting for us. As it was there was some evidence that 2 submarines might be in the vicinity. But we were not spotted at all. The plan was that the fighters should go in at 0600 and strafe the airfields and shoot up any aircraft that attempted to take off. Exactly at 6 a.m. we saw gun flashes ashore showing the A/A was engaging our fighters. We could clearly see them against the Eastern sky with shell bursting all round them. Soon we saw a most encouraging blaze on the aerodrome which showed that at least one or more aircraft had been set on fire. The A/A was intermittent as we approached with my flagship leading the 4 battleships, the 5 cruisers away to my left closing the shore to engage their targets and ahead two lots of destroyers including one party led by Dick Onslow which was going right inside the harbour to roar it up. At 6.55 a.m. we opened fire and soon saw huge shell-bursts on the harbour, barracks, etc. with immense volumes of smoke and dust. Away to the left the cruisers were flattening out a wireless station and some coast batteries. No-one fired at the battleships at all – too afraid to draw their fire perhaps. Dick Onslow's party went in in the most gallant manner, heavy shells from

[1]Capt R. G. Onslow, Capt (D).

the battleships falling not far from them and then white splashes as some of the shore batteries opened up on them. They roared up the harbour a fair treat but were a little too ardent and were still well inside range of the coast batteries as the battleships ceased fire. As a result they got a bit of a dusting as they were coming out. However they had very few killed, only 2 actually of which one was the poor Gaumont British press chap and the other a P.O. About 6 wounded, including one officer. It was a very nice bit of work and pretty to watch. I longed to be in it myself. During our retirement a couple of Jap aircraft tried to attack but were shot down by our fighters who had already got 4 on the ground. Apart from that we had no come-back until this evening when about 12 Jap aircraft tried to get at us. The conditions were difficult for fighter interception owing to cloud and approaching darkness. However the fighter boys shot down 4 of them and after hanging about for some time and giving me a bit of headache, the rest of them were driven off and now at 9.30 p.m. I think it's unlikely they will find us. So ends a nice day enjoyed by all except the Japs. We made a proper mess of Sabang by all accounts and I doubt if it will be much further use to the Japs as a Naval base.

Certain of the Corsair pilots came on board *Queen Elizabeth* later and reported that a number of the Zekes failed to open fire even when they were in a favourable position to do so; the Zekes can out-manoeuvre the Corsairs very easily but these Zekes appeared to be a very green lot and had it not been for the cover afforded by the cloud, the Corsairs think they might well have bagged the lot.

395. *To Cunningham*

27 July 1944

I am glad to report that at the series of Cs-in-C's meetings held at SEAC HQ in Kandy before I left for operation CRIMSON, agreement was reached with regard to the planning organisation.

2. In effect this corresponds very closely indeed to the N African organisation and provides an integrated planning staff with members of both the Cs-in-C's and SAC's staffs working together. There will be 4, or possibly 5, Directors of Plans; Duncan Hill[1] will act as the Naval Director of Plans for the time being, and possibly continue as such if large scale amphibious operations are intended in this Theatre and a Flag Officer is appointed as Force Commander.

[1]Capt Duncan C. Hill: Cdr 1935; EO *Vindictive* 1939; *Royal Arthur* (Skegness) Sept 1939; Capt June 1942; TORCH staff Aug 1942; SO Eastern F Jan 1944; DP (N) SEAC July 1944; NA Moscow 1945.

3.   The SAC assured us that he had such an organisation in mind for some time past, but owing to the strong opposition of the Americans and his own staff he had been reluctant to bring this into operation until he had been able to convince these opponents that it would be the best in the circumstances. He said that in this he had not been successful and he was now making a change in direct opposition to the advice of his COS, Deputy COS and other senior members, including representatives of General Stilwell and also General Stratemeyer.[1] He pointed out that it was a serious step for him to take such action and he hoped that we would appreciate how difficult a decision it had been for him to make.

4.   Giffard, Peirse and myself were somewhat sceptical in regard to this statement; we, of course, appreciate that Pownall, Wedemeyer, Langley and the rest have always been most anxious to see the Supreme Commander control everything personally through his staff. We also feel that had it not been for our opposition to this proposed Supreme set up, we should undoubtedly have had by now a MacArthur model firmly established.

7.   I am very glad indeed that this agreement has been reached before Fraser's arrival because it would have been most unsatisfactory to have left him with this mess to clear up. The impression I informed you of in a previous letter that my letter to the Admiralty on the subject had brought things to a head, is, I believe, correct. This letter was not, however, referred to in any way at any of the meetings in Kandy.

8.   Operation CRIMSON went off without a hitch and exactly according to plan. . . .

9.   The party did everyone a world of good, and especially some of the big ships who had not had a chance to fire their main armament in action previously in this war. As a matter of interest, the *Queen Elizabeth* is one of these ships, since her last action was at the Dardanelles when Bill Norman[2] was in her as a Midshipman and myself as Fleet Wireless Officer.

396. *Desk diary, 1944*

29 July

3.   A signal from the Admiralty to say that no Swordfish Mk 3 would be available for Eastern Fleet A/U carriers, but Avengers would prove quite

---

[1]Gens Pownall & Wedemeyer. Maj-Gen George Stratemeyer USAAF was C-in-C US 10th Air Force, based in China.
[2]H. G. Norman: Capt 1938; IDC 1939; *President* 1940; *Nile* 1941; *Queen Elizabeth* 1943.

suitable in the *Smiter* class.[1] All my A/U Escort Captains prefer the Swordfish and are most doubtful about operating Avengers at night in this Theatre; the Admiralty, however, say that in practice this presents no difficulty. I feel myself that with the light winds experienced here or alternatively the strong winds and a good deal of motion on the ship, there is a great deal to be said for the Swordfish.

397. *From Mountbatten*

30 July 1944

Best congratulations on going off with a real good SA-BANG.

398. *From Admiral Nimitz*

29 July 1944

My warm congratulations on the aggressive and effective attack on Sabang by your forces.

399. *Desk diary, 1944*

1 August

4. Generally speaking the views of the conference [of SAC and Cs-in-C] was that all these proposed operations, with the exception of Plans Y and Z, were not definitely linked up with further movements or any general strategic plan. In my mind they bear the continual impress of an endeavour to conduct major operations with minor forces, in order to achieve something in this Theatre, whether that something is likely to be of ultimate value or not.

3 August

Howe arrived at 1000 and Captain H. W. U. McCall[2] called on me; he reports that he still has trouble with his evaporators and requires at least 7 days to effect repairs. I understand these defects are due to faulty design in baffle plates and are common to the whole class; it is most unfortunate, however, that such defects were not attended to before sending this ship to the tropics.

---

[1]*Smiter* class: CVE, US-built, 1943, 11,420t, 20 a/c, 2×5in, 16k.
[2]Capt H. W. U. McCall: Capt 1937; NA S America 1938; *Dido* Sept 1940; Cdre, BAD Feb 1943; *Howe* March 1943.

2. The Captain of the *Richelieu*[1] called on me and emphasised the good effects which operation CRIMSON had had on his officers and men; he expressed the hope that there would be further opportunities for *Richelieu* to engage the enemy as he felt this was quite the most important factor in maintaining the morale and contentment of his people.

5. My staff are at the moment examining plans for bombardment or air strikes at Akyab, Car Nicobar, Padang and one or two other places, but none of these plans can of course, be implemented until we have some idea of what the strategy is to be in this Theatre. The cement works at Padang are, however, an exception and will be suitable for a carrier borne air strike but not for a bombardment.

4 August

I proceeded on board *Howe* and addressed the ship's company. I observed shower baths and a canvas screened washing place had been established on the upper deck and was informed by the Captain that the ship's bathrooms below decks were almost untenable in this climate owing to poor ventilation and at sea they had to be closed down for protection. I was also informed that nearly 1½ miles of additional ventilation had been fitted before the ship sailed for the East, but that in spite of this the conditions below were still very bad indeed. It seems to me that our constructors are lamentably behind the times in regard to this important matter of ventilation and I should have thought that a study of American methods in their later construction would have been profitable.[2]

7 August

3. Whilst on board *Maidstone* [at Trincomalee] I was able to see the ship's company of *Storm* who had just returned from a very successful patrol in which she had entered the harbour in broad daylight on the surface and sunk 2 A/S vessels by gunfire; subsequently she attacked and sank 4 small MV's including one laden with ammunition for Rangoon. *Storm* is commanded by Lt-Cdr Young, RNVR. . . .

---

[1]Capitaine G-M-J Merveilleux de Vignaux (1897–1964): ensign April 1917; *Jean Bart*; *Tirailleur* Aug 1918; Lt de V 1923; Gun Sch; GO *Jeanne d'Arc* (Darlan i/c) Aug 1927; *Siroco* i/c 1936; staff & gunnery appts; *Malin* i/c May 1941; fought against Allied landings Casablanca Nov 1942; refloated *Albatros* Dec 1942; Capt de V Aug 1943; *Richelieu* April 1944; N Sea; Indian O; RA Dec 1945; Cdt Oran 1946; Ret List May 1949. Somerville thought he had 'a great sense of humour and buoyant spirits'; in other words, a man after his own heart.

[2]British ships were still designed primarily for northern waters; moreover, the RN's attitude to creature comfort was still somewhat Nelsonian.

9 August

A report from Trincomalee at 0230 reported that *Valiant* was afloat and was being towed clear of the dock, but that the latter had sunk. It appears that at 2230 the dock was dried out all but 2 feet when cracks appeared before the butt strap of the after section and the after end started to break off. The dock finally listed 10° to port and all lights and power failed. When the after end finally sank the trim of the remainder of the dock was such that *Valiant*'s quarter deck was almost awash at the after end with her bows high and dry; power was eventually obtained to operate the flooding valves fore end and list and trim were corrected, and the fore part eventually sank. *Valiant* is holed forward but not badly and her propellor shafts appear to be bent.

2.　A telegram from SAC suggests that Plan Z is now being backed at the expense of CULVERIN and everything else. A signal from General Stilwell to SAC says that Peirse does not consider that an assault on Malaya could take place under cover of carrier borne aircraft and that consequently N Sumatra must be taken initially. Stilwell says that SEAC Joint Planners consider that Japanese air power is likely to deteriorate and if we are to take any worthwhile part in the war against Japan in this Theatre, speed with the acceptance of reasonable risks is essential. I am rather inclined to agree with this point of view more especially as we appear to have over-estimated Japanese air power consistently.

10 August

Latest reports of damage to *Valiant* show that the flooding forward was strictly controlled and is not very serious, but the damage to propellors, shafts, A brackets and rudders appears to be serious and may put her out of action a long time.

6.　I ordered a board of enquiry to investigate the sinking of AFD 23 with Rear Admiral Walker as President.[1]

7.　Our submarines' bag for July was:–

Sunk	1 Jap U-boat
	1 4000 ton MV
	8 small MV approximating 1480 tons
	16 junks approximating 5876 tons
Damaged	2 MVs approximating 3100 tons
	3 Mvs　　　"　　　1050 tons
	1 junk　　　"　　　20 tons

[1]Rear Adm H. T. C. Walker: Capt Dec 1931; Flag Capt & CSO to Layton, *Barham*, Med F Jan 1939; Cdre Portsmouth Barracks April 1940; RA Aug 1941; DPS Nov 1941; 5CS *London* Eastern F May 1944; VA, FO 3BS & 2nd-in-C E Indies F Dec 1944.

Also   56 mines were laid, 2 special operations completed and 2 bombardments carried out.

15 August

Report from Force 66 that diesel oil is still rising to the surface at the spot at which the submarine was attacked by *Findhorn* and this coupled with sighting of 'suspicious objects' appears to confirm the U-boat was sunk.[1]

22 August

3. Admiral Fraser arrived at 1845 in a York accompanied by Cdre de Pass[2] and one or two members of his staff; he looked very fit and well and was met by myself, C-in-C Ceylon, GOC Ceylon and representatives from SEAC HQ.
4. I drove with him to C-in-C Ceylon's house where we had a short talk; he told me that he had not taken part in any of the discussions regarding future operations in this Theatre, but had been told we had made an offer of the main units of the Eastern Fleet to the US, to be used in the Pacific. Fraser understood it is considered unlikely that Admiral Nimitz will agree to using the Fleet in the Northern Pacific since he believes that both he and Admiral King do not wish to see any British participation in the final attack on Japan proper. On the other hand General MacArthur was anxious to have a British Task Force in his area and this was backed up by Mr Curtin who also wished to see British Naval Forces based on Australia in order to counter balance to some extent American domination . . .

23 August

Admiral Fraser's flag was hoisted in *Relentless* at 0800 and he assumed command of Eastern Fleet. My flag in *Caradoc*[3] was hauled down at sunset.
2. I spent the forenoon discussing my turn over notes with Admiral Fraser and giving him my views on various senior officers out here and on certain changes which I thought were necessary. In this connection I expressed doubts as to whether Power was suitable to command the Fleet if Fraser decided that the C-in-C must remain ashore and that Fleet operations must be conducted by another Admiral. Fraser told me he

---

[1]*Findhorn*: 1943, 1460t, 2×4in, 20k; she sank *U198* in company with HMIS *Godavari*: 1943, 1340t, 6×4in, 18k.
[2]Avro York: transport, 1942, 298mph. Cdre Daniel de Pass: Capt 1934; *Cossack* 1937; DPS 1940; Patrol Services C Depot April 1941; Ret List Jan 1944; COS to Fraser 1944.
[3]*Caradoc*: 1917, 4120t, 5×6in, 2×3in, 8tt, 29k; probably a base ship by this date.

believed that Admiral H. B. Rawlings[1] was considered a potential relief for Power; I expressed some doubts as to whether Rawlings had the requisite capacity; it is not easy to choose a suitable Vice-Admiral senior to Miles who I believe might prove the best choice in spite of his lack of recent sea experience.

6. Discussing with Geoffrey Layton, that evening, the question of somebody to relieve him, he suggested that Berty Ramsay might be a good choice; with this I quite agree and said I would sound Fraser on the matter.[2]

24 August

2. The SAC returned from the UK at 1540 and called to see me. He confirmed that the main units of the EF had been offered to the US and said that he was sure that Admiral King would not agree to their participation in an attack on Japan proper. In this connection he said that whereas we could only mount 3 amphibious divisions, the Americans could mount some 20; under these circumstances our military participation could only be a token one. My comment was that the EF might well prove of material assistance in the final assault and it seemed a great pity it could not be used for this purpose. SAC said he felt sure MacArthur would jump at the offer of the Fleet; I told him that in this case it was absolutely essential we should have some stipulation that the Flag Officer commanding the Fleet should be consulted with regard to the employment of the Fleet and the preparation of Naval plans in this connection. SAC's comment was that much as I might have disliked his proposed set up at Kandy, he felt convinced I would dislike still more MacArthur's set up at Brisbane; this of course has been a matter of discussion between us for some time and it was the first time I have heard SAC openly criticise the MacArthur set up.

3. Referring to VANGUARD[3] the SAC stated that it must be fully staged and every effort made to ensure success; the PM however still hankered after CULVERIN but both the SAC and myself agreed that by the time CULVERIN could be mounted we should be in a position to go straight to the Kra Peninsula or to any other points selected for the recapture of Malaya.

---

[1]Vice Adm Sir H. Bernard Rawlings: Capt 1930; *Valiant* Aug 1939; RA 1BS, Med F Dec 1940; Inshore Sqdn, Med 1941; RA 7CS May 1941–Jan 1942; ACNS (F) 1942–3; VA & FO Levant & E Med July 1944; 2nd-in-C & operational cdr BPF 1945.

[2]Ramsay remained ANCXF in NW Europe. Layton went home at this time to become C-in-C Portsmouth. There was little need for another C-in-C Ceylon.

[3]Presumably another projected combined operation.

25 August

I proceeded to Ratmalana aerodrome at 0710 where I was joined by my Chief of Staff, Secretary, SOP, Valet and Wren Stenographer, and found a large party of officers assembled to see me off; unfortunately a deluge of rain came down which made the runway unserviceable until 0900 so goodbyes had to be said at 8 o'clock.[1]

400. *From the Admiralty*

19 August 1944

On the occasion of hauling down your flag the Board of Admiralty wish to express to you their high appreciation of your service as C-in-C Eastern Fleet. My Lords recall that you assumed this command at a critical period when Japanese menace in Eastern Theatre was grave and the task of Eastern Fleet at that time was vital but unspectacular and maintenance of high morale in such circumstances was a prime factor.

My Lords appreciate how much your personal example and inspiration contributed to the fine spirit and high standard of efficiency which have throughout pervaded the Fleet under your command and which have been amply demonstrated in recent operations against the enemy which you have so successfully conducted.

401. *To the Admiralty*

20 August 1944

I am most sincerely grateful for Their Lordships' appreciation.

Anything that we have been able to achieve in this Theatre has been due to the fine team work of my Flag and Commanding Officers afloat and ashore and to the unremitting service rendered by my staff under the direction of Commodore Edwards.

With such support my task has been lightened in no small degree.

---

[1] Cdre Edwards, Capt Laybourne, Cdr Edden, valet CPO Steward Redman, WRNS PA Maureen Stuart Clark, who later became his Flag Lt (as a 3O WRNS) in Washington. The party flew home via Karachi, Cairo, Alexandria, Malta & Naples, enabling Somerville to meet senior officers of all services; moreover, at Naples he met his daughter Rachel, a 2O WRNS, with whom he visted Capri.

PART IV

THE BRITISH ADMIRALTY DELEGATION WASHINGTON, D.C.

January 1944–December 1945

INTRODUCTION

Early in 1944, Somerville received from his old friend, Admiral of the Fleet Sir Andrew Cunningham, an unwelcome and unexpected message [399]. The First Sea Lord asked him to leave a post which was just about to become immensely rewarding for a shore appointment far from the frontline. Somerville was invited to become the head of the British Admiralty Delegation in Washington, D.C., a component part of the British Joint Staff Mission established in 1941; the head of BAD served also as the First Sea Lord's representative on the Combined Chiefs of Staff, who were based in Washington. The Delegation had an extensive remit; it acted as a liaison office, it exchanged information with the US Navy, participated in joint projects, monitored supplies of equipment, munitions, aircraft and ships under Lend-Lease, and engaged in technical discussions with the Americans. Though the head of BAD had overall responsibility for these activities, in practice most of the sections ran themselves and there were always at least two other flag officers to look after the principal sectors. The head of the Delegation, therefore, was principally concerned with maintaining good relations with the Navy Department and other branches of the US Government, co-ordinating the work of his service with the Army and RAF representatives, and discussing future strategy on the Combined Chiefs of Staff Committee. He had to be a full Admiral with substantial, successful and relevant high level experience during the war. The first incumbent was Admiral Sir Charles Little, Second Sea Lord from 1938 to 1941. He was followed in the spring of 1942 by Cunningham, whose prestige and obstinacy were required to combat the US Chief of Naval Operations, Admiral King, widely regarded by the British, not always justly, as an obstructive figure and an Anglophobe. When Cunningham left in the autumn of 1942 to command the naval forces involved in operation TORCH, he was succeeded by Admiral Sir Percy Noble, until that time C-in-C, Western Approaches and therefore the man best acquainted with the Battle of the Atlantic, the most pressing naval issue of the day. Noble was due to retire in the summer of 1944 and in any case the crisis of the U-boat war had long passed. Furthermore, the appointment was as wearing in its own way as any of the major combat commands and Noble served longer than either Little or Cunningham.

As the nature of the sea war changed and as our situation *vis-à-vis* the Americans altered, so a new head of the Delegation better fitted to deal with the current and likely future issues was required. By 1944, the focus of the naval war was shifting to the Far East and it made good sense, therefore, to have a head of Delegation who was well acquainted with the war against Japan. From the latter part of 1943, ironically the point at which Cunningham succeeded Pound as First Sea Lord, the United States Navy had become, indisputably, the largest navy in the world and the British were increasingly supplicants in Washington, pleading for as large a share of the vast American output of ships, landing craft, planes and other articles of war as they could obtain. As the US Navy took ever firmer hold of Neptune's trident, so it seemed to British observers[1] that Admiral King became more obdurate and anti-British. What was now required as the head of BAD was an Admiral of high repute, seasoned in battle, enjoying the full confidence of Cunningham and equal to Admiral King in forthrightness and doggedness. As Cunningham pointed out, Somerville had all the necessary qualities; moreover, no one else could match his experience in the east or his redoubtable personality [401, 402].

Somerville declared dutifully that he would accept the appointment if Cunningham really wished him to do so but he made it clear that he had no desire for a shore post, that he felt unsuited to the kind of work involved and that he was concerned about the financial implications [400, 403]. The Treasury, worried by the shortage of US dollars, imposed strict limits on allowances for those serving in the USA; Cunningham and Noble had evidently paid for some of the entertaining considered necessary in Washington out of their own pockets. Somerville, who hoped after the war to maintain the family estate at Dinder, was understandably reluctant to make a major contribution from his own funds to what he considered to be activities in the national interest. However, Cunningham reassured him on the financial aspect and by the spring of 1944, resigned to seeing out his career in a desk job far away from the fighting and in an appointment for which he had absolutely no enthusiasm, he was making the necessary staff arrangements [404].

At that point, however, he was just embarking on the final, offensive phase of his time with the Eastern Fleet. His successful carrier attacks on

---

[1] See Noble to Cunningham, 12 Jan & 20 Feb 1944; Cunningham to Noble, 6 Feb 1944, all in Cunningham papers, BM Add. Mss. 52571; Cunningham, diary, 9 June 1944, BM Add Mss 52577.

Japanese bases, one of the few aggressive blows dealt by our forces in that Theatre, naturally attracted the interest of the Prime Minister, who was always keen to endorse and encourage boldness and the offensive spirit. He raised objections to Somerville's imminent translation to Washington and throughout April and May 1944 carried on a running fight with the First Lord, Alexander, and Cunningham. Ironically, each success of Somerville's fleet gave Churchill more ammunition to resist his replacement. The Admiralty patiently explained, again and again, why Somerville was the only man for the post and why it was desirable to install a new commander of what was to become our principal fleet, eventually to carry the war to Japan in the Pacific. Still Churchill stalled; he put forward Tovey and Fraser as possible heads of BAD but ultimately Alexander and Cunningham prevailed. Somerville was relieved by Fraser in August 1944 and, after a rare and brief spell in Britain, left for Washington late in October [405–10]. It should be noted that he was not removed from command of Eastern Fleet because of his dispute with Mountbatten; Cunningham would never have stomached an attempt to replace him on those grounds, though it seems likely that Mountbatten would have persuaded Churchill not to extend his appointment.[1]

Somerville never enjoyed his time in Washington, though he made many American friends and experienced some happy occasions. Quite apart from feeling constitutionally unsuited to the kind of duties embraced by his new post, he loathed the constant round of parties, the political intrigues (not all of them conducted by professional politicians), the endless negotiating, the wearing encounters with King and those of his subordinates who took their cue from the Chief of Naval Operations, and the management of a vast and varied empire, all far from the smell of action and the moody sea[2] [412, 424, 427].

Upon his arrival, Somerville lost no time in making himself known to the leading figures in Washington – the President, his Chief of Staff (Admiral Leahy), Secretary of the Navy Forrestal,[3] Admiral King and his senior associates [411–13, 417]. His relationship with King was crucial and he was fortunate that he had met King once before, when he had visited Washington with others from India in May 1943; on that occasion, he had got on well with the singular American Admiral [403]. King seems to have been chameleon-like in his behaviour; like everyone else, Somerville could never judge beforehand how he would behave. While

---

[1]Roskill, *Churchill and the Admirals*, p. 259.
[2]Macintyre, pp. 255–9.
[3]James V. Forrestal (1892–1949): Dem poln; investment banker; naval aviator, 1917–18; spl admin asst to Press June 1940; USec Navy Aug 1940; Sec Navy May 1944; Sec Defense July 1947–March 1949; fell out with Pres Truman; took his own life.

King was usually cordial in a personal sense, he quickly reverted to stern obduracy when Somerville requested ships, aircraft, other equipment or information [411, 412]. With the US Navy's drive across the Pacific now assuming a triumphal character and with Japan's home islands on the fleet's horizon and already under constant air attack, King was increasingly opposed to making matériel and dockyard facilities available to the Royal Navy, though there were occasions on which he was thoroughly amenable [412, 413, 414, 415, 417, 421, 428, 430, 432, 457, 459]. Somerville realised that he must use a combination of his own prestige, his salty humour, his gift of anecdote and his own not inconsiderable capacity for sheer bloodymindedness to deal effectively with King [421, 422, 423, 427, 428, 436, 460]. King came to respect and like Somerville and certainly Cunningham's belief that his old friend was the man best fitted to deal with King in the final stages of the war was handsomely confirmed.[1]

Somerville seems to have found some other senior officers in the Navy Department relatively easy to deal with and, on their own initiative, forthcoming with assistance and information. Somerville had complained frequently when in the Eastern Fleet of the American reluctance to keep him properly informed of plans and events in the Pacific and he made it an early priority to request a better flow of information to the Admiralty, a subject on which King, as usual, blew hot and cold, though in general efforts were made to meet Somerville's wishes [413, 417, 428, 430]. Of equal concern to Somerville was the need to improve the publicity about the British war effort, especially that of the Royal Navy and more particularly the British Pacific Fleet and he urged Cunningham and the Ministry of Information to despatch a well-qualified naval publicity team to Washington [420, 422, 428, 430, 431, 433]. Otherwise, the British contribution to the war, particularly in SE Asia and the Far East would not be impressed upon the Americans. Somerville, though not by nature a publicity seeker, manfully undertook a one-man campaign to publicise British achievements and in particular those of Mountbatten and South East Asia Command [414, 421, 422].

It was not to be expected that Somerville would have much contact with the President but such meetings as they did have seem to have been most amicable and informal, though Somerville noted, as did many others, Roosevelt's rapid physical decline after the election of 1944 and was not surprised when he heard of FDR's death in April 1945 [417,

---

[1]Roskill, who was a Cdr and CSO (Admin) at BAD at the time, considered that Somerville was 'the most successful of all British Admirals in handling "Ernie" King', *Churchill and the Admirals*, pp. 270–1.

428, 434]. He found Admiral Leahy most congenial and helpful [411, 428] and he established a cordial relationship with Admiral Nimitz [430, 468], King's successor as Chief of Naval Operations.

Somerville reported frequently and informally to Cunningham [420, 438, 459, 460, 465, 466, 467] and kept up a substantial correspondence with other military figures round the world, notably Mountbatten [414, 416, 418, 419, 423, 427, 429, 431, 433]. One of Somerville's duties was to inspect British units in the United States [421], and especially establishments of the Royal Canadian Navy [434, 465]. The Canadians had an ambivalent relationship with the British and many seemed better disposed towards the Americans; there were hints of French-Canadian animus against Britain and an American observation on the fraught relations between the two Commonwealth Navies. Somerville paid three short visits home, one of which, sadly, was to the bedside of his dying wife and another was on his return from the summit conference at Yalta in the Crimea (held in February 1945) [428, 459, 464].

Much of Somerville's time at Yalta was concerned with the related issues of oil and shipping. Both were in short supply in Britain and the British had to go cap in hand to the Americans, who drove a hard bargain, in part because they did not believe Britain's circumstances were as straitened as she claimed and because they faced insatiable demands from their own forces in the Pacific. Somerville worked energetically to secure a fair share of both shipping and oil, with a degree of success, despite having a case which was far from watertight [428, 430, 436, 459].

From time to time Somerville noted interesting differences between American organisation and methods and those of the Royal Navy. It seemed evident to him that, despite the autocratic rule of King in Washington, the Navy Department exercised far less control over fleet and station commanders overseas than did the Admiralty and was often as much in the dark about distant water operations as America's allies [413]. Many of his discussions, naturally enough, were about carrier operations, a subject to which he had given considerable if not systematic thought (lack of time prevented him from much more than occasional soliloquies and observations on operations) and he must have been intrigued by an American officer's strictures on 'air admirals' [413]. It was equally interesting to discover that, just as the British were abandoning armoured flight decks for fleet carriers in favour of greater aircraft capacity, the Americans, impressed by the effects of kamikazes on their unarmoured ships, were adopting them for new fleet carriers [425]. Comparisons between the two services were inevitable and

Somerville's observations and reports suggest that the honours were about even[1] [412, 413, 421, 425, 428, 430, 459, 460, 462, 463, 465].

Somerville was also deeply involved in joint strategic planning, the provision of resources for future operations and naval co-operation in general. While the Atlantic Theatre was now generally safe, there was a late alarm over the new, fast, schnorkel-equipped U-boats which seemed likely once again to cause high shipping losses [428]. Rather more of the strategic and resource issues related to South East Asia Command, where Mountbatten was trying desperately to fulfil his directive to carry out significant Allied combined operations in conjunction with overland offensives and long range bombing, despite his acute shortage of materials, especially shipping and landing craft. Somerville strove hard to obtain a higher priority for Mountbatten's command but with little success. Mountbatten tried to boost his naval forces by proposing the diversion of reinforcements for the British Pacific Fleet, and even the Fleet itself, to operations within his own command; these bids were ill-received by Cunningham and by the high command in general [428, 430, 431, 437, 444, 451].

Much the most important aspect of Somerville's work in Washington was his role as a major facilitator of resources and operations for the British Pacific Fleet. From the moment he arrived, he was involved in a constant battle with King and many of his subordinates both to secure a fair share of the final operations against Japan for the British task force and for the aircraft, support ships, supplies and bases necessary to permit them to play a significant part in the last round. He was well aware, long before he went to Washington, that King and many of his senior colleagues did not want the British Fleet to operate in the Pacific and, having lost the battle to exclude it, were now determined to divert it to the geographical and strategic margins.[2] Somerville grasped all opportunities to stress the substantial contribution the British fleet could make to victory in the Pacific [411]. Many senior British figures (though *not* the First Sea Lord) were prepared to send the fleet to the South West Pacific to operate under MacArthur's command, and this was evidently supported by the General himself and other American commanders [413, 415, 423]. Somerville was more willing to adapt to American practices than Cunningham.[3] When King attempted to block Fraser's appointment

---

[1]The US Navy was far ahead in engineering, aircraft, A/A, fleet train, and refuelling; the British led in radar, sonar and carrier take off and landing technical development.

[2]Marder, vol. 2, pp. 343–514 is especially good on RN operations against Japan after Somerville left Eastern Fleet.

[3]On Cunningham's rather parochial and traditional views, see R. Humble, *Fraser of North Cape*, pp. 259–60, 283.

because he was senior to US admirals, Somerville moved quickly to bolster Fraser's position [415, 417] and, as he forecast, any potential wrangles were dispelled when Fraser met Nimitz and came to an agreement with him which King was compelled to accept [425]. The issue of when, where and how the British task force should be employed was not resolved until the fleet reached the Pacific in March 1945 [413, 415, 423, 425, 428, 430, 431]. Once it began to operate alongside the main US carrier task forces, however, it performed well [428, 435], though it continued to have supply difficulties and was inferior to the American carrier force in efficiency and endurance [425, 426, 428, 430, 431, 463]. Nevertheless, the armoured decks of the British carriers proved their worth, though in circumstances wholly unexpected – defence against *kamikazes*. Suicide planes had been a major Japanese weapon against American warships since the Philippines campaign in the autumn of 1944 but they were at their most numerous and destructive in the operations off Okinawa and Iwo Jima. The problem was one to which there was no easy or readily available solution and opinion clearly differed on how to handle them. [411, 423, 425, 428, 430, 435, 454]. American casualties in ships and men were extremely heavy; fleet carriers were frequently put out of action, while British carriers were able to return to operations within hours of being hit, though with reduced capacity [437, 452]. Somerville's concerns from the spring of 1945 were in securing recognition for the fleet's achievements and finding a mutually acceptable forward base for its operations, on which King was by turns amenable and obstructive [433, 435, 436, 452, 453, 455–60, 462]. Resolution of the issue came only at the end of the war, just before the dropping of the atomic bombs and Japan's request for peace, on both of which Somerville had some interesting observations. How little was understood about the destructive effect of nuclear weapons, especially long term radiation, was revealed in his diary, together with his belief that the Japanese would not otherwise have surrendered [462–64].

It was at that point that Somerville was called home, where his wife lay critically ill; she died just after VJ-Day and he returned to Washington some three weeks later to clear up his business. There was considerable comfort for him in that his daughter Rachel was posted to BAD at that time. He found the three US Chiefs of Staff all war-weary and anxious to retire, especially as the American Government was about to set up a Department of Defense which would reduce the autonomy of the three services [466, 467]. By mid-December, Somerville's work was done and he handed over to Admiral Moore, his successor as head of BAD[1] and left

---

[1]Adm Sir Henry Moore, formerly C-in-C, Home Fleet.

for home and retirement. He took with him the sincere good wishes of his American colleagues – King included [468, 469].

On VE-Day, Somerville had received the ultimate accolade for an officer in the Royal Navy, elevation to the rank of Admiral of the Fleet, having been restored to the Active List a few months earlier. The promotion, a just reward for the immensely successful discharge of three high commands during the war, was a most effective riposte to the naval surgeons who had compelled his retirement in 1939 on medical grounds. Many tributes poured in on and after 8 May 1945, as full of humour as they were of congratulations [442–51] but none as sparkling or as well known as the exchange of signals between BAD and the Admiralty on the occasion of VE-Day [439–41].

Somerville never pretended to like his sojourn in Washington. It was of vital importance, its value not diminished by the shift in strategic concern from Europe to Asia, and he invested it with his characteristic energy and clarity of vision. In particular, he gained the respect and co-operation of Admiral King as probably no other British admiral could have done. His liveliness, geniality and capacity to get on well with almost everyone made him many genuine friends in America. He worked diligently to meet the First Sea Lord's, Mountbatten's and Fraser's needs and he took numerous initiatives, not least in publicising Britain's part in the war, especially in the east and even more so that of the Royal Navy.

CONCLUSION

Within a few months of leaving Washington, Somerville retired finally from active service after serving for almost half a century. During that time he had become one of the Navy's leading communications specialists and the prime mover in the early days of Naval radar. He was already a Captain when he gained command of a ship but quickly made an outstanding reputation as a battleship Captain. During the 1930s, much of his time was spent on personnel matters, where he once more adapted to new demands with vigour and speed. His first sea-going command as a flag officer made two immediate and enormous demands on his stamina, character, adaptability, skill and, not least, his charm. He had to succeed the formidable Andrew Cunningham, widely regarded as *the* destroyer man and he had to deal with the chaos resulting from the Spanish Civil War. He dealt with these challenges with aplomb, only to have his promising flag career cut short by a disputed medical decision. It was his, and his country's, great good fortune that the Second World War provided almost immediately a means of reviving his career and of reaching the highest honour the Service could offer. After strenuous activity in the field of radar and 'miscellaneous weapons and devices' during the 'phoney war', he plunged, of his own volition, into the Dunkirk evacuation operations, providing invaluable assistance to Admiral Ramsay. His experience and availability led to the command of the hastily assembled Force H, formed in the wake of France's collapse and which began its life in the most distressing fashion by attacking the fleet of our late ally at Mers-el-Kebir. Force H then proceeded to earn laurels for itself and plaudits for its commander with a series of successful convoys to Malta, coupled with attacks on Italian bases, brushes with bombers and submarines and, on two occasions, with the Italian fleet. Furthermore, it should not be forgotten that Force H had the unique burden of defending both the western Mediterranean and the western central Atlantic. The disasters to British arms in the Far East at the end of 1941 were the prelude to Somerville's two and a half years in command of the Eastern Fleet. Its strength see-sawed as other theatres drained it of ships but, beginning by avoiding the superior Japanese air and sea forces, Somerville ended his command of the Eastern Fleet by leading it on several successful carrier strikes against Japanese bases. His final appointment was one he would not have chosen and was loath to accept. A sense of duty and loyalty to his old friend, Andrew Cunningham, now First Sea Lord, prompted him to take up the post of head of the British Admiralty Delegation. In Washington, he fought many battles with Fleet Admiral King, the C-in-C, US Fleet, and Chief of Naval Operations, especially in support of the British Pacific Fleet. It was fitting that his career should be capped by his restoration to the Active List and his promotion to Admiral of the Fleet.

Sir James Somerville had great technical interest and ability in a variety of fields. Not only that, he was, by common consent of those who served with him, a masterly fleet handler and a first-rate and demanding trainer of ships, planes and men. He demonstrated a keen concern for the welfare of those who served under him and was to be seen frequently visiting his ships and shore establishments, as well as flying with his air crews. In truth, he deserves the title of our leading air admiral of the time, giving more attention to the handling of the fleet's air component than any of his contemporaries. None of his three great wartime commands was a sinecure, and he did not spare himself in the discharge of his duties. He experienced the loneliness and pressures of high command but bore the burdens with good humour and apparent ease. It was not his good fortune to be identified with a successful, classic sea battle, unlike other Admirals of the Fleet – Andrew Cunningham and Matapan, Tovey and the *Bismarck*, Fraser and the *Scharnhorst* – but he was responsible for handing *Bismarck* to Tovey almost on a plate, he was as important as Cunningham in maintaining Britain's Mediterranean position and in the Eastern Fleet he trained many of the ships and men who went on with Fraser to the final round in the Pacific. He made few errors – he should not have allowed *Strasbourg* to escape from Mers-el-Kebir, and he should have ensured that the signal detaching *Sheffield* to shadow *Bismarck* was repeated to *Ark Royal*. On two occasions he enjoyed good fortune – the fruits, perhaps, of great boldness – in avoiding potentially disastrous encounters with superior fleets – the Italians after the bombardment of Genoa and the Japanese off Ceylon. His career in the Second World War was full of action and variety and demonstrates the many aspects of sea power; much of a navy's time at sea is spent in lonely but vital vigil and consists of humdrum but essential duties – convoying, inspecting neutrals for contraband, rescuing survivors, patrolling – in which there is little apparent dash and glory, yet on such duties diligently and efficiently performed does the success of other arms and the battle fleets depend. Admiral of the Fleet Sir James Somerville recognised, as these papers demonstrate, the multi-faceted nature of sea power and practised the arts of admiralty both ashore and afloat with a consummate professionalism worthy to be remembered with the great admirals of the past.

402. *From Cunningham*

29 January 1944

Noble has asked to be relieved in Washington in June due to his impending retirement.

2. You know well the importance we attach to this appointment and how difficult it is to find an officer who has the necessary qualities to fill it with success. Although we should very much regret your departure from the Eastern Fleet, after much thought it has been decided to offer it to you. We consider that there is no one who would fill it so adequately. Your outstanding war service and knowledge of Eastern Waters makes you particularly suitable at this time when the war in the Far East is becoming of primary importance.

3. We shall be very grateful if you find yourself able to accept.

4. It is proposed that Fraser should relieve you as C-in-C, EF.

403. *To Cunningham*

30 January 1944

I do not really feel that this proposed appointment is at all up my street and I have a personal dislike for it. But I will of course go if you consider I ought to accept.

2. No one could ask for a better relief than Bruce Fraser.

3. I assume that Percy is not leaving in order to avoid bankruptcy.

404. *From Cunningham*

February 1944

The intention in offering you the Washington appointment was in no way a suggestion that it was time you were relieved in Eastern Fleet.

You must however realise that officers who are qualified to fill this appointment adequately are very scarce.

I would not have allowed you finally to accept appointment without setting the financial position squarely before you. . . .

405. *From Cunningham*

10 March 1944

D.   I don't know what you think about Washington. From the monetary angle my wife thinks it would be all right provided you did not do too much entertaining in your own house. I got a good deal more but I returned £160 to the Treasury and paid for all my own entertaining, which, at about £90 a big cocktail party, fair walked off with the dollars.

I cannot pretend that it is an attractive post unless you like a continual scrap. Our friend has become very difficult and if you don't take it God only knows where we shall get someone of the necessary calibre to deal with him.

E.   As I read your letters you have no wish to return to the Active List and on the whole I think you are wise unless you want another stripe and less money.

406. *To Cunningham*

c. end of March 1944

4.   Re. Washington, it is certainly a most unattractive proposition, but whilst I was there last year I got on fairly well with old Ernie King – however, whether he will be as forthcoming when I am BAD, I can't say. . . .

5.   As regards returning to the Active List, I wanted to make it quite clear that I have no desire at all to take advantage of my being retired, but if it is for the good of the Service that I should return to the Active List I am quite prepared to do so. Mollie[1] is apparently very keen for me to go back on the Active List and I suppose in some ways it is a bit of an anomaly, and does not perhaps do the Service much good for me to go from one important job to another as a retired Admiral, which has been my lot during the war. . . .

[1]Lady Somerville.

407. *Paymaster Captain W. McBride to Paymaster Captain Alan Laybourne*[1]

British Admiralty Delegation,
Washington, DC,
10 April 1944

. . . The BAD set-up is very similar to a duplicate Admiralty. The Head of BAD represents the First Sea Lord and the Admiralty generally and is, of course, the Representative on the Combined Chiefs of Staff Committee. The Second and Fourth Sea Lords are represented by BAMR (Admiral French), the Controller and Director of Dockyards by BASR (Rear Admiral Waller), and the Fifth Sea Lord by Captain John. Le Maitre represents the Secretary of the Admiralty. As the new construction is rapidly dwindling the work in BAD is lessening every day in certain respects, and we are about to reorganise it so that BASR and BAMR will be brought under one head – Admiral Waller. This should be working before you arrive.[2]

The Head of the Delegation is in the CCS building, where of course your office is, and the rest of the BAD is in the Arlington Hotel, about 10 minutes away by car.

Admiral Somerville's staff will consist of:–

Chief of Staff – Cdre A.W. Clarke
Secretary to Chief of Staff – Paymaster Lt-Cdr J.D. Trythall
Director of Plans (Washington) – Captain L.E. Porter (Note: also member of Combined Staff Planners)
Plans (Strategic) – Cdr H.B.C. Gill

[1] Paymr-Capt W. McBride: Paymr-Cdr 1933; Temp Paymr-Capt & Sec to C-in-C China (Noble) 1939–41; *Eaglet* (Liverpool) 1941–2; Actg Paymr-Capt BAD 1943–4.

Paymr-Capt Alan Laybourne: Paymr-Lt-Cdr & Sec to Cdre, Portsmouth Barracks Oct 1932; Paymr-Cdr & Sec to RA (D), Med F (Somerville) 1936; Sec to VA T. H. Binney, FOIC, Scapa Flow Aug 1939; Tempy Paymr-Capt & Sec to C-in-C, Eastern F Feb 1942; Actg Capt (S) 1944; BAD 1944–5.

[2] Vice Adm (Ret) Sir Wilfred F. French: Capt 1917; RA 1929; VA Feb 1934; Ret List Oct 1938; Admy Feb 1941; BAD July 1942.

Rear Adm John W. A. Waller.

Capt (later Adm of the Fleet Sir) Caspar John (1903–84): son of Augustus John, the artist; ent RN 1916; pilot 1926; passionate advocate of naval aviation; *Hermes* 1925–7; tec involvement 1930s; Lt-Cdr 1933; Cdr 1936; NAD 1937; EO *York*, NAWI Sta 1939; Actg Capt, Dir Gen N Dev & Prodn, Min A/C Prodn May 1941; Capt June 1941; NA Mexico & C Am & Asst NA (Air) Washington, June 1943; *Ocean* May 1945; IDC 1947; CO Lossiemouth 1948; DC N Air Eqpt & Dir Air Org & Trng; RA 1951; Min Supply 1952–4; FO (A) Home, Lee & VA 1954; VCNS & Adm 1957; 1SL 1960–3; Adm of F 1962; pub svc.

Mr A. S. Le Maitre: Actg Prin Asst Sec, Admy 1941; Dep Sec Admy June 1941; Under Sec Admy, N America 1944; Prin Asst Sec June 1945.

Plans (Q) – Cdr G.M.D. Hutcheson
Staff Officer (Air) – Cdr C.E. Fenwick (Note: also combines this with
duties of Staff Officer (Operations))*
Staff Officer (Trade) – Captain H.W. Morey*
   * These officers have offices in the Navy Department, which is across
the road from the CCS building.
DNI (Washington) – Captain T.C.T. Wynne, with three assistants
Signal Officer – Captain K.M. Walter, with one Lieut (S) as assistant.[1] . . .

The Joint Staff Mission – which consists of Field Marshal Sir John
Dill and the three Heads of the British Services – meets once a week and
on the following day, they meet the American Chiefs of Staff, when all
matters for decision are discussed and decided upon. . . .

408. *Alexander to Churchill*

15 April 1944

. . . I would like to set out the reasons why the First Sea Lord and I consider that the proposed appointment of Admiral Somerville to
Washington and of Admiral Fraser to command the Eastern Fleet should
be made now.
1.   We feel that it is very necessary that Admiral Noble should be
relieved as soon as possible not only because of his age but because he
has now had two years of hard and strenuous work. Admiral Noble has
been very successful in Washington but the appointment is, as the First
Sea Lord has mentioned to you, most uncongenial and wearing, and we

[1]Cdre A. W. Clarke: Capt, Admy 1939; Asst NA Washington July 1940; *Sheffield* Aug
1941; COS to C-in-C Med, Malta Jan 1943; Cdre & COS, BAD Jan 1944. Paymr-Lt-Cdr J.
D. Trythall: Paymr-Lt1936; *Achilles* 1939; *Eaglet* (Liverpool) Feb 1941; Actg Paymr-Lt-
Cdr, BAD Nov 1942; Paymr-Lt-Cdr Jan 1944; Lt-Cdr (S), Sec to RA 11th A/C Carrier
Sqdn, *Venerable* March 1945. Actg Capt L. E. Porter: Cdr 1937; SO(I), China Sta, *Kent*
1937; *Suffolk* Nov 1940; Actg Capt, BAD Nov 1942. Cdr H. B. C. Gill: Lt-Cdr 1938;
Suffolk 1939; *Devonshire* 1940; *Drake* April 1941; *Dryad* (Nav Sch, Portsmouth) April
1942; Cdr June 1942; BAD June 1943; *Leander* 1945. Actg Cdr (Ret) G. M. D. Hutcheson:
Lt-Cdr, Ret List Jan 1938; *Raleigh* (Torpoint) April 1941; *Asbury* (LC base ship) May
1943; BAD Jan 1944. Obsvr Lt-Cdr C. E. Fenwick: Lt 1933; Lt (O) *Daedalus* (Lee) 1939;
Lt-Cdr Feb 1941; CO 710 Sqdn *Albatross* April 1941; Lt-Cdr (O) *Stalker* April 1942; SO
(Air & O) BAD Aug 1943. Actg Capt (Ret) H.W. Morey: Lt 1908; Cdr Ret List Dec 1926;
TD Aug 1939; Actg Capt BAD May 1942. Actg Capt T. C. T. Wynne: Cdr June 1933; EO
Orion July 1938; NID June 1942; Actg Capt BAD April 1943; CO Inshore Sqdn *Byrsa* Jan
1945. Actg Capt Keith M. Walter: Cdr 1938; Tac Sch 1939; SD Aug 1939; *Aurora* May
1942; Actg Capt BAD Nov 1943. One should also mention here Cdr Stephen W. Roskill
(1903–1982): Cdr 1938; TSD 1939; *Leander* Dec 1941–Jan 1943; *Onslaught* 1943; RNZN
June 1943; Actg Capt BAD March 1944; Capt June 1944; CSO (Admin & Weapons); after
the war, the official historian of the war at sea.

feel that the appointment of a man of Admiral Somerville's type, rank and prestige will be of the utmost value.

2.   You have already agreed that the principal Naval command is that of the Eastern Fleet and that Admiral Fraser shall go out there. The First Sea Lord and I agree that it is important that he should get there as soon as possible, and transfers of this kind inevitably take time. While we appreciate the need for firm decisions on strategy we do not think that it will make any difference if Admiral Fraser left before they were taken. It would however have been six weeks before he could leave.

The First Sea Lord and I would therefore be very grateful if you could see your way to agree to these changes now.

409.   *Churchill to Alexander*

29 April 1944

Admiral Somerville has added new claims to our confidence by his brilliant attack at Sabang while the main Japanese Fleet was at Singapore. Why do we want to make a change here at all?

It seems to me he knows the theatre, has right ideas about it and is capable of daring action. Does he want to go to Washington and give up his fighting command?

410.   *Alexander to Churchill*

3 May 1944

2.   Admiral Somerville certainly conducted a brilliant operation in the bombing of Sabang but there is no reason to suppose that Admiral Fraser will show a less aggressive spirit. . . .

3.   Admiral Somerville has no desire to go to Washington. No Admiral does desire to take up this most uncongenial and expensive appointment. Those there previously have gone against their inclinations and it is considered desirable to set a term to the appointment of BAD. Sir Percy Noble has been there since November 1942 and expressed a desire to be and was told he would be relieved in the summer. No other officer of the rank and experience in war required to impress the Americans is available except Admiral Somerville. He has the knowledge and the good humour necessary to deal with Admiral King.

4.   Sir James Somerville has now been in command of the Eastern Fleet since March 1942 and it is an undoubted fact that prolonged service in the tropics is liable to impair the vitality of officers and as time goes on

increased efforts on their part are necessary to maintain their efficiency. He will be 62 in July.

5.   We are planning for an Eastern war which may last for two or three years. We feel strongly that the change which will be inevitable before that time lapses is better made now than at a time when critical operations may be in progress.

411.   *Churchill to Alexander*

21 May 1944

1.   Since I last minuted you on this subject, Admiral Somerville has brought off the excellent Sourabaya operation. His telegrams about it show him keen and sprightly in the last degree. I do not therefore wish to make a change at the present time unless Admiral Somerville desires to be relieved or it is thought by the doctors that he is failing physically.

2.   Admiral Fraser is well placed at Scapa. The *Tirpitz* has yet to be destroyed or prevented from returning home. The Russian convoys must be resumed as soon as the press of OVERLORD is over. In both cases I think you have the right man in the right place. As Admiral King is so difficult, why not let him be dealt with by other channels than through our Admirals. We shall soon probably have the American Chiefs of Staff over here. It would seem a great pity to throw away all the knowledge of this eastern theatre which Admiral Somerville has gained. I am very reluctant therefore to make the changes you desire.

412.   *Alexander to Churchill*

24 May 1944

So far as I am aware, Admiral Somerville is in excellent health, otherwise I should not, of course, propose to send him to such an exacting post as that at Washington.

The Home Fleet is now so much reduced that it is no longer necessary to keep an officer of Admiral Fraser's seniority and ability in command there. The second in command – Vice Admiral Moore – who has actually been carrying out the operations against *Tirpitz* is considered a very suitable relief for him and it is proposed to make this change at an early date.

It is not feasible to deal with Admiral King in any other way than through the Admiral appointed to the CCS organisation. Many naval subjects which concern the Admiralty and the Navy Department alone are dealt with direct through this Admiral, and it is essential to have an officer of rank and experience. It is just Admiral Somerville's experience in Eastern Waters which will make him so valuable in Washington at the present time.

For these reasons as well as those given in my minute of 3 May (especially para. 5)[1] we continue at the Admiralty to hold strongly the opinion that these changes should be made now, and it is considered necessary for the effective prosecution of the war against Japan.

413. *Churchill to Alexander*

27 May 1944

I do not think it right to remove Admiral [Sir] James Somerville from his post. He has acquired special knowledge of all the conditions in the Indian Ocean and he is apparently in the best of health. Finally, he does not wish to go. To send this officer on this great command to Washington would be a squandering of our war power. Why do you not send Admiral Fraser to Washington, if the Home Fleet is no longer a fit charge for him? Or, alternatively, there is Admiral Tovey who can go from the Nore, to Washington.

2.   I do not think that you should say to me that your particular view about the movement of these Admirals is 'necessary for the effective prosecution of the war against Japan'. It might well be that in six months I should take a different view. But this idea of moving Admirals,when they are on the top of their form, from the theatres where they are acting with success, in order that they should dance attendance on Admiral King in Washington is, in my opinion, entirely wrong. Admiral Tovey would put up a splendid fight there.[2]

414. *BAD desk diary, 1944*

30 October

Admirals King and Cassady

Called on Admiral King; Vice Admirals Cooke and Edwards[3] also

---

[1] No. 410.

[2] Tovey, no great favourite of Churchill when he was C-in-C Home Fleet, was currently C-in-C Nore.

[3] Vice Adm Richard S. Edwards (1885–1956): US N Acad 1903–06; battleships & destroyers 1906–12; s/m *C3* i/c 1913; Cdr 1st Grp, S/M Flo, Atl F; battleships with Grand F 1917–19; Bat Sqdn GO 1919–21; *Wood* i/c 1924–6; staff & gun duties 1930–4; N War Coll 1934–5; S/M Div, Sqdn & Base cmds 1937–40; *Colorado* 1940; Cdr, S/M, Patrol Force Oct 1940 & Atl F S/M Feb 1941; DCOS, C-in-C Fleet Dec 1941–Aug 1942; DC-in-C Fleet & DCNO Oct 1944; Adm April 1945; VCNO Oct 1945; Cdr W Sea Frontier Jan 1946; Pac Res F Jan 1947; Ret List July 1947.

present. King very genial and expressed pleasure at my return to Washington. . . . King referred to suicide attacks by Japanese air which now seemed to be increasing and which he considered a serious menace. . . . I referred to *Saratoga*'s association with the Eastern Fleet and King said *Saratoga* had had a great time with us and enjoyed every minute of it.

After leaving King [I] called on Admiral Cassady who is now Deputy to Admiral Fitch;[1] he took me in to see the latter and we talked generally about carrier operations but not for long.

1 November

Admiral Leahy and the British Pacific Fleet

I saw Admiral Leahy at 10 o'clock; he was very cordial. Describing the Pacific action he said there was no doubt about it that quite a lot of Japanese ships got away all right and would turn up again. Furthermore a good many American ships suffered damage which would take some little time to repair.[2] I suggested that the British Fleet would be useful in such a situation and Leahy said smiling – yes, but it's a pity it can't be there now. I gather from him that he, at any rate, was by no means averse to the participation of the British Fleet in Pacific operations since he agreed with me that no Admiral could have too many ships in view of the unexpected hazards in modern naval warfare. . . .

415. *To Cunningham*

British Admiralty Delegation,
Washington, DC,
4 November 1944

Nothing has occurred during the week that I have been here to change my opinion that this is a bloody awful job and Washington is a bloody awful place, needless to say this must be perfectly stale news to you, though perhaps you may be surprised I should obtain confirmation so quickly.

---

[1]Vice Adm Aubrey W. ('Jake') Fitch (1883–1948): wide range of ships & stas 1907–11; PE Instr US N Acad 1911–13; Atl F 1914; GO *Wyoming* Grand F 1917–19; Cdr M/L Div 1920–2; pilot 1930; A/C carriers i/c 1931–7; NW Coll 1937–8; Cmd NAS Pensacola 1938–40; RA CarDiv 1 Nov 1940; Cdr Air TF *Lexington*, Coral Sea May 1942; Cdr US NA Forces, Pac F June 1942; VA Dec 1943; DCNO (Air) Aug 1944; Supt US N Acad Aug 1945; US Navy 1947; Adm & Ret List July 1947.

[2]Operations off the Philippines, known collectively as the Battle of Leyte Gulf.

Ernie King and the rest were all very friendly and nice when I paid my initial call on them but when I asked Ernie yesterday if he could get a hustle on the US Chiefs of Staff about a reply to the Hospital ship question he was his usual curt and off-hand self. ...

... the demonstration of the artificial harbours[1] has gone extremely well here and proved the greatest success; I attended one session and from the remarks made to me by various American officers, I could judge how impressed they were with this all-British job and the way it was handled. It does not appear to have any total application to the Pacific, but the Americans seemed to think that some of the bits and pieces and the methods employed might be copied by them to advantage.

416. BAD desk diary, 1944

6 November

Secretary of the Navy Forrestal

... an appointment had been made for me to call on Mr Forrestal at 4.30 but [I] was unable to see Captain Markey[2] before doing so. The Secretary was extremely friendly and used a phrase which a number of other people have used here to the effect that I was very welcome because I was a 'fighting Admiral'; what exactly qualifies one for this description is not quite clear. In conversation the Secretary emphasised the need for complete frankness between Allies and also the avoidance of criticism over small matters or differences of opinion which tend to become magnified. ...

Mr Forrestal said he was most anxious that officers, such as Admiral Cassady, who had served with the British Fleet, should continue to gain further experience with the British Fleet since he felt this was the surest way of securing a common view point which was essential not only during this war but subsequently. It seems quite clear that Admiral Cassady has been at pains to emphasise the good relations which existed between his task force and the Eastern Fleet and I feel I am largely indebted to him for the friendly reception I have had from so many quarters.

---

[1]Mulberries, as used off Normandy.
[2]Capt Gene Markey, USNR: b 1895: US Army 1916–19; novelist, playwright, film producer; Lt-Cdr USNR Oct 1938; Navy Dept 1941–2; Cdr Dec 1942; staff Cdr S Pac 1942–3; staff appts, Med & ME, India & Ceylon May 1943–July 1944; Spl Asst to Sec Navy & Dir N Photo Services July 1944–Nov 1945; Cdre, Ret List 1945.

Captain Markey on Admiral King

After leaving Mr Forrestal I had a very much 'off the record' talk with Captain Markey. He said that Admiral King was undoubtedly dictator over the Navy and that any attempt to upset or usurp his authority would be resisted by him most violently. On the other hand occasions might well arise when the President would insist on asserting his position as C-in-C, and he had in fact done so on certain occasions in the past. Markey considered that generally speaking on Naval matters the President and Admiral Leahy thought together and were frequently opposed in such thoughts by Admiral King, but it was only on occasions that a show down occurred.

7 November

Admiral Edwards and Co-operation

Admiral Edwards called on me in the afternoon and asked whether there were any little difficulties he could help over. I referred to the question of the holding back of the three repair ships now being completed for British use, but which I had just been informed the Americans now state they must keep for themselves. Admiral Edwards said he did not think the decision was final although he knew it had been under discussion, but the trouble was that they had so many ships damaged in the Philippines. In reply to a suggestion from me that it seemed improbable these repair ships, which would not be in service until April at the earliest, could be of much use in dealing with repairs of ships damaged in a recent action, the Admiral then said that it was not the action damages which were worrying them but the current damages in the operations now being undertaken by the Navy against land based air, about three ships a day being damaged by bombs and the position was beginning to look rather serious. . . .

I then suggested to the Admiral that it would be much easier for me and other senior officers of the BAD if we were kept more fully informed on such matters as damage to American ships, and in fact the general trend of operations. I pointed out that the first account of the night action I had been able to see anywhere was contained in current weekly news summary, and asked him what further information they had. Edwards replied that they themselves had very little information and that this report of the night action was probably far from accurate . . . I pointed out to the Admiral that in London not only had Admiral Stark access to the operations rooms at the Admiralty but he also had a British Admiral – Admiral Blake, to supply him with any information he might require. In comparison with London I felt we in Washington were on a very poor wicket.

The Admiral said he quite appreciated this and would take steps to look into the matter and see if something could not be done about it but he again emphasised the fact that they did not have full information in the Navy Department concerning events in the Pacific.

It seems to me that the Navy Department does not exercise anything like the same extent of control which the Admiralty exercise over the British Navy and that once having allocated forces to say Admiral Nimitz the Navy Department more or less washes its hands of the party and Admiral Nimitz just tells the Navy Department as much or as little as he likes about what has happened.

8 November

HMS Nelson

Captain Matheson of the *Nelson* called on me and stated that the US Authorities had cut down all work on *Nelson* to an absolute minimum. Referring to bombardments on the Normandy coast he said that the blast damage was considerable and it was due to necessity for firing on forward bearings.[1] . . .

Air Admirals

In the evening I dined with Cdre Clarke; Captain Dayton Clark, my former USNLO, was also present. Clark was critical of the American practice of putting their air Admirals in command of task forces. He considered that not only had this been overdone, but that it was easier for a surface force commander to have good tactical appreciation of the possibilities of use of air, rather than vice versa; he considered that the lack of 'follow up' by American surface forces in the previous encounters with the Japanese was due to the air Admirals not knowing how to handle surface forces.

10 November

General MacArthur and the British Pacific Fleet

General Lumsden[2] came to see me, said MacArthur was most anxious to have the British Fleet attached to him if possible as he had always

[1]Capt A. F. Matheson: Lt-Cdr June 1935; FGO, China Sta *Kent* March 1938; *Excellent* April 1940; Cdr June 1941; SO(O), 15CS, Med F *Cleopatra* April 1942; Actg Capt *Nelson* Sept 1943. *Nelson & Rodney* had all of their main armament forward of the bridge.
[2]Gen Sir Herbert Lumsden RA: 2Lt 1916; W Front 1916–18; Capt 1925; Maj 1931; staff appts 1930s; Lt-Col 1938; Brig 1940; PM's personal rep on MacArthur's staff.

been starved of ships, especially carriers. He said that if British Fleet was attached to MacArthur he felt quite certain the British Admiral could make his own conditions with MacArthur in regard to operations of the Fleet and general control of naval forces. He informed me confidentially that Admiral King had been anxious to replace Kinkaid by an Admiral who would be senior to any British Admiral that came out but Nimitz and others had protested at this and apparently the matter was allowed to drop.

He considered that Kinkaid's personal antagonism to MacArthur was responsible for many delays and lack of finish in the conduct of operations in the SW Pacific. King was determined that the war in the Pacific should be won by the American Navy; he had no personal motives in the matter but according to MacArthur, King would put the American Navy before the Army, or Air and even before the American Nation; it had to come first in every respect.

Lumsden thought it improbable that Nimitz would ever act contrary to King's wishes; I had suggested that when Fraser and Nimitz met that a good many difficulties would be smoothed out and they would no doubt arrange matters on a practical basis which King might have to accept. . . .

RCN in the Pacific

Referring to the Canadian Naval detachment of 2 cruisers, 2 light fleet carriers, 11 destroyers and 38 frigates to the Eastern Fleet, [Rear Admiral] Reid said the size of this force was governed by the number of men available, viz. 13,500[1] . . .

Tactics and Signals in the Pacific

Captain K. Walter, Signal Officer on my staff, called on me on his return from the UK. He said that the question of the British Fleet in the Pacific going 'all American' with regard to tactics and signals was now under consideration; he felt that Admiral Fraser realised it might be necessary for this to be done eventually but that both he and the CNS were averse to [doing] anything too hasty in this direction. It seems to me, however, that we shall have to go all American once we get to the Pacific and the sooner training to this effect takes place the better. I have not

---

[1]Rear Adm Howard E. Reid, RCN: Cdr 1933; Cdr-in-Chg, Halifax, NS 1938; Capt 1939; HQ, Ottawa 1941; Cdre 1 Cl, *Avalon* & FO, Newfoundland Force 1943; RA & NMCS Washington Dec 1943.

As the RCN bore a considerable share of the Battle of the Altantic, this was a very sizeable force for a country with a small population & resources to supply.

found the American tactical instructions easy to follow and I dislike many of their dispositions but on the other hand I do not feel it would be possible for the two fleets to work in tactical co-operation unless they adopt the same methods.

417. To Mountbatten

10 November 1944

. . . I, of course, had to give a press conference soon after my arrival and took occasion to refer to these inaccuracies[1] and, at the same time, emphasised the fact that it was lack of craft, men and material which had hitherto prevented you from conducting amphibious operations and reminding them of the figures recently published concerning the scale of operations in Burma and the large bag of Japanese resulting from these operations. I think the publication of those figures was most valuable since apparently Americans have realised for the first time the extent to which we have been engaged with the Japanese and the fact that in round figures we have accounted for more Japanese than all their much advertised operations in the Pacific.

So far as the provision of landing craft, etc., is concerned, you are certainly up against rather a brick wall because the Americans undoubtedly consider that the Pacific must have priority over SEAC. From one angle I can accept their argument up to a point in as much as the Philippine operations are proving pretty expensive and are not quite as expected. MacArthur's communiques have aroused some comment in civilian circles on the scale that they are too optimistic; you may remember that about a week ago he talked about mopping up final elements of Japanese resistance in Leyte and only two days later had to confess that the Japanese had landed another 30,000 men. . . .

418. BAD desk diary, 1944

13 November

British Fleet in the Pacific

Received a signal from Admiral King to First Sea Lord in which he stated he did not agree with the appointment of Fraser as C-in-C EF since

---

[1]Presumably the US tendency to allege that the British never did anything in SE Asia and that the Americans earned all the glory.

it was a new departure to have more than one Naval C-in-C in any particular area. Furthermore King stated it had been his intention when the units of the Fleet first arrived to place these under Kinkaid for working up and that it was a matter for him to decide later whether the British Fleet would operate under Kinkaid or Nimitz. This is obviously going to cause a stir in the Admiralty since so far as I am aware it has always been considered that the Admiral in charge of the British Fleet would come under a Supreme Commander, not necessarily under an American Admiral; in this instance of course Fraser is senior in rank to Kinkaid. I sent a signal to the First Sea Lord asking for his reactions on this signal, in particular whether or what stipulations he had with regard to the appointment of the Fleet either as detached units to American task forces, as British Task Forces, or as a concentrated British Force, and also his views on whether Fraser could properly work under Kinkaid's orders. As I said previously, MacArthur would certainly welcome the British Fleet working under his orders and with a British Admiral in command so as not to be tied up too closely to Admiral King.

14 November

Repair Ships

In regard to the three repair ships, the Admiralty reiterates that these are essential for the maintenance of the British Fleet in the Pacific, but Admiral King has now put in a memorandum in which he shows that the Americans have only 9 ARs to support 180 heavy ships whereas the British had provisionally allocated 8 ARs for 72 ships. Of course King makes no reference to any shore based repair facilities at forward bases and no doubt this statement is somewhat special pleading. My appreciation at the moment is that probably the American need is greater than ours up to and including July 1945, and that we are not on a particularly good wicket to contest the assignment of these ships to the US. King's memorandum has been telegraphed to the Admiralty and I must await their remarks.

419. *From Mountbatten*

SEAC HQ,
Kandy,
Ceylon,
14 November 1944

Thank you so much for your letter on 24 October, written at sea. It is typically thoughtful of you to have written to commiserate on the cancellation of DRACULA.[1] We always seem to have our amphibious operations cancelled in October, just like Stilwell always gets sacked every October by the Generalissimo![2]

However, as you will have observed from our SEACOS telegrams, I was sent off to Cairo, where the PM, Foreign Secretary, CIGS and Pug Ismay held a meeting with me, at which I was invited to put up new proposals for a reduced amphibious operation, which has resulted in my suggesting the Arakan in a couple of months, followed by the Kra Isthmus a couple of months later.

You probably heard that while I was in London in August, I did my best to persuade the Prime Minister that we did not require the battle fleet in SEAC, provided he left enough carriers and escort vessels to enable amphibious operations to take place, and perhaps one or two old battleships to help with the bombardment. I hope, and rather think, I was able to tip the scales in favour of the battle fleet going to the Pacific, and all I hope now is that they do not take away elements which are vital to the success of amphibious operations in SEAC.

The Foreign Secretary made a great point of of the need for reconquering the British Empire with mainly British force of arms.

Did you know that General Hurley the President's representative in Chungking, told poor Walter Moyne not long before he was killed,[3] that unless the British reconquered Singapore by themselves he did not think the Americans would agree to give it back to us at the peace table!!!

The Foreign Secretary said that the British Government point of view was that we must get back at least Singapore and Rangoon by mainly British force of arms before Japan was defeated by mainly American

---

[1] A projected amphibious & airborne assault on Rangoon, finally carried out in the spring of 1945.

[2] This time the sacking was permanent.

[3] Gen Patrick Hurley: Sec of War 1929–33; Pres Roosevelt's personal rep with Chiang.

Lord Moyne (Walter E. Guinness, 1880–1944): Suffolk Yeo, S Af War; Con MP 1907–31; Lt-Col Middle E 1914–18; business, nat sci, travel, philanthropy; USec State for War 1922; Fin Sec Treasy 1923, 1924–5; Minr of Ag 1925–9; baron 1932; Sec State for Cols & Leader of Lords 1941; Dep Minr of State Middle E 1942; Res Minr 1944; assassinated Cairo 6 Nov 1944 by Stern Gang.

effort, and since it was quite clear that no British forces were really going to be allowed to play a spectacular role in the ultimate defeat of Japan, this policy was all the more important. No doubt Anthony Eden gave you the same views himself. . . .

420. *BAD desk diary, 1944*

16 November

US Information

. . . Admiral Thebaud[1] called on me during the afternoon and said he felt that possibly I was not as much in the picture as I would like to be, and he would be very glad to give me all the information possible so far as it lay 'within his instructions'. It seems clear that the American staff have received orders to put me in the picture.

C-in-C, British Pacific Fleet

Today I received a copy of a signal from the First Sea Lord to COM-INCH setting out the position as the First Sea Lord viewed it with regard to Admiral Fraser's appointment in the Pacific; it struck me as an extremely well worded and discreet signal which laid emphasis on the fact that any difficulties in this connection could quickly be solved when Fraser had a chance to talk matters over with Nimitz and MacArthur. . . .

18 November

Meeting with President Roosevelt

At 12 o'clock I called on the President; he expressed real pleasure on my return and then informed me in confidence of the name of the new Head of the British Missions which had been proposed by the PM that morning.[2] . . .

---

[1]Rear Adm Leo H. Thebaud US Navy: b 1890; US N Acad 1909–13; battleships 1913–17; *Paul Jones* i/c 1917–18; further destroyer service 1918–21; Cmncns Div, ONO 1921–2; Instr N Acad 1922–5; *Paulding* i/c 1926–8; staff & NA duties; *Clark* i/c 1936–8; Exec N Acad 1938–40; Cdr DD Sqdn 27 & 13 1940 & Cdr US Escort Control & SUSNO Londonderry March 1942; *Boise*, Med 1943; Cru Div 10, Pac F 1943–4; Asst COS C-in-C Fleet & DNI Sept 1944–Sept 1945; NA France & Bel 1945–6; Inspr 1946–9; Cdt 1st N Dist 1950–1; Ret List March 1952.

[2]Field Marshal Sir Henry (later Lord) Maitland Wilson ('Jumbo', 1881–1964): Rifle Bde 1900; Ladysmith; India 1907; Capt 1908; W Front 1915–18; Staff Coll 1919; Lt-Col 1919; NW Frontier; Col 16 Inf Bde 1934; Maj-Gen 1935; 2 Div 1937; GOC Egypt & Lt-Gen 1939; Army of the Nile 1940; Greece 1941; GOC Palestine 1941; Middle E 1941–4, C-in-C 1943 & SAC 1944; FM 1944; Head Br Mil Missn Jan 1945–April 1947.

The President then proceeded to discuss the question of another meeting of the Big Three . . . but he added he was averse to using any Black Sea port for the meeting since he understood that whilst the Prime Minister and himself might be safeguarded from the lice, all others attending would certainly suffer from them. He felt it was no use having a conference on board a ship since Stalin disliked ships and frankly confessed he knew nothing about them or the Navy and could never understand them.[1]

Referring to the Philippine operations he said the US Navy had done a grand job and expressed pleasure that agreement had been reached for Fraser to take the British Fleet there. I felt it unwise to probe the President at all regarding his ideas on how the Fleet should be employed, . . .

20 November

Repair Ships

Received a reply from the Admiralty concerning repair ships. They consider we must have these repair ships in order to implement the OCTAGON decision that the British Fleet would be self supporting and point out that Admiral King's memorandum on the subject does not give proper weight to the relative availability of shore based facilities. The Admiralty quote figures which show that the total shore based British facilities available do not amount to those available at a single Royal dockyard. Although American resources at Pearl Harbor, Espirito Santo, etc., are not known, it can be assumed they must be very largely in excess of the British resources, and that in consequence any suggestion of comparing the number of repair ships with the ships they are to service is misleading.

In conclusion the Admiralty point out that if only the Americans would agree to pooling resources there would be no further difficulty and they would raise no objection to the re-assignment of the three repair ships. . . .

21 November

Airborne Early Warning Radar

Air Vice Marshal Tait and Air Commodore Lang called on me; Tait is endeavouring to obtain a supply of the AEW for the FAA and RAF but

---

[1]Stalin was, of course, head of the Soviet Navy as well as everything else.

considered the prospects at present were not too good. The AEW consists of a very high powered radar carried in an aircraft which remains over a ship or other receiving point and transmits to her a radar picture of what she can pick up. By this means it is hoped that low-flying aircraft, i.e. at 300 feet would be picked up at ranges between 40 and 50 miles and that surface ships might well be registered up to 150 miles.[1]

421.   *From Mountbatten*

22 November 1944

. . . Today is the day on which Bruce Fraser forms the British Pacific Fleet and Arthur John Power takes over the East Indies Fleet. As a matter of fact Fraser tells me that the East Indies Fleet is going to be numerically considerably bigger than the Pacific Fleet when one includes all the landing craft and landing ships and their crews. He also pointed out to me that it will bring the Fleet much closer to SEAC than was the case before. Previously the C-in-C EF had such a large separate responsibility in looking after the Japanese Battle Fleet with his own Battle Fleet, and such a small responsibility to me in the absence of any landing craft that we never had any Service reasons for getting really close together on the operational side beyond the making of vague plans which never seemed to come off. Now, he pointed out, the East Indies Fleet will be 90% engaged in connection with SEAC amphibious operations, since the Japanese Fleet is unlikely to reappear in SEAC.

I know you will be delighted to hear that the Joint Planning Staff works a fair treat and since their introduction there have been no more arguments with the Cs-in-C.[2] . . .

422.   *To Auchinleck*

22 November 1944

. . . Jack Dill's death came as great shock to everyone, but the American authorities went out of their way to give him a really impressive and dignified funeral; Marshall in particular said the nicest things about him and so did the President when I saw him last week.[3] Jumbo

---

[1] Only about 40 sets were available in total; not unnaturally, the Americans retained these.

[2] There had been wholesale changes in the high command and staff in the theatre, which helped to make things work more smoothly.

[3] Dill had been ailing for some months; he had done a superb job of cementing the Anglo-American alliance and in particular made close frineds with Gen Marshall; see A. Danchev, *Very Special Relationship* (London: Brassey, 1986).

Wilson will have a difficult job to fill his place, but on the other hand from what I have heard, I think he will be well received in Washington. . . .

So far as SEAC is concerned, it is quite clear that the US authorities consider the Pacific should and must have priority over SEAC in regard to landing craft and material generally. We have a constant fight trying to get any agreement to a reasonable quota for our own operations.

423. *From Cunningham*

28 November 1944

. . . Dill's death is a great loss. His friendship with Marshall was a great asset and I doubt if anyone can fill his place in that respect. You will have seen that Jumbo Wilson has been appointed to take his place. The PM has gone all Army – neither of the other Services mean anything to him at the moment and I think he looks on all admirals as half-wits – it may be that he knows that they are mostly independent minded. But Jumbo is a very good man, wise and experienced, who allows nothing to rattle him. I'm sure you will like him.

We have been trying to get together a good party to go to Washington to work under you and Butler[1] to see that the Navy gets a proportionate share of publicity in the Pacific war. . . . today we are informed by the Ministry of Information . . . that one ex-officer in Washington is all that is required. Of course this is quite ridiculous . . .

I think King's signal was a bit of a try on, but I am sure that when Fraser gets in touch with Nimitz, what now appears to be a very uncomfortable situation will clear up. . . .

. . . The US losses may certainly make them want us to help them. I have always been sure of it. . . .

You appear to have got on well with the press. I did not find them bad fellows, but rather inclined to see double meanings in what I told them.

424. *BAD desk diary, 1944*

29 November

Naval Barracks, New York City

I inspected the Naval Barracks at Pier 92 commanded by Captain W.N. Pashley, USN. At these barracks both RN and USN ratings are

---

[1]Embassy Information Officer.

accommodated; the barracks are beautifully clean and equipped on a scale far superior to anything attempted in the UK. Our men appear to be well satisfied with all the arrangements except in regard to the messing. In answer to an enquiry I was told 'they don't give you roast beef and duff regular 'ere, Sir, like you gets at 'ome; they keeps choppin' and changin' about every day'. It is odd to find the conservatism in this respect, and he apparently ignored the benefits of a varied and well balanced diet which included many items of food unobtainable in England since the war began.

On leaving Pier 92 I inspected the Combined RN and US barracks at Brooklyn and walked round the Naval Hospital and Dental Establishment. At the latter I found some 30 dental officers were installed and as usual the equipment was on a lavish scale.

The COs of both establishments emphasised that our men appear to get on very well with their men, that our own men were generally speaking far more experienced than the very raw recruits that formed the bulk of the USN personnel passing through the establishments. . . .

1 December

Repair Ships

After having avoided me for some time I was at last able to have an interview with Admiral King in the Navy Department. I found him to be most friendly and forthcoming. Discussing the question of the allocation of repair ships in the Pacific he described at some length the difficulties with which they were faced owing to damage sustained in the Philippine operations, and made it clear that in his opinion whatever agreement had been reached in regard to allocation of repair ships, circumstances had now made it necessary to reconsider such allocations in the light of the necessities of the moment. On my pointing out the difficulties of relating repair ships and land based repair facilities to the number of ships to be maintained, he agreed that a pooling of resources in the sense that repair facilities should be elastic so as to enable the maximum number of ships whether British or American to be maintained in the forward area of operations, was desirable and necessary; he said he would be prepared to consider proposals on this subject if put forward by me. . . .

7 December

Unfreezing Admiral King

I lunched with Admiral King at his mess in the Navy Department; the Admiral sat at the head of the table with some 8 or 9 other Admirals present and the atmosphere was exactly like that of a prep school with the Headmaster in the Chair. None of the Admirals opened their mouths except to reply to Ernie, so to break this up I started a discussion on Jutland, followed this up with some remarks about the mutiny at Invergordon and finally gave an account of some records I had discovered at the Admiralty when I was DPS which dealt with statements of British seamen who deserted from the British Navy to the American Navy and subsequently returned to the British Navy. I am glad to say this had the desired effect and conversation became general. On leaving Admiral King said to me 'Don't forget, Admiral, the door is on the latch'.

I have to address the Overseas Writers' Club tomorrow and I intend giving Dickie a good boost since he undoubtedly has had a bad and undeserved press out here.

We are having a meeting with the US Chiefs of Staff tomorrow – the first since I arrived, and that only as a result of a special request from us – and I hope we shall get them to appreciate the real seriousness of the shipping situation, and the need for an over-all survey of the shipping in all Theatres; the Pacific is obviously the sponge which wants squeezing. . . .

425. *To Cunningham*

7 December 1944

. . . I am glad to hear that MOI have now withdrawn their objections to our PR team, and I feel the sooner they get going the better. American Naval publicity in the papers is so bad that I have been at pains to discover why something is not done about it. The excuses put up are as follows:–

(a) the Navy Department will not release enough news.
(b) the American public as a whole is not interested in the Navy or Navy-minded.

Whilst there are some grounds for (a), I think the real reason lies in (b); the greater part of America is so far removed from the sea that the people have little or no understanding of sea matters and don't wish to learn. . . .

Touching the matter of Ernie King . . . I had a good interview with him which was followed by an invitation to go over and have lunch in his mess at the Navy Department whenever I felt inclined. . . .

The Americans seem to be really concerned about the Jap suicide attacks and if our fellows have any suggestions to make in regard to dealing with them I am sure these would be very well received over here. Fitch and one or two others seem to think that our armoured flight decks would restrict the damage considerably and I rather hoped that Nimitz would have pressed for an early arrival of our party in the Pacific. As matters now stand this will not be the case owing to the operation against 'P';[1] I examined this operation with John Cassady of the *Saratoga* and it seemed to us that it was hardly profitable in view of the distances involved, mountains, etc. Our estimate of the possible bomb load for all four of the carriers was 40 tons which does not seem much of a strike against so large a target. . . .

426. *To Mountbatten*

13 December 1944

. . . Strangely enough Ernie King and I appear to be hitting it off; he dodged me for about three weeks but now we have got to the point where I have a standing invitation to lunch at his mess in the Navy Department, and no doubt we shall soon be 'Ernie' and 'James'. This does not mean to say that he is any the easier to deal with except that I don't think he does things of malice aforethought to trip me up; nevertheless he can be very tiresome.

In so far as the Pacific is concerned, I am hoping very much that Fraser and Nimitz will come to a good understanding, because if they do I feel there is a reasonable chance of any proposals they make being implemented in Washington. I believe MacArthur is very keen to have our Fleet allotted to him in order that he may be relieved of having to go cap in hand to Nimitz every time he wants some ships. Whether or not this will appeal to Nimitz I cannot say, or also whether our battleships and carriers would be suitably employed if engaged only on mopping up operations in the Philippines and NEI. . . .

427. *To Joan Bright Astley*

14 December 1944

. . . I still loathe it. I loathe all this wire pulling & manoeuvring but apparently I have a very good press in the Navy Department & in Washington as a whole. Exactly why I don't know. . . . frankly I hate it all. Seems to me that an oily tongue is all you want coupled with some sex appeal – my notion of the latter has expired. . . .

I have a good skiff but all this fat living & being so far from the war does no-one any good. I yearn for the discomfort of my bridge & my sea cabin & for the joy of seeing a Fleet in good order do their stuff.

[1]Carrier air attacks on Palembang, Sumatra, Jan 1945.

Spend a lot of effort in boosting Dickie Mount B's shares & people listen quite attentively. He's got a bad press here due I think to his initial flamboyancy & attempts to parade[?]. You've got to establish yourself first before you can get away with that sort of thing.

428. BAD desk diary, 1944

18 December

Magnificent work of Ark Royal

Captain Ring, USN, who had served in the rank of Lt-Cdr as Observer in the *Ark Royal* in 1940 and '41, called on me and said he had been at pains to impress on people in his service the great achievements of the British Navy in the early years of the war when they had practically no reserves and were fighting single handed. He referred in particular to the magnificent work of the *Ark Royal* and of her handful of fighters who would make sortie after sortie and work under conditions which would be regarded as quite unacceptable nowadays; he said that people were inclined to forget this great achievement and he felt highly privileged that he had been there himself to see what could be done. . . .

22 December

Fraser's meeting with Nimitz

. . . Signals have been received from Admiral Fraser reporting a very cordial meeting with Admiral Nimitz; that Manus would be used as a forward base and that the British Fleet would certainly participate in the most advanced operations. He proposes to adopt US signalling in the British Fleet forthwith and was considering using the *Lothian* as his HQ ship. The Fleet will operate as a task force under Halsey or Spruance[1] but

---

[1]*Lothian*: ex-*City of Edinburgh*, 1938, 8036gt, 4×4in; hired as LS 1944.

Adm (later Fleet Adm) William F. ('Bull') Halsey, jr, US Navy (1882–1959): N Acad 1900–4; Great White Fleet 1907–9; Lt 1909; destroyer cmds, incl Queenstown force 1918; Lt Cdr 1916; ONI 1921–2; NA N Eur 1922–4; Capt 1927; N War Coll 1932–3; Army War Coll 1933–4; pilot 1935; *Saratoga* 1935–7; Cmdt Pensacola NAS 1937–8; RA 1938; carrier sqdn cmds, Pac F 1938–43; Adm Nov 1942; C-in-C S Pac 1943; 3rd F June 1944; Fleet Adm Dec 1945; Ret List 1947; a controversial, extrovert, aggressive FO, in thick of Pac campaigns.

Adm Raymond A Spruance US Navy (1886–1969): N Acad 1903–6; Great White Fleet 1907–09; elec specialist; Lt-Cdr 1917; *Aaron Ward* & *Osborne* i/c; Bu Eng; NWColl 1926–7 & later on staff; *Mississippi* 1938; RA & Cdr 10th N Dist 1940–1; cru div Pac F 1941–2; Cdr, carrier TF, Midway; COS & DC-in-C Pac F; VA 1943; 5th F Aug 1943; Adm March 1945; Iwo Jima & Okinawa; C-in-C Pac F Nov 1945; Pres, N War Coll 1946–8; Ret List; Amb Philippines 1952–5.

he considers our logistic resources are inadequate for the service required.

No mention has been made of MacArthur or the possibility of the British Fleet being attached to him so I presume this is no longer on the map.

Escort Carriers

The Admiralty now offer to COMINCH 4 CVEs as ferries until April 1945, but subsequently are prepared to offer the *Royalist*[1] with 4 or 5 CVEs for operations from April to August on the understanding that these assault loaded CVEs will not in fact be used for ferries and ferrying purposes.

27 December

US Escort Carriers

Cdr Hopkins,[2] who is an observer in the Pacific, called on me and gave me some interesting information. He criticises the design of the US CVEs on the score that the flight decks are much too light and these are penetrated by the falling engines of suicide bombers after the latter have been shot to pieces in the air. Through the holes made by the engines burning oil runs down into the hangars and causes the fires which have been so prevalent after all these attacks.

British Carrier Raids in Indian Ocean

In regard to our own air operations in the Indian Ocean, the Americans criticise the fact that we only make tip and run raids instead of remaining on the spot and continuing the attacks as have been done recently in the case of Formosa. They appear to have overlooked the fact that in these operations we only had two carriers and furthermore weather conditions made any fuelling at sea hazardous especially in regard to strikes directed against Sabang.

---

[37] *Royalist*: 1943, 5770t, 8×5.25in, 6tt, 33k; cmd ship of a CVE group.
[38] Lt-Cdr F. H. E. Hopkins: Lt 1933; O Lt RNAS Ford 1939; 816 Sqdn *Formidable* Nov 1940; Matapan; Lt-Cdr 830 Sqdn, Malta Dec 1941; BAD July 1942; NLO, US Pac F Jan 1945; Cdr June 1945.

Fuelling at Sea

The US have developed a technique to a great extent, of fuelling at sea and transferring personnel and stores by means of the breeches buoy when the ships are steaming at 15 to 20 knots. Hopkins expresses grave doubts of the ability of our carriers in the Pacific Fleet to keep pace with the Americans unless we definitely allot a number of escort carriers to act continually as ferries to replace carriers. . . .

29 December

American Fleet Carriers

. . . Captain Roger Williams, of the Newport Shipbuilding Company . . . informed me that the new American Fleet Carriers are to have armoured decks which is somewhat remarkable since I learnt a few days ago that [in] the staff requirements of the new British carriers we appear to be abandoning armoured flight decks for the lighter weight wood covered decks hitherto used by the Americans. . . .

429. *To Cunningham*

28 December 1944

. . . Cdr Hopkins, a very bright lad who has just returned from the Pacific . . . expresses grave doubts whether the replacement aircraft for our carriers are sufficient to allow the latter to operate for the period which is regarded as normal for American carriers. The wastage has been excessive and a large number of aircraft returning damaged are pushed straight over the side in order to allow sufficient room for returning aircraft to operate from flight decks not yet damaged. All this suggests that there may be a good case for our armoured flight decks though, of course, these would probably be quite ineffective if the Japanese used still larger aircraft and heavier bombs for the suicide attacks . . . .

Although the discussions between Nimitz and Fraser appear to have been most friendly, it is not quite clear yet what results were actually achieved in connection with such matters as the maintenance of our ships in the Pacific, and the question of fuelling. Whatever agreements may have been reached about this previously, it seems quite clear that the Americans are prepared to abrogate such agreements on the plea that circumstances have altered so much since they were made. . . .

430. *To North*

28 December 1944

P.S. I still consider this is a bloody awful place & a bloody awful job. Actually I seem to be on easy terms personally with Ernie King & the other US COS & also with Forrestal, Gates, etc. But that makes little odds when it comes to dealing with them collectively. . . .

431. *BAD desk diary, 1945*

1 January

Organisation of British and American Pacific Fleets

We received today a very good signal from Admiral Fraser giving the organisation of the Pacific Fleet. This consists of:–

(a)   a fast carrier force which includes the fast battleships
(b)   a close support force which includes the old battleships and assault carriers, and
(c)   the amphibious assault force.

It was intended that the BPF should be included in (a) working under either Halsey or Spruance and would form another support task force available for forward operations. Fraser referred to the fact that the Fleet remains at sea in the combat area for several weeks at a time and he doubts very much whether the arrangements made for the maintenance of the British ships will prove adequate; this is especially the case in connection with replacement of aircraft in the carriers for which a number of CVEs will be required which should be fully operational as regards flying staff.

3 January

Security of Ultra

Group Captain Winterbotham[1] called; he is concerned with security of Ultra etc. and complained of the lax organisation which prevailed in American HQ in Australia and also the SW Pacific. He informed me that a case came to his notice of a press correspondent releasing the fact that General MacArthur read Japanese messages.

[1]Grp Capt F. W. Winterbotham RAFR: Grp Capt June 1940; Sec, Directorate of Intelligence & i/c ULTRA security.

Lt-Cdr Douglas Fairbanks, Jr, USNR[1]

Lt-Cdr Fairbanks called on me and gave me an interesting account of what he had been doing in the Mediterranean in connection with deception plans and also of his work in connection with Anglo-American relations prior to American entry into the war. Referring to Admiral King he said he was convinced that he was not anti-British but that he was anti-British Navy for the following reasons – up to date the British Navy had been the one Navy in the world, with a consistent history of successes and with a reputation of being the one really strong efficient fleet in the world. King considered that the American Navy had now caught up and passed the British Navy not only in numbers but also in technical efficiency and consequently he was determined that this should be recognised by everyone. In consequence of this he was jealous of British Navy participation in any Theatre where the American Navy was operating unless it was absolutely essential; he was also inclined to be unduly critical of any deficiencies on our part and to magnify these in order to put us in a bad position *vis à vis* the American Navy. According to Fairbanks the officers in the American Navy put their Navy before America and King's attitude in this connection was reflected right through the service. . . .

4 January

Admiral Leahy

. . . Talking to Grew and Bliss[2] after dinner they considered that Admiral Leahy was only a figurehead on the CCS and that he was too old to be effective. I disagreed with this opinion and pointed out that whilst the Admiral undoubtedly failed on occasions to grasp all the details of the more intricate problems, yet on the other hand when really important matters were under discussion he was fully in the picture in regard to the essentials and took a broad view and not merely a parochial Navy, Army or Air angle. I considered, however, his greatest asset was that he introduced a touch of humour now and then which went a long way towards sweetening the atmosphere and which I did my best to encourage. It was somewhat interesting that later in the evening Admiral Leahy in conversation with me said he felt that our conferences were perhaps less formal than they used to be and he considered this was a good thing since it made it far more easy to reconcile differences when they arose.

---

[1] Lt-Cdr Douglas Fairbanks, jr, USNR: b 1909; Lt (j.g.) April 1941; staff, TF 39, Atl & Med 1942; staff, Amphib Ops 1942–3; staff, N Forces, NW Africa May 1943–Sept 1944; Lt-Cdr Oct 1943; ONO Oct 1944–Jan 1945; Cdr Oct 1945; HQ, C-in-C Fleet 1945–6; Capt Oct 1954; Ret List July 1969; actor, writer, producer; special dip envoy.

[2] Joseph C. Grew: career diplomat; friend of FDR; Amb Japan 1931–1941 (memoirs *Ten Years in Japan*); USec, State Dept 1942. Bliss not identified.

5 January

Repair of HMS Sheffield

Cdr Liddell[1] of the *Sheffield* called on me and reported that work was being held up owing to lack of sufficient priority of labour; he had reason to believe that one of the cruisers damaged in the Pacific is arriving at Boston and that she will apparently have priority over *Sheffield*. I have instructed Liddell to get in touch with Admiral Waller immediately on this matter. . . .

8 January

DRACULA

. . . There has been some discussion about the assignment of resources for operation DRACULA; the Americans consider it is most unlikely this operation could be staged in December 1945 and are therefore most reluctant to assign equipment which they maintain is required in the Western and Pacific theatres for immediate operations. We are asking the COS to confirm that the December date still holds and furthermore that the scale of operations remains unchanged.

9 January

Death of General Lumsden

. . . Signal received from Admiral Fraser reporting that General Lumsden and Sub-Lt (S) Morton had been killed by enemy action in the Philippines but that he and other officers and British ratings were unhurt; I learnt later that Fraser and the others were on board the *New Mexico* when she was struck by a suicide aircraft in the Lingayen Gulf.[2] . . .

Utility of Heavy Ship Bombardment

Officers of the Navy Department are inclined to question the utility of these heavy ship bombardments prior to landing since apparently they inflict little damage on the defences, cause few casualties as the Japanese always withdraw, and are very expensive in ammunition.

---

[1]Cdr J. Liddell: Lt-Cdr 1934; FS & W/TO, Med F March 1939; Port Sig O, Chatham Jan 1941; Cdr June 1941; Sig Est, Haslemere July 1942; *Sheffield*; *Newfoundland* 1945.
[2]They were killed instantly when a *kamikaze* struck the bridge of USS *New Mexico* on 6 Jan 1945, off the Philippines; Fraser miraculously escaped unhurt. Actg Sub-Lt (S) Morton was Fraser's Secretary.

10 January

Burrough to replace Ramsay

. . . A signal received from PM states that he [is considering a proposal?] to appoint Admiral Burrough to replace Admiral Ramsay, who was recently killed. I saw Admiral King about this and after enquiring about Burrough's background he stated he would raise no objection to the appointment.

Pacific information for Admiralty

I then raised the question of supplying the Admiralty with more information about the general organisation in the Pacific, composition of task forces, operations on which they were engaged and so forth, about which the Admiralty have at present so little knowledge and which they feel they should have in view of the forthcoming participation of British units. Admiral King became very aggressive at first and said this was pure curiosity on the part of the Admiralty and his test in furnishing information was 'Do they need to know it?' – in his opinion the Admiralty had no need to have this information. I pointed out to King that by keeping the Admiralty properly informed it would be possible for them to do a great deal towards assisting Admiral Nimitz; if the British Fleet was required in the Pacific, and I had every reason to believe that it was, then it was essential to keep British authorities fully in the picture so that they could adjust priorities and in cases foresee requirements which were bound to arise. Admiral King settled down a bit after this, became much more friendly and finally said that he would look into the matter, but he did not wish to burden Admiral Nimitz's wireless communications with additional signals since he is already hard put to it to handle the present traffic. I told the Admiral that the Admiralty would be quite satisfied providing the Navy Department furnished all the information they had available. I referred to a paragraph in the Admiralty signal which stated that attempts to get this information hitherto had been unsuccessful and told the Admiral this was in fact [because] he was a hard-hearted old beggar (spelt somewhat differently) and they hoped I would get some change out of him. At this he laughed and said he would do his best to meet the Admiralty's wishes. My personal impression is that the Navy Department are very sore about not getting enough information from the Pacific themselves and Admiral King feels perhaps that he has overplayed decentralisation too much. . . .

11 January

Suicide attacks

... Battle reports from Flag and Commanding Officers engaged in the Philippine operations show some divergence of opinion as to how suicide attacks are best dealt with; one Flag Officer considers that drastic manoeuvring should be carried out and should take priority over either opening A arcs or giving the guns a fair chance. Other Flag and Commanding Officers advocate giving guns every possible assistance to shoot down the target during its final dive.

12 January

Shipping survey

... The shipping survey has now been completed and a meeting was held attended by Mr Law, Nicholson, Heads of Missions and Staff Officers to consider the report. The report states fairly decisively that the deficiencies which have been disclosed are not manageable but the shipping representatives appear to think that in fact these deficiencies can be met without necessarily curtailing current or projected military operations. My own impression is that we are working on a very narrow margin and that it will be essential to consider the shipping situation before embarking on more extended operations, especially in the Pacific.

U-boat situation

We received a memorandum from the First Sea Lord on the U-boat situation in which he points out that the new 1700-ton boats with their fast underwater speed and greater underwater endurance and also with the advantage of the Schnorkel may cause a serious recrudescence of losses from U-boat attack. It is a matter of speculation whether the Germans will revert to pack tactics or merely accentuate their inshore operations but he points out that the losses rising as high as 70 ships a month cannot by any means be excluded. The new U-boats have overcome to a considerable extent the disabilities which the earlier type suffered from slow underwater speed and necessity to surface a certain number of hours each day in order to recharge batteries.[1]

---

[1]Cunningham was rightly concerned about the threat as no effective counter-measures were available, other than extensive mining and intensifying air and surface escorts. Fortunately, the Schnorkel boats sank few ships, though they themselves were difficult to detect and destroy, and very few of the fast boats got to sea before the war ended.

13 January

Scientific Research

... Admiral Furer,[1] who is co-ordinator of Naval scientific research, called on me and discussed American current investigations; he acknowledged very fully that the larger proportion of new ideas emanated from the UK but that America with her tremendous resources had been able to implement these ideas more rapidly than the British; he was much in favour of continued exchange of scientific information but said that American authorities in general wanted to strike an equal balance in regard to such exchanges and he felt this was quite impractical. ...

19 January

Admiral King on Pacific

... He said there was no objection to my referring [in press conference] to the set up in the Pacific, that the British Fleet would be allotted by him for service with either Nimitz or MacArthur, but at the mention of MacArthur's name he said

> that man is never satisfied; he is always complaining he is being robbed of ships. He seems to think that the Fleet will be used to mop up the Philippines and in that he is much mistaken; the assault forces now in the Philippines are required for other operations and MacArthur must train Filipinos and other people to do the mopping up; he certainly won't have the Fleet to help him.

I asked if by this King suggested the Philippines should now be bypassed and to this he replied 'certainly, in the same way as we bypassed New Guinea and Rabaul'. It is quite clear to me that MacArthur's name is like a red rag to a bull in King's presence.

29 January

Discussion with First Sea Lord

The American and British Chiefs of Staff arrived [at Malta] during the afternoon; the First Sea Lord is staying at Admiralty House. We dis-

---

[1]Rear Adm Julius A. Furer US Navy (1880–1963): N Acad 1897–1901; Constructor Corps; sci management pioneer; prominent in sub-chaser programme 1917–18; Fleet N Constr, Pac F 1919; Bur Con & Rpr; Cavite NY, Phil. Is, 1928–30; Philadelphia NY 1930–5; Asst NA London July 1935–Dec 1937; N sci research 1944.

cussed the submarine campaign; shipping situation and other matters. He informed me he had proposed offering Hamilton the appointment of ACNB and that Shelley would be going to Paris as Naval Attache.[1] First Sea Lord complained that Fraser was asking for too much for the Pacific, and that it was impossible to meet his requirements; I suggested that Fraser was probably trying to get the British Fleet up to the maintenance and operating standard of the US Fleet, and that to do so he would probably require all that he had asked for.

1 February

Pacific Operations

At the CCS meeting in the afternoon Admiral King gave a clear account of the proposed Pacific operations which indicated the intention to establish bases forward of Formosa from which a closer blockade could be established and air bases formed to increase the scale of air attack on Japan proper.

3 February

Yalta

We were taken to tents and given vodka, small eats and hot tea and I was introduced to Mr Molotov[2] and other Russian officials. At 1130 I left in car with the Field Marshal, Colonel Chapman Walker[3] and 3/O Stuart Clark for Alupka which is just west of Yalta. It was a 5 hour drive with only moderate roads which had sentries posted about every 150 yards. The country at first was flat and uninteresting and most of the villages and small towns were in ruins; as we approached the coast we climbed through a pass over the mountains at about 3000 feet and the scenery became more interesting. At Yalta there appeared to be a great deal of destruction and hardly a house standing intact; as we proceeded to Alupka we noticed that nearly all the fine villas had been wrecked and were told later that this had been methodical destruction on the part of the Germans to prevent the Russians from establishing winter quarters in

[1]Vice Adm Sir Louis H. K. ('Turtle') Hamilton: Capt 1932; Capt, RN Coll, Greenwich 1937; *Aurora* Feb 1940; RA Jan 1941; *Tyne* Feb 1941; led Vaagsö raid 1941; 1CS *Norfolk* Feb 1942; *Kent* June 1943; VA, Malta & FOC Med Dec 1943; Actg Adm, 1st N Mem, Commonwealth N Bd, Aust. June 1945.

Rear Adm R. Shelley: Capt 1934; NA Berlin 1939; Capt of F *Warspite* Feb 1940; *Queen Elizabeth* 1941; *Suffolk* 1942; RA & FO E Af 1942–4; NA Paris 1945.

[2]Vyacheslav Molotov, the durable & often inscrutable Soviet Foreign Sec.

[1]Col P. J. F. Chapman-Walker: Herts Regt (TA); Lt 1929; Maj 1943; Temp Lt-Col 1945.

the Crimea. We arrived finally at the Villa Voronthoz, an extraordinarily ugly building of mixed Moorish and Gothic design, built about 1830 and somewhat hastily adapted for the senior members of the British Delegation. ...

5 February

Carrier strike on Palembang

A report on the strike by our carriers at Palembang suggests that the operation was quite successful; two strikes were carried out and apart from oil installations, some 78 Japanese aircraft were either destroyed or damaged for the loss of 9 of our own. A second attack was made two days later ... This time the target was Soeng Gerong where hits were obtained on the cracking plants starting intensive fires. Twenty-two Japanese aircraft were destroyed for the loss of 15 of our own of which 8 crews were recovered.

Shipping and Petroleum

At the COS meeting this morning it was decided we must accept the 'basic undertaking', in regard to shipping for civil purposes as put forward by the US. BAD reports that US authorities are quite adamant with regard to reduction of our oil stocks so it looks as if this will have to be referred to the highest for decision.

After lunch the First Sea Lord, D of P[1] and myself had a conference in regard to supply of Corsairs, repair ships for the Pacific Fleet, forward bases for the Fleet, etc., ...

8 February

Petroleum

Results of the oil conference were discussed at the COS meeting and First Sea Lord expressed concern at not being able to obtain definite agreement to the 1.1 m. tons of black oil for the Admiralty, but both Leathers and I are convinced that the Admiralty black oil situation is really quite satisfactory if account is taken of the extra quantity of this oil now allocated for merchant ships etc.

[1]Capt Guy Grantham.

9 February

British Pacific Fleet and repair ships

First Sea Lord and I proceeded to Livadia and had a conference with Admiral King on repair ships, employment of BPF, information concerning operations in the Pacific and other matters. King was quite friendly and forthcoming and said he would be willing to return one of the repair ships at present assigned to the US Navy. In regard to future operations in the Pacific he said he had not yet made up his mind with regard to whether the British Fleet would be required for Stage 2 of the operations but he felt it was unlikely they would be used for Stage 1. On the other hand he suggested there was a possibility they might be required to assist MacArthur in connection with possible operations against either Hainan or Borneo. This is of interest since at Washington he was most emphatic that MacArthur would not conduct any further operations outside the Philippines and I judge now that King's views on this matter have been over-ruled.

CCS meeting

This meeting was followed by a CCS meeting to pass the report for the President and Prime Minister which was subsequently presented at a Plenary Meeting attended by both the latter. The President appeared to me to be looking very ill and much worse than when I last saw him about three weeks ago at the White House.[1]

13 February

British Pacific Fleet

Discussed with Syfret [at the Admiralty] maintenance of BPF and Fraser's request to use ships of Force X[2] in connection with the Fleet train and other purposes. Syfret appeared to think Fraser was asking for too much but I expressed the view that if he did not use these ships he would find it very difficult to operate and that in particular the personnel ship was essential to avoid cramming men into cruisers and other ships for passage to and from rear base in Australia.

---

[1]The President's health had been deteriorating for a year; he had good days and bad days but was only a few weeks away from death at this time.

[2]Probably naval auxiliaries.

15 February

Assignment of Aircraft

I discussed with 5th Sea Lord[1] the question of Corsair assignment and general aircraft situation. I pointed out that so long as we appeared to have a considerable number of inactive reserve aircraft there were certain to be suggestions from the Americans that we should reduce such reserves until such time as we had spare groups formed, in fact until our situation was more or less the same as theirs, that is a small number of aircraft in reserve and a much larger number in reserve but manned by spare groups.

Public Relations

I called on the Minister of Information[2] at 1230 and found he was strongly in favour of the Naval PR team being sent out as soon as possible and felt quite confident he would be able to persuade the PM that this was essential. I referred to the little use that had been made of the members of the Missions in connection with PR and the great need to use this material and above all to see that members of the Missions were properly briefed in regard to current events, more especially in connection with newspaper articles criticising the British. Mr Bracken said he would send out to Washington and New York two of his best people to look out for this side of the matter and he welcomed very heartily the proposal to use members of the Missions for this important work.

20 February

British Pacific Fleet

Discussing the employment of the BPF with the First Sea Lord [at the Admiralty] he suggested that unless something concrete was proposed by Admiral King by 1 or 2 March I should tackle him about this matter and obtain if possible some definite indication of his intentions; First Sea Lord is by no means convinced that King is not trying to put us off with minor operations for our Fleet.

---

[1]Vice Adm Sir Denis Boyd.

[2]Brendan R. (later Viscount) Bracken (1901–53): Con MP 1929; well travelled, publr & fin jnlst, philanthropist; assoc with Churchill 1920s; PPS Admy 1939–40; PPS to PM 1940; Minr of Info 1941–5; 1st Lord May 1945; Vsct 1952.

Somerville was extremely unhappy with the indifferent attitude of the MOI staff in Washington.

432. *To Mountbatten*

Washington,
23 February 1945

. . . The most recent accounts of the Iwo Jima operation suggest very heavy casualties in regard to landing craft which fill me with concern as I feel sure that this will add to our difficulties in getting a proper build up, especially on spares, in your part of the world.

As we are frequently drawn into discussions in regard to operations in the SEA [Command], and the priority they should have, I should be grateful if you would arrange that any appreciations you make on this subject are communicated to us in Washington either directly or indirectly, as these may provide us with useful ammunition. A great deal can often be done 'off the record' in discussions on such matters and a good background built up which becomes useful at CCS meetings here. . . .

433. *BAD desk diary, 1945*

23 February

Convoy PQ 17

During the afternoon I was shown an article which appeared in the *New York Times* that day on the Russian convoy in July 1942 which suffered severe losses. A survivor who has just been repatriated had alleged that the convoy was deserted by the escort. On looking up Battle Summary 22 it was clear that there was no question that the convoy was 'deserted' and I therefore signalled to the Admiralty suggesting that a disclaimer should be issued as soon as possible.[1] . . .

26 February

Convoy PQ 17

The papers publish the Admiralty account of what occurred to the Russian July '42 convoy. I consider this account is very poor in as much as it does not make clear by whom the order was given to disperse the convoy, and although it suggests that the Home Fleet was at sea, there is

[1]This is still a hotly debated issue but it resulted from a disastrous decision by Pound to withdraw the convoy's close escort and scatter the merchantmen in the face of a possible sortie by *Tirpitz*; the Home F heavy ships were kept well away from U-boat and bomber concentrations off Norway.

no indication as to why this Fleet was not able to participate in the protection of the convoy. . . .

27 February

Convoy PQ 17

New York Times publishes quite a good leading article on the Russian convoy but against this other papers carry stories from other survivors which tend to support a mutual allegation that the convoy was deserted by its escort. . . .

28 February

SEAC

We have now received Mountbatten's proposed plans for future operations; he states that Singapore is his next objective after Rangoon; with a view to minimum intermediate landings he proposes these should be confined to Phuket which would require 2 divisions plus in early June, and that in October a landing would be effected in the Port Swettenham area for which 4 divisions would be required. Singapore might be reached between December and March '46. Phuket would act as a staging area whereas Port Swettenham would be area for deployment.

He has considered an attack via the Sunda Straits but this had been discarded owing to lack of naval facilities for operations so far from Ceylon.

Escorts for American Troop Ships in East Indies

I had an interview with Admiral King this morning to discuss the question of escorting American troopships in the Indian Ocean. C-in-C EI has stated that in his opinion this was no longer necessary and escorts were not being provided for British troopships in this area. King stated he quite appreciated that at the moment escorts were not essential, but for political reasons he had to request that they should be continued for American ships. Having been told by some of his staff that King was not prepared to let me see certain special intelligence reports I tackled him on the subject and handed him a personal letter. After reading this he said I must certainly have the information and whoever had suggested it should not be made available was quite wrong; the trouble lies I think in the fact that King is such an autocrat his subordinates are afraid to approach him and consequently this sort of misunderstanding occurs.

British Pacific Fleet

On his own initiative King referred to employment of the BPF and said that at the moment they were awaiting the return of Admiral Carter[1] in order that the latter might give an opinion as to the possibility of reopening the N Borneo oil fields within a reasonable period. I agree with King that if this could be done within 6 to 9 months the operation to recapture these was well worth while. King then said that if the operation took place MacArthur was anxious to use the BPF for the purpose and he, King, felt this would be a very useful initial operation for them to undertake. With this view I fully agreed. King added finally that he hoped no one would think he was holding back the British Fleet from operations in the Pacific because it was his firm intention to use every available ship to the greatest possible extent; he was friendly and co-operative throughout the interview. . . .

1 March

Oil

. . . At the JSM meeting the oil situation was discussed, Wilkinson[2] and other oil experts being present. The COS say we are now down to 5.2 m.t. and will soon reach 4.5 m.t. if tankers are not made available. Wilkinson agreed that although para. 8 of the agreement might be construed as giving Americans a right to build up stocks in the Pacific at our expense he did not necessarily think this would be done and he was quite sure General Somervell[3] and others appreciated that the spirit of the agreement was that the stock level in the UK should be kept at approx. 6.25 m.t. unless shortages elsewhere made some reduction necessary. The matter is being investigated at present by the oil experts. . . .

5 March

Admiral Nimitz

I dined in the *Dauntless*[4] and sat next to Admiral Nimitz. He said that continual seagoing affected ships' companies to some extent but that he

---

[1]Rear Adm Worrall R. ('Nick') Carter US Navy (1885–1975): Great White Fleet 1907–09; s/m *C5* i/c 1911; A/S Devices Aide, Sims's staff, London 1918; Cdr 1923; ONI; *Osborne* i/c 1927; *Marblehead* 1936; Cdt Guantanamo NB 1938–40; S/M Sqdn 4, Hawaii 1940; COS, Bat Force 1941–2; major logistics cmds, Pac 1942–5; RA Ret List 1947.

[2]Possibly Engr-Rear Adm B.J.H. Wilkinson: Capt (E) 1936; FEO, Med F July 1939; Engr-RA Nov 1943; *Victory* June 1944.

[3]Lt-Gen Brehon B. Somervell US Army: engr; Brig, supply, Gen Staff Nov 1941; chief, Army Service Forces.

[4]*Dauntless*: ex-*Delphine*, 1921, 1363t; t/o US Navy Jan 1942; a steam yacht and King's preferred residence while CNO.

considered maintenance of morale at its present standard was largely due to continual action, plenty of work, good food and plenty of sweet stuffs for the younger men. It was a good test of Flag and Commanding Officers and whilst some could not stand up to it, others became acclimatised and philosophical and are unaffected by these long periods at sea. The Admiral stressed the need to be frank in admitting mistakes when they were made, and furthermore said the officers must not get in the habit of regarding notice of such mistakes being taken by senior officers as necessarily conveying a reprimand. He was rather concerned at the views expressed by Fraser initially on the time the BPF could remain at sea and felt that this would have created a good deal of criticism in the US Fleet had such views been maintained. Referring to suicide attacks he said that these do affect morale to some extent and the main thing was to have as few men as possible on the upper deck and exposed to such attacks. It was the sight of subsequent casualties which seemed to upset officers and men more than anything else. *Saratoga*'s heavier flight deck undoubtedly saved her after she had been hit by 4 suiciders.

Referring to the casualties sustained during the typhoon[1] he admitted these were due to lack of seamanship and should have been avoided; officers at present place far too much dependence on weather reports and are not weatherwise as in the old days. American CVLs are somewhat tender and require careful handling in bad weather. . . .

SACSEA and BPF

Signal received from SACSEA suggests that BPF should be used to support attack for operation ROGER, operating from the Gulf of Saigon; he stated that Admiral Cooke had raised this matter on his recent visit and said he, Cooke, thought the CCS would support this suggestion. I feel sure this proposal will not be at all well received by the COS.

7 March

British Pacific Fleet

There are further press comments from Australia on Fraser's statement.[2] They suggest that the Americans do not intend to use the British Fleet or if they do only for mopping up.

First Sea Lord signals to me that the action of Cooke in suggesting the

---

[1] In S China Sea; much structural damage done; 3 destroyers capsized, defective stability.

[2] The future employment of the BPF was still in doubt but it was resolved on 17 March.

co-operation of BPF for operation ROGER is most improper and that I should represent this to King when a suitable opportunity occurs. This was followed by a COS signal in which they repudiate the proposal to use the BPF and send a fairly strongly worded message to the JCS calling attention to the need for an early pronouncement concerning intentions in regard to the BPF.

I went to see King and raised the whole matter with him. He told me that he personally was very much against the BPF being used for ROGER[1] and furthermore expressed grave doubts whether this operation was feasible in view of the strong Japanese forces in the Malayan Peninsula.

8 March

Oil Stocks

During the afternoon I saw Admiral Leahy, explained the oil situation and pointed out that as I knew operations in the Pacific were now being planned I felt very strongly that the JCS should bear in mind constantly the need for oil economy until after the middle of the current year when the tanker situation will be easier. Leahy thanked me for bringing this to his notice and said he would pass it on to the JCS; it was obviously of vital importance that General Eisenhower's operations should not be restricted in any way on account of fuel.

9 March

British Pacific Fleet

Reports on Nimitz's press conference appear today. He gave a promise that the British Fleet would be used at the time and in the manner to give the best material assistance in the final defeat of Japan, and denied that any political considerations entered into its employment. . . .

I lunched with the Ambassador[2] in order to meet General Hurley. H.E. said Nimitz had told him there were no difficulties at all between him and Fraser and in a few days' time there would be information concerning the proposed employment of the BPF. . . .

---

[1]The planned seizure of Phuket Is., off Siam; not carried out.
[2]The Earl of Halifax (Edward F. L. Wood, 1881–1959): Fellow of All Souls; Con MP 1910–25; W Front 1914–17; USec Cols 1921–2; Pres, Bd of Educn 1922–4; Minr Ag 1925; Viceroy of India 1925–31; Pres Bd of Educn 1932; Sec State for War 1935; Ld Privy Seal 1935; Ld Pres 1937; For Sec Feb 1938–Dec 1940; Amb US Jan 1941–May 1946; earl 1944.

10 March

Oil Situation

The JSM held a meeting to consider the oil situation; Wilkinson reported that the US petroleum board have agreed to a fairly drastic cut in the Pacific and that this in conjunction with the cut in the Mediterranean should bring our stocks up in the UK to 5 m.t. fairly soon. After June the situation should be easier owing to an increased number of tankers going into the pool.

11 March

Gyro Sights

. . . At the BAMSR meeting Roskill stated that the US now think our gyro sight better than theirs. An odd situation has arisen since we are pressing the US to give us their gyro sight and they are now pressing us to give them ours. . . .

13 March

British Pacific Fleet

. . . In reply to a request by me that statements concerning the BPF to the effect that it could only steam 15 knots, that it was designed for the protection of the British Isles, etc. should be contradicted, the Admiralty say they do not agree and these must be allowed to die a natural death. Personally I think this is a mistake as the statements have been repeated more than once and our PR people in New York and elsewhere are being continually asked about this matter. . . .

434. *To Mountbatten*

27 March 1945

British Pacific Fleet

By the time this letter reaches you I hope that the BPF will be in the news and that all these wild stories that it is unable to operate alongside the American Fleet will be disposed of. But I fear very much that our poor representation by camera and press men will once again let us down, and that we shall never get a proper acknowledgment on this side of what the Fleet does.

Shipping

The Re-deployment Teams are busy at work, and their first cockshy suggests we may be able to reach agreement. Although nothing definite has been said on the matter, we rather feel the Americans may press for SEAC operations to be curtailed should operations in the Pacific be held up owing to lack of shipping. I only mention this because I think you should know about it, but it does not necessarily follow by any means that such curtailment will be necessary. The shipping situation is undoubtedly tight and will continue tight for some time after the collapse of Germany, but I feel myself that with better management by the Americans of their shipping in the Pacific it ought to be possible to make both ends meet. After all, over a million tons of new shipping comes into the pool every month, and with submarine losses down to the 100,000 tons per month figure we ought to be able to compete. . . .

435. *Pocket diary, 1945*

27 March

. . . Macready[?] & I to Navy Dept to tackle Ernie about refusal to allow our technical people to visit works making VT fuzes. E obviously had no knowledge of this and said he'd have it looked into at once. Papers give poor prominence to RN landing craft used for Rhine crossing.

29 March

. . . Communique from C-in-C Pacific re strike by BPF on Sikushima; to be issued today.[1] Admiral Fouroux[?] to see me; would include [–?] French ships for Pacific. Hoping French & Brit. officers will get together more in Washington. COS objected strongly to Eisenhower's new plan to strike across centre of S Germany instead of taking N & W German ports. Went to see King about this and found he agreed!! Raised question of CVEs. . . .

5 April

. . . To Brooklyn Navy Yard where I was met by a guard and band and taken round by Admiral Daubier[?] and Kennedy[?]. Went on board *Coral Sea* the new 59,000 ton carrier. Armoured flight deck being fitted. Drove round yard and saw two *Essex* class on the slips.[2]

[1]The first operations, against Japanese airfields in the vicinity of Okinawa.
[2]*Coral Sea*: 1946, 45,000t, 137 a/c, 18×5in, 33k; Somerville's figure is no doubt the full load displacement. *Essex* class: 1943+, 27,100t, 100 a/c, 12×5in, 33k; main US fleet carrier.

6 April

. . . Nimitz and MacArthur appointed joint commanders in the Pacific which is rather amusing.

7 April

. . . News that *Yamato*,[1] 2 CL & 8 destroyers sortied & were attacked by TF 58 carriers. All sunk except 3 destroyers. US have lost 3 destroyers sunk at Okinawa & other ships damaged but Jap all out attack seems to have been a flop.

8 April

. . . Apparently BPF had little opposition at Sikushima but lost a good many aircraft operationally i.e. 2 in combat & 14 from other causes for 5 Japs shot down. . . .

436.   *BAD desk diary, 1945*

9 April

. . . Copies of [report?] of Ad. King. Not a single reference to British Fleet. 'We did it all ourselves' is the obvious suggestion.

Information that Japanese want Germans to send them U-boats. Hitherto Germans have been unwilling to do so. . . .

10 April

In reply to request from Fraser that BPF should have more forward base and suggesting Subic, King now proposes Brunei in N Borneo & says he intends to carry out operations against N Borneo quite soon.

437.   *Pocket diary, 1945*

10 April

. . . Left at 9.40 a.m. in car for Patuxent Air Station where we arrived at 11.15. Large party of foreign NAs including Chinese Admiral & Norwegian Commodore. Capt. Stacey[?] took us round & we inspected various types and then saw demonstrations of fighters. They included a Seafire and Mosquito. Helicopters on view & I went up & took over controls – most amusing. Lunch in the Mess & then had demonstrated cannon, rockets, smoke screen, [–?] & assisted take off. . . .

---

[1]*Yamato*: 1941, 63,215t, 9×18in, 12×6.1in, 12×5.1in, 27k; sunk by US naval a/c 7 April 1945.

12 April

. . . At JSM attitudes of US in respect of assignments again discussed & need for joint action at COS level. Question of priority for SEAC also requires immediate settling. . . . Ships sunk & damaged at Okin[awa] rather formidable though not many sunk. At 5.45 heard that President Roosevelt had died suddenly. Great shock to US but in view of Yalta I must confess I was not altogether surprised. . . .

13 April

. . . To HMCS *York*, RCNVR training depot [at Toronto]. Saw march past & addressed men. . . .

14 April

. . . To office & found there had been a CCS meeting yesterday at which future operations in SW Pacific were discussed. US would like to turn area over to us. . . .

438. *BAD desk diary, 1945*

17 April

. . . To Navy Dept where I was given latest news of Okinawa and saw picture of 1 man V bomb used by Japs. Over 135 ships (including 3 BB, 3 CV & 22 DD damaged) have now been damaged or sunk at Okinawa. Although some 1300 Jap planes destroyed some ND fellows believe at least another 2500 or more available and that all could be committed to suicide. . . .

19 April

In personal signal FSL says he considers the Brunei proposal is merely attempt to [head?] off BPF from main operations directed against Japan. As regards turning over SW Pacific to us he feels we have not sufficient resources to [cope?] without US help. Feels if Ernie really wanted he could find us a base in Philippines. In reply I pointed out we had rather a weak case as Ernie did not ask.

Signal of appreciation from Spruance to Rawlings about way BPF are starting to [hit?] targets and [launching?] strikes.

20 April

. . . FSL sends copies of signals from Fraser about Brunei, Darwin. Latter presses for Subic – says Darwin no better than Manus & much further back. Argues BPF should take part in Borneo operations. Considers

SW Pacific should not be in SEAC command, in fact considers not suitable to be made separate theatre.

439. *Pocket diary, 1945*

21 April

... Had a most explosive interview with Ernie King about Brunei. He said BPF quite unable to support itself. I also exploded but we cooled off & ended friendly. K said Brunei were [–?] stressed and he was quite ready to consider another place.

2 May

... Mussolini's death confirmed also Germans in N Italy have surrendered. Hitler's own death announced & that Admiral Dönitz is now Führer & he urges Germans to continue fighting Russians.[1] Landings of Australians & US in N Borneo.

3 May

... Rangoon entered by our troops which is a nice surprise. ... Score for April is 125,000 tons lost, half by U-boats but 27 of latter sunk. ...

440. *BAD desk diary, 1945*

7 May

CTF 57 reports [attack on] airfield in Salewan [island?] group. *Formidable* hit by suicide making hole in flight deck 2' square ... splinter entered boiler room. ... Speed reduced temporarily to 10 knots but soon fully operational and full speed. 10 Japs destroyed. We lost 16 including 10 Avengers & 1 Corsair by suicide hit on *Formidable*.[2]

Dickie maintains he can attack Singapore in year and [make it a useful] base if Light Fleet Carriers made available.[3] Signal from Germany to the U-boats to cease hostilities and return to base. C-in-C BPF says in view of plans for attack on Kyushu does not believe forward base can be organised in time. Proposes to use Manus and asks for Fleet Train to be augmented.

---

[1]Grand-Adm Karl Dönitz: head of German Navy S/M arm to 1943; succeeded Raeder as head of navy; chosen by Hitler as his successor.

[2]All the British carriers were hit by suicide bombers at some point, some more than once; the armoured decks proved their worth, however, and, despite suffering casualties to men and planes, they were able to resume operations within a few hours.

[3]Four of these new carriers were being sent out to the Pacific; they joined the BPF just as the war ended.

441.   *To Joan Bright Astley*

8 May 1945

... He's [Cunningham] certainly a bit critical & always has been. We are good friends but he gets very annoyed when I tell him he's damn well wrong about people & just because he gives an opinion it isn't necessarily right.

442.   *Admiralty to AGM Home and Abroad*

8 May 1945

Splice the mainbrace.

443.   *British Admiralty Delegation to the Admiralty*

8 May 1945

Poor BAD can splice no brace
Because of rum there is no trace.

444.   *Admiralty to British Admiralty Delegation*

8 May 1945

Although no Admiral of the Fleet
Should ever take his sippers neat
You'll look VE-Day in the eyeball
With neat Rye Whiskey in your highball[1].

445.   *From Fleet Admiral Leahy*

7 May 1945

The welcome news of your impending promotion [to Admiral of the Fleet] reached me today ...

I think it is altogether fitting that you, who have played such an active and important part in this long struggle, should receive this final promotion which marks the final culmination of our efforts in the war against the Nazis. ...

[1] All poems by Anon, though Adm Somerville's son says that the verse from BAD 'is very characteristic of the doggerel style that JFS enjoyed to demonstrate' ...

446. *From Captain Kaye Edden*[1]

Gunnery Division,
Admiralty,
9 May 1945

My warmest congratulations on today's grand news of your elevation . . .

London yesterday, VE Day, was a good sight. The crowds, although
naturally not so great as those at Coronation time, were terrific outside
Buckingham Palace, in the Mall, Whitehall, Parliament Square and also
in Piccadilly and its Circus. But all very well behaved, due largely no
doubt to the scarcity of alcohol! . . .

I hope to visit Germany soon on the scout for ideas and a 'look see'.
But we already have our teams of 'experts' over there combing through
the vast haul of equipment, drawings and 'professors' (the latter two
being the more important).

. . . we are doing all we can to help the BPF, and EIF, but the allocation
of resources in UK is a complicated problem; and clearly the Merchant
Navy must rank high on the list. . . .

447. *From Cunningham*

9 May 1945

Your old class mate is so delighted about your rise to A.F.!! My very
heartiest congratulations, the whole Service will rejoice with me, I have
had so many enquiries as to whether it was going to happen.

These are great times. A terrific day yesterday starting with a Board
meeting to drink a bottle of Waterloo brandy which Albert [Alexander]
produced. The PM basking and expanding under showers of applause.

Well he deserves it – trying as he is sometimes.

. . . I will not say that there will not be a tripartite meeting sometime
about then [*c.* 10 June]. The bear is very bearish and no one sees any way
out of our present difficulties except as a result of a meeting of the big
three. The General Election is also a difficulty. Between ourselves the
powers would like to call it off but the Labour party must come to heel.
My own view is that Labour may win if it comes off. No bad thing, they
won't last long. . . .

P.S. I get so fed up with Dickie trying to pinch the BPF.

---

[1]Capt (later Vice Adm Sir) W. Kaye Edden (1905–90): Cdr N Ordnance Depot 1938;
London Sept 1940; SO(P) Eastern F March 1942; Capt June 1944; DDGD (A) Nov 1944;
completed career as Adm Cmdg Reserves.

448. *From Admiral Burnett*

10 May 1945

Our warmest congratulations. I refer 3 certain persons at Chatham in 1939 to Job 13 Verse 4.[1]

449. *To Burnett*

11 May 1945

Thank you Bob. For sale one Bath chair.

450. *From Fraser*

10 May 1945

I send my heartiest congratulations on your promotion together with those of your old staff now in the BPF.

451. *To Fraser*

10 May 1945

Thank you Bruce and please thank the boys who I hope are behaving nicely.

452. *From Mountbatten*

10 May 1945

Heartiest congratulations from all of us in SE Asia Command.

453. *To Mounbatten*

11 May 1945

I much appreciate the congratulations of my old comrades of SE Asia Command.

---

[1]But ye are forgers of lies, ye are all physicians of no value.

454. *To Cunningham*

15 May 1945

Thank you so much for a very charming letter which I value greatly coming as it does from you. I must confess however that I never felt I had any real claim to join the Super Old Bastards and can only hope that no one else's nose has been put out of joint.

. . . As my signals will have told you the JCS are very much at sixes and sevens about the Pacific. It would do that party a world of good to meet the COS and talk this matter out. I have a conviction that there is wonderful logistic organisation but damn little operational imagination at present. Some new blood is wanted in that party.

I agree about Dickie and the Fleets. Our name would certainly stink if we took ships away from the BPF for mopping up in SEAC. . . .

455. *BAD desk diary, 1945*

10 May

. . . Bruce offers CINCPAC 1500 RMEs for airfield construction. . . .

Signal from Bruce that on 9th TF attacked by group [of] suicides. *Victorious* [hit on] flight deck, for'd lift, accelerator and 10% aircraft out of action. Can operate a few aircraft at reduced handling speed. *Formidable* hit [on] flight deck setting aircraft alight, 2 pom-poms hit but ship operational.

12 May

. . . Signal from Bruce . . . Says US are using many facilities in Australia, 6 of our CVEs. Four salvage ships diverted to Rangoon. No call on US yet for [assistance?]. Good co-operation. All essential parts self supporting.

14 May

. . . JCS adhere to developing Brunei and consider Manus too far away. Say this will not preclude BPF operating anywhere in [Pacific?] – no available site in Philippines. Consider problem is basic integration of British Base resources.

456.   *Pocket diary, 1945*

14 May

. . . To see Ernie King about JCS reply re Brunei. Said if he would give OK at US bases to help us all would be well. E referred to trouble with MacA but seemed inclined to co-operate. Discussed future strategies for Japan. I suggested our COS views should be obtained. Serious differences of opinion among JCS on this. . . .

457.   *BAD desk diary, 1945*

15 May

List from Navy Dept. of suicide [resume?] Oct – April includes: Attempts 521; Hits 253; Near Miss 70; Ships hit 222; Sunk 34. . . .

17 May

. . . Fraser reports CINCPAC plans for BPF are 1 or if possible 2 fast carrier groups for China in August if it [is to be attacked] and 2 groups for Rykyu in Nov.
. . . 10,000 ton Jap cruiser sighted by *Shah*'s aircraft and sunk by *Saumarez* and other destroyers off Penang.[1]

18 May

Signal from ABC that question of Mosquitoes for Pacific might be left to CAS. I sent ABC a signal yesterday to say Colyer told me suggestion not well received & hoped we could meet US wishes as it would strengthen our position.

458.   *Pocket diary, 1945*

22 May

. . . BF reports *Formidable* had serious fire & accident in hangar. 25 Corsairs & 7 Avengers unserviceable . . . BF reports *Quilliam*[2] collided [with] *Indom*[*itable*] in fog & is being towed back to Leyte at 5½ knots.

26 May

. . . Orders that convoy in Atlantic to cease on 29th. Ships to burn

---

[1]*Haguro*: 1929, 13,000t, 10×8in, 8×5.1in, 16tt, 33.5k. She was sunk by 5 'V' class destroyers, led by *Saumarez* (Capt M. L. Power) in a classic destroyer action. *Saumarez* (L): 1943, 1730t, 4×4.7in, 8tt, 36k. 'V' class: 1944, 1710t, 4×4.7in, 8tt, 36k.
[2]*Quilliam* (L): 1942, 1750t, 4×4.7in, 8tt, 34k.

lights. Signal from ABC asking me to return to charge about base in Philippines. So far as I can see darn few anchorages which are suitable so asked him which he had in mind.

28 May

. . . ABC replied re bases in Philippines but not much help. He again asks for Subic and some others which have no facilities. Went to see Ernie who was quite amenable and said he would ask Nimitz for his views. Also said off the record that there were political objections to British having a base in Philippines.

459. *BAD desk diary, 1945*

30 May

ABC comments on my signal re interview with King that best arrangement would be for us to share a base with US using our facilities to supplement theirs. Does not feel any advantage from Bruce and Nimitz getting together until King made up his mind.

460. *Pocket diary, 1945*

4 June

Saw Ernie King about my going to Forrestal re Research co-ordination. E quite agreeable. Showed me reply from Nimitz re bases which was what I expected i.e. that Brunei best. Re submarines Ernie said this was a matter for Nimitz. Sent signal to ABC & again pointed out that obvious thing was for Fraser & Nimitz to get together. . . . Germans report only 6 U-boats now unaccounted for & think they must have been sunk. Freeman to see me about operational research. I suggested close analysis of suicides. . . .

461. *BAD desk diary, 1945*

6 June

Annapolis for graduation exercises. Ad. Beardall. Good show. V.g. speech by Forrestal. Referred to democratic nature of US Navy – not an [Aristocratic?] Club. Ernie King son of a railway worker and all others lowly origin.

ABC returns to charge about bases & asks me to try again with Ernie but no fresh arguments really.

7 June

. . . CCS meeting. Coasters. King tried to establish absolute priority for N Pacific. He retracted and agreed he'd fought for Pacific rights when Normandy [operation?] was on. . . . King said Nimitz was suggesting Eniwetok as base for Fraser.

462.   *Pocket diary, 1945*

7 June

ISM at 10 a.m. Discussed coaster situation which is tricky – we have not too good a case. . . . Had quite a good CCS meeting. Allocation of 30 coasters was main item. Ernie stubborn & [–?] but gave way later & we finally got 15 which was much better than we expected.

10 June

. . . To Admiralty[1] at 9.45 & saw Syfret. . . . M[ollie] & I to the Cunninghams for tea. Talked to A. about Fraser getting in touch with Nimitz – seems more inclined to agree. Complained that Bruce had got dug in too much at Sydney . . .

13 June

. . . to Admiralty. Found Alan & Maureen there and large pile of paper & signals. . . . long one from Ernie about bases in which he still presses Brunei but says US bases available for forward operations of BPF. Lunched with Betty Stark & ABC, Ghormley, Delrose[?] there as well. Long discussion with Andrew, Bellairs and Grantham[2] over reply to Ernie about bases and other matters. . . . *Trenchant* sank a cruiser of *Ashigara* class in Java Sea.[3] . . .

16 June

. . . To Admiralty early. Saw Cronyn[4] about battle reports & need to promulgate lessons learnt. Saw ABC later who agreed. . . .

[1]He flew home on 8 June.

[2]Capt Laybourne & WRNS 3O M. Stuart Clark. Adm Stark, Adm Cunningham; Delrose unknown. Vice Adm Robert L. Ghormley US Navy (1883–1958): early service in cruisers; GO *Nevada* 1916–18; *Sands* i/c E Med 1920–2; EO *Oklahoma*; Capt *Nevada* 1935–6; staff appts; NW Coll 1937–8; Dir War Plans Div, ONO 1938–9; Asst CNO 1939–40; RA 1938; A-Am naval talks Aug 1940; VA Sept 1941; Cdr S Pac Area June 1942; Guadalcanal landings Aug 1942; N Dept; Cdr 14th N Dist, Pearl Harbor Feb 1943; Cdr US N Forces, Germany Dec 1944–Dec 1945; Chm Gen Bd Jan 1946; Ret List Aug 1946. Rear Adm (Ret) R. M. Bellairs: Br N Rep, Permt Advi Cmn, League of Nations 1932–9; mission to US 1942; Admy 1939–45.

[3]*Ashigara*: 1929, 13,000t, 10×8in, 8×5.1in, 16tt, 33.5k. *Trenchant*: 'T' class s/m, 1943.

[4]Capt St J. Cronyn: Cdr 1937; Trng Cdr *Victory* 1939; *Niger* April 1940; Actg Capt *Miranda* Sept 1940; *Revenge* 1942; Capt July 1943; TSD 1944.

22 June

... Johnny Durnford to see me about visit of Training Staff to USA. Had a long talk with Wake Walker about VT fuses, Blind fire markings/mountings[?] & directors etc. & suggested we had failed to keep in touch with US policy. WW admitted that our gunnery development was the least satisfactory of anything here.[1]

23 June

... Found signal from BF in which he says he might use E Australia as main base & [Noumea?] as intermediate, etc. Says he will see Nimitz in July & sees no advantage in earlier meeting. All very unsatisfactory. ...

2 July

... Went to see Ernie King on usual subject of bases, etc. Found him very friendly & apparently wishing to be helpful & did not get much change. He volunteered it would be a good thing when Fraser & Nimitz met. Goodeve & Wright[2] to see me; seems good chance of continued research etc. co-operation. Had a long session with Stevens about CNI matters.[3] ...

4 July

... Haley[?] from *KGV* & Cdr [–?] from DNO to see me with Roskill. Gave interesting account of their doings in BPF. Said our ships having no blind fire were much more liable to damage in night air attacks. Oerlikons now looked on as of very little value. ...

463. *To Cunningham*

9 July 1945

There is not much I can add to my signal in regard to the interview I had with King about Pacific bases. As I see the situation, the possible bases outside the Philippines are either completely congested or will be before long, and in the Philippine bases it seems to me the great trouble is that MacArthur and Nimitz are at loggerheads, and the USN appar-

---

[1]Rear Adm John W. Durnford: Capt 1935; *Suffolk* 1939; Cdre, 2nd N Mem, Aust. N Bd June 1941; *Resolution* June 1942; RA July 1943; Dir RN Staff Coll Oct 1943; DNT Dec 1944. Wake Walker was 3SL & Controller.

[2]C. S. Wright was Admy Dir Sci Research since 1938. Charles Goodeve was a civilian scientist, att. Admy, June 1940.

[3]Capt E. B. K. Stevens, head of RN PR team sent to Washington in 1945 as a result of Somerville's pressure: Cdr 1933; *Imogen* 1937; Capt Dec 1939; *Havelock* Jan 1940; *Greenwich* Aug 1941; *Pakenham* 1942; Cdre 1 Cl *Nile* (Addnl COS to C-in-C Levant, J.H.D. Cunningham) 1943; COS (A) Med Dec 1943; BAD 1945.

ently took great exception at having to go to MacArthur cap in hand for anything they want.

I met John McCloy,[1] the Under-Secretary for War, at the Embassy last week, and in the Ambassador's presence, he invited me to state any views I had on the Pacific operations. I referred to the obvious lack of harmony between the two Supreme Commanders, i.e. Nimitz and MacArthur and said the ideal solution appeared to be for Eisenhower to go out as Supreme Commander since he had such a talent for pulling people together and making them co-operate. I also suggested that Nimitz should relieve King as COMINCH since, whilst I fully appreciated King's efficiency and judgment, I felt that the autocratic rule he exercised over his subordinates was most detrimental and furthermore his obsession to put the American Fleet on the map as the first, in fact the only worthwhile, Fleet in the world frequently obscures his judgment. I then referred to the almost complete delegation of authority to the Commander on the spot which the Americans practise, which I thought was very much overdone though I also added that my personal views were that we perhaps at times kept too tight a hold on our Cs-in-C. ...

King was very close mouthed about the typhoon during the first part of June; he said an enquiry had been ordered and he would not express an opinion about the matter until he got their report. I think King is very sensitive about anything which suggests American seamanship and fleet handling is not up to standard; as I told McCloy, King always seems to be so nervous that he is wearing the wrong sort of tie at a dinner party. I rubbed into King that we did not pretend to be very experienced in the matter of typhoons since the bulk of our Fleet had been operating in Theatres where these are never encountered; it was of very great importance that we should have full information of what happened so that we could profit by their experience. After reading recent battle reports I am more impressed than ever with the necessity for a really good operational research team to tackle the subject of defence of the Fleet and anchorages against air attack and especially suicide attacks. I keep on suggesting to King, Finch [Fitch?] and others that they should ask our people to assist; they all agree that it is desirable but no action is taken, so perhaps you could give King a prod on the subject at TERMINAL.

---

[1] John J. McCloy (1895–1990): attorney; Asst & USec of War 1941–5; Pres, World Bank 1947; US High Cmnr for Germany 1949.

464. *BAD desk diary, 1945*

9 July

... Douglas Fairbanks [Jr] to see me. Discussing regular USN officers said chief [–?] mass of them from middle or lower middle classes. Those of good family tried to hide it! Jealous of British RN [who?] were considered socially superior. Also all had private means!

10 July

... Letter from Admiralty re allocation of German Fleet. We are most anxious to have it all scrapped but if this is not acceptable [definitely?] to do our utmost to keep control of the bulk of submarines. German ships were of little or no value in Pacific war on account of spares, ammunition etc. Sent précis to King and will discuss it with him. ...

465. *Pocket diary, 1945*

11 July

... Cdr Mitchell[1] to see me on way to Pacific. Flight deck expert. Says US flight deck drill better than ours. ... Saw Ernie King about allocation of German Navy. His views coincide with ours.

16 July

... Nimitz agreed to give facilities at Manus. Rumours that Japs trying to initiate peace proposals at Moscow. ...

19 July

... Papers give good leaders for British bombardments of Jap coast towns with US fleet. Japs seem to make no effort at all to strike back. ... Papers also discuss possible peace feelers by Japan. ...

20 July

... Letters from TERMINAL[2] show that JCS do not take kindly the proposal COS should participate to greater extent in Pacific strategy. We have dug our toes in however. After welcoming proposal for 5 divisions JCS beginning to raise logistics & other difficulties. ...

---

[1]Actg Cdr (Ret) J. E. M. Mitchell: Lt-Cdr *Cochrane* (Rosyth) 1940; *Lanka* (Mine Ctr-Measures) 1941; *Orlando* (Greenock) 1943; Actg Cdr *President III* (Windsor) May 1944.

[2]The Potsdam conference between Stalin, Pres Harry S. Truman and Churchill (replaced by the new PM, Attlee, half way through).

21 July

... No particular news from TERMINAL. Asked him [Ambassador] afterwards about story that Bill Leahy was anti-Brit. Said he had no evidence but thought that at White House things might be a shade more difficult for us & we should miss Harry Hopkins. ...

466. BAD desk diary, 1945

1 August

... Tupper Carey[1] to see me. Said Fleet Train making good progress but US thought we were always too conservative and turned down things as impracticable without sufficient justification.

2 August

Japs still making peace feelers at Moscow but as they will ... not accept unconditional surrender it does not seem likely to come to anything.

6 August

... Evening papers report dropping of first atomic bomb on Japan. Radio full of this all evening.

467. Pocket diary, 1945

7 August

... Papers very full of atomic bomb & its development. Results not yet observed owing to enormous cloud of dust and smoke. At 11.0 Sir James Chadwick[2] gave us a talk on development of bomb & answered questions about future development & said radio activity would make area dangerous to life & health for at least 3 weeks. ...

9 August

... Second atomic bomb dropped on Nagasaki. At 4.14 I had a call from Rachel to say Mollie critically ill & could I come home.[3] ...

---

[1]Capt P. C. S Tupper Carey: Cdr 1939; NID 1940; *Warspite* May 1942; FNO, Eastern F July 1943; Capt & Master of F, BPF, *Howe*, June 1945.
[2]Sir James Chadwick (1891–1974): physicist; FRS 1927; Nobel Prize 1935; Prof, Liverpool 1935; head of Br Atomic Missn, Washington 1943–6; Master of Caius Coll, Cambridge 1948–58.
[3]He flew home at once; Lady Somerville died at Dinder on 18 August.

15 August

[At Dinder] . . . 7.0 news said Japs accept peace terms . . . Radio full of VJ Day rejoicings. . . .

468. *To Rt Hon Malcolm MacDonald*[1]

12 October

. . . Rear Admiral H Thebaud, USN, late DNI, . . . had detected an undoubted irritation on the part of the Canadians in respect of what they considered to be the treatment meted out to them in their dealings with the British . . . in general they appeared to arise from what Canadians alleged to be the 'superior' attitude adopted by the British in their dealings with them. . . .

So far as the Canadian Navy was concerned he had found there was a tendency on their part to lean towards America, i.e. to adopt US material and methods rather than British. . . .

. . . The Admiral went on to refer to his service as Captain of a Destroyer Flotilla in Londonderry during '42 and '43. He stated that, somewhat to his surprise, he found it generally fell to him to reconcile differences between British and Canadian Naval Officers. He would have expected it to be the other way about, i.e. the Canadian Navy would act as intermediary between the US and British allies. He felt that in many cases friction which arose was due to hypersensitiveness on the part of Canadian Naval Officers, but at the same time he also felt that in certain instances British Naval Officers had failed to take due account of Canadians' sensitiveness or the fact that they were a young Navy lacking the experience of the British.

This statement of Admiral Thebaud's bears out a conversation which is reported to have taken place between Vice Admiral Jones[2] and another US officer whose identity I am not aware of; it was to the effect that British Naval authorities were unsatisfactory to deal with and that in general they were 'high hatted' and seemed to think Canadian Naval Officers were amateurs. Admiral Jones also expressed annoyance that the fact that British equipment, and particularly radar, supplied to

[1]Malcolm MacDonald (1901–81): 2nd son of James Ramsay MacDonald, 1st Lab PM; Lab MP 1929; USec Dominions 1931; Sec St Doms & Cols 1935–40; Minr Health 1940; H Cmnr Canada 1941–6; Govr-Gen Malaysia; UK Cmnr Gen, SE Asia; H Cmnr India 1955–60; Laos Conf, Geneva 1961–2; Govr Kenya 1963–4 & H Cmnr 1964–5; Spl Rep of Br Govt in Africa 1967–9; Pres, R Commonwealth S 1971 & other pub svc.

[2]Vice Adm G. C. Jones, RCN: Capt Aug 1938; Ottawa 1939; Cdre 1 Cl i/c Can. DF *Assiniboine* 1941; RA Dec 1941; *Stadacona* (RCN Barracks, Halifax) 1942; VA, HQ Ottawa May 1944.

Canadian ships was not of the latest pattern and not up to the standard
of American equipment. It is also understood to express the view that
the Canadian Navy should look to America rather than Britain in the
future. . . .

On my recent visit to Montreal, Ottawa, Toronto, Vancouver and
Esquimalt[1] I have received every sign of outward friendliness and great
hospitality from Canadian naval officers of all ranks.

469. *To Cunningham*

13 October 1945

. . . I tried to get Ernie King to talk about postwar Navies in relation to
new developments, e.g., atomic bombs, guided missiles, etc. He would
not open up at all but merely generalised that the US must never be
caught unprepared again and it was their business to see that they always
had a strong navy. Furthermore, he did not at the moment envisage any
radical alteration to the types of Naval vessels which would be required
in the future. . . .

It seems to me that Ernie King is worn out and is waiting for the
moment when he can turn all his headaches over to someone else; who
that is to be is not yet clear, but in spite of the new regulations concerning age for retirement, I feel that Nimitz is the most likely runner-up.[2]

470. *To Cunningham*

12 November 1945

. . . The battle between the Army and Navy over here in connection
with an integrated defence force continues at full speed and is causing
really bitter feeling everywhere. It is very difficult to forecast what the
result is likely to be since politics and votes inevitably enter into the matter. On the whole I am inclined to think that Jim Forrestal's plan, which
quite clearly approximates to the set up we have, has a good chance of
being accepted; but in the meanwhile every sort of fatuous argument as
to who really won the war in the Pacific and who is likely to win wars in
the future, is being advanced.[3]

Ernie [King], George [Marshall] and Hap [Arnold] are all straining at

---

[1]Esquimalt was the principal Canadian naval station on the Pacific coast.
[2]Nimitz did indeed succeed King.
[3]The setting up of a Dept of Defense, in which the Depts of War and the Navy would be
subsumed; HQ at the Pentagon.

the leash to get shot of their jobs and away out of a controversy which they all dislike but feel they must wage so long as they are in the saddle. . . .

471. *From Fleet Admiral Nimitz*

Navy Department
Washington, DC,
3 December 1945

. . . It is with regret that I hear that you are leaving on 15 December. I know that you will take with you the friendship and respect of all your associates in the United States Navy.

472. *Pocket diary, 1945*

14 December

. . . Jumbo & I to White House at 1045 to see Ernie & to receive DSM.[1] . . . At 3.0 saw President[2] at White House to say goodbye. Discussed Press and atomic energy. . . . At 3.30 heard Harry Moore was arriving by air. To Anacostia at 4.30 & waited half an hour. Ad. Edwards there. Harry looked very well.

15 December

Attended Embassy meeting but only to introduce Harry & say goodbye. . . . To Navy Dept to say goodbye to Jim Forrestal who was very nice. Took Harry to Navy Dept at 12.0 to meet Nimitz & King. Had quite a long talk. Nimitz pleasant about Philip Vian & Rawlings. Ernie at his very smartest. . . . Special Service Dept presented me with a lovely model of *Renown* which they'd made.[3]

[1] An American decoration of high standing.
[2] President Harry S. Truman (1884–1972): small businessman, Missouri, jnr officer, AEF 1917–18; Dem Sen, Mo. 1935–44; Chm, Sen Cttee on war effort; VPres March 1945; succ to Pres on d of FDR April 1945; elec in own right Nov 1948; left office Jan 1953; devotee of history & music; virtually unknown, catapulted to most powerful & responsible office on earth; historians differ violently on his standing.
[3] Left New York aboard *Queen Mary*, 18 Dec; Rachel remained in Washington with Joint Staff Mission.

DOCUMENTS AND SOURCES

Public Record Office, Kew, London

Records of the Admiralty:–

(a) War History Collection (ADM 199/391, ADM 199/1187)
(b) Papers of the First Sea Lord (ADM 205)

National Maritime Museum, Greenwich, London

The Papers of Admiral Sir William G. Tennant (TENN)

The Imperial War Museum, London

The Papers of Mrs Joan Bright Astley (Astley Papers)

The British Library, The British Museum, London

The Papers of Admiral of the Fleet Viscount Cunningham of Hyndhope
(BM Add. Mss. [CUNN] 52563, 52566).

The Churchill Archives Centre, Churchill College, Cambridge

(a) The Papers of Admiral of the Fleet Sir James Somerville (SMVL)
(b) The Papers of Admiral Sir Dudley North (NORTH)
(c) The Papers of Admiral Sir Ralph Edwards (REDW).

PART I

1.	To his wife	31 July 1936	SMVL 3/19
2.	To his wife	6 August 1936	SMVL 3/19
3.	To his wife	7 August 1936	SMVL 3/19
4.	To his wife	8 August 1936	SMVL 3/19
5.	To Admiral Sir Dudley Pound	9 August 1936	SMVL 5/5
6.	To his wife	17 August 1936	SMVL 3/19
7.	To Pound	21 August 1936	SMVL 5/5
8.	To Senior Spanish Naval Officers	24 August 1936	SMVL 5/5
9.	To his wife	21 May 1937	SMVL 3/20
10.	From Commanding Officer, HMS *Grenade*	24 June 1937	SMVL 5/5

44.	Report of Proceedings	6–11 July 1940	ADM 199/391
45.	To his wife	10 July 1940	SMVL 3/22
46.	To Pound	13 July 1940	SMVL 7/28
47.	To his wife	24 July 1940	SMVL 3/22
48.	Report of Proceedings	11–30 July 1940	ADM 199/391
49.	To his wife	2 August 1940	SMVL 3/22
50.	To his wife	5 August 1940	SMVL 3/22
51.	Report of Proceedings	30 July–9 August 1940	ADM 199/391
52.	Notes of a meeting held in the First Sea Lord's room	11 August 1940	SMVL 7/28
53.	Subjects of Interest to Senior Officer, Force H	August 1940	SMVL 7/28
54.	Report of Proceedings	10–25 August 1940	ADM 199/391
55.	Report of Proceedings	30 August– 3 September 1940	SMVL 7/4
56.	To Blake	4 September 1940	SMVL 7/28
57.	Report of Proceedings	4–10 September 1940	SMVL 7/4
58.	Report of Proceedings	11–14 September 1940	SMVL 7/4
59.	To his wife	12 September 1940	SMVL 3/22
60.	To his wife	14 September 1940	SMVL 3/22
61.	To his wife	17 September 1940	SMVL 3/22
62.	Report of Proceedings	15–20 September 1940	SMVL 7/4
63.	Report of Proceedings	20–23 September 1940	SMVL 7/4
64.	To Blake	24 September 1940	SMVL 7/28
65.	To his wife	24 September 1940	SMVL 3/22
66.	To his wife	25 September 1940	SMVL 3/22
67.	To his wife	26 September 1940	SMVL 3/22
68.	Report of Proceedings	27–28 September 1940	SMVL 7/4
69.	To his wife	28 September 1940	SMVL 3/22
70.	To his wife	29 September 1940	SMVL 3/22
71.	To his wife	30 September 1940	SMVL 3/22
72.	To his wife	1 October 1940	SMVL 3/22
73.	To his wife	2 October 1940	SMVL 3/22
74.	To his wife	4 October 1940	SMVL 3/22
75.	To his wife	5 October 1940	SMVL 3/22
76.	Report of Proceedings	29 September–7 October 1940	SMVL 7/4
77.	To the Admiralty	7 October 1940	SMVL 7/25
78.	To his wife	8 October 1940	SMVL 3/22

79.	To his wife	9 October 1940	SMVL 3/22
80.	From the Admiralty	15 October 1940	SMVL 7/26
81.	Naval Attaché, Madrid, to Staff Officer (I), Gibraltar	10 September 1940	SMVL 7/25
82.	The Admiralty to Admiral North	15 October 1940	SMVL 7/25
83.	To his wife	25 October 1940	SMVL 3/22
84.	To the Admiralty	25 October 1940	SMVL 7/26
85.	To his wife	26 October 1940	SMVL 3/22
86.	Memorandum by Admiral North	29 October 1943	SMVL 7/25
87.	Memorandum by Admiral North	29 October 1943	SMVL 7/25
88.	To his wife	12 October 1940	SMVL 3/22
89.	Report of Proceedings	7–14 October 1940	SMVL 7/4
90.	To Blake	17 October 1940	SMVL 7/28
91.	To Blake	22 October 1940	SMVL 7/28
92.	Report of Proceedings	14–20 October 1940	SMVL 7/4
93.	Report of Proceedings	22 October– 7 November 1940	SMVL 7/4
94.	Report of Proceedings	7–11 November 1940	SMVL 7/5
95.	To his wife	10 November 1940	SMVL 3/22
96.	Report of Proceedings	11–19 November 1940	SMVL 7/5
97.	To his wife	15 November 1940	SMVL 3/22
98.	To his wife	17 November 1940	SMVL 3/22
99.	To his wife	20 November 1940	SMVL 3/22
100.	Report of Proceedings	19–29 November 1940	SMVL 7/5
101.	To his wife	25 November 1940	SMVL 3/22
102.	To his wife	28 November 1940	SMVL 3/22
103.	To his wife	30 November 1940	SMVL 3/22
104.	Report of Proceedings	29 November– 3 December 1940	SMVL 7/5
105.	To his wife	4 December 1940	SMVL 3/22
106.	To his wife	6 December 1940	SMVL 3/22
107.	To his wife	7 December 1940	SMVL 3/22
108.	To the Admiralty	6 December 1940	SMVL 7/21
109.	From the Secretary of the Admiralty	10 January 1941	SMVL 7/21
110.	From Lord Cork	7 December 1940	SMVL 7/21
111.	To his wife	8 December 1940	SMVL 3/22
112.	To his wife	11 December 1940	SMVL 3/22
113.	To Cunningham	8 January 1941	CUNN 52563
114.	Finding of the Board of Inquiry	December 1940	SMVL 7/21

147.	Report of Proceedings	1–8 March 1941	SMVL 7/7
148.	Report of Proceedings	8–23 March 1941	SMVL 7/7
149.	Report of Proceedings	24–31 March 1941	SMVL 7/7
150.	Report of Proceedings	1–4 April 1941	SMVL 7/7
151.	To North	7 April 1941	NORTH 2/8
152.	Report of Proceedings	4–16 April 1941	SMVL 7/7
153.	Report of Proceedings	16–24 April 1941	SMVL 7/7
154.	Report of Proceedings	24–28 April 1941	SMVL 7/7
155.	Report of Proceedings	28 April–12 May 1941	SMVL 7/8
156.	To his wife	9 May 1941	SMVL 3/24
157.	To North	14 May 1941	NORTH 2/8
158.	To North	23–28 May 1941	NORTH 2/8
159.	To his wife	24–27 May 1941	SMVL 3/24
160.	Report of Proceedings	23–29 May 1941	SMVL 7/9
161.	To C-in-C, Home Fleet	4 June 1941	ADM 199/1187
162.	Report of Proceedings	29 May–7 June 1941	SMVL 7/9
163.	To North	15 June 1941	NORTH 2/8
164.	Report of Proceedings	7–15 June 1941	SMVL 7/9
165.	To Cunningham	11 June 1941	CUNN 52563
166.	Report of Proceedings	16–22 June 1941	SMVL 7/10
167.	Report of Proceedings	22 June–1 July 1941	SMVL 7/10
168.	To Cunningham	2 July 1941	CUNN 52563
169.	Statement on First Year of Force H's Operations	9 July 1941	SMVL 7/28
170.	To North	13 July 1941	NORTH 2/8
171.	To Force H and SUBSTANCE Convoy	20 July 1941	SMVL 7/24
172.	Report on Operation SUBSTANCE	4 August 1941	SMVL 7/24
173.	To North	30 July 1941	NORTH 2/8
174.	Report of Proceedings	27 July–4 August 1941	SMVL 7/11
175.	To North	5–6 August 1941	NORTH 2/8
176.	Report of Proceedings	5–14 August 1941	SMVL 7/11
177.	To Cunningham	10 August 1941	CUNN 52563
178.	Report of Proceedings	15–26 August 1941	SMVL 7/12
179.	Orders for Operation MINCEMEAT	20 August 1941	SMVL 7/12
180.	To North	26 August 1941	NORTH 2/8
181.	Report of Proceedings	26 August–14 September 1941	SMVL 7/13
182.	To Cunningham	7 September 1941	CUNN 52563
183.	To North	8 September 1941	NORTH 2/8
184.	Report of Proceedings	14–24 September 1941	SMVL 7/14

PART III

216.	To Pound	2 March 1942	SMVL 8/1
217.	To Pound	2 March 1942	REDW 2/8
218.	Pocket diary, 1942	3–7 March 1942	SMVL 3/31
219.	To his wife	8 March 1942	SMVL 3/31
220.	Pocket diary, 1942	9–10 March 1942	SMVL 3/31
221.	To the Admiralty	10 March 1942	REDW 2/8
222.	To Pound	11 March 1942	SMVL 8/1
223.	To his wife	14 March 1942	SMVL 3/31
224.	Pocket diary, 1942	19 March 1942	SMVL 3/31
225.	The Chiefs of Staff to Wavell	19 March 1942	REDW 2/8
226.	To his wife	20 March 1942	SMVL 3/31
227.	Pocket diary, 1942	28 March 1942	SMVL 3/31
228.	To his wife	26–28 March 1942	SMVL 3/31
229.	Pocket diary, 1942	29–31 March 1942	SMVL 3/31
230.	To his wife	1–3 March 1942	SMVL 3/31
231.	From Cdre Edwards's diary	4 April 1942	REDW 2/7
232.	To his wife	4–6 April 1942	SMVL 3/31
233.	From Cdre Edwards's diary	6 April 1942	REDW 2/7
234.	To his wife	7 April 1942	SMVL 3/31
235.	To the Admiralty	8 April 1942	REDW 2/8
236.	To the Admiralty	8 April 1942	REDW 2/9
237.	From Layton	9 April 1942	REDW 2/9
238.	To his wife	9 April 1942	SMVL 3/31
239.	Pocket diary, 1942	9 April 1942	SMVL 3/31
240.	To North	10 April 1942	NORTH 2/8
241.	To the Admiralty	11 April 1942	REDW 2/8
242.	Pound to Alexander	6 June 1942	ADM 205/14
243.	Alexander to Churchill	10 June 1942	ADM 205/14
244.	Pocket diary, 1942	11 April 1942	SMVL 3/31
245.	To his wife	15 April 1942	SMVL 3/31
246.	To the Admiralty	16 April 1942	REDW 2/9
247.	From the Chiefs of Staff	16 April 1942	REDW 2/8
248.	Pocket diary, 1942	17–21 April 1942	SMVL 3/31
249.	From Wavell	20 April 1942	SMVL 8/7
250.	To Wavell	21 April 1942	SMVL 8/7
251.	To his wife	22 April 1942	SMVL 3/31
252.	To his wife	25 April 1942	SMVL 3/31
253.	Pocket diary, 1942	27–28 April 1942	SMVL 3/31
254.	To the Admiralty	29 April 1942	REDW 2/9
255.	From Pound	1 May 1942	REDW 2/9
256.	To Pound	2 May 1942	REDW 2/9
257.	Pocket diary, 1942	3 May 1942	SMVL 3/31
258.	To his wife	3 May 1942	SMVL 3/31
259.	Pocket diary, 1942	5–7 May 1942	SMVL 3/31
260.	To the Admiralty	9 May 1942	REDW 2/10
261.	Alexander to Churchill	15 May 1942	ADM 205/13

262.	To his wife	18 May 1942	SMVL 3/31
263.	Pocket diary, 1942	20–23 May 1942	SMVL 3/31
264.	To North	27 May 1942	NORTH 2/8
265.	To his wife	28 May 1942	SMVL 3/31
266.	From the Admiralty	2 June 1942	REDW 2/10
267.	Pocket diary, 1942	31 May–11 June 1942	SMVL 3/31
268.	Churchill to Pound	10 June 1942	ADM 205/14
269.	Pound to Churchill	10 June 1942	ADM 205/14
270.	To his wife	13 June 1942	SMVL 3/31
271.	Pocket diary, 1942	21 June 1942	SMVL 3/31
272.	To Joan Bright Astley	23 June 1942	Astley Papers
273.	To Pound	29 June 1942	SMVL 8/1
274.	Pound to Churchill	11 July 1942	ADM 205/14
275.	Churchill to Pound	c.12 July 1942	ADM 205/14
276.	Alexander to Churchill	14 July 1942	ADM 205/14
277.	To Joan Bright Astley	12 July 1942	Astley Papers
278.	To Pound	15 July 1942	SMVL 8/1
279.	Pocket diary, 1942	15–22 July 1942	SMVL 3/31
280.	Pound to Churchill	18 July 1942	ADM 205/14
281.	To North	20 July 1942	NORTH 2/8
282.	To his wife	31 July–3 August 1942	SMVL 3/31
283.	To Joan Bright Astley	11 August 1942	Astley Papers
284.	Pocket diary, 1942	5–31 August 1942	SMVL 3/31
285.	To Pound	1 September 1942	SMVL 8/1
286.	Pocket diary, 1942	3–10 September 1942	SMVL 3/31
287.	To his wife	10 September 1942	SMVL 3/31
288.	To his wife	25 September 1942	SMVL 3/31
289.	Pocket diary, 1942	26 September 1942	SMVL 3/31
290.	To North	27 September 1942	NORTH 2/8
291.	To Cunningham	9 October 1942	CUNN 52563
292.	Pocket diary, 1942	11 October 1942	SMVL 3/31
293.	To his wife	11 October 1942	SMVL 3/31
294.	Pocket diary, 1942	13 October–11 November 1942	SMVL 3/31
295.	To Pound	7 November 1942	SMVL 8/1
296.	To North	24 November 1942	NORTH 2/8
297.	Pocket diary, 1942	27 November–21 December 1942	SMVL 3/31
298.	To Pound	28 December 1942	SMVL 8/1
299.	Pocket diary, 1943	7 January–17 February 1943	SMVL 3/31
300.	To North	22 February 1943	NORTH 2/8
301.	To his wife	23 February 1943	SMVL 3/31

| 302. | To Pound | 11 March 1943 | SMVL 8/1 |
| 303. | Pocket diary, 1943 | 26 February–
8 March 1943 | SMVL 3/31 |
| 304. | To Joan Bright Astley | 7 March 1943 | Astley Papers |
| 305. | To North | 8 March 1943 | NORTH 2/8 |
| 306. | Report of Proceedings | 18 March–7 April
1943 | SMVL 8/5 |
307.	Pocket diary, 1943	8 April–5 July 1943	SMVL 3/31
308.	To the Admiralty	3 July 1943	REDW 2/10
309.	From Royle	25 May 1943	SMVL 8/4
310.	To Royle	17 July 1943	SMVL 8/4
311.	Pocket diary, 1943	8 July–23 August
1943	SMVL 3/31
312.	Report of Proceedings	24 July–26 August
1943	SMVL 8/5
313.	To Pound	27 August 1943	SMVL 8/3
314.	From Mountbatten	2 September 1943	SMVL 8/3
315.	Pocket diary, 1943	16 September 1943	SMVL 3/31
316.	Eastern Fleet War Diary	September 1943	ADM199/643
317.	To Pound	19 September 1943	SMVL 8/1
318.	To his wife	30 September 1943	SMVL 3/31
319.	To his wife	5 October 1943	SMVL 3/31
320.	Desk diary, 1943	6–11 October 1943	SMVL 2/2
321.	To Tennant	23 October 1943	TENN 25
322.	To Cunningham	27 October 1943	SMVL 8/2
323.	Desk diary, 1943	29 October 1943	SMVL 2/2
324.	Eastern Fleet War Diary	October 1943	ADM199/643
325.	To his wife	29 October 1943	SMVL 3/31
326.	Desk diary, 1943	31 October–
11 November 1943	SMVL 2/2
327.	To Mountbatten	13 November 1943	SMVL 8/3
328.	Churchill to Cunningham and
Ismay	17 November 1943	ADM 205/27
329.	Cunningham to Churchill	20 November 1943	ADM 205/27
330.	From Mountbatten	24 November 1943	SMVL 8/3
331.	To Cunningham	4 December 1943	SMVL 8/2
332.	From Cunningham	19 December 1943	SMVL 8/2
333.	To his wife	3 December 1943	SMVL 3/31
334.	Desk diary, 1943	20 November 1943	SMVL 2/2
335.	Eastern Fleet War Diary	November 1943	ADM199/643
336.	To his wife	6 December 1943	SMVL 3/31
337.	Desk diary, 1943	8 December 1943	SMVL 2/2
338.	To his wife	8 December 1943	SMVL 3/31
339.	To his wife	21 December 1943	SMVL 3/31
340.	Desk diary, 1943	31 December 1943	SMVL 2/2
341.	Desk diary, 1944	2 January 1944	SMVL 2/2

342.	To Cunningham	3 January 1944	SMVL 8/2
343.	Desk diary, 1944	4–18 January 1944	SMVL 2/2
344.	To his wife	18 January 1944	SMVL 3/31
345.	To Mountbatten	18 January 1944	SMVL 8/3
346.	Desk diary, 1944	19 January 1944	SMVL 2/2
347.	To Tennant	22 January 1944	TENN 25
348.	Desk diary, 1944	27–31 January 1944	SMVL 2/2
349.	To Cunningham	1 February 1944	CUNN 52563
350.	VCNS to Cunningham	12 February 1944	CUNN 52563
351.	VCNS to Cunningham	12 February 1944	CUNN 52563
352.	From Cunningham	10 March 1944	SMVL 8/2
353.	To his wife	1 February 1944	SMVL 3/31
354.	To Cunningham	3 February 1944	SMVL 8/2
355.	Desk diary, 1944	6–8 February 1944	SMVL 2/2
356.	To his wife	8 February 1944	SMVL 3/31
357.	Desk diary, 1944	9–12 February 1944	SMVL 2/2
358.	From Ismay	12 February 1944	SMVL 8/4
359.	Desk diary, 1944	13–16 February 1944	SMVL 2/2
360.	From Mountbatten	17 February 1944	SMVL 8/3
361.	Desk diary, 1944	21–23 February 1944	SMVL 2/2
362.	To Mountbatten	23 February 1944	SMVL 8/3
363.	Desk diary, 1944	24–29 February 1944	SMVL 2/2
364.	To Cunningham	29 February 1944	SMVL 8/2
365.	Desk diary, 1944	1–11 March 1944	SMVL 2/2
366.	To Mountbatten	11 March 1944	SMVL 8/3
367.	Desk diary, 1944	12–26 March 1944	SMVL 2/2
368.	To his wife	27 March 1944	SMVL 3/31
369.	Desk diary, 1944	31 March–24 April 1944	SMVL 2/2
370.	To Mountbatten	24 April 1944	SMVL 8/3
371.	To Tennant	25 April 1944	SMVL 8/7
372.	To his wife	2 May 1944	SMVL 3/31
373.	Desk diary, 1944	2–4 May 1944	SMVL 2/2
374.	To Admiral Fraser	6 May 1944	SMVL 8/4
375.	Desk diary, 1944	6–15 May 1944	SMVL 2/2
376.	To his wife	16 May 1944	SMVL 3/31
377.	Desk diary, 1944	17–18 May 1944	SMVL 2/2
378.	To his wife	18 May 1944	SMVL 3/31
379.	To General MacArthur	c.19 May 1944	SMVL 8/5
380.	To his wife	20 May 1944	SMVL 3/31
381.	Desk diary, 1944	20–24 May 1944	SMVL 2/2

382.	To his wife	24 May 1944	SMVL 3/31
383.	To his wife	25 May 1944	SMVL 3/31
384.	Desk diary, 1944	28 May–6 June 1944	SMVL 2/2
385.	To Cunningham	12 June 1944	SMVL 8/2
386.	Desk diary, 1944	12–27 June 1944	SMVL 2/2
387.	To his wife	25 June 1944	SMVL 3/31
388.	To Cunningham	27 June 1944	SMVL 8/2
389.	Desk diary, 1944	29 June–18 July 1944	SMVL 2/2
390.	To Cunningham	18 July 1944	SMVL 8/2
391.	Desk diary, 1944	19–21 July 1944	SMVL 2/2
392.	From Mountbatten	22 July 1944	SMVL 8/3
393.	Desk diary, 1944	22–27 July 1944	SMVL 2/2
394.	To his wife	25 July 1944	SMVL 3/31
395.	To Cunningham	27 July 1944	SMVL 8/2
396.	Desk diary 1944	29 July 1944	SMVL 2/2
397.	From Mountbatten	30 July 1944	SMVL 8/7
398.	From Admiral Nimitz	29 July 1944	SMVL 8/7
399.	Desk diary, 1944	1–25 August 1944	SMVL 2/2
400.	From the Admiralty	19 August 1944	SMVL 8/7
401.	To the Admiralty	20 August 1944	SMVL 8/7

PART IV

402.	From Cunningham	29 January 1944	SMVL 9/1
403.	To Cunningham	30 January 1944	SMVL 9/1
404.	From Cunningham	February 1944	SMVL 8/2
405.	From Cunningham	10 March 1944	SMVL 8/2
406.	To Cunningham	c.end of March 1944	SMVL 8/2
407.	Capt (P) McBride to Capt (P) Laybourne	10 April 1944	SMVL 9/1
408.	Alexander to Churchill	15 April 1944	ADM 205/35
409.	Churchill to Alexander	29 April 1944	ADM 205/35
410.	Alexander to Churchill	3 May 1944	ADM 205/35
411.	Churchill to Alexander	21 May 1944	ADM 205/35
412.	Alexander to Churchill	24 May 1944	ADM 205/35
413.	Churchill to Alexander	27 May 1944	ADM 205/35
414.	BAD desk diary, 1944	30 October–1 November 1944	SMVL 2/3
415.	To Cunningham	4 November 1944	CUNN 52563
416.	BAD desk diary, 1944	6–10 November 1944	SMVL 2/3
417.	To Mountbatten	10 November 1944	SMVL 9/2

418.	BAD desk diary, 1944	13–14 November 1944	SMVL 2/3
419.	From Mountbatten	14 November 1944	SMVL 9/2
420.	BAD desk diary, 1944	16–21 November 1944	SMVL 2/3
421.	From Mountbatten	22 November 1944	SMVL 9/2
422.	To Auchinleck	22 November 1944	SMVL 9/4
423.	From Cunningham	28 November 1944	CUNN 52563
424.	BAD desk diary, 1944	29 November–7 December 1944	SMVL 2/3
425.	To Cunningham	7 December 1944	CUNN 52563
426.	To Mountbatten	13 December 1944	SMVL 9/2
427.	To Joan Bright Astley	14 December 1944	Astley Papers
428.	BAD desk diary, 1944	18–29 December 1944	SMVL 2/3
429.	To Cunningham	28 December 1944	CUNN 52563
430.	To North	28 December 1944	NORTH 2/8
431.	BAD desk diary, 1945	1 January–20 February 1945	SMVL 2/3
432.	To Mountbatten	23 February 1945	SMVL 9/2
433.	BAD desk diary, 1945	23 February–13 March 1945	SMVL 2/3
434.	To Mountbatten	27 March 1945	SMVL 9/2
435.	Pocket diary, 1945	27 March–8 April 1945	SMVL 1/36
436.	BAD desk diary, 1945	9–10 April 1945	SMVL 2/4
437.	Pocket diary, 1945	10–14 April 1945	SMVL 1/36
438.	BAD desk diary, 1945	17–20 April 1945	SMVL 2/4
439.	Pocket diary, 1945	21 April–3 May 1945	SMVL 1/36
440.	BAD desk diary, 1945	7 May 1945	SMVL 2/4
441.	To Joan Bright Astley	8 May 1945	Astley Papers
442.	The Admiralty to AGM Home and Abroad	8 May 1945	SMVL 9/3
443.	BAD to the Admiralty	8 May 1945	SMVL 9/3
444.	The Admiralty to BAD	8 May 1945	SMVL 9/3
445.	From Fleet Admiral Leahy	7 May 1945	SMVL 9/3
446.	From Captain Edden	9 May 1945	SMVL 9/3
447.	From Cunningham	9 May 1945	SMVL 9/3
448.	From Admiral Burnett	10 May 1945	SMVL 9/3
449.	To Burnett	11 May 1945	SMVL 9/3
450.	From Fraser	10 May 1945	SMVL 9/3
451.	To Fraser	10 May 1945	SMVL 9/3
452.	From Mountbatten	10 May 1945	SMVL 9/3
453.	To Mountbatten	11 May 1945	SMVL 9/3
454.	To Cunningham	15 May 1945	CUNN 52563

455.	BAD desk diary, 1945	10–14 May 1945	SMVL 2/4
456.	Pocket diary, 1945	14 May 1945	SMVL 1/36
457.	BAD desk diary, 1945	15–18 May 1945	SMVL 2/4
458.	Pocket diary, 1945	22–28 May 1945	SMVL 1/36
459.	BAD desk diary, 1945	30 May 1945	SMVL 2/4
460.	Pocket diary, 1945	4 June 1945	SMVL 1/36
461.	BAD desk diary, 1945	6 June 1945	SMVL 2/4
462.	Pocket diary, 1945	7 June–4 July 1945	SMVL 1/36
463.	To Cunningham	9 July 1945	CUNN 52563
464.	BAD desk diary, 1945	9–10 July 1945	SMVL 2/4
465.	Pocket diary, 1945	11–21 July 1945	SMVL 1/36
466.	BAD desk diary, 1945	1–6 August 1945	SMVL 2/4
467.	Pocket diary, 1945	7–15 August 1945	SMVL 1/36
468.	To Malcolm MacDonald	12 October 1945	CUNN 52563
469.	To Cunningham	13 October 1945	CUNN 52563
470.	To Cunningham	12 November 1945	CUNN 52563
471.	From Fleet Admiral Nimitz	3 December 1945	SMVL 9/4
472.	Pocket diary, 1945	14–15 December 1945	SMVL 1/36

INDEX

673

Navy Records Society
(Founded 1893)

The Navy Records Society was established for the purpose of printing unpublished manuscripts and rare works of naval interest. Membership of the Society is open to all who are interested in naval history, and any person wishing to become a member should apply to the Hon. Secretary, c/o BZW Limited, 1st Floor, St Mary's Court, 100 Lower Thames Street, London EC3R 6JN, United Kingdom. The annual subscription is £30, which entitles the member to receive one free copy of each work issued by the Society in that year, and to buy earlier issues at reduced prices.

A list of works in print, available to members only, is shown below; very few copies are left of those marked with an asterisk. Prices for works in print are available on application to Mrs. Annette Gould, 5, Goodwood Close, Midhurst, West Sussex GU29 9JG, United Kingdom, to whom all enquiries concerning works in print should be sent. Those marked 'TS' and 'SP' are published for the Society by Temple Smith and Scolar Press, and are available to non-members from the Ashgate Publishing Group, Gower House, Croft Road, Aldershot, Hampshire GU11 3HR. Those marked 'A & U' are published by George Allen & Unwin, and are available to non-members only through bookshops.

Vols. 1 and 2. *State Papers relating to the Defeat of the Spanish Armada, Anno 1588* Vols I & II, ed, Professor J. K. Laughton. TS

Vol. 11. *Papers relating to the Spanish War, 1585–87*, ed. Julian S. Corbett. TS.

Vol. 16. *Logs of the Great Sea Fights, 1794–1805*, Vol. I, ed. Vice-Admiral Sir T. Sturges Jackson.

Vol. 18. *Logs of the Great Sea Fights, 1794–1805*, Vol. II, ed. Vice-Admiral Sir T. Sturges Jackson.

Vol. 20. *The Naval Miscellany*, Vol. I, ed. Professor J. K. Laughton.

Vol. 31. *The Recollections of Commander James Anthony Gardner, 1775–1814*, ed. Admiral Sir R. Vesey Hamilton and Professor J. K. Laughton.

Vol. 32. *Letters and Papers of Charles, Lord Barham, 1758–1813*, Vol. I, ed. Sir J. K. Laughton.

Vol. 38. *Letters and Papers of Charles, Lord Barham, 1758–1813*, Vol. II, ed. Sir J. K. Laughton.

Vol. 39. *Letters and Papers of Charles, Lord Barham, 1758–1813*, Vol. III, ed. Sir J. K. Laughton.

Vol. 40. *The Naval Miscellany*, Vol. II, ed. Sir J. K. Laughton.

Vol. 41. *Papers relating to the First Dutch War, 1652–54*, Vol. V, ed. C. T. Atkinson.

Vol. 42. *Letters relating to the Loss of Minorca in 1756*, ed. Captain H. W. Richmond.

Vol. 43. *The Naval Tracts of Sir William Monson*, Vol. III, ed. M. Oppenheim.

Vol. 45. *The Naval Tracts of Sir William Monson*, Vol. IV, ed. M. Oppenheim.

*Vol. 46. *The Private Papers of George, Second Earl Spencer*, Vol. I, ed. Julian S. Corbett.

Vol. 47. *The Naval Tracts of Sir William Monson*, Vol. V, ed. M. Oppenheim.

Vol. 49. *Documents relating to Law and Custom of the Sea*, Vol. I, ed. R. G. Marsden.

Vol. 50. *Documents relating to Law and Custom of the Sea*, Vol. II, ed. R. G. Marsden.

Vol. 52. *The Life of Admiral Sir John Leake*, Vol. I, ed. G. A. R. Callender.

Vol. 53. *The Life of Admiral Sir John Leake*, Vol. II, ed. G. A. R. Callender.

Vol. 54. *The Life and Works of Sir Henry Mainwaring*, Vol. I, ed. G. E. Manwaring.

Vol. 60. *Samuel Pepys's Naval Minutes*, ed. Dr. J. R. Tanner.

Vol. 65. *Boteler's Dialogues*, ed. W. G. Perrin.

Vol. 66. *Papers relating to the First Dutch War, 1652–54*, Vol. VI, ed. C. T. Atkinson.

Vol. 67. *The Byng Papers*, Vol. I, ed. W. C. B. Tunstall.

Vol. 68. *The Byng Papers*, Vol. II, ed. W. C. B. Tunstall.

Corrigenda to *Papers relating to the First Dutch War, 1652–54*, ed. Captain A. C. Dewar.

Vol. 70. *The Byng Papers*, Vol. III, ed. W. C. B. Tunstall.

*Vol. 71. *The Private Papers of John, Earl of Sandwich*, Vol. II, ed. G. R. Barnes and Lt Cdr J. H. Owen.

Vol. 73. *The Tangier Papers of Samuel Pepys*, ed. Edwin Chappell.

Vol. 74. *The Tomlinson Papers*, ed. J. G. Bullocke.

Vol. 77. *Letters and Papers of Admiral The Hon. Samuel Barrington*, Vol. I, ed. D. Bonner-Smith.

Vol. 79. *The Journals of Sir Thomas Allin, 1660–1678*, Vol. I, ed. R. C. Anderson.

Vol. 80. *The Journals of Sir Thomas Allin, 1660–1678*, Vol. II, ed. R. C. Anderson.

Vol. 89. *The Sergison Papers, 1688–1702*, ed. Cdr R. D. Merriman.

Vol. 104. *The Navy and South America, 1807–1823*, ed. Professor G. S. Graham and Professor R. A. Humphreys.

Vol. 107. *The Health of Seamen*, ed. Professor C. C. Lloyd.

Vol. 108. *The Jellicoe Papers*, Vol. I, ed. A. Temple Patterson.

*Vol. 109. *Documents relating to Anson's Voyage round the World, 1740–1744*, ed. Dr. Glyndwr Williams.

Vol. 111. *The Jellicoe Papers*, Vol. II, ed. A. Temple Patterson.

Vol. 112. *The Rupert and Monck Letterbook, 1666*, ed. Rev. J. R. Powell and E. K. Timings.

Vol. 113. *Documents relating to the Royal Naval Air Service*, Vol. I, ed. Captain S. W. Roskill.

Vol. 114. *The Siege and Capture of Havana, 1762*, ed. Professor David Syrett.

*Vol. 115. *Policy and Operations in the Mediterranean, 1912–14*, ed. E. W. R. Lumby.

Vol. 116. *The Jacobean Commissions of Enquiry, 1608 & 1618*, ed. Dr. A. P. McGowan.

Vol. 117. *The Keyes Papers*, Vol. I, ed. Dr Paul G. Halpern.

Vol. 119. *The Manning of the Royal Navy: Selected Public Pamphlets 1693–1873*, ed. Professor J. S. Bromley.

Vol. 120. *Naval Administration, 1715–1750*, ed. Professor D. A. Baugh.

Vol. 121. *The Keyes Papers*, Vol. II, ed. Dr Paul G. Halpern.

Vol. 122. *The Keyes Papers*, Vol. III, ed. Dr Paul G. Halpern.

Vol. 123. *The Navy of the Lancastrian Kings: Accounts and Inventories of William Soper, Keeper of the King's Ships 1422–1427*, ed. Dr Susan Rose.

Vol. 124. *The Pollen Papers: The Privately Circulated Printed Works of Arthur Hungerford Pollen, 1901–1916*, ed. Dr Jon. T. Sumida. A & U.

Vol. 125. *The Naval Miscellany*, Vol. V, ed. N. A. M. Rodger. A & U.

Vol. 126. *The Royal Navy in the Mediterranean, 1915–1918*, ed. Professor Paul G. Halpern. TS.

Vol. 127. *The Expedition of Sir John Norris and Sir Francis Drake to Spain and Portugal, 1589*, ed. Professor R. B. Wernham. TS.

Vol. 128. *The Beatty Papers*, Vol. I, 1902–1918, ed. Professor B. McL. Ranft. SP.

Vol. 129. *The Hawke Papers: A Selection: 1743–1771*, ed. Dr. Ruddock F. Mackay. SP.

Vol. 130. *Anglo-American Naval Relations 1917–1919*, ed. Michael Simpson. SP.

Vol. 131. *British Naval Documents 1204–1960*, ed. John B. Hattendorf, R. J. B. Knight, A. W. H. Pearsall, N. A. M. Rodger and Geoffrey Till. SP.

Vol. 132. *The Beatty Papers*, Vol. II, 1916–1927, ed. Professor B. McL. Ranft. SP.

Vol. 133. *Samuel Pepys and the Second Dutch War*. Transcribed by William Matthews and Charles Knighton, ed. Robert Latham. SP.

Occasional Publications:

Vol. 1, *The Commissioned Sea Officers of the Royal Navy, 1660–1815*, ed. Professor David Syrett and Professor R. L. DiNardo. SP.